1001 JAVA PROGRAMMER'S TIPS

By Mark C. Chan, Steven W. Griffith, and Anthony F. Iasi

JAMSA
P·R·E·S·S
...a computer user's best friend®

1001 JAVA PROGRAMMER'S TIPS

Published by
Jamsa Press
2975 S. Rainbow Blvd., Suite I
Las Vegas, NV 89102
U.S.A.

http://www.jamsa.com

For information about the translation or distribution of any Jamsa Press book, please write to Jamsa Press at the address listed above.

1001 Java Programmer's Tips

Printed in the United States of America.
98765432

ISBN 1-884133-32-0

Publisher
  Debbie Jamsa

Director of Publishing Operations
  Janet Lawrie

Composition
  James Rehrauer
  Nelson Yee

Cover Design
  Marianne Helm

Copy Editors
  Heather Grigg
  Rosemary Pasco

Technical Advisor
  Phil Schmauder

Proofers
  Heather Grigg
  Rosemary Pasco
  Jeanne Smith

Indexer
  John Bianchi

Cover Photograph
  O'Gara/Bissell

Production Manager
  Rick Pearson

Dedications

To the memory of my grandmothers, their love shall be with me always. To my wife, Audrey, for her patience and staying up late all those nights during the writing of this book. To my dad, mom and my in-laws for their caring and support throughout the years. — **Mark C. Chan**

To my loving wife, Mary, for her patience and unending support and our cats, Izzy and Moses, for keeping us amused during the grind. — **Steven W. Griffith**

To my wonderful mom, Elena, who thinks Java is cool but would much rather enjoy a cup of hot Italian cappuccino with me. — **Anthony F. Iasi**

Acknowledgments

We would like to thank Bob Matlin whose heroic efforts frequently transformed gibberish into readable English. Without Bob, we would have missed our deadline. We also thank the entire staff at Digital West Media, especially Terry Reim and Lynn Bremner whose professionalism kept us organized and made sure we kept our tip numbers straight. Also, Al Servati who pulled together the right people at the right time to make this project a success. And last but not least, the publisher who pushed us to the edge and helped us to discover those late night and early morning hours we thought we never had. Thanks Kris!

Table of Contents

Contents

OBJECT-ORIENTED PROGRAMMING

DEFINING YOUR OWN CLASS

JAVA PROGRAMMING IN DETAIL

DIFFERENCES BETWEEN JAVA AND C/C++

LANGUAGE BASICS

MATH FUNCTIONS IN JAVA

DATE FUNCTIONS IN JAVA

MULTIMEDIA PROGRAMMING

3-D GRAPHICS

TABLE OF CONTENTS

NETWORK PROGRAMMING

MEMORY MANAGEMENT

JAVA DATABASE CONNECTIVITY (JDBC)

OBJECT SERIALIZATION

JAVA SECURITY

DEBUGGING JAVA

BUILDING CUSTOM CONTROLS

PUTTING IT ALL TOGETHER

FINISHING UP

JAVA IS A PROGRAMMING LANGUAGE   1

Java is an object-oriented programming language that was designed to be portable across multiple platforms and operating systems. Developed by Sun Microsystems, Java is modeled after the C++ programming language and includes special features that make it ideal for programs on the Internet. Still, you may be wondering why Java is suddenly receiving so much hype, and what possible improvements could have been made to this new language so as to push aside a well-established language such as C++.

First and foremost, Java makes it easy to put interactive graphics and other special effects on a World Wide Web page. As with any programming language, Java lets you write programs. Special Java programs, called *applets*, execute inside a Web page with a capacity matching that of any traditional program. Furthermore, when you run a Java applet, the remote server transmits the applet to your browser across the Internet. So, rather than going out to a computer store to buy software, Java applets let you download applications automatically when you need them.

Java is a very young programming language with room for improvement in both the language itself and the tools used to develop it. This book will help you get started with Java quickly by giving you 1001 tips you can put to immediate use. As Java's support and popularity increases, along with the explosive growth of the Internet, you will be able to use these tips to help you build the next generation of computer software.

HOTJAVA IS A BROWSER (LIKE NETSCAPE NAVIGATOR)   2

Programmers often mention the name "HotJava" in the same breath as Java. Whereas Java is a programming language, *HotJava* was the first Web browser that could download and play (execute) Java applets. *HotJava*, created by Sun, is simply a browser, much like the *Netscape Navigator* or *Microsoft's Internet Explorer*.

Although *HotJava* was the first browser to support Java applets, many browsers now support or will soon support applets. Starting with Netscape Navigator 2.0, for example, you can play Java applets for many platforms (Windows 95, the Mac, and so on). Another distinguishing feature of HotJava is that unlike most browsers which are written in C/C++, the HotJava browser is written with the Java programming language. Figure 2 illustrates the *HotJava* browser, which you can download from Sun's Web site at *http://www.javasoft.com/nav/download/index.html#browser*.

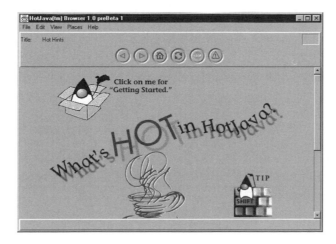

Figure 2 The HotJava browser.

3 JAVA IS OBJECT ORIENTED

Java is an object-oriented programming language which means you can use Java to develop your programs in terms of data and the methods (functions) that operate on the data. In Java, a *class* is a collection of the data and methods which describe an object with which your program works. Think of an object as a "thing," such as a graphics image, a dialog box, or a file.

Java applets can arrange classes in a hierarchical fashion which means you can build new classes from existing classes, improving upon or extending the existing class' capabilities. Everything in Java, except for a few primitive types such as numbers, characters, and boolean (true and false) types, is an object. Java comes with an extensive set of classes that you can use in your programs. In fact, a Java applet itself is a Java class.

4 JAVA IS PLATFORM INDEPENDENT

When you write and compile a Java applet, you end up with a platform-independent file called a *bytecode*. Like a standard program, a bytecode consists of ones and zeros. Unlike a standard program, however, the bytecode is not processor specific. In other words, the bytecode does not correspond to an Intel Pentium or a Motorola processor. Instead, after the server downloads the bytecode to your browser, special code within the browser reads and interprets the bytecode, in turn running the applet. To run the bytecode in this way, the interpreter translates the platform-independent ones and zeros into ones and zeros your computer's processor understands. In other words, it maps the bytecode to ones and zeros that correspond to the current processor, such as a Pentium.

Each computer platform (Mac, Windows, and so on) can have its own Java interpreter. However, the bytecode file that the server downloads to each browser is identical. In this way, you use the same bytecode on a browser running on a Mac, a PC, or a Silicon Graphics workstation. The multi-platform bytecode file is just one aspect of Java's portability. Java's designers also took the extra effort to remove any platform dependence in the Java language. Thus, you will not find any hardware specific references in Java.

5 JAVA IS SECURE

A computer virus is a program written by someone who wants to maliciously damage the files you have stored on your disks or your computer's disk itself. To encounter a virus from across the Internet, you must download and run a program. Unfortunately, with Java applets, a remote server downloads the applet to a browser on your system which, in turn, runs the applet. At first glance, these downloaded Java applets are an ideal way for malicious programmers to create viruses. Luckily, the Java developers designed Java with networking in mind. Therefore, Java has several built-in security defenses which reduce a programmer's ability to use Java to create a virus.

First, Java applets cannot read or write local files that reside on your disk. In this way, the applet cannot store the virus on your disk or attach the virus to a file. The applet simply cannot perform disk input and output. Second, Java applets are "blind" to your computer's memory layout. Specifically, Java applets do not have pointers to memory, and programmers cannot use this traditional back door to your computer. Third, Java cannot corrupt memory outside its own memory space. By building these precautions into the programming language itself, the Java developers have greatly impaired Java's use in creating and transmitting computer viruses.

JAVA IS ROBUST 6

When people talk about code being *robust*, they are referring to the code's reliability. Although Java has not eliminated unreliable code, it has made writing high-quality software easier. To begin, Java eliminates many of the memory problems that are common in languages such as C and C++. Java does not support direct access to pointers to memory. As a result, a Java applet cannot corrupt your computer's memory. Also, Java performs run-time checks (while the applet is running) to make sure that all array and string references are within each item's bounds. In other programming languages, many software bugs result from the program not freeing memory that ought to be freed or freeing the same memory more than once. Java, on the other hand, performs automatic garbage collection (which releases unused memory), eliminating the program's need to *free* unused memory.

Next, Java is more strongly typed than C++ and requires explicit method declarations, which reduces the potential for type-mismatch errors. Finally, Java institutes an error trapping method known as *exception handling*. When a program error occurs, Java signals the program with an *exception*, which provides the program with a chance to recover from the error and warns the user that something caused a specific operation to fail.

JAVA IS EASY TO LEARN 7

If you are already familiar with C/C++, you will find that Java is actually a simpler language to master. Java incorporates the basic tenets of object-oriented design, yet it eliminates some of the more complicated constructs of the other languages, such as multiple inheritance and templates. Many of the language keywords are the same or have only minor differences, which increases portability.

If you are a C programmer dreading the seemingly inevitable push toward C++, you may rejoice over Java's cleaner approach to object-oriented programming. In fact, you may want to skip C++ altogether and learn Java instead. Java's manageable selection of predefined classes are both useful and easy to understand. Many of the common operations that may take you hundreds or thousands of lines of code are already done for you. For example, you can write a simple network chat program without having to know much about sockets, protocols, and other low-level network issues.

JAVA FOR THE INTERNET 8

Sun designed Java from the start to fit hand-in-glove on the Internet. *Applets* are special Java programs that execute from within a Web browser. In contrast, a Java application (an application program as opposed to an applet) does not run within a browser. As it turns out, Java applets are not much different from standalone Java applications. You can start developing your Java program from either an applet or an application and cross over any time. For example, assume that you are writing a new Java-based application that is initially designed as a standalone (non-Internet) game for Mac computers. At the end of your program's development cycle, you decide that you want it to run on Web browsers. Your task to make it into a Web-based applet involves very trivial changes, and the addition of some simple HTML code. At the same time, you will find that the game will also run on computers other than Macs! The point you need to remember is that Java applets run within browsers across the Web, whereas Java application programs do not.

9 JAVA FOR INTRANETS

An *intranet* is an in-house version of the Internet. An intranet uses the same technologies, software, and equipment that the Internet uses (primarily TCP/IP). Whereas the Internet has information servers miles away controlled by other organizations, your company controls the servers and client computers inside your office in an intranet. During the past year, intranets have experienced explosive popularity growth because they offer a very low cost way for companies to maintain and distribute internal information in an easy-to-use format.

Because intranets work like the Internet, Java also finds a home on company intranets. All the techniques that you will learn and, in fact, the same applets that you will use for the Internet, may be applied in your intranet. You may find that Java applets will help you solve special software problems within the intranet. You can use applets to provide a friendly interface to company databases, documentation stores, equipment controls, and so on, while running on any computer from a Mac to a PC to a UNIX workstation.

10 INSTALLING THE JAVA DEVELOPER'S KIT FROM THE CD-ROM

The Java Developer's Kit (JDK) is a collection of software from Sun that contains everything you need to create Java applets. Specifically, the JDK contains the Java compiler, a debugger, and an appletviewer with which you can run Java applets outside of a browser, as well as documentation and sample applets. You can download the JDK for many different platforms from Sun's Web, as discussed in Tip 11. If you are programming in the Windows 95 or Windows NT environment, you can install the JDK from the CD-ROM that accompanies this book.

Installing the Java Developer's Kit (JDK) from this book's companion CD-ROM is very easy. To begin, Sun provides the JDK in a single, self-exacting, executable file whose name we have simplified on the CD as *JDK102.EXE*. When you run the program, it will extract all the files for the Java Developer's Kit (from itself) into a directory named Java on your hard disk. To install the JDK, perform these steps:

1. If you are using Windows 95, select the Start menu Run option. Windows 95, in turn, will display the Run dialog box. Type **command** and press <ENTER>.

2. If you are using Windows NT, select the Program Manager's File menu Run option. Windows NT, in turn, will display the Run dialog box. Type **command** and press <ENTER>.

3. From the command prompt, use the following change directory command to select the root directory as your current directory:

```
C:\WINDOWS> CD \ <ENTER>
```

4. Insert the CD-ROM from the 1001 Java Tips into your CD-ROM drive.

5. Without changing your current drive from your hard drive, type in the program name JDK102 preceded by your CD-ROM drive letter, a colon, and a back slash, then press <ENTER>. For example, if your CD-ROM drive is drive D:, you would type the following:

```
C:\> D:\JDK102 <ENTER>
```

*Note: When you install the **Java Developer's Kit** on your hard disk, the installation program will create the Java directory within your current directory. In most cases, you will want to put the Java directory within your disk's root directory. If, for some reason, you install Java into the wrong directory, simply remove the Java directory using the DELTREE command and run the JDK102.EXE a second time, but in the correct directory.*

Note: If you download the **Java Developer's Kit** from Sun, the name of your self-extracting file will differ from the name **1001 Java Programmer's Tips** uses on the CD. If you are using Windows 95 or Windows NT, the file will use a long filename.

As the program runs, it will place all the Java Developer's Kit files onto your hard drive. Specifically, the program will create the subdirectories listed in Table 10.

Subdirectory	Contents
java	The main directory.
java\lib	Contains the Java class libraries, primarily the file *classes.zip* from which the Java compiler extracts classes during compilation.
java\bin	Contains the executable Java programs, such as the compiler, debugger, and the appletviewer.
java\include	Contains header files that correspond to various Java classes.

Table 10 *Subdirectories which the Java installation creates on your disk.*

After you install the Java Developer's Kit onto your hard disk, you need to modify the two environment variables before you can use the JDK's programs:

PATH   Use the PATH command to add the directory C:\JAVA\BIN to your command path.

HOME   Use the SET command to assign the HOME entry to the drive and directory that contains the JAVA directory files such as: SET HOME= C:\

Edit your system's AUTOEXEC.BAT file and update the PATH command to include the C:\JAVA\BIN directory. Next, add a SET command that assigns the HOME variable to the directory path of your Java files.

Note: Sun offers a very liberal license agreement with respect to your rights to use and distribute the **Java Developer's Kit**. Read the license agreement closely. We've included a copy of the agreement on the CD-ROM in a file named LICENSE.TXT.

DOWNLOAD THE JDK FROM THE INTERNET 11

The Java Developer's Kit (JDK) is available from Sun Microsystems. In addition to including the Java compiler, the JDK provides several essential programming utilities (such as a debugger and appletviewer), as well as the source code for many sample applets. Specifically, the JDK helps you perform the following operations:

- Develop applets that conform to the standard Java API

- Create applets that run in all Java-enabled browsers

- Develop Java applications

- Experiment with the debugger API

You can obtain a copy of the JDK for your computer (such as Windows-, Mac-, or Unix-specific JDK) by using your browser to connect to Sun's Web site:

`http://java.sun.com/java.sun.com/products/JDK`

This Web site will present you with an up-to-date list of supported platforms:

- SPARC Solaris (2.3 or higher)
- Intel x86 Solaris
- Windows 95 and Windows NT
- MacOS (PowerMac or, at least, a 68030/25Mhz processor with System 7)

At this Sun Web site, you will also find a list of current JDK releases; click on the hyperlink for the latest release. As you follow this series of hyperlinks, the site will ask you to specify the type of computer on which you will be developing. After you specify your system type, the server will download the appropriate JDK to your computer.

Note: *Java requires Windows 95 or Windows NT. You cannot use the* **Java Developer's Kit** *for Windows 3.1.*

12 INSTALLING THE JDK ON THE MACINTOSH PLATFORM

After you download the Macintosh JDK, you will need to decompress the file. Use the *Stuffit* program to decompress the MacBinary format file. Use the *DeHQX* or *BinHex4* programs to decompress the *hqx* format. After you decompress the files, you can run the installation program which will create a folder on your Macintosh with the default name *JDK-1.0.2-mac* that contains a series of subfolders. To run the *Applet Viewer*, perform the following steps:

1. Open the folder *Sample Applets*
2. Open the folder *WireFrame*
3. Drag and drop the file *example1.html* onto the application *Applet Viewer*

13 INSTALLING THE JDK ON SUN SOLARIS MACHINES

After you download the Solaris JDK, you can unpack the release files using the *tar* command:

```
%/usr/bin/zcat JDK-1_0_2-solaris2-sparc.tar.Z | tar xf <ENTER>
```

The *tar* command will create a new *java* directory or will overwrite a similarly-named directory, if one exists. Should you need to keep the old directory, rename it before you run the *tar* command. The *java* directory will contain several subdirectories and files. After you run the *tar* command to unpack the files, you can run the *appletviewer* by performing these steps:

1. Add java/bin to your command path
2. Use the change directory command (**cd**) to select a directory that contains an HTML file:

```
% cd java/demo/TicTacToe    <ENTER>
```

3. Run the *appletviewer* specifying the desired HTML file:

```
% appletviewer example1.html    <ENTER>
```

Note: *If, when you run* **java,** **javac,** *or the* **appletviewer,** *you get the fatal error message,* **Exception in thread NULL,** *you should reset your CLASSPATH environment variable to include only the latest version of the JDK class library. For example:*

```
% setenv CLASSPATH .:/usr/local/java/lib/classes.zip
```

JAVA INTEGRATED DEVELOPMENT ENVIRONMENTS FOR THE MAC 14

Presently, there are three main contenders for Mac Java Integrated Development Environments (IDE). If you are already developing code using an established IDE, such as that from Symantec or Metrowerks, you may want to stay with the same IDE for Java. Both of these products now support Java compiling, program building, and full-source debugging. These products have been around for years supporting C and C++ development. Both have an excellent track record and should continue to improve the Java environment, with time. In fact, Metrowerks provides a low cost version of their IDE just for Java, called *Discover*.

Roaster from Natural Intelligence is a newcomer when compared to Symantec and Metrowerks. Natural Intelligence has the distinction of being the first to incorporate Java on the Macintosh and, as of this writing, they are ahead in features and reliability when compared to the IDEs from Symantec and Metrowerks. You can learn more about each of these products at the Web sites shown below.

Figure 14.1 http://www.symantec.com/

Figure 14.2 http://www.Metrowerks.com/

Figure 14.3 http://www.roaster.com/

JAVA INTEGRATED DEVELOPMENT ENVIRONMENTS FOR PCs 15

An integrated development environment (IDE) is a collection of programs which combines a source-code editor, compiler, debugger, and other tools such as a profiler, pretty printer, and so on, that provide you with all the tools you need to develop programs. A user environment that lets you use each of these tools is an integrated program environment.

If you have a PC running Windows 95 or NT, you have several integrated development environments to choose from. Table 15 provides the URLs for Web sites at which you can obtain a full description of each product, as well as ordering information:

Company	Product	URL
Symantec	Cafe for 95/NT	http://cafe.symantec.com
Symantec	Just-In-Time compiler	http://cafe.symantec.com
Kalimantan	Kalimantan	http://www.real-time.com/java/kalimantan/index.html
Innovative Software	OEW for Java	http://www.isg.de/OEW/Java
ModelWorks Software	JPad	http://www.modelworks.com/express
Metroworks	CodeWarrior Java	http://www.Metrowerks.com/
Rogue Wave	Jfactory	http://www.roguewave.com/products

Table 15 Java IDEs for Windows. (Continued on next page.)

Company	Product	URL
Borland	BC++5.0/Java	http://www.borland.com/Product/java
Sun	Java Workshop	http://www.sun.com/developer-products/java
Soft As It Gets	Java IDE	http://www.getsoft.com

Table 15 *Java IDEs for Windows. (Continued from previous page.)*

16 UNDERSTANDING JAVA'S LICENSING ISSUES

To increase the size of the Java user community, Sun offers a very liberal license agreement with respect to your rights to use and distribute the Java Developer's Kit (JDK). However, if you plan to distribute Java or its related tools, you should read the license agreement closely. You will find a file (normally named *COPYRIGHT*) within the Java files you install on to your disk. In addition, you can find guidelines for using and licensing the Java technology at Sun's Web site (*http://java.sun.com/java.sun.com/licensing-FAQ.html*), shown in Figure 16. Also, if you have specific questions regarding the license, you can e-mail Sun at *licensing@java.sun.com*.

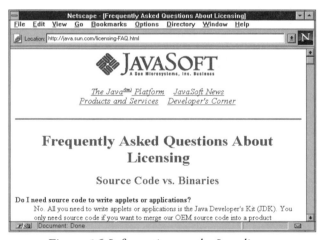

Figure 16 *Information on the Java license.*

17 UNDERSTANDING THE APPLET HTML TAGS

After you create an applet, you make the applet available to other users by placing the applet on a Web page. As you may already know, designers describe Web pages using a markup code called *HTML* (the hypertext markup language). Designers represent a Web page using a file that contains HTML entries. An HTML file uses keywords, known as *tags*, which define the page's appearance to a browser. For example, the designer uses HTML entries to define the appearance of text and where and what images the browser displays on the Web page. When the Web page uses Java applets, the designer uses a special *<APPLET>* tag that provides the browser with information about the applet.

Using the *<APPLET>* tag, the designer can specify (to the browser) a set of attributes that describe such items as the applet filename, the size and location of the applet window, and so on. The complete syntax of the *<APPLET>* tag is as follows:

```
<APPLET   [CODEBASE=URL path]   CODE=filename   WIDTH=pixelWidth
HEIGHT=pixelHeight   [ALT=text]   [NAME=name]   [ALIGN=alignment]
[VSPACE=verticalSpace]   [HSPACE=horizontalSpace]>
[<PARAMETER_NAME=param   VALUE=value> ...]   </APPLET>
```

Within the *<APPLET>* tag, the items shown in brackets are optional. Table 17 provides a brief description of each attribute.

Attribute	Purpose
CODEBASE	Specifies the directory or URL containing the applet classes
CODE	Required. Specifies the applet class filename
WIDTH	Required. Specifies the applet's initial window width
HEIGHT	Required. Specifies the applet's initial window height
ALT	Specifies text a non Java-enabled browser displays
NAME	Gives a name to the applet instance
ALIGN	Sets the applet's alignment on the page
VSPACE	Sets the margin above and below the applet
HSPACE	Sets the margin on either side of the applet
PARAM	Passes named values to the applet

Table 17 Summary of APPLET tag attributes.

The following statements illustrate an example of an *<APPLET>* tag:

```
<APPLET CODE="MyFirst.class" ALIGN=LEFT
VSPACE=50 HSPACE=20 WIDTH=300 HEIGHT=200>
<PARAM name="rate" value="100"></APPLET>
```

In this case, the HTML *<APPLET>* entry passes a parameter named *rate* to the applet whose value is 100.

In this example, the browser will display the applet window 20 pixels from the browser window's left edge, with 50 pixels of space above and below the applet. In addition, this passes a parameter named *rate*, whose value is 100, to the applet.

Setting Applet Size

18

Java applets run within their own window. Within your HTML file, you set the size of an applet window, using the *<APPLET>* tag's *WIDTH* and *HEIGHT* attributes. The size values you specify for each attribute are in pixels. For example, the following *<APPLET>* entry creates an applet window that is 30 pixels tall by 100 pixels wide:

```
<APPLET CODE=clock.class WIDTH=100 HEIGHT=30> </APPLET>
```

Setting an Applet's Height and Width as a Percentage

19

As you learned in Tip 18, you use the *<APPLET>* tag *WIDTH* and *HEIGHT* attributes to specify the pixel size of an applet window. In addition to letting you specify the applet window size in terms of pixels, many browsers let you specify the applet window's size as a percentage of the browser's window's size. You do this by specifying a percentage value for the *HEIGHT* and *WIDTH* attributes within the *<APPLET>* tag. For example, the following *<APPLET>* entry creates an applet window based on 50% of the height and 100% of the width of the browser's window:

```
<applet code=test.class width=100% height=50%> </applet>
```

Note: *Be careful when using percentages to express the applet window size—not all browsers may support percentages.*

20 ALIGNING AN APPLET USING THE *HTML ALIGN* ATTRIBUTE

Within an HTML *<APPLET>* tag, you use the *ALIGN* attribute to adjust the applet's position relative to the other items on the page. Although several alignment values are available, it may be easier if you keep in mind that there are two types of alignment situations: in one case, the applet is a block that text flows around and, in the other case, the applet flows with the text as if the applet were a big character.

When the applet is a block, you use two alignment values: *LEFT* and *RIGHT*. When the applet flows with the text, you use the remaining alignment values. Table 20 summarizes how the browser positions the applet based on the alignment values.

Alignment value	Behavior
LEFT	Applet appears on the left edge of page. Text fills in on the right.
RIGHT	Applet appears on the right edge of page. Text fills in on the left.
TOP	The top of the applet appears at the top of the text.
BOTTOM	The bottom of the applet appears at the bottom of the text.
TEXTTOP	The top of the applet appears at the top of the text.
MIDDLE	The middle of the applet appears at the baseline of the text.
ABSMIDDLE	The middle of the applet appears at the middle of the text.
BASELINE	The bottom of the applet appears at the baseline of the text.
ABSBOTTOM	The bottom of the applet appears at the bottom of the text.

Table 20 *Summary of alignment values.*

The following *<APPLET>* tag illustrates the use of the *ALIGN* attribute:

```
<APPLET CODE="MyFirst.class" ALIGN=LEFT WIDTH=300 HEIGHT=300></APPLET>
```

Unfortunately, the *ALIGN* attribute is one of those HTML features that requires some experimentation. Occasionally, setting alignment options may have surprising results and may look different when running on different browsers. You may have to experiment with the settings several times before you arrive at a page that looks just right.

21 CONTROLLING AN APPLET WINDOW'S SPACING

Within an HTML *<APPLET>* tag, you use the *VSPACE* and *HSPACE* attributes to specify the amount of space, in pixels, the browser places between the applet and its surrounding objects. The *VSPACE* attribute sets the vertical space (above and below), and the *HSPACE* attribute sets the horizontal space (left and right). You may want to use these attributes if your applet appears crowded with other items, such as text, on the Web page. The following *<APPLET>* tag illustrates the use of the *VSPACE* and *HSPACE* attributes:

```
<APPLET CODE="MyFirst.class" ALIGN=LEFT VSPACE=80 HSPACE=10
WIDTH=300 HEIGHT=200></APPLET>
```

In this example, the browser will display the applet 10 pixels from the page's left edge with an 80-pixel space above and below the applet window.

USING THE *ALT* ATTRIBUTE FOR NON-JAVA BROWSERS 22

Not all browsers support Java. When a non-Java-enabled browser encounters a Java applet within an HTML file, the browser has two choices. First, the browser can simply ignore the *<APPLET>* tag. Second, the browser can display a message to users that tells them it has encountered an applet that it will not run. Within an HTML *<APPLET>* entry, you use the *ALT* attribute to specify the message the user's non-Java-enabled browser should display when it encounters the *<APPLET>* tag. The browser displays your message when it cannot play the applet. Using the *ALT* attribute, for example, you may direct the browser to display text to users that tells them that they are missing out on a great applet! The following <APPLET> entry illustrates the use of the *ALT* attribute:

```
<APPLET CODE="MyFirst.class" ALT="Java applet not shown!"
   WIDTH=300  HEIGHT=300></APPLET>
```

In this case, if a browser is not Java-enabled, the browser will display the message *Java applet not shown*, when the browser encounters the *<APPLET>* tag.

USING *CODEBASE* TO SPECIFY AN APPLET'S LOCATION 23

The Java applets your browser executes reside in a file with the *.class* extension. When you create a Web page, you can store your Java *.class* files in a directory which is different from the directory that contains the page's HTML files. Within the HTML *<APPLET>* tag, you can use the *CODEBASE* attribute to specify the directory within which the applet's *.class* files reside. The *CODEBASE* location can be a directory on the same computer or a directory at another computer. The *CODEBASE* attribute specifies (to the browser) the base URL (relative or specific) of the directory that contains the *.class* files. If an *<APPLET>* tag does not use the *CODEBASE* attribute, the browser uses the current directory (the one containing the HTML file) to locate the *.class* files. The following *<APPLET>* tag directs the browser to look for the applet files in the directory called */server_a/applets*:

```
<APPLET CODE="MyFirst.class" CODEBASE="/server_a/applets"
   WIDTH=300  HEIGHT=300></APPLET>
```

RUNNING JAVA APPLETS USING THE APPLETVIEWER 24

Most Java development environments include a special program called an *appletviewer*. Using the *appletviewer*, you can execute your applet just as if it were running within a Web page displayed by a browser. In most cases, the *appletviewer* can run your applet faster than a browser, making the *appletviewer* convenient for testing your applet. As you develop your applet, you will want to run it each time you add features. By using the *appletviewer*, you can quickly try out your applet without starting your Java-enabled Web browser. You run the *appletviewer* that accompanies Sun's Java Developer's Kit from the command line, specifying the name of the HTML file that contains the *<APPLET>* entry for the applet you want to view:

```
C:\> appletviewer  SomeFileName.HTML  <ENTER>
```

Figure 24, for example, illustrates a Java applet running within Sun's *appletviewer*.

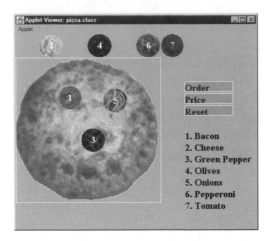

Figure 24 Running a Java applet within the appletviewer.

25 JAVA IS COMPATIBLE WITH ALL SERVERS BUT NOT ALL BROWSERS

When a Java applet runs over a network, two sides are at work. One is the server, which is responsible for maintaining and handling browser requests for the various files it controls. On the server side, a Java applet is just a file like any other file that an HTTP server already handles. You do not need any special server software for Java since the real work of executing the Java applet is performed by the browser, not the server.

On the other side is the client, or browser, which requests, receives, and interprets files from the server. The browser is responsible for displaying the Web page, playing sounds, running animations and, in general, determining the type of data the server is sending and handling that data accordingly.

When a Web page contains a Java applet, the page's HTML file will contain an *<APPLET>* entry. If the browser is Java-enabled, the browser will request the applet file from the server. The server, in turn, will send the applet's bytecode to the browser, which will start its Java interpreter to execute the code.

26 BROWSERS THAT SUPPORT JAVA APPLETS

Software developers continually update browsers to support Java and new Java features. To find out if your browser is Java-enabled, visit your browser developer's Web site. The ubiquitous *Netscape Navigator* and *Microsoft Internet Explorer* both fully support Java. To stay current on Java and Java browsers, you should visit the Web sites shown in the figures below.

Figure 26.1 http://www.netscape.com/

Figure 26.2 http://java.sun.com

Figure 26.3 http://www.microsoft.— com/ie/ie.htm

DOWNLOADING NETSCAPE NAVIGATOR 27

The *Netscape Navigator* browser by Netscape Communications, Inc. was one of the first browsers to provide full Java support. You can easily obtain the *Netscape Navigator*, free of charge, from the Internet. *Netscape Navigator Version 3* provides Java support for most computers. Because Netscape frequently updates the browser, you will need to consult their Web site on a regular basis to remain current with the latest version available for your computer. To download the *Netscape Navigator*, visit the Netscape Web site at *http://www.netscape.com/comprod/mirror/index.html*, shown in Figure 27.1, and follow the steps discussed in Tip 23. Figure 27.2 illustrates a Java applet running within the *Netscape Navigator*.

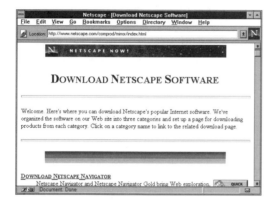

Figure 27.1 *The Netscape Web site.*

Figure 27.2 *Running a Java applet within the Navigator.*

INSTALLING NETSCAPE NAVIGATOR 28

Depending on the type of computer on which you will be installing Netscape, the installation process is relatively straightforward. For Windows, you will simply double click your mouse on the *.exe* file which you downloaded from Netscapc. This program, in turn, will unpack the installation files and produce a *setup.exe* file. Next, by running the *setup.exe* program, you will install Netscape on your system. The Mac-based installation is also very easy and entails double-clicking on the *.sea* (self-extracting archive) file.

Depending on which Netscape package you download, you may receive a series of special files called *plug-ins*. The Netscape installation places these files within a subdirectory (beneath the Netscape directory) named *plugins*. These plug-in programs let you add new capabilities to the *Netscape Navigator*. For example, to view Apple's *Quicktime* movies, you simply place the *Quicktime* movie player into the plug-ins directory, and restart Netscape. If a Web page contains a *Quicktime* movie and you have the plug-in properly installed, you can view the movie from within the Netscape browser.

CONFIGURE NETSCAPE FOR JAVA 29

The *Netscape Navigator* is one of the most widely used browsers in the world. The *Navigator* fully supports Java, and you can get the *Navigator* for both Windows and the Mac. After you install the *Netscape Navigator* on your system, make sure that Java is enabled. Do this by selecting the *Network Preferences* item in the *Options* menu. A dialog box will appear with various tabs running across the top. Select the *Languages* tab. You will then see a checkbox with the words *Enable Java*. If this box is not checked, check it now. If you cannot check it, or the *Enable Java* checkbox does not appear, your version of the browser does not support Java. You will have to download the latest version from Netscape's Web site, as discussed in Tip 27.

30 RUNNING JAVA APPLETS USING NETSCAPE

After you properly configure the *Netscape Navigator*, you can run Java applets by accessing sites that have Java applets on their Web pages, or you can run applets that reside locally on your own computer. Typically, most Java development environments come with an *appletviewer* which you can use to test your applets. However, a better test of an applet is to make sure it runs within the Netscape browser. You can do this easily by following these steps:

1. Within the Netscape Navigator, select the *File* menu *Open File in Browser* option. Netscape, in turn, will display a *Source* dialog box.

2. Within the *Source* dialog box, select an HTML file that refers to your applet.

3. Select Open.

Netscape, in turn, will use the HTML file to access (and execute) the applet specified by the HTML file's *<APPLET>* tag. If Netscape has trouble finding your applet, make sure the applet's *.class* file is present. As you have learned, you can use the *CODEBASE* attribute within the *<APPLET>* tag to specify a directory where the *.class* file is located. In any case, if Netscape can successfully execute your applet, you can be assured that your applet will work just as well when another user accesses your applet within the Netscape browser from anywhere around the world! In addition to using the File menu Open option to access local HTML files, you can also specify the file within the location field. For example, the following URL directs the *Netscape Navigator* to open an HTML file named named *Demo.html* that resides in the *Test* directory on drive C:

```
file://C:\Test\Demo.html
```

31 DOWNLOADING MICROSOFT'S INTERNET EXPLORER

If financial analysts were concerned that Microsoft was sleeping through the "Internet explosion," Microsoft's *Internet Explorer* Web browser put their fears to rest. Although Netscape had seemingly conquered the browser market with *Netscape Navigator*, Microsoft quickly rebounded with a very powerful Web browser—one that provides features you can't find within Netscape's industry-leading browser. To download the Microsoft *Internet Explorer*, visit Microsoft's Web site at *http://www.microsoft.com/ie/*, as shown in Figure 31.

*Figure 31 Download the Microsoft **Internet Explorer**.*

INSTALLING INTERNET EXPLORER · 32

In Tip 31, you learned how to download Microsoft's *Internet Explorer*. When you download the Explorer, you actually download a program that will install the Explorer on your system. Using the Windows 95 Start menu Run option, you run this program to install the Explorer on your system. When the installation completes, delete the file that you downloaded to free up disk space. Figure 32 illustrates the *Internet Explorer*.

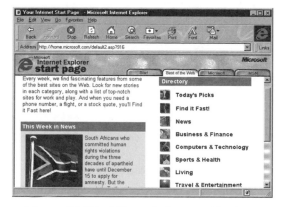

Figure 32 The Microsoft Internet Explorer.

CONFIGURE INTERNET EXPLORER FOR JAVA · 33

After you have the *Internet Explorer* up and running, it is ready to run Java applets. To take the *Internet Explorer* for a Java test drive, run the *Magnify* applet which you will find at the Jamsa Press Web site at *http://www.jamsa.com/catalog/javalib/applet/ex.htm*, as shown in Figure 33.

Figure 33 Running a Java applet within the Internet Explorer.

RUNNING JAVA APPLETS USING INTERNET EXPLORER · 34

As you learned in Tip 33, running Java applets within the *Internet Explorer* is quite easy—you simply specify the URL of the HTML that corresponds to the applet within the browser's *Address* field. As you create Java applets throughout this book, you will want to test each applet within the *Internet Explorer*. To do so, you must specify the location of a local HTML file that resides on your hard disk. To open a local HTML file, select the File menu Open option. The *Internet Explorer*, in turn, will display a dialog box within which you can type the file's pathname.

In addition to using the File menu Open option to access local HTML files, you can also specify the file within the browser's *Address* field. For example, the following URL directs the *Internet Explorer* to open an HTML file named named *Demo.html* that resides in the *Test* directory on drive C:

```
file://C:\Test\Demo.html
```

35 UNTRUSTED JAVA APPLET WINDOW WARNING

If you use Netscape to browse a homepage that uses Java objects and you get the message "Untrusted Java Applet Window," the message is telling you that the Java applet is trying to create one or more separate windows (windows that are separate from the browser) and that several security restrictions exist. In other words, the message occurs when your applet creates a window from within Netscape. Because Netscape applies high-security restrictions to applets, Netscape will inform you each time the applet generates a window.

Consider, for example, a case in which you are running an applet, and a window suddenly pops up asking for your bank account PIN number. Some users may unknowingly enter that information thinking it will gain them access to their account. Instead, the person who designed the applet is using the window as a way to grab personal information from the user. The "Untrusted Java Applet Window" is a red flag that users should not ignore.

36 UNDERSTANDING THE CLASSFORMATERROR EXCEPTION

Although Java-related errors within the *Netscape Navigator* and *Internet Explorer* are becoming fewer and farther apart. You may still encounter errors. One command error occurs when Netscape cannot access the class file that corresponds to a Java applet. For example, if you connect to a server to access a Java applet and you get a *ClassFormatError*, as shown next, Netscape is having trouble reading the data contained within the applet's *.class* file:

```
#Applet exception: error: java.lang.ClassFormatError
```

Within Netscape, *ClassFormatError* exceptions occur several reasons:

1. The HTPP server is not serving *.class* files as *application/octet-stream*. In such cases, check the server's configuration files, if you have accesss.

2. The *.class* file may be corrupted. Try to rebuild it by recompiling the applet, and test it locally with an *appletviewer*.

3. Netscape may have cached a different version of the applet. Go into Netscape's Options menu and clear the disk and memory caches. You may want to quit and restart Netscape, and then try the applet again.

37 NETSCAPE'S APPLET NOT INITIALIZED ERROR

In Tip 36, you learned that there may be times when Netscape cannot access a Java applet's *.class* file because the file is corrupted or because of a server error. There may be times when the server simply can't locate the applet's class file. In such cases, Netscape displays the "Applet not initialized" error message. When this error message occurs, you may want to check that your system's CLASSPATH environment variable points to the directory that contains the class file. Within a UNIX environment, you assign the CLASSPATH variable as follows:

```
setenv CLASSPATH my_class_directory
```

Within the Windows environment, you must add the following line to your *AUTOEXEC.BAT* file:

```
SET CLASSPATH=C:\JDK\JAVA\CLASSES;
```

If the class is part of a package, you must place the package file in the appropriate subpath of the CLASSPATH directory.

BEWARE OF ALPHA AND BETA VERSIONS OF JAVA APPLETS 38

Not all Java-enabled browsers are created equal. For example, Java-enabled versions of Netscape 2.0 will only run beta and *Java 1.0.2* applets that were created with the *1.0.2 Java Developers Kit* (JDK). Many Web pages still use applets created with the alpha version of the JDK. If, as you browse the Web, you cannot access an applet that you think you should be able to run, the applet may be an alpha applet. In such cases, you can find out by looking at the HTML file. Alpha applets use the *<APP>* tag, whereas the beta applets use the *<APPLET>* tag. Likewise, when you use a Java environment, make sure you are using the latest version. Otherwise, you may wind up creating applets that some browsers cannot access.

UNDERSTANDING JAVA, J++, OPENJ BUILDER (LATTE), AND CAFÉ 39

If you are familiar with programming languages such as C/C++, you are well aware that many software manufacturers provide their own compilers. For example, Microsoft, Borland, Symantec, and many others provide C++ compilers and programming environments. Although the Java programming language is still quite young, software manufacturers have already jumped on the Java bandwagon. Microsoft, for example, now offers Visual J++, a Java IDE based on Microsoft's very popular visual programming environment. Similarly, Borland offers OpenJ Builder (Latte) and Symantec offers Café. For more information on these products, visit the following Web sites.

Figure 39.1 http://www.microsoft.—com/visualj/

Figure 39.2 http://www.borland.—com/openjbuilder/

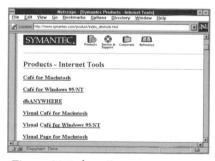

Figure 39.3 http://www.symantec.—com/product/index—_devtools.html

HOW TO GET DOCUMENTATION ON JAVA 40

Across the Web, a slew of sites provide information on Java. As a rule, you should visit Sun's Javasoft site (*http://java.sun.com/doc/programmer.html*) on a regular basis. At this site, you will find a wide range of documentation, including white papers, API specifications, a programmer's guide, and sample applets. In addition to the Javasoft site, the following list contains some of the Web's best sources of Java documentation:

```
http://www.acme.com/java/software/
http://www.km-cd.com/black_coffee/
http://members.aol.com/opensolinc/opensolution.html
http://www.sdsu.edu/~boyns/java/
```

```
http://www.cupojoe.com/
http://www.gamelan.com/index.shtml
http://wwwipd.ira.uka.de/~espresso/
http://www.dannyg.com/javascript/
http://www.surinam.net/java/java.html
http://ncc.hursley.ibm.com/javainfo
http://www.csn.net/express/
http://www.ve.com/javachart/
http://www.cc.gatech.edu/grads/k/Colleen.Kehoe/java/local.html
http://www.xs4all.nl/~dgb/java.html
http://ng.netgate.net/%aronoff/JavaLinks.html
http://www.teamjava.com:80/links/
http://www.next.com/WebObjects/Java.html
```

41 UNDERSTANDING THE PROGRAM DEVELOPMENT PROCESS

Depending on what development package you use to create your Java programs, you will go about compiling, organizing, and testing your programs in different ways. However, the general development process is mostly the same no matter which package or platform you use.

As discussed, the end result of the Java program development process is a *bytecode* file which the server downloads to the browser for interpretation and execution. When you compile your Java source file, you are creating a bytecode file. Java *source-code* files, on the other hand, contain the class definitions and program statements you write using the Java language. In addition to the Java source-code files, you must create a small HTML file, which the browser uses to invoke your applet.

After the compiler creates the bytecode and you create an HTML file, you can test your applet using either your browser or an *appletviewer*. If your applet contains errors, many Java development environments provide a *debugger* program that you can use to track down the errors. When you are ready to release your applet to the public, you must place the applet and a corresponding HTML file on a Web server.

Therefore, the general development cycle of a Java applet includes the creation of source-code and HTML files, compiling the sources into bytecode, testing the bytecode through an *appletviewer*, detecting and removing any errors from the applet using a *debugger* and, finally, releasing the applet for use on a Web server.

42 UNDERSTANDING THE FILE TYPES

When you create Java source-code files that contain classes and methods, you need to be aware of the Java file-naming convention. Each Java source-code file must end with the *.java* extension. In addition, the file's name must match the name of the public class the file defines. For example, if your source-code file creates a class named *MorphaMatic*, your source-code file must use the name *MorphaMatic.java*. As you can see, the letters of the source-code file name must match the class name exactly, including the use of upper and lowercase letters.

The HTML file that you use to run the applet can have any name. As a rule, however, you should use the standard extension for your system, typically *.html* or *.htm*. Also, to help organize your files, you may want to use a name similar to that of your applet for the HTML file name, such as *MorphaMatic.html*.

Finally, the bytecode file the Java compiler creates will have the *.class* extension. In this case, the bytecode file will have the name *MorphaMatic.class*. As discussed, the *.class* file is the file the Web server downloads to your browser which, in turn, interprets and executes the file's contents.

UNDERSTANDING JAVA'S SYSTEM CONSOLE 43

To run a Java applet, you can use a Web browser or the Java *appletviewer*. For simplicity, you will normally use the *appletviewer* to test and debug your applets. When you use the *appletviewer* to run a Java applet, the applet can display its output within a window (which is most common) and also to the *system console*. In the days of mini computers, the system console corresponded to a printer that stood next to the computer. When programs sent messages to the console, a computer operator (a person) would read the message and respond. Such console messages might ask the operator to mount a magnetic tape or a specific disk drive.

For PCs running an operating system such as Windows 95, Windows NT, or even Mac computers, the console corresponds to a window containing the messages generated from your applet while running the appletviewer. As you will learn, you will normally use display messages to the system console to help you test and debug your programs. When you use the common browsers (such as Netscape) to run the applet, the messages the applet writes to the system console normally do not appear. Figure 43.1 illustrates an applet running within the *appletviewer*. In a similar way, Figure 43.2 illustrates the contents of the system console window as the applet executes.

Figure 43.1 *An applet within the appletviewer.*

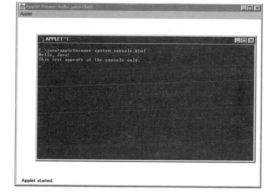

Figure 43.2 *The system console window.*

CREATING AN ASCII SOURCE FILE 44

To create a Java source file, you can use any ASCII editor such as *EDIT* (MS-DOS), *Notepad* (Windows), or *vi* (UNIX). When you create your *.java* source-code files, you must name the file after the public class the file contains, followed by a *.java* extension. The following is a sample Java source-code file named *MyFirst.java*:

```
import  java.applet.*;
import  java.awt.*;

public  class  MyFirst  extends  Applet    // the applet class definition
  {
     //   variables and statements go here

     public void init( ) // an initialization method
       {
```

```
              // The method's statements go here
    }
 }
```

This class (*MyFirst*) contains a method called *init*. As you will learn, Java predefines a series of methods which your applets can derive or improve (extend) upon. A Java applet automatically calls the optional *init* method when the applet starts. In this example, you would place statements within the *init* method that you want the applet to execute once, as the applet first starts executing.

Before you can run this program, you must compile it with a Java compiler. In doing so, you will create a file called *MyFirst.class* which contains the bytecode instructions that Java interpreters can use to execute the applet.

45 CREATING AN HTML SOURCE FILE

When you create the HTML file for a Web page that will execute a Java applet, you will need to insert an *<APPLET>* entry with the HTML file. As you will learn, adding a Java applet to an existing HTML file is relatively easy. To include a Java applet within an HTML file, you don't have to make many changes to the file's HTML entry. In fact, simply use the *<APPLET>* entry to tell the browser the name of the applet's bytecode file and where on the Web page to display the applet window. The following HTML *<APPLET>* entry illustrates how you would add the *MyFirst.class* Java applet to a Web page:

```
<APPLET CODE="MyFirst.class" WIDTH=300 HEIGHT=300></APPLET>
```

As you can see, this *<APPLET>* entry specifies the applet's bytecode filename (which in this case is *MyFirst.class*), as well as the pixel size of the applet window. When your browser encounters the *<APPLET>* entry, your browser will request the server to download the bytecode files, which the browser will then interpret and execute.

46 COMPILING JAVA USING THE JAVAC COMPILER

If you are using Sun's *Java Developer's Kit* (JDK), you may compile your Java sources from the command line using the *javac* compiler provided in the JDK. For example, to compile the Java source-code file, *MyFirst.java*, you would run the *javac* compiler from the command line, as shown here:

```
C:\JAVACODE> javac MyFirst.java    <ENTER>
```

In this case, *C:\JAVACODE>* corresponds to the system's command-line prompt. As you can see, the *javac* command includes the *MyFirst.java* source filename. In this case, if the *javac* command successfully compiles the applet, the compiler will create the bytecode file, *MyFirst.class*, which you can execute using the *appletviewer* or your browser. Before you can run the applet, however, you must create an HTML file that contains an *<APPLET>* entry that corresponds to the applet.

Note: *To access a system prompt within Windows 95, select the Start menu and choose Run. Windows 95, in turn, will display the Run dialog box. Within the Run dialog box, type* **Command** *and press <ENTER>. To access the system prompt from within Windows NT, select the Program Manager's File menu and choose Run.*

UNDERSTANDING THE JAVAC COMPILER   47

As discussed in Tip 46, Sun's Java compiler, *javac*, compiles your Java source code and creates a bytecode file. The *javac* compiler has the following command-line format:

```
javac [ options ] filename.java ...
```

The *javac* compiler expects your source-code files to use the *.java* extension. For every class your source-code files define (you can pass more than one source-code file within the *javac* command line), the *javac* compiler stores the resulting bytecode files with the class name *.class* extension. By default, the *javac* compiler places the resulting *.class* files in the same directory as the corresponding *.java* file, unless your command line uses the *-d* option to specify a different target directory.

The *javac* compiler supports a variety of options. You may want to consult the JDK documentation guide for a full explanation of each option. Table 47 summarizes the *javac* command-line options:

Option	Summary
-classpath path	Sets the source-code directory where *javac* looks for class files
-d directory	Sets the class target directory where *javac* writes *.class* bytecode files
-g	Enables generation of debugging tables for use by debuggers
-nowarn	Turns off compiler warnings
-O	Optimizes code by inlining static, final, and private methods
-verbose	Prints messages showing which source code file is being compiled

Table 47 Summary of javac compiler options.

WHAT IS JAVAC_G?   48

As you have learned, the *javac* compiler examines your source-code files and produces the bytecode *.class* files. As your Java applets become more complex, it may become difficult for you to locate errors (bugs) within your code. To help you locate such errors, most Java development environments provide a special debugger program. In the case of the Sun's Java Developer's Kit, the debugger program is named *jdb* (for Java debugger). To provide *jdb* with more information to work with, the Sun's JDK provides a special version of the compiler named *javac_g*. Sun designed the *javac_g* compiler for use with debuggers. Essentially, *javac_g* is a non-optimized version of the *javac* compiler which places tables of information within the bytecode that the debugger can use to track down errors. To compile a Java applet using the *javac_g* compiler, you simply specify the applet source-file name within the *javac_g* command line, as shown here:

```
C:\JAVACODE> javac_g SomeFile.java    <ENTER>
```

COMPILING JAVA SOURCES ON WINDOWS AND UNIX   49

Most of the Java integrated development environments (IDEs) for Windows (such as Visual J++) are menu driven. In such cases, to compile your applet, you simply select the Compile option from a menu. Figure 49, for example, illustrates Microsoft's Visual J++ programming environment.

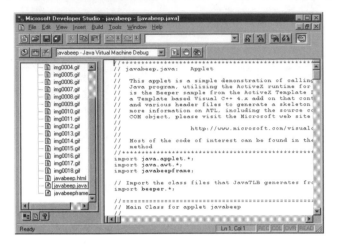

Figure 49 *Compiling a Java applet within Microsoft's Visual J++.*

If you are using Sun's *Java Developer's Kit* (JDK), on either a Windows-based or UNIX-based system, you compile your Java sources by using the program *javac*:

```
C:\> javac MyFirst.java    <ENTER>
```

50   COMPILING JAVA ON THE MAC PLATFORM

If you are using a Java integrated development environment (IDE) from Symantec, Metrowerks, or Natural Intelligence, you simply select the Compile option from a pull-down menu. If the compiler successfully compiles your applet, it will create a *.class* file. Figure 50 illustrates the Mac programming environment.

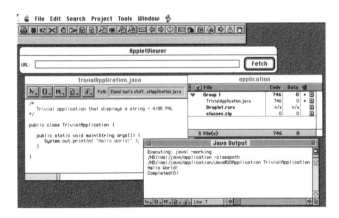

Figure 50 *Compiling a Java applet within Mac.*

If you are using Sun's *Java Developer's Kit* (JDK), you compile your Java sources by using the program *javac* as discussed in Tip 49.

51   UNDERSTANDING COMPILER WARNINGS AND ERRORS

All languages, from English, to French, to German, and programming languages such as C/C++, Basic, and even Java have a grammar that defines the rules you must follow when you use the language. When you violate a rule of a programming language, the compiler will generate one or more syntax error messages.

When your program contains one or more syntax errors, the Java compiler will display error messages on your screen and will not create the bytecode (*.class*) file. In such cases, you must edit your source code to correct the syntax errors and then recompile.

At other times, the Java compiler may display one or more *warning messages* to your screen, but will still create the bytecode file. As a rule, when the compiler displays a warning message, edit your source file and try to determine the cause of the compiler's complaint and correct it. Although the compiler warnings may never cause an error during your program's execution, some warnings leave open the opportunity for errors that are very difficult to debug later. Remember, the compiler displays warning messages for a purpose—the compiler is warning you that you have done something "not quite right."

OPTIMIZING JAVAC OUTPUT 52

When you compare the performance of a Java program against that of a C/C++program, you will find that the current generation of Java programs can be as much as *twenty times slower* than their C/C++ counterparts. This performance loss is due mostly to the fact that the browser must *interpret* the Java bytecode and convert it into the computer's native code (such as a Pentium- or Motorola-specific code) before the code can run. In C/C++, the code is in the processor's native format to begin with, so this time-consuming translation step is not required. Remember, however, that Java's generic bytecode allows the same Java code to run on multiple platforms.

The Java designers are working on various solutions to speed up Java. In the meantime, you can use the *-O* compiler switch with *javac*, which may increase the applet's performance. The *-O* switch directs *javac* to optimize its bytecode by "inlining" *static*, *final*, and *private* methods. For now, don't worry what "inlining" such code means other than it may improve your applet performance. Unfortunately, when you use inlining, you may increase the size of your bytecode file, which will increase the applet's download time. The following *javac* command illustrates how you use the *-O* switch:

```
C:\JAVACODE> javac -O MyFirst.java    <ENTER>
```

PUTTING YOUR JAVA APPLET ON A SERVER 53

When you are finally ready to release your applet for use by others, you simply place your applet and its corresponding HTML file on a Web (HTTP) server. You do not need to do anything special to your pre-existing HTTP server to allow browsers to access Java applets on the server. Instead, as discussed, you simply need to create an HTML file for the Web page that contains the *<APPLET>* tag. As you will recall, the *<APPLET>* entry tells the browser the location of the Java bytecode (*.class*) file and specifics the location and spacing of the applet window. For example, the following HTML file directs the browser to look for the applet file, *MyFirst.class*, in the server-based directory named *applets*:

```
<APPLET CODE="MyFirst.class" CODEBASE="applets"
WIDTH=100 HEIGHT=300></APPLET>
```

In this case, the browser will first request the HTML file from the server. When the browser encounters the *<APPLET>* tag within the HTML file, the browser will then request the corresponding class file (the bytecodes) from the server. The browser's request to the server for the file will specify the applet's directory.

54 BEWARE OF TOO MANY LOCAL VARIABLES

Version 1.0.2 of the *javac* compiler will not compile methods (functions) that contain over 63 local variables. If you experience errors related to a method that uses this many local variables, either break up the method into several methods, or use arrays to store your data. In any case, Sun considers this limit a bug which it may address in a later release. However, most software engineers will consider this local-variable limit a "good bug" because it will very likely improve code readability. As it turns out, a large number of local variables increase a function's complexity which, in turn, makes the function more difficult for other programmers to understand. If your function requires an excessive number of variables, your function is probably doing more than one thing, which is a good indicator that you need to break the corresponding tasks into multiple pieces.

55 WINDOWS 95 AND NT MAY HAVE TROUBLE WITH CASE

If you are using Microsoft Windows 95 or NT and you have class names which are identical except for the case of the letters, the *javac* compiler may errantly ignore the case, assuming the two names are the same. For example, the *javac* compiler will return an error for the following code:

```
/* file Test.java */
class Test {
    // class definition here
}


/* file test.java */
class test {
    // class definition here
    void function(Test t)  {
        // do some work here
    }
}
```

This name confusion is a compiler bug, which Sun should fix in a future release. For now, you should not rely on the case of letters to distinguish class names. As before, many software engineers will consider this to be a "good bug," because it may make your applets easier to understand. If the compiler is confused by your choice of function names, many programmers, who have to read, understand, and possibly modify your code, may be confused as well.

56 JAVA APPLETS VERSUS APPLICATIONS

With Java, you can create two types of programs: an *applet* or an *application*. As you have learned, a Java applet is a program that executes from within a Web browser. A Java application, on the other hand, is a program that is independent of the browser and can run as a standalone program.

Because an applet is run from within a Web browser, it has the advantage of having an existing window and the ability to respond to user interface events provided through the browser. In addition, because applets are designed for network use, Java is much more restrictive in the types of access that applets can have to your file system than it is with non-network applications.

As you will learn, when you write a Java application, you must specify a *main* method (much like the C/C++ *main*), which the program executes when it begins. Within the *main* method, you specify the functionality that your application performs. With an applet, on the other hand, you need to write additional methods that respond to events which are an important part of the applet's life cycle. These methods include *init, start, stop, destroy,* and *paint.* Each of these events has a corresponding method and, when the event occurs, Java will call the appropriate method to handle it.

When you write your first Java programs, you can write them as if they were applets and use the *appletviewer* to execute them. As it turns out, you can later convert your applet to an application by replacing your *init* method with a *main* method.

STRUCTURE OF A SIMPLE JAVA APPLET 57

To create an applet, you create a subclass of the *applet* class which Java predefines and stores in the *java.applet* package (Java terminology refers to libraries as packages). The *applet* class provides the capability to handle a variety of user-interface events and screen drawing operations. Because your applet will need to use these methods from the *applet* class, you must *import* the *java.applet* package into your applet. In short, importing a package makes it more convenient for your applet to refer to (use) classes and methods contained within the package. To import a package, your applets use the *import* keyword. The following statement, for example, illustrates how your applet imports the *applet* class:

```
import java.applet.*;
```

Following the import statements, you specify your applet's name (without the *.java* extension) using the following format:

```
public class MyClassName extends Applet
```

Depending on the operations your applet needs to perform, the applet must respond to a variety of events. The *applet* class provides you with default method implementations (functions) for major events, but you can override those methods in your class. Five of the more important methods include *init, start, stop, destroy,* and *paint.*

If you decide that you need to override any of these methods, you may do so by defining them as methods within the public class. You may also write your own methods, of course. In addition, the file containing the public class may also contain private classes which you define to perform special tasks. The tips that follow will examine classes, the difference between *private* and *public* classes, and where you place your class methods within an applet.

A "HELLO, WORLD" JAVA APPLET 58

In most computer books that teach you a new language, the first program that you learn is called "Hello, World." It is generally a simple program which prints the phrase "Hello, World" to your computer screen. By creating the same applet in Java, you can place your applet on the Internet to literally greet the entire world! The following applet, *Hello.java,* is a complete Java applet which displays the "Hello, World" message:

```
import java.applet.*;
import java.awt.*;

public class Hello extends Applet
```

```
{
    public void paint(Graphics g) // Java automatically calls paint
    {
        g.setColor(Color.red);
        g.drawString("Hello, World!",5,10);
    }
}
```

This applet displays the message "Hello, World" within an applet window in red! As it turns out, each time Java must display or update the applet window, Java calls the *paint* method. By using the *setColor* method from the *Graphics* class, the applet changes the drawing color to red. Next, using the *Graphics* class *drawString* method, the applet displays text within the applet window.

Remember, when you name the file containing this source code, name the file *Hello.java*, which matches the name of the applet's *public* class. You can view this applet either through a Java-enabled Web browser, or through an applet viewer utility. Before you do, however, you must create a small HTML that contains an *<APPLET>* tag, as shown:

```
<APPLET  CODE="Hello.class"  WIDTH=300  HEIGHT=300></APPLET>
```

59 RUNNING THE "HELLO, WORLD" APPLET

To run the "Hello, World" applet that resides in the class file *Hello.class*, you must create an HTML file as discussed in Tip 58. In this case, you can name that file *Hello.html*. Next, from the command prompt, you can run the *appletviewer* as shown here:

```
C:\> appletviewer   Hello.html   <ENTER>
```

The appletviewer, in turn, will display the applet's output as shown in Figure 59.

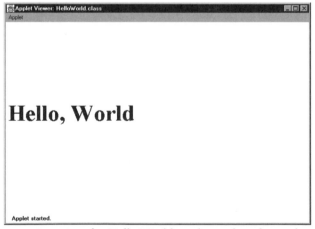

Figure 59 Running the Hello World applet within the appletviewer.

60 UNDERSTANDING THE KEY APPLET FUNCTIONS

When you view an applet, several events occur automatically as your applet comes to life and later disappear when you decide to quit or surf to another page. As it turns out, you control each of these "automatic operations" by defining special functions within your applet.

When you first open the Web page that contains the applet (the HTML file), Java calls the applet's optional *init* method, within which your applet performs its one-time startup operations, such as creating and initializing objects, getting parameter values from the HTML file, and other operations the applet should perform one and only one time.

After Java calls the *init* method, Java calls the *start* method. (As it turns out, Java actually calls the *start* method each time the user returns to applet's Web page after visiting another Web site.) The key difference between the *init* method and the *start* method is that Java only calls the *init* method once during the life of the applet. On the other hand, Java may call the *start* method many times as the user surfs to and from the applet.

Of course, if there is a *start* method, there must be a *stop* method. As it turns out, each time the user leaves the applet's Web page, Java calls the *stop* method. Within the *stop* method, for example, you might turn off music that you had playing in the background as your applet runs. In this way, the music won't continue as the user surfs other sites.

As the applet runs, many user interactions and related events may occur. For example, the user may size, move, or cover the window. As you will learn, you must write methods that respond to user induced events such as window resizing, mouse clicking, and menu selections. At this point in its life cycle, the applet is at its full glory.

Finally, when the user decides to quit the applet, Java calls the *destroy* method to release specific resources or clean up whatever items the applet has allocated during its lifetime. As you examine applets throughout this book, you will find that applets make extensive use of these common methods.

STRUCTURE OF A SIMPLE JAVA APPLICATION 61

As you have learned, a Java application is a program that is independent of the browser and can run as a standalone program. When you write a Java application, you must define a *main* method, which executes when the program starts. From the *main* method, you can specify the functionality that your program performs.

Unlike a Java applet which begins with a class definition that extends the *applet* class, a Java application begins with a *public class* definition whose name matches that of the file within which the class is defined. For example, the following statement starts the definition of a Java application named *MyApplication*:

```
public class MyApplication
```

In addition, the application must define a *main* method, which Java calls when the program starts:

```
public static void main(String args[])
```

Note that the *main* method receives a parameter of type *String*, which is an array of command-line items that the user may have supplied when the program was invoked. Using this array, your program can access the command-line parameters within the *main* method. Tip 64 illustrates a complete Java application that displays the "Hello, World" message.

A "HELLO, WORLD" JAVA APPLICATION 62

The following Java application, *Hello.java*, displays the words "Hello, World" on the screen:

```
public class Hello
  {
```

```
public static void main(String args[])
{
    System.out.println("Hello, World!");
}
}
```

To start, you may want to compare this application to its applet counterpart shown in Tip 58. As you can see, the application uses a *main* method. Within *main*, the application uses the *System.out.println* method to display the "Hello, World" string to a console window (as opposed to an applet's graphics window). As your applets become more complex, you may use the *System.out.println* method as a handy debug tool with which you can print the values of variables from within a program to the console window.

As you will recall, Java applications do not run within a browser. Instead, as discussed in Tip 64, you run standalone programs using the *java* command.

63 RUNNING A JAVA APPLICATION

Java applications do not run within the Web browser, or within the *appletviewer*. Instead, after you compile the application using the *javac* compiler, you use the Java interpreter (that your development environment provides) to run the application. For example, if you are using Sun's *Java Developer's Kit* (JDK), you first compile the application's source code using the *javac* compiler, as shown here:

    C:\JAVACODE> java HelloWorld.java   <ENTER>

Next, you use the java command to interpret and execute the application's bytecode:

    C:\JAVACODE> java MyFirst.class   <ENTER>
    Hello, World!

64 UNDERSTANDING THE JAVA INTERPRETER

As discussed in Tip 63, Sun's Java interpreter, *java*, executes an application's bytecodes. The command-line format of Sun's *java* interpreter is as follows:

    C:\JAVACODE> java [options] application_name [arguments]   <ENTER>

If the user specifies a command line, *java* passes the arguments as an array of command-line arguments to the *main* method. The *java* interpreter supports a variety of options. You may want to consult the JDK documentation for a full explanation of each option. Table 64 provides a summary of the *java* command-line options:

Switch	Summary
-debug	Attaches the *jdb* debugger
-cs, -checksource	Auto compiles changed source-code files
-classpath path	Sets the directory that contains the application's class source files
-mx x	Sets the application's maximum memory size

Table 64 Summary of java command-line switches. (Continued on next page.)

Switch	Summary
-ms x	Sets the application's maximum startup memory size
-noasyncgc	Turns off asynchronous garbage collection
-ss x	Sets maximum stack size for C code in threads
-oss x	Sets maximum stack size for Java code in threads
-t	Prints a trace of executed instructions
-v, -verbose	Prints message to *stdout* every time a class file is loaded
-verify	Runs the verifier to examine all code
-veriftremote	Runs the verifier on all code that is loaded via a classloader
-noverify	Turns verification off
-verbosegc	Prints messages whenever the garbage collector frees memory
-D*propertyname=newvalue*	Allows you to redefine property names

Table 64 *Summary of java command-line switches. (Continued from previous page.)*

65

USING THE CS (CHECK SOURCE) SWITCH

When you develop Java code using Sun's JDK, you normally compile your sources by using the *javac* compiler. If no compile errors exist, you then run your application using the *java* interpreter. As a shortcut, you can specify the *-cs* command-line switch when you invoke the *java* interpreter. The *java* command, in turn, will automatically compile out-of-date (modified) source-code files for you.

By using the *-cs* switch, you can make changes to your sources and immediately execute the *java* interpreter without having to manually run the *javac* compiler yourself. The *java* interpreter knows which files it needs to recompile by comparing each file's modification dates against the corresponding class' modification date. Normally, programmers use the *-cs* option when they have made a minor change to the source files and know that the files contain no compilation errors. The following command illustrates the use of the *-cs* switch:

```
C:\JAVACODE> java -cs MyProgram <ENTER>
```

66

UNDERSTANDING THE MAIN METHOD

As you have learned, you only use the *main* method within a Java application and not in a Java applet. When you run your compiled Java class using the Java interpreter, the *main* method is the first code in the application to execute. The *main* method can contain any program statements you need, including variable declarations, looping statements, and even calls to other methods. The following Java application, *PrintArgs.java*, uses a *for* loop to display each of its command-line arguments to the console window:

```java
class PrintArgs
  {
    public static void main(String args[ ])
     {
       for (int j= 0; j < args.length; j++)
          System.out.println("Arg #" + j + "-> " + args[j]);
     }
  }
```

As you can see, the *main* method receives one parameter, an array of strings each of which corresponds to a command-line argument. Using a *for* statement, the program loops through the array of command-line arguments. The program uses the *args.length* attribute to determine the number of elements in the array.

After you compile this application using *javac*, you can run the application using the java interpreter, as shown here:

```
C:\JAVACODE> java PrintArgs 1 hello "hi there"
```

The application, in turn, will display the command line arguments, as shown here:

```
C:\JAVACODE> javac -O MyFirst.java    <ENTER>
Arg #0-> 1
Arg #1-> hello
Arg #2-> hi there
```

As you can see, if you group arguments within quotes ("hi there") the Java interpreter treats the arguments as one parameter.

67 UNDERSTANDING STATEMENTS

A Java program consists of a list of instructions that you want the computer to perform. Within a Java applet, you use statements to express these instructions in a format the Java compiler understands. If you are already familiar with C/C++, you will discover that Java statements are very similar. For example, the following statements produce a program which prints the words "Hello, Java!" in an applet window:

```java
import java.applet.*;
import java.awt.Graphics;

public class hello_java extends Applet
   {
     public void paint(Graphics g)
      {
         g.drawString("Hello, Java!", 20, 20);
      }
   }
```

68 UNDERSTANDING CODE BLOCKS

A *code block* is a series of related Java statements or declarations you surround with a pair of matching braces { }. For example, the following program uses two code blocks, one that corresponds to the class *print_number* and a second that corresponds to the *init* method. The program displays it's output to the console window:

```java
import java.applet.*;

public class print_number extends Applet
   {
     int block1_number = 1;
```

```
    public void init()
      {
        int block2_number = 2;
        System.out.println("Blocks:" + block1_number +
          block2_number);
      }
  }
```

Code blocks provide two important features: code readability and the convenience of controlling the scope of variable declarations. By blocking code, your code becomes easier for another programmer to read and understand. In addition, variables your program declares within a block are valid for that block and not available outside the block (in other words, Java restricts the variable's scope to that block).

However, unlike C/C++, you cannot declare two identically named variables in two different blocks within the same method. In the code block example, the code declares the variables *block1_number* and *block2_number* at the start of their respective blocks. As you will learn, Java lets you declare variables at any location within a block and not just at the start of the block.

ADDING STATEMENTS TO YOUR JAVA PROGRAM 69

By adding statements to your Java program, you extend the program's features. You may use any of the examples on this book's companion CD-ROM or, for that matter, any pre-existing Java program, as well as add additional statements. Before your computer can run the program, you must first save your changes and compile the program. The Java compiler, in turn, converts your statements into bytecodes that your browser interprets and executes. If your new statements contain errors, the compiler will display error messages, and you will have to correct the errors and re-compile your source-code before you can run your new program.

UNDERSTANDING STYLE AND INDENTATION 70

As you write Java programs, you will discover that you have considerable flexibility in how you line up your statements and indent lines. Some editor programs help you line up indented lines and indent new blocks, for example. If you have already programmed in another language, you probably have your own style of indentation. Java does not impose any specific style. However, you may want to be consistent with your own style and always be conscious that a well-formatted program is easier to read and maintain. For example, the following two programs function equivalently. However, one is much easier to read than the other:

```
import java.applet.*;public class am_i_readable extends
Applet{public void init(){System.out.println("Can you guess what I
do?");}}
```

```
import java.applet.*;

public class am_i_readable extends Applet
   {
     public void init()
```

```
    {
        System.out.println("Can you guess what I do?");
    }
}
```

71   UNDERSTANDING THE SEMICOLON

As you have learned, a Java program consists of a list of instructions that you want the computer to perform. Within a Java program, you use semicolons to separate one instruction from the next. The Java language's use of the semicolon is similar to that of C/C++. The following example separates two statements using semicolons, placing the statements on individual lines:

```
int width = 10;
int height = 20;
```

Java, however, does not care that your statements appear on individual lines. You could have written the previous example on one line as follows:

```
int width = 10; int height = 20;
```

Because the Java compiler ignores comments, you do not need to place a semicolon after a comment:

```
int width = 10; int height = 20; // Two distinct statements
```

Likewise, you don't need to place a semicolon after the right brace that ends a code block. When you compile your applets, the Java compiler will tell you (sometimes not explicitly) when it expects a semicolon that your code has omitted. If such an error occurs, you must edit your source code, add the semicolon, and then recompile the code before your application will run.

72   SIMPLE DEBUGGING MESSAGES WITH SYSTEM.OUT.PRINTLN

When your programs do not run as you expect, you will need to debug (remove the errors from) your program. One way to detect errors within your code is to display the values of variables at different locations in your program. To display values to the console window, you can use the *System.out.println* method, as shown here:

```
int x = 5;
int y = 10;
System.out.println("Debug: x=" + x " y=" + y);
```

Within the *System.out.println* output, the text that appears within quotes appears just as it appears in the function call. The plus sign (+), when used within the *println* method, is a *concatenation* operator that "glues" together the quoted text with the value of the variable (or number) that follows the plus sign. The *System.out.println* function automatically converts numbers to strings for display. For example, the previous function call will display the following output:

```
Debug: x=5 y=10
```

Remember, the *System.out.println* does not display characters to the applet window. Instead, the function displays the output to the text-based console window.

JAVA IS CASE SENSITIVE 73

As you type in your Java programs, you must keep in mind that Java considers upper and lowercase characters as different. The following program, for example, uses the uppercase *V* in the keyword *void*. Therefore, the program will not successfully compile:

```java
import java.applet.*;

public class bad_case extends Applet
   {
      public Void init()
        {
            System.out.println("This program does not compile.");
        }
   }
```

When you compile this program, your compiler will display an error message regarding the uppercase *Void*. To correct the error, edit the source-code file and change the uppercase *Void* to lowercase *void*. After you save the changes to your source code, you must then compile the code for your changes to take effect.

UNDERSTANDING LOGIC ERRORS (BUGS) 74

As you learned in Tip 73, Java's case sensitivity will cause the compiler to display a syntax error when you use the incorrect case. When syntax errors occur, the compiler will not generate an applet you can run. To correct such syntax errors, you must edit the source-code file, correct the error, and then recompile. At other times, your program will successfully run, but does not correctly perform the task you desire. For example, assume that you want the following program to display its output on two lines in the console window:

```java
import java.applet.*;

public class one_line extends Applet
   {
      public void init()
        {
            System.out.print("This is line one.");
            System.out.println("This is the second line.");
        }
   }
```

Because the program does not violate any of Java's syntax rules, the program will successfully compile. When you execute the program, however, it does not display its output on two lines but, instead, displays the output on one line, as shown:

This is line one.This is the second line.

When your program does not work as you desire, the program contains *logic errors* or *bugs*. When your program contains a logic error (and eventually your programs will), you must try to figure out the cause of the error and correct it. The process of removing logic errors from your program is called *debugging*. In the case of the program in this example, the bug is that the first statement uses the *print* instead of the *println* method, as shown:

```
System.out.println("This is line one.\n");
```

75 UNDERSTANDING THE PROGRAM COMPILATION PROCESS

When you create programs, you will normally follow the same steps. To begin, you will use an editor to create your source file. Next, you will compile the program using a Java compiler. If the program contains syntax errors, you must edit the source file, correct the errors, and re-compile.

After the program successfully compiles, the compiler generates a new file, known as bytecode. By using a Java interpreter, or *appletviewer*, you can execute the bytecode to test if it runs successfully. If the program does not work as you expected, you must review the source code to locate the error. After you correct the error, you must compile the source code to create a new bytecode file. You can then test the new program to ensure that it performs the desired task. Figure 75 illustrates the program development process.

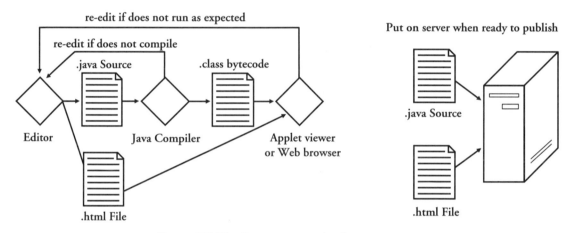

Figure 75 The Java program development process.

76 UNDERSTANDING CLASS FILE TYPES

When you create a Java applet, you will encounter files that use a variety of extensions. You start your program development by placing your program statements in a source-code file with the same name as the *public class*, followed by the *.java* extension. For example, assume that the applet's *public class* is defined as follows:

```
public class hello_java extends Applet
```

In this case, you must name the source-code file as *hello_java.java* (for this name, you must use all lowercase letters). After you have successfully compiled your Java program, in this case *hello_java.java*, your compiler will create a bytecode file ending in the *.class* extension, or *hello_java.class* for example. The *.class* file which the compiler creates contains binary (1's and 0's) code, called bytecode, that your browser or the *appletviewer* executes.

Every Java applet you examine will start with one or more *import* statements. In short, these *import* files tell the compiler that your applet will use a package, or library, of previously compiled code. This library code contains additional code the program uses to perform specific tasks. As you will learn, Java extracts this precompiled code from a special compressed file named *classes.zip*. If you examine the directories that contain the Java development files (such as the compiler), you will find the *classes.zip* file.

Finally, for a browser to execute your Java applet's *.class* file, you must create an HTML file that contains an *<APPLET>* entry. Normally, the HTML file's extension is either *.html* or *.htm*.

UNDERSTANDING THE CLASSES.ZIP FILE 77

Most Windows 95 or Mac Java development environments use a file named *classes.zip* to store the default Java library (packages) in a compressed format. When you use the *import* statement within an applet to reference a specific package, the Java compiler extracts the package code from the *classes.zip* file. For example, the following *import* statement directs the Java compiler to use the code contained in the *AudioClip* package:

```
import  java.applet.AudioClip;
```

The Java development environment compresses the *classes.zip* to save disk space. If you "unzip" the *classes.zip* file, you will find that it contains a series of files all ending in the *.class* extension. If you have sufficient disk space, you can speed up your compiles by unzipping the class files. To unzip the *classes.zip* file, you will need to use a utility such as WinZip, which you can download from *http://www.winzip.com/winzip/winzip/download.htm*.

UNDERSTANDING THE IMPORT STATEMENT 78

The Java *import* statement is an optional statement that lets you later abbreviate references to classes, methods, and variables without typing in their full pathnames. Using the *import* statement and abbreviating names makes your code more legible and also saves you typing time. Do not compare the Java *import* statement to the C/C++ *#include* statement. The *import* statement does not "read in" or load any file. It merely tells the compiler the classes to which your program is referring. For example, if you do not use the *import* statement, you will have to type in the full pathname of every external class, such as the following:

```
java.util.Hashtable my_table = new java.util.Hashtable();
```

By using the *import* statement, you can refer to classes directly, without typing in the full package name:

```
import  java.util.Hashtable; // import this class

Hashtable my_table = new java.util.Hashtable(); // this is shorter
```

Within your programs, you may have as many *import* statements as you need to specify the libraries your program is using. Each *import* statement, however, must appear after the optional *package* statement and before the first class or interface definition in the file.

As you will learn, you will base much of your Java development on previously written code. Also, most of your *import* statements will specify standard packages contained in the *classes.zip* file which is part of the Java Developer's Kit. However, you can also include classes from other developers or from packages that you have previously written.

USING THE * SHORTCUT WITH THE IMPORT STATEMENT 79

If you are using packages from the Java Developer's Kit (JDK), you can use the asterisk (*) to eliminate your need to enumerate each class. For example, the following *import* statements list several classes explicitly:

```
import java.awt.Color;
import java.awt.Dialog;
import java.awt.Font;
import java.awt.Graphics;
```

As you can see, each of these classes resides within the *java.awt* package. Rather than forcing you to specify each class in this case, you can simplify your program by replacing the class names with the asterisk, as shown here:

```
import java.awt.*;
```

In this case, the *import* statement tells the Java compiler that your program is using zero or more classes defined within *java.awt*. As you examine Java programs, you will find that most programs use the asterisk in this way for simplification.

80 SPEEDUP COMPILES BY SEPARATING CLASSES

As you know, programmers consider it a good programming practice to separate class source code into separate files. By creating smaller class-specific files instead of putting all of the applet code in one large file, the project will be easier to maintain, reuse, easier for other programmers to understand, and will build faster.

However, to make your classes easier for other applets to use, you may want to organize multiple class files into *packages* (often called *class libraries*). You create a Java package by specifying the *package* keyword at the top of your class file. For example, the following statement creates a package named *SpecialPurposePackage*:

```
package SpecialPurposePackage;
```

When you need to access those classes from another applet source file, you use the *import* statement, as shown here:

```
import SpecialPurposePackage.*;
```

81 UNDERSTANDING JAVA KEYWORDS

The Java programming language defines several keywords that have special meaning to the compiler. As you choose variable names and create your own methods, you cannot use these keywords. Table 81 briefly describes the Java keywords:

Keyword	Meaning
abstract	Defines an abstract method or class
boolean	A *boolean* type (1 bit)
break	Terminates (breaks) a loop or *switch* statement's processing
byte	An 8-bit integer type
case	Indicates a choice within a *switch* statement
catch	Traps an exception
char	A Unicode character type (2 bytes)

Table 81 Java Keywords. (Continued on following page.)

Keyword	Meaning
class	Defines a class type
const	Reserved for future use—not currently used in Java
continue	Continues a loop's execution with the next iteration
default	Indicates the default choice within a *switch* statement when no other cases match
do	Starts a *do/while* loop
double	A double-precision floating number type (8 bytes)
else	Specifies an *if* statement's alternative clause
extends	Defines the parent class of a class the code is defining
final	Specifies a variable is a constant, class cannot be subclassed, and a method cannot be overridden
finally	Specifies the part of a *try* block Java always executes
float	A single-precision floating point type (4 bytes)
for	Starts a *for* (counting) loop
future	Reserved for future use—not currently used in Java
generic	Reserved for future use—not currently used in Java
goto	Reserved for future use—not currently used in Java
if	Specifies a conditional statement
implements	Specifies that a class implements (defines the methods for) the named interface or interfaces
import	Identifies packages (class libraries) the program uses
inner	Reserved for future use—not currently used in Java
instanceof	Returns true if the specified object is an instance of a class
int	An integer type (4 bytes)
interface	Defines an abstract type with methods that a class can implement
long	A long integer type (8 bytes)
native	Specifies that the method is implemented elsewhere in C, or in some other platform-dependent fashion
new	Allocates a new object or array
null	Specifies a variable that does not refer to any object—is not considered equal to zero, as in C
operator	Reserved for future use—not currently used in Java
outer	Reserved for future use—not currently used in Java
package	A collection of classes (a class library)
private	Modifier that indicates only members of this class can access the object
protected	Modifier that indicates only members of this class, its subclasses, and other classes within the package can access the object
public	Modifier that indicates methods of all classes can access the object
rest	Reserved for future use—not currently used in Java

Table 81 Java Keywords. (Continued on following page.)

Keyword	Meaning
return	Returns control from a function to the caller
short	A short integer type (2 bytes)
static	Modifier that indicates an object's uniqueness to a class, but not to objects of its class
super	Refers to the superclass object or constructor
switch	Used with one or more *case* statements to create a conditional statement
synchronized	Locks a class or section of code to prevent concurrent modification by threads
this	Refers to the instance of the current object
throw	Directs the program to signal that an exception has occurred
throws	Lists the exceptions that the method can throw
transient	Reserved for future use—not currently used in Java
try	Specifies a block of code that traps exceptions
var	Reserved for future use—not currently used in Java
void	Specifies that a method does not return a value
volatile	Specifies that a variable changes asynchronously and the compiler should not attempt to optimize the variable's use
while	Specifies the start of a *while* loop

Table 81 Java Keywords. (Continued from previous page.)

82   UNDERSTANDING NON-QUALIFIED VERSUS QUALIFIED NAMES

When you use a class from another package, you use the *import* statement to indicate what class you are referring to, or you may refer to any member of the class by using its full directory path, that is, its *fully qualified name*. A fully qualified name is composed of three parts: the package name, the class name, and the field name. Table 82 shows you how to combine these components to create several qualified names:

Package name	Class name	Field name	=	Qualified name
java.io.	InputStream.	close		java.io.InputStream.close
java.awt.	List.	addItem		java.awt.List.addItem
java.net.	URL.	getFile		java.net.URL.getFile
java.util.	Stack.	pop		java.util.Stack.pop

Table 82 Examples of fully qualified names.

If you or your company develops your own package, you may define your own package names. Sun recommends that you use your company's Internet domain name written in reverse order as your package name prefix. For example, if your domain name is *www.mycompany.com*, your package name prefix would be *COM.mycompany*. Assuming that you have written a new 3-D graphics class, you may come up with a fully qualified name for a particular method such as *COM.mycompany.firstpackage.3Dgraphics.drawBox*. If you decide to use your new method in a program, you may invoke it by using the qualified name, as follows:

```
COM.mycompany.firstpackage.3Dgraphics.drawBox(boxCoordinates);
```

However, as you have learned, the *import* statement lets you eliminate the package name, thereby providing you the option to use unqualified class names:

```
import COM.mycompany.firstpackage;

// some intermediate code
3Dgraphics.drawBox(boxCoordinates);
```

AMBIGUOUS NAME REFERENCES CAUSE COMPILE ERRORS 83

When you use *import* statements, you can refer to individual classes directly by their class name, without spelling out the entire qualified name. However, when you import many different packages (especially from a variety of vendors), you increase the chances that two or more classes will have the same name—which will result in an error. In such cases, your solution is to use the fully qualified names for each of the ambiguous classes. For example, assume that your company creates a package with a class called *Date*. If you import that class along with the *java.util.Date* class, your program will have to use fully qualified names for references to either *Date* class:

```
import COM.mycompany.test;
import java.util.*;

// intermediate statements go here
java.util.Date today = new java.util.Date();
COM.mycompany.test.Date today2 = new COM.mycompany.test.Date();
```

ADDING COMMENTS TO YOUR PROGRAM 84

As a rule, each time you create a program you need to ensure that you include comments throughout the program to explain the processing the program performs. The Java compiler ignores comments; thus, comments have no effect on your applet's code. However, your comments are very useful to another programmer who needs to work on your program and expand its capability (or to yourself should you need to modify the code several weeks or months after you last worked on it). Also, properly commented Java classes are more likely to be correctly used by other developers. Java currently provides three ways in which you can add comments to your code. To start, you can comment over several lines by using the /* and */ pair of characters, as shown:

```
/*
This comment covers several lines in the program file. The Java
compiler will completely ignore the contents within these lines.
Use this style of comments when you need to use several lines in
the file for documentation.
*/
```

You can also use the double slash (//) to comment your code. The double slash directs the compiler to consider everything to the right of the slashes (on that same line) as a comment. Programmers often use this approach to comment individual lines of code, as shown:

```
int fontsize = 30;    // sets the title font size
int fontsize_2 = 20;  // sets the label font size
```

The general technique behind commenting code is not to state the obvious, but to explain how, why, and what. In the previous example, the double-slash comments add meaning to statements which would otherwise cost a programmer several minutes to determine.

Finally, within a Java program, you can use a special comment notation that starts with /** and ends with */ to generate automatic documentation with the *javadoc* utility. You can also use the *javadoc* program to produce HTML files from your program file.

85 Using Comments to Exclude Program Statements

As you develop more complex code, you may find it necessary to temporarily exclude lines of code that may have become obsolete or that you need only for debugging. The best way to disable code without deleting the statements from your program is to use the double slashes to "comment out" individual lines. For example, the following statements comment out the first *fontsize* declaration and assignment:

```
//int fontsize = 30; // set the title font size
int fontsize = 40; // set the title font size—new version
```

In this case, the first statement appears to have two comments. As it turns out, Java lets you place one set of comment slashes to the left of a second set, as shown.

Within your programs, there may be times when you want to comment out several consecutive lines of code. In such cases, you can use the /* and */ pair to comment out several large blocks of code. If your applet uses the /* and */ comment characters, you need to be more careful about embedded comments. Specifically, Java allows the double slash comments within the /* and */ pair but does not allow another pair of /* and */ comment characters. For example, the following comments with embedded double slashes are legal:

```
/*
Save this old line of code when we test for the 13" monitors
// int fontsize = 30; // set the title font size
*/
```

However, the following embedded comments are not legal:

```
/*
Save this old line of code when we test for the 13" monitors
// int fontsize = 30; /* set the title font size */
*/
```

86 Understanding Variables (Identifiers)

To perform useful work, programs must store information, not only within a file such as a document that you edit over multiple computer sessions, but also internally. As you know, each time you run a program, the operating system loads your program's instructions into the computer's memory. As the program runs, it stores values in memory locations. For example, assume that you have a program that prints a document. Each time you run the program, it displays a message asking you the name of the file, as well as the number of copies you want to print. As you type in this information, the program stores the values you enter in specific memory locations. To help your program track the memory locations in which it has placed data, each memory location has a unique *address*, such as location 0, 1, 2, 3, and so on. Because there can be millions of such addresses, you can guess that keeping track of the individual storage locations can become very difficult. To simplify the storage of information, programs define *variables*, which are simply names that the program associates with specific locations in memory. As the word *variable* implies, the value that the program stores in these locations can change or vary throughout the program's lifetime.

Each variable has a specific *type*, which tells the computer how much memory the data requires and the operations that can be performed on the data. Given the previous example, the program might use a variable named *filename* (that stores the name of the file you want to print) and one named *count* (that stores the number of copies you want to print). Within your program, you reference variables by name. Therefore, you should assign meaningful names to each variable. Within your Java programs, you can declare your variables at the beginning of any block. Typically, you declare variables at the beginning of a class or method, as shown:

```
public void init()
  {
    String filename;      // filename to print
    int count;            // number of copies to print

    // Other program statements go here
  }
```

NAMING RULES FOR JAVA IDENTIFIERS

 87

Each variable your program uses must have a unique name. To name a variable within a Java program, you must declare the variable by specifying the variable's type followed by the variable's name. The following statements illustrate several variable declarations:

```
short disk_track_number;
double radio_frequency;
int width, height;          // declares two int variablesfloat
pressure_in_psi = 32.361;   // initializing the variable
```

When you name a variable within a Java program, you must not use any reserved Java keywords. See Java Tip 81 for a list of Java keywords. Java variable names are essentially unlimited in length and case is significant (Java considers upper and lowercase letters as different). You must begin your variable name with a letter after which it can contain both letters and digits. A letter is defined as any of the characters 'A' to 'Z', 'a' to 'z', '_', '$', and any Unicode character that is a letter in a language. A digit is defined as '0' to '9' and any Unicode character that denotes a digit. You cannot use symbols like '©' or '+' inside your variable names.

GOOD NAMING PRACTICES

 88

When you declare variables in your programs, you should choose meaningful variable names that describe the variable's use. Because Java encourages the reuse of classes, you will frequently include classes written by other programmers. Likewise, your classes may find their way to other programmers. Should anyone need to study the original source code, or need to enhance its capabilities, well-named variables will make the program's flow easier to follow.

Programmers follow several techniques when naming variables. Some use the underscore character to separate words within a variable name, for example, *file_name_length*. Other programmers like to capitalize the individual words, as in *FileNameLength*. Windows programmers use a technique known as *Hungarian notation* which involves the use of a prefix code to indicate variable type. For example, the name of a file stored in a zero-terminated string (*sz*) would be named *szFileName*. Table 88 shows several Hungarian prefixes. Whatever technique you choose, make sure that you use it consistently.

Prefix	Data Type
c	char
by	byte
n	short or int
i	int
b	boolean
w	4 byte int (word)
l	long
s	string

Table 88 Hungarian notation.

89 COMMENT VARIABLES AT DECLARATION

Even though you may have explicitly named your variables so they describe their purpose within the program, you should always add a comment that follows the variable's declaration. You will find that you can effectively document the purpose of a variable within a short sentence. Remember, other programmers may need to work on your code and, thus, need to understand each variable's use. In addition, if you should come back to your own code several months later, you will appreciate the value of good documentation. The following statements illustrate how you should use the double slash method for commenting variables:

```
int ButtonCount;   // Number of buttons along window bottom
Image Background;  // Background image set by user preference
boolean AutoSave;  // Set from bit 6 in file attributes flag
```

90 UNDERSTANDING BINARY NUMBERS

Everyone is familiar with the base 10 number system, which is the numbers 0, 1, 2, 3, 4, 5, 6, 7, 8, and 9. Along with the base 10 system is a system of rules on how to add, subtract, multiply, and divide numbers within the same system. In all probability, it was based on the fact that humans have 10 fingers and toes. In contrast, computers only have two states, 0 and 1, so a new set of rules was developed to add, subtract, multiply, and divide using these two numbers.

When you write Java code, you will generally not be required to work with binary numbers. However, in some cases, you may have to brush up on your binary arithmetic. For example, you may need to work with binary numbers if you are using the bitwise operators, such as & or |.

A binary number is arranged in a set of bits. 8 bits is known as a *byte*, and each bit within the byte has a numeric value based upon its position in the byte. For example, the byte "00110001" has three bits which are 1. For those bits, you would add the values 2^5 plus 2^4 plus 2^0, or 32 + 16 + 1, or 49, as shown in the following example:

0	0	1	1	0	0	0	1
2^7	2^6	2^5	2^4	2^3	2^2	2^1	2^0

In Java, many variable types such as *int*, *char*, *short*, *long*, *float*, and *double* are larger than a single byte. The same rules for binary arithmetic apply to those types as well. The only difference is that many more bits represent the value.

ASSIGNING A VALUE TO A VARIABLE 91

A variable is a name that your program associates with a storage location in memory. After you declare a variable within your program, you can assign it a value. In the Java language, you assign a value to a variable using the equal sign (called the *assignment operator*). The following statements show how several variables are assigned values:

```
// the following assigns the graphics context
g = getGraphics();


// the following assigns several window variables
window_height = 50; // maximum height of main window
window_width = 100; // maximum width of main window
```

You may assign values to variables within any program block after the program has declared the variable (or at the same time as it is declared).

UNDERSTANDING JAVA PRIMITIVE DATA TYPES 92

When you declare variables within your programs, you must tell the Java compiler the variable's name and type. Java is a strongly typed language, meaning every variable must have a declared type. A type defines the set of values that the variable can store, as well as the set of operations the applet can perform on the data. Java supports eight primitive types.

Integer types are used for numbers without fractional parts. The four integer types each store a different range of values:

Type name	Size	Range
long	8 bytes	-9,223,372,036,854,775,808L to 9,223,372,036,854,775,807L
int	4 bytes	-2,147,483,648 to 2,147,483,647
short	2 bytes	-32,768 to 32,767
byte	1 byte	-128 to 127

The two floating-point types store numbers with fractional parts:

Type name	Size	Range
double	8 bytes	±1.79769313486231570E+308 (15 significant digits)
float	4 bytes	±3.40282347E+38 (7 significant digits)

The *char* type stores alphanumeric and Unicode characters:

Type name	Size	Range
char	2 bytes	65,536 possible characters

The boolean type is used in logical testing:

Type name	Size	Values
boolean	1 bit	*true* or *false*

93 DECLARING MULTIPLE VARIABLES OF THE SAME TYPE

When you declare a variable within your program, you must tell the Java compiler the variable's name and type. The following statements declare three variables of type *int* and two of type *boolean*:

```
int age;
int weight;
int height;
boolean smokes;
boolean exercises;
```

When you declare variables of the same type, Java lets you list the variable names on one or more lines, with each variable name separated by commas, as shown:

```
int age, weight, height;
boolean smokes, exercises;
```

94 ASSIGNING VALUES TO VARIABLES AT DECLARATION

After you declare a variable within your program (specify the variable's type and name), you can use the Java assignment operator (the equal sign =) to assign a value to the variable. As it turns out, Java lets you assign a value to a variable within the variable's declaration. Programmers refer to the process of assigning a variable's first value as *initializing* the variable. For example, the following statements declare and initialize several variables:

```
// set the user's age, weight in lbs, and height in inches
int age = 21;
int weight = 150;
int height = 69;


// the following assigns a font variable
Font font = new Font("TimesRoman", Font.BOLD, 20);
```

95 UNDERSTANDING JAVA LITERALS

Literals correspond to a specific value in your Java program. For example, if you type the number 7 (the literal number 7) in a Java program, Java will treat the value as an *int* type. If you use the character *x* within single quotes ('x'), Java will treat it as a *char* type. Likewise, if you place the literal *x* within double quotes ("x"), Java will treat it as a *String*. Depending on the literal you are using, Java provides special rules for hexadecimal, octals, characters, strings, and boolean values. As you will learn, you can force a literal to be a certain type. For example, Java will treat the number 1 as an *int*. But you can force Java to treat the value as the type *long* by appending the L character to the literal number: 1L.

USING HEXADECIMAL OR OCTAL INTEGER LITERALS 96

Integer literals come in several forms. If you type the value **16** in your program, Java will treat it as an *int*. However, because the number 16 can fit within a type *byte* or *short*, you can force Java to treat it as a type other than *int* by appending a special character to the value. If your number is larger than what an *int* can hold, Java automatically assumes that it is a type *long*, as shown.

```
x1 = 16;            // Compiler assumes 16 is an int
x2 = 16L;           // Code forces compiler to treat 16 as a long
x3 = 3000000000;  // Compiler assumes 3000000000 is a long
```

Within an applet, you can express literal integer values as a hexadecimal or an octal number. To specify a hexadecimal number, precede the value with a leading *0x*. To specify an octal number, precede the value with a leading *0*. The following assignment statements illustrate the use of octal and hexadecimal literal values:

```
int my_octal = 0007;   // assigns an int an octal value
int my_hex = 0x000A;   // assigns an int a hex value
```

UNDERSTANDING SIGNED VALUES 97

Because most variables in Java are *signed* (except for boolean and char), you should understand the fundamentals behind a signed number. A single byte can represent an unsigned number from decimal 0 (binary 00000000) to 255 (binary 11111111). In this case, the unsigned number can only be a positive value.

With a signed value, on the other hand, a byte's leftmost bit (bit number 7) indicates the value's sign, where 0 represents a positive value and 1 negative value. For a signed byte value, positive numbers may range from 0 (binary 00000000) to +127 (binary 01111111) and negative signed numbers may range from -1 (binary 11111111) to -128 (binary 10000000).

You can convert from a positive number to a negative number (and vice versa) by using a technique known as taking the number's two's complement. To determine the number's two's complement, simply invert the bits (that is, convert the value's 1 bits to 0's and 0 bits to 1's) and then add a 1. For example, to convert a positive 1 (binary 00000001) to a negative 1, follow these steps:

1. Invert the bits: 00000001 becomes 11111110

2. Add one: 11111110 plus 1 equals 11111111

As you have discovered, the binary equivalent of -1 is 11111111, also known as the two's complement of 00000001. In Java, many variable types, such as *int, char, short, long, float,* and *double* are larger than a single byte. In those cases, the same rules for signed values apply.

UNDERSTANDING OVERFLOW 98

When you choose your variables, you must not only choose the appropriate type of variable (floating point or integer, for example), but you must also decide on how many digits you need to hold your value (the maximum or minimum value the variable will hold). *Overflow* occurs when you perform an arithmetic operation that results in a number that is too big or too small for your variable to hold. When overflow occurs, Java will truncate the value and your program will produce incorrect results. For example, consider the following integer types:

Type name	Size	Range
long	8 bytes	-9,223,372,036,854,775,808L to 9,223,372,036,854,775,807L
int	4 bytes	-2,147,483,648 to 2,147,483,647
short	2 bytes	-32,768 to 32,767
byte	1 byte	-128 to 127

Table 98 The range of integer types.

If you have determined that your integer variable will never hold a number larger than 1,000, you should consider using a *short*. As you can see in Table 98, to store a value of 1,000 or less, you can actually use any of the integer types, except for *byte*, which only hold positive numbers up to 127. However, by choosing the type that "best fits" the variable's value, you improve your applet's performance and memory use.

99 USING FLOATING-POINT LITERALS

A floating-point literal value is a number such as 3.1415 or 1001.3333. When you use floating-point literals within your applet, Java stores the values as the type *double*. If, however, your applet does not require double precision for the value (in other words, single precision is accurate enough) you can direct the compiler to treat the value as type *float* instead of a *double* by appending *f* or *F* to the value. For example, the following statement directs the compiler to treat the literal 3.1415f as a single-precision floating-point value:

```
if (3.1415f == pi_float)
   // Other statements here
```

100 USING DOUBLE LITERALS

As you learned in tip 99, by appending an *f* or *F* to a floating-point literal value, you can direct the Java compiler to treat the literal value as type *float*. In a similar way, by appending *d* or *D* to a floating-point literal value, you direct the compiler to store the literal as type *double*. By appending the *d* or *D* to a literal value in this way, you ensure that the compiler and other programmers who are reading your code understand that your applet is treating the literal as type *double*. For example, the following statement directs the compiler to treat the value 91D as type double:

```
scaled_magnification= 91D * factor;
   // Other statements here
```

101 USING CHARACTER LITERALS

You may express character literals by enclosing a single character within single quotes. Java stores literal characters as 2 byte Unicode characters (using two bytes per character lets Java easily represent the character sets of all languages worldwide), as shown in the following statement:

```
my_char= 'a';
```

Within a Java applet, you may use character literals to represent special escape codes such as a formfeed or newline character. In addition, character literals can specify non-printable characters, as well as Unicode characters. Turn to Tip 117 (Understanding Escape Sequences for Character and String Literals) for more information on using character literals in this way.

USING STRING LITERALS

 102

A *String* literal is a combination of characters enclosed by double quotes. Unlike strings in C or C++, Java strings are class objects containing methods that let you compare and test the string. To declare a string, you use the *String* type. For example, the following statement declares a *String* object named *city* and assigns the object the *String* literal "San Diego":

```
String  city = "San Diego";
```

You may use the concatenation operator, +, to join two strings together. For example, the following statements use the concatenation operator to assign a city and state to the *String* object *location*:

```
String comma = ", ";
String state = "California";
String location = city + comma + state;
```

In this case, the string *location* will contain the value "San Diego, California." You can also use the concatenation operator for non-string objects, such as a numeric value, for which Java will automatically convert the value to a string:

```
String address = location + " " + 92128;
```

In this case, the statement will assign the string *address* the value "San Diego, California 92128." The *String* class provides you with many useful methods to operate on strings. For more examples of the *String* class, refer to the *String's* section of this book.

UNDERSTANDING THE PRIMITIVE TYPE BYTE

 103

A *byte* is a primitive Java data type that uses eight bits to represent a number ranging from -128 to 127. The following statements declare two *byte* variables. The first variable, *flag_bits*, can store one value. The second byte variable, *data_table*, is an array, capable of holding four values. In this case, the Java compiler will preassign the array elements using the values specified between the left and right braces:

```
byte flag_bits;
byte data_table = { 32, 16, 8, 4 };   // Creates an array
```

UNDERSTANDING THE PRIMITIVE TYPE SHORT

 104

The type *short* is a primitive Java data type that uses two bytes to represent a number in the range -32768 to 32767. The Java type *short* is identical to the two-byte type *int* in many C/C++ compilers. The following statements declare two variables of type *short*:

```
short age;
short height, width;
```

105 UNDERSTANDING THE PRIMITIVE TYPE INT

The type *int* is a primitive Java data type that uses four bytes to represent whole numbers in the range from -2,147,483,648 to 2,147,483,647. If you are porting (migrating) C++ code to Java, you need to be aware that Java uses four bytes to represent an *int*, whereas many C++ compilers use only two bytes (which would be equivalent to a Java *short*). The following statements declare two variables of type *int*:

```
int dollar_sales;
int max_memory = 250000;
```

106 BEWARE OF OVERFLOWING INTEGERS

When your applet uses integer variables, you need to be aware of overflow errors which occur when the applet tries to assign a larger (or smaller) value than the variable can hold. When overflow occurs, you will be unaware of the error. In other words, an overflow error is a silent logic error (a bug). To avoid overflow errors, you must ensure that you select an integer type that is large enough to hold all conceivable values that your program may generate for a given variable. The following Java program, *OverflowDemo.java*, illustrates overflow errors:

```
class OverflowDemo
  {
    public static void main(String argv[])
      {
        short a = 20000;
        short b = 30000;
        short result = a;

        result += b;

        System.out.println("Result is: " + result);
      }
  }
```

When you compile and later execute this program, your screen will display the following output:

```
C:\> java OverflowDemo <ENTER>
Result is -15536
```

As you can see, because of overflow, the results of the arithmetic operations are not what you would expect.

107 UNDERSTANDING THE PRIMITIVE TYPE LONG

The type *long* is a primitive Java data type that uses eight bytes to represent whole numbers in the range from -9,223,372,036,854,775,808 to 9,223,372,036,854,775,807. If you are porting (migrating) code from C++ to Java, it is important to note that Java uses eight bytes to represent the type *long*, whereas most C++ compilers use only four. The following statement declares a variable of type *long* named *atom_count*:

```
long atom_count;
```

UNDERSTANDING THE PRIMITIVE TYPE FLOAT

The type *float* is a primitive Java data type that uses four bytes to represent a single-precision floating-point number in the range ±3.40282347E+38 to ±1.40239846E-45. The type *float* provides seven significant digits. The class *java.lang.Float* defines these minimum and maximum limits as constants. The following statement declares a variable named *intensity_percentage* of type *float*:

```
float  intensity_percentage;
```

UNDERSTANDING THE PRIMITIVE TYPE DOUBLE

The type *double* is a primitive Java data type that uses eight bytes to represent a number in the range ±1.79769313486231570E+308 to ±4.94065645841246544E-324. The type *double* provides 14 significant digits. The class *java.lang.Double* defines these minimum and maximum limits as the constants *java.lang.Double.MAX_VALUE* and *java.lang.Double.MIN_VALUE*. The following statement defines a variable of type *double* named *stellar_distance*:

```
double  stellar_distance;
```

UNDERSTANDING PRECISION

When you use floating point numbers within a Java applet, you need to be aware of how much precision (numeric accuracy) a given variable can provide. Precision refers to the number of accurate decimal digits a floating-point type can provide. The *float* type only has seven digits of precision (also known as single precision). The type *float's* seven digits of accuracy may be enough to represent the price of a new car, but may not be enough to represent precise numbers such as 1.23456789. The type *double* can represent fourteen significant digits. You should use the type *double* when you need precise floating-point values. Table 110 summarizes floating point precision and the range of values that the variable may hold:

Type name	Precision	Range
double	15 digits	±1.79769313486231570E+308
float	7 digits	±3.40282347E+38

Table 110 The range of values the types **float** *and* **double** *can store.*

UNDERSTANDING THE PRIMITIVE TYPE CHAR

The type *char* is a primitive Java data type that uses two bytes to store a Unicode character. Unlike the *String* type, you represent character literals within single quotes. For example, the following statement declares a variable of type *char* named *alpha*:

```
char alpha = 'A';
```

Java uses two bytes for type *char* to support multiple languages. You can express them by using the '\u' escape sequence followed by a two-byte character code. For example, the following statement assigns a Unicode character to the variable *unialpha*:

```
char unicode_unialpha = '\u0041';
```

112 UNICODE IN JAVA

The Unicode two-byte character code supports the diverse set of characters that make up the written text of the world's languages. In Java, the two-byte *char* type supports Unicode characters. Within a Java applet, you express Unicode characters using the '\u' escape code and values in the range '\u0000' to '\u00FF' which is identical to the standard ASCII/ANSI character code that you are already familiar with.

Fortunately, you will not need to make any changes to the way you code characters. You only need to be aware that a character occupies two bytes. If you need to give your Java program the ability to display output in other languages, the Unicode standard is already in place to provide built-in support. The only shortcoming today is the poor availability of fonts that can display all the characters that Unicode provides.

113 UNDERSTANDING THE PRIMITIVE TYPE BOOLEAN

The type *boolean* stores a true or false value. The *boolean* type only requires 1 bit and you cannot cast a boolean value to any other type. Because a *boolean* variable is only 1 bit, you cannot assign a boolean the value of 0 or 1 as you can in C or C++. In addition, all tests that require a *boolean* must ultimately result in a test against *true* or *false*. The following statements illustrate how you can convert values between *boolean* and *int* variables:

```
int i;
boolean b;


b = (i != 0);      // converts an int value to a boolean value
i = (b) ? 1 : 0; // converts a boolean value to an int value
```

114 ASSIGNING INITIAL VALUES DURING A VARIABLE'S DECLARATION

When you declare a variable, you may also assign the variable an initial value, as shown in the following statements:

```
boolean first_time = true;
char init_char = 'A';
float nominal_temperature = 98.6;
```

However, if you do not initialize your variables, Java guarantees that the compiler will automatically assign a default value. Table 114 lists the defaults for the various primitive data types:

Type	Default value
boolean	false
char	\u0000

Table 114 *Default initial values for variables. (Continued on following page.)*

Type	Default value
byte	0
short	0
int	0
long	0
float	0.0
double	0.0

Table 114 Default initial values for variables. (Continued from previous page.)

WHEN YOU DO NOT NEED TO CAST PRIMITIVE TYPES

 115

Casting a value is the process of converting a value of one type to a value of another type. Generally, you do not need to use any explicit casting notation when you assign a smaller type primitive to a larger type primitive. For example, the following statement assigns a *byte* value (which ranges from -128 to 127) to a *short* value (which ranges from -32768 to 32767) without the need of a cast:

```
short some_short;
byte some_byte = 100;


some_short = some_byte; // Java automatically casts for you
```

The following summarizes some of the assignments which do not require an explicit cast in Java. A type may be assigned to any of the types to the right of it. For example, *long* may be assigned to *int*, *short*, or *byte*.

```
double <- float <- long <- int <- short <- byte
```

HOW TO CAST PRIMITIVE TYPES

 116

As discussed in Tip 115, *casting* is the process assigning a value of one type to a value of another type. When you assign a larger type to a smaller type (such as assigning a value of type *double* to a value of type *float*), you must perform an explicit cast since this form of assignment may result in loss of precision. By performing an explicit cast, you inform the Java compiler that you intend to convert the number (and accept the consequences of any lost precision). The general form of a cast is:

```
(typename) value_to_cast
```

To perform an explicit cast, you simply group the type of the target variable within parenthesis such as (float). For example, the following statements cast a value of type *double* to a value of type *float*:

```
float result;
double starting_value = 0.123456789;

result = (float) starting_value;
```

117 ESCAPE SEQUENCES IN CHARACTER AND STRING LITERALS

Within a Java applet, you use escape sequences to represent special characters such as a carriage-return or linefeed, as well as the non-printable characters such as a bell and characters from the Unicode character set. Table 117 lists the escape sequences you can assign to variables of type *char*, *String*, and within character and string literals.

Escape	Meaning
\b	Backspace
\n	Newline
\t	Tab
\r	Carriage return
\f	Formfeed
\\	Backslash
\'	Single quote
\"	Double quote
\ddd	The character representing the octal value ddd
\udddd	Unicode character
\xdd	Hexadecimal

Table 117 Java escape sequences.

118 DISPLAYING PRIMITIVE DATA TYPES WITH SYSTEM.OUT.PRINTLN

As you develop and later debug your code, you will find it necessary to display the values of variables at different locations throughout your program. To display such values, you will find the *System.out.println* very convenient. As you have seen, the *System.out.println* function displays its output to the console window (not within a Java applet window), thereby keeping your debugging information in a separate window.

When you use the *System.out.println* function in conjunction with the concatenation operator (+), you can easily print out your variables with very little effort. Because the concatenation operator automatically converts and appends its operands to strings, you can use it within *System.out.println* to display numeric values. The following example shows how you can display a variety of primitive types using the *System.out.println* function:

```
short s = 15431;
int i = 123456;
float f = 3.14159;

System.out.println("short: " + s + "int: " + i + "float: " + f);
```

When you use *System.out.println* in this way, your applet will display the output to the console window.

BASIC JAVA MATH OPERATION

Within an applet, you use arithmetic operators to perform addition, subtraction, multiplication, and so on. Java has five basic arithmetic operators, as shown in Table 119.

Operator	Purpose	Example	
+	addition	5 + 25	
-	subtraction	23 - 7	
*	multiplication	6.3 * 3.14	
/	division	3.2 / 2.2	
%	modulus	7 % 2	// Remainder of 7 divided by 2

Table 119 *Basic arithmetic operators.*

When you use an arithmetic operator, Java will generally return a type that is big enough to hold the result. For example, if you multiply a *float* by an *int*, Java will return a value of type *float*. Most of the Java arithmetic operands behave as you would expect. The exception is the division operator. By default, if you perform a division operation using integer values, Java will return an integer result. In other words, if you divide 7 by 2, Java will return the value 3. When you perform a division operation and you want a floating-point result, you must make sure that the operands are either type *float* or *double*:

```
int result;
float answer;

result = 10 / 4;    // result is 2
answer = 10f / 4f;  // answer is 2.5
```

USING THE ASSIGNMENT OPERATORS

Assignment operators let you combine an operation with an assignment. For example, the following statement multiplies the variable *number* by five, assigning the result of the multiplication back to the variable *number*:

```
number = number * 5;
```

Using an assignment operator, you can simplify this multiplication operation, as shown:

```
number *= 5;
```

Java provides a variety of assignment operators, as summarized in Table 120:

Operator	Example	Meaning of operator
=	x= y + z;	simple assignment
+=	x+= y;	x= x + y addition
-=	x-= y;	x= x - y subtraction
/=	x/= y;	x= x / y division

Table 120 *More arithmetic operators.(Continued on following page.)*

Operator	Example	Meaning of operator	
*=	x*= y;	x= x * y	multiplication
%/	x%/ y;	x= x % y	modulus
^=	x ^= y;	x= x^ y	bitwise XOR
&=	x &= y;	x= x & y	bitwise AND
|=	x |= y;	x= x | y	bitwise OR
<<=	x <<= y;	x= x << y	left shift
>>=	x >>= y;	x= x >> y	right shift
>>>=	x >>>= y;	x= x >>> y	zero fill right shift

Table 120 More arithmetic operators. (Continued from previous page.)

121 CHAINING MULTIPLE ASSIGNMENT OPERATORS IN ONE STATEMENT

When Java encounters an arithmetic expression, Java evaluates the right-hand side of the expression first. Consequently, you can chain a series of expressions together. For example, the following statements assign the value zero to a series of variables by chaining the assignment statements:

```java
int a, b, c, d;

long x, y;

x = y = a = b = c = d = 0;
```

122 BE AWARE OF INTEGER DIVISION

By default, if you perform a division operation with integer operands, Java returns an integer result. For example, the following statements assign the result of the integer division (10/3 = 3) to the floating-point variable answer:

```java
float answer;

answer = 10 / 3;   // result is 3.0
```

To return a floating-point value from a division operation, you must make sure that the operands are type *float* or *double*:

```java
float answer;

answer = 10f / 4f;   // results in a 2.5
```

123 ARITHMETIC OPERATIONS IN VARIABLE DECLARATIONS

As you have learned, when you declare variables in Java, you can assign an initial value to the variables at the same time. As it turns out, within your assignment, you may use an arithmetic expression, as shown:

```java
float circumference = 2f * 3.14f * 3.4f;
```

In addition to using literal values within the expression, you can also use variables. For example, the following statement initializes the variable *total* to the result of the expression *circumference * 2..3*:

```
double total = circumference * 2.3;
```

UNDERSTANDING MODULO ARITHMETIC

 124

As you have learned, if you perform a division operation using integer operands, Java will return an integer result and will drop the fractional remainder. To determine the remainder of an integer division, you use the modulus operator (%). For example, the following statements illustrate the use of the integer division and modulus operator:

```
int integer_part, remainder;

integer_part = 10 / 3;   // results in a 3

remainder = 10 % 3;      // results in a 1
```

Java applets often use the modulus operator to determine if a value is odd or even. For example, if the remainder of a number modulo 2 is 0, the value is even. Likewise, if the result is 1, the value is odd.

UNDERSTANDING JAVA'S INCREMENT OPERATOR

 125

Within Java applets, you will find that a common operation is to increment, by one, the value of an integer variable. For example, you might use a variable as a loop counter, or to index elements within an array. As you know, one way to increment a value is to use the assignment statement, as shown:

```
number = number + 1;
```

Likewise, using an assignment operator, you can also increment a variable's value by one:

```
number += 1;
```

Also, like C and C++, Java provides an increment operator (++) that you can use to increase a variable's value by one. For example, the following statement uses the increment operator to add the value one to the variable *count_up*:

```
int count_up = 100;

count_up++;   // count_up is now 101
```

Java also lets you use the increment operator with floating point numbers. For example, the following statements increment the value of the floating-point variable *ratio* by one:

```
float ratio = 100.95;

ratio++;   // ratio is now 101.95
```

As you will learn in Tip 127, Java lets you precede a variable with the prefix-increment operator (++variable) or follow the variable with the postfix-increment operator (variable++). Depending on the expression within which you use the prefix and postfix operators, your choice of operators will change the expression's result.

126   UNDERSTANDING JAVA'S DECREMENT OPERATOR

Just as there are many times within an applet when you need to increment a variable by one, there are also times when you must decrement a variable's value by one. As you might guess, you can use an assignment statement similar to the following to decrement a variable's value:

```
number = number - 1;
```

Likewise, you can also use an assignment operator to decrement the variable's value:

```
number -= 1;
```

Just as Java provides an increment operator (++) which you can use to increase a variable's value by one, Java also provides a decrement operator (--). The following statement, for example, uses the decrement operator to decrease the variable *count_down's* value by one:

```
int count_down= 100;

count_down--;   // count_down is now 99
```

Java also lets you use the decrement (--) operator with floating point numbers and, as you will learn in Tip 127, Java supports a prefix-decrement operator (--variable) and a postfix-decrement operator (variable--).

127   UNDERSTANDING PRE AND POST INCREMENT/DECREMENT

As you have learned in Tips 125 and 126, Java provides increment (++) and decrement (--) operators with which you can add or subtract one from a variable's value. Java provides two versions of each operator, a prefix operator (++variable or -- variable) and a postfix operator (variable++ or variable --). The difference between the prefix and postfix operators is *when* Java increments or decrements the variable. When you use the prefix operator, Java will first increment or decrement the variable *and then* use the variable's value. For example, in the following statements, Java will first increment the *age* and then use the variable's value. Likewise, Java will first decrement the variable *years_til_retirement* and then use the variable's value:

```
int age = 35;
int years_til_retirement = 65 - age;

// Assuming it's your birthday, you increment your age and decrease
// your years til retirement

System.out.println("My age is now: " + ++age); // My age is now 36
System.out.println("I must work: " + --years_til_retirement +
    " years");                          // I must work 29 years
```

In this case, because the applet uses the prefix operators, Java first increments or decrements the corresponding variable, and then uses the variable's value.

On the other hand, if the applet uses the postfix operators (variable++ or variable --), Java will first use the variable's value and then increment or decrement the variables. The following statements illustrate the use of the postfix operators:

```
int current_value = 10
int previous_value = current_value++; // previous_value is now 10
                                       // current value is 11


int big_value = 100;
int new_value = --big_value;                // new_value is 99
                                            // big_value is 99
```

When you choose to use a prefix or postfix operator, you must first determine when you want Java to increment or decrement the variable's value. If you want Java to increment or decrement the variable's value before Java uses the variable, use the prefix operator. Otherwise, if you want Java to first use the variable's value and then increment or decrement the variable, use the postfix operator.

DISPLAYING HEXADECIMAL OR OCTAL VALUES

 128

As you work with numeric values to perform arithmetic operations, there will be times when your applets need to display the decimal equivalent of hexadecimal or octal value. Frequently, programmers display values in octal or hexadecimal when they debug their code. The easiest way to achieve this is by using the *System.out.println* function. The following *init* function illustrates the use of *System.out.println* to display a hexadecimal and an octal value as decimals:

```
public void init()
  {
     System.out.println("hex=" + 0xffff + " octal=" + 07777);
  }
```

If you place this *init* function into a Java applet and then execute the applet, your screen will display the following decimal values:

```
hex=65535  octal=4095
```

UNDERSTANDING PRECEDENCE AND ASSOCIATIVITY

 129

When you use a series of operators within a Java expression, keep in mind the order in which Java performs the operations. For example, consider the following assignment:

```
answer = 2 + 3 * 4;
```

As you may know, in Java, as in most programming languages, the multiplication operation takes precedence over addition, which is why this example yields an answer of 14, instead of 20. The term *precedence* refers to operator ordering. When Java encounters an equation with multiple operators, Java will first perform the operation with the higher precedence.

In some cases, however, all of the operators will have the same precedence. In Java, several operators share the same precedence order; for example, the operators *, /, and % have equal precedence. When an expression's operators have the same precedence, you need to use another rule called *associativity* to determine which operator must be performed before the others. Consider the following expression which contains operators that share the same precedence:

```
answer = 5 * 4 / 3 / 2;
```

For Java, multiplication and division both share the same precedence and have an associativity rule which states that Java perform the operations from left to right. Therefore, in the previous example, Java will start with 5 * 4, divide by 3 and, finally, divide by 2. If you are interested, the answer is 3. Remember, Java assumes integer division when you use integers.

Table 129 summarizes Java'a operator precedence and associativity. Those operators with the precedence of 1 are performed first. An associativity of "L" indicates that operators of the same precedence are evaluated from left to right, whereas "R" indicates that they are evaluated from right to left.

Precedence	Operator	Associativity
1	++ -- ~ !	R
	+ - (unary)	
	(type cast)	
2	* / %	L
3	+ -	L
	+ (concat)	L
4	>>>	L
	>> <<	L
5	< <= > >=	L
	instanceof	L
6	== !=	L
7	&	L
8	^	L
9	|	L
10	&&	L
11	||	L
12	?:	R
13	= *= /= %=	R
	+= -=	
	<<= >>=	
	>>>= &= ^=	
	|=	

Table 129 *Operator precedence and associativity.*

130 FORCING ORDER OF OPERATOR EVALUATION WITH PARENTHESES

As you have learned, Java uses operator precedence and associativity to determine the order in which it performs operations. Sometimes, however, the order you want Java to perform operations in does not match Java's precedence and associativity rules. In such cases, you can use parentheses to specify the order in which you want Java to perform the operations. The following statements illustrate the use of parentheses to override Java's rules of precedence:

```
answer1 = 2 + 3 * 4;     // assigns the value 14
answer2 = (2 + 3) * 4;   // assigns the value 20
```

If you place multiple operations within your parenthesis, say *(4 + 2 * 5)*, Java will use its rules of precedence and associativity within the parenthesis to determine the order in which it performs operations.

UNDERSTANDING THE BITWISE OR OPERATOR

131

The bitwise OR operator (|) works on any of Java's integer types and performs a logical OR on the bits that make up the values. A logical OR returns a one at each bit position when either of the two values have one in the same bit position. If both bits are zero, the operator returns a zero. The following statements illustrate the use of a logical OR operation:

```
int source_bits = 6; // binary 00000000 00000000 00000000 00000110
int flag_bits = 4;   // binary 00000000 00000000 00000000 00000100
int answer = (source_bits | flag_bits);   // 0000 . . .     00000110
```

You can also use the bitwise OR operator with *boolean* types and with conditional expressions, such as *if (boolean_a | boolean_b)*. For *boolean* values, the bitwise OR operator fully evaluates both operands, even if the result of the condition may already be known after evaluating the left-hand operand (if the left-hand side is true, the condition is true). This "side-effect" is important to understand because in some cases you may need to ensure that Java evaluates the right-hand side of the operation—the right-hand *boolean* may be the result of a function Java must call. If you do not want Java to "needlessly evaluate" the right-hand operand, you should use the logical OR operator (||) instead. When the logical OR operator knows the condition is true (after evaluating the left-hand condition), the logical OR operator directs Java to "short circuit" the condition, skipping the operation on its right-hand side.

UNDERSTANDING THE BITWISE AND OPERATOR

132

The bitwise AND operator (&) works on any of Java's integer types and performs a logical AND on the bits that make up the values. A logical AND operator returns a one at each bit position for which the two values both have a one in the same bit position. If either of the two values has a zero in the bit position, the logical AND operator returns the value zero. For example, the following statements perform a logical AND on two integer values:

```
int source_bits = 6; // binary 00000000 00000000 00000000 00000110
int test_bits = 4;   // binary 00000000 00000000 00000000 00000100
int result = (source_bits & test_bits);   // 000 . . .     00000100
```

You can also use the bitwise AND operator with *boolean* types and with a conditional expression, such as *if (boolean_a & boolean_b)*. For *boolean* values, the bitwise AND operator fully evaluates both operands, even if the result of the condition may already be known after evaluating the left-hand operand (if the left-hand side is false, the condition is false). This "side-effect" is important to understand because in some cases you may need to ensure that Java evaluates the right-hand side of the operation—the right-hand *boolean* may be the result of a function Java must call. If you do not want Java to "needlessly evaluate" the right-hand operand, you should use the logical AND operator (&) instead. When the logical AND operator knows the condition is false (after evaluating the left-hand condition), the logical AND operator directs Java to "short circuit" the condition, skipping the operation on its right-hand side.

UNDERSTANDING THE BITWISE EXCLUSIVE XOR OPERATOR

133

The bitwise XOR operator (^) works on any of Java's integer types and performs a logical XOR on the bits that make up the values. A logical XOR returns a one at each bit position when the two values have opposite values in the same bit position. For example, the following statements perform a logical XOR on two integers:

```
int source_bits = 7;  // binary 00000000 00000000 00000000 00000111
int test_bits = 4;    // binary 00000000 00000000 00000000 00000100
int result = (source_bits ^ test_bits);    // 000 . . .    00000011
```

134 UNDERSTANDING THE BITWISE INVERSE OPERATOR

The bitwise NOT operator (~) works on any of Java's integer types and inverts the bits that make up a value. In other words, the bitwise NOT inverts the bit value of one to zero and vice versa. The following illustration demonstrates a bitwise NOT operation:

```
0 0 0 0 0 1 1 0    The original value

1 1 1 1 1 0 0 1    The new value after the bitwise NOT operator
```

In Java, you use the bitwise NOT operator as follows:

```
new_value = (~ original_value);
```

135 PERFORMING A BITWISE SHIFT

When you work with the bits that make up a number, there are many operations that require you to shift the bit values to the right or to the left. In Java, you can perform a left bitwise shift by using the << operator, or a right bitwise shift by using the >> operator. Unlike the inconsistencies found in some implementations of C/C++, Java always preserves the sign bit (the leftmost bit) after performing the right bitwise shift. *Arithmetic shift* or *sign-extension* are terms used to describe bit-shift operations that preserve the sign bit. The following statements shift a value two bits to the left and then two bits to the right, using Java's bitwise shift operators:

```
int original = -3;
int left_shift = original << 2;
int right_shift = left_shift >> 2;
System.out.println(original + " " + left_shift + " " + right_shift);
```

This code fragment will produce the following results:

```
-3  -12  -3
```

Note that Java automatically keeps track of the integer value's leftmost bit, which stores the number's sign. If Java did not preserve the sign bit, the previous statements would not have resulted in the original value of -3 three because the negative sign bit would have been lost. To shift a variable's value "in-place," you can use shift and assignment operators, as shown here:

```
left_shift >>= 2;
```

136 USING THE >>> OPERATOR

The >>> operator does a right shift just like the >> operator. The one difference is that the >>> operator does not preserve the left-most sign bit. In other words, the operator always sets the leftmost bit to zero. In contrast, the >> operator shifts one bit into the leftmost value for negative numbers, thereby keeping the number negative. You normally use the >>> operator when your operand does not represent a signed quantity, but instead, a bit mask of some type for which you don't care about the operand's sign bit. The following example uses the >>> operator to shift the value 256 two bits to the right, yielding 64, as shown:

```
int bit_mask = 256;            // 1000000
int answer = bit_mask >>> 2;   // 0010000 or the value 64
```

To shift a variable's value "in-place," you can use shift and assignment operators, as shown:

```
bit_mask >>>= 2;
```

BEWARE OF THE >>> ANOMALY WITH SHORT AND BYTE TYPES 137

The >>> shift operator does not work properly for *short* and *byte* values. As you learned in Tip 136, the >>> operator shifts bits to the right by filling the leftmost bit with a zero (even if the value had a sign bit of one). Unfortunately, Java promotes the types *short* and *byte* to *ints* before the shift takes place. This means that the *byte* you thought was only 8 bits long is actually 32 bits long as far as the shift operator is concerned. For example, consider shifting a *byte* value of -1 by 10, as shown:

```
byte byte_value = -1;
byte_value >>>= 10;
```

You would expect that shifting a *byte* (containing 8 bits) by 10 bits to the right would "empty out" the byte, yielding a zero. However, because Java promotes *byte_value* to an *int* before it performs the shift, the operation actually shifts 10 bits of a 32-bit number. And even worse, Java truncates that 32-bit number back to an 8-bit byte. For this example, a 32-bit value of -1 shifted 10 places produces a *byte* result of -1!

TESTING A CONDITION WITH THE IF STATEMENT 138

As your applets become more complex, they will need to make decisions based on specific conditions and then execute the proper statements accordingly. To make such decisions, your applets use the *if* statement. In short, an applet uses the *if* statement to test a condition. If the condition is true, the applet will execute a statement (or block of related statements). On the other hand, if the condition is false, the applet may execute a different set of statements as specified by an *else* clause. The basic form of an *if* statement is as follows:

```
if (condition)
  {
     // True statements here
  }
```

For example, the following statements use an *if* statement to test if the variable *rpm* contains a value that is greater than 9000. If the variable contains a value greater than 9000, the *if* statement's condition evaluates as true, and the applet will perform the statements that follow. In this case, if the variable *rpm* contains a value such as 12000, the condition evaluates as true and the applet will assign the variable *overload* the value true and then display a message to the system console warning the user that the engine is about to overheat:

```
if (rpm > 9000)    // this is the conditional test
  {
```

```
    overload = true;
    System.out.println("Warning! Engine is about to overheat!\n");
}
```

Should the condition evaluate as false, the applet will continue its execution at the statement that follows the *if* statement. In Tip 141, you will learn how to use an *else* clause with an *if* statement to direct your applet to perform an alternate set of statements when the condition evaluates to false.

139 TESTING FOR EQUALITY

As your programs become more complex, they will compare a variable's value to known conditions and then execute the proper statements accordingly. The *if* statement is one way your programs can make such decisions. The format of the *if* statement is as follows:

```
if (condition)
    statement;
```

Most *if* statements will test if a variable's value is equal to a specific value. For example, the following *if* statement tests whether the variable *age* contains the value 21:

```
if (age == 21)
    statement;
```

Java uses the double equal signs (==) in tests for equality. When you write tests for equality, make sure you use double equal signs (==), as opposed to the single equal sign (=) that Java uses for an assignment.

Just as there are times when your programs test for equality, there will also be times when they must test whether two values are unequal. Java uses the symbol != to test inequality. The following statement tests whether the variable *age* is not equal to 21:

```
if (age != 21)
    statement;
```

140 PERFORMING RELATIONAL TESTS (> < >= <=)

As your programs become more complex, you may need to test whether a value is greater than, less than, greater than or equal to, or less than or equal to another. To perform such tests, Java provides you with a set of relational operators, as shown in Table 140.

Operator	Function
>	Greater-than operator
<	Less-than operator
>=	Greater-than-or-equal-to operator
<=	Less-than-or-equal-to operator

Table 140 Java relational operators.

TESTING A CONDITION WITH IF-ELSE

141

As your programs become more complex, there will be times when the program must perform one set of instructions if one condition is true and, possibly, other instructions for another. For example, your program might have different instructions for different age groups. When a program performs (or does not perform) instructions based on a specific condition, the program is performing *conditional processing*. To perform conditional processing, the program evaluates a condition that results in a true or false. For example, the condition *age is 25* is true or false. One of the statements that Java provides to help your programs perform conditional processing is the *if-else* statement. The *if-else* statement has this format:

```
if (condition)
  {
    // Statement block1
  }
else
  {
    // Statement block2
  }
```

If the *boolean* condition that follows the *if* keyword is true, Java performs the statements that immediately follow. If the condition is false, Java performs the statements that follow the *else* keyword. The following example illustrates the use of the *if-else* statement:

```
if (age == 21)
    System.out.println("Cool—no more getting carded.\n");
else
    System.out.println("Oh, I wish I was 21—don't you\n");
```

TESTING MULTIPLE CONDITIONS WITH ELSE-IF

142

When your program performs a series of conditional tests, you may find that you need to test against several criteria. For example, your program may test for several age groups and execute a series of statements based on a specific age. To test multiple conditions, your programs use the *else-if* clause within an *if-else* statement, as shown:

```
if (age <= 18)
   age_group = kids;
else if ((age > 18) && (age < 65))
   age_group = adults;
else if (age >= 65)
   age_group = elderly;
```

BEWARE OF THE IF-IF-ELSE STATEMENT

143

When your program uses *if-else* statements, a sneaky logic error can cause you much frustration if you don't keep track of which *else* statement corresponds to which *if*. For example, consider the following code fragment:

```
test_score = 100;
current_grade = 'B';

if (test_score >= 90)
  if (current_grade == 'A')
    System.out.println("Another A for an A student\n");
else
  System.out.println("Should have worked harder\n");
```

The first *if* statement tests whether the student's test score was greater than or equal to 90. If so, a second *if* statement tests whether the student already has an A grade and, if so, prints a message. Based upon the indentation, you would expect the *else* statement to display its message when the score was less than 90. Unfortunately, that's not how this program works. When you place an *else* statement within your program, Java associates the *else* with the first *else*less if. Therefore, although the test score was 100, the previous code fragment would print out a message telling the student: should have worked harder! In other words, the fragment executes the statements, as follows:

```
if (test_score >= 90)
  if (current_grade == 'A')
    System.out.println("Another A for an A student\n");
  else
    System.out.println("Should have worked harder\n");
```

To prevent Java from associating the *else* statement with the wrong *if* statement in this way, place the second *if* statement within braces, forming a *compound statement*, as shown:

```
if (test_score >= 90)
  {
    if (current_grade == 'A')
      System.out.println("Another A for an A student\n");
  }
else
  System.out.println("Should have worked harder\n");
```

144 ASSIGNING THE RESULT OF A CONDITION

Several of the tips in this section have presented different conditions that evaluate to a true or false *boolean* value within a conditional statement such as *if, while,* or *for.* You may find that some of your tests are repetitious and are re-used in several conditional statements. In these cases, you may want to perform the test once, assign it to a *boolean*, and then use the *boolean* in the various conditional statements. For example, rather than continually evaluating expressions such as *(temperature > 100),* the code fragment assigns the condition's *boolean* result to the variable *hot,* and then uses the variable *hot* throughout its processing:

```
boolean hot = (temperature > 100);
boolean humid = (humidity > 88);

if ((hot) && (humid))
    // Statements
else if (hot)
    // Statements
```

WATCH OUT FOR INCORRECT USE OF BOOLEANS

When you work with conditional statements that require a *boolean*, you may use any expression as long as Java resolves the expression to a *boolean*. In Java, 0 is not the same as false and 1 is not the same as true. For example, the following statements *are illegal* in Java (unlike C/C++):

```
int hot = 1;

if (hot)
   // Statements
```

In Java, you must use a *boolean* or an expression that resolves to a *boolean*. For example, the following statements are legal in Java:

```
int hot = 1;

if (hot == 1)
   // Statements
```

PERFORMING LOGICAL AND TO TEST TWO CONDITIONS

As you have learned, Java's *if* statement lets your programs test various conditions. As your programs become more complex, they will eventually need to test for multiple conditions. For example, you may want an *if* statement to test whether a user has a dog and, if so, whether that dog is a Dalmatian. In most cases, when you want to test if two conditions are true, you can use Java's conditional AND operator (&&). Consider the following *if* statement:

```
if ((user_has_dog == true) && (dog == Dalmatian))
   {
      // Statements
   }
```

When Java encounters an *if* statement that uses the logical AND operator (&&), Java evaluates the conditions from left to right. If you examine the parentheses, you will find that the previous *if* statement is in the following form:

```
if (condition)
```

Within this statement, the condition is actually two conditions connected with the &&:

```
((user_has_dog == true) && (dog == Dalmatian))
```

For a condition that uses the logical AND (&&) to evaluate as true, both conditions must evaluate as true. If either condition is false, the resulting condition evaluates as false. In this example, if *user_has_dog* were false, Java would not waste time evaluating the second expression—performing a "short circuit" evaluation.

However, if you use the bitwise AND operator (&) instead, Java will evaluate all expressions in the condition. Directing Java to execute all the expressions in a condition becomes important if the right-hand expression calls a function or performs other tasks that may introduce a "side effect."

147 PERFORMING LOGICAL *OR* TO TEST TWO CONDITIONS

As you know, Java's *if* statement lets your program test conditions. As your programs become more complex, you will eventually need to test for multiple conditions. For example, you may want an *if* statement to test whether a user has a dog, or whether the user has a computer. In cases when you want to test whether either of two conditions is true (or if both are true), you use the logical OR operator. Java represents the logical OR operator with two vertical bars (||). Consider the following *if* statement:

```
if ((user_has_dog == true) || (user_has_computer == true))
  {
    // Statements
  }
```

When Java encounters an *if* statement that uses the logical OR operator (||), Java evaluates the conditions from left to right. If you examine the parentheses, you will find that the previous *if* statement is in the following form:

```
if (condition)
```

In the previous example, the condition is actually two conditions connected with the logical OR:

```
(user_has_dog == true) || (user_has_computer == true)
```

For the condition based on a logical OR to evaluate as true, only one of the conditions must evaluate as true. If either condition (or both) is true, the resulting condition evaluates as true. If both conditions evaluate as false, the result is false. In this example, if the condition *user_has_dog* is true, Java will not waste time evaluating the second expression—performing a "short-circuit" evaluation which improves your program's performance.

However, if you use the bitwise OR operator (|) instead, Java will evaluate all expressions in the condition. Having Java execute all the expressions in a condition becomes important if the right-hand expression calls a function or performs other tasks that may introduce a "side effect."

148 PERFORMING LOGICAL *NOT* TO TEST TWO CONDITIONS

When your programs use the *if* statement to perform conditional processing, the *if* statement evaluates an expression that yields a *true* or *false* result. Depending on your program's processing, you may only want the program to perform a set of statements when the condition evaluates as *false*. For example, assume you need a program to test whether the user has a dog. If the user does not have a dog, the program should display a message telling him or her to buy a Dalmatian! If the user has a dog, the program should not do anything. When you want your program to perform one or more statements when a condition is *false*, you should use the NOT operator, which Java represents with the exclamation mark (!). Consider the following *if* statement:

```
if (! user_has_dog)
    System.out.println("You need to buy a Dalmatian!\n");
```

In this case, if the user does not have a dog, the program will display a message telling the user to buy a Dalmatian.

UNDERSTANDING THE LOGICAL OPERATOR 149

Logical operators, as opposed to bitwise operators, will only evaluate as many operands as minimally needed to determine a result. For example, when a Java program performs a logical OR (||) operation, Java will not evaluate the right-hand operand if the left-hand operand is true because, in a logical OR operation, if the left-hand operand is true, the condition is true. When Java skips the evaluation of the right-hand operand in this way, Java "short circuits" the condition. Programming languages use "short circuit" (sometimes called "lazy") evaluation to improve your program performance by eliminating unnecessary operations. It is important that you understand such "short circuit" evaluations because one day you may have a function call on the right-hand side of a condition that Java must evaluate:

```
if (condition_a && some_critical_function(4.5, 3.2))
```

In this case, if Java evaluates *condition_a* as false, which makes the entire condition false, Java will short circuit the condition and will not invoke the function that appears on the right-hand side of the logical AND operator. For cases when you must ensure that Java evaluates the right-hand operator, use the bitwise OR (|) or the bitwise AND (&) operators.

UNDERSTANDING CONDITIONAL TERNARY OPERATORS 150

Java provides a convenient way for you to test a *boolean* expression and execute either of two expressions based on the *boolean* test's true or false result. The *conditional ternary operator* (? :) uses the following form:

```
(variable) = (boolean expression) ? (any operand) : (any operand)
```

If the *boolean* expression is *true*, Java assigns the operand that follows the question mark (?) to the variable. On the other hand, if the *boolean* expression is false, Java assigns right-most operand, which follows the colon, to the variable. The following statements, for example, assign the value false to the *boolean* variable *done*:

```
boolean done;
int count= 4;

done = (count > 10) ? true : false;
```

In this way, the conditional ternary operator is equivalent to the following *if-else* statement:

```
if (count > 10)
   done = true;
else
   done = false;
```

JAVA GUARANTEES MINIMAL EVALUATION OF LOGICAL EXPRESSIONS 151

When your program uses the logical AND (&&) or logical OR (||) operators within an expression, Java will evaluate the minimum number of conditions it needs to decide whether the entire condition is true or false. In addition, Java will evaluate those conditions from left to right. For example, in the following expression, Java only needs to check the first leftmost condition to determine that the entire logical AND is false:

```
boolean first_test = false;
boolean second_test = true;
boolean third_test = true;

if (first_test && second_test && third_test)
   System.out.println("If statement evaluates to true\n");
```

In this case, because the expression *first_test* is false, the condition can never be true, no matter what the values of the other conditions. Thus, to save time, Java will not test the other conditions.

You can always rely on Java's minimal evaluation for the logical AND (&&) and logical OR (||) operators. When your conditions use more complex expressions, you don't want Java to stop its evaluation as soon as it knows the condition's result. For example, the following statement calls a function within a conditional expression:

```
if (first_test && second_test && call_me_if_you_must())
   System.out.println("If statement evaluates to true\n");
```

In this case, Java only evaluates (calls) the function *call_me_if_you_must* when the conditions *first_test* and *second_test* are true. If you truly need the function to execute every time, replace the logical AND (&&) operators with bitwise AND (&) operators, as shown:

```
if (first_test & second_test & always_call_me())
   System.out.println("If statement evaluates to true\n");
```

152 DECLARING VARIABLES WITHIN COMPOUND STATEMENTS

A *compound statement* is one or more statements grouped within left and right braces {}. Many of the Java examples you have seen so far have used compound statements. For example, the following code fragment makes use of compound statements within an *if* statement:

```
int velocity;

// Code to set the velocity is here

if (velocity > 1000)
  {
    int message = SHUT_DOWN;
    int urgency_level = HIGH;
    System.out.println("Over the limit. Shutting down!\n");
     engine.sendMessage(message, urgency_level);
  }
```

If you examine this code closely, you will find that the code declares two variables, *message* and *urgency_level*, within the compound statement. Declaring variables within a compound statement is a feature Java borrowed from C/C++. As is the case in C/C++, variables you declare within a compound statement (a code block) in this way are only valid within that block. As an additional feature, you may actually declare variables *anywhere* within the block (not just at the beginning).

As you create your programs, one of the best ways you can improve your program's readability is to use indentation. As a rule, each time your program uses a brace (such as at the start of a compound statement), you should consider indenting the code that follows the brace two spaces. For example, consider the following program:

```java
import java.applet.*;

public class dogs extends Applet
  {
    public void init()
     {
        int age = 10;
        boolean user_has_dog = false;

        if (age == 10)
          {
             System.out.println("Dogs are important pets\n");
             if (! user_has_dog)
                 System.out.println("You should get a dalmatian\n");
          }
         System.out.println("Happy, is a dalmatian\n");
     }
  }
```

By examining the indentation only, you can quickly get a feel for related program statements. Indentation is meaningless to the Java compiler. To the compiler, the following program is identical to the one just shown:

```java
import java.applet.*;
public class dogs extends Applet
{
public void init()
{
int age= 10;
boolean user_has_dog= false;

if (age == 10)
{
System.out.println("Dogs are important pets\n");
if (! user_has_dog)
System.out.println("You should get a dalmatian\n");
}
System.out.println("Happy is a dalmatian\n");
}
}
```

As you can see, the indentation makes the first program much easier to understand.

154 TESTING FLOATING-POINT VALUES

Several of the tips this section presents have used *if* statements to test a variable's value. For example, the following statements test two integer variables:

```
if (age == 21)
  // Statements

if (height > 73)
  // Statements
```

When you work with floating-point values, however, you need to be careful when you test a variable's value. For example, the following statement tests a floating-point variable named *sales_tax*:

```
if (sales_tax == 0.065F)
   // Statements
```

As you may recall from earlier tips, *float* and *double* values provide a certain level of precision which is based on the limited number of bits the computer uses represent floating-point variables. For example, if your program calculates the value of the variable *sales_tax*, the computer may actually represent the 0.065 value you expected as 0.0649999. As a result, the previous *if* statement will never evaluate as true. To prevent such errors within your program, do not test for exact floating-point values. Instead, test for an acceptable range of values as shown here:

```
if ((sales_tax >= 0.064F) && (sales_tax <= 0.066F))
   // Statements
```

In this case, the *if* statement will allow the *sales_tax* to vary between .064 and .066 to evaluate the condition as *true*.

155 USING THE WHILE LOOP

Within an applet, one of the operations you will perform on a regular basis is to loop, repeating a set of instructions until a specific condition becomes true. For example, your applet might repeatedly prompt the user to type in an age until the user enters a value in the range of 1 to 125. Or, the applet might loop until the user types a valid menu option.

To repeat statements in this way, Java programs use the *while* statement. The general format of the *while* statement is:

```
while (condition)
  {
    // Statements to repeat here
  }
```

When Java encounters a *while* statement, Java will examine the specified condition. If the condition is true, Java will execute the loop's statements and then retest the condition. As long as the condition remains true, Java will continue to execute the loop's statements. When the condition is false, Java continues its execution at the first statement that follows the *while* loop.

The following *while* statement, for example, loops as long as the variable *index* contains a value that is greater than 0:

```
int index = 5;

while (index > 0)
  {
    System.out.println("Value of index is: " + index-);
  }
```

If you execute this loop, it will display the following output:

```
Value of index is 5
Value of index is 4
Value of index is 3
Value of index is 2
Value of index is 1
```

Unlike C/C++, the condition you specify within a *while* loop must evaluate to a *boolean* (true or false), as opposed to a one or a zero. Therefore, the following statement, which is valid in C/C++, will not compile within Java:

```
int index = 5;

while (index--) // Does not evaluate to a boolean
  {
    // code goes here
  }
```

To correct the syntax error, you must change the condition to evaluate to a *boolean*, as shown:

```
int index = 5;

while (index-- > 0) //  Evaluates to a boolean
  {
    // code goes here
  }
```

USING THE FOR LOOP

156

As you learned in Tip 155, the *while* statement lets your program loop as long as a specific condition is true. In many cases, however, your program will need to perform a set of statements a specific number of times. For example, your program might calculate the test scores for 30 students, determine the highs and lows for 100 stock quotes, or even sound your computer's speaker three times. To help your programs repeat one or more statements a specific number of times, Java provides the *for* statement, whose format is as follows:

```
for (starting_value; ending_condition; increment_value)
  {
    // Statements to execute
  }
```

When your program repeats (loops through) statements a specific number of times, you will normally use a variable, called the *control variable*, to count the number of times the loop has performed the statements. The *for* statement consist of four parts. The *starting_value* section assigns the control variable its initial value, which is normally 0 or 1.

The *ending_condition* section normally tests the control variable's value to determine if the loop has executed the desired number of times. The *increment_value* section normally adds the value 1 to the control variable each time the loop executes. Finally, the *for* loop's fourth section is the set of statements the loop executes with each iteration. Consider the following *for* loop that displays the values 1 through 10 to the console window:

```java
for (int counter = 1; counter <= 10; counter++)
  {
     System.out.println("Counter: " + counter);
  }
```

In this case, *counter* is the loop's control variable. The *for* statement first assigns the variable the value 1. Next, the *for* loop immediately tests whether or not *counter's* value is less than or equal to 10 (the loop's ending condition). If *counter* is less than 10, the *for* loop begins immediately executing its first statement which, in this case, is the function call to *System.out.println* which displays the *counter* variable's value. Next, the *for* statement performs its increment section, adding one to the variable counter. The *for* statement then repeats its test. If *counter's* value is still less than or equal to 10, the loop continues. If, however, *counter's* value now exceeds 10, the loop ends and Java continues your program's execution at the first statement that follows the loop.

As you will learn, Java *for* loops do not restrict you to using integer values as the control variable. The following *for* loop, for example, uses a control variable of type *char* to display the letter A through Z:

```java
for (char letter = 1; letter <= 10; letter++)
  {
     System.out.println(" " + letter);
  }
```

Likewise, the following *for* statement uses a control variable of type *float*:

```java
for (float value = 0; value <= 1.0; value += 0.1)
  {
     System.out.println("Value: " + value);
  }
```

157 PARTS OF THE FOR STATEMENT ARE OPTIONAL

As you have learned, the general format of the *for* loop is as follows:

```java
for (initializers; condition; increments)
  {
    // Statements
  }
```

As it turns out, you can omit each part of the *for* loop. In other words, the loop's *initializers*, *condition*, or *increments* parts can be empty statements—that is, you simply include a semicolon with no statement or expression. For example, the following for loop has no *initializers* or *increments*:

```java
boolean found_it = false;

for ( ; found_it == false ; )
  {
    // Statements
  }
```

Note that although the *for* statement does not provide *initializers* and *increments*, the loop still provides the semicolons. In this case, when Java first executes the *for* statement, Java has no initializations to perform, so it immediately evaluates the loop's condition. If the condition is true, Java executes the loop's statements. With each iteration of the loop, Java has no variable's to increment. As such, Java again immediately evaluates the loop's condition to determine whether or not it should repeat the loop's statements.

DECREMENTING VALUES IN A FOR STATEMENT

 158

As you have learned, programs use a *for* statement to repeat a set of statements a specific number of times. The following *for* statement, for example, displays the numbers 1 through 10:

```
for (int count = 1; count <= 10; count++)
  {
     System.out.println("count: " + count);
  }
```

As you can see, the *for* statement increments the variable *count* by one with each iteration. Java, however, does not require that you increment a variable with each iteration. Instead, you can omit the increment portion of the *for* statement, or you can even decrement a variable. For example, the following *for* statement displays the values 10 down to 1 by decrementing the variable *count* with each iteration:

```
for (int count = 10; count > 0; count--)
  {
     System.out.println("count: " + count);
  }
```

CONTROLLING THE FOR LOOP INCREMENT

 159

Within a *for* statement's increment, Java does not require that you increment or decrement a variable's value by one. Instead, Java lets you perform just about any operation you need. For example, you might add 5 to a value with each iteration, or you might multiply a value by 10. The following *for* statement displays the values 5, 10, 15, and so on up to 100 by incrementing the variable *count* by 5 with each iteration:

```
for (int count = 5; count <= 100; count += 5)
  {
     System.out.println("count: " + count);
  }
```

DECLARING VARIABLES WITHIN A FOR LOOP'S STATEMENTS

 160

As with any block of compound statements, you may declare additional variables within the braces that define a *for* loop. The variables may be of any data type, and Java limits their scope to the loop. The following example declares and uses variables within a *for* loop:

```
for (int index = 1, boolean found_it = false;
     (index <= 100) && (found_it == false); index++)
  {
```

```
        char char_code;
        boolean reached_limit = false;

        // Additional statements go here
}
```

161 UNDERSTANDING THE INFINITE LOOP

As you have learned, the *for* loop lets you repeat one or more statements a specific number of times. When the *for* loop's ending condition is met, your program continues its execution at the statement which immediately follows. When you use *for* loops, you need to ensure that the loop's ending condition *can be* met. Otherwise, the loop will continue to execute forever. Such unending loops are called *infinite loops* because they will continue forever. In most cases, infinite loops occur as the result of a programming error. For example, consider the following loop:

```
for (int count = 0; count < 100; count--)
  {
     // Statements
  }
```

If you look closely at the *for loop*'s third component, you can see that the *count* variable is being decremented each time through the loop. However, *count* started out initialized to 0 and, as a result, it will always be less than 100. Since the loop will only terminate if count reaches 100, this loop will loop forever.

Actually, the previous loop won't execute forever because eventually, if you continue to decrement the integer variable *count*, the variable's value will *overflow* and become a large positive value, causing the loop to end.

The bug, in this case, is that the programmer probably meant to increment the *count* variable and not decrement the variable:

```
for (int count=0; count < 100; count++)
```

There are many other situations that can produce an infinite loop. Generally, if your computer "locks up," and you are using loops, you may want to check your loop conditions to make sure that they can meet their ending condition.

162 BREAKING INFINITE LOOPS

As you have learned earlier, the *for* loop has several optional items. The general format of the *for* loop is as follows:

```
for (initializers; condition; increments)
  {
     // Statement block
  }
```

The *for* loop's initializers, condition, and increments parts may all be empty statements, that is, you can simply include two semicolons between the parentheses, as shown:

```
for ( ; ; )
  {
     // loop body goes here
  }
```

When your *for* loop has all empty statements, as shown above, it will loop forever unless you provide additional code within the loop body that terminates the loop, such as a *break* statement which continues the program's processing at the first statement that follows the *for* loop:

```
for ( ; ; )
   {
      if (done_looping == true)
         break; // get out of the loop
   }

// processing continues here after executing the break statement
```

If you use the *for* loop in this way, you may want to consider using a *while* loop instead, since the *while* loop accomplishes the same thing in a cleaner way, as shown:

```
while (done_looping == false)
   {
      // Statements
   }
```

USING COMMAS IN A FOR LOOP

 163

Unlike C/C++, Java does not support the comma operator within all sections of the *for* loop. If you are familiar with C, you know that you can place multiple expressions in various sections of the *for* statement. Java lets you use multiple comma-separated expressions in the initialization and increment sections, but not the condition section, of the loop. The general format of the *for* loop is:

```
for (initializers; condition; increments)
   {
      // statement block
   }
```

The following statements illustrate the use of multiple comma-separated expressions within a *for* statement:

```
int index;
String name;

for (index = 0, name = "Anthony"; (index<25) && (name.length() >=1);
     index++, name.some_function())
   {
      System.out.println(name);
   }
```

Within a Java *for* loop, you cannot mix variable declarations with other expressions and separate them with a comma. For example, by declaring *index* within the *for* loop, *int index=0,* the initialization section now contains a declaration and an assignment. If you try to include the comma operator, the compiler will generate an error:

```
String name;
```

```
for (int index = 0, name = "Anthony";     // Do not mix types
    (index < 25) && (name.length() >=1); index++, name.a_function())
{
    System.out.println(name);
}
```

164 USING THE DO LOOP

As you have learned, Java's *while* statement lets you repeat one or more statements until a specific condition is true. Likewise, Java's *for* statement lets you repeat one or more statements a specific number of times. In addition, Java provides the *do* statement, which lets you execute one or more statements *at least one time*, and then, if necessary, repeat statements. The form of the *do* statement is as follows:

```
do {
    // Statement block
} while ( condition );
```

You should consider using the *do* loop whenever you need to execute one or more statements at least one time. The following statements illustrate the use of the *do* loop:

```
int index= 100;

do {
    System.out.println(index);
    index++;
} while (index <= 10);
```

In this case, for example, if *index* starts with the value 100, the loop will execute once, print the index, and stop. The *do* loop is very convenient for menu processing for which you want to display a menu of options at least one time, possibly redisplaying the menu options based on the user's menu selections.

165 UNDERSTANDING THE CONTINUE STATEMENT

As you have learned, the *for, while,* and *do* statements let your programs repeat one or more statements until a specific condition is met. Depending on your program's purpose, there may be times, based on a specific condition, when you will want to skip the current iteration. Java's *continue* statement lets you do just that.

If Java encounters a *continue* statement within a *for* loop, Java will immediately execute the loop's increment portion and then perform the ending condition test. If Java encounters a *continue* statement within a *while* or *do* loop, Java will immediately perform the ending condition test. If you are familiar with C, you will find that the *continue* statement behaves the same way in Java as it does in C.

For example, the following code fragment illustrates how you may use the *continue* statement to continue the program's execution at the next iteration of a loop whenever an odd number is encountered. By using the *continue* statement in this way, the loop only prints even numbers:

```
for (int count= 1; count<= 100; count++)
  {
    if (count % 2) // odd number
      continue;      // skip to the bottom of the loop

    System.out.println(count);   // display the even number
  }
```

Unlike C/C++, you can use a label with the Java *continue* statement that allows you to specify the loop you would like the program's execution to continue. Without a label, *continue* will skip to the end of the surrounding loop. The following example illustrates the use of a label with the *continue* statement:

```
outer_loop: while (!done_one)
  {
    while (!done_two)
      {
        // Statements

        if (done_one)
          continue outer_loop;  // continue on to the outer loop
      }
  }
```

In this case, the *continue* statement's label directs the program to exit the inner loop and jump to the outer loop that corresponds to the label.

*Note: If a labeled loop contains a **finally** clause, Java will execute the corresponding statements before it jumps to the corresponding label.*

ENDING A LOOP WITH THE BREAK STATEMENT

166

As you have learned, the *for, while,* and *do* statements let your programs repeat one or more statements until a specific condition is met. Depending on your program's purpose, there may be times, based on a specific condition, when you will want the loop to end immediately and your program to continue processing at the statement that follows the loop. Java's *break* statememt lets you do just that.

If Java encounters a *break* statement, the loop's execution will immediately end. The next statement to execute is the statement that immediately follows the loop. If you are familiar with C/C++, you will find that Java's *break* statement behaves the same way. For example, the following code fragment illustrates how you may use the *break* statement to jump out of a loop when a certain condition occurs:

```
for (int count= 1; count<= 100; count++)
  {
    if (count == 50)   // stop counting when 50 is reached
      break;                // skip to first statement outside the loop

    System.out.println(count);
  }

// Execution continues here following the break statement
```

Unlike C/C++, Java lets you use a label with the *break* statement that specifies exactly which loop you want to break out of. Without a label, the *break* statement directs Java to continue its execution at the first line that follows the surrounding loop. The following example illustrates the use of a label with the *break* statement:

```
outer_loop: while (!done_one)
  {
    while (!done_two)
      {
        // Statements
        if (done_one)
          break outer_loop;   // break out of the outer loop
      }
  }
```

Note: *If a labeled loop contains a* **finally** *clause, Java will execute the corresponding statements before it jumps to the corresponding label.*

167 TESTING MULTIPLE CONDITIONS WITH THE SWITCH STATEMENT

As you have learned, Java's *if-else* statements let you test multiple conditions. For example, the following program excerpt uses *if-else* statements to determine the price of a shoe, based on the variable *shoe_size*:

```
if (shoe_size == 6)
    price = 25.00;
else if (shoe_size == 8)
    price = 35.00;
else if (shoe_size == 11)
    price = 45.00;
```

In cases where your program tests the same variable for multiple possible values, Java provides a *switch* statement whose format is the same as it is for C/C++. By using the *switch* statement, you can rewrite the previous example as follows:

```
switch (shoe_size)
  {
    case 6: price = 25.00;
            break;
    case 8: price = 35.00;
            break;
    case 11: price = 45.00;
             break;
  }
```

Within a *switch* statement, the *break* statement separates the statements that correspond to one case from another. Normally, you will place a *break* statement after each case's last statement to direct the program's execution (the program's flow) to the first statement that follows the *switch* statement. In other words, the *break* statement breaks (or ends) the program's processing of the *switch* statement.

SELECTING THE TYPE CHAR IN A SWITCH STATEMENT   168

You can use the Java *switch* statement to select choices based on the type *byte*, *char*, *short*, *int*, or *long*. To use *switch* statements with values of type *char*, simply specify the character you want to test within single quotes, as follows:

```
switch (letter_grade)
 {
   case 'A': points = 100;
            break;
   case 'B': points = 90;
            break;
   case 'C': points = 80;
            break;
 }
```

UNDERSTANDING BREAK WITHIN A SWITCH STATEMENT   169

As is the case with the *for*, *while*, and *do* statements, the *break* statement causes execution of the *switch* statement to immediately end and the program processing to continue at the first statement that follows the *switch*. As discussed, you normally place *break* statements at the end of each *case* within a *switch* statement. As it turns out, once Java finds a matching case, Java considers all the cases that follow as true. If you don't include the *break* statement, Java will execute the statements for all matching cases (all the cases that follow the matching case). For example, consider the following program snippet:

```
switch (letter_grade)
 {
   case 'A': points = 100;
            break;
   case 'B': points = 90;
            break;
   case 'C': points = 80;
            break;
 }
```

In this example, based on the value of the variable *letter_grade*, the statements will assign the variable *points* the value 100, 90, or 80. After the switch statement finds a match, it should not execute the other cases. By using the *break* statement, your program will exit out of the *switch* statement and continue its processing at the first statement that follows the *switch*.

In some cases, you may want to remove the *break* statement. In doing so, the program will continue stepping through each *case's* statements until it reaches the end of the *switch* block, or until a *break* is found. For example, the following fragment tests for various *letter_grades*, all of which receive the same treatment:

```
switch (letter_grade)
 {
   case 'A':
```

```
        case 'B':
        case 'C': status = PASS;
                  break;
        case 'D':
        case 'F': status= FAIL;
    }
```

In this case, the processing for grades *A*, *B*, and *C* falls through to the PASS assignment after which the *break* statement continues the program's execution at the statement that follows the *switch* statement. In a similar way, the letter grades D and F both receive the same processing. Allowing a *switch* statement's processing to "fall through" in this way is handy when you have multiple values for which the program executes the same statements.

170 USING THE DEFAULT CASE IN A SWITCH STATEMENT

As you have learned, Java's *switch* statement lets you perform conditional processing. When you use the *switch* statement, you specify one or more cases that you want Java to match. As you use the *switch* statement, you might find that you want Java to perform specific statements when none of the other cases match. To do so, you simply include a *default* case, as shown:

```
switch (letter_grade)
  {
     case 'A':
     case 'B':
     case 'C': status= PASS;
               break;
     default:  status= FAIL;
               break;
  }
```

In this case, the grades *A*, *B*, and *C* each receive a passing status. All other grades, which are not listed, execute the *default* case, which results in a failing status.

171 WHEN YOU SHOULD USE IF-ELSE RATHER THAN SWITCH

A significant limitation of Java's *switch* statement is that you can select choices based only on the types *byte*, *char*, *short*, *int*, and *long*. Within a *switch* statement, you cannot use the larger primitive types, such as value of type *long* and *float*, *String*, as well as other objects, nor can you test for any relationship other than equality (such as whether a value is greater than another value). If you need to perform more complex tests such as these, you must use the *if-else* statement.

172 USING FUNCTIONS TO PERFORM SPECIFIC TASKS

As you create your applets, you should break apart complex tasks into smaller more manageable pieces called *functions*. In general, a function is a group of Java statements that perform a specific task. For example, you might create a function that returns the larger of two values, or a function that computes the sales tax on a purchase, and so on. For example, the following statements create a function named *maximum* that returns the larger of two values:

```
int maximum(int a, int b)
  {
    if (a > b)
      return(a);
    else
      return(b);
  }
```

Each function you create has a unique name, such as *maximum*. As you can see, you group the function's statements within left and right braces {}. After you create a function, you call the function by specifying the function's name and passing values to the function that you group within parentheses. The following statement, for example, uses (calls) the maximum function to determine the larger of two values:

```
int result = maximum(1, 1001);    // Call the function
System.out.println("The larger value is " + result);
```

FUNCTIONS NORMALLY RETURN A VALUE

 173

As you have learned, functions let you group related statements that perform a specific task. Normally, when a function completes its processing, the function will return a value to its caller (the location in your program that invoked the function). In Tip 172, for example, the *maximum* function compared two values and then returned the larger value. To return a value to the caller, a function uses a *return* statement, as shown:

```
if (a > b)
   return(a);
else
   return(b);
```

Functions must return one type of value, such as a value of type *int* or *float*. When you declare a function, you must specify the function type. For example, the following declaration informs the Java compiler that the *maximum* function returns a value of type *int*:

```
int maximum(int a, int b)
```

PASSING PARAMETERS TO FUNCTIONS

 174

As you have learned, a function groups related statements that perform a specific task. To make the statements more "generic" or applicable to a wider range of operations, Java lets you pass values to a function when you call the function. For example, in the *maximum* function, you passed the function the two values you wanted the function to compare. The values you pass to a function are *parameters*. Within the function header (the first line of the function declaration), you must specify the number and type of each parameter. In addition, you must specify the name the function will use to refer to each parameter. The following function header tells the compiler that the *maximum* function will receive two parameters of type *int*:

```
int maximum(int a, int b)
```

Within the function statements, the function will refer to its two parameters using the names *a* and *b*.

175 UNDERSTANDING A FUNCTION'S SCOPE

A function's *scope* defines the locations within your program where the function is known. In other words, a function's scope defines the program locations that can call (use) the function. When you create functions within a Java applet, the functions, by default, are known only to the class within which they are defined. In other words, Java restricts the function's scope to its class, so, your program cannot call the function from another class. In later tips, you will learn that Java programmers normally refer to class functions as *methods*. Most programmers, therefore, will use the terms methods and functions interchangeably. You will also learn how you can change a function's scope by using the *public*, *private*, and *protected* modifiers.

176 UNDERSTANDING LOCAL VARIABLES

As you have learned, when your program calls a function, your program can pass information to the function using named parameters. Within the function statements, the function refers to each parameter by name. To perform its processing, the function may require other variables. For example, the following implementation of the *minimum* function uses a variable named *result* to perform its processing:

```java
int minimum(int a, int b)
  {
     int result;

     result = (a > b) ? a: b;

     return(result);
  }
```

In this case, the variable *result* is a local variable that is known only within the *minimum* function. In other words, Java restricts the variable's scope to the *minimum* function. If your program uses a variable named *result* somewhere else, the two variable names will not conflict.

177 UNDERSTANDING CALL BY VALUE

In Java, there are two classifications of variables. The first is the primitive types (also known as built-in types), which include the types *float*, *boolean*, *int*, *char*, and so on. The second is the non-primitive types, which are objects and arrays. It is important that you understand the distinction between the two as it affects how they behave when Java passes them as parameters to a method and when Java assigns them to other variables.

When you pass primitive types as parameters in a method call, you are actually passing a copy of the variable's value. To pass a parameter by value in this way, Java makes a copy of the variable's value in a memory location, known as the stack. The method your program is calling has access only to the value copy stored in the stack, as opposed to the variable itself. Therefore, the method cannot change the original variable's value. For example, the following applet, *TestApplet.java*, sets some variables and then calls a method by value. Within the method, the statements change the parameter values. However, because the method is working only with copies of the values, the original variable's value remains unchanged when the method ends:

```java
import java.applet.Applet;
```

```
public class TestApplet extends Applet {

    void PassByValue(int x, int y)
     {
        x += 100; // do whatever you like, originals are unchanged
        y += 100;
        System.out.println("Changed to "  + x + " and " + y);
     }


    public void init()
     {
        int x= 1;
        int y= 2;
        System.out.println("Original "  + x + " and " + y);
        PassByValue(x, y);
        System.out.println("Original "  + x + " and " + y);
     }
}
```

This applet takes two variables and adds 100 to the values within the *PassByValue* method. When the method ends, however, the original values of these parameters remain unchanged. The program will display the following output:

```
Original 1 and 2
Changed to 101 and 102
Original 1 and 2
```

WHY CALL BY VALUE PREVENTS PARAMETER VALUE CHANGE 178

When you pass primitive types such as the types *float*, *boolean*, *int*, and *char* to a method, Java passes the variables by value. In other words, Java makes a copy of the original variable which the method can access and the original remains unchanged. Within a method, the code can change the values as much as it needs because Java created these values as copies of the originals.

Whenever you pass a primitive type as a parameter to a method, Java copies this parameter to a special memory location known as the *stack*. The stack maintains information about variables used by the method while the method executes. When the method is complete, Java discards the stack's contents and the copies of the variables that you passed into the method are gone forever.

Because Java copies your original primitive type parameters, there is never any danger of a method altering your original values. Remember, this only applies to primitive types which are automatically passed by value. Objects and arrays are not passed by value (instead they are passed by reference), and they *are* in danger of being changed!

HOW TO USE CALL BY REFERENCE IN JAVA 179

As you have learned, there are two classifications of variables: primitive types which include the types *float*, *boolean*, *int*, and *char*, and non-primitive types which are objects and arrays. It is important to understand the distinction between the two as it affects how they behave when Java passes them as parameters to a method or assigns them to other variables. In Java, you can only pass primitive types by value. Likewise, Java always passes the non-primitive types by reference.

When you use non-primitive types as parameters in a method call, you are actually passing in a *reference* to the variable. If you are familiar with C/C++, you know that you can take an address of a variable using the address (&) operator, and you can "dereference" an address using the * and -> operators. These operators do not exist in Java. Instead, all objects and arrays are automatically passed by reference, and you do not need to use any special notation.

When you call a method by value, Java copies the variable passed to a methodon to the stack, and the original is not altered. When you call a method by reference, Java passes the variable to the method and any changes the method makes to the variable are permanent, even after the method completes. The following applet, *TestReference.java*, passes an array object to a method which, in turn, changes the first two array elements. When the method ends, its changes to the array remain in effect:

```java
import java.applet.Applet;

public class TestReference extends Applet {

    void PassByReference(int a[ ])
    {
        a[0]= 0; // change the referenced array
        a[1]= 0;
    }

    public void init()
    {
        int z[] = {9, 7};  // declare an array with some values
        System.out.println("Original "  + z[0] + " and " + z[1]);

        PassByReference(z);
        System.out.println("Changed to "  + z[0] + " and " + z[1]);
    }
}
```

As you can see, the applet passes the array to the *PassByReference* method. The method, in turn, assigns zeros to the array's first two elements. Because Java passes arrays by reference, the original array is affected by the method's alterations. The applet will display the following output:

```
Original 9 and 7
Changed to 0 and 0
```

180   UNDERSTANDING STATIC VARIABLES

When you declare a class, you define variables (and methods) for that class. When you later instantiate the class (create a class object), Java assigns a fresh set of variables to the new object. No matter how many instances of that class you create, each object's variables will be independent from the variables of the other objects.

However, if you declare a variable using the *static* modifier, Java will share that variable with each instance of the class. Furthermore, your programs can access *static* variables using an instance of the class, as well as by using the class name. In contrast, your programs can only access non-*static* variables through an object instance. To declare a *static* variable, simply use the *static* keyword, as shown:

```
public class RememberMe
  {
      public static int SharedValue;
  }
```

The following statements show that you can access a *static* class variable using either an object instance or by referring to the class name itself:

```
public class RememberMe
  {
      public static int SharedValue;
  }


// access the static through the class name
System.out.println(RememberMe.SharedValue);

RememberMe inst = new RememberMe();            // create an instance

// access the static through an instance
System.out.println(inst.goodMemory);
```

You will examine how you use static variables to share information in later tips. For now, simply remember that Java shares *static* class member variables among each instance of the class (every class object) and that you can access a *static* class member variable using the class name.

UNDERSTANDING RECURSION 181

As you have learned, Java lets you divide your program into smaller pieces using methods and classes. By organizing your code using methods, your program becomes easier to understand, program, and test. In addition, you can often reuse the methods you create for one class within other classes. As your programs execute, one method may call another method, which calls another, which may in turn call several other methods. As it turns out, Java lets a method call itself!

A *recursive method* is a method that calls itself to perform a specific operation. The process of a method calling itself is *recursion*. As the complexity of your programs increases, you may find that many operations are easily defined in terms of themselves. For such cases, you might want to create a recursive method.

Many programming books, use the factorial problem to illustrate how recursion works. The factorial of the value 1 is 1. The factorial of the value 2 is 2*1. The factorial of the value 3 is 3*2*1. Likewise, the factorial of the value 4 is 4*3*2*1. This process can essentially go on forever. If you take a close look at the processing that the factorial performs, you will find that the factorial of 4, for example, is actually 4 times the factorial of 3 (3*2*1). Likewise, the factorial of 3 is actually 3 times the factorial of 2 (2*1). The factorial of 2 is 2 times the factorial of 1 (1). Table 181 illustrates the factorial processing.

Value	Calculation	Result	Factorial
1	1	1	1
2	2*1	2	2*Factorial(1)

Table 181 Factorial processing. (Continued on following page.)

Value	Calculation	Result	Factorial
3	3*2*1	6	3*Factorial(2)
4	4*3*2*1	24	4*Factorial(3)
5	5*4*3*2*1	120	5*Factorial(4)

Table 181 Factorial processing. (Continued from previous page.)

To create a method to compute factorials recursively, you create a method that calls itself, as shown:

```
public int factorial(int value)
  {
    if (value == 1)
       return(1);
    else
       return(value * factorial(value - 1));
  }
```

As you can see, if the method receives the parameter value 1, the method returns the value 1 (remember, the factor of the value 1 is 1). However, if the parameter value is not 1, the method returns the result of the current value times the factorial of the value minus 1 (this is where the method calls itself). For a recursive method to work successfully, the method must have an ending condition. In this case, the ending condition is the factorial of the value 1.

182 USING RECURSIVE METHODS IN JAVA

As you learned in Tip 181, a recursive method is one that calls itself to perform its processing. Recursive methods in Java require no special changes in the way you declare or call them. However, Java does allow two variations of recursion. As you saw in the previous tip, your method can call itself directly. This is called *direct recursion*. The second type of recursion is called *indirect recursion*. This is where a method calls another method which, in turn, calls the first method. The important point to note for either type of recursion is that the methods must define an ending condition. Otherwise, the methods would continue to call themselves forever. Actually, the methods won't actually call themselves forever because Java will eventually run out of stack space (the area where Java stores parameter information during a method call), and the program will end with an error.

183 OVERLOADING METHODS

Within your programs, you should assign meaningful names to your methods that describe the processing the method performs. For example, if your program uses a method that returns the square root of a value, you might call that method *square_root*. As you have learned, the parameter values you pass to a method are a specific type, such as *int* or *float*. Assume, for example, that your program needs to determine the square root of an integer value such as 9, as well as a floating-point value such as 3.84. In other programming languages, programmers would need to create two differently named functions to perform this processing, such as *int_square_root* and *float_square_root*. Java, however, lets you create two methods, both named *square_root*, whose parameter types differ—meaning one of the functions support the type *int* and the second supports the type *float*.

Method overloading is the process of assigning several methods the same name, distinguishing between the methods by their number or types of parameters. When your program calls one of the methods, the Java compiler examines the number of parameters and the parameter types to determine which method you really want to call. The following class defines several overloaded methods each distinctive in that they all have different parameters:

```
class Screwdriver_blades {
    int blade_size(float width, float thickness, float height)  { }
    int blade_size(float width) { }
    int blade_size(int ansi_standard_index) { }
}
```

To call any of the three methods, you simply provide the appropriate parameters. Java, in turn, will automatically call the right one:

```
screwdriver.blade_size(3.5, 0.2, 5.1);
screwdriver.blade_size(3.5);
screwdriver.blade_size(135);
```

OVERRIDING METHODS 184

In the previous tip, you learned that Java lets your programs overload a method by providing several different implementations of the method that vary by the number or type of parameters. In addition to letting your programs overload a method, Java also lets your programs override methods. The most notable difference between method overloading and method overriding is that the method signatures are identical in method overriding. In other words, when you override a method, you define a new method that uses the same number and type of parameters as an existing method.

In other words, overridden methods have not only identical names, but also identical parameters. Another difference between overridden and overloaded methods is that you do not declare overridden methods within the same class; instead, you declare them in separate classes.

When you declare a class that contains its own methods and derive another class from that class, you may have identically named (and parameterized) methods in both the two classes. Consider the following example, which derives the *Tomato* class from the *Vegetable* class:

```
class Vegetable {
    int peel_it(double rate) {}
}

class Tomato extends Vegetable {
    int peel_it(double rate) {}
}
```

Because the *Tomato* class is derived from the *Vegetable* class, and both have identical method signatures for the *peel_it* method, Java must make a decision on which of the *peel_it* methods to call. The rule is simple. Java uses the method defined in the class of the most current object. If it's an object of the subclass, Java uses the subclass method. If it's an object of the superclass, Java uses the superclass object. The following statements illustrate how Java decides on which method to call, based on what the current object is:

```
class Sample {
    public static void main(String args[])
    {
        Vegetable generic = new Vegetable();
        Tomato bigboy = new Tomato();
```

```
        generic.peel_it(1.2);        // calls the Vegetable peel_it
        bigboy.peel_it(1.6);         // calls the Tomato peel_it
        generic = bigboy;            // change the current object
        generic.peel_it(2.2);        // calls the Tomato peel_it
    }
}
```

As you can see, Java calls the *peel_it* method based on the object *generic* or *bigboy*. Notice that the *generic* object started as a *Vegetable*. However, when the statements assign the *generic* object the *bigboy* object, Java will then use the *Tomato* class *peel_it* method.

To distinguish between method overloading and method overriding, think about what you are trying to achieve. If you want to define multiple methods that differ by parameters, you are overloading a method. If you want Java to use a new method definition, you are overriding an existing method.

185 UNDERSTANDING VARIABLE SCOPE AND CONTROL STRUCTURES

As you have learned, the term *scope*, as it applies to variables, refers to the locations throughout your program where a variable is known. It is important that you understand the scope of a variable because if you try to access a variable that is out of scope (unknown to the current section of your code), you may either get a compile error or, in some cases, an execution error when you run your Java program.

As it turns out, Java's variable scoping rules are very similar to the scoping rules in C++. The general rule to remember is that Java restricts a variable's scope to inside the block within which you declared the variable. In the following example, the variables *scope_loop* and *scope_inside* are available inside the loop block, and the variable *scope_outside* is declared outside of the loop:

```
int scope_outside;

for (int scope_loop = 0; scope_loop < 10; scope_loop++)
   {
     int scope_inside;
     // both scope_loop and scope_inside are available inside here
   }

// only scope_outside is available here
```

If you declare variables within a compound statement or block that have the same name as variables defined outside of the compound statement or block, the Java compiler will use the newly declared variables within the compound statement (overriding the existing variable) and the original variables outside of the statement.

186 A CLASS DATA STRUCTURE GROUPS DATA AND OPERATIONS

Java is an object-oriented programming language based on classes. A *class* is a programming data structure within which you can group an object's data with the methods that operate on the data. For example, the data within a *window* class might contain the window's size and screen location. Likewise, the methods within the *window* class might include functions that display, size, and move the window. When you create a Java applet, you can define your own classes within the applet, or you can use existing classes from a class library (*packages*) that resides within a file on your disk.

One of the features that makes the Java programming language so powerful is that you can use the objects you create for one applet within another. In addition, your Java applets can use classes written by other programmers. Programmers store existing classcs within class libraries. In fact, each Java applet you create will use a special *Applet* class.

AN OBJECT IS A CLASS VARIABLE

187

In the simplest sense, an *object* is a *thing* or a real-world entity. When programmers create programs, they write instructions that work with different things such as variables or files. Different things have different *operations* that your programs perform on them. For example, given a *file* object, your program might perform such operations as reading, writing, or printing the file. As you will learn, Java programs define objects in terms of a class. An *object class* defines the data the object will store and the functions that operate on the data. Java programs often refer to the functions that manipulate the class data as *methods*. Most of your Java programs have already used the *System.out* object. In the case of this object, the I/O stream was the *thing*, and the method, *System.out.println*, performed an operation with the object, in this case, displaying screen output.

Within a Java program, think of a class as defining a template for variable declarations. In other words, a class defines a data type that contains data and related operations. An object, on the other hand, is a variable of the class type, which programmers often refer to as an *instance* of the class.

UNDERSTANDING OBJECT-ORIENTED PROGRAMMING

188

To programmers, an *object* is a collection of data, and *methods* are a set of operations that manipulate the data. *Object-oriented programming* provides a way of looking at programs in terms of the objects (things) that make up a system. After you have identified your system's objects, you can determine the operations normally performed on the object. If you have a *document* object, for example, common operations might include printing, spell-checking, faxing, or even discarding.

Object-oriented programming does not require a special programming language such as Java. You can write object-oriented programs in such languages as C++ or FORTRAN. However, as you will learn, languages described as "object-oriented" normally provide class-based data structures that let your programs group the data and methods into one variable. Object-oriented programming has many advantages, primarily object reuse and ease of understanding. As it turns out, you can often use the objects that you write for one program in another program. Rather than building a collection of function libraries, object-oriented programmers build *class libraries*. Likewise, by grouping an object's data and methods, object-oriented programs are often more readily understood than their non-object-based counterparts.

UNDERSTANDING ABSTRACTION

189

Abstraction is the process of looking at an object in terms of its methods (the operations), while temporarily ignoring the underlying details of the object's implementation. Programmers use abstraction to simplify the design and implementation of complex programs. For example, if you are told to write a word processor, the task might at first seem insurmountable. However, using abstraction, you begin to realize that a word processor actually consists of objects such as a document object that users will create, save, spell-check, and print. By viewing programs in abstract terms, you can better understand the required programming. In Java, the *class* is the primary tool for supporting abstraction.

190 UNDERSTANDING ENCAPSULATION

As you read articles and books about object-oriented programming and Java, you might encounter the term *encapsulation*. In the simplest sense, encapsulation is the combination of data and methods into a single data structure. Encapsulation groups together all the components of an object. In the "object-oriented" sense, encapsulation also defines how your programs can reference an object's data. Because you can divide a Java class into *public* and *private* sections, you can control the degree to which class users can modify or access the class data. For example, programs can only access an object's *private* data using *public* methods defined within the class. Encapsulating an object's data in this way protects the data from program misuses. In Java, the *class* is the fundamental tool for encapsulation.

191 UNDERSTANDING INHERITANCE

Java lets objects of one type call and access objects of a different class type. In addition, Java lets you build one object using another. For example, assume that you have defined a *disk_drive* class, a *keyboard* class, a *screen* class, and a *mouse* class. By combining all four classes, you could create a *computer* class. As the number of classes you create within Java programs increases, you may find that many of your newer classes are simply extensions of classes you have already created. To help you reuse your existing classes (saving you considerable programming time), Java lets you combine objects to build a new class.

192 UNDERSTANDING METHODS

If you have programmed in another object-oriented language such as C++, you are already familiar with methods. If you have programmed in a language such as C or Pascal, think of a method as a function or procedure. A *method* is simply a function that belongs to a class. Java methods have the following general form:

```
modifier type name(parameters)
  {
     // implementation
  }
```

The *modifier* section can be a variety of optional keywords such as *public*, *private*, or *protected*. The *type* specifies the type of value the method returns to the caller. The parameters are comma-separated arguments to the method. Finally, the implementation defines the statements that make up the method. The following statements, for example, define a method named *sum* which adds (sums) three variables of type *int*:

```
int sum(int a, int b, int c)
  {
     int result;                 // Local variable

     result = a + b + c;
     return(result);
  }
```

In this case, the method does not use any modifiers. The *int* that presents the method's name tells you the method returns a value of type *int*. In this case, the method uses three parameters of type *int*, whose names are *a*, *b*, and *c*.

UNDERSTANDING METHOD SIGNATURES

193

When you design methods for your classes, you may want to use a technique known as *overloading* to create multiple methods by the same name. As you learned in Tip 183, Java lets your programs overload methods, so the Java compiler will decide which function to invoke, depending on the number or type of parameters passed to the method.

When you overload a method, the methods all have the same name, but different signatures. The method's *signature* is the combination of the method's name, return type, and parameters. The following methods all have different signatures, and the first three are overloaded:

```
int measure_it(int width, int height) { }
int measure_it(int length) { }
float measure_it(int length) { }
float size_it(int length) { }
```

UNDERSTANDING CONSTRUCTOR METHODS

194

When your program creates an object instance, the program will normally assign initial values to the object data members. To simplify the process of initializing object members, Java supports a special function called a *constructor*, which automatically executes when the instance is created. The constructor function is a *public* method that uses the same name as the class. The general form of a constructor method is as follows:

```
classname(parameters)
{
    // Implementation
}
```

For example, using the *Book* class, the constructor function would have the name *Book*, as shown:

```
class Book {
    String title;
    String publisher;
    float price;

    // The following method is the constructor
    Book(String title, String publisher, float price);
    void print_book_info()  {  /* Implementation here */ }
};
```

Your programs can define the constructor method's statements within the class itself or outside of the class. For the previous example, assume that the code was implemented elsewhere in the source file. When your program later declares an object, the program can pass parameters to the constructor function, as shown:

```
Book tips = new Book("1001 Java Tips", "Jamsa Press", 49.95);
```

The constructor method will execute automatically and fill in the class member variables with the initial data passed into the constructor. You should keep the following rules in mind about Java constructors:

- A constructor has the same name as the class.

- A constructor is always called with the *new* keyword.

- Constructors may have zero or more parameters.

- Constructors do not need to return an explicit type.

195 OVERLOADING CONSTRUCTOR METHODS

As you learned in Tip 194, a constructor method is a special class method that Java automatically executes when your program creates an instance of an object. Also, as you know, Java lets your programs overload methods so the Java compiler will decide which function to invoke, depending on the parameters passed. Constructor methods are no exception. The following *Book* class provides two constructors, each with different parameters:

```
class Book {
    String title;
    String publisher;
    float price;
    // Constructor methods
    Book(String title, String publisher, float price);
    Book(String title, float price);
    void print_book_info()  {   /* Implementation here */ }
};
```

In this case, your program has two ways to declare a *Book* object. One way is to specify the title, publisher, and price, as shown:

```
Book tips = new Book("1001 Java Tips", "Jamsa Press", 49.95);
```

The second constructor lets you create a *Book* object when you do not know the publisher:

```
Book tips = new Book("1001 Java Tips", 49.95);
```

The two previous examples combine the declaration and instantiation of the new object into one statement. Many programmers like to use this technique. However, you may also separate the declaration from the instantiation, as follows:

```
Book tips;   // the declaration
tips = new Book("1001 Java Tips", 49.95);   // the instantiation
```

196 UNDERSTANDING POLYMORPHISM: THE OVERLOADING TYPE

Polymorphism is a term used to describe a situation where one name may refer to different methods. In Java, there are two types of polymorphism: the *overloading type* and the *overriding type*.

The overloading type of polymorphism occurs when you have the same method names within a class. You are allowed to do this as long as the methods have different numbers of parameters or different types of parameters. Having different return types does not count toward "disambiguating" methods and won't help you if you need two methods that have the same names and parameters, but different return types. As you create your polymorphic class methods and write code to access them, Java will determine which of the methods will be called at compile time. This is also known as *early binding*.

The following statements demonstrate a class containing several overloaded methods and illustrate a type of polymorphism:

```
class Screwdriver {
    int blade_size(float width, float thickness, float height)  { }
    int blade_size(float width) { }
    int blade_size(int ansi_standard_index) { }
}
```

UNDERSTANDING POLYMORPHISM: THE OVERRIDING TYPE 197

Polymorphism is a term that describes a situation where one name may refer to different methods. In Java, there are two types of polymorphism: the *overloading type* and the *overriding type*.

When you override methods, Java determines the proper methods to call at the program's run time, not at compile time. To determine which methods to call, Java must consider not just the methods within one class, but also the methods in the parent classes. Overriding occurs when a class method has the same name and *signature* (number, type, and order of parameters) as a method in a parent class (or superclass). In the case where the methods have the same name and signature, the method in the derived class will always override the method in its parent class.

The following example shows a derived class with a method (*operate_it*) that uses the same name as a method within the parent class:

```
class Tool {     // this is the superclass
    void operate_it()
    {
        System.out.println("Generic");
    }
}

class Screwdriver extends Tool {   // this is the subclass
    void operate_it()
    {
        System.out.println("Screwdriver");
    }
}

class Do_It {

    public static void main (String args[])
    {
        Tool generic = new Tool();
        Screwdriver phillips = new Screwdriver();

        generic.operate_it();    // calls the generic method
        phillips.operate_it();   // calls the screwdriver method

        generic = phillips;
        generic.operate_it();    // calls the screwdriver method !!!
    }
}
```

As you can see, the method call *generic.operate_it* will call the derived class method instead of the generic parent class method. By assigning the generic object to a more specific object, *phillips*, Java selects the derived method for the object at run-time. In this way, the *generic* object changes forms (is polymorphic) during the program's run-time.

198   UNDERSTANDING AN ABSTRACT CLASS

When you design a program in Java or with any other object-oriented language, you generally start with a high-level description of what your program needs to do. Object-oriented languages make it easier for you to model (or represent) the problem your program needs to solve because you can use classes to represent the "things" which make up your solution. Consider, for example, creating a program that draws life-like simulations of various insects. You would probably start by defining which insects you want to draw and what features they will have.

Let's say you would like to start by modeling an ant and a tarantula, and you create classes for each of these insects. As you develop the classes, you will quickly realize there are certain characteristics that are common to the ant and the tarantula. For example, both of these insects crawl and you will need to write a method (presumably named *crawl*) for each of them. Java provides you with a special type of class, called an *abstract class*, which can help you organize your classes based on common methods. An abstract class lets you put the common method names in one abstract class (without having to write the actual implementation code). Later, as you create new classes, such as the *ant* and *tarantula* classes, you can derive them from an abstract class that has a series of required methods (such as *crawl*) already defined.

Abstract methods have only a method name followed by a parameter list (also known as a *signature*). They do not have the code which implements the method—that is left to subsequently derived subclasses. Other key points about abstract methods are:

- Classes which contain abstract methods are called *abstract classes*.

- A program cannot instantiate an abstract class as an object.

- Abstract classes may contain a mixture of non-abstract and abstract methods. Non-abstract methods implement the method statements.

- Any subclass which extends the class containing abstract methods must provide the implementation for all of the abstract methods, otherwise the subclass itself becomes an abstract class.

For example, the following statements create an abstract class named *CrawlingInsects*:

```
public abstract class CrawlingInsects {
    public abstract int crawl( float   speed);
    // Other methods can go here
}
```

Notice that the abstract class contains a method without an implementation. When you create classes for crawling insects, such as ants and tarantulas, you must provide the implementation at that time. As you have learned, abstract classes, in a way, force you to create and use the methods they define. The following *ant* class demonstrates how you can use the *CrawlingInsects* abstract class:

```
public class Ant extends CrawlingInsects {

    String species_name;
```

```
public int crawl (float speed)
    {
        // Implementation to make the ant crawl goes here
    }
}
```

INHERITANCE IN JAVA 199

Inheritance is one of the most important features of object-oriented programming. In the simplest sense, inheritance is the process of building upon a class that is already defined, extending the existing class in some way. By understanding how inheritance works, you can design and derive new Java classes that are incrementally different from pre-existing classes. Inheritance will give you access to the information contained within any of the parent classes throughout the inheritance chain.

In Java, almost everything is an object. All of the classes you write, except for the special case of interfaces, are automatically subclasses of Java's built-in root class called *Object*. Just by creating your own first class, you've already used inheritance. Inheritance lets your subclasses build upon classes that are provided by the Java environment, other vendors and programmers, and those that you create yourself.

The best way to think about inheritance is to think of a hierarchy tree. Figure 199 illustrates a basic class hierarchy where the classes near the bottom are derived from classes above:

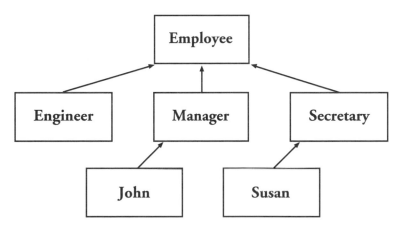

Figure 199 A class hierarchy.

A subclass inherits all of the methods and variables from all of its parent classes. When you write a derived subclass, it is as if you had retyped all of the *public* methods and variables that are present in the parent classes. Of course, Java does this for you; all you need to do is to create different methods and variables that the new subclass needs and its parents do not provide.

Unlike other object-oriented languages, such as C++, Java permits you to derive from only one parent class. You cannot derive a new subclass from two or more parent classes. *Multiple inheritance* is the process of deriving a class from two or more parents—and it is one of the features that the Java designers left out in order to keep Java simple. Fortunately, as you will learn in the next tip, Java provides a much cleaner alternative to multiple inheritance using something called an *interface*.

200   UNDERSTANDING INTERFACES

In Java, a class can have only one superclass (parent class). As you have learned, you can create new classes by deriving them from other classes, thereby inheriting the variables and methods of the parent class. This is a powerful technique that lets you add incremental functionality while keeping your classes as simple as possible. It also forces you to think about the design of your program and helps you organize its layout and flow.

However, there may be times when you would like to derive features from more than one parent class. This may come about from the nature of the problem you are trying to solve, for example: how to represent your solution in terms of classes. Java does not permit multiple inheritance, that is, the ability to derive a class from more than one class. However, Java has a way for you to declare a special kind of class that permits an unlimited number of derivations. This special class is called an *interface*, and it gives you most of the benefits of multiple inheritance with none of the complexities.

An *interface* is much like a class in that they both are declared one to a file, and they both have the same general format. Also, you can derive an *interface* from other *interfaces*. However, the major differences between an *interface* and a *class* are:

- An *interface* class, like an *abstract* class, supplies the method names but does not provide the method implementation.

- Any class may implement several interface classes, in a way, overcoming Java's multiple-inheritance restriction.

- A program cannot instantiate an *interface* class.

- All methods in an interface class are implicitly *public* and *abstract*. No other types are allowed.

- All variables in an interface class are implicitly *public*, *static*, and *final*. No other types are allowed.

- All methods must be implemented by the class using the *interface*.

- An *interface* class does not have an ultimate root parent leading to the *Object*. Instead, *interface* classes are in a separate hierarchy which you can freely apply to any part of your class tree.

An *interface* buys you the flexibility of declaring a set of methods and variables that may be implemented by any class in your hierarchy tree. An example of an *interface* is as follows:

```
public interface LiquidQualities {
    float viscosity;
    public void pour_it(float rate);
}
```

To use this *interface* in your class, you must use the *implements* keyword in your class declaration:

```
class OrangeJuice extends Beverages implements LiquidQualities {
    // Must implement all the interface methods here
    public void pour_it(float rate) { /* implement here */ }
}
```

Notice that the statements derive the *OrangeJuice* class from the *Beverages* class. At the same time, the statements use the *implements* keyword to access methods and variables from an *interface* class. If you need to, you may implement a class using several *interface* classes, as shown:

```
class OrangeJuice extends Beverages implements LiquidQualities,
    TasteQualities, ColorQualities {
        // Other class statements here
    }
```

USING INTERFACE FOR GLOBAL CONSTANTS

 201

As you learned in Tip 200, using interfaces you provide a way for one class to derive characteristics from more than one parent class. In addition, you can use an *interface* to provide a set of constants that any of your classes can access directly. The following statements, for example, show you how to set up an *interface* class that defines a set of constants:

```
public interface DateConstants {
    public static final String base_month = "January";
    public static final int months_per_year = 12;
}
```

To use these constants from any class, you simply use the *implements* keyword within the class definition and then reference the constants directly. For example, the following statements implement the *DateConstants* class which lets the *MyCalendar* class access the constants:

```
public class My_Calendar implements DateConstants {
    public static void main(String argv[ ])
     {
        int total_months = months_per_year;
        System.out.println("Start month is " + base_month);

        // Other statements here
    }
}
```

UNDERSTANDING WHEN TO CHOOSE INHERITANCE ("IS A?")

 202

As you design new programs and as you build up your class hierarchy (increase the number of classes you can reuse in other programs), you will need to decide when to derive new subclasses from pre-existing classes. If you are not careful, you may wind up using inheritance when it is not needed. A good rule of thumb when deciding whether you should derive a class from another class is to ask the "Is a?" question.

For example, assume that you have a *Cheese* class and a *Brie* class, and you are trying to decide whether you should derive the *Brie* class from the *Cheese* class. If you can say, "Brie is a Cheese," you can use inheritance and derive *Brie* from *Cheese*.

A common mistake programmers make who are new to object-oriented program is to ask the "Has a?" question instead of "Is a?" For example, a car "has a" steering wheel, but a car is not a steering wheel. Therefore, you would not use inheritance within the *car* class to implement the *steering_wheel* class. Tip 203 discusses "Has a?" relationships in more detail.

203 UNDERSTANDING WHEN TO CHOOSE CONTAINMENT ("HAS A?")

In many cases, you will need to instantiate (create) an instance of a class from within your class by using the *new* operator. In fact, when you see the terms *container class* or *containment*, the terms refer to a class which contains declarations of other classes. As you learned in Tip 202, to determine if you should derive one class from another, you can ask the "Is a?" question. Similarly, you can ask the "Has a?" question to determine if one class should contain another.

For example, assume that you have a *Brie* class and a *WhiteCrust* class, and you are trying to decide whether the *Brie* class should contain the *WhiteCrust* class. If you can say, "Brie has a WhiteCrust," you can use containment and instantiate a *WhiteCrust* object from within the *Brie* class.

204 RESTRICTING EXTENSIONS OF METHODS AND CLASSES

As a class designer, you may want to restrict another programmer from extending (or deriving from) a particular class or method. For example, you may provide a class with a series of methods that should not be overridden. By using the *final* keyword, you can control which methods can be extended further. For example, the following class definition uses the *final* keyword within the *set_password* method definition to prevent another programmer from overriding the method:

```
class SystemSettings {
    public final int set_password(String pw) { }
}
```

If you use the *final* keyword at the start of the class declaration, another programmer cannot extend the class itself. For example, the following statements place the *final* keyword within the *LastStand* class definition to prevent another programmer from extending the class:

```
final class LastStand {
    public int do_not_override_me(int x) { }
}
```

205 FORCING METHOD AND CLASS EXTENSIONS

When you define a class, you use the *abstract* keyword to force other programmers who use the class to implement a specific class method. Normally, you use the *abstract* keyword when you design a generic class that requires a programmer who uses the class to define specific methods. In other words, the *abstract* keyword tells the Java compiler and programmers who are using your code that the program must implement one or more of the class methods. You should also provide the *abstract* keyword at the beginning of each individual method that needs an implementation. For example, the following statements create an abstract class named *Stove*. Within the class, another programmer who is using the class must implement the *set_heating_value* method:

```
abstract class Stove {
    abstract void set_heating_value(int value);
}
```

For another programmer to use the *Stove* class, they must implement the abstract *set_heating_value* function.

USING AN INTERFACE TO CREATE CALLBACK METHODS 206

Callbacks are methods that are frequently called by Graphical User Interfaces (GUIs) in response to an event related to screen redraw operations, mouse clicks, typing, and so on. In general, you can think of callbacks as event handlers—software that responds to specific events. You can use callback functions in any situation for which you need the program to call a method based on some event.

You may already be familiar with a technique used in C/C++ in which a program passes a callback function as a pointer to another caller function. Using the function pointer, the function which receives the pointer can invoke the callback function. As Java does not have pointers, you can use a technique involving interfaces to create a callback function. To start, you must define an interface that the callback method will implement. For example, the following statements define an *interface* named *EventHandler*:

```
public interface EventHandler {
   public void handleIt();
}
```

Next, you must implement the interface (in this case the *handleIt* function) within your callback method:

```
public class CallMeBack implements EventHandler {
   private EventSender sender;   // class that will
                                 // do the calling
   public CallMeBack ()
     {
        sender= new EventSender(this); // pass ourself
                                       // to the sender
     }

   public void handleIt()
     {
        // do whatever you want here
     }
}
```

Finally, your code that actually calls the callback may look something like this:

```
public class EventSender {

   private EventHandler handler;
   private boolean call_it_now;
   public EventSender(EventHandler new_handler)
     {
        handler = new_handler;     // save the handler for
                                   // later use
        call_it_now = false;       // set to true at some
                                   // other place

     }
```

```
public void InvokeIt()
  {
    if (call_it_now)            // set true somewhere in
                                // your code
      {
          handler.handleIt();   // invoke the interface's
                                // method
      }
  }
}
```

207 OBJECT-ORIENTED VERSUS PROCEDURAL PROGRAMMING

When you compare object-oriented programming (OOP) to the traditional procedural program methodology, you will find that object-oriented programming provides a new framework with which you look at programming problems. In a procedural methodology, programmers write functions to solve pieces of a problem. If another programmer has written functions to solve specific problems, your programs can use (call) these functions. In traditional procedural programming, programmers spend more time on functions rather than the problem the program should solve.

As you have learned, object-oriented programming provides a way of looking at programs in terms of data and the methods which operate on the data. In object-oriented programming, your focus shifts away from thinking about functions and toward thinking about the things (objects) that make up your program. The basic difference between object-oriented programming and a procedural approach comes from four key principles: abstraction, encapsulation, inheritance, and polymorphism.

Abstraction is the process of temporarily ignoring an object's underlying details and, instead, focusing on the problem or object so you can extract the object's essential characteristics. For example, if you think about car tires, an abstract tire may have a brand name, size, price, and an ideal amount of air. These characteristics apply to all tires. Using abstraction, you can focus on these key (common) characteristics, as opposed to details about a specific tire type.

Encapsulation is the process of grouping an object's abstracted information with the operations (methods) that a program may perform on the data. For example, a *class* is an encapsulation of an object's data and methods.

Inheritance is a framework with which you can create new classes by introducing new features or changes to pre-existing classes. Inheritance frees you from C's chore of rewriting functions when you need to make small changes.

Finally, *polymorphism* is the ability of an object to take on different forms. The term *poly* stands for "many," and *morphism* means "forms." For example, within a program, a polymorphic telephone object can change forms to become a touch-tone, a rotary dial phone, or even a cellular phone.

208 DEFINING YOUR OWN CLASS

You have made extensive use of existing Java classes in many of the previous tips. As your programs become more complex, you will make extensive use of your own classes. To define your own class within an applet, you specify the *class* keyword followed by the name of the class, as shown:

```
class MyNewClass {
    // Statements here
}
```

You store each new class you create in a file with the *.java* extension. You may have multiple classes defined in such a file; however, you may only have one *public* class per *.java* file. A *public* class is a class which is available outside of the package—that is, other programs can use the class. When you name the class file, you must use the same name for the file as for the class itself. For example, you would store the following *OliveTree* class in the *OliveTree.java* file:

```
public class OliveTree {
    // Statements here
}
```

As you will learn, you can use several additional keywords to modify the class. For example, if the *OliveTree* class is a subclass based on the *Trees* superclass, you would use the *extends* keyword, as follows:

```
public class OliveTree extends Trees {
```

For now, don't worry about such terms as subclass, superclass, or even the *extends* keyword. You will examine each of these topics throughout the remainder of this book.

CREATING A SIMPLE CLASS OBJECT 209

After you have a class that you would like to use, you can *instantiate* (create) an instance of that class. An instance of a class is also known as an *object*. To better understand the process of instantiating an object, consider this simple *Fruit* class:

```
public class Fruit {
    // Statements here
}
```

For now, you can ignore the contents of the *Fruit* class (its methods and member variables). Next, you can create an instance of the *Fruit* class by declaring an object variable and assigning it to an object your program creates using the new operator:

```
Fruit apple;            // Declare an object variable

apple = new Fruit(); // Make apple point to new object
```

As it turns out, Java lets you combine the previous two lines into one line, which declares and instantiates the object in one step:

```
Fruit apple = new Fruit();  // Declare and instantiate
```

ADDING VARIABLES TO YOUR SIMPLE CLASS 210

As you may already know, functions in C and methods in C++ and Java let you declare variables within the function or method. These *local variables* are visible only within the function or method, but not outside it. In other words, the program can only access (use) the variables within the function or method. In a similar way, you can also declare local variables inside a class definition. These class-based local variables are sometimes called *instance variables* or *member variables* because each instance of the object gets its own copy of the variables.

For example, the following statements add two local variables to the *Fruit* class:

```
public class Fruit {
    float price;
    String variety;

    // Other statements
}
```

Your program can now use the variables *price* and *variety* to store unique information for each instance of the *Fruit* object that you create. For example, assume that your program instantiates an *apple* object, as shown:

```
Fruit apple = new Fruit();   // declare and instantiate
```

Now, your program can access the *apple* object's variables by using the object variable followed by a dot and the name of the instance variable. For example, the following statements assign values to the *apple* object's member variables:

```
apple.price = 0.85F;
apple.variety = "McIntosh";
```

Remember that the instance-variable values are unique for each object instance that you create using the *new* operator. You can instantiate other fruits, assign prices and varieties, and each will have their unique values maintained independently. For example, the following statements create an *orange* object and assign values to the member variables:

```
Fruit orange = new Fruit();   // Declare and instantiate
                              // an object

orange.price = 0.35F;
orange.variety = "Valencia";
```

At this point, the program now has two objects, *apple* and *orange*, each with a unique price and variety name.

211 JAVA ASSIGNS DEFAULT VALUES TO CLASS MEMBER VARIABLES

If you do not initialize the local variables that your programs declare within methods and classes, Java will assign a default value to the variable based on the variable's type. Table 211 lists Java default values.

Type	Default value
boolean	false
char	\u0000
byte	0
short	0
int	0
long	0
float	0.0
double	0.0

Table 211 Default initial values for variables.

212

In Java, Constant Local Variables Are Not Legal

As you create variables within a Java applet, you may want to create a constant value within the class. To create a constant within Java, you precede the variable declaration with the *final* keyword, as shown:

```
final String title  = "1001 Java Programmer's Tips";
```

Within a class, however, you cannot use the *final* keyword when you declare local variables inside a method. If you do so, the Java compiler will display a syntax error message. The following statements illustrate legal and illegal uses of the *final* keyword:

```
final int isGood = 100;     // outside a method and legal

public void paint(Graphics g)
  {
      final int notGood = 200;    // this is illegal here
  }
```

213

Using the Static Variables Initialization Block

When your programs work with multiple objects of the same type, there may be times when the objects need to share information. In such cases, you can use the *static* keyword to direct the Java compiler to share the variable. When you declare a class member as *static*, you tell the Java compiler that you want only one copy of the variable associated with the class, rather than multiple copies of the variables associated with each instance. You may initialize the *static* variable as you would any other non-static (or instance) variable by assigning a value to it. The following statements create a shared member variable name, *pounds*:

```
public class Weight {
    public static int pounds = 155;

    // Statements here
  }
```

To access the *static* variable (also called a class variable because the variable's value is class specific, rather than instance specific), simply use the class name and variable, as shown:

```
System.out.println("Current weight is " + Weight.pounds);
```

In this case, if your program has multiple *Weight* objects, each object will share the value of the *pounds* variable. Should one object change the variable's value, each object will see the change.

214

Adding Methods to Your Simple Class

Methods define an object's behavior by providing various operations that the object can perform during its lifetime. You must declare methods within the class that owns them. For example, the following statements add two methods to the *Fruit* class:

```java
public class Fruit {
    float price;
    String variety;

    Fruit(float p, String v)
      {
        price= p;
        variety= v;
      }

    void displayIt()
      {
        System.out.println("Variety: " + variety +
          ",Price: " + price);
      }
  }
```

The first method, *Fruit*, has the same name as the class itself. This is a special method known as a constructor. As you will learn, Java calls the class constructor method each time the program instantiates an object. Normally, the constructor performs initializing chores, assigning values to the class-member variables. For example, by using the *Fruit* constructor method, the program can declare, instantiate, and identify a new fruit all in one line, as shown:

```java
Fruit apple = new Fruit(0.85F, "McIntosh");
```

By using the object variable (*apple*), you can invoke individual methods. For example, the following statement invokes the *Fruit* class *displayIt* method:

```java
apple.displayIt();
```

The previous statement will display the current values of the instance variables, as follows:

```
Variety: McIntosh, Price: 0.85
```

Note: *You cannot invoke constructors directly—instead, Java invokes the constructor methods automatically during object creation.*

215 OVERLOADING CLASS METHODS

When you create class methods, Java lets you declare two or more methods with the same names which differ by the number of parameters or types of parameters they support. When the Java compiler examines your code, it will determine which of the methods to call based on the parameters a function call uses. For example, the following statements add another constructor method that supports just one parameter:

```java
public class Fruit {
    float price;
    String variety;

    Fruit(String v)
      {
        price = 1.00F;
        variety = v;
      }
```

```
    Fruit(float p, String v)
      {
        price = p;
        variety = v;
      }

    void displayIt()
      {
        System.out.println("Variety:" + variety + ",Price:"
          + price);
      }
    }
```

In this case, the class *overloads* the *Fruit* constructor method. Depending on the parameters you supply, Java will decide which method to call. For example, the following line, which creates a new *banana* object, does not assign an explicit price. Instead, the program relies on the default price of 1.00, which is set by the class constructor:

```
Fruit banana = new Fruit("Dole");
```

Of course, if you know the price, you can call the other constructor specifying a price and name, as shown:

```
Fruit apple = new Fruit(0.85F, "McIntosh");
```

USING INHERITANCE TO BUILD CLASSES 216

After you create a class, you may find it necessary to extend the class capabilities. When you need to extend a class, Java lets you create new classes which use variables and methods from an existing class, while adding new variables and methods of its own. For example, consider the following *Fruit* class:

```
public class Fruit {
    float price;
    String variety;

    Fruit(float p, String v)
      {
        price= p;
        variety= v;
      }

    void displayIt()
      {
        System.out.println("Variety:" + variety + ",Price:"
          + price);
      }
    }
```

This *Fruit* class is very basic, designed so that programs can apply it to all presently conceivable fruits. However, because it is so simple, you may find it necessary to extend it further when the program needs to support a new fruit. To add new features to the class, you can create new classes which extend (or build upon) the *Fruit* class. For example, the following class definitions each extend the *Fruit* class, adding new members:

```
public class Apple extends Fruit {
    boolean sliced;
}

public class Orange extends Fruit {
    boolean wedged;
}
```

In this case, the statements create the *Apple* and *Orange* classes (note the uppercase letters to distinguish these classes from the *apple* and *orange* instances you created earlier).

As you can see, the two new classes add specific qualities to the *Apple* and *Orange* classes which did not (and should not) exist in the original *Fruit* class. By keeping the *Fruit* class generic, you can create subclasses which add new features to a derived class.

The power behind inheritance is that you can access all of the parent's public variables and methods as if they were typed into the subclass. This time, to create the *Apple* instance, you simply instantiate the derived class rather than the parent class:

```
Apple GreatApple = new Apple(0.85F, "McIntosh");

GreatApple.sliced = true;
```

Because the *Apple* class did not define a constructor method, Java will invoke the next constructor in the chain which, in this case, is the *Fruit* constructor.

217 IMPLEMENTING INHERITANCE AND POLYMORPHISM IN JAVA

When you extend a class and create a new subclass that contains additional variables and methods, you are telling Java that the subclass contains all of its parent's public variables and methods, as well as the ones within the subclass itself. At times, you may have methods in your subclass with the same name as the methods in the parent class itself. In the case where the methods have the same name and signature, the method in the derived class will always override the method in its parent class. For example, consider again the *Fruit* class and the extended *Apple* class:

```
public class Fruit {
    float price;
    String variety;

    Fruit(float p, String v)
      {
        price= p;
        variety= v;
      }

    void displayIt()
      {
        System.out.println("Variety:" + variety + ",Price:"
          + price);
      }
  }


public class Apple extends Fruit {
    boolean sliced;
```

```
    Apple(float p, String v) { super(p, v); }
    void displayIt()
      {
        System.out.println("Variety:" + variety + ",Price:"
          + price + ",Sliced: " + sliced);
      }
    }
```

Because the *Apple* class is derived from the *Fruit* class, and both have identical method signatures (method names and parameter usage) for the *displayIt* method, Java must decide which of the *displayIt* methods to call. The rule Java follows is to use the method defined in the most current object. The following example illustrates how Java decides which method to call based on the current object:

```
class Sample {
    public static void main(String args[])
      {
        Fruit banana = new Fruit(0.55F, "Banana");
        Apple greatApple = new Apple(0.85F, "McIntosh");
        greatApple.sliced = true;

        banana.displayIt();         // calls the Fruit displayIt
        greatApple.displayIt();     // calls the Apple displayIt
      }
    }
```

As shown by the program's output which follows, Java calls the *displayIt* method based on the object *banana* or *greatApple*. For the *banana* object, Java invokes the *Fruit* class method. For the *apple* object, Java invokes the *Apple* class method.

```
Variety:  Banana,Price:  0.55
Variety:  McIntosh,Price:  0.85,Sliced:true
```

WHAT IS A SUPERCLASS? 218

When you derive one class from another in Java, you establish relationships between the various classes. The parent class (or the class that is being derived from) is often called the *superclass* or *base class*. The superclass is really an ordinary class which is being extended by another class. In other words, you do not need to do anything special to the class in order for it to become a superclass. Any of the classes you write may some day become a superclass if someone decides to create a new subclass derived from your class.

Of course, you can prevent a class from becoming a superclass (that is, do not allow it to be extended). If you use the *final* keyword at the start of the class declaration, the class cannot be extended.

UNDERSTANDING JAVA'S THIS REFERENCE 219

When your programs work with objects, you may need to refer to the class object itself. For example, a class method may need to pass itself to another function. Likewise, a method may need to return the object itself to the function's caller, so the caller knows which object it was manipulating.

In such cases, your programs can use Java's *this* keyword to refer to the object itself. You do not need to declare the *this* keyword or do anything special because *this* is always available and always returns you a reference to the current object.

Your programs use the Java *this* keyword much like any other object—by using the object name and dot operator. The following statement, for example, assumes you need to pass the current object as a parameter to the method *someMethod*:

```
this.someMethod(this);
```

In a similar way, to access the current object's instance variables, you can prefix the variable names with Java's *this* keyword:

```
this.someVariable = 5;
```

Within a class method, the *this* keyword is implicit, meaning most class methods omit it. In other words, the following statements are identical:

```
this.someVariable = 5;      // Uses this keyword

someVariable = 5;           // Omits implied this
```

Another situation for which Java's *this* keyword is useful is when both an instance variable and a method variable have the same name. By using the Java's *this* keyword, you can distinguish between the two. For example, the following *printMe* class method uses a local variable named *copy* which conflicts with the class member variable named *copy*. By using Java's *this* keyword, the *printMe* method can distinguish between the local and class member variables:

```
class ThisTest {
   int copy = 5;

   void printMe()
     {
       int copy = 10;
       System.out.println("Inst=" + this.copy + ", Local="
          + copy);
     }
 }
```

These statements will display the following output:

```
Inst=5,  Local=10
```

Yet another use for *this* is to call a constructor method from within another constructor of the same class. To accomplish this, you must follow specific rules:

1. You must use *this* in the first line of a constructor.

2. You must use the form *this (constructor arguments)*.

The following example shows how a constructor can call another constructor within the same class:

```
class Telephone {
    public Telephone()          // First constructor
    {
        this(getValue());    // Call the other constructor
    }

    public Telephone(int reset_value)   // Called from above
    {
        // Statements here
    }
}
```

By having a reference to the current object, you can use *this* for a variety of situations, including accessing instance variables as a return value to identify the object to a caller, or as an argument to a method. Finally, class methods declared with the *static* keyword cannot use *this*.

UNDERSTANDING THE SUPER KEYWORD

 220

When Java calls the constructor method for a subclass, Java will automatically call the superclass default constructor. As it turns out, Java provides a default constructor for all classes which allocates the object's memory and initiates the object. The *default constructor* is a constructor that has no parameters. If your subclass constructor does not explicitly call the superclass constructor, Java will call the superclass default constructor. If you want your subclass constructor to call a specific superclass constructor, you need to use the *super* keyword.

The *super* keyword gives you access to the superclass object and lets you invoke a specific superclass constructor, as well as other methods found in the superclass. For example, the following subclass constructor explicitly calls a specific superclass constructor:

```
public class HazelNut extends Nuts {

    public HazelNut (int size) // subclass constructor
    {
        super(size);   // call the superclass constructor
        // Statements here
    }
}
```

To call a superclass constructor in this manner, the *super* constructor method must be the first statement inside the subclass constructor.

USING SUPER TO CALL A PARENT'S CLASS METHOD

 221

As you have learned in Tip 220, the *super* keyword gives a subclass access to the superclass constructor. Another way programs use the *super* keyword is to access the variables and methods of a superclass. For example, assume that your program uses a *Nuts* class, as shown:

```
public class Nuts {
   int nutsize;

   printNuts()
     {
         // Statements here
     }
   // Additional statements
 }
```

Next, assume you create a *PineNut* class as a subclass of the *Nut* class, as shown:

```
public class PineNut extends Nuts {

   public PineNut (int size)       // subclass constructor
     {
        super.nutsize = size;      // assign to the superclass
                                   // variable
        super.printNuts();         // call printNuts in the
                                   // superclass

     }
 }
```

By using the *super* keyword, you can access the superclass variable *nutsize* and method *printNuts* from within the *PineNuts* subclass.

222 UNDERSTANDING THE NEW KEYWORD

When you create a Java program, you define a set of classes. Classes are, for the most part, templates for objects the program will create. As you have learned, programs use the *new* keyword to create an object based on a specific class. In fact, the *new* operator actually allocates the memory that will hold the object, and then assigns the object to the corresponding memory location. Next, the *new* operator directs Java to invoke the object's class constructor function. Using the object variable, your program can reference the object's memory locations. For example, the following statement declares and instantiates an object variable named *my_dialog*:

```
java.awt.Dialog my_dialog = new java.awt.Dialog(parent, modal);
```

In other words, to create an object, you use the *new* keyword followed by the object's class and optional parameters within parentheses. Java will pass the parameters to the class constructor method, which initializes the object after the object has been created.

223 UNDERSTANDING THE INSTANCEOF KEYWORD

Within your programs, you may need to know if one object is an instance of a specific class. For example, if you store different types of objects within an array, you may need to examine the array elements to determine the type of object the array contains. In such cases, your programs can use the *instanceof* operator, which will return *true* if the object on its left-hand side is an instance of the class specified on its right-hand side. In addition, your programs can use the *instanceof* operator to indicate whether the object on the left-hand side implements an *interface* specified on the right-hand side. For example, the following statements use the *instanceof* operator to determine if the variable *some_class* contains an object that is an instance of the Java *Font* type. You can also use *instanceof* within a boolean statement, as shown:

```
if (some_class instanceof java.awt.Font)
    // yes it is, execute some statements
```

As you will learn in Tip 224, the *instanceof* operator comes in handy when you are about to cast an object. By checking whether the object is an instance of a particular class, you can cast that object to the class type without the risk of generating an exception.

CASTING CLASS TYPES  224

Just as there are times when you need to cast variables from one type to another, there may be times when you must cast Java objects. The object form of the cast operation is similar to the one you used for variables. One restriction is, however, that the class of the object you are casting and the class of the object you are casting it to must be related by inheritance as superclasses or subclasses. For example, to cast the *turkey* object to the *Bird* class, you would use the following statements:

```
turkey = (Bird) thanksgiving_food[1];
```

The previous statement demonstrates a situation in which an array of *thanksgiving_food* may contain a variety of foods; thus, casting is required for Java to make the proper assignment.

Generally, you can easily assign an object to a superclass variable by following the inheritance chain and making the object more general. However, if you assign an object to a subclass variable that is lower in the hierarchy, you are giving the object attributes it does not have and does not have any way to identify. In these cases, Java may generate an exception (an error). Before your program casts an object, you should always use the *instanceof* operator to check if the object is an instance of the class you are casting. For example, the following statements test whether the object in the *thanksgiving_food* array is an instance of the *Bird* class. If so, the statements cast the object to the *Bird* class:

```
if (thanksgiving_food[1] instanceof Bird)
    turkey = (Bird) thanksgiving_food[1];
```

COMPARING OBJECTS WITH == REALLY COMPARES REFERENCES 225

When you use Java's equality (==) and not equals (!=) operators with objects, you are actually testing whether the two variables refer to the same object. As you work with objects, you must always remember that when you assign objects to variables, or pass objects as arguments to methods, you are passing *references* to the objects, not the objects themselves. So, when you try to perform an equality comparison using the object variables, you are simply comparing the references.

If you need to compare the actual contents of the objects, you must use some other approach. The *String* class, for example, provides you with the *equals* method, which actually compares the objects, that is, the strings.

226 UNDERSTANDING INFORMATION HIDING

Information hiding is the process of hiding underlying implementation details of a method, program, or class. Information hiding lets programmers treat methods and classes as *black boxes*. In other words, if a programmer passes a parameter to a method, the programmer knows a specific result will occur. The programmer does not need to know how the result is calculated, but simply that the method works. For example, most programmers don't know the mathematics behind the *tanh* function, which returns an angle's hyperbolic tangent. However, the programmers know that if they pass a specific value to *tanh*, a known result will occur. To use the method, the programmer only needs to know the input parameters and the values returned.

In object-oriented programming, an object has underlying implementation details. For example, in the case of a document, the data must be stored in Word, Excel, or some other format. To use the document object, however, the program should not need to know the format. Instead, the program should be able to perform read, write, and even fax operations without knowing the object details. To help programmers hide an object's underlying details, Java lets you divide a class definition into *private* and *public* parts. The program can directly access the class *public* data and methods, while the program cannot access the *private* data methods.

As you design your classes, you will have to decide which variables and methods you should make a part of the class, and which should be *public* or *private*. As you make these decisions, you define how other users will access your class.

227 AVOID USING TOO MANY BASIC TYPES IN YOUR CLASS

As you design your class, you should keep an eye out for a "build up" of basic variable types. For example, consider the case where you are designing a *Letter* class for which you need to represent all the usual properties associated with a letter, such as the sender and receiver's name, street, city, and so on. The variable declaration section within this class may look something like:

```
private String senderName;
private String senderStreet;
private String senderCity;
private String senderState;
private String senderZip;
private String receiverName;
private String receiverStreet;
private String receiverCity;
private String receiverState;
private String receiverZip;
```

In this case, you should consider creating a second *Address* class. Then, you can use the *Address* class to represent a sender's or receiver's address. After you define the *Address* class, you can use it in the *Letter* class, as shown:

```
Address sender;
Address receiver;
```

By encapsulating basic types into additional classes in this way, you make your classes easier to use and maintain.

UNDERSTANDING THE ABSTRACT CLASS MODIFIER

228

As you have learned, Java lets you extend an existing class with a subclass. Over time, you may start to develop your own class libraries whose classes you anticipate other programmers will extend. For some classes, there may be times when it does not make sense to implement a method until you know how a programmer will extend the class. In such cases, you can define the method as abstract, which forces a programmer who is extending the class to implement the method.

When you use the *abstract* keyword within a class, a program cannot create an instance of that class. As briefly discussed, abstract classes usually have abstract methods which the class did not implement. Instead, a subclass extends the abstract class, and the subclass must supply the *abstract* method's implementation. To declare a class abstract, simply include the *abstract* keyword within the class definition, as shown:

```
public abstract class SomeAbstractClass {
```

UNDERSTANDING THE FINAL CLASS MODIFIER

229

As you have learned, Java lets one class extend another. When you design a class, there may be times when you don't want another programmer to extend the class. In such cases, by including the *final* keyword within a class definition, you prevent the class from being subclassed. The following statement illustrates the use of the *final* keyword within a class definition:

```
public final class TheBuckStopsHere {
```

UNDERSTANDING THE PUBLIC CLASS MODIFIER

230

As you learned in Tip 226, information hiding is the process of hiding the "inner workings" of a function or class. As you develop Java programs, there may be times when you create classes that you don't want the code outside of the class package (the class file) to access, or even to have knowledge of.

When you use the *public* keyword within a class declaration, you make that class visible (and accessible) everywhere. A non-public class, on the other hand, is visible only to the package within which it is defined. To control access to a class, do not include the *public* keyword within the class declaration. Java only lets you place one *public* class within a source-code file. For example, the following statement illustrates the use of the *public* keyword within a class:

```
public class ImEverywhereYouWantMeToBe {
```

UNDERSTANDING THE PUBLIC FIELD MODIFIER

231

A *variable's scope* defines the locations within a program where the variable is known. Within a class definition, you can control a class member variable's scope by preceding a variable's declaration with the *public*, *private*, or *protected* keywords. A *public* variable is visible (accessible) everywhere in the program where the class itself is visible (accessible). To declare a variable *public*, simply use the *public* keyword at the start of the variable declaration, as shown:

```
public int seeMeEveryWhere;
```

232 UNDERSTANDING THE PRIVATE FIELD MODIFIER

As you learned in Tip 231, to control a class member variable's scope, you can precede the variable's declaration with the *public, private,* or *protected* keywords. A *private* variable is only visible within its class. Subclasses cannot access *private* variables. To declare a variable *private,* simply use the *private* keyword at the start of the variable declaration, as shown:

```
private int InvisibleOutside;
```

233 UNDERSTANDING THE PROTECTED FIELD MODIFIER

As you learned in Tip 231, to control a class member variable's scope, you can precede the variable's declaration with the *public, private,* or *protected* keywords. A *protected* variable is one that is only visible within its class, within subclasses, or within the package that the class is part of. The difference between a *private* class member and a *protected* class member is that a *private* class member is not accessible within a subclass. To declare a variable *protected,* simply use the *protected* keyword at the start of the variable declaration, as shown:

```
protected int ImProtected;
```

234 UNDERSTANDING THE PRIVATE PROTECTED FIELD MODIFIER

As you learned in Tip 231, to control a class member variable's scope, you can precede the variable's declaration with the *public, private,* or *protected* keywords. A *private protected* variable is only visible within its class and within subclasses of the class. The difference between a *protected* class member and a *private protected* variable is that a *private protected* variable is not accessible within its *package.* To declare a variable *private protected,* simply use the *private protected* keyword at the start of the variable declaration, as shown:

```
private protected int ImPrivateProtected;
```

235 UNDERSTANDING THE STATIC FIELD MODIFIER

As you have learned, class member variables are often called *instance variables* because each instance of the class, each object, gets its own copy of each variable. Depending on your program's purpose, there may be times when the class objects need to share information. In such cases, you can specify one or more class variables as shared among the objects. To share a variable among class objects, you declare the variable as *static,* as shown:

```
public static int ShareThisValue;
```

In this case, if one object changes the value of the *ShareThisValue* variable, each object will see the updated value.

UNDERSTANDING THE final FIELD MODIFIER

 236

When you declare a variable in a class *final*, you tell the compiler that the variable has a constant value that program should not change. To define a *final* variable, you must also include an initializer that assigns a value to the constant. For example, the following statement creates a constant value named MAX_KEYS, to which the program assigns the value 256:

```
protected static final int MAX_KEYS = 256;
```

UNDERSTANDING THE transient FIELD MODIFIER

 237

When you declare a variable in a class *transient*, you tell Java that the variable is not part of the object's persistent state. Currently, Java does not use the *transient* keyword. However, future (persistent) versions of Java may use the *transient* keyword to tell the compiler that the program is using the variable for "scratch pad" purposes and that the compiler does not need to save the variable to disk. The following statement illustrates the use of the *transient* keyword:

```
transient float temp_swap_value;
```

UNDERSTANDING THE volatile FIELD MODIFIER

 238

When you compile a program, the compiler will examine your code and perform some "tricks" behind the scenes that optimize your program's performance. Under certain circumstances, you may want to force the compiler not to optimize a variable. Optimization can make certain assumptions about where and how memory is handled. If, for example, you are building an interface to a memory-mapped device, you may need to suppress optimization. To protect a variable from being optimized, you should use the *volatile* keyword, as shown:

```
volatile double system_bit_flags;
```

UNDERSTANDING DEFAULT CONSTRUCTORS

 239

When you create your classes, you should always provide one or more constructor methods. However, if you do not specify a constructor, Java will provide a default constructor for you. Java's default constructor will allocate memory to hold the object and will then initialize all instance variables to their defaults. Java will not provide a default constructor, however, if your class specifies one or more constructors for the class.

UNDERSTANDING THE public METHOD MODIFIER

 240

As you have learned, using the *public*, *private*, and *protected* keywords, you can control a variable's scope. In a similar way, Java lets you use these attributes with class methods as well. A *public* method is visible everywhere that the class is visible. To declare a method as *public*, simply precede the method header with the *public* keyword, as shown:

```
public float myPublicMethod();
```

241 Understanding the private Method Modifier

As you have learned, using the *public*, *private*, and *protected* keywords, you can control a variable's scope. In a similar way, Java lets you use these attributes with class methods as well. A *private* method is only visible within its class. Subclasses cannot access *private* methods. To declare a method as *private*, simply precede the method header with the *private* keyword, as shown:

```
private int myPrivateMethod();
```

242 Understanding the protected Method Modifier

As you have learned, using the *public*, *private*, and *protected* keywords, you can control a variable's scope. In a similar way, Java lets you use these attributes with class methods as well. A *protected* method is only visible within its class, within subclasses, or within the class package. To declare a method as *protected*, simply precede the method header with the *protected* keyword, as shown:

```
protected int myProtectedMethod();
```

243 Understanding the private protected Method Modifier

As you have learned, using the *public*, *private*, and *protected* keywords, you can control a variable's scope. In a similar way, Java lets you use these attributes with class methods as well. A *private protected* method is only visible within its class and within subclasses of the class. The difference between a *protected* method and a *private protected* method is that a private protected method is not accessible throughout the class *package*. To declare a method as *private protected*, simply precede the method header with the *private protected* keyword, as shown:

```
private protected int myPrivateProtectedMethod();
```

244 Understanding the static Method Modifier

When you declare a method in a class *static*, you do not need an instance of the class to use the method. Also known as *class methods*, programs use *static* methods for cases when the program should not have to create an object in order to call the method. You can use *static* methods to access other *static* members of the class, however, you cannot use the *static* method to access any non-static variables or methods. To declare a method as *static*, simply precede the method header with the *static* keyword, as shown:

```
public class Sample {
   public static int CallMeAnytime()
    {
        // Statements here
    }
 }
```

To call a *static* method, you must specify the class name and dot operator, as shown:

```
Classname.StaticMethodName(parameters);
```

For example, using the *Sample* class previously shown, you would call the *static CallMeAnytime* method, as follows:

```
x = Sample.CallMeAnytime();
```

UNDERSTANDING THE FINAL METHOD MODIFIER

 245

As you have learned, Java lets you extend one class (the superclass) with another (the subclass). When a subclass extends a class, the subclass can override the superclass methods. In some cases, depending on a method's purpose, you may want to prevent a subclass from overriding a specific method. When you declare a class method as *final*, another class cannot override the methods. Methods which you declare *static* or *private* are implicitly *final*. To declare a method as *final*, simply precede the method header with the *final* keyword, as shown:

```
public final CannotOverrideThisMethod();
```

UNDERSTANDING THE ABSTRACT METHOD MODIFIER

 246

When the *abstract* keyword precedes a class method, you cannot create an instance of the class containing the method. Abstract methods do not provide an implementation. Instead, your abstract method definition only indicates the arguments and return type. When a subclass extends the class containing the abstract method, the subclass is required to supply the implementation for the abstract method. To declare a method *abstract*, simply provide the *abstract* keyword, as follows:

```
public abstract void implementMeLater(int x);
```

ILLEGAL ABSTRACT METHODS

 247

As you have learned, a class does not implement *abstract* methods. Instead, a subclass that extends the class must provide the method implementation. If you were to declare an *abstract* method with either the *private* or *final* modifiers, the Java compiler would issue a syntax error because the *abstract* modifier tells the compiler that a subclass will implement the class. However, the *private* and *final* modifiers tell the compiler that the method cannot change. For example, the following two method declarations are illegal:

```
private abstract void BadMethod();        // Illegal combination

final abstract void ReallyBadMethod();    // Illegal combination
```

UNDERSTANDING THE NATIVE METHOD MODIFIER

 248

As your programs become more complex, there may be times when your Java program will call a routine written in another language, such as C/C++. Although using code written in another programming language reduces your code portability, you may need to use such code in situations where you need high-performance code. The *native* modifier tells the Java compiler that the method is implemented elsewhere. Therefore, *native* methods do not have a Java implementation. The following statement illustrates the use of the *native* keyword:

```
static native void outsider(int x);
```

249 UNDERSTANDING THE SYNCHRONIZED METHOD MODIFIER

As you have learned, Java supports multiple threads of execution which appear to execute simultaneously within your program. Depending on your program's processing, there may be times when you must guarantee that two or more threads cannot access a method at the same time. To control the number of threads that can access a method at any one time, you use the *synchronized* keyword. When the Java compiler encounters the *synchronized* keyword, the compiler will include special code that locks the method as one thread starts executing the method's instructions, and later unlocks the method as the thread exits. Normally, programs synchronize methods that access shared data. The following statement illustrates the use of the *synchronized* keyword:

```
synchronized void refreshData()
```

250 JAVA PASSES PRIMITIVE-TYPE CLASS VARIABLES BY VALUE

When you use primitive types as parameters in a method call, Java passes the parameters by value—meaning the Java passes a copy of the variable's value. As you have learned, primitive types (also known as built-in types) include the types *float*, *boolean*, *int*, and *char*. To pass a parameter by value, Java makes a copy of the value and places the copy in a memory location, known as the *stack*. Because the method receives a copy of the variable's value, the method cannot change the variable's value. Therefore, when the method exits, the original values of the parameters will not have been changed. When a class passes a primitive-type member variable to a method, Java will use call by value in this way. Java passes non-primitive member variables, such as arrays or objects, by reference.

251 UNDERSTANDING THE INIT METHOD

When a Web browser (or an appletviewer) runs a Java applet, the applet's execution starts with the *init* method. Think of the Java *init* method as similar to the *main* function in C/C++, at which the program's execution starts. However, unlike the C/C++ *main* function, when the Java *init* method ends, the applet does not end. Most applets use *init* to initialize key variables (hence, the name *init*). If you do not supply an *init* method within your applet, Java will run its own default *init* method which is defined in the *Applet* class library. The following statements illustrate the format of an *init* method:

```
public void init()
  {
    // statements
  }
```

The *public* keyword tells the Java compiler that another object (in this case, the browser) can call the *init* method from outside of the *Applet* class. The *void* keyword tells the Java compiler that the *init* method does not return a value to the browser. As you can see from the empty parentheses following the method name, *init* does not use any parameters. (Note that unlike C/C++, Java does not use the *void* keyword within the parentheses to indicate no parameters. Instead, you simply use the empty parameters, as shown.)

UNDERSTANDING THE START AND STOP METHODS 252

As you have learned, the *init* method is the first code within your applet that Java runs. After the *init* method ends, Java calls the *start* method. Java also calls the *start* method whenever a user returns to the Web page that contains the running applet (assuming the user left the applet's Web page with the applet running to view other pages). Unlike the *init* method which runs only once, the *start* method may be called repeatedly. The *start* method is optional, which means you do not need to implement the *start* method within your applet. If, for example, your applet needs to restart its processing (such as a thread that controls an animation), you will find that the *start* method is well suited for restarting tasks that have been stopped.

In a similar way, Java calls the *stop* method whenever the user moves off the Web page that contains the applet, without ending the applet. By implementing the *stop* method, you can detect that the user is no longer viewing the applet. In that case, the applet should take steps to turn off time-consuming tasks such as animations or background sounds which the user should only hear when viewing the applet.

Because Java calls the *start* and *stop* methods for you, you should never call these methods yourself. As you become more familiar with how Java uses threads, you will find that the *start* and *stop* methods are indispensable when you use them together with thread objects. For example, the following *start* method uses the *new* operator to create and start a thread object:

```
public void start()
  {
    my_thread= new Thread(this);     // Create the thread
    my_thread.start();               // Start the thread
  }
```

To stop the thread's execution, you can use the *stop* method, as shown:

```
public void stop()
  {
    my_thread.stop();                       // Stop the thread
  }
```

UNDERSTANDING THE PAINT METHOD 253

When you run a program or Java applet within a window, you can size, move, or cover the window's contents with a different window. When you later display the window, the program, or Java applet, must redraw the window's contents. Depending on the window's contents, the steps the program must perform to redraw the window will differ. However, in general, your programs will probably contain graphics and text that must be redrawn periodically.

As it turns out, each time an applet must redraw its applet-window contents, the *Applet* class calls a special method named *paint*. When you define the *paint* method, the applet can control what items it redraws within the applet window. For example, if you need the applet to print the text "Hello, world", you can have the paint method do this for you automatically whenever the applet window needs to be redrawn. The following code fragment illustrates the use of the *paint* method:

```
import  java.applet.*;
import  java.awt.Graphics;
```

```
public class Hello extends Applet {
    public void paint(Graphics g)
    {
        g.drawString("Hello, world", 20, 20);
    }
}
```

The *paint* method receives one parameter from Java, a *Graphics* object, which defines the graphics context which contains attributes such as the current window color, font, font size, and so on.

254 UNDERSTANDING THE DESTROY METHOD

Each time your applet ends, Java automatically calls the *destroy* method to free up memory the applet was using. The *destroy* method is the compliment of the *init* method. However, you normally do not need to override the *destroy* method unless you have specific resources that you need to remove, such as large graphical files or special threads that your applet has created. In short, the *destroy* method provides a convenient way to group your applet's "clean up" processing into one location, as shown:

```
public void destroy()
{
    // Statements here
}
```

255 HOW TO CREATE RESIZABLE APPLETS FOR NETSCAPE BROWSERS

As you have learned, Java executes the *start* method when a user runs an applet or returns to the applet's Web page. Likewise, Java executes the *stop* method when a user leaves the Web page. Within these methods, you include code to perform whatever chores the applet requires for this situation. Many applets, for example, terminate their thread processing within the *stop* method.

As it turns out, Netscape browsers also call the *start* and *stop* methods when the user resizes the browser window. This means that if you include code in the *stop* method to terminate applet processing, your applet will terminate its processing if the user resizes the browser window. Most of the time, stopping the applet's threads for resize operations is not what you want to happen.

To solve this problem, you must write additional Java code that supports users with Netscape browsers. When a user resizes a Netscape browser window that contains an applet, the browser will always perform the following steps:

    1. Call the *stop* method

    2. Call both *resize* methods (*resize*(int,int) and *resize*(dimension))

    3. Call the *start* method

If your applet stops, processes, or threads within the *stop* method, you will have to redesign your code so the thread is suspended, instead of being terminated. At that point, the *start* method should resume with an existing thread instead of starting a new one. For example, the new *start* and *stop* methods may look like the following:

```
public void stop()                    // Called if resized or left the page
  {
    if (theThread!= null)             // Check if a thread is running
     {
        if (theThread.isAlive)
           theThread.suspend();        // Suspend the current thread
     }
  }

public void start()  // Called if resized or returned to the page
  {
    if (theThread!= null)             // Check if a thread was active
        theThread.resume();           // Resume the suspended thread
    else
        theThread = new Thread(); // Create the first thread
  }
```

When a thread is suspended in "applet space," you must perform some extra processing to kill the thread when the applet no longer needs it. In this example, the suspended threads are still holding their resources. If the user leaves this page and surfs off across the Web without returning, the applet threads are left in a suspended state.

Leaving the threads in a suspended state may become a significant problem in a complex applet that uses many threads. One solution to the suspended threads is to kill them within the *destroy* method. Likewise, the applet can set a timer to kill the threads after they have been suspended for a specified period of time. In any case, the following statements illustrate how you would stop the thread in the *destroy* method:

```
public void destroy()
  {
    if (theThread!= null)
     {
        theThread.stop();
        theThread = null;
     }
  }
```

DISPLAYING A STRING IN THE STATUS LINE 256

The status line is a small area at the bottom of the applet window within which your applet can display messages to the user. For example, if your program is loading a large graphic file, you may want to display a message to the user that indicates the status of the load operation. To display a message within the status line, you can use the *showStatus* method. The following statement illustrates the use of the *showStatus* method to display a message to the user:

```
getAppletContext().showStatus("Loading the file BigImage.gif");
```

The statement uses the *getAppletContext* method to get the applet's graphics context. Next, using the *showStatus* method, the applet displays the status-line message.

257 GETTING AN APPLET'S INPUT PARAMETERS

As you learned, users can pass information to standalone Java programs using the command line. With a Java applet, on the other hand, you can pass parameters to the applet from the HTML file. To do so, you place one or more *<PARAM>* tags in your HTML file between the *<APPLET>* and *</APPLET>*. The format of the <PARAM> tag is as follows:

```
<PARAM name=NameString value=ValueString>
```

An applet can access the *NameString* and *ValueString* items by calling the *getParameter* method. Both *NameString* and *ValueString* items are strings. If the items contain strings, you must surround them with double quotes. The following HTML entries illustrate the use of the *<PARAM>* entry to provide parameter information to an applet:

```
<APPLET class=my_args width=450, height=230>
<PARAM name="first arg" value="test">
<PARAM name=second value="100">  </APPLET>
```

To access the HTML parameters from within your applet, you will use the *getParameter* method, as shown:

```
String s = getParameter("first arg");      // s is the String "test"

String s2 = getParameter("second");        // s2 has the String 100
int second_value = Integer.parseInt(s2); // convert s2 to a number
```

To access an HTML parameter, you pass the parameter's name to the *getParameter* method which, in turn, will return a *String* value that contains the parameter's corresponding value. In this case, because the first parameter's value is a *String*, the applet can use the value immediately after the call to *getParameter*. The second parameter is an integer value of 100. By using the *parseInt* method, the applet can convert the *String* "100" to the number 100.

If your program invokes the *getParameter* method with the name of an HTML parameter that does not exist, *getParameter* will return the *null* value. Within an applet, your program can test for the *null* value, as shown:

```
String param = getParameter("Some Parameter");

if (param == null)
   param = "Default value";
```

In this case, the statements use the *getParameter* method to get the value for the "Some Parameter" HTML parameter. Next, the statements test if the *getParameter* method returned the value *null*, which indicates the HTML file did not define the parameter. As such, the statements assign a default value to the variable *param*.

258 PROVIDING APPLET AUTHOR INFORMATION

When users view your applet with a browser, you may want them to know that you were the applet's author, or you may want to specify copyright information. As it turns out, most browsers include a provision that lets users display this type of information. By overriding the *getAppletInfo* method, you can provide information about your applet:

```
public String getAppletInfo()
  {
    return "MyGreatApplet Copyright © 1997 John Smith";
  }
```

Figure 258 illustrates this author information within the Netscape Navigator.

Figure 258 *Displaying author information within the Appletviewer.*

PROVIDING APPLET PARAMETER INFORMATION  259

Many Web browsers allow the user to display information about the types of parameters the applet supports. You can define your applet's legal parameters so that Web page designers, who may want to use your applet in their own Web pages, will know which options they can use within the HTML *<PARAM>* entries. To provide this information, you must override the *getParameterInfo* method, as shown:

```
public String[][] getParameterInfo()
{
  String[][] info = {
     {"Color", "An integer color value", "sets line color"},
     {"Speed", "A value from 1 to 10", "sets animation rate"},
     {"Chunky", "A boolean value", "sets low resolution mode"}
  };
  return info;
}
```

The parameter information is organized in arrays in which the first item is the parameter name, the second indicates the type information, and the third is its description. Figure 259 illustrates the parameter information within the Netscape Navigator.

Figure 259 *Displaying parameter information within the Appletviewer.*

260 JAVA DOES NOT SUPPORT THE GOTO STATEMENT

For years, programmers have been taught the evils of using the *goto* statement. In general, the criticism of the *goto* statement has evolved because of programmer misuses and abuses of *goto*, which produced code that was difficult to read. In reality, however, the *goto* statement itself is not inherently evil and, in fact, use of the *goto* can often produce code that is very easy to understand. Despite the fact that proper use of the *goto* statement can produce understandable, well-structured code, the *goto* statement has never been popular in C/C++. In any case, Java does not use the *goto* statement. However, *goto* is a reserved word so that the compiler can catch any stray uses of the *goto* construct.

261 JAVA SUPPORTS LABELED BREAK AND CONTINUE STATEMENTS

As you learned in Tip 260, Java does not support the *goto* statement. However, the tip also mentioned that a "branching statement" such as the *goto* has valid uses. Java, therefore, provides labeled *break* and *continue* statements to replace some of the *goto* statement's legitimate uses. For example, you can specify a label with the *break* statement so, when the code reaches the *break*, Java will continue the program's processing at the corresponding label. For example, using a labeled *break* statement, a program can branch out of a series of nested loops, as shown:

```
go_here: for (i= 0;  i < 10; i++) {
   while (j < 100) {
      if (z == 10)
         break go_here;
   }
}
```

In this case, if Java encounters the labeled *break* statement, Java will branch the program's execution out of the *while* loop, continuing the program's execution at the start of the *for* loop.

Likewise, if your program uses a label with a *continue* statement, Java will jump to (continue its execution with) the next iteration of the current loop, as shown:

```
go_here: while (i < 10) {
   while (j < 100) {
      if (z == 10)
         continue go_here;
   }
}
```

262 JAVA DOES NOT SUPPORT POINTERS

In C/C++ programs, pointers store an object's memory address. Using pointers, C/C++ programs can directly access objects within memory. To determine an object's address, C/C++ programs use the address (&) operator. To access the value stored at the memory location, the programs use the * and -> operators to "dereference" the address. In C/C++, the primary use of pointers is to let functions change parameter values (programmers refer to the process of passing the address of parameters to a function as a *call by reference*). These address and dereference operators do not exist in Java.

Although pointers are a key element in C/C++, many programmers find the use of pointers difficult and error prone. In addition, the errant or malicious use of pointers yield errors which are unacceptable in the "network environment" of the World Wide Web. Thus, Java has done away with pointers to eliminate one of the biggest sources of bugs found in C/C++ programs. Furthermore, by eliminating pointers, Java becomes more secure.

Unfortunately, because Java does not support pointers, a Java function cannot change the value of a parameter (programmers refer to a function that cannot change parameter values as a *call by value*).

JAVA DOES NOT SUPPORT A PREPROCESSOR 263

Before the C/C++ compiler examines a program's statements, the compiler first runs a special program called the *preprocessor*. In general, the C/C++ preprocessor examines the source code and performs special processing (preprocessing the code before the compiler examines the code), such as substituting constants and macros throughout the source code. Within a C/C++ source file, the programmer can place preprocessor support directives, such as *#define*, *#ifdef*, and *#include*, which control the preprocessor's processing.

Java, however, does not have a preprocessor of any kind. Instead, you will learn that Java provides alternatives to the preprocess directives which allow you to achieve similar results. For example, in the past, you may have created a constant using the C/C++ *#define* preprocessor directive. In Java, on the other hand, you use the following statement to create a constant named *MAX_ITEMS*:

```
protected static final int MAX_ITEMS = 1000;
```

JAVA PASSES ARRAY AND OBJECT PARAMETERS BY REFERENCE 264

As you learned in Tip 262, Java does not support pointers. Therefore, Java functions *normally* cannot change a parameter's value. In other words, Java normally passes parameters to functions using *call by value*. As it turns out, Java does pass non-primitive types, such as objects and arrays, by reference—which lets a function change the parameter. However, keep in mind that the C/C++ &, *, and -> operators do not exist in Java. Instead, Java automatically passes all objects and arrays by reference so your Java programs do not need to use any special pointer notation.

COMMAND-LINE ARGUMENTS DIFFER BETWEEN JAVA AND C/C++ 265

When you run a program from a system prompt (also known as the command line), the information you type becomes the program's command line. If you are familiar with C/C++, you know that you access the command-line arguments (the individual items within the command line) using two parameters (*argc* and *argv*), which you access as parameters to the *main* function:

```
void main(int argc, char *argv[])
```

The *argc* parameter contains a count of the number of command-line arguments. The *argv* parameter is an array of character strings whose elements contain the individual command-line arguments.

In Java, you only access command-line arguments when you create standalone programs which use the function *main*, as shown:

```
public static void main(String argv[])
```

As you can see, Java passes the command-line arguments to *main* as a *String* array. Java replaces the C/C++ *argc* parameter, which specifies the number of command-line arguments, with the *length* member of the *argv String* object *argv.length*. Also, another difference between Java's command-line processing and that of C/C++ is that the first item in the Java array is not the name of the Java program.

The following Java program, *ShowCmd.java*, displays its command-line arguments:

```
class ShowCmd {
    public static void main(String args[])
    {
        for (int index = 0; index < args.length; index++)
            System.out.println("Arg" + index + " is " + args[index]);
    }
}
```

As you can see, the *main* method receives one parameter—an array of strings each of which corresponds to a command-line argument. Using a *for* statement, the program loops through the array of command-line arguments. The program uses the *args.length* attribute to determine the number of elements in the array. After you compile this application using *javac*, you can run the application using the java interpreter, as shown:

```
C:\JAVACODE> java ShowCmd Hello there "Big Guy"
```

The application, in turn, will display the command line arguments, as shown:

```
C:\JAVACODE> javac -O ShowCmd.java    <ENTER>
Arg 0 is Hello
Arg 1 is there
Arg 2 is Big Guy
```

As you can see, if you group arguments within quotes ("Big Guy") the Java interpreter treats the arguments as one parameter.

266 JAVA TYPE CHAR IS 16 BITS TO SUPPORT UNICODE

Both Java and C/C++ support the type *char*. In C/C++, the type *char* is one byte, allowing variables of type *char* to represent 256 different characters. Java's type *char*, on the other hand, is two bytes long, which allows variables of type *char* to represent 65,536 different characters. Java's expanded *char* supports the Unicode two-byte character code, which supports the diverse written text of all world languages.

267 JAVA DOES NOT SUPPORT THE UNSIGNED KEYWORD

In C/C++, programs use the *unsigned* modifier to specify that the variable does not use its most significant bit to represent the values sign. Unsigned variables cannot represent negative numbers. Normally, programmers use the unsigned modifier to increase the range of positive values the variable can store. In Java, on the other hand, all integral types are signed, except for *char*. Java does not support the *unsigned* keyword.

CONVERSION BETWEEN BOOLEAN AND INTEGER TYPES 268

As you have learned, the Java *boolean* type lets a variable store a true or false value. Java represents a *boolean* variable's type using only one bit. C/C++, on the other hand, represents false with the value 0 and true with *any* non-zero value. Within a Java program, you cannot assign a *boolean* variable the value of 0 or 1 as you can in C/C++. The following statements illustrate how a program can convert *boolean* and *int* values:

```
int some_int;
boolean some_boolean;

// convert an int value to a boolean value
some_boolean = (some_int != 0);

// convert a boolean value to an int value
some_int = some_boolean ? 1 : 0;
```

JAVA PROGRAMS FREE ALLOCATED MEMORY AUTOMATICALLY 269

Java uses a technique called *garbage collection* to detect when your program is no longer using an object and then to deallocate the object's memory automatically. Unlike C/C++, you do not need to make explicit calls to the *delete* or *free* functions. Instead, when you use the *new* keyword to allocate memory in Java, rest assured that Java will automatically free that memory when the object is no longer in use.

JAVA LOOP CONDITIONS MUST BE TYPE BOOLEAN 270

As you have learned, Java represents the type *boolean* using only one bit. Therefore, Java will not let a program assign a *boolean* variable the value of 0 or 1, as does C/C++. In addition, all conditions in Java that require a *boolean* test must ultimately result in a test against *true* or *false*. For example, because the following C/C++ condition does not test a true or false condition, the condition is not valid in Java:

```
int count = 100;
while (!count)
```

Instead, in Java you must form a *boolean* expression, as shown:

```
int count = 100;
while (count != 0)
```

JAVA IS MULTITHREADED 271

Multithreading is the ability to have various parts of a program perform program steps seemingly at the same time. For example, many Web browsers let users view various pages and click on hot links while the browser is downloading various pictures, text, sounds, and while drawing objects on the screen. The Java design began with the goal of supporting multiple threads of execution. Java lets programs interleave multiple program steps through the use of *threads*. Many of the tips presented throughout this book discuss threads in detail.

272 JAVA HAS A SYNCHRONIZED STATEMENT TO CONTROL THREADS

When a program makes use of multiple threads, the program may need a way to control the thread's operation, preventing multiple threads from acting on the same piece of code at the same time. For example, consider a piece of code that prints the numbers 1 to 10, incrementing a counter as it goes along. If another thread runs the counter code at the same time, the two threads will errantly increment the counter by twos. To control the execution of multiple threads, Java programs use the *synchronized* keyword to control access to a block of code. For example, the following function uses the *synchronized* keyword which directs Java to allow only one thread of execution to run the function's statements at any given time:

```
public synchronized void count_up_by_one()
  {
     counter++;
      System.out.println(counter);
  }
```

273 JAVA DOES NOT SUPPORT STRUCTURES OR UNIONS

C/C++ programs use structures to group related variables. In addition, C/C++ programs use unions to let a variable store any one of a number of value types. In Java, classes replace *structures* and subclassing replaces *unions*.

274 JAVA DOES NOT SUPPORT THE *VOID* * TYPE

Java uses the type *void*, as does C/C++, to indicate that a method does not return a value:

```
void some_function(int value)   // Valid in C/C++ and Java
  {
      // Statements here
  }
```

C/C++ also uses the type *void* to specify that a method receives no arguments:

```
int some_function(void)   // Use of void is valid in C/C++, not Java
  {
      // Statements here
  }
```

Java, however, does not use the *void* type to specify a function uses no arguments. Instead, a Java function uses empty parentheses, as shown:

```
int some_function()   // Java function with no arguments
  {
      // Statements here
  }
```

Finally, because Java does not support pointers, Java does not support the *void* * type.

JAVA DOES NOT SUPPORT THE SIZEOF OPERATOR 275

C/C++ programs use the *sizeof* operator to determine the amount of memory (in bytes) an object consumes. Because Java does not let your programs manipulate pointers directly, or let your programs access internal structures, Java does not support the *sizeof* operator.

JAVA PREVENTS THE = AND == OPERATOR MIXUP 276

In C/C++, programmers often use the result of an assignment statement within a *boolean* condition. For example, the following statement assigns the value 100 to the variable *test_me* and then tests the variable's value within an *if* statement's condition:

```
if (test_me = 100)
```

In this case, after the C/C++ program assigns the value 100 to the variable, the condition will test wether the variable contains a true (nonzero) or false (zero) value. In other words, the following statements are identical to the previous statement:

```
test_me = 100;

if (test_me)
```

Although the first statement lets programmers combine two statements into one, the statement often confuses programmers in that they are unsure whether the original programmer's goal was to assign the value 100 to the variable *test_me* or if the programmer actually wanted to test if the variable was equal to 100, as shown:

```
if (test_me == 100)
```

Java eliminates the possibility of errors that arise from the use of the assignment operator (=) when the programmer meant to test for equality (==). The Java compiler will report this very common, and occasionally difficult to find, bug as an error.

CREATING AN OBJECT 277

When you write a Java program, you define a series of classes. As you have learned, you use classes within your program to create instances of objects. In other words, a class defines what an object looks like, specifying the fields and methods your program can use. For most classes, you create an object of the class using the *new* operator. For example, the following statements create a *String* object and a *DemoClass* object using the *new* operator:

```
String name= new String();
DemoClass MyObject= new DemoClass("Sample text");
```

Note that these statements combine the object declaration and instantiation (use of the *new* operator). Many programmers like to use this technique. However, Java does let you separate the declaration from the instantiation, as shown:

```
String name;            // the declaration
name = new String();    // the instantiation
```

When you create an object, you may need to supply arguments between the parentheses. The number and type of arguments are determined by the constructor method associated with the class. When you use *new*, you are actually calling the constructor method which has the same name as the class itself.

278 OBJECT WRAPPER FOR PRIMITIVE DATA TYPES

In Java, primitive type variables (such as variables of type *float, boolean, int, char, long,* and *double*) are not objects. So you may find that the primitive types do not fit well with some of your other objects. In such cases, your programs can convert these primitive types into objects by using a special set of classes. These classes reside in the *java/src/lang library* and are named as follows:

Primitive type	Corresponding class
boolean	Boolean
char	Character
int	Integer
long	Long
float	Float
double	Double

Table 278 *Classes in the java/src/lang library.*

Types for *byte* and *short* do not have their own class because you can cast the *Integer* class for these types. The following statements create a variable of type *long* and a *Long* object, illustrating how you can convert values between the two.

```
Long long_object;
long long_primitive = 10L;


long_object = new Long(long_primitive);      // Convert long to object
long_primitive = long_object.longValue();    // Convert object to long
```

279 COMPARING OBJECTS VERSUS COMPARING PRIMITIVE DATA TYPES

Java supports two classifications of variables: The first class of variables includes the primitive (or built-in) types, which include: *float, boolean, int, char,* and so on. The second class of variables are the non-primitive types which are objects and arrays. It is important to understand the distinction between the two because this difference determines how you compare them. When you compare primitive types, you are actually comparing the value of the variable. You can use, for example, the == operator to test for equality:

```
int test;

if (test == 5) // Use == for primitive data types
```

When your programs use non-primitive types, you are actually using an address, a *reference*, to the variable. Unless you are interested in comparing the addresses of two variables (which is unlikely), you should not use the == operator. Instead, most classes provide specific methods that let your programs compare objects. For example, to compare *String* objects, you would use the *String* class *equals* method, as shown:

```
String str1, str2;
str1 = "Hello";
str2 = "Hello";

test = str1.equals(str2);   // Do not use == to compare objects
```

CREATING A CHARACTER OBJECT

280

Throughout Java programs, you will make extensive use of *String* objects that provide a set of methods which let you manipulate the object's characters. In a similar way, there may be times when your programs need more control over character variables. For example, your programs may want to determine if a character contains a digit such as '0' through '9,' is upper or lowercase, and so on. In such cases, you may want to use the *Character* class type as opposed to the primitive type *char*. The following statements, for example, create a *Character* object and assign the object the letter *A*:

```
Character letter = new Character;

letter = 'A';
```

DETERMINING WHETHER A CHARACTER IS A DIGIT

281

When your programs work with characters or character arrays, you may need to determine if a character is a digit, such as '0', '1', and so on, through '9'. In such cases, you can use the *Character* class *isDigit* method to perform a test. The following statements, for example, test whether the variable *value* contains a digit:

```
Character value = new Character('5');

if (value.isDigit())
   System.out.println("The digit is: " + value);
```

As you have learned, your applets can call *static methods* (also known as *class methods*) even if your program does not have an instance of the class. The *isDigit* method is such a method. You may invoke this method at any time through its class name, *Character*:

```
if (Character.isDigit(some_variable))
```

DETERMINING WHETHER A CHARACTER IS LOWER OR UPPERCASE

282

When your programs work with characters, there may be times when you need to determine if a character is upper or lowercase. In such cases, if you are using the *Character* class, you can use the *isLowerCase* or *isUpperCase* methods to perform the test. The following statements use the *isUppercase* method to determine if a *Character* object contains an uppercase letter:

```
Character letter = new Character('5');

if (letter.isUppercase())
   System.out.println("The letter is uppercase");
```

Like other class variables, you can use these methods without an object by referring to the *Character* class name, as shown:

```
if (Character.isLowerCase(some_variable))
```

283 DETERMINING WHETHER A CHARACTER IS A SPACE

When your programs work with characters, there may be times when you need to determine if a character is a space. If you are using *Character* objects, your programs can use the *isSpace* method to perform the test. The following statements use the *is Space* method to determine if a *Character* is a space.

```
Character letter = new Character(' ');

if (letter.isSpace())
  System.out.println("The letter is a space");
```

Like other class variables, you can use these methods without an object by referring to the *Character* class name, as shown:

```
if (Character.isSpace(some_variable))
```

284 CONVERTING A CHARACTER TO A NUMERIC VALUE

As you have learned, you can use the *Character* class *isDigit* method to determine if a character is a digit. Next, to convert the character representation of the digit to its numeric equivalent, your programs can use the *Character* class *digit* method. The following statements, for example, convert the character '3' to the numeric value 3, using the *digit* method:

```
int number;
Character three = new Character('3');
number = Character.digit(three);
```

As it turns out, the *digit* method lets you convert a value from octal, decimal, or hexadecimal by specifying a radix of 8, 10, or 16. For example, the following statements convert a digit containing the hexadecimal value 'F' (a decimal 15) to a numeric value:

```
int number;
Character hex_value = new Character('F');
number = Character.digit(hex_value);
```

285 COMPARING CHARACTER OBJECTS

When your programs compare values of type *char* (the primitive type), your programs compare actual values. To perform such a test, your programs use the equality operator (==), as shown:

```
char theChar = 'A';

if (theChar == 'A')
```

When your programs work with a non-primitive *Character* type, your programs compare the object's contents using the *Character* class *equals* method, as shown:

```
Character char_A, char_B;
char_A = new Character('A');
char_B = new Character('B');


if (char_A.equals(char_B))
   // come here if the two objects are equal
```

If your programs use the equality operator with *Character* objects, Java will not compare the values the objects store, but rather, the object's memory location.

UNDERSTANDING THE DIFFERENCE BETWEEN CLONE AND COPY 286

As you work with objects within a Java applet, there will be times when you will need to make an exact, yet independent, copy of an instance. For simpler classes, you could probably copy an object instance in one or two lines of code. For example, the following statements duplicate the contents of a *String* object:

```
String orig = "CopyMe";
String copy_of_orig = orig.toString();   // new object created
```

Although these statements correctly duplicate the *orig* object using the *toString* method, not all classes have a method to conveniently duplicate an object. What's worse, some newcomers to Java may fall into the trap of making a copy of the instance variable, as follows:

```
String orig = "CopyMe";
String copy_of_orig = orig;   // this is a copy of the
                              // reference only!
```

The above lines perform a copy of the instance reference only—in other words, the statements do not create a second object! In this case, you have two variables both referring to the one object. You can access the "CopyMe" *String* through either of the two variables. Because reference types are not passed by value, assigning one object to another in Java does not copy the value of the object. It only assigns a reference to the object.

Now that you have learned that a simple variable copy does not duplicate an object, you may be wondering what does. As you saw with the first example in this tip, you can copy objects yourself. However, Java provides a method called *clone* that is available in several classes for this purpose.

The *clone* method is available in classes that implement the *Cloneable* interface. If you are designing your own class and would like to give users of your class the ability to duplicate an instance, you should consider implementing a *clone* method for the class.

DUPLICATING AN OBJECT WITH THE CLONE METHOD 287

As you learned in Tip 286, a *clone* method is a function with which an applet can duplicate an object quickly. If a class implements a *clone* method, you can duplicate an instance of that class very easily. For example, consider a case where you have created a *Vector* object and you need a second copy of the instance. The *Vector* class implements a *clone* method for you, so you can use it as follows:

```
Vector orig = new Vector;
Vector copy_of_orig = orig.clone();   // make a copy now
```

288 JAVA DOES NOT PROVIDE A DEFAULT CLONE METHOD

As you have learned, a *clone* method lets an applet duplicate a specific object instance quickly. To use a class *clone* method, you need to make sure that the class you want to *clone* actually implements the *clone* method. As you will learn, Java defines a *Cloneable* interface with which you can implement a *clone* method for any class. To determine if a class is *Cloneable*, examine the class definition and look for a *clone* method, as well as the words *implements Cloneable* in the class header. For example, the words *implements Cloneable* within the following class definition tells you that the Vector class implements the *clone* method:

```
public class Vector extends Object implements Cloneable {
```

If a Java applet calls the *clone* method for an object that does not implement the method, Java will generate (throw) the *CloneNotSupportedException* exception.

289 CREATING A STRING OBJECT

When you work with character strings in Java, you use instances of the *java.lang.String* class. Unlike character strings in C/C++, Java *String* objects are not null terminated (terminated with an ASCII zero). For Java strings, you don't need to know about the terminator character. In fact, Java will not give you a way to examine the termination character or what comes after it. In addition, Java will perform run-time bounds checking on all string and array accesses, preventing you from stepping outside the bounds of the memory occupied by the *String*.

When Java encounters a string literal surrounded by double quotes, Java will automatically create a *String* object. Likewise, you can create a *String* object by simply declaring a *String* variable and assigning any double quoted string to it. For example, the following statements create a character string named *title* and assigns to the string object the text "1001 Java Programmer's Tips":

```
String title;
title = "1001 Java Programmer's Tips";
```

For convenience, you can also create *String* objects with a single line:

```
String title = "1001 Java Programmer's Tips";
```

290 UNDERSTANDING IMPLICIT AND EXPLICIT STRING DECLARATIONS

When you use a string literal in your Java program, Java automatically creates a *String* object containing the value within the quotes. For example, the following statement creates a string object named *publisher* and assigns the object the text "Jamsa Press":

```
String publisher = "Jamsa Press";
```

This *implicit* declaration of a *String* object is unlike the declaration of other classes for which you must explicitly create an object by using the *new* operator. In a similar way, you can create a *String* object *explicitly*, just as you would create any other object—by using the *new* operator:

```
String publisher = new String("Jamsa Press");
```

As it turns out, Java treats a literal character string as a *String* object, which means your applets can use the *String* class methods, as shown here:

```
int len = "Jamsa Press".length();   // assigns the length of 11
```

CONVERTING A CHARACTER ARRAY TO A STRING

 291

Unlike C/C++ which uses character arrays to store strings, Java programs store strings with *String* objects. Depending on the task the program performs, however, the program may need to work with either a *String* object or character array. For example, if you are writing a graphics-based program to rotate (or spin) the letters of a company name, you may want to access each letter by storing the letters within an array. For other tasks, however, you will want to represent the company name as a *String* object. Luckily, Java makes it easy for your programs to convert a character array to a *String*. For example, the following statements use the *String* object constructor method to convert a character array to a *String*:

```
char char_array[] = {'A', 'B', 'C'};

String s = new String(char_array);
System.out.println("My new string is " + s);
```

The *String* class has a variety of *overloaded* constructors that your applets can use to convert objects into *Strings*. In this case, the constructor converts a character array into a *String* object and the statements will display the following output:

```
My new string is ABC
```

CONVERTING A STRING TO A CHARACTER ARRAY

 292

As you learned in Tip 291, Java makes it easy for your applets to convert character arrays to *String* objects and vice versa. To convert a *String* object to a character array, your applets can use the *String* class *toCharArray* method. For example, the following statements convert the *String* "ABC" into a character array:

```
char char_array[] = "ABC".toCharArray();
System.out.println("Middle character is " + char_array[1]);
```

As you can see, after the statements convert the String object into a character array, the statements can then use the array to access individual characters easily and will display the following output:

```
Middle character is B
```

COPYING A STRING

 293

As your Java programs become more complex, you will find that programs often copy the contents of one string object to another. To copy a *String* object, you must actually create another *String* object. As briefly discussed in Tip 286, you must avoid the trap of using the assignment operator (=) to copy a *String* object, because doing so will create two variables that point to the same *String* object. For example, the following statements will result in two variables that refer to one *String* object:

```
String s1, s2;
s1 = "ABC";      // s1 references a new ABC object
s2 = s1;         // s2 references the same ABC object
```

Because the statements use the assignment statement without first creating a new *String* object, the statements do not make a second copy of the *String*. If you actually need to create a second independent *String* object, you must use the *new* operator, as shown:

```
String s1, s2;
s1 = "ABC";
s2 = new String(s1); // A second String has been created
```

In this case, the *s2* variable is a *String* object separate from *s1*. Both objects, however, contain the same characters: "ABC".

294 CONCATENATING ONE STRING TO ANOTHER

String concatenation is the process of appending one string's contents to another's, joining each string's characters. Using *String* objects, Java programs can concatenate one *String's* contents to another using the *concat* method, as shown:

```
String s1, s2;
s1 = "ABC";
s2 = "XYZ";

s1 = s1.concat(s2); // Concatenates s2's contents to s1
```

In this case, the operation creates a new *s1* object that contains the characters "ABCXYZ". Following the operation, the variable *s1* no longer references the *String* object that contained the characters "ABC". Therefore, Java's automatic garbage collection will deallocate the memory that contained the object.

295 USING THE "+" OPERATOR TO CONCATENATE STRINGS

As you learned in Tip 294, Java programs can use the *String* class *concat* method to concatenate one string's contents to another's. In addition to the *concat* method, Java programs can also use the concatenation operator (+) to concatenate *Strings* (and a variety of other types). For example, the following statements illustrate the use of the concatenation operator to join to character strings:

```
String s1 = "ABC";
String s2 = "XYZ";
String s3 = s1 + " to " + s2;
```

As you can see, the statements take three *String* objects and concatenates them to form the fourth *String* object referenced by the variable *s3*. Remember, Java automatically converts the string literal " to" into a *String* object. The *s3* object, in this case, will contain the value "ABC to XYZ".

COMPARING TWO STRINGS 296

Within Java applets, a common operation is the comparison of one character string to another. For example, your applet may compare a user's input to a specific filename. When your applets compare *Strings*, you need to carefully consider the two types of comparisons that you may perform. As you have learned, *String* variables refer to (are references) to strings of characters that reside somewhere in your computer's memory. By comparing two strings using the equality operator (==), you actually compare whether the two *String* objects refer to the same memory location in your computer, that is, whether the two *Strings* are the same object. If you want to compare whether the two *Strings* have the same characters, you must use the *String* class *equals* method. For example, the following statements illustrate how these two comparisons differ:

```
class ComparingStrings {
    public static void main(String args[])
    {
        String s1, s2;
        s1 = "ABC";
        s2 = s1;  // variable refer to the same String
        System.out.println("Same object? " + (s1 == s2));

        s2 = new String(s1);  // create a new object copied from s1
        System.out.println("Same object? " + (s1 == s2));
        System.out.println("Same value? " + s1.equals(s2));
    }
}
```

As you can see, this program initially uses an assignment statement, *s2= s1*, which makes the *s2* variable refer to the same object as the *s1* variable. By using the == operator, the statements then compare whether the two objects are the same. The program next creates a new *String* named *s2*, which is a different object that contains the same set of characters. In this case, the program will display the following output:

```
Same object? true
Same object? false
Same value? true
```

DETERMINING IF TWO STRINGS ARE EQUAL 297

Within your programs, you will often need to determine whether two strings are equal (contain the same characters). To test two *Strings* for equality, you can use the *equals* method as follows:

```
String name = "Anthony";
String thing = "Apple";

if (name.equals(thing))          // true, if the strings are equal
```

In this case, you use the *equals* method to determine if the contents of the *name String* are equal to the contents of the *thing* object. Because Java treats literal strings as *String* objects, you can also use the *equals* method to compare a literal string to another string, as shown:

```
String thing = "Apple";
if ("Anthony".equals(thing))   // true, if the strings are equal
```

298 DETERMINING IF TWO (CASELESS) STRINGS ARE EQUAL

As you learned in Tip 297, to test whether two strings are equal, you can use the *String* class *equals* method. When you use the *equals* method to compare strings, you need to understand that the *equals* method considers upper and lowercase letters as different. In some cases, however, you may want to ignore the case of the two *Strings* you are comparing. To perform a case insensitive comparison, use the *equalsIgnoreCase* method, as shown:

```
String nameLower = "Anthony";
String nameUpper = "ANTHONY";

if (nameLower.equalsIgnoreCase(nameUpper)) // true
```

299 DETERMINING IF SECTIONS OF TWO STRINGS ARE EQUAL

When you compare strings within a program, there will be times when you will want to compare substrings that reside within strings. For example, if you ask the user to type in a complete filename, you may only want to compare the file's extension to a string such as "html". In other words, you don't want to examine the entire string (such as, *SomeFilename.html*). Java's *String* class provides two overloaded methods called *regionMatches* which permit you to compare a section of two strings. The method format is as follows:

```
boolean regionMatches(int toffset, String other, int ooffset,
    int len);

boolean regionMatches(boolean ignoreCase, int toffset, String other,
    int ooffset, int len);
```

The *toffset* and *ooffset* arguments specify the zero-based starting point of the comparison, that is, the number of characters into the two strings. The *len* argument specifies the number of characters to compare. For example, the following statements compare the string "ABC" to the three character substring that starts at offset 2 within the string "XYZABCD":

```
String s1, s2;
s1 = "ABC";
s2 = "XYZABCD";

boolean matches= s1.regionMatches(0, s2, 2, 3);  // returns true
```

As you can see, one of the *regionMatches* methods supports a first parameter that allows you to turn case sensitivity on or off.

300 GETTING AN INDIVIDUAL CHARACTER FROM A STRING

As you learned in Tip 299, Java provides functions that let your programs work with substrings. For example, the *regionMatches* function lets your programs compare substrings from within two strings. In a similar way, the *charAt* method lets your programs determine the individual character at specific (zero-indexed) locations within a *String*.

For example, the following statements use the *charAt* method to determine the character at offset 1 within the *String* object *s*, which in this case is the letter *B*:

```
String s = "ABC";
char c = s.charAt(1);   // returns the letter B
```

GETTING THE LENGTH OF A STRING

 301

As you work with character strings within your programs, there will be many times when you will need to know the number of characters the *String* object contains. In such cases, your programs can use the *length* method, as shown:

```
String s = "ABC";
int len = s.length();   // returns the length of 3
```

GETTING A SECTION OF A STRING

 302

As you work with strings, there will be times when you will need to extract a part of a string (a substring). For example, if a string contains a URL such as *http://www.jamsa.com*, you may want to extract the substring that defines the URL's protocol (in this case, http). To extract a substring from a string object, you can use the *String* class *substring* method, as shown:

```
String substring(int beginIndex);
String substring(int beginIndex, int endIndex);
```

As you can see, the *String* class provides two different *substring* methods that differ by the number of parameters. The first method returns the substring that starts at the character location specified by the *beginIndex* parameter, and includes all the characters that follow to the end of the string. If you want to extract a substring from within the middle of a string, you can use the second method that adds the *endIndex* parameter which specifies the location of the string's first character that *you do not want in the substring*. Remember, Java Strings are zero-based, which means the first character is located at offset zero. The following statements illustrate the use of the *substring* method:

```
String s1 = "Bananas";
String s2 = s1.substring(2,6);
System.out.println(s2);
```

These statements copy characters starting at the third character of the word *bananas* through the sixth character, which causes the program to print the characters *nana*. Note that the function does not specify the offset five, which corresponds to the third letter *a* in bananas. Instead, the function specifies offset 6 which corresponds to the letter *s*. The function uses the index location in this way so applets can take the difference between the *beginIndex* and *endIndex* to compute the total number of characters that are copied. In the previous example, 6 - 2 is 4 characters copied.

REPLACING CHARACTERS OF A STRING

 303

As you work with strings, there may be times when you will need to replace one character in the string with another. To replace each occurrence of one character in a string with another, your applets can use the *String* object's *replace* method. For example, the following statements use the *replace* method to replace each occurrence of a lowercase letter *o* with its uppercase equivalent:

```
String name = "CooLTooLS";
name = name.replace('o', 'O');
System.out.println(name);
```

304 FINDING A STRING'S FIRST OCCURRENCE OF A CHARACTER

As you work with strings, there may be times when you need to locate the first occurrence of a character. For example, if you are working with a string that contains a URL, you might want to determine the location of the colon (:) that follows the prototype (such as http:). In such cases, you can use the *String* class *indexOf* method. The *indexOf* method returns the *String* index of the first occurrence of the specified character. The following statement uses the *indexOf* function to locate the first occurrence of the letter *o* within the string "CooLTooLs":

```
String name = "CooLTooLS";
System.out.println(name.indexOf('o'));   // Displays the value 1
```

These statements will display the value 1 which corresponds to the first occurrence of the character *o*. If the character does not exist within the string, the *indexOf* function returns the value -1.

305 FINDING A STRING'S LAST OCCURRENCE OF A CHARACTER

In Tip 304, you learned that your applets can use the *indexOf* function to find the first occurrence of a specified character. In a similar way, there may be times when your programs need to determine the rightmost (or last) occurrence of a character within a string. In such cases, your programs can use the *lastIndexOf* method. For example, the following statement uses the *lastIndexOf* method to locate the rightmost occurrence of the character *o* within the string "CooLTooLS":

```
String name = "CooLTooLS";
System.out.println(name.lastIndexOf('o'));   // Display the value 6
```

These statements will display the value 6, which corresponds to the rightmost (last) occurrence of the character *o* within the string. If the character does not exist within the string, the *indexOf* function returns the value -1.

306 FINDING THE FIRST OCCURRENCE OF A STRING INSIDE A STRING

In Tip 304, you learned that the *String* class *indexOf* function returns the first (leftmost) occurrence of a character within a string. If your program passes a string parameter to the function, as opposed to a character, the *indexOf* method will return the character location of the first occurrence of the specified substring. In other words, the *String* class overloads the *indexOf* method to support character and *String* parameters. The following statements, for example, display the first occurrence of the substring *oo* within the string "CoolTooLS":

```
String name = "CooLTooLS";
System.out.println(name.indexOf("oo"));   // Displays the value 1
```

These statements will display the value 1 which corresponds to the first occurrence of the substring within a string. If the substring does not exist within the string, the *indexOf* method returns the value -1.

FINDING THE LAST OCCURRENCE OF A STRING INSIDE A STRING 307

As you work with strings, there may be times when your programs need to locate the rightmost occurrence of a string. For example, if you are working with a URL, such as *http://www.somesite.com/html/index.html*, you might want to locate the rightmost occurrence of the substring "html". To determine the rightmost occurrence of a string, your programs can use the *lastIndexOf* method. For example, the following statements use the *lastIndexOf* method to determine the last (rightmost) occurrence of the substring "oo" within the string "CooLTooLS":

```
String name = "CooLTooLS";
System.out.println(name.lastIndexOf("oo"); // Displays the value 5
```

These statements display the value 5, which corresponds to the last occurrence of the substring within the string. If the substring does not exist within the string, the function returns the value -1.

CHECKING STRING PREFIX 308

When you work with strings, there may be times when you need to determine if a string starts with a specific substring. For example, if your string contains a URL, you may want to know if the string starts with the substring "http" or "ftp". To determine if a string starts with a particular substring, you can use the *String* class *startsWith* method. For example, the following statements use the *startsWith* method to determine if the *URL* object starts with the characters "http":

```
String URL = "http://www.jamsa.com";
System.out.println(URL.startsWith("http"));       // prints true
```

The *startsWith* function returns a *boolean* (true or false) value. If you specify a zero-based index as the second parameter to *startsWith*, the function will start checking for the substring at that character. Using an index value in this way is useful when you know that the prefix actually starts a known number of characters into the string. For example, the following statement uses the *startsWith* function to determine if the substring "www" starts at offset 7 of the *URL* object:

```
System.out.println(URL.startsWith("www", 7));     // prints true
```

CHECKING STRING SUFFIX 309

In Tip 308, you learned that by using the *String* class *startsWith* method, your applets can determine if a string starts with a specific substring. In a similar way, there may be times when your programs need to determine if a string ends with a specific substring. To determine if a *String* ends with a particular substring, you can use the *endsWith* method. The following statements, for example, use the *endsWith* method to determine if the *URL* object ends with the substring "html":

```
String URL = "http://www.jamsa.com/file.html";
System.out.println(name.endsWith("html"));     // prints true
```

The *endsWith* function returns a *boolean* (true or false) value.

310 CONVERTING A STRING TO LOWER OR UPPERCASE

Within your programs, there will be times when you need to convert a *String's* contents to upper or lowercase. The *String* class provides you with a method to make a *String* uppercase or lowercase. For example, the following statements use the *toLowerCase* function to convert the String "CooLTooLS" to lowercase "cooltools":

```
String name = "CooLTooLS";
name = name.toLowerCase();
```

To convert a character string to uppercase, your programs can use the toUppercase method, as shown here:

```
name = name.toUpperCase();
```

311 REMOVING LEADING AND TRAILING WHITESPACES FROM A STRING

When you work with strings, there may be many times when you will need to remove leading and trailing whitespace characters (such as spaces and tabs) from the string. In such cases, your programs can use the *String* class *trim* method. For example, the following statements use the *trim* function to remove whitespace from the character string:

```
String password = "     OpenMe   ";
password = password.trim();
System.out.println("Password is:" + password);
```

These statements remove the leading and trailing spaces of the *password* object. If you use the *trim* function on *Strings* that have embedded spaces, the *trim* function will remove only the leading and trailing spaces.

312 CONVERTING PRIMITIVE DATA TYPES TO STRING

As you work with primitive data types (such as the types *int*, *float*, and *double*), there will be times when you must convert the value to a *String* object. In such cases, you can use the *String* class *valueOf* method. The *String* class overloads the *valueOf* method to support each of the Java primitive types, as shown:

```
String valueOf(char[] data);
String valueOf(char[] data, int offset, int count);
String valueOf(boolean b);
String valueOf(char c);
String valueOf(int i);
String valueOf(long l);
String valueOf(float f);
String valueOf(double d);
```

To use the *String* class *valueOf* method, you specify the class name and method, such as *String.valueOf(1001)*. The following statements create new *String* objects from various primitive types using the *valueOf* method:

```
String s1 = String.valueOf(4);      // convert an int to a String
String s2 = String.valueOf(true);   // convert a boolean to a String
```

```
String s3 = String.valueOf(3.1415); // convert a float to a String
String s4 = String.valueOf('A');     // convert a char to a String
```

UNDERSTANDING STRING REFERENCE, IMMUTABILITY, AND SHARING 313

Strings, like any other object, make use of references. When you assign objects to variables, or pass objects as arguments to methods, you are passing references to those objects, not the objects themselves, nor copies of those objects. For example, consider the following example:

```
String s1, s2;        // declare the variables
s1 = "Something";     // create a String object
s2 = s1;              // two variables share a reference
```

At this point, the statements have created one *String* object (which contains "Something") and two references, *s1* and *s2*. By assigning *s2* to *s1*, the statements simply create another reference to a pre-existing object in memory. Both of the references refer to the same object. You can use either the *s1* variable or the *s2* variable to perform operations on the string. To create two separate *String* objects (as opposed to references), you must use the *new* operator, as shown:

```
s2 = new String(s1);
```

Using the *new* operator in this way creates two objects, each containing the same contents—that is, both have their own copy of the text "Something".

In Java, *String* objects are *immutable*, that is, once you create a *String*, you cannot make changes directly to that object. Instead, when you assign different characters to a *String* object, Java allocates new memory locations to hold the characters and then points the object to the new memory locations. Then, Java's automatic garbage collection deallocates the original memory locations for you.

To make it easier for you to change your character string, Java provides a class called *StringBuffer*. The *StringBuffer* class can be used as a temporary "scratchpad" for you to make changes to your string before it is copied to a new immutable *String* object. Tip 314 discusses the *StringBuffer* class in detail.

HOW JAVA USES THE STRING AND STRINGBUFFER CLASSES 314

As you have learned, Java strings are immutable, which means after you create a *String* object, you cannot change that object's contents. The Java designers found that most of the time, programmers do not need to change a string after it is created. By making *String* objects immutable, Java can provide better error protection and more efficient handling of strings. However, in case you do need to change the *String*, you can use a class called *StringBuffer* as a temporary "scratchpad" which you use to make changes. In short, your programs can change the *String* objects you store within a *Stringbuffer* and later copy the buffer's contents back to the *String* object after your alterations are complete.

In short, you should use *String* objects for "frozen" character strings whose contents you don't expect to change. In contrast, you should use the *StringBuffer* class for strings you expect to change in content or size. Within your programs, you can take advantage of features from both classes because both provide methods to easily convert between the two.

315 CREATING A NEW STRING USING THE STRINGBUFFER CLASS

As you learned in Tip 314, your programs should use a *StringBuffer* to hold the contents of character strings that you expect to change during your program's execution. Within a Java program, you can create a *StringBuffer* object from any *String* object. For example, the following statements create two *StringBuffer* objects, one using a *String* object (*orange_str*) and another directly from the *StringBuffer* class:

```java
String orange_str = "Orange";
StringBuffer orange_buff = new StringBuffer(orange_str);
StringBuffer kiwi_buff = new StringBuffer("Kiwi");
```

316 CONVERTING A STRINGBUFFER TO STRING

As briefly discussed, Java makes it easy for your programs to convert a *String* object into a *StringBuffer* object and vice versa. To convert a string object into a *StringBuffer* object, you simply use the *new* operator to create a *StringBuffer* instance based on a *String* object as shown in Tip 315. To convert the *StringBuffer* object into a *String*, you can simply use the *toString* method, as shown:

```java
StringBuffer kiwi_buff = new StringBuffer("Kiwi"); // Create object
String kiwi_string = kiwi_buff.toString();          // Convert object
```

317 APPENDING AND INSERTING TEXT TO A STRINGBUFFER

The *StringBuffer* class allows your programs to manipulate the contents of a string. For example, the *StringBuffer* class provides methods that let you add a variety of primitive types to the end of the string (the *append* methods), as well as methods to insert the primitive types at a specified position within the string (the *insert* methods). The following statements illustrate the use of the *StringBuffer* primitive-type append and insert methods:

```java
StringBuffer kiwi_buff = new StringBuffer("Kiwi");

kiwi_buff.append(" Fruit ");    // concatenate a string
kiwi_buff.append(1.49F);        // concatenate a float
kiwi_buff.insert(11, '$');      // insert a $ at position 11

System.out.println(kiwi_buff.toString());
```

The statements begin by creating a *StringBuffer* containing the text "Kiwi". By using the *append* methods, the statements then concatenate a string named *Fruit* and a value of type *float*. Next, the *insert* method places a dollar sign at the eleventh character position. Remember that Java indexes characters starting at zero. Finally, the program prints the following line:

```
Kiwi Fruit $1.49000
```

THE DIFFERENCE BETWEEN STRINGBUFFER CAPACITY AND LENGTH 318

As you place text within a *StringBuffer* using the *append* and *insert* methods, there may be times when you need to know the buffer's current length, as well as the buffer's capacity. Using the *StringBuffer* class *length* and *setLength* methods, your programs can determine the buffer's size and capacity. The buffer's capacity refers to the maximum number of characters the buffer can store. For example, the following statement creates a *StringBuffer* object that contains fourteen characters:

```
StringBuffer call_sign = new StringBuffer("CBS Television");
```

At this point, if you were to use the *capacity* method to determine the *StringBuffer's* capacity, the method would return a value one greater than the number of characters, or fifteen:

```
System.out.println(call_sign.capacity());    // Displays the value 15
```

Now, assume you use the *StringBuffer* class *setLength* method to reduce the size of the *StringBuffer's* contents to three characters, as shown:

```
call_sign.setLength(3);
```

At this time, the *StringBuffer* object now has a size of three (which the *length* function will return, as discussed in Tip 319), but the *object's* capacity has not changed.

CHECKING AND SETTING A STRINGBUFFER'S LENGTH 319

After you create a *StringBuffer* object, you can determine how many characters your object is holding by using the *length* method. Also, as you learned in Tip 318, you can adjust the size of a *StringBuffer* object using the *setLength* method. The following statements illustrate the use of the *StringBuffer length*, *setLength*, and *toString* methods:

```
StringBuffer kiwi_buff = new StringBuffer("Kiwi Fruit");
System.out.println(kiwi_buff.length());    // Displays the value 10

System.out.println(kiwi_buff.toString()); // Displays Kiwi Fruit
kiwi_buff.setLength(4);

System.out.println(kiwi_buff.length());    // Displays the value 4
System.out.println(kiwi_buff.toString()); // Displays Kiwi
```

As you can see, the *StringBuffer* length is initially equal to the number of characters in the *String* object "Kiwi Fruit" causing the first invocation of the *length* method to return the value 10. Next, the statements use the *setLength* function to limit the buffer's contents to four characters, which causes the second invocation of the *length* method to return the value 4.

320 CREATING A BOOLEAN OBJECT

As you learned in Tip 277, Java provides a special set of classes that correspond to each of the primitive types. If, for example, you need to manipulate a boolean variable, you may want to create a *Boolean* object, as shown:

```
Boolean boolean_object;
boolean_object = new Boolean(true);   // to object
```

The Boolean class is useful when your programs need to pass a *boolean* parameter to a method by reference.

321 CONVERTING THE "TRUE" AND "FALSE" STRING TO BOOLEAN

If your Java programs work with character strings, there may be times when a string contains characters such as "True" or "False" that represent a boolean value. Within your programs, you can use the *Boolean* class *valueOf* method to convert the text to a *boolean*. Because *valueOf* is a static method, you do not need to create an instance of the class to perform the conversion. For example, the following statements illustrate the use of a static function call to the *valueOf* method:

```
System.out.println(Boolean.valueOf("TRUE"));
System.out.println(Boolean.valueOf("True"));
System.out.println(Boolean.valueOf("true"));
System.out.println(Boolean.valueOf("FALSE"));
System.out.println(Boolean.valueOf("False"));
System.out.println(Boolean.valueOf("false"));
```

322 CONVERTING A BOOLEAN TO "TRUE" AND "FALSE" STRINGS

In Tip 321, you learned that the *Boolean* class *valueOf* function lets your programs convert a character-string representation of a true or false value into an actual *boolean* value. In the opposite manner, your programs may need to convert a *Boolean* object's true or false value into a character string. To convert the value, your programs can use the *Boolean* class *toString* function, as shown:

```
Boolean boolean_object = new Boolean(true);
String boolean_string = boolean_object.toString();
```

In this case, the statements will assign the *String* object *boolean_string* the value "true".

323 USING THE BOOLEANVALUE METHOD

As you have learned, within a condition such as an *if* or *while* statement, the condition must evaluate to a primitive true or false *boolean* value. If you are using a *Boolean* object, you need a way to determine the object's underlying *boolean* value. To get the corresponding primitive *boolean* value, use the *Boolean* class *booleanValue* method, as shown:

```
Boolean boolean_object = new Boolean(true);
if (boolean_object.booleanValue())
    // true case goes here
```

CREATING AN INTEGER OBJECT 324

As you learned in Tip 277, Java provides a special set of classes that correspond to each of the primitive types. To help you convert values to or from the type *int*, Java defines the *Integer* class. The following statements create an *Integer* object:

```
Integer integer_object;
integer_object = new Integer(5);   // to object
```

The *Integer* class is useful when you need to pass an *int* value to a function by reference.

CONVERTING AN INTEGER TO OTHER DATA TYPES 325

Within a program, you may need to convert a value of type *int* to a value of a different primitive type such as *float*, *long*, or *double*. The following statements illustrate how you would use the *Integer* class method to convert a value of type *int* to other types:

```
Integer integer_object;
integer_object = new Integer(5);              // Create an object

float f = integer_object.floatValue();
long l = integer_object.longValue();
double d = integer_object.doubleValue();
```

HOW TO COMPARE INTEGER OBJECTS 326

When you use *Integer* class objects, do not mistakenly compare two objects using the equality operator (==). Instead, to compare *Integer* class objects, you must use the *Integer* class *equals* method. If you use the equality operator, your program will compare the object references (the object addresses in memory, as opposed to the object values). The following statements use the *Integer* class *equals* method to compare to *Integer* objects:

```
Integer Int1 = new Integer(5);
Integer Int2 = new Integer("5");
System.out.println(Int1.equals(Int2));
```

These statements create two *Integer* objects. The first statement creates an *Integer* object using the number 5, while the second statement creates an object using the character string "5". Finally, the *equals* method compares the two objects and returns *true*.

327 CONVERTING OTHER DATA TYPES TO INTEGER OBJECTS

Because the *Integer* class has a constructor that accepts a *String* object, you can supply any *String* and the *Integer* class will attempt to make it into an *Integer* object. Likewise, the *Integer* class has a static class method named *valueOf* that also will create an *Integer* object. Because *valueOf* is a static method, you do not need a pre-existing *Integer* object to invoke it.

In any case, after you have a *String* object that represents an integer number, your program can convert the *String* object to an *Integer* object. At other times, you may need to convert other types of values into an *Integer* object. For example, assume you want to convert a *float* to an *Integer*. Because the *Integer* class accepts *Strings* for conversion and your programs can easily convert a value of type *float* to a character string, your programs can perform the *float*-to-*Integer* conversion, as follows:

```
String f_str = Float.toString(1.0F);        // float to String
Integer f_Int = Integer.valueOf(f_str);     // String to float
```

If the value of type *float* is not a whole value, such as 1.3333, the conversion generates an exception (java.lang.NumberFormatException) indicating that you cannot convert the value directly to an *Integer*.

328 GETTING A NUMERIC OBJECT'S MINIMUM AND MAXIMUM VALUES

Java derives its numeric object types, such as *Double, Float, Integer,* and *Long,* using the *java.lang.Number* class library. As it turns out, these four numeric object types all provide the *MAX_VALUE* and *MIN_VALUE* attributes that contain the maximum or minimum values that the particular class can represent. For example, the following statements use the attributes to display the largest and smallest values that the *Integer* class can represent:

```
System.out.println(Integer.MAX_VALUE);
System.out.println(Integer.MIN_VALUE);
```

In this case, the statements will display the values 2147483647 and -2147483648.

329 DEALING WITH FLOATING-POINT NUMBER OBJECTS

As you learned in Tip 277, Java provides a special set of classes that correspond to each of the primitive types. To help you convert values to or from the type *float* or *double*, Java defines the *Float* and *Double* classes. The following statements create *Float* and *Double* objects:

```
Float  float_object;
Double double_object;

float_object = new Float(5.0F);    // Create a Float object
double_object = new Double(5.0);   // Create a Double object
```

These statements create two floating point objects, one referenced by *float_object*, and the other by *double_object*. These two classes are useful when you need to pass a *float* or *double* value to a function by reference.

THE LIMITATIONS OF JAVA'S FLOATING-POINT TO STRING CONVERSION 330

To convert floating-point numbers directly to *String* types, you can use Java's *Float, Double,* or *String* classes to perform the conversion. These classes have *static* conversion methods that your program can call without having to create an instance of that class. Using the *Float* and *Double* classes, your programs can use the *toString* method. Using the *String* class, your programs can use the *valueOf* method. The following statements illustrate the use of these methods to perform a *float*-to-*String* conversion and vice versa:

```
float f = 1.123456789F;

System.out.println("float = " + Float.toString(f));
System.out.println("float = " + String.valueOf(f));
```

The shortcoming of both these methods is that both will round your floating-point number after the fifth decimal place. For instance, the above example converts a *float* with nine digits to the right of the decimal point to a *String* displaying only five digits:

```
float = 1.12346
float = 1.12346
```

BUILDING YOUR OWN FLOATING-POINT NUMBER FORMATTING CLASS 331

Java's immense flexibility lets you build handy methods to pick up where the language itself leaves off. For example, consider a case where you might need a general purpose class to format floating-point numbers. You can write a class which formats an amount by adding a dollar sign, a percent sign, the ability to support caller-specified precision, and to properly add a negative sign when needed.

The following class, *DoubleFormat,* is not part of the Java library. Instead, you must create a new file (named *DoubleFormat.java*) and type the class in yourself. You may want to do this now, as the next two tips contain additional methods that you can add to this class to expand its functionality.

```
class DoubleFormat {
    public static String toString(double inValue, int precision) {
        return toString(inValue, precision, false);
    }

    public static String toString (double inValue, int precision,
        boolean use_comma)
    {
        boolean trailing_zero;
        double absval= Math.abs(inValue); // get positive portion

        if (precision < 0)
          {
            precision = -precision;
            trailing_zero = false;
          }
```

```
    else
        trailing_zero = true;

    String signStr = "";

    if (inValue < 0)
        signStr= "-";

    long intDigit = (long) Math.floor(absval);  // get integer part

    String intDigitStr = String.valueOf(intDigit);

    if (use_comma)
      {
          int intDigitStrLen= intDigitStr.length();
          int dig_index= (intDigitStrLen - 1) % 3;

          dig_index++;

          String intCommaDigitStr = intDigitStr.substring(0,
            dig_index);

          while (dig_index < intDigitStrLen)
            {
              intCommaDigitStr += "," +
                  intDigitStr.substring(dig_index, dig_index+3);

              dig_index+= 3;
            }
          intDigitStr= intCommaDigitStr;
      }

    String precDigitStr= "";

    long precDigit= Math.round((absval - intDigit) *
          Math.pow(10.0, precision));

    precDigitStr= String.valueOf(precDigit);

    // pad zeros between decimal and precision digits
    String zeroFilling= "";

    for (int i= 0; i < precision-precDigitStr.length(); i++)
        zeroFilling += "0";

    precDigitStr= zeroFilling + precDigitStr;

    if (!trailing_zero)
      {
          int lastZero;

          for (lastZero = precDigitStr.length() - 1;
              lastZero >= 0; lastZero—)
            if (precDigitStr.charAt(lastZero)!= '0')
                break;
```

```
                 precDigitStr= precDigitStr.substring(0, lastZero + 1);
       }

    if (precDigitStr.equals(""))
       return signStr + intDigitStr;
    else
       return signStr + intDigitStr + "." + precDigitStr;
  }
}
```

Note: *Rather than typing in this class, you can obtain the class source code from the companion CD-ROM that accompanies this book.*

FORMATTING DOLLAR VALUE FLOATING-POINT NUMBERS 332

In Tip 331, you learned how to build a general purpose class for formatting floating-point numbers. To make that class more useful, you may want to add the following methods to the class to help you format dollar values:

```
public static String toDollarString(double inValue, int precision)
 {
    return "$" + toString(inValue, precision, true);
 }

public static String toDollarString(double inValue)
 {
    return "$" + toString(inValue, 2, true);
 }
```

The first method, *toDollarString*, takes a floating-point number and a precision value that indicates how many digits of precision you would like to see in the output. It returns a *String* formatted along with the $ sign. The second method is similar, except that it assumes you want two digits of precision.

FORMATTING PERCENT VALUE FLOATING-POINT NUMBERS 333

In Tip 331, you learned how to build a general purpose class for formatting floating-point numbers. To make that class more useful, you may want to add the following methods to the class to help you format percent values:

```
public static String toPercent(double inValue, int precision)
 {
    return toString(inValue, precision, true) + "%";
 }

public static String toPercentString(double inValue)
 {
    return toString(inValue, 2, true) + "%";
 }
```

The first method, *toPercent*, takes a floating-point number and a precision value which indicates how many digits of precision you would like to see in the output. It returns a *String* formatted along with the % sign. The second method is similar, except that it assumes you want two digits of precision.

334 GETTING THE ABSOLUTE VALUE OF A NUMBER

Java's *java.lang.Math* class provides a variety of static methods for exponentiation, floating-point trigonometry, min and max functions, as well as other operations. Because they are all static methods, your programs can reference them by the class name without having to create an instance of the class. Several of the following tips discuss these mathematical methods in detail.

To return the absolute value of a number, the *Math* class provides four overloaded methods all named *abs*. The methods support the four numeric types, *int*, *long*, *float*, and *double*:

```
public static int abs(int a);
public static long abs(long a);
public static float abs(float a);
public static double abs(double a);
```

For example, to return the absolute value of a *float*, you can use the *abs* method, as shown:

```
float num = -5.8F;
num = Math.abs(num);   // Assigns the value 5.8F
```

335 USING THE SQRT METHOD

When your programs perform arithmetic operations, there will be times when you will need to take the square root of a value. In such cases, your programs can use the *Math* class *sqrt* method. The format of the *sqrt* method is as follows:

```
public static double sqrt(double a) throws ArithmeticException;
```

The following statements, for example, use the *Math* class *sqrt* method to return the square root of the value 7.9:

```
float num = 7.9F;
num = (float) Math.sqrt(num);   // return the square root value
```

Notice that this statement uses an explicit cast to assign the return value to a *float* because the *sqrt* method returns a *double*. In this case, the variable *num* will have a value of 2.81069 after the assignment.

336 USING THE COS METHOD

For a triangle, the cosine of an angle is the ratio of the angle's adjacent edge to the hypotenuse. The *Math* class *cos* method returns the cosine of an angle expressed in radians. The declaration of the *cos* function is as follows:

```
public static double cos(double a);
```

To return the cosine of an angle, you can use the *cos* method, as shown:

```
double num, angle = 0.785398D;   // angle in radians
num = Math.cos(angle);           // return the cosine of the angle
```

In this case, the statements will assign the variable *num* the value of 0.707107.

USING THE SIN METHOD

In a triangle, the sine of an angle is the ratio of the angle's opposite edge to the hypotenuse. The *Math* class *sin* method returns the sine of an angle expressed in radians. The declaration of the *sin* method is as follows:

```
public static double sin(double a);
```

To return the sine of an angle, you can use the *sin* method, as shown:

```
double num, angle = 0.785398D;    // angle in radians, 1/4
num = Math.sin(angle);            // return the sine of the angle
```

In this case, the statements will assign the variable *num* a value of 0.707107.

USING THE TAN METHOD

In a triangle, the tangent of an angle is the ratio of the angle's opposite edge to the adjacent edge. The *Math* class *tan* method returns the tangent of an angle expressed in radians. The declaration of the *tan* method is as follows:

```
public static double tan(double a);
```

To return the tangent of an angle, you can use the *tan* method, as shown:

```
double num angle = 0.785398D;     // angle in radians, 1/4
num = Math.tan(angle);            // return the tangent of the angle
```

In this case, the statements will assign the variable *num* the value of 1.0.

USING THE ACOS METHOD

The arccosine is the ratio between the hypotenuse of a right triangle and the leg adjacent to a given angle; the inverse of the cosine of an angle. If y is the cosine of θ, then θ is the arccosine of y. The *Math* class *acos* method returns the arccosine of an angle specified in radians. The declaration for the *acos* function is as follows:

```
public static double acos(double a);
```

To return the arccosine of a number, you can use the *acos* method, as shown:

```
float num = 0.707107F;
num = (float) Math.acos(num);  // return the arccosine
```

Notice that these statements use an explicit cast to assign the result to a *float* because the *acos* method returns a *double*. In this case, *num* will have a value of 0.785398 radians after the assignment.

340 USING THE ASIN METHOD

The arcsine is the ratio between the hypotenuse of a right triangle and the leg opposite a given acute angle; the inverse of the sine of an angle. If *y* is the sine of θ, then θ is the arcsine of *y*. The *Math* class *asin* method returns the arcsine of the number as a *double*. The declaration of the *asin* method is as follows:

```
public static double asin(double a);
```

To return the arcsine of a number, you can use the *asin* method, as shown:

```
float num = 0.707107F;
num = (float) Math.asin(num);   // return the arcsine
```

Notice that these statements use an explicit cast to assign the return to a *float* because the *asin* method returns a *double*. In this case, *num* will have a value of 0.785398 radians after the assignment.

341 USING THE ATAN METHOD

The arctangent is the ratio between the leg adjacent to a given acute angle and the leg opposite it in a right triangle; the inverse of the tangent of an angle. If *y* is the tangent of θ, then θ is the arctangent of *y*. The *atan* method in the *Math* class returns the arctangent of the number as a *double*. The declaration of the *atan* method is as follows:

```
public static double atan(double a);
```

To return the arctangent of a number, you can use the *atan* method, as shown:

```
double num = 1.0D;
num = Math.atan(num);   // return the arctangent
```

342 CONVERTING RECTANGULAR TO POLAR COORDINATES

In the rectangular coordinate system, the coordinates (x, y) locate a point *x* units along the *x*-axis and *y* units along the *y*-axis. In the polar coordinate system, the coordinates (r, θ) locate a point *r* units from the origin and at an angle θ measured from a reference line. If you have the (x, y) rectangular coordinates and would like to convert them to polar coordinates (r, θ), you can use the following equations:

$$r = sqrt(x^2 + y^2)$$

$$\theta = arctan(y/x)$$

To implement these equations in Java, use statements similar to the following:

```
float x = 10F, y = 20F;

float r = (float) Math.sqrt(Math.pow(x, 2) + Math.pow(y, 2));
float theta = (float) Math.atan(y/x);

System.out.println(r + ", " + theta);
```

ROUNDING A FLOATING-POINT VALUE TO AN INTEGER 343

The Java *Math* class provides two methods for rounding a number. The first rounds values of type *float* to *int*, and the second rounds values of type *double* to *long*:

```
public static int round(float a);
public static long round(double a);
```

The following statements illustrate the use of the *round* method:

```
float f1 = 3.8F, f2 = 3.2F;
int i, j;

i = Math.round(f1);
j = Math.round(f2);
```

These statements assign the variable *i* the value 4, and the variable *j* the value 3.

USING THE FLOOR METHOD 344

When you work with floating-point numbers, you may need to round down the value to the next lower integer. For such cases, the Java *Math* class provides the *floor* method whose format is as follows:

```
public static double floor(double a);
```

Unlike the *round* methods which round up or down to an integer, the *floor* method rounds down the floating-point number and returns a type that is also a floating point. For example, the following statements illustrate the use of the *floor* method:

```
float ff = 3.8F;
float jj = (float) Math.floor(ff);

System.out.println(ff + " after floor is —> " + jj);
```

These statements will display the following output:

```
3.20000 after floor is —> 3
```

USING THE CEIL METHOD 345

When you work with floating-point numbers, you may need to round up the value to the next higher integer. For such cases, the Java *Math* class provides the *ceil* method, the format of which is as follows:

```
public static double ceil(double a);
```

Unlike the *round* methods which round up or down to an integer, the *ceil* method rounds up the floating-point number and returns a type that is also a floating point. The following statements illustrate the use of the *ceil* function:

```
float ff = 3.2F;
float jj = (float) Math.ceil(ff);

System.out.println(ff + " after ceil is -> " + jj);
```

In this case, because the *ceil* method returns the type *double* and the statements use a variable of type *float*, the statements use an explicit cast. The statements will display the following output:

```
3.20000 after ceil is -> 4
```

346 ROUNDING A FLOATING-POINT VALUE UP OR DOWN

As you learned in Tip 343, Java's *round* method will round a floating-point number to an integer. Depending on your program's purpose, you may want to round the number to another floating-point value. To obtain a floating-point value from the *round* method, you simply use an explicit cast to a value of type *float* or *double*, as shown:

```
float f = (float) Math.round(3.8F);
double d = (double) Math.round(3.2F);
```

These statements will assign the variable *f* the value 4.0 and the variable *d* the value 3.0.

347 WORKING WITH EXPONENTIALS

When your programs perform complex mathematical operations, there may be times when you need to calculate the exponential of e^x. In such cases, your programs can use the *Math* class *exp* method. The following statement illustrates the use of the *exp* function to determine the result of $e^{0.4}$:

```
double value = Math.exp(0.4);     // computes to 1.49183
```

348 GETTING THE VALUE OF E OR PI

Java's *java.lang.Math* class provides two predefined constants. One for *e* and the other for PI. To obtain these values, specify the *Math* class name followed by the name of the constant, as shown:

```
System.out.println("e is: " + Math.E);
System.out.println("PI is: " + Math.PI);
```

These statements, for example, will display the following output:

```
e is: 2.71828
PI is: 3.14159
```

FINDING THE REMAINDER OF A FLOATING-POINT DIVISION

As you have learned, the modulo operator (%) returns the remainder of an integer division. Depending on your program's purpose, you may want to know the remainder of floating-point division. In such cases, the *Math* class provides the *IEEEremainder* method to divide two floating-point values, returning the remainder as a floating-point value. The form of the *IEEEremainder* method is as follows:

```
public static double IEEEremainder(double f1, double f2);
```

For example, if you invoke *IEEEremainder* with the values 10.0 and 3.0, the function will return the value 1.0 (10 divided by 3 is 3 with a remainder of 1). The following statements, for example, will display the floating-point remainder to the screen:

```
double n = 10.0;
double d = 3.0;

System.out.println(Math.IEEEremainder(n, d));
```

CALCULATING NATURAL LOG

The natural logarithm of a number is the power to which the value *e* must be raised to equal the given number. To help your programs determine the natural log, the *Math* class provides the *log* method, which returns the natural logarithm of a floating point value. The following statement illustrates the use of the *log* function:

```
double d = Math.log(7.0);   // returns 1.94591
```

DETERMINING MAXIMUM AND MINIMUM VALUES

When your programs compare two numbers, there will be times when you will want to know the minimum or maximum of two values. For such cases, the *Math* class provides the *min* and *max* methods. You can use these methods to compare values of type *int*, *long*, *float*, and *double*. For example, the following statements use the *min* and *max* functions to determine the minimum of two values of type *float* and the maximum of two values of type *double*:

```
float min = Math.min(3.5F, 4.8F);     // Assigns the value 3.5F
double max = Math.max(Math.PI, 3.0);  // Assigns the value Math.PI
```

CALCULATING THE RESULT OF X^N

One of the most common mathematical operations your programs will perform is to raise a value to a given power. For such cases, the *Math* class provides the *pow* method, which returns the result of a value raised to a given power. The format of the *pow* method is as follows:

```
public static double log(double a, double b) throws
    ArithmeticException;
```

If the result of the value raised to the given power results in overflow, Java will throw an exception of type *ArithmeticException*. The *pow* method takes two *doubles* as parameters; the first parameter is the base value and the second is the power to which the method raises the base. The following statement illustrates the use of the *pow* function:

```
double ans = Math.pow(3, 2);   // returns 3 to the 2, or 9
```

353 CREATING RANDOM FLOATING-POINT NUMBERS

Depending on your program's purpose, you may need to generate one or more random numbers. In such cases, your programs can use the *Math* class *random* function. The format of the *random* function is as follows:

```
public static synchronized double random();
```

The following statements illustrate the use of the *random* method:

```
double rand;

rand = Math.random();
```

The *random* function returns a value in the range 0 to 1.0. By multiplying the function's result by a value such as 100 or 1000, your programs can change the range of values.

354 UNDERSTANDING PSEUDO RANDOM VERSUS TRUE RANDOM

When Java, or most other computer languages, needs to produce a random number, a special calculation is made based on a given input value called a *seed* number. The calculation will always produce the same number when the same *seed* number is given. Because the function's result is always predictable, it is called a *pseudo-random* number. A *true-random* number is not predictable.

The fact that the *pseudo-random* number is predictable does not mean that it cannot make a good random number. The *seed* number in Java is 64 bits long and the algorithm which uses it to create a random number produces a good distribution of values.

A big advantage of *pseudo-random* numbers is that your program is easier to debug when it uses the same sequence of random numbers. After you release your software to users, you can ensure good randomness by using a different *seed* for each program run. For example, the *seed* could be based on the time, user keystrokes, network activity, or any other random phenomena.

355 SEEDING A RANDOM NUMBER GENERATOR

Java provides the *java.util.Random* class which facilitates your program's implementation of a pseudo-random number generator. By default, the class methods uses the current time as the *seed* value. However, you can use the *setSeed* method or the class constructor to specify a *seed* value of your own. You may want to do this when, for example, you need to debug code which uses random numbers, and you need a repeatable sequence of numbers. For example, you can use the *Random* class and set a starting *seed* value as follows:

```java
import java.util.*;

class Randomize {
    public static void main(String args[])
    {
        Random r = new Random(123456); // set an initial seed
        System.out.println("Random 1 is " + r.nextInt());

        r.setSeed(654321);   // reset the seed to something else
        System.out.println("Random 2 is " + r.nextInt());
    }
}
```

The program first sets a *seed* when it creates the *Random* class object. Next, within the call to the *System.out.println* function, the program calls the *nextInt* method, which returns the next integer in the random number sequence.

Normally, you do not need to set a new *seed* more than once within your programs. However, should you need to do so, you can call the *setSeed* method, as shown. This program produces the following output:

```
Random 1 is 1774763047
Random 2 is 129127415
```

CREATING RANDOM FLOATING-POINT NUMBERS 356

As shown in Tip 355, you can generate random numbers by using an instance of the *Random* class. You also learned that the *nextInt* function returns the next integer in a range of random numbers. In a similar way, the *Random* class contains a method called *nextFloat*, which produces a new random floating-point number for each call. The following statements illustrate the use of the *nextFloat* method:

```java
Random r = new Random();    // use a default initial seed
System.out.println("Random float is " + r.nextFloat());
```

CREATING RANDOM NUMBERS WITH GAUSSIAN DISTRIBUTION 357

When you create random numbers, you may need better control over the range of numbers that the random number generator creates. As it turns out, you can produce a set of random numbers based on a Gaussian distribution, that is, a distribution having a mean of 0.0 and a standard deviation of 1.0. To get numbers based on the Gaussian distribution, you use the *Random* class *nextGaussian* method, as shown:

```java
Random r = new Random(); // use a default initial seed
System.out.println("Random 1 is " + r.nextGaussian());
```

358 CONTROLLING THE RANGE OF RANDOM INTEGERS

As you have learned, Java programs can generate random integers by using an instance of the *Random* class. The *Random* class contains a method called *nextInt*, which produces a new random *int* for each call. Depending on your program's purpose, you may need to produce random numbers in a specific range. To control the range of integer values a random-number generator creates, you can use the modulus operator (%). For example, if you need numbers in the range -100 to 100, you can get the remainder of the random number divided by 100, as shown:

```
Random r = new Random();      // use a default initial seed
System.out.println("Random int is " + r.nextInt() % 100);
```

Likewise, if you need to restrict the range of numbers to positive values, say 0 to 100, your programs can use the *Math* class *abs* function, as shown:

```
Random r = new Random();      // use a default initial seed
System.out.println("Random int is " + Math.abs(r.nextInt() % 100));
```

359 CREATING RANDOM INTEGERS FOR A SPECIFIC RANGE

The *Random* class methods for generating random numbers produce values in the ranges indicated in Table 359:

Method name	Range of output
nextFloat	0.0 to 1.0
nextDouble	0.0 to 1.0
nextInt	-2147483648 to 2147483647
nextLong	-9223372036854775808 to 9223372036854775807

Table 359 Range of random numbers.

As you learned in Tip 358, by performing simple math operations, you can manipulate the random numbers to produce a desired range. The following example shows you how you might limit the range of floating-point random numbers from 0 to 100:

```
Random r = new Random();    // create a Random object
float f = r.nextFloat();    // get a random value (0.0 to 1.0)

float v = (f * 100);        // multiply by a factor to get 0 to 100
```

360 GETTING THE CURRENT DATE WITH THE DATE CLASS

Within your programs, there may be times when your programs will need to work with the current date and time. As it turns out, Java's *Date* class, *java.util.Date*, provides various methods to represent and manipulate dates and times. If your program calls the *Date* constructor with no arguments, a *Date* instance is initialized with the current date and time.

Because different parts of the world represent dates in different formats, the *Date* class provides a convenient method which formats the current date into the local style. The *toLocaleString* method will take the date information in the instance and create a *String* object. For example, the following statements use the *Date* class methods to display the current date and time within the United States:

```
import java.util.Date;

class PrintTheDate {
   public static void main(String arg[] )
    {
       Date today= new Date();
        System.out.println(today.toLocaleString() );
    }
 }
```

The above code will print the date and time, for example:

```
Tuesday, 26 November, 1996   10:02:17 PM
```

BEWARE OF SPECIFYING DATES BEYOND 2000

 361

When your programs work with dates, you need to be careful with dates beyond 2000. When you use the *setYear* method or any of the constructors that take a year, you are indicating a year by the number of years since 1900—rather than the century's last two digits. Therefore, to set the date to the year 2000, you would use the value 100, as follows:

```
Date future_date= new Date(100, 2, 29);
```

Note: Some versions of the Java compiler may have a problem representing years beyond 2035. You may want to test your compiler's ability to process years beyond 2035.

CREATING YOUR OWN DATE/TIME WITH THE DATE CLASS

 362

Within your programs, you can construct a *Date* class object using the *Date* method either with parameters (to get the current date and time), or without parameters. If you call the *Date* constructor with parameters, you may set a specific date and time. You may also set a particular date and time after the *Date* instance is created by calling a specific series of *Date* class methods.

You may want to create a *Date* object with a date or time different than the current date or time for a variety of situations. For example, you may need to store dates for specific items in a database, or perhaps you may need to compare two dates. In any case, the *Date* class offers several methods your programs can use to change dates and times, as shown in Table 362:

Method	Purpose
setDate(int date)	Set the date (day of the month)
setHours(int hours)	Set the hours
setMinutes(int minutes)	Set the minutes
setMonth(int month)	Set the month minus one (zero-based)

Table 362 Summary of methods for changing date and time. (Continued on following page.)

Method	Purpose
setSeconds(int seconds)	Set the seconds
setTime(long time)	Set the date based on number of milliseconds since 1/1/1970
setYear(long year)	Set the year as a number since 1900

Table 362 Summary of methods for changing date and time. (Continued from previous page.)

For example, to create a *Date* object with the date, May 31, 1997, you would use the following statement:

```
Date start_date= new Date(97, 4, 31);
```

363 USING THE DATE CLASS TO FIND THE DAY OF THE WEEK

After you create a *Date* object, either with the current date and time, or with some other date and time, you can obtain the day of the week using the *getDay* method. The *Date* class represents the day of the week as a zero-based number, with Sunday equal to zero and Saturday equal to six. The following statements will display the day of the week that corresponds to the date, May 31, 1997—which turns out to be 6 (a Saturday):

```
Date start_date = new Date(97, 4, 31);
System.out.println(start_date.getDay());
```

364 BE AWARE OF DATE CLASS ZERO-BASED OBJECTS

The *Date* class provides several functions you can use to get or set the current date. When you use the *getDay, getMonth, setDay,* or *setMonth* methods, be aware that these methods use zero-based dates. In other words, the first day of the week and the first month of the year use the number 0. For example, the first day of the week, Sunday, is represented by a 0. The first month of the year, January, is also represented by a 0. Likewise, the last day of the week, Saturday, is represented by a 6 and the last month, December, is 11.

365 GETTING THE CURRENT TIME WITH THE DATE CLASS

Within your programs, there will be many times when you need to determine the current time. If your program calls the *Date* constructor with no arguments, the constructor will initialize the *Date* object with the current date and time. To determine the current time using the *Date* class, you can use several different techniques. For example, the following statements display the current time using the *toGMTString* (to Greenwich Mean Time) *getHours,* and *getMinutes* methods:

```
import java.util.Date;

class PrintTheTime {
   public static void main(String arg[])
    {
      Date now= new Date();

        System.out.println(now.toGMTString().substring(12));
        System.out.println(now.getHours() + ":" + now.getMinutes());
    }
 }
```

The *toGMTString* method uses the current *Date* information to return a *String* representing the Greenwich Mean Time. By using the *substring* method, you can "chop off" the date information and just report the time, as shown here:

```
06:37:16  GMT
```

To display the current time using a 24-hour format, your program can concatenate the result of the *getHours* and *getMinutes* methods. For example, the previous statements will display the following output:

```
23:41
```

WHAT IS THE EPOCH DATE?

 366

Within a Java program, you can create a *Date* object by specifying a year, month, date and, optionally, the hour, minute, and second as parameters to the constructor function. You can also create a *Date* object with no arguments to the constructor, in which case the *Date* object will contain the current date and time. Finally, you can create a *Date* object by specifying the number of milliseconds since the *epoch* date, which is midnight GMT, January 1, 1970. The *Date* class uses the *epoch* date as a reference point which lets your programs refer to subsequent dates in terms of a single *long* integer. You cannot set a year before 1970.

GETTING CURRENT TIME IN MILLISECONDS

 367

Within your programs, there will be times when you need to compare two dates. One way to compare dates is to convert the dates to milliseconds since a specific date, such as seconds since the *epoch* date (discussed in Tip 366). The *Date* class *getTime* method returns the number of milliseconds since the *epoch* date, midnight GMT, January 1st, 1970. The following statements illustrate how you can use the *getDate* method to compare two dates:

```java
import java.util.Date;

class CompareDates {
   public static void main(String arg[])
    {
      Date now = new Date();
      Date future = new Date(97, 3, 15, 12, 30);

      long difference = future.getTime() - now.getTime();

      System.out.println("Current date: " + now.getHours() +
         ":" + now.getMinutes());

      System.out.println("Future date: " + future.getHours() +
         ":" + future.getMinutes());

      System.out.println("Difference (ms): " + difference);
   }
}
```

368 MEASURE CODE EXECUTION SPEED WITH THE *getTime* METHOD

As you examine your program's performance, there may be times when you want to time a particular section of your code. You can time blocks of code within your programs simply by using the *getTime* method before and after the section of code you want to time. For example, the following statements use the *getTime* method to determine how much time the *for* loop's processing consumes:

```
Date now = new Date();

long startTime= now.getTime(); // begin time count

for (long m=0; m < 1000000; m++)
   ; // do some time consuming task

now = new Date();
long endTime = now.getTime();   // end the time count

System.out.println("Milliseconds=" + (endTime-startTime));
```

These statements will display the time it takes the program to perform the *for* loop, as follows:

```
Milliseconds=1616
```

369 COMPARING DATES WITH AFTER, BEFORE, AND EQUALS METHODS

Java provide several methods to compare two *Date* objects: *after*, *before* and *equals*. The following statements create two *Date* objects, each with a different date. The statements then determine if one date is before or after the other, or whether they are the same date:

```
Date startDate= new Date();
Date endDate= new Date(120, 4, 31);

System.out.println(startDate.toLocaleString() );
System.out.println(endDate.toLocaleString() );
System.out.println("Is start date after " +
   startDate.after(endDate));
System.out.println("Is start date before " +
   startDate.before(endDate));
System.out.println("Are dates equal " + startDate.equals(endDate));
```

These statements will display the following output:

```
Saturday, 31 August, 1996  01:10:39 AM
Sunday, 31 May, 2020  12:00:00 AM
Is start date after false
Is start date before true
Are dates equal false
```

CONVERTING STRING TO DATE

370

The *Date* class provides a very convenient constructor that takes a *String* representation of a date and converts the string into a *Date* object by assigning values to the various time and date fields. The following statements illustrate the use of the *Date* class *String*-based constructor:

```
Date someDate= new Date("Dec 25, 1996");

System.out.println(someDate.toLocaleString() );
someDate= new Date("Dec 25, 1996 1:56 PM");
System.out.println(someDate.toLocaleString() );
```

In this case, the statements successfully convert the two *Strings* into *Date* objects and display the following dates:

```
Wednesday, 25 December, 1996   12:00:00 AM
Wednesday, 25 December, 1996   01:56:00 PM
```

CALCULATING THE DAYS BETWEEN TWO DATES

371

Because the *Date* class lets your programs express dates in terms of milliseconds from a known *epoch* date, you can determine the number of milliseconds between two dates very easily. After you have the number of milliseconds between dates, you can determine the number of days between those dates. The following statements, for example, convert milliseconds to days by dividing the milliseconds by 86400000, that is, the number of milliseconds per day:

```
import  java.applet.*;
import  java.awt.*;
import  java.util.*;

public class daysBetween   extends Applet {
    public long days(Date startDate, Date endDate)
    {
         return(Math.abs(endDate.getTime() -
            startDate.getTime())/86400000);
    }

    public void init()
    {
       Date startDate = new Date(96, 8, 4);
       Date endDate = new Date(96, 8, 6);

       System.out.println("Diffence = " + days(startDate, endDate));
    }
}
```

In this program, the *days* method takes two *Date* objects and returns the number of days between them.

372 CREATING A DAYSINMONTH METHOD

Within your programs, you can use the *Date* class to determine the number of days in any month. The following *DaysInMonth* method takes a *Date* object and returns the number of days in the date's month. The method works by determining how many days there are from the specified date to the first of the following month.

```
short DaysInMonth(Date thisDate)
  {
   long diff;
   Date tempDate = new Date();
   tempDate.setTime(thisDate.getTime());   // copy the date

   if (thisDate.getMonth()!= 11)
     {
        tempDate.setMonth(thisDate.getMonth() + 1);
     }
   else
     {    // special case of December
       tempDate.setMonth(0);
       tempDate.setYear(thisDate.getYear() + 1);
     }

   tempDate.setDate(1);
    diff=Math.abs(tempDate.getTime()-thisDate.getTime())/86400000;
   diff+= thisDate.getDate();
   return((short)(diff-1));
   }
```

373 UNDERSTANDING DIFFERENT DATE STANDARDS

The basis for standard time throughout the world is the meridian at Greenwich, England. You can specify the time for any location in the world in terms of the number of hours from Greenwich Mean Time, or simply GMT. Java uses midnight GMT, January 1st, 1970 for its epoch date.

Java provides methods you can use to express the time based on two time locations: the time at Greenwich and your local time. Of course, the classes determine the time based on your computer's clock and time-zone settings. Thus, you must make sure that both your system's time and time-zone settings are correct. When you need to express the time and date in terms of GMT, you can use the *Date* class *toGMTString* method. If you need the time expressed in the local time, use *Date* class *toLocaleString* method.

The *Date* class *getTimezoneOffset* method determines the local time-zone offset, which is the number of minutes your program must add to Greenwich Mean Time to give the local time zone. This value includes the correction, if necessary, for daylight savings time.

BEWARE WHEN RELYING ON DATE FORMATS

 374

When you work with the *Date* class object, be aware that Sun has reported several bugs in the *Date* class. One bug involves the *toString* method, which gives different output on different platforms. If your program parses the string or relies on the presence of specific fields, you should carefully verify that the strings contain the text you expect. For example, on a Sun Solaris computer, calling the *Date* class *toString* method will result in this output:

```
Tue Sep 10 12:22:56 PDT 1996
```

On Microsoft Windows NT and Windows 95, the *toString* method produces the following date string:

```
Tue Sep 10 12:22:56 1996
```

USING THE DOS TZ ENVIRONMENT VARIABLE

 375

If you use a Windows-based system, you can set the time-zone variable, TZ, by placing a SET command within your system's *AUTOEXEC.BAT* file. The format of the TZ entry is as follows:

```
SET TZ=SSS[+/-]h[h][DDD]
```

The SSS field contains the standard time zone name (such as EST or PST), and the [+/-]h[h] specifies the difference in hours between the standard time zone and GMT. Finally, the DDD field specifies the name of the daylight savings time zone (such as PDT). The following entry sets the time zone for the West Coast when daylight savings time is active:

```
SET TZ=PST8PDT
```

When daylight savings time is not active, omit the time zone name, as shown:

```
SET TZ=PST8
```

If you do not specify a TZ entry, the default is EST5EDT.

UNDERSTANDING ARRAYS

 376

Throughout this book's tips, you have learned how to create variables for individual objects. Sometimes, however, you will need to manipulate a series of related objects within an array object. Arrays let your programs work conveniently with a group of related objects. In short, an array simply lets you store and access a set of objects of the same type within the same variable. For example, you can use an array to keep track of grades for fifty students or to store a series of filenames.

Even though Java arrays are similar in syntax to C/C++ arrays, they have subtle differences. In Java, an array is basically an object that points to a set of other objects or primitive data types. The only visible difference between arrays and objects is that arrays have a special syntax to make them behave like the arrays found in other languages. Unlike C and C++, however, Java arrays cannot change in size, nor can a program use an out-of-bounds index with a Java array. Also, you declare and create arrays in Java very differently than in C/C++. The following tips describe how to create and use arrays in Java.

377 DECLARING AN ARRAY IN JAVA

As you have learned, creating an object is a two-step process. To start, you must first declare the object. Then, you must make an instance of that object. In Java, arrays are objects. Therefore, you must first declare an array, and then create it.

In Java, you can declare an array in two ways. The first format places the bracket [] on the variable name. The following code demonstrates an integer array declaration:

```
int myarray[];
```

The alternative declaration format places the bracket [] on the variable data type. The following code demonstrates the brackets after the type name:

```
int[] myarray;
```

Notice that the size of the array is not part of the declaration. You define an array's size when you create the array.

378 CREATING AN ARRAY OF PRIMITIVE DATA TYPES

In Tip 377, you learned how to declare an array. Your next step is to create the array object. As you have learned, in Java you create objects with the *new* keyword. When you create an array, you follow the *new* keyword with the object type followed by the size of the array in bracket. A primitive array is an array of one of the primitive numeric, *char*, or *boolean* types. The following statements demonstrate how to create various primitive arrays.

```
int myarray1[] = new int[100];
double myarray2[] = new double[100];
boolean myarray3[] = new boolean[100];
```

In this case, the statements do not initialize the contents of the arrays. However, by default, Java initializes the primitive numeric data type arrays to zero and *boolean* arrays to false.

379 INITIALIZING AN ARRAY OF PRIMITIVE DATA TYPES

Just as with C/C++ and other programming languages, you can initialize numeric arrays when you declare the arrays. When you specify initial values within an array declaration, Java performs the *new* operation and defines the array size for you. The following statements demonstrate the declaration and initialization of a numeric array and a *boolean* array:

```
int myarray1[] = { 1, 2, 3, 4, 5 };

boolean myarray2[] = { true, false, true };
```

In these examples, Java creates one array object that holds five integers and a second array that holds three *boolean* values. Java also initializes the arrays with the specified values. Notice that you surround the array values with braces {}, and separate each value with a comma.

UNDERSTANDING ARRAY INDEXING 380

Each value of an array is called an *array element*. To access an array element, you specify the name of the array with the index of that element placed between bracket []. Java array indexing is similar to that of C/C++. The following code demonstrates a loop that cycles through all the elements of an array and displays each value to the screen:

```
int myarray[] = { 1, 2, 3, 4, 5 };

for (int index = 0; index < 5; index++)
 {
    System.println(myarray[index]);
 }
```

In this example, the size of the array is five. In Java, the index of the first element of an array is zero, and the last location is the size of the array minus one. Therefore, to loop through all the members of the array, the program uses the loop variable values 0 to 4.

When you index a Java array, Java checks that the index value is greater than or equal to zero and less than the size of the array. If the index is less than zero or greater than or equal to the size of the array, then Java will generate an *IndexOutOfBoundsException* error and terminate your program. (An exception is how Java flags an error condition You will learn about the exceptions in later tips.)

ASSIGNING AN ARRAY ELEMENT 381

Within your programs, you can use an array element just like any other variable. For example, you can use the assignment operator to change the array element's value anywhere within the class that defines the array. Likewise, you can access the element's value from any location within the class. The following statements declare the array *myarray* to store five integer values. Then, within the *for* loop, the program assigns values to the array elements and then accesses (uses) the element's value within the *System.out.println* function call:

```
int myarray[] = new int[5];      // Initializes array to all zeros

for (int index=0; index < 5; index++)
  {
    marray[index] = index + 1;            // Assign a new value
     System.out.println(myarray[index]); // Use the value
  }
```

FINDING THE LENGTH OF AN ARRAY 382

In Java, an array is an object. The only member variable of an array object is the *length* variable which contains the size of the array. You will find the array object *length* variable useful for looping through the elements of an array. The *length* variable is *read only* because the size of an array object cannot change after you create the array. The following code demonstrates the use of the *length* variable within a *for* loop that cycles through all the elements of an array:

```
int myarray[] = { 1, 2, 3, 4, 5 };

for (int index=0; index < myarray.length; index++)
  {
      System.out.println(myarray[index]);
  }
```

383 UNDERSTANDING ARRAY REFERENCES

As you have learned, Java uses references to point to an object. Array references are no different from those that you use for other types of objects. For example, you can point to one array object with an array reference, and later point to another array object using the same reference. The following statements use the *myarray* reference to access two different arrays:

```
public class arrayReference {

  static public void main(String args[])
    {
       int myfirst[] = { 1, 2, 3, 4 };
       int mysecond[] = { 5, 6, 7, 8, 9, 10 };
       int myarray[];

     myarray = myfirst;

      System.out.println("First Array:");

      for (int index=0; index < myarray.length; index++)
        {
           System.out.println(myarray[index]);
        }

     myarray = mysecond;

      System.out.println("Second Array:");

      for (int index=0; index < myarray.length; index++)
        {
           System.out.println(myarray[index]);
        }
    }
}
```

384 CREATING AN ARRAY OF OBJECTS

In Tip 377, you learned how to create arrays of primitive data types. As your programs become more complex, there will be many times when you will want to create an array of objects, such as an array of *String* objects. The first two steps in creating an array of objects are the same as creating an array of primitives. The following statement, for example, creates an array of *Rectangle* objects:

```
Rectangle myarray[] = new Rectangle[5];
```

When you create an array of primitive types, Java initializes the array to all zeros. However, when you create an array of objects, Java initializes the array to *null* to indicate that the array does not yet contain any objects. You must create the members of the array and assign them to the proper array element. The following code demonstrates how to assign *Rectangle* objects to an array:

```
Rectangle myarray[] = new Rectangle[5];

    for (int index=0; index < myarray.length; index++)
    {
        myarray[index] = new Rectangle(0,0,10,10);
    }
```

UNDERSTANDING MULTIDIMENSIONAL ARRAYS 385

Each of the arrays you have created in the preceding tips have contained a single list of array elements. Sometimes, however, you will find it convenient to use multidimensional arrays to organize data that is indexed by two or more parameters. You can visualize a two-dimensional array as a row-column table. You access elements within the table by specifying a particular row and column. Think of a three-dimensional array as a stack of tables, each on a different piece of paper. You access elements within the three-dimensional array by specifying a page, row, and column. Figure 385 illustrates ways you can visualize multidimensional arrays.

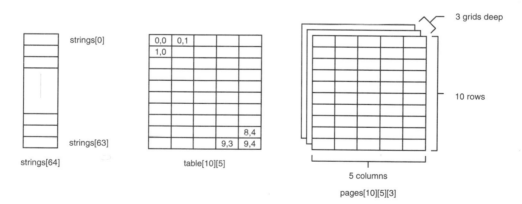

Figure 385   Multidimensional arrays.

DECLARING MULTIDIMENSIONAL ARRAYS 386

Tip 385 discussed multidimensional arrays. To declare a multidimensional arrays within a Java program, you simply specify additional sets of brackets. For example, to declare a two-dimensional array, you declare the array with two sets of brackets, as shown:

```
int TicTacToe[][];
```

You can also use the alternative declaration syntax that you learned in Tip 377 to declare multidimensional arrays by placing the extra brackets after the primitive or object type. The following code demonstrates an alternative declaration of a two-dimensional array:

```
int[][] TicTacToe;
```

You may even mix the two types of declarations, as demonstrated by the following code:

```
int[] TicTacToe[];
```

Each of these examples declares an equivalent two-dimensional array reference.

387 CREATING MULTIDIMENSIONAL ARRAYS

In Tip 378, you have learned how to create single-dimensional array objects. To create a multidimensional array object, you simply specify additional array brackets that specify the dimension's size information. For example, to create an array to keep track of fifty student's grades for five tests, you can create a 50x5 array. The following statement demonstrates how to create a multidimensional array:

```
Integer myarray[][] = new Integer [50][5];
```

As you have learned, because this statement defines an array of *Integer* objects, this code only initializes the array elements to null. To finish making the array, you must assign values to the proper array elements.

388 LOOPING THROUGH MULTIDIMENSIONAL ARRAYS

In Tip 380, you learned how to use a *for* statement to loop through a single-dimensional array. To loop through a multidimensional arrays, you can use a *for* loop for each array dimension. For example, to cycle through all the members of a two-dimensional array, you use two *for* loops. The inner *for* loop executes once (in its entirety) for each iteration of the outer *for* loop. The following statements demonstrate how you loop through a two-dimensional array:

```
public class arrayLooping
   {
     static public void main(String args[])
       {
         Integer myarray[][] = new Integer [50][5];

         for (int i=0; i < myarray.length; i++)
           {
             for (int k=0; k < myarray[i].length; k++)
               {
                 myarray[i][k] = new Integer(i*10 + k);
                 System.out.println(myarray[i][k]);
               }
           }
       }
   }
```

The outer *for* loop, in this case, loops through the 50 rows of the array. The inner *for* loop, on the other hand, loops through the array's 5 columns. Notice that the outer loop determines the number of rows in the array using *myarray.length*. Likewise, the inner loop determines the number of columns in each row using *myarray[i].length*, where the index *i* corresponds to the current row.

UNDERSTANDING UNBALANCED ARRAYS

So far, the two-dimensional arrays that you have created have been rectangular. Rectangular arrays are like tables. All of the rows are of the same length, and all of the columns are of the same length. Java's multidimensional arrays are actually arrays of arrays. Each dimension does not have to be a fixed length, but dimensions must be specified left to right. For example, the following declaration is legal because the elements are specified from left to right:

```
/* legal dimension specification */
boolean legal_ex[][] = new boolean[2][];
```

On the other hand, this array declaration is illegal because it specifies elements from right to left:

```
/* illegal dimension specification */
boolean illegal_ex[][] = new boolean[][5];
```

Consider an example of a two-dimensional unbalanced array. Suppose, for example, you use a two-dimensional array to keep track of a set of bowling pins. Each row has a different number of pins. So, the size of the array for each row is different, and the array is triangular instead of rectangular. To create a triangular array, you first must declare it. For a set of bowling pins, the first dimension will be 4, representing the number of rows:

```
/* declare only the first dimension */
boolean down_pins[][] = new boolean[4][];
```

After you declare the array, you then create an array for each row. The following code demonstrates how to create a triangular array:

```
public class arrayPins {

    static public void main(String args[])
      {
        /* declare only the first dimension */
        boolean pins_fell [][] = new boolean[4][];

        /* create the second dimension */
        for (int i=0; i< pins_fell.length; i++)
          {
            pins_fell [i] = new boolean[i + 1];
          }

        /* print the contents of the array to the screen */
        for (int i=0; i< pins_fell.length; i++)
          {
            for (int k=0; k< pins_fell[i].length; k++)
              {
                System.out.print(pins_fell[i][k] + " ");
              }
```

```
            System.out.println("");
        }
    }
}
```

As you can see, the program allocates columns for each row of the array. Later, the program displays the contents of the two-dimensional array. When you compile and execute this program, your screen will display the following output:

```
false
false false
false false false
false false false false
```

390 INITIALIZING MULTIDIMENSIONAL ARRAYS

As you have learned, when you create a single-dimensional array, you can initialize the array by placing the values between right and left braces {}. In a similar way, you can initialize a two-dimensional array at its declaration by using additional braces {} to distinguish each dimension. For example, the following code demonstrates how to initialize a two-dimensional array of integer values:

```
int myarray[][] = {{ 1, 2, 3 },
                   { 4, 5, 6 },
                   { 7, 8, 9 }};
```

Notice that the statements separate each row with a comma. In addition, the declaration does not specify an array size. Instead, the Java compiler determines the array size based on the values you specify.

You can also initialize unbalanced multidimensional arrays at their declaration. For example, the following code demonstrates how to initialize a triangular array of integers:

```
int myarray[][] = {{ 1 },
                   { 2, 3 },
                   { 4, 5, 6 },
                   { 7, 8, 9, 10 }};
```

391 SEARCHING AN ARRAY FOR A SPECIFIC VALUE

One operation your programs will commonly perform on arrays is to search for a specific value. There are two classic types of search techniques, sequential and binary. In a sequential or linear search, you search through the array elements one by one, starting from the first location until you find a match. You can easily implement a sequential search with a *for* loop. The following program code, for example, demonstrates how you would perform a linear search:

```
public class arrayLinear {

    public static int lsearch(int array[], int value)
    {

        for (int i=0; i < array.length; i++)
        {
```

```
        if (array[i] == value)
           return(i); // return index;
      }

    return(-1);
  }

  public static void main(String[] args)
  {
    int array[] = new int[100];

    for (int i=0; i < array.length; i++)
      {
        array[i] = i;
      }

    System.out.println("Result " + lsearch(array, 67));
    System.out.println("Result " + lsearch(array, 33));
    System.out.println("Result " + lsearch(array, 1));
    System.out.println("Result " + lsearch(array, 1001));
  }
}
```

As you can see, the *lsearch* method loops through the array elements until it locates a matching value. If your search does not find a match, the method returns the value -1. If your search successfully locates the value, the method returns the index value that corresponds to the value's location within the array.

UNDERSTANDING THE BINARY SEARCH

 392

In the previous tip, you learned that you can find an element in an array by searching each element of the array one by one. Unfortunately, sequential searches are very inefficient for large arrays. If your array is sorted, you can use a binary search instead to locate a value within the array. A binary search repeatedly subdivides the array until it finds your desired element. For example, you have undoubtedly searched for a word in a dictionary. A sequential search is equivalent to searching each word one by one, starting from the very first word. If the word is much past the first page, this type of search is a very inefficient process.

A binary search is equivalent to opening a dictionary in the middle, and then deciding if the word is in the first half or second half of the book. You then open the next section in the middle and decide if the word is in the first half or second half of that section. You can then repeat this process of dividing the book in half until you find the word for which you are looking. If you have never tried, pick a word and try to find it in a dictionary using a binary search technique. You might be surprised at how few divisions it takes to get very close to the word you are looking for. A binary search is very efficient. However, the array must be sorted for it to work.

USING A BINARY SEARCH

 393

A binary search is an efficient algorithm for searching through a sorted array. To demonstrate the binary search technique, the following program looks through an array of integers for various values. As the program executes, it prints messages that describe the process of the search. Also, at the end of the search, the program displays the number of steps it required to find the desired value:

```java
public class arrayBinary {

    public static int bsearch(int array[], int value)
      {
         boolean found = false;
         int high = array.length - 1;
         int low = 0;
         int cnt = 0;
         int mid = (high + low)/2;

         System.out.println("Looking for " + value);

         while (!found && (high >= low))
           {
              System.out.print("Low " + low +  " Mid " + mid);
              System.out.println(" High " + high);

              if (value == array[mid])
                {
                   found = true;
                }
              else if (value < array[mid])
                 high = mid - 1;
              else
                 low = mid + 1;

              mid = (high + low)/2;

              cnt++;
           }

         System.out.println("Steps " + cnt);

         return((found) ? mid: -1);
      }

    public static void main(String[] args)
      {
         int array[] = new int[100];

         for (int i=0; i < array.length; i++)
           {
              array[i] = i;
           }

         System.out.println("Results " + bsearch(array,67));
         System.out.println("Results " + bsearch(array,33));
         System.out.println("Results " + bsearch(array,1));
         System.out.println("Results " + bsearch(array,1001));
      }
}
```

From this program's output, you can see how a binary search sub-divides an array. The program uses the *high*, *mid*, and *low* variables to keep track of the ranges for each step of the search. The following tips describe how to sort an array, so that you may use the binary search technique.

SORTING AN ARRAY

 394

You have learned that arrays let your programs manipulate a series of objects of the same type. One operation your programs may often need to perform is sorting the array's objects. A program can sort an array of numbers from smallest to largest (ascending order) or largest to smallest (descending order). In a similar way, a program can sort an array of *Strings* alphabetically. In fact, any array with objects that can be compared with a greater, equal, or less than result can be sorted. Your program can use many techniques to sort an array. Each technique makes a trade-off between complexity and efficiency. The following tips describe some useful array-sorting techniques.

UNDERSTANDING THE BUBBLE SORT

 395

Just as "Hello, World" is the first program many programmers write, the bubble sort is the first sorting technique most programmers learn. Because it is simple, the bubble sort is not very efficient. For large arrays, the bubble sort can be very slow. However, for small arrays of 30 or less elements, it performs adequately.

To use a bubble sort to place array values in ascending order (smallest to largest), the bubble sort works through the array and moves the largest value to the top of the array. It repeats this process until no more values are left. For example, suppose you have three children that must be lined up by height for school pictures. To start, you can compare the first to second child and switch them if necessary. Then, you compare the second to third, again switching if necessary. After this first pass, the tallest child will be third. You then compare the first to the second and switch if necessary. That is it. The children will be in the correct order. Figure 395. illustrates the bubble sort technique for an array of integers.

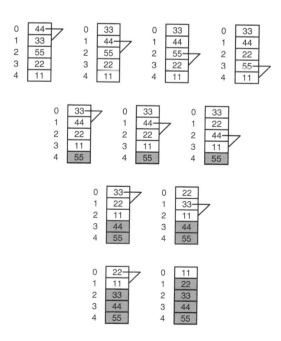

Figure 395 Iterations of a bubble sort.

396 PUTTING THE BUBBLE SORT TO USE

In the previous tip, you learned that the bubble sort is a simple sorting technique that can be used on small arrays. The following code, *arrayBubble.java*, demonstrates the use of a bubble sort to sort an array of 30 random integers:

```java
public class arrayBubble {

  public static void bubble_sort(int array[])
    {
      int i = array.length;

      while (—i >= 0)
        {
          for (int j = 0; j < i; j++)
            {
              if (array[j] > array[j+1])
                {
                  /* swap  values */
                  int temp = array[j];
                  array[j] = array[j+1];
                  array[j+1] = temp;
                }
            }
        }
    }

  public static void main(String[] args)
    {
      int array[] = new int[30];
      System.out.println("Before Sort");

      for (int i=0; i<array.length; i++)
        {
          array[i] = (int)(Math.random() * 30.0);
          System.out.println(array[i]);
        }

      bubble_sort(array);

      System.out.println("After Sort");

      for (int i=0; i<array.length; i++)
        {
          System.out.println(array[i]);
        }
    }
}
```

The bubble sort is suitable only for small arrays. The next tip covers a more sophisticated sorting technique that is much more processor efficient.

UNDERSTANDING QUICK SORT 397

For large arrays, you need an efficient sorting technique. One of the most efficient techniques is the *quick sort*. The quick sort technique takes the middle element of an array and sub-divides the array into two smaller arrays. One array will contain elements greater than the middle value of the original array. Conversely, the other array will contain elements that are less than the middle value. The quick sort will repeat this process for each new array until the final arrays contain only a single element. At this point, the single element arrays are in the proper order, as shown in Figure 397.

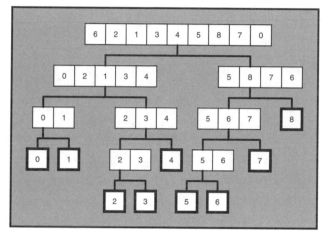

Figure 397 *Iterations of a quick sort.*

PUTTING THE QUICK SORT TO USE 398

In the previous tip, you learned that the quick sort is an efficient technique that you can use to sort an array. The following code demonstrates how to quick sort an array of 1,000 random integers.

```java
public class arrayQsort {

  static void qsort(int array[], int first, int last)
  {
      int low = first;
      int high = last;

      if (first >= last)
         return;

      int mid = array[(first + last)/2];

      do {
          while (array[low] < mid)
             low++;

          while (array[high] > mid)
             high--;
```

```java
                if (low <= high)
                  {
                     int temp = array[low];
                     array[low++] = array[high];
                     array[high--] = temp;
                  }
            } while (low <= high) ;

        qsort(array, first, high);
        qsort(array, low, last);
    }

public static void main(String[] args)
  {
     int array[] = new int[1000];

     System.out.println("Before Sort");

     for (int i = 0; i < array.length; i++)
       {
          array[i] = (int)(Math.random() * 1000.0);
          System.out.println(array[i]);
       }

     qsort(array, 0, array.length-1);

     System.out.println("After Sort");

     for (int i = 0; i < array.length; i++)
       {
          System.out.println(array[i]);
       }
    }
}
```

Note: *The previous quick sort function sorts an array from lowest to highest. To change the order of the sort, you simply change the comparisons in the **while** loops, as the following code illustrates:*

```java
while (array[low] > mid)
   low++;

while (array[high] < mid)
   high--;
```

399 USING ARRAYCOPY ON AN ARRAY OF PRIMITIVE DATA TYPES

As you work with arrays, you may sometimes need to copy the array's contents. To help simplify an array copy operation, Java provides the *arraycopy* method. You have learned that creating an array of primitive data types is slightly different than creating an array of objects. You will find that *arraycopy* also works somewhat differently for arrays of primitive data types andof objects.

When you copy an array of primitive data types, *arraycopy* works as you would expect—the method copies the entire array to a different array. The target array must already exist, and it must be large enough to hold the copy. After the copy, the two arrays are independent. Figure 399 illustrates how to visualize an *arraycopy* of primitive data types.

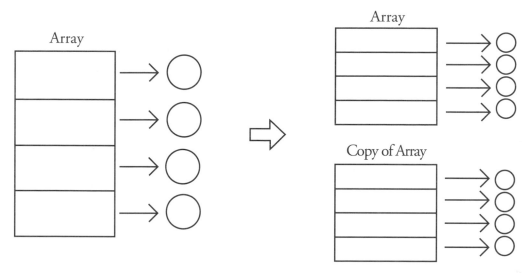

Figure 399 *Copying an array of primitive data types.*

The following code, *arrayCopyPrim.java*, demonstrates how to use the *arraycopy* method to copy an array of integers.

```java
public class arrayCopyPrim {

  public static void main(String[] args)
   {
     int array1[] = { 0, 1, 2, 3, 4 };
     int array2[] = new int[5];

     System.arraycopy(array1, 0, array2, 0, array1.length);

     array2[2] = 200; // modify second array

     System.out.print("Array 1: ");

     for (int i = 0; i < array1.length; i++)
        System.out.print(array1[i] + " ");

     System.out.println();
     System.out.print("Array 2: ");

     for (int i=0; i<array2.length; i++)
        System.out.print(array2[i] + " ");

     System.out.println();
   }
}
```

When you compile and execute this program, your screen will display the following output.

```
Array 1: 0 1 2 3 4
Array 2: 0 1 200 3 4
```

In this example, after the program copies the array, the program modifies the third element of the second array. When the program later displays the contents of both arrays, notice that the first array is unchanged. In other words, after you use the *arraycopy* method, the arrays are independent.

Within your programs, you do not have to copy an entire array with the *arraycopy* method. If you examine the arguments to the *arraycopy* method, you will find that you can copy a range of elements into another array.

400 USING ARRAYCOPY ON AN ARRAY OF OBJECTS

You learned in the previous tip that when you copy an array of primitives, the copy is physically different from the original. However, when you copy an array of objects, only the object *references* are copied to the new array. The objects that make up the elements of the source array are not duplicated. When you modify an object that is an element of one array, you actually modify the corresponding element of the other array. Figure 400 illustrates how to visualize an *arraycopy* of objects.

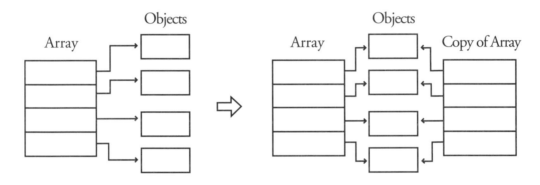

Figure 400 *Copying an array of objects.*

The following code demonstrates how to copy an array of objects:

```java
public class arrayCopyObject {

  public static void main(String[] args)
    {
      StringBuffer array1[] = new StringBuffer[5];
      StringBuffer array2[] = new StringBuffer[5];

      for (int i=0; i<array1.length; i++)
        array1[i] = new StringBuffer(Integer.toString(i));

      System.arraycopy(array1, 0, array2, 0, array1.length);

      array2[2].append("00"); // modify second array

      System.out.print("Array 1: ");
```

```
      for (int i=0; i<array1.length; i++)
        System.out.print(array1[i] + " ");

    System.out.println();
    System.out.print("Array 2: ");

      for (int i=0; i<array2.length; i++)
         System.out.print(array2[i] + " ");

    System.out.println();
  }
}
```

When you compile and execute this program, your screen will display the following output.

```
Array 1: 0 1 200 3 4
Array 2: 0 1 200 3 4
```

In the previous example, after the program copies the array, the program modifies the third element of the second array. After the program displays the contents of both arrays, notice that both arrays have been modified. Clearly, both arrays point to the same list of objects.

STORING DIFFERENT OBJECTS IN AN ARRAY 401

The arrays you have created in the previous tips contain only a single type of object. As it turns out, you can also create arrays that hold many different types of objects. The most generic array that you can declare in Java is of type *Object*. Every Java object is a subclass of the *Object* class. Within an array, you can store any Java object's reference. However, to retrieve and use an object from an *Object* array, you must use the *instanceof* operator. The following code demonstrates how you can store images and rectangles in a single array:

```java
import java.awt.*;
import java.awt.image.*;
import java.applet.*;

public class arrayOfObjectsApplet extends Applet {

    Object array[] = new Object[4];

    public void init()
      {
        array[0] = getImage(getCodeBase(), "a.gif");
        array[1] = getImage(getCodeBase(), "b.gif");
        array[2] = new Rectangle(0,26,26, 26);
        array[3] = new Rectangle(26,0,26, 26);
      }


    public void paint(Graphics g)
      {
```

```
        g.setColor(Color.black);

    for (int i = 0; i < array.length; i++)
      {
        if (array[i] instanceof Image)
          {
            Image img = (Image) array[i];
             g.drawImage((Image)array[i],i*26,i*26,this);
          }
        else if (array[i] instanceof Rectangle)
          {
            Rectangle r = (Rectangle) array[i];
            g.fillRect(r.x, r.y, r.width, r.height);
          }
      }
  }
}
```

As you have learned, Java applets use interfaces to allow one class to access the data and methods of another. Sometimes, you will find it more convenient to create an *interface* that all objects in an array implement. In this way, you can then call the methods of the *interface* without having to know what the objects are.

402 UNDERSTANDING EVENT-DRIVEN PROGRAMS

The "Hello World" program is an example of a simple Java program. The program has just one purpose: to display a string to the screen. As you will learn, most Java programs are much more complex and must respond to a variety of events. An *event-driven program* is a program that waits for someone (or something) to tell it to do something. For example, assume the program resizes the applet window. The browser, in turn, will generate an event that tells the applet to resize the window. The applet, in turn, will call the *paint* function to redraw the window.

As you will learn, a user, the operating system, or other programs can generate events. When an event-driven program does something in response to an event, the program is said to have "handled the event." For example, suppose you want your program to quit when a user presses the "Q" key. You would write your program so that it detects and handles all *keydown* events. If the user presses the "Q" key, you can end the program. As your Java programs become more complex, they will make extensive use of events. To simplify your programming, Java predefines an *Event* class.

403 UNDERSTANDING THE EVENT CLASS

As you will learn, Java generates an *Event* object when something happens (an event occurs) to which the applet must respond. An *Event* object is an instance of the *Event* class and stores information about the event. For example, when you click the mouse, Java generates an event object that contains the mouse screen coordinates. Likewise, when you press a keyboard key, Java generates a keyboard event that contains the key's ASCII code. When an event occurs, Java calls a series of methods based on the event type. Table 403 shows some of the information stored in the *Event* object.

Type	Name	Description
int	id	Contains the event type identifier
Object	target	Object where event occurred
int	clickCount	Multiple mouse click flag
int	key	Key code for keyboard events
int	modifiers	Modifier keys state when event occurred
long	when	Time when event occurred
int	x,y	Coordinates of mouse events

Table 403 *Event class variables.*

Not all events have valid data for all the variables in the *Event* object. For example, it does not make sense to check the *clickCount* variable for a *keydown* event—the *clickCount* variable corresponds to mouse double-click operations. The following tips will show you how to use the *Event* class data.

UNDERSTANDING CONVENIENCE METHODS 404

In most event-driven programming languages, the program sits in a loop waiting for events to occur. Within this *event loop* you place code that decides which part of your program should receive the event. Based on your code, the program dispatches events by calling appropriate methods.

Within a Java applet, Java provides this event-processing loop behind the scenes for you. Also, Java defines a set of *convenience methods* to help your program distinguish between events. A convenience method is how Java tells your program that a particular type of *Event* has occurred. For example, if a user clicks the mouse, Java will call the *mouseDown* convenience method.

Java declares convenience methods in the *Component* class. You will learn the details of the *Component* class in later tips. For now, you just need to know that the *Applet* class is a subclass of the *Component* class which defines many of component objects every program needs (such as the convenience methods). Consequently, you can use the convenience methods in any class you extend from the *Applet* or *Component* classes.

Within your applet, you can have more than one object that extends from the *Component* class. Each of these objects can have its own convenience methods. Java will call the correct methods based on the type of event that occurred.

USING THE MOUSEDOWN METHOD 405

As your applets become interactive, they will need to respond to mouse and keyboard events. One of Java's convenience methods is the *mouseDown* method, which your programs can use to detect when a user has held down the mouse button. The following program, *mouseDownApplet.java*, displays the mouse-screen coordinates every time the user clicks the mouse (causing Java to call the *mouseDown* method):

```
import java.awt.*;
import java.applet.*;

public class mouseDownApplet extends Applet {
```

```
public boolean mouseDown(Event evt, int x, int y)
  {
    System.out.println("Mouse Down (" + x + "," + y + ")");
    return(true);
  }
}
```

The *mouseDown* method's first argument is the *Event* object. The second and third arguments are the (*x* and *y*) screen coordinates of the mouse pointer at the time the user clicked the mouse. The screen coordinates specify the distance in pixels from the upper-left corner of the display to the mouse pointer's location. In the previous example, the applet window's upper-left corner is location (0, 0).

Note that the *mouseDown* method returns true. When you create an event handler within your applets, your method should return the value true to tell Java that you have "handled the event." If Java receives the true value, Java will not call any other convenience methods to handle the event. If your event handler returns false, Java will call another event handler to process the event.

406 USING THE MOUSEUP METHOD

In the previous tip, you learned about the *mouseDown* event which Java calls when the user holds down the mouse button. Conversely, Java provides the *mouseUp* event when the user releases the mouse button. If you are not familiar with writing graphical user interfaces, you may wonder why there are two mouse-click events. A common use of the mouse-down event is to highlight a control, such as a button, that the user has selected. If the user releases the mouse button over the control, the program knows the user has accepted the button. However, if the user moves the mouse off the control before the mouse is released, the program knows the user did not select the button.

The following program, *mouseUpApplet.java*, displays a message to the screen every time the user holds down the mouse button and also when the user releases the button. The program also displays the mouse-screen coordinates for each event:

```
import java.awt.*;
import java.applet.*;

public class mouseUpApplet extends Applet {
   public boolean mouseDown(Event evt, int x, int y)
     {
        System.out.println("Mouse Down (" + x + "," + y + ")");
        return(true);
     }

   public boolean mouseUp(Event evt, int x, int y)
     {
        System.out.println("Mouse Up (" + x + "," + y + ")");
        return(true);
     }
 }
```

Take time now to run this applet. Next, move and click the mouse both from within and outside of the applet window to learn how Java responds to such mouse operations.

USING THE MOUSEDRAG METHOD

In the previous tips, you have learned how to detect and respond to mouse-down and mouse-up events. There may be times, however, when you need to track how a mouse moves between mouse-down and mouse-up events—in other words, how the user drags the mouse. For example, many graphical programs use a bounding box which shows users the screen area they are selecting. To help your programs process mouse-drag operations, Java provides the *mouseDrag* convenience method which lets the applet track the mouse from the mouse-down event to the mouse-up event.

The following program, *mouseDragApplet.java*, does three things. First, the applet displays a message to the screen every time the user holds the mouse button down. Next, the applet displays a message as the user moves the mouse. Finally, the applet displays a message when the user releases the mouse button.

```java
import java.applet.*;
import java.awt.*;

public class mouseDragApplet extends Applet {

    public boolean mouseDown(Event evt, int x, int y)
      {
         System.out.println("mouseDown:(" + x + "," + y + ")");
         return(true);
      }

    public boolean mouseUp(Event evt, int x, int y)
      {
         System.out.println("mouseUp:(" + x + "," + y + ")");
         return(true);
      }

    public boolean mouseDrag(Event evt, int x, int y)
      {
         System.out.println("mouseDrag:(" + x + "," + y + ")");
         return(true);
      }
}
```

When you run this applet, do not expect equal time intervals between calls to the *mouseDrag* method. The frequency Java uses to call the *mouseDrag* method depends both on the operating system and the machine's speed.

USING THE MOUSEMOVE METHOD

In Tip 407, you learned that the *mouseDrag* method lets your applets track mouse movement when the user is holding down the mouse button. However, there may be times when you will need to track mouse movements when the user is not holding the mouse button down. For example, suppose you want to display the mouse's screen coordinates as the user moves the mouse around a drawing area. For such cases, you can use the *mouseMove* method to display the coordinates. The following program, *mouseMoveApplet.java*, demonstrates how to track the mouse movements using the *mouseMove* method:

```
import java.applet.*;
import java.awt.*;

public class mouseMoveApplet extends Applet {

    public boolean mouseDown(Event evt, int x, int y)
      {
        System.out.println("mouseDown:(" + x + "," + y + ")");
        return(true);
      }

    public boolean mouseUp(Event evt, int x, int y)
      {
        System.out.println("mouseUp:(" + x + "," + y + ")");
        return(true);
      }

    public boolean mouseMove(Event evt, int x, int y)
      {
        System.out.println("mouseMove:(" + x + "," + y + ")");
        return(true);
      }
}
```

As was the case with the *mouseDrag* method, you cannot expect equal intervals between calls to the *mouseMove* method. However, you can expect that Java will call the method often enough to give the user an adequate response.

409 DETECTING DOUBLE-CLICKS WITH CLICKCOUNT

In the previous tips, you have learned how to detect when the user has pressed the mouse button. In many cases, your programs must respond to a mouse double-click operation, which is simply two quick clicks of the mouse. As you have learned, the *Event* class contains information about an event. One piece of information the *Event* class contains for mouse events is the *clickCount* variable. Your applets can use the *clickCount* variable to detect double-click operations. The following program, *doubleClick.java*, displays a message to the screen each time the user double-clicks the mouse:

```
import java.applet.*;
import java.awt.*;

public class doubleClick extends Applet {

    public void init()
      {
        resize(400, 300);
      }

    public boolean mouseDown(Event evt, int x, int y)
      {
        if (evt.clickCount == 1)
          System.out.println("mouseDown: single click");
```

```
      else if (evt.clickCount == 2)
         System.out.println("mouseDown: double click");
      else if (evt.clickCount == 3)
         System.out.println("mouseDown: triple click");
      else if (evt.clickCount > 3)
         System.out.println("mouseDown: many clicks");

      return(true);
   }
}
```

AN ALTERNATIVE WAY TO DETECT DOUBLE-CLICKS 410

In Tip 409, you learned how to detect double-click operations using the *Event* class *clickCount* variable. Unfortunately, depending on your release of Java, you may find that *clickCount* does not always contain the correct value. An alternative way to detect double-click mouse operations is to determine the time interval between clicks yourself. To do this, you can check the *Event* class *when* variable. If two mouse clicks occur within a specific interval of time, your applet can treat the mouse clicks as a double-click operation. The following program, *altDoubleClick.java*, demonstrates how you might check the interval between *mouseDown* events using the *when* variable:

```java
import java.applet.*;
import java.awt.*;

public class altDoubleClick extends Applet {

    static int lastclick = 0;
    static long maxdelay = 100;
    static int doubleclick = 0;

    public void init()
      {
         resize(400, 300);
      }

    public boolean mouseDown(Event evt, int x, int y)
      {
         long delay = evt.when - lastclick;

         if ((delay > maxdelay) || (doubleclick == 0))
            doubleclick = 1;
         else
            doubleclick++;

         if (evt.clickCount == 1)
            System.out.println("mouseDown: single click");
         else if (evt.clickCount == 2)
            System.out.println("mouseDown: double click");
         else if (evt.clickCount == 3)
            System.out.println("mouseDown: tripple click");
```

```
        else if (evt.clickCount > 3)
            System.out.println("mouseDown: many clicks");

        return(true);
      }
  }
```

On most operating systems, a user can set the sensitivity for double clicks. However, the *when* variable technique in this tip has no way to adjust sensitivity based on the operating-system settings.

411 DETECTING MOUSE-CLICK MODIFIER KEYS

From the time of the first graphical-user interface, there have been mouse-click and key combinations that users perform for special purposes. For example, in many graphical programs, drawing with the SHIFT key depressed causes an oval tool to draw circles.

To detect a mouse-click modifier key within a Java applet, you check the *Event* class *modifiers* variable. Java defines a set of constants in the *Event* class that your programs can use to check for a specific modifier key such as *SHIFT_MASK*, *CTRL_MASK*, and *ALT_MASK*. To determine if the user has pressed a specific key, you perform a bitwise AND operation of the corresponding constant and the modifier variable. The following program, *singleModifier.java*, demonstrates how your programs detect that a user modified the mouse operation by holding down the SHIFT key:

```
import java.awt.*;
import java.applet.*;

public class singleModifier extends Applet {

    public boolean mouseDown(Event evt, int x, int y)
    {
        if ((evt.modifiers & Event.SHIFT_MASK) != 0)
            System.out.println("mouseDown and Shift key pressed");
        else
            System.out.println("mouseDown");
        return(true);
    }
}
```

412 UNDERSTANDING THE MULTI-BUTTON MOUSE PROBLEM

In the previous tips, you have learned how to detect when the user clicks the mouse. On some platforms, the mouse has more than one button. Unfortunately, Java does not provide a clear way to distinguish between mouse buttons. In fact, to date, only undocumented techniques exist—which might not work in future versions of Java. Also, if you create a program that requires more than one mouse button, your program will be platform dependent. Until a solution is built into the language, we recommend that you just assume that there is only one mouse button. With that said, the following program, *multiMouse.java*, will now demonstrate an undocumented technique for detecting the second and third mouse button:

```
import java.applet.*;
import java.awt.*;

public class multiMouse extends Applet {

   public void init()
   {
       resize(400, 300);
   }

   public boolean mouseDown(Event evt, int x, int y)
   {
      if ((evt.modifiers & Event.ALT_MASK) > 0)
          System.out.println("mouseDown: middle button");
      else if ((evt.modifiers & Event.META_MASK) > 0)
          System.out.println("mouseDown: right button");
      else
          System.out.println("mouseDown: left button");

      return(true);
   }
}
```

As you can see, the program detects the other mouse buttons by checking the modifier keys. Currently, the other mouse buttons are equivalent to a standard mouse click with a modifier key pressed. Remember, however, these techniques may not work in future versions of Java.

USING MOUSEENTER AND MOUSEEXIT 413

You have learned that your applets can handle *mouseMove* events when a user moves a mouse around the screen. Within your programs, you can use the event coordinates to manually check when a mouse enters a window or control. However, Java has two functions that can do this for you: *mouseEnter* and *mouseExit*. Java calls the *mouseEnter* when a mouse enters a component. Likewise, Java calls the *mouseExit* when the mouse leaves that component. For example, you might use these methods to display a pop-up help message that tells a user about a particular control or button. The following program, *mouseEnterExit.java*, demonstrates how your programs can detect when a mouse enters and leaves an applet window:

```
import java.awt.*;
import java.applet.*;

public class mouseEnterExit extends Applet {

   public boolean mouseEnter(Event evt, int x, int y)
   {
       System.out.println("mouseEnter");
      return(true);
   }

   public boolean mouseExit(Event evt, int x, int y)
   {
```

```
        System.out.println("mouseExit");
        return(true);
    }
}
```

The first message will cause the status window (the window that displays the message "mouseEnter") to be in front of the applet. For the *mouseEnter* and *mouseExit* methods to work, you must click the applet so that it becomes the front-most window.

414 UNDERSTANDING KEYBOARD EVENTS

In the previous tips, you learned about the events that are generated by the mouse. As you will learn, another set of important events is generated from the keyboard. When Java generates a keyboard event, it passes an *Event* object that contains information about the key pressed. Java recognizes normal keys, modifier keys, and special keys. For normal keys, the event object contains the key's ASCII value. For the function, arrow, and other special keys, there are no ASCII codes, so Java uses special Java-defined codes. In Tip 411, you learned how to detect modifier keys. The modifier keys are stored in the *modifiers* variable in the *Event* object. The following tips describe how to handle various keyboard events.

415 USING THE KEYDOWN METHOD

As you have learned, Java provides convenience methods that make capturing mouse events easy. For example, when the user holds down the mouse button, Java will call the *mouseDown* method. Similarly, when the user presses a keyboard key, Java will call the *keyDown* convenience method. The arguments to the *keyDown* method are the *Event* object and a key code. The following program, *keyDownApplet.java*, demonstrates how to capture key strokes and display them within the status window:

```java
import  java.applet.*;
import  java.awt.*;

public class keyDownApplet  extends Applet {

    public boolean keyDown(Event evt, int code)
    {
        System.out.println("keyDown:" + (char)code);
       return(true);
    }
}
```

416 USING THE KEYUP METHOD

As you have learned, Java provides separate events for mouse-down and mouse-up operations. Thus, it should not surprise you that Java provides separate events for key-down and key-up operations. When the user releases a keyboard key, Java calls the *keyUp* convenience method. The arguments to the *keyUp* method are the *Event* object and a key code. The following program, *keyUpApplet.java*, demonstrates how to detect a key-up event:

```
import java.applet.*;
import java.awt.*;

public class keyUpApplet extends Applet {

   public boolean keyDown(Event evt, int code)
     {
        System.out.println("keyDown:" + (char) code);
        return(true);
     }

   public boolean keyUp(Event evt, int code)
     {
        System.out.println("keyUp:" + (char) code);
        return(true);
     }
 }
```

DETECTING MULTIPLE MODIFIER KEYS  417

In Tip 414, you learned that Java supports three types of keyboard characters. The first type are normal keys, which you learned to handle in the previous two tips. Another type of keys is the modifier keys. In Tip 415, you learned how to detect that the user has pressed a modifier key during a mouse click. Now, you will learn how to detect that multiple modifier keys were pressed at the same time.

The *Event* class *modifiers* variable is a bit field that lets a variable contain multiple flags. Within the *modifiers* variable, Java sets one bit for each of the SHIFT, CTRL, and ALT keys. Within your program, you can test which modifiers are set by performing a bitwise AND operation of the modifier constant and the *modifiers* variable. The following program, *multipleModifier.java*, demonstrates how to detect the SHIFT and CTRL modifier keys when a normal key has been pressed:

```
import java.applet.*;
import java.awt.*;

public class multipleModifier extends Applet {

    public void init()
      {
         resize(400, 300);
      }

    public boolean keyDown(Event evt, int key)
      {
         if (((evt.modifiers & Event.SHIFT_MASK) > 0) &&
             ((evt.modifiers & Event.CTRL_MASK) > 0))
           System.out.println("SHIFT and CTRL pressed");

         return(true);
      }
 }
```

418 AN ALTERNATIVE WAY TO DETECT KEYBOARD MODIFIER KEYS

In the previous tip, you learned how to detect keyboard modifier keys by examining the *Event* class *modifiers* variable. An alternative way to check for modifier keys is to use the methods built into the *Event* class: *controlDown*, *metaDown*, or *shiftDown*. You can use these methods instead of performing a bitwise AND operation of the modifier constants with the *modifiers* variable. The following program, *altModifierKey.java*, demonstrates how to check for modifier keys using the built-in *Event* class methods:

```java
import java.applet.*;
import java.awt.*;

public class altModifierKey extends Applet {

    public void init()
      {
         resize(400, 300);
      }

    public boolean keyDown(Event evt, int key)
      {
         if (evt.controlDown() && evt.shiftDown())
           System.out.println("SHIFT and CTRL pressed");
         return(true);
      }
}
```

419 DETECTING SPECIAL KEYS

You have learned how to detect normal and modifier keys. For special keys, such as the keyboard arrow and function keys, you must check the key code as you did for normal keys. However, instead of using the ASCII codes, you use the special key constants defined in the *Event* class. Table 419 lists the *Event* class special key constants.

Special Keys	Description
F1, F2, F3, F4, F5, F6	Function keys
F7, F8, F9, F10, F11, F12	Function keys
Left, Right	Left and right arrow keys
Up, Down	Up and down arrow keys
Home, End	Home and End keys
PgUp, PgDown	PageUp and PageDown keys

Table 419 Event class key constants.

The following program, *testApplet.java*, demonstrates how to detect special keys.

```java
import java.applet.*;
import java.awt.*;
```

```
public class testApplet extends Applet {

    public void init()
      {
          resize(400, 300);
      }

    public boolean keyDown(Event evt, int key)
      {
        switch (key) {
            case Event.UP:     System.out.println("Up arrow");
                               break;
            case Event.DOWN:   System.out.println("Down arrow");
                               break;
            case Event.LEFT:   System.out.println("Left arrow");
                               break;
            case Event.RIGHT:  System.out.println("Right arrow");
                               break;
        }
        return(true);
      }
}
```

USING THE HANDLEEVENT METHOD

 420

Each of the Java programs you have examined, thus far, have handled keyboard and mouse events using the convenience methods. As you have learned, the convenience methods separate events by type. Another way your programs can handle events is to capture the events using the *handleEvent* method.

As it turns out, before Java passes an event to a convenience method, Java first passes the event to the *handleEvent* method. If you handle the event (and return true) within the *handleEvent* method, Java will not call the convenience method.

In other words, if you handle mouse events within the *handleEvent* method, you do not have to use the *mouseDown* method. However, using the *mouseDown* method is a better way to organize your code, because the name clearly identifies the event.

On the other hand, to handle events that do not have convenience methods, you must capture the events within the *handleEvent* method. Within the *handleEvent* method, you check the *id* variable against the constants defined in the *Event* class to distinguish event types. The following program, *handleEventApplet.java*, captures events and displays their names:

```
import java.applet.*;
import java.awt.*;

public class handleEventApplet extends Applet {

    public void init()
      {
          resize(400, 300);
      }
```

```
    public boolean handleEvent(Event evt)
  {
    if (evt.id == Event.WINDOW_DESTROY)
      System.out.println("WINDOW_DESTROY");
    else if (evt.id == Event.WINDOW_EXPOSE)
      System.out.println("WINDOW_EXPOSE");
    else if (evt.id == Event.WINDOW_ICONIFY)
      System.out.println("WINDOW_ICONIFY");
    else if (evt.id == Event.WINDOW_DEICONIFY)
      System.out.println("WINDOW_DEICONIFY");
    else if (evt.id == Event.WINDOW_MOVED)
      System.out.println("WINDOW_ MOVED");
    else if (evt.id == Event.KEY_PRESS)
      System.out.println("KEY_PRESS");
    else if (evt.id == Event.KEY_RELEASE)
      System.out.println("KEY_RELEASE");
    else if (evt.id == Event.MOUSE_DOWN)
      System.out.println("MOUSE_DOWN");
    else if (evt.id == Event.MOUSE_UP)
      System.out.println("MOUSE_UP");
    else if (evt.id == Event.MOUSE_MOVE)
      System.out.println("MOUSE_MOVE");
    else if (evt.id == Event.MOUSE_ENTER)
      System.out.println("MOUSE_ENTER");
    else if (evt.id == Event.MOUSE_EXIT)
      System.out.println("MOUSE_EXIT");
    else if (evt.id == Event.MOUSE_DRAG)
      System.out.println("MOUSE_DRAG");
    else
      System.out.println(evt); // print other events

    return(super.handleEvent(evt));
  }
}
```

421 How *NOT* to Handle an Event

Each of the *Event*-based examples presented so far have focused on handling events. After handling an event, each method has notified Java that it handled the event by returning *true*. Sometimes, however, there will be events that your programs do not handle. Either your program will not know how to handle the event or it may be more appropriate for another method to handle it. To ensure that an alternative method gets a chance to handle an event, you should use the following *return* statement:

```
return (super.handleEvent(evt)); // evt is the Event object
```

The reason you don't simply return *false* is that the proper path for events to travel is through the inheritance tree. When you don't handle an event in the *handleEvent* method, you want Java to try one of the convenience methods to see if it can handle the event. If you return *false* from the *handleEvent* method, the convenience methods will not be checked. The following code demonstrates how your programs return from an event they do not handle:

```
import java.applet.*;
import java.awt.*;

public class badHandleEvent extends Applet {

   public boolean mouseDown(Event evt, int x, int y)
     {
       /* this method is never called! */
       System.out.println("mouseDown:(" + x + ", " + y + ")");
       return(true);
     }

   public boolean handleEvent(Event evt)
     {
       return(false); // never do this!
     }
   }
```

Note: If your **handleEvent** *method does not handle an event, do not return the value false because Java will not call the corresponding convenience method.*

MAKING SURE YOU CAN QUIT YOUR APPLICATIONS 422

Most operating systems wrap your Java application inside a standard window frame. Within these frames, a menu or icon usually lets the user close a window (ending the program). When you select this item, the operating system generates a *WINDOW_DESTROY* message. Unless your program handles the *WINDOW_DESTROY* message, your application will not quit. In fact, if your application is simple, you might not have any way to quit your application. If you are using UNIX, you could kill the process, but that is a little drastic. Instead, your program should always handle the *WINDOW_DESTROY* event. Your application can then quit easily and naturally. The following program, *quitApplication.java*, shows how to handle a *WINDOW_DESTROY* event:

```
import java.awt.*;
class quitApplication extends Frame {

   public quitApplication(String label)
     {
       setTitle(label);
       resize(100,100);
     }

   public boolean handleEvent(Event evt)
     {
       if (evt.id == Event.WINDOW_DESTROY)
         System.exit(0);                    // Quit the application
       return(super.handleEvent(evt)); // Don't handle other events
     }
```

```
   public static void main(String[] args)
     {
        testApplication f = new testApplication("Window quit test");
        f.show();
     }
}
```

423 DETECTING WHEN A WINDOW IS ICONIFIED

You have learned how to catch many events. Another pair of events that a Java application receives are *WINDOW_ICONIFY* and *WINDOW_DEICONIFY*. You should note that icon events are platform dependent because not all operating systems iconify applications. You may find it useful to handle icon events if you wish to disable a graphics intensive program from updating while it is "iconified." There usually is no reason to update a window that is not visible. The following code demonstrates how to disable the *paint* method if an application is iconified:

```java
import java.awt.*;

class iconifyApplication extends Frame {
   boolean icon = false;

   public iconifyApplication(String label)
     {
        setTitle(label);
        resize(100,100);
     }

   public boolean handleEvent(Event evt)
     {
        System.out.println("here");
        if (evt.id == Event.WINDOW_DESTROY)
          System.exit(0); // quit application
        else if (evt.id == Event.WINDOW_ICONIFY)
          icon = true;
        else if (evt.id == Event.WINDOW_DEICONIFY)
          icon = false;
        return(super.handleEvent(evt)); // Don't handle other events
     }

   public void paint(Graphics g)
     {
        if (!icon)
          System.out.println("update");
        else
          System.out.println("don't update");
     }

   public static void main(String[] args)
     {
```

```
        iconifyApplication f = new iconifyApplication ("iconify");
        f.show();
    }
}
```

UNDERSTANDING THE ABSTRACT WINDOWING TOOLKIT (AWT)

424

In the early days of the computer age, developing a graphical application often required detailed knowledge of the underlying graphics hardware. Just imagine having to program at the register level or having to map between memory addresses and screen coordinates! Even today, creating a graphics program that runs on different platforms can still be a challenge. For example, you will have to learn the Windows API (Application Programming Interface) to program on the Microsoft Windows platform and, perhaps, MOTIF on an X-Window platform.

By contrast, one of the strengths of Java is that it is platform independent. Java's Abstract Windowing Toolkit (AWT) package provides a set of platform-independent classes that handle graphics operations. For example, you can create a command button using the *Button* constructor, regardless of the platform on which the Java code is going to run. The actual button may be implemented through native codes and look a little different on each platform, but you do not have to program differently.

The AWT package includes classes for drawing lines, and creating command buttons, pull-down menus, dialog boxes, and so on. To use Java's Abstract Windowing Toolkit package, you must import it using the following *import* statement:

```
import java.awt.*;
```

Although you can specify the package each time it is used, it is much more convenient to use the import statement. The following tips in this section will show you how to use the classes in Java's AWT package.

LOOKING AT THE AWT CLASS HIERARCHY

425

As you learned in the previous tip, Java's Abstract Windowing Toolkit provides a collection of methods your programs can use to perform graphics operations. Figure 425 shows the AWT class hierarchy. This hierarchy should give you a good idea of the AWT's rich set of graphics features available.

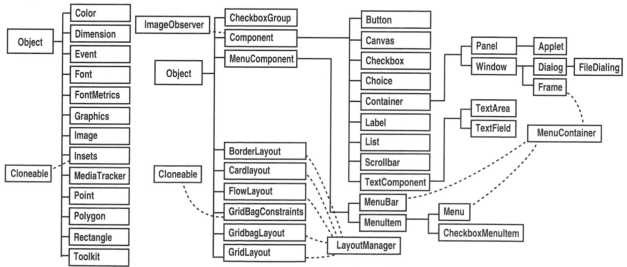

Figure 425 *AWT class hierarchy.*

426 UNDERSTANDING GRAPHICS OBJECTS

Before your applets can draw lines or text on the screen, you must first obtain the *Graphics* object. In fact, much of Java's graphics operations are *Graphics* class methods. Your program can obtain the *Graphics* object (the graphics context) from the parameter passed through the *update* or *paint* method. The *Graphics* object contains the current color, font, origin location, and so on. Java will use the *Graphics* object in each of its drawing operations. The following statements illustrate the use of the graphics context within the *paint* method:

```
public void paint(Graphics g)
  {
    // display entire string
    g.drawString("1001 Java Programmer's Tips", 5, 10);
  }
```

427 UNDERSTANDING JAVA'S COORDINATE SYSTEM

Before you examine Java's Abstract Windowing Toolkit, you should first understand Java's coordinate system. Many of the AWT class methods use an *x-y* coordinate system to position the item to be drawn. For example, to draw a line using the *drawLine* method, your programs use the parameters *x1*, *y1*, *x2*, *y2* to specify the line's starting and ending coordinates. The default location of the origin (0, 0) on the screen is at the top-left corner with positive *X* extending to the right and positive *Y* extending to the bottom, as shown in Figure 427.

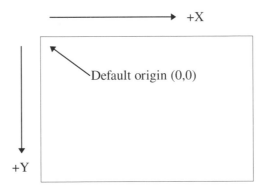

Figure 427 Default Java coordinate system.

428 DRAWING A STRING

As you have learned, you can display a *String* object on the screen using the *drawString* method. The *drawString* method, as shown, lets you display a *String* at the position specified by the *x-* and *y* -parameters:

```
drawString(String str, int x, int y);
```

To display a *String* object at the correct location, you must understand the meaning of each of the *drawString* parameters. The *drawString* method *x* parameter specifies the position of the *String* object's left side. The *y* parameter controls the position of the *String* object's baseline. For instance, if you try to position the String at location (0,0), you will find that much of the String is drawn outside of the visible window. Figure 428 shows the effect of the *x* and *y* parameters on string placement:

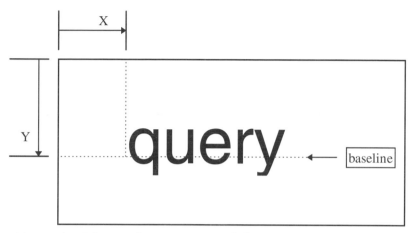

Figure 428 The x-and y -position specified in the **drawString** *method.*

DRAWING CHARACTERS 429

Depending on your applet's purpose, there will be times when your program works with *String* objects while, at other times, your program will work with character arrays. As you learned in Tip 428, you can display a *String* object's contents using the *drawString* method. To draw a character array, on the other hand, you can use the *Graphics* class *drawChar* method:

```
drawChar(char data[], int offset, int length, int x, int y);
```

As you can see, within the *drawChar* method, you specify the drawing location using the *x* and *y* parameters. In addition, using the *offset* and *length* parameters, you can specify the characters in the array that you want to display. The following program, *draw_char.java*, uses the *drawChar* method to display the character array "1001 Java Tips":

```
import java.applet.*;
import java.awt.*;

public class draw_char extends Applet {

    final static char mystring[] =
        {'1','0','0','1',' ','J','a','v','a',' ','T','i','p','s'};

    public void paint(Graphics g)
      {
        // display entire string
        g.drawChars(mystring, 0, mystring.length, 0, 25);
        // display the substring  "Java"
        g.drawChars(mystring, 5, 4, 0, 50);
      }
  }
```

As you can see, the paint function receives as a parameter, the *Graphics* object *g*, which contains the graphics context. Using this object, the function displays characters to the applet window. As discussed, the graphics context contains such items as the current font, font size, color, window coordinates, and so on. Figure 429 illustrates the program's output within the Java *appletviewer*.

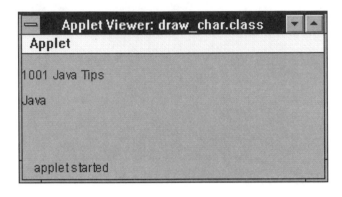

Figure 429 *The output of the **draw_char** applet.*

430 SETTING THE ORIGIN WITH THE TRANSLATE METHOD

As you have learned, Java's default origin for graphics operations is the top-left corner of the applet window. Using the *Graphics* class *translate* method, however, you can reposition Java's graphics origin. The format of the *translate* method is as follows:

```
translate(int x, int y);
```

For example, the following statement moves Java's graphics origin to the *x* and *y* coordinates 100,50:

```
g.translate(100, 50);
```

Figure 430 illustrates the effect of the previous translate method:

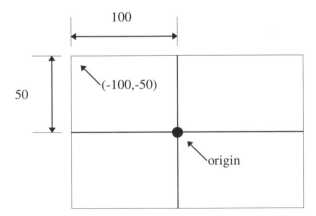

Figure 430 *Translating the origin.*

DRAWING A LINE 431

Within a Java applet that performs graphics operations, you can draw simple and complex graphics using line-based graphics. To draw a line within the applet window, you can use the *Graphics* class *drawLine* method. The format of the *drawLine* method is as follows:

```
drawLine(int x1, int y1, int x2, int y2);
```

For example, the following *paint* method uses the *drawLine* method to draw a line from the coordinates(0,0) to coordinates (160,80):

```
public void paint(Graphics g)
  {
     g.drawLine(0, 0, 160, 80);
  }
```

If you place this *paint* method within an applet, the applet will draw a line similar to that shown in Figure 431.

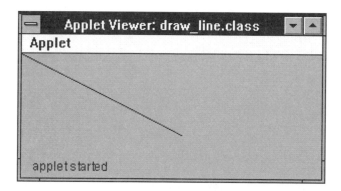

Figure 431 A line drawn from (0,0) to (160,80).

DRAWING A RECTANGLE 432

In Tip 431, you learned that using the *drawLine* method, your applets can draw a line from one set of coordinates to another. In a similar way, to draw a rectangle on the screen, you can use the Graphics class *drawRect* method. The format of the *drawRect* is as follows:

```
drawRect(int x, int y, int width, int height);
```

The *x* and *y* parameters specify the location of the top-left corner of the rectangle. Likewise, the *width* and *height* parameters specify the rectangle's size. For example, the following statements draw a 10x10 rectangle (in pixels relative to the 0,0 origin) within the applet window:

```
public void paint(Graphics g)
  {
     g.drawRect(0, 0, 10, 10);
  }
```

433 DRAWING A ROUNDED RECTANGLE

In Tip 432, you learned how to draw a rectangle with the *drawRect* method. Depending on your applet's purpose, there may be times when you will need to display a rectangle that uses rounded corners. To draw a rectangle with rounded corners, your programs can use the *drawRoundRect* method, as shown:

```
drawRoundRect(int x, int y, int width, int height,
    int arcWidth, int arcHeight);
```

The *arcWidth* and *arcHeight* parameters specify the size of the rectangle's rounded corners, as shown in Figure 433.1:

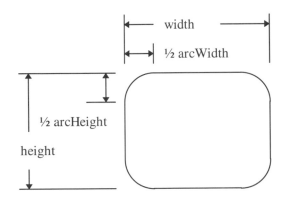

Figure 433.1 *Parameters of the **drawRoundRect()** method.*

For example, the following *paint* method uses *drawRoundRect* to draw the rounded rectangle shown in Figure 433.2:

```
public void paint(Graphics g)
  {
    g.drawRoundRect(0, 0, 160, 80, 50, 25);
  }
```

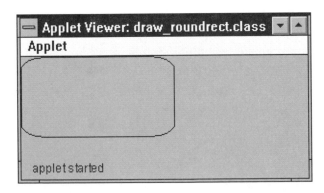

Figure 433.2 *A rectangle with **arcWidth** of 50 and **arcHeight** of 25.*

DRAWING A CIRCLE WITH THE DRAWROUNDRECT METHOD — 434

As you learned in Tip 433, you can draw a rectangle with rounded corners using the *drawRoundRect* method. In a similar way, your programs can draw a circle using the *drawRoundRect* method. As discussed, the format of the *drawRoundRect* method is as follows:

```
drawRoundRect(int x, int y, int width, int height,
    int arcWidth, int arcHeight);
```

To draw a circle using the *drawRoundRect* method, you simply specify an *arcWidth* that is equal to the *arcHeight*, as shown:

```
drawRoundRect(0, 0, 80, 80, 80, 80);
```

In this case, the *drawRoundRect* method will draw a circle with a radius of 40 pixels, as shown in Figure 434.

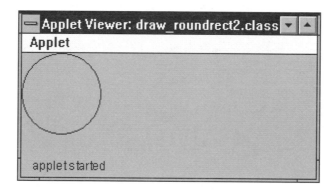

*Figure 434 A circle drawn with the **drawRoundRect** method.*

Using a rounded rectangle is just one of the ways to draw a circle; Tip 443 will show a better solution using the *drawOval* method.

DRAWING WITH COLORS — 435

Unless your Java program will only run on a monochrome monitor, which isn't likely, you will need the ability to change the program's drawing color. Within your applets, you can use the *Graphics* class *setColor* method to change the current color. Conversely, your applets can use the *getColor* method to obtain the current color. Java will use the current color for drawing text, lines, and filling interiors. The following applet, *color_textline.java*, illustrates the use of the *setColor* method and results in the screen shown in Figure 435.

```
import java.applet.*;
import java.awt.*;

public class color_textline extends Applet {
```

```
    public void paint(Graphics g)
     {
        // draw black text
        g.setColor(Color.black);
        g.drawString("A line of text in black", 5, 30);


        // draw red text
        g.setColor(Color.red);
        g.drawString("A line of text in red", 5, 60);


        // draw magenta text
        g.setColor(Color.magenta);
        g.drawString("A line of text in magenta", 5, 90);
     }
 }
```

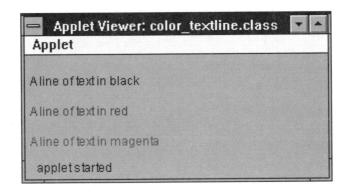

Figure 435 *Text and lines drawn with different colors.*

436 USING PREDEFINED COLORS

In Tip 435, you learned how to use the *Graphics* class *setColor* method to set the current color. When you use the *setColor* method, you can use the following color constants:

black	blue	cyan	darkGray
gray	green	lightGray	magenta
orange	pink	red	white
yellow			

For example, the following program, *ColorConstants.java*, illustrates the use of several color constants within the *setColor* method:

```
import java.applet.*;
import java.awt.*;

public class ColorConstants extends Applet {
```

```
    public void paint(Graphics g)
      {
        g.setColor(Color.yellow);
        g.drawString("Yellow Yellow Yellow", 5, 30);

        g.setColor(Color.blue);
        g.drawString("Blue Blue Blue", 5, 60);

        g.setColor(Color.green);
        g.drawString("Green Green Green", 5, 90);
      }
    }
```

CREATING A NEW COLOR

437

As you learned in Tip 436, Java provides several predefined color values. However, depending on your program's purpose, there may be times when you need a color outside of Java's predefined colors. In such cases, you can create any color you want using the *Graphics* class *Color* constructors, as shown:

```
Color(int r, int g, int b);
Color(int rgb);
Color(float r, float g, float b);
```

The following applet, *rgb_shades.java*, illustrates the use of the *Graphics* class *Color* constructor by creating eight different shades of red, green, and blue, as shown in Figure 437.

```
import java.applet.*;
import java.awt.*;

public class rgb_shades extends Applet {

    public void paint(Graphics g)
      {
        // shades of red
        for(int i=1; i<=8; i++)
          {
            Color color = new Color(i*32 - 1, 0, 0);
            g.setColor(color);
            g.fillRect(i*30 + 2, 2, 28, 28);
          }

        // shades of green
        for(int i=1; i<=8; i++)
          {
            Color color = new Color(0, i*32 - 1, 0);
            g.setColor(color);
            g.fillRect(i*30 + 2, 32, 28, 28);
          }
```

```
    // shades of blue
    for(int i=1; i<=8; i++)
      {
        Color color = new Color(0, 0, i*32 - 1);
        g.setColor(color);
        g.fillRect(i*30 + 2, 62, 28, 28);
      }
    }
  }
```

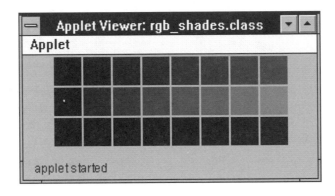

*Figure 437 An applet illustrating the use of the **Color** constructor.*

438 CHANGING THE DEFAULT APPLET BACKGROUND

Each of the previous Java applets in this section has used the same (default) background color. By default, Java uses a light gray background color for the Windows 95 and Windows NT *appletviewer*. Using the *Component* class *setBackground* method, you can change the background color. Your applets can use the *Component* class methods because *Applet* is a subclass of the *Component* class. The following applet, *background.java*, changes the background color to black, as shown in Figure 438.

```
import java.applet.*;
import java.awt.*;

public class background extends Applet {

  public void init()
    {
      setBackground(Color.black);
    }

  public void paint(Graphics g)
    {
      g.setColor(Color.white);
      g.drawString("White text on black background", 5, 50);
    }
  }
```

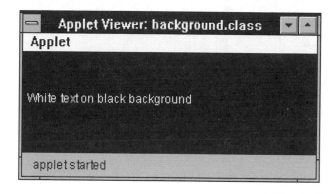

Figure 438 An applet illustrating the use of the
setBackground method.

DRAWING A FILLED RECTANGLE

439

As you learned in Tip 432, you can draw a rectangle using the *Graphics* class *drawRect* method. As you also learned, the *drawRect* method draws an empty rectangle. Depending on your applet's purpose, there may be times when you will need to draw a filled rectangle. To draw a rectangle with a filled interior, your applets can use the *Graphics* class *fillRect* method. The format of the *fillRect* method is as follows:

```
fillRect(int x, int y, int width, int height);
```

The *fillRect* method is similar to the *drawRect* method in that the *x* and *y* parameters specify the location of the rectangle's top-left corner; the *width* and *height* parameter specify the rectangle's dimension. When you draw a filled rectangle, Java uses the color defined by the *setColor* method.

DRAWING A FILLED ROUNDED RECTANGLE

440

As you have learned in Tip 439, you can draw a filled rectangle using the *fillRect* method. Just as the *Graphics* class *drawRoundRect* method lets you draw a rounded rectangle, your applets can use the *fillRoundRect* method to draw a filled rectangle. The format of the *fillRoundRect* method is as follows:

```
fillRoundRect(int x, int y, int width, int height,
    int arcWidth, int arcHeight);
```

The following *paint* method illustrates the use of the *fillRoundRect* method to draw the filled rectangle shown in Figure 440. As is the case with the *Graphics* class *fillRect* method, the *fillRoundRect* method uses the color defined by the *setColor* method:

```
public void paint(Graphics g)
  {
     g.fillRoundRect(0, 0, 160, 80, 50, 25);
  }
```

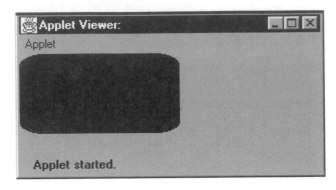

*Figure 440 A filled rectangle with **arcWidth** of 50 and **arcHeight** of 25.*

441 BUILDING A SIMPLE BAR CHART

Whether you are writing a book or a Java-based program, a picture is worth a thousand words. Within your applets, charts provide an effective means for presenting data as pictures. Based on what you have learned from previous tips, you can use the *Graphics* class *drawString*, *drawLine*, and *fillRect* methods to create a bar chart. The following applet, *bar_chart.java*, will display the bar chart shown in Figure 441.

```java
import java.applet.*;
import java.awt.*;

public class bar_chart extends Applet {
    final static int data_set[] = { 50, 85, 32, 65 };
    final static String data_label[] = { "93", "94", "95", "96" };

    int Graph_offset = 20;              // graph offset from origin
    int Graph_Height = 150;
    int Y_Tick_Height = Graph_Height / 5; // 5 Y-axis divisions;
    int Graph_Width = 240;
    int X_Tick_Width = Graph_Width / data_set.length; // 4 X-axis
                                                      // divisions

    public void paint(Graphics g)
      {
        g.setColor(Color.black);

        // draw y axis
         g.drawLine(Graph_offset + Graph_Width, Graph_offset,
            Graph_offset + Graph_Width, Graph_offset + Graph_Height);

        // draw y-tick labels
        for(int i=0; i<=5; i++)
          {
```

```java
        g.drawString(String.valueOf(i*20),   // 20 units per tick
            Graph_offset + Graph_Width + 10,
            Graph_offset + Graph_Height -(i*Y_Tick_Height));

        // draw grid line
        g.drawLine(Graph_offset,
            Graph_offset + Graph_Height -(i*Y_Tick_Height),
            Graph_offset + Graph_Width + 5,
            Graph_offset + Graph_Height -(i*Y_Tick_Height));
    }

// draw x axis
 g.drawLine(Graph_offset, Graph_offset + Graph_Height,
            Graph_offset + Graph_Width, Graph_offset +
            Graph_Height);

// draw x-tick lables
 for(int i=0; i<data_set.length; i++)
  {
      g.drawString(data_label[i],
          Graph_offset + X_Tick_Width*i + X_Tick_Width/2,
          Graph_offset + Graph_Height + 20);

      // draw x-tick lines
      g.drawLine(Graph_offset + X_Tick_Width*i +
          X_Tick_Width/2,
          Graph_offset + Graph_Height,
          Graph_offset + X_Tick_Width*i + X_Tick_Width/2,
          Graph_offset + Graph_Height + 5);
  }

// draw data(bar lines)
g.setColor(Color.red);
for(int i=0; i<data_set.length; i++)
  {
    int bar_height = data_set[i] * Graph_Height / 100;

    g.fillRect(Graph_offset + X_Tick_Width*i +
      X_Tick_Width/4,
      Graph_offset + Graph_Height - bar_height,
      X_Tick_Width/2,  bar_height);
  }
 }
}
```

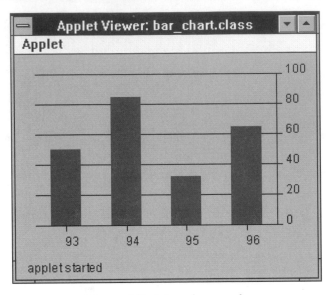

Figure 441 A bar chart applet.

442 DRAWING AN OVAL

Within your applets, there will be times when you need to draw ovals and circles. To draw an oval, your programs can use the *Graphics* class *drawOval* method. The format of the *drawOval* method is as follows:

```
drawOval(int x, int y, int width, int height);
```

For example, the following *paint* method uses the *drawOval* class to draw an oval with dimensions of 90 x 60 pixels at location(0,0), as shown in Figure 442.

```
public void paint(Graphics g)
   {
     g.drawOval(0, 0, 90, 60);
   }
```

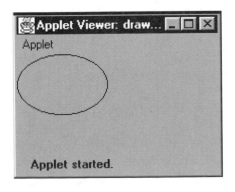

Figure 442 A 90 x 60 pixels oval at location (0,0).

DRAWING A CIRCLE USING THE DRAWOVAL METHOD  443

In Tip 434, you learned how to draw a circle using a rectangle with rounded corners. A better way to draw circles, however, is to use the *drawOval* method with equal width and height. For example, the following statement uses the *drawOval* method to draw a circle with a diameter of 100 pixels:

```
drawOval(0, 0, 100, 100);
```

DRAWING A FILLED OVAL 444

As you learned in Tip 443, your applets can draw an oval using the *drawOval* method. As you have also learned, the *drawOval* method draws an empty oval. Depending on your applet's purpose, you may want to draw a filled oval. In such cases, your programs can use the *fillOval* method. The format of the *fillOval* method is as follows:

```
fillOval(int x, int y, int width, int height);
```

The *fillOval* method uses the color specified by the *setColor* method. The following applet, *fill_oval.java*, uses the *fillOval* method to draw several filled ovals of various sizes and shapes, as shown in Figure 444:

```java
import java.applet.*;
import java.awt.*;

public class fill_oval extends Applet {
   public void paint(Graphics g)
    {
       g.fillOval(0,   30, 50, 20);
       g.fillOval(70,   0, 20, 80);
       g.fillOval(140, 0, 75, 75);
    }
 }
```

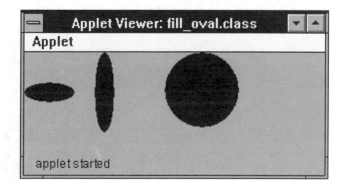

*Figure 444 Several filled ovals drawn with the **fillOval** method.*

445   DRAWING AN ARC

When your programs perform graphics operations, there may be times when you need to draw an arc. In such cases, your programs can use the *Graphics* class *drawArc* method. The format of the *drawArc* method is as follows:

```
drawArc(int x, int y, int width, int height, int startAngle,
    int arcAngle);
```

Figure 445.1 shows how the method's *width*, *height*, *startAngle*, and *arcAngle* parameters control the shape of the arc:

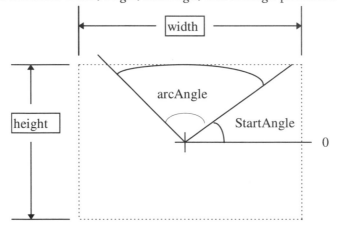

Figure 445.1 *Parameters of the* **drawArc** *method.*

The following program illustrates the use of the *drawArc* method. Figure 445.2 illustrates the program's output:

```java
import java.applet.*;
import java.awt.*;

public class draw_arc extends Applet {
    public void paint(Graphics g)
     {
        g.drawArc(10,  20, 50, 30, 30,  90);
        g.drawArc(80,  10, 30, 80,  0, 135);
        g.drawArc(150, 10, 60, 60, 120,300);
     }
}
```

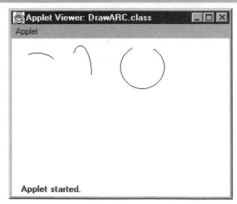

Figure 445.2 *A series of arcs drawn by the* **drawArc** *method.*

DRAWING A FILLED ARC   446

As you learned in Tip 445, your programs can draw an arc using the *Graphics* class *drawArc* method. Depending on your applet's purpose, you may want to draw a filled arc. In such cases, your programs can use the *fillArc* method. The format of the *fillArc* method is as follows:

```
fillArc(int x, int y, int width, int height, int startAngle,
    int arcAngle);
```

The *fillArc* method uses the color specified by the *setColor* method. The following applet, *fill_arc.java*, draws several filled arcs of various sizes and shapes, as shown in Figure 446:

```
import java.applet.*;
import java.awt.*;

public class fill_arc extends Applet {
    public void paint(Graphics g) {
        g.fillArc(10,  20, 50, 30, 30,  90);
        g.fillArc(80,  10, 30, 80,  0, 135);
        g.fillArc(150, 10, 60, 60, 120,300);
    }
}
```

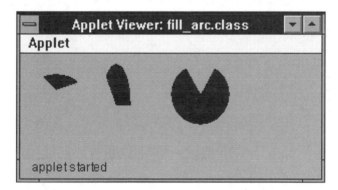

*Figure 446 Several filled arcs drawn with the **fillArc** method.*

DRAWING A PIE CHART   447

In Tip 446, you learned how to draw filled arcs using the *Graphics* class *fillArc* method. Likewise, in Tip 441, you learned how to draw bar charts. In a similar way, by using pie-shaped filled arcs, your programs can create pie charts. The following applet, *pie_chart.java*, displays the chart shown in Figure 447.

```
import java.applet.*;
import java.awt.*;

public class pie_chart extends Applet {

    final static int data_set[] = { 20, 40, 32, 8 };
```

```
    final static String data_label[] =
      {"Apple","Orange","Banana","Other"};

    final static Color data_color[] =
      {Color.red, Color.blue, Color.yellow, Color.green};

    int Graph_offset = 20;            // Graph offset from origin
    int Graph_Diameter = 150;

    public void paint(Graphics g)
      {
        int start_angle, pie_size;
        int sub_total = 0;

        start_angle = 0;
        for(int i=0; i < data_set.length; i++)
          {
            // draw pie
            sub_total += data_set[i];
            pie_size = sub_total * 360 / 100 - start_angle;
            g.setColor(data_color[i]);
             g.fillArc(Graph_offset,  Graph_offset, Graph_Diameter,
                        Graph_Diameter, start_angle,  pie_size);

            start_angle += pie_size;

            // draw legend
            g.fillRect(Graph_offset + Graph_Diameter + 10,
                        Graph_offset + i * 20, 15, 15);
            g.setColor(Color.black);
            g.drawString(data_label[i], Graph_offset +
                          Graph_Diameter + 10 + 20,
                          Graph_offset + i * 20 + 15);
          }
      }
}
```

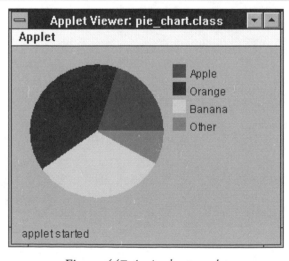

Figure 447 A pie chart applet.

DRAWING A POLYGON

A *polygon* is a closed plane figure bounded by straight lines. As the graphics your applet must draw become more complex, there may be times when you can represent the shape as a polygon. Graphics-based programs normally represent a polygon using two arrays. One array contains the polygon's *x* coordinates, while the second array contains the *y* coordinates. To draw a polygon within your applet, you can use the *Graphics* class *drawPolygon* method. The formats for the *drawPolygon* method are as follows:

```
drawPolygon(int xPoints[], int yPoints[], int nPoints);
drawPolygon(Polygon p);
```

Be aware that Java does not close off the polygon automatically. To draw a closed polygon, the last point in the polygon must be the same as the first point. The following applet, *draw_poly.java*, uses the *drawPolygon* method to draw several polygons, as shown in Figure 448:

```java
import java.applet.*;
import java.awt.*;

public class draw_poly extends Applet {
    int poly1_x[] = {  40,  80,   0,  40 };
    int poly1_y[] = {   5,  45,  45,   5 };

    int poly2_x[] = { 140, 180, 180, 140, 100, 100, 140 };
    int poly2_y[] = {   5,  25,  45,  65,  45,  25,   5 };

    int poly3_x[] = { 240, 260, 220, 260, 220, 240 };
    int poly3_y[] = {   5,  65,  85,  25,  25,   5 };

    public void paint(Graphics g)
      {
        g.drawPolygon(poly1_x, poly1_y, poly1_x.length);
        g.drawPolygon(poly2_x, poly2_y, poly2_x.length);
        g.drawPolygon(poly3_x, poly3_y, poly3_x.length);
      }
  }
```

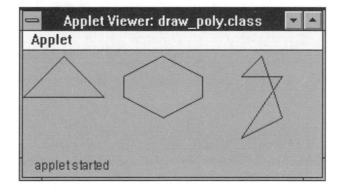

*Figure 448 Polygons drawn using the **drawPolygon** method.*

449 DRAWING A FILLED POLYGON

In Tip 448, you learned how to draw polygons using the *Graphics* class *drawPolygon* method. In a similar way, your applets can draw filled polygons using the *fillPolygon* method. Unlike the *drawPolygon* method, the *fillPolygon* method will automatically close off the end of the polygon, even if the last point is not the same as the first point. The *fillPolygon* method uses the color specified by the *setColor* method. The following program, *fill_poly.java*, uses the *fillPolygon* method to draw the filled polygons, as shown in Figure 449:

```java
import java.applet.*;
import java.awt.*;

public class fill_poly extends Applet {
    int poly1_x[] = {  40,  80,   0,  40 };
    int poly1_y[] = {   5,  45,  45,   5 };

    int poly2_x[] = { 140, 180, 180, 140, 100, 100, 140 };
    int poly2_y[] = {   5,  25,  45,  65,  45,  25,   5 };

    int poly3_x[] = { 240, 260, 220, 260, 220, 240 };
    int poly3_y[] = {   5,  65,  85,  25,  25,   5 };

    public void paint(Graphics g)
      {
        g.fillPolygon(poly1_x, poly1_y, poly1_x.length);
        g.fillPolygon(poly2_x, poly2_y, poly2_x.length);
        g.fillPolygon(poly3_x, poly3_y, poly3_x.length);
      }
 }
```

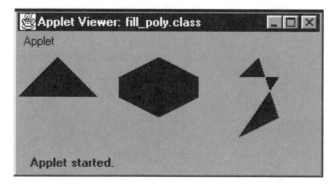

*Figure 449 Filled polygons drawn using the **fillPolygon** method.*

450 DRAWING 3-D RECTANGLES

Almost all graphical user interfaces designed today have a three-dimensional look. Command buttons appear to rise off the page, and when you click on a button, the button appears to push in. You can create this 3-D look by using a simple highlight and shadow. Assuming that light comes from the top-left, by applying highlight on the top and left side together with shadow on the right and bottom side, you can create a raised look. Similarly, by placing a shadow on the top and left side together with highlight on the right and bottom side, you can create a pushed-in look. Figure 450 shows a raised and a pushed-in rectangle.

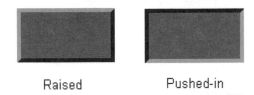

Raised   Pushed-in

Figure 450 *Raised and pushed-in rectangles using highlights and shadows.*

The Java AWT provides the *draw3DRect* with which you can draw a 3-D rectangle:

```
draw3DRect(int x, int y, int width, int height, boolean raised);
```

The *draw3DRect* method is very similar to the *drawRect* method, but includes the extra *raised* parameter. You create a raised rectangle by specifying *true* or a pushed-in rectangle by specifying *false*.

DRAWING A FILLED 3-D RECTANGLE 451

In Tip 450, you learned that you can draw a 3-D rectangle using the *draw3DRect* method. Depending on your program's design, there may be times when you will want a filled 3-D rectangle. To display a filled 3-D rectangle, your programs can use the *fill3DRect* method, the format of which is as follows:

```
fill3DRect(int x, int y, int width, int height, boolean raised);
```

The *fill3DRect* method uses the same set of parameters as the *draw3DRect* method. To create a raised rectangle, use the value *true* for the *raised* parameter. Likewise, to display a pushed-in rectangle, use the value *false*.

IMPLEMENTING YOUR OWN 3-D RECTANGLE 452

In Tip 450 and Tip 451, you learned how to draw 3-D rectangles using the *draw3DRect* and *fill3DRect* methods. If you use these methods within your program, you may find the 3-D effect very hard to see. The problem with the built-in methods is that Java only draws the highlight and shadow borders one pixel wide. The following applet, *three_d_rect.java*, implements better *draw3DRect* and *fill3DRect* methods with borders that are three pixels wide, as shown in Figure 452:

```java
import java.applet.*;
import java.awt.*;

public class three_d_rect extends Applet {
```

```
    public void draw3DRect(Graphics g, int x, int y,
       int width, int height, boolean raised)
    {

       g.draw3DRect(x, y, width-1, height-1, raised);
       g.draw3DRect(x+1, y+1, width-3, height-3, raised);
       g.draw3DRect(x+2, y+2, width-5, height-5, raised);
    }

    public void fill3DRect(Graphics g, int x, int y,
       int width, int height, boolean raised)
    {

       g.draw3DRect(x, y, width-1, height-1, raised);
       g.draw3DRect(x+1, y+1, width-3, height-3, raised);
       g.draw3DRect(x+2, y+2, width-5, height-5, raised);
       g.fillRect(x+3, y+3, width-6, height-6);
    }

    public void paint(Graphics g)
    {

       g.setColor(Color.gray);
       draw3DRect(g, 10, 5, 80, 40, true);
       draw3DRect(g, 130, 5, 80, 40, false);
       fill3DRect(g, 10, 55, 80, 40, true);
       fill3DRect(g, 130, 55, 80, 40, false);
    }
}
```

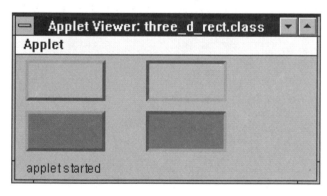

Figure 452 Drawing 3-D rectangles.

453 USING THE DARKER AND BRIGHTER METHODS

In Tip 452, you learned that you can create a 3-D effect using highlights and shadows. The *Color* class *darker* and *brighter* methods can help you obtain the highlight and shadow colors. You can also use these methods to create special effects like the one shown Figure 453, which was created by the *bright_dark.java* applet, as shown:

```java
import java.applet.*;
import java.awt.*;

public class bright_dark extends Applet {

    Color dark_red = new Color(4, 0, 0);
    Color light_gray = new Color(250, 250, 250);

    public void paint(Graphics g)
      {
        Color color;
        // brighter colors
        color = dark_red;
        for (int i = 0; i < 16; i++)
          {
            g.setColor(color);
            g.fillRect(0, i*5, 300, 5);
            color = color.brighter();
          }

        // darker colors
        color = light_gray;
        for(int i = 16; i < 32; i++)
          {
            g.setColor(color);
            g.fillRect(0, i*5, 300, 5);
            color = color.darker();
          }
      }
}
```

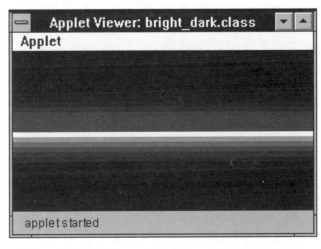

Figure 453 Gradient color effects using the **Color** class
bright and **dark** methods.

454 FINDING SCREEN REGIONS THAT NEED UPDATING

When an area of a Java program needs to be redrawn, Java will automatically call the *update* and *paint* methods. If only a portion of the drawing area needs updating, Java will try to find the smallest rectangle that encloses the required area and set it as the Graphics object's *clipping region*. Java then passes the *Graphics* object to the *update* and *paint* methods. The *update* and *paint* methods ignore all drawings outside of the clipping rectangle, which allows faster screen updates.

In most Java programs, programmers override the *paint* or *update* method to draw the entire applet. To improve your program's performance, you can determine the clipping region that needs updating and then redraw only that portion of the window. To determine the clipping area, your programs can call the *getClipRect* method. The following applet, *get_cliprect.java*, displays the clipping area that needs updating. Experiment with this applet by hiding and exposing part of the applet window with another application.

```java
import java.applet.*;
import java.awt.*;


public class get_cliprect extends Applet {

    public void paint(Graphics g)
      {
        // draw a X on the screen
        g.drawLine(0, 0, 300, 100);
        g.drawLine(300, 0, 0, 100);

        // print clipping rectangle to standard out
        System.out.println("Clipping Rect:" + g.getClipRect());
      }
}
```

455 CREATING A RECTANGLE

As you learned in Tip 454, the *getClipRect* method returns a *Rectangle* object that defines the current clipping region. Depending on your applet's purpose, you may need to create your own *Rectangle* object. For example, you may want to define a clickable region within which the user can click the mouse to select different objects. To create a *Rectangle* object, use one of the following *Rectangle* constructors:

```java
Rectangle();
Rectangle(int x, int y, int width, int height);
Rectangle(int width, int height);
Rectangle(Point p, Dimension d);
Rectangle(Point);
Rectangle(Dimension);
```

These constructors create the *Rectangle* object and initialize the *x, y, width,* and *height* fields which define the rectangle's size and location.

UNDERSTANDING THE POINT AND DIMENSION CLASS 456

Within an applet that performs graphics operations, there will be many times when you need to store *x* and *y* coordinates. In such cases, your programs can use the *Point* class to create an object to store a point's coordinates. To create a *Point* object, use the following constructor:

```
Point(int x, int y);
```

In a similar way, there will be times when your programs need to store information about a graphic object's width and height. To store such information, your programs can create a *Dimension* object using one of the following constructor methods:

```
Dimension();
Dimension(Dimension d);
Dimension(int width, int height);
```

The first constructor, with no argument, creates a *Dimension* object of zero width and zero height. The second constructor, with a *Dimension* argument, creates a copy of the specified dimension. The third constructor creates a *Dimension* object with the specified width and height.

CHECKING WHETHER A POINT IS INSIDE A RECTANGLE 457

Within a graphics-based program, you may need to determine whether a point (*x* and *y* coordinates) resides within a rectangle's coordinates. To determine whether a point is within a rectangle, your programs can use the *Rectangle* class *inside* method. The following applet, *click_rect.java*, implements two clickable rectangular regions using a *Rectangle* object. When the user clicks his or her mouse within a region, the applet will display a message so stating:

```
import java.applet.*;
import java.awt.*;

public class click_rect extends Applet {

    Rectangle a_rect = new Rectangle(10,  10, 80, 40);
    Rectangle b_rect = new Rectangle(100, 10, 80, 40);

    public boolean mouseDown(Event e, int x, int y)
      {
        if (a_rect.inside(x,y))              // rectangle A clicked
           System.out.println("A clicked.");

        if (b_rect.inside(x,y))              // rectangle B clicked
           System.out.println("B clicked.");

        return true;
      }
```

```
public void paint(Graphics g)
  {
      // draw the 2 clickable rectangles
      g.setColor(Color.yellow);
      g.fillRect(a_rect.x, a_rect.y, a_rect.width,
        a_rect.height);
      g.fillRect(b_rect.x, b_rect.y, b_rect.width,
        b_rect.height);

      g.setColor(Color.black);
      g.drawString("A", a_rect.x + a_rect.width/2,
                   a_rect.y + a_rect.height/2);
      g.drawString("B", b_rect.x + b_rect.width/2,
                   b_rect.y + b_rect.height/2);
  }
}
```

Figure 457 shows a screen shot from the *click_rect.java* applet. As you can see, the applet defines two clickable rectangular regions: *A* and *B*. When the applet detects a mouse click, the applet will check if the click location is inside one of these two rectangles. If the click location is inside *A* or *B*, the applet will display a message to the console window.

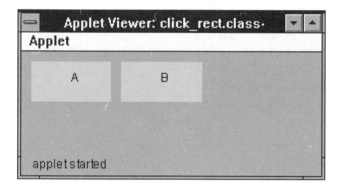

Figure 457 An applet with two clickable rectangles.

 458 CHECKING WHETHER TWO RECTANGLES INTERSECT

Within a graphics-based program, there may be times when you need to test whether two rectangle objects intersect. To determine whether two *Rectangle* objects intersect, your programs can use the *Rectangle* class *intersects* method. A game program, for example, might use the *intersects* method to detect whether a missile has hit a spaceship. The following applet, *intersects.java*, illustrates the use of the *intersects* method. Take time to experiment with the rectangle coordinates, and test whether the rectangles intersect.

```
import java.applet.*;
import java.awt.*;

public class intersects extends Applet {

    Rectangle g_rect = new Rectangle(10,  10, 80, 40);
    Rectangle y_rect = new Rectangle(20, 20, 80, 40);
```

```
    public void paint(Graphics g)
      {
        // draw the rectangles
          g.setColor(Color.yellow);
           g.drawRect(y_rect.x, y_rect.y, y_rect.width,
          y_rect.height);

           g.setColor(Color.green);
            g.drawRect(g_rect.x, g_rect.y, g_rect.width,
           g_rect.height);

        g.setColor(Color.black);
        if (y_rect.intersects(g_rect))
           g.drawString("The two rectangles intersect.", 10,90);
      }
    }
```

USING THE INTERSECTION AND UNION METHODS 459

When your program uses *Rectangle* objects, you may need to determine the screen region that holds both objects, or if two *Rectangle* objects intersect. To find the intersection or the union of two rectangles, you can use the *Rectangle* class *intersection* and *union* methods. The *intersection* method returns the area where two *Rectangle* objects overlap. That is, the *intersection* method returns the area that two *Rectangle* objects have in common.

The *union* method, on the other hand, behaves differently than you might expect. The *union* method returns the smallest rectangle that encloses two *Rectangle* objects, instead of returning just the area covered by both objects. Figure 459 illustrates the behavior of the *intersection* and *union* methods.

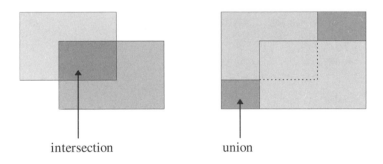

intersection   union

Figure 459 The intersection and union of two rectangles.

CREATING A POLYGON 460

To define complex shapes like triangles and pentagons, your programs can use a *Polygon* object. To create a *Polygon* object, use one of the following constructor methods:

```
Polygon();
Polygon(int xpoints[], int ypoints[], int npoints);
```

If you use the *Polygon* constructor without arguments, you will need to use the *addPoint* method to define the polygon's points. The companion disk that accompanies this book, contains the applet *poly_object.java* that creates two polygons using each constructor. Figure 460 illustrates how the *Graphics* class *fillPolygon* method displays polygons.

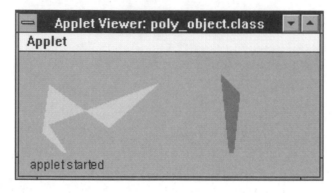

Figure 460 An applet with 2 polygons.

461 CHECKING WHETHER A POINT IS INSIDE A POLYGON

In Tip 460, you learned how to check whether a specific point resides within a *Rectangle* object. In a similar way, there may be times when you need to know whether a point resides within a *Polygon* object. For example, depending on the shapes that appear within the applet window, you may want to create a clickable region that is defined by a polygon. The following applet, *click_poly.java*, creates three clickable triangles of different colors.

```java
import java.applet.*;
import java.awt.*;

public class click_poly extends Applet {

    int a_xpoints[] = { 40, 10, 70 };
    int a_ypoints[] = { 20, 50, 50 };
    int a_len = a_xpoints.length;

    int b_xpoints[] = { 120, 90, 150 };
    int b_ypoints[] = { 20, 50, 50 };
    int b_len = b_xpoints.length;

    Polygon a_poly = new Polygon(a_xpoints, a_ypoints, a_len);
    Polygon b_poly = new Polygon(b_xpoints, b_ypoints, b_len);

    public boolean mouseDown(Event e, int x, int y)
      {
        if (a_poly.inside(x,y))        // Polygon A clicked
          System.out.println("A clicked.");

        if (b_poly.inside(x,y))        // Polygon B clicked
          System.out.println("B clicked.");

        return true;
      }
```

```
public void paint(Graphics g)
    {
        // draw the 2 clickable polygons
        g.setColor(Color.yellow);
        g.fillPolygon(a_poly);
        g.setColor(Color.red);
        g.fillPolygon(b_poly);

        g.setColor(Color.black);
        g.drawString("A", 30, 45);
        g.drawString("B" , 110, 45);
    }
}
```

FINDING THE BOUNDING BOX OF A POLYGON

462

In some drawing programs, such as CorelDRAW, when you select an object, the program creates a box to enclose the object which has handles that let you resize or move the object. In Java, a *bounding box* is the smallest box that contains a given polygon. The *Polygon* class *getBoundingBox* method returns the bounding box for a *Polygon* object. The following applet, *boundbox.java*, draws a *Polygon* object and then uses the *getBoundingBox* method to draw a bounding box. In addition, the program uses the *draw_handle* method to add editing handles.

```
import java.applet.*;
import java.awt.*;

public class boundbox extends Applet {

    int xpoints[] = {30, 90,140, 80, 90, 60};
    int ypoints[] = {30, 10, 40, 70, 50, 30};
    int num_pts = ypoints.length;

    Polygon poly = new Polygon(xpoints, ypoints, num_pts);

    void draw_handle(Graphics g, int x, int y)
    {
        g.fillRect(x-3, y-3, 7, 7);
    }

    public void paint(Graphics g)
    {
        // draw the polygons
        g.setColor(Color.red);
        g.fillPolygon(poly);

        Rectangle bbox = poly.getBoundingBox();
        g.setColor(Color.black);
        g.drawRect(bbox.x, bbox.y, bbox.width, bbox.height);
        draw_handle(g, bbox.x, bbox.y);
        draw_handle(g, bbox.x + bbox.width, bbox.y);
```

```
        draw_handle(g, bbox.x, bbox.y + bbox.height);
        draw_handle(g, bbox.x + bbox.width, bbox.y + bbox.height);
    }
}
```

Figure 462 shows the output of the *boundbox.java* applet. Although this program does not allow any actual editing, you can use the program as the basis of your own drawing program.

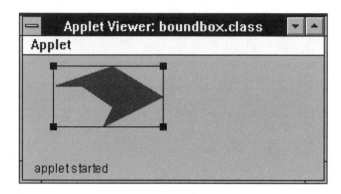

*Figure 462 An applet illustrating the **getBoundingBox** method.*

463 CREATING FONTS

In previous tips, you have learned how to draw text to the screen. In each case, the program drew the text using the default font. Within your programs, you can change the current font by creating new *Font* objects of different names, styles, and point sizes using the *Font* constructor, the format of which follows:

```
Font(String name, int style, int size);
```

The *name* parameter specifies the font name, such as "Courier" or "TimesRoman"; Tip 464 will show you how to get a list of available fonts. The second parameter specifies the font style, which can be *Font.PLAIN*, *Font.BOLD*, *Font.ITALIC*, or the combination of *BOLD* and *ITALIC*, such as *Font.BOLD + Font.ITALIC*. The third parameter specifies the font's point size. For example, the following method call creates a 14 point bold Courier font:

```
Font myFont = new Font("Courier", Font.BOLD, 14);
```

464 FONTS AVAILABLE IN JAVA

Java defines five platform-independent font names which you should find available on all platforms. You may use these names as the first parameter to the *Font* constructor: *Courier, Dialog, Helvetica, TimesRoman,* and *Symbol.* When an applet creates a *Font* object, Java maps the font to a platform-dependent font. For example, Java maps the *Helvetica* font to the Arial font under Microsoft Windows. You may choose to specify a font name other than the five standard ones. However, if the font you specify is not available, Java will automatically pick an available one for you.

DRAWING WITH DIFFERENT FONTS

In Tip 463, you learned how to create a *Font* object. To use a *Font* object to display text, you must use the *Graphics* class *setFont* method to select the font. The following applet, *fonts.java*, draws several lines of text using different font names, styles, and point sizes, as shown in Figure 465.

```java
import java.applet.*;
import java.awt.*;

public class fonts extends Applet {

    Font f1 = new Font("Helvetica", Font.PLAIN, 18);
    Font f2 = new Font("Helvetica", Font.BOLD, 10);
    Font f3 = new Font("Helvetica", Font.ITALIC, 12);
    Font f4 = new Font("Courier",   Font.PLAIN, 12);
    Font f5 = new Font("TimesRoman", Font.BOLD + Font.ITALIC, 14);
    Font f6 = new Font("Dialog", Font.ITALIC, 14);

    public void paint(Graphics g)
      {
        g.setFont(f1);
        g.drawString("18pt plain Helvetica", 5, 20);

        g.setFont(f2);
        g.drawString("10pt bold Helvetica", 5, 43);

        g.setFont(f3);
        g.drawString("12pt italic Helvetica", 5, 58);

        g.setFont(f4);
        g.drawString("12pt plain Courier", 5, 75);

        g.setFont(f5);
        g.drawString("14pt bold & italic Times Roman", 5, 92);

        g.setFont(f6);
        g.drawString("14pt italic Dialog", 5, 111);
    }
}
```

Figure 465 An applet illustrating the use of various font names, styles, and point sizes.

466 GETTING A LIST OF AVAILABLE FONTS

As you have learned, to display text using a specific font, your applets must create a *Font* object, and then use the *setFont* method to select the font. Before your applet selects a font, you may want to determine if the font is available. To get a list of available fonts, your programs can use the *Toolkit* class *getFontList* method. The following applet, *font_list.java*, illustrates the use of the *getFontList* method:

```java
import java.applet.*;
import java.awt.*;

public class font_list extends Applet {

    public void paint(Graphics g)
      {
        String fontlist[] = getToolkit().getFontList();

        for(int i = 0; i < fontlist.length; i++)
          {
            Font f = new Font(fontlist[i], Font.BOLD, 14);
            g.setFont(f);
            g.drawString(fontlist[i], 5, i * 20 + 20);
          }
      }
}
```

467 FINDING INFORMATION ON A FONT

When your programs display text, there will be times when you need to get information about the current font. For example, before you display text, you may need to test the current font size to make sure the text will fit within the window region you desire. To learn specifics about the current font, your programs must first use the *Component* class *getFont* method to get the current *Font* object. Next, to get information about the current font, your program can use the *Font* class methods listed in Table 467.

Method	Purpose
getName	Returns the name of the font
getSize	Returns the point size of the font
getStyle	Returns the style of the font
isBold	Returns true if it is a bold font
isItalic	Returns true if it is a italic font
isPlain	Returns true if it is a plain font

Table 467 Font class methods that return information about a font.

The following *init* method displays the name, style, and size of the current font:

```
public void init()
  {
    Font f = getFont();
    System.out.println("Name: " + f.getName());
    System.out.println("Style: " + f.getStyle());
    System.out.println("isBold: " + f.isBold());
    System.out.println("isItalic: " + f.isItalic());
    System.out.println("isPlain: " + f.isPlain());
    System.out.println("Size: " + f.getSize());
  }
```

UNDERSTANDING FONT METRICS 468

In Tip 467, you learned how to use *Font* class methods to obtain the current font's point size. Before you learn how to gather more information about the current font metrics, such as the *baseline* and *character width*, you need to better understand several key terms. Later, to correctly place text on the screen, or to align text with other objects, you will need to take advantage of several font characteristics. Figure 468 will help you understand several key font metrics.

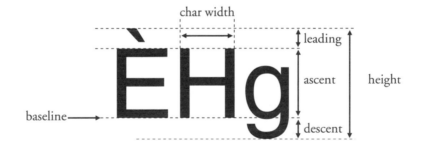

Figure 468 Font metrics parameters.

HOW TO GET FONT METRICS INFORMATION 469

In Tip 468, you learned about several key font characteristics. Using a *FontMetrics* object, your applets can get several of these metrics for the current font. To create a *FontMetrics* object, you can use either the *getFontMetrics* method or the *FontMetrics(Font)* constructor. Then, you can use the *FontMetrics* class methods to find about specifics about the current font. Table 469 lists several of the *FontMetrics* methods.

Method	Purpose
getAscent()	Returns the ascent of the font
getDescent()	Returns the descent of the font
getLeading()	Returns the leading of the font
getHeight()	Returns the height of the font

*Table 469 Several **FontMetrics** methods. (Continued on following page.)*

Method	Purpose
charWidth(char ch)	Returns the width of the character specified
bytesWidth(byte data[], int off, int len)	Returns the width of the byte array
stringWidth(String str)	Returns the width of the String

*Table 469 Several **FontMetrics** methods. (Continued from previous page.)*

For example, the following creates a *FontMetrics* object for the current font, and then uses the *charWidth* method to return the pixel width of the 14-point Courier font letter *C*:

```
Font f = Font("Courier", Font.BOLD, 14);
FontMetrics fmetrics = new FontMetrics(f);
int len = fmetrics.charWidth('C');
```

470 UNDERLINING YOUR TEXT

Although the Java AWT library lets you create new fonts that use the bold and italic style, Java does not support underlined text. However, using the *FontMetrics* class *stringWidth()* method, you can find the width of a string and underline the text yourself. The following applet, *underline.java*, underlines a string, as shown in Figure 470:

```
import java.applet.*;
import java.awt.*;

public class underline extends Applet {

    Font f1 = new Font("TimesRoman", Font.PLAIN, 14);
    String str =  "This line is underlined";

    public void paint(Graphics g)
      {
         int strlen = getFontMetrics(f1).stringWidth(str);

         g.setFont(f1);
         g.drawString(str, 5, 30);

         // draw line to underline string
         g.drawLine(5, 30 + 1, 5 + strlen, 30 + 1);
      }
  }
```

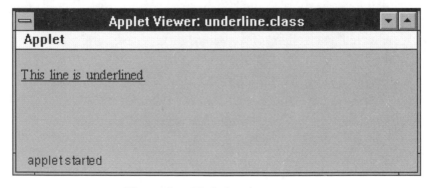

Figure 470 Underlined text string.

Although Java lets you select different fonts for drawing text, it is a more challenging task if you want to display text using different fonts or if you want to draw two strings of the same font on the same line. After you display the first string, you must find its ending screen location, and position the second string at that point. The following applet, *two_string.java*, uses the *stringWidth* method to find the width of a string, and then uses the width information to draw a line of text using multiple fonts, as shown in Figure 471:

```java
import java.applet.*;
import java.awt.*;

public class two_string extends Applet {

    Font f1 = new Font("Helvetica", Font.BOLD, 18);
    Font f2 = new Font("Courier", Font.PLAIN, 12);
    Font f3 = new Font("TimesRoman", Font.BOLD + Font.ITALIC, 12);

    String s1 = "18pt-Bold Helvetica ";
    String s2 = "and ";
    String s3 = "12pt-Bold-Italic Times Roman ";

    public void paint(Graphics g)
      {
        int x = 5;

        g.setColor(Color.blue);
        g.setFont(f1);
        g.drawString(s1, x, 50);
        x += getFontMetrics(f1).stringWidth(s1);

        g.setColor(Color.black);
        g.setFont(f2);
        g.drawString(s2, x, 50);
        x += getFontMetrics(f2).stringWidth(s2);

        g.setColor(Color.red);
        g.setFont(f3);
        g.drawString(s3, x, 50);
      }
  }
```

As you can see, the program increments the variable *x*, using the variable to position each new string of text.

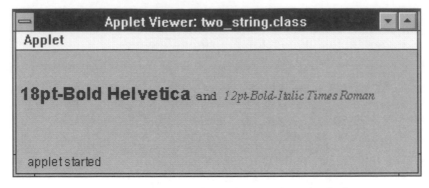

Figure 471 Drawing a line of text with multiple fonts.

472 ALIGNING YOUR TEXT

Using the *FontMetrics* methods you examined in Tip 469, you can align your text horizontally and vertically. In fact, as you will learn, having a reusable class for drawing aligned text is quite handy. The following code, *AlignedText.java*, shows you how to build such a class. In this case, the code creates the *AlignedText* class, which you can use within your other applets:

```java
import java.awt.*;

public class AlignedText {
    // Define constants for setting text alignment
    public static final int LEFT = 0x00;
    public static final int RIGHT = 0x01;
    public static final int CENTER = 0x02;
    public static final int BASELINE = 0x00;
    public static final int TOP = 0x04;
    public static final int BOTTOM = 0x08;

    private int     alignmentType;

    public AlignedText()
      {
        alignmentType = LEFT | BASELINE; // default alignment
      }

    public void set_alignment(int alignment_type)
      {
        alignmentType = alignment_type;
      }

    public void drawString(Graphics g, String aString , int x, int y)
      {
        FontMetrics fmetrics = g.getFontMetrics();
        int len =  fmetrics.stringWidth(aString);

        if ((alignmentType & RIGHT) != 0)
          x -= len;        // offset x for right alignment

        else if ((alignmentType & CENTER) != 0)
          x -= len/2;    // offset x for center alignment
```

```
            if ((alignmentType & TOP) != 0)
              y += fmetrics.getAscent();        // offset y for top alignment

            else if((alignmentType & BOTTOM) != 0)
              y -= fmetrics.getDescent();  // offset y for bottom
                                           // alignment
            g.drawString(aString, x, y);
        }
    }
```

The *AlignedText* class lets you set the text alignment using the *set_align* method. You can set horizontal alignment with *aligned_text.LEFT*, *aligned_text.RIGHT*, or *aligned_text.CENTER*, as well as the vertical alignment with *aligned_text.TOP*, *aligned_text.BOTTOM*, and *aligned_text.BASELINE*. You can then draw text using the *AlignedText* class *drawString* method.

The following applet, *aligntext_test.java*, illustrates the use of the *AlignedText* class and draws several text strings with different alignments, as shown in Figure 472:

```
import java.awt.*;
import java.applet.*;

public class aligntext_test extends Applet {

    AlignedText aligned_txt = new AlignedText();

    public void paint(Graphics g)
      {
        aligned_txt = new AlignedText();

        g.setColor(Color.black);
        g.drawLine(50, 0, 50, 100);
        g.setColor(Color.blue);
         aligned_txt.set_alignment(aligned_txt.LEFT);
        aligned_txt.drawString(g, "left", 50, 30);

         aligned_txt.set_alignment(aligned_txt.CENTER);
        aligned_txt.drawString(g, "center", 50, 60);
         aligned_txt.set_alignment(aligned_txt.RIGHT);
        aligned_txt.drawString(g, "right",  50, 90);

        g.setColor(Color.black);
        g.drawLine(100, 50, 300, 50);
        g.setColor(Color.blue);
         aligned_txt.set_alignment(aligned_txt.BOTTOM);
        aligned_txt.drawString(g, "bottom", 100, 50);

         aligned_txt.set_alignment(aligned_txt.BASELINE);
        aligned_txt.drawString(g, "baseline", 160, 50);
         aligned_txt.set_alignment(aligned_txt.TOP);
        aligned_txt.drawString(g, "top", 220, 50);
    }
}
```

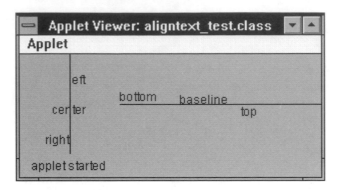

Figure 472 *Text strings with different alignments.*

473 GETTING A *GIF* IMAGE FILE FROM THE WEB

The days of text-only Web pages are long gone. Today's Web pages are loaded with *GIF* and *JPEG* images. You can also display *GIF* and *JPEG* image files within your Java applets. Displaying an image file in Java involves two steps: getting the image and drawing the image. To get a *GIF* or *JPEG* image file within a Java applet is a simple a matter of calling one of the following *getImage* methods:

```
Image getImage(URL url);
Image getImage(URL url, String name);
```

Within the first *getImage* method, the *url* parameter must be a Uniform Reference Locator (URL) that points to an image file on the Web. The *getImage* method returns an *Image* object that your program can later use to reference the GIF or JPEG image. For example, the following statement creates an *Image* object for the file *sample.gif* which resides on the server at, *http://www.myserver.com*:

```
Image img = getImage(new URL("http://www.myserver.com/sample.gif"));
```

Notice the hardcoded pathname in this example. As a rule, it is not good programming to hardcode the server's name within the source file. Should you later need to move the image file to a different server, you will need to change the source code to match the server's location and recompile. Instead, your applet can use the *getCodeBase* method to locate an image file. With the second *getImage* method, the *url* parameter points to the location where the image file is and the *name* parameter specifies the name of the image file. For example, the following statement uses the *getCodeBase* method to get the server and directory location that corresponds to the applet file and then uses that location to locate the file *sample.gif*:

```
Image img = getImage(getCodeBase(), "sample.gif");
```

Be aware that neither of these *getImage* methods actually loads the image. Instead, your applet loads the image when it is first needed in the applet.

474 DRAWING AN IMAGE

As you learned in Tip 473, the *getImage* method returns an *Image* object for the specified *GIF* or *JPEG* image file. To display the *Image* object, your applets can use the *drawImage* method:

```
boolean drawImage(Image img, int x, int y, ImageObserver observer);
```

The *x* and *y* parameters specify the location of the upper-left corner of the image. The following applet, *draw_image.java*, displays a *GIF* image file named *cow.gif*, as shown in Figure 474:

```java
import java.applet.*;
import java.awt.*;

public class draw_image extends Applet {

    Image img;

    public void init()
      {
        img = getImage(getCodeBase(), "cow.gif");
      }

    public void paint(Graphics g)
      {
        g.drawImage(img, 0, 0, this);
      }
}
```

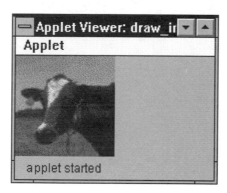

*Figure 474 An applet that displays a **GIF** image file.*

STRETCHING AN IMAGE IN JAVA 475

In Tip 474, you learned how to display an image within a Java applet. However, if the size of the display area is different from the size of the image, you may want to stretch or shrink the image to fit the area. As it turns out, there is another form of the *drawImage* method that lets you specify the image *width* and *height*:

```java
boolean drawImage(Image img, int x, int y, int width,
    int height, ImageObserver observer);
```

When your programs use the *drawImage* method, the method draws to scale using the specified width and height. The following applet, *stretch_image.java*, shown in Figure 475, displays the same GIF image as in Tip 474, but it is stretched to fill the entire applet area:

```java
import java.applet.*;
import java.awt.*;
```

```
public class stretch_image extends Applet {

    Image img;

    public void init()
      {
        img = getImage(getCodeBase(), "cow.gif");
      }

    public void paint(Graphics g)
      {
        g.drawImage(img, 0, 0, 200, 100, this);
      }
}
```

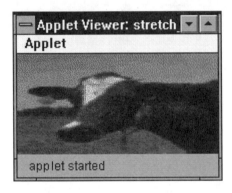

Figure 475 An *applet that displays a stretched image.*

476 MATCHING JAVA BACKGROUND COLOR TO THE HTML

As you have learned, you embed statements that correspond to your Java applet within an HTML document. At times, you may want the background color of your applet to be the same as the background color of the HTML document. Unfortunately, Java does not automatically match the background colors, nor does it provide a transparent background color for the applet. To match the following HTML document's background colors, perform the following steps:

1. Pass a parameter to the applet that specifies the HTML document's RGB background color.

2. Create a matching RGB color in Java using the *Color* constructor.

3. Assign the background color using the *setBackground* method.

The following HTML statements pass the RGB color FFCFCF as an HTML parameter named *BGCOLOR*:

```
<HTML><BODY  bgcolor="#FFCFCF"  >
<APPLET  CODE="match_back.class"  WIDTH=300  HEIGHT=100>
<param  name=BGCOLOR    value="FFCFCF"></APPLET>
</BODY></HTML>
```

The following Java statements use the *getParameter* method to determine the HTML background color. Next, the statements use the *setBackgruond* method to set the background color:

```
public void init()
  {
    String arg = getParameter("BGCOLOR");
    int bgColorVal = Integer.valueOf(arg, 16).intValue();
    setBackground(new Color(bgColorVal));
  }
```

MATCHING JAVA BACKGROUND PATTERN TO THE HTML PAGE 477

In Tip 476, you learned how to match a Java applet's background color with the Web page's background. However, some Web pages use tiled image files for the background. Instead of changing the background color using the *setBackground* method, your applet can draw the background by tiling the image. The following HTML statements specify parameter values that specify the image file and its dimensions. Using the *getParameter* method, your program can access these values from the HTML file.

```
<HTML><BODY  BACKGROUND="pattern.gif">
<APPLET  CODE="tile_back.class"  WIDTH=300  HEIGHT=100>
<param  name=BACKGROUND  value="pattern.gif">
<param  name=BGWIDTH  value="40">
<param  name=BGHEIGHT  value="40">
</BODY></HTML>
```

The following *init* method uses the *getParameter* method to get the HTML parameter values. Then, the statements tile the image as specified by the parameters.

```
Image img;
int bg_width, bg_height;

public void init()
  {
    String arg = getParameter("BACKGROUND");
    System.out.println("BACKGROUND=" + arg);
    img = getImage(getCodeBase(), arg);
    arg = getParameter("BGWIDTH");
    bg_width = Integer.valueOf(arg, 16).intValue();
    arg = getParameter("BGHEIGHT");
    bg_height = Integer.valueOf(arg, 16).intValue();
  }

public void paint(Graphics g)
  {
    int x, y;

    // draw background pattern
    y = 0;
    while(y < size().height)
      {
        x = 0;
```

```
        while(x < size().width)
          {
             g.drawImage(img, x, y, this);
             x += bg_width;
          }


        y += bg_height;
     }
  }
```

When you use this technique for matching background patterns, you should use random and seamless patterns. Otherwise, the discontinuity of the pattern between the Web page and the applet will form a visible edge. In this example, the size of the pattern image is passed to the applet in parameters. Alternatively, in later tips you will learn how to inquire about an image's size, rather than having to specify a size.

478 CLEARING AN AREA OF THE SCREEN

In previous tips, you learned how to draw images within the applet window; however, there may also be times when you want to erase part of the drawing. One way to erase an image is to cover part of a drawing with a rectangle filled with the background color. To do so, first set the drawing color to match the background color using the *setColor* method. Then, draw a filled rectangle over the region you want to erase using the *fillRect* method. An easier way to clear an area of the screen is to use the *Graphics* class *clearRect* method, the format of which is as follows:

```
void clearRect(int x, int y, int width, int height);
```

As shown in Figure 478, the following applet, *clear.java*, illustrates the *clearRect* method by drawing a few shapes and clearing a rectangular area in the middle:

```java
import java.applet.*;
import java.awt.*;

public class clear extends Applet {

   public void paint(Graphics g)
     {
       /* draw a few shapes */
       g.setColor(Color.red);
       g.fillRoundRect(10, 10, 160, 80, 50, 25);
       g.setColor(Color.blue);
       g.fillOval(80, 40, 100, 80);
       g.setColor(Color.green);
       g.fillRect(150, 20, 50, 50);
       /* clear a rectangular area */
       g.clearRect(90, 50, 80, 40);
     }

}
```

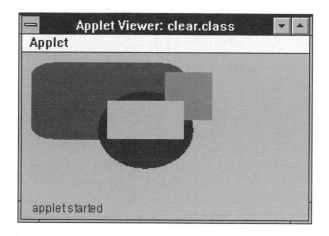

*Figure 478 An applet illustrating the **clearRect** method.*

USING THE REPAINT METHOD 479

Although Java calls the *update* and *paint* methods automatically when it needs to update the display, there may be times when you want to force a screen-redraw operation. To trigger the screen redraw operation, your programs can call the *repaint* method. Java, in turn, will call the *update* and *paint* methods. The following applet, *click_repaint.java*, toggles the display between the text string "circle" and a drawn circle each time the user clicks the mouse. The applet calls the *repaint* method to redraw the screen each time the applet detects a mouse event:

```
import java.applet.*;
import java.awt.*;

public class click_repaint extends Applet {

    int display_page = 0;

    public boolean mouseDown(Event e, int x, int y)
      {
        if (display_page == 0)
          display_page = 1;
        else
          display_page = 0;

        repaint();
        return true;
      }

    public void paint(Graphics g)
      {
        if (display_page == 0)
          g.drawOval(10, 10, 80, 80);
        else
          g.drawString("Circle", 30, 50);
      }
  }
```

480 COPYING AN AREA OF THE SCREEN

When your programs perform graphics operations, there may be times when you have drawn something on the screen which you want to duplicate in another area of the screen. Instead of repeating the drawing operation, you can simply copy the area and draw it in a different location using the *Graphics* class *copyArea* method, the format of which is as follows:

```
void copyArea(int x, int y, int width, int height, int dx,
    int dy);
```

The *x, y, width,* and *height* parameters specify the position and size of the area you want to copy. The *dx* and *dy* parameters specify the destination location's offset position from the source. Be aware that the *dx* and *dy* parameters specify an offset from the source region, and not the absolute location on the display.

The following applet, *copy_area.java,* draws a small pattern and then duplicates it to fill the entire background, as shown in Figure 480:

```java
import java.applet.*;
import java.awt.*;

public class copy_area extends Applet {

    int PATTERN_SIZE = 40;

    public void paint(Graphics g)
      {
        // draw a pattern
        g.setColor(Color.red);
         g.fillOval(0,0, PATTERN_SIZE, PATTERN_SIZE);
        g.setColor(Color.black);

        g.drawLine(0, 0, PATTERN_SIZE-1, PATTERN_SIZE-1);
        g.drawLine(0, PATTERN_SIZE-1, PATTERN_SIZE-1, 0);

        // duplicate the pattern
        for (int y=0; y<4; y++)
          for (int x=0; x<8; x++)
              g.copyArea(0, 0, PATTERN_SIZE, PATTERN_SIZE,
              x*PATTERN_SIZE, y*PATTERN_SIZE);
      }
  }
```

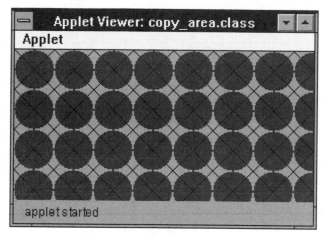

Figure 480 *Duplicating an image using the* **copyArea** *method.*

USING THE GETGRAPHICS METHOD 481

As you have learned, to draw an image within the applet window, you need to get a *Graphics* object. Most applets perform their drawing operations using the *paint* or *update* methods within which they can easily get a *Graphics* object from the parameter Java passes to the methods. However, there may be times when you want to draw outside of the *paint* and *update* methods. To do so, you can also get a *Graphics* object by using the *Component* class *getGraphics* method, the format of which is as follows:

```
Graphics getGraphics();
```

The following applet, *mouse_draw.java*, draws a circle at the location where the user clicks on the applet. The applet illustrates the use of the *getGraphics* method by placing a call to the *drawOval* method within the *mouseDown* event handling method.

```
import java.applet.*;
import java.awt.*;

public class mouse_draw extends Applet {

   public boolean mouseDown(Event e, int x, int y)
     {
        Graphics g = getGraphics();
        g.setColor(Color.red);
        g.drawOval(x-2, y-2, 4, 4);
        g.dispose();
        return true;

     }
 }
```

482 USING THE XOR PAINT MODE

Normally, when you perform a drawing operation such as using a *fillRect* method to draw a rectangle, Java's default drawing mode simply overwrites the current background using your image. To provide you with better control over how Java displays one object on top of another, the *Graphics* class also offers the XOR (exclusive-or) paint mode. You set the painting mode to XOR by calling the *Graphics* class *setXORMode* method, the format of which is as follows:

```
void setXORMode(Color c1);
```

Programs use the exclusive-or mode when they need to display and later erase an image. For example, the first time your program displays an image using the XOR mode, the program will display the object. However, if the program then displays the image at the same location, again using the XOR mode, the image will disappear. Programs that create animations by drawing a series of images use the XOR mode to draw an image, and then to erase the image when they are ready to draw the next image.

To restore Java's painting mode to overwrite mode, your applet calls the *setPaintMode* method with no parameters, as shown:

```
void setPaintMode();
```

The following applet, *xor_mode.java*, illustrates the use of the XOR painting mode, creating the image shown in Figure 482:

```java
import java.applet.*;
import java.awt.*;

public class xor_mode extends Applet {

    public void paint (Graphics g)
      {
         g.setColor (Color.yellow);
         g.fillRect (0, 0, 150, 100);
         g.setXORMode (Color.red);
         g.fillRect (50, 25, 200, 50);
      }
 }
```

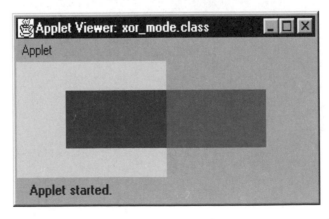

Figure 482 Drawing an image using the XOR painting mode.

SETTING YOUR OWN RECTANGULAR CLIPPING REGION

In Tip 454, you learned that you can get the applet's clipping area using the *getClipRect* method. As you also learned, before Java calls the *update* or *paint* methods, Java sets the clipping area to the screen region that the applet needs to update. There may be times, however, when you want to set your own clipping region to limit a drawing to a specified area. By using the *Graphics* class *clipRect* method, your applet can set its own rectangular clipping region. The format of the *clipRect* method is as follows:

```
void clipRect(int x, int y, int width, int height);
```

The *x* and *y* parameters specify the upper-left corner of the clipping area. The *width* and *height* parameters specify the clipping region's size. The following applet, *clip_area.java*, illustrates the use of the *clipRect* method by defining a clipping region and then drawing several shapes over the region. Figure 483 shows the effect of the program's clipping. As you will see, Java restricts the applet's display of graphics images to those images that fit within the clipping region. Java clips (ignores) the graphics images that fall outside of the clipping region:

```java
import java.applet.*;
import java.awt.*;

public class clip_area extends Applet {

    public void paint(Graphics g)
      {
        g.clipRect(90, 50, 80, 40); // set clipping rectangle

        g.setColor(Color.blue);       // draw a few shapes
        g.fillOval(90, 50, 100, 80);

        g.setColor(Color.red);
        g.fillRoundRect(10, 10, 150, 70, 50, 25);

        g.setColor(Color.green);
        g.fillRect(150, 20, 50, 50);
      }
  }
```

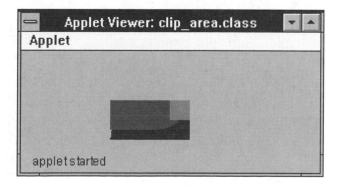

Figure 483 An applet illustrating the effect of a clipping rectangle.

484 USING THE CREATE METHOD TO COPY A GRAPHICS OBJECT

In the previous tip, you learned how to change the applet's clipping region using the *clipRect* method. Unfortunately, there is a problem with the way the program sets the clipping area. When you try to move the clipping region to a different position by using the *clipRect* method again, you will find that the resulting clipping is actually the overlapping area of the first and second clipping rectangles. It turns out that each time an applet calls the *clipRect* method, Java sets the new clipping rectangle as the intersection of the current clipping rectangle and the clipping rectangle specified in *clipRect*. To get around this problem, your applet can make a new copy of the *Graphics* object using the *create* method each time it sets a clipping rectangle. The following applet, *multi_clip.java*, as shown in Figure 484, sets the clipping rectangle to three different locations and sizes:

```java
import java.applet.*;
import java.awt.*;

public class multi_clip extends Applet {

   void draw_shapes(Graphics g)
     {
       /* draw a few shapes */
       g.setColor(Color.blue);
       g.fillOval(90, 50, 100, 80);
       g.setColor(Color.red);
       g.fillRoundRect(10, 10, 150, 70, 50, 25);
       g.setColor(Color.green);
       g.fillRect(150, 20, 50, 50);
     }

   public void paint(Graphics g)
     {
       /* set clipping rectangle*/
       Graphics g1 = g.create();
       g1.clipRect(90, 50, 80, 40);
       draw_shapes(g1);
       g1.dispose();

       /* set another clipping rectangle*/
       Graphics g2 = g.create();
       g2.clipRect(40, 0, 50, 50);
       draw_shapes(g2);
       g2.dispose();

       /* set the third clipping rectangle*/
       Graphics g3 = g.create();
       g3.clipRect(160, 20, 80, 40);
       draw_shapes(g3);
       g3.dispose();
     }
 }
```

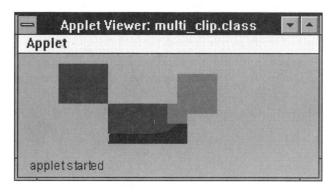

Figure 484 *An applet illustrating multiple clipping rectangles.*

THE IMPORTANCE OF DISPOSING GRAPHICS OBJECT

485

You may notice in Tip 484 that the applet calls the *dispose* method after it uses the *Graphics* object returned by the *getGraphics* and *create* methods. In Java, you normally do not have to free allocated memory as you would in C/C++. Instead, the Java garbage-collection mechanism will do that for you automatically. However, you still need to inform Java to free up the system resources used by a *Graphics* object by using the *dispose* method. If you do not call *dispose*, applets running on some platforms may stop working when the system runs out of resources. In general, when you are done using a *Graphics* object returned by either *getGraphics* or *create*, you should call the *dispose* method, as shown in the following code:

```
Graphics g;
g = getGraphics();   // or create();


// graphics operations here


g.dispose();             // call dispose to free up system resources
```

Note: *You should not dispose of the* **Graphics** *object passed as parameter to the* **paint** *and* **update** *methods, as that object corresponds to the applet's original graphics context.*

UNDERSTANDING AWT COMPONENTS

486

Although you can create a graphical user interface using only line, rectangle, and text drawing methods, most programs normally utilize more complex interface elements, such as buttons, text-entry fields, lists, and dialog boxes. For suchneeds, the AWT library includes a set of user-interface elements within the *Component class*. As you will learn, the *Button, Scrollbar*, and other classes are all subclasses of the *Component* class.

Bear in mind that although you cannot create an instance of the *Component* class itself, you can use the methods defined in the *Component* class through the subclass objects. For example, you can disable a button or a scrollbar using the *Component* class *disable* method. Subsequent tips in this section will show you how to use these methods.

487 CREATING A LABEL

The *Label* class lets objects display static (unchanging) text on the screen. As the name suggests, applets use *Label* objects to label other components. *Label* objects do not allow any user interaction. To create a text label on your screen, your applet can use one of the following *Label* constructor methods:

```
Label();
Label(String label);
Label(String label, int alignment);
```

To add a *Label* object to the applet window, you use the *Container* class *add* method. The following applet, *label_test.java*, illustrates the use of the *Label* class to display the text "Label object" within the window:

```
import java.applet.*;
import java.awt.*;

public class label_test extends Applet {

   Label label = new Label("Label object");

   public void init()
    {
       add(label);
    }
 }
```

When you run this applet, your screen will display the *Label* object as shown in Figure 487.

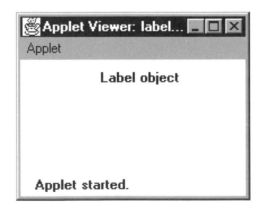

Figure 487 *Displaying a* **Label** *object.*

488 UNDERSTANDING APPLET LAYOUT

In Tip 488, you learned that you can display a *Label* object within the applet window using the *Container* class *add* method. You may have noticed in the previous applet that you do not have to specify the label's screen position. Instead, Java automatically places the *Label* object centered at the top of the applet window.

The size of a component, such as a label, may differ from one platform to another. For instance, because the default font size on the Windows platform and a UNIX platform may be different, the size of a *Label* component with the same label string may also be different. If you were to place components at absolute *x* and *y* coordinates, a layout that looks good on one platform may have components overlapping each other on a different platform.

To solve the layout differences between platforms, Java places components inside a subclass of the *Container* class. As you will learn, *Panel* and *Window* are subclasses of the *Container* class, and *Applet* is a subclass of *Panel*. Java determines the arrangement of an *Applet's* components on the screen using both the "Layout Manager" and the order that the applet adds the components to the screen. The "Layout Manager" is software that specifies how the components will be arranged. The default layout for an *Applet*, or *Panel*, is *FlowLayout*, which arranges the components from left to right and then top to bottom, as shown in Figure 488. Using *FlowLayout*, Java will put as many components as it can in a row before going on to the next row. In addition to *FlowLayout*, Java provides *BorderLayout*, *CardLayout*, *GridLayout*, and *GridBagLayout*. Subsequent tips in this section will cover these layout styles in detail.

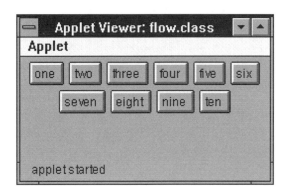

*Figure 488 Displaying screen components using **FlowLayout**.*

SETTING LABEL ALIGNMENT 489

In Tip 488, you created a *Label* object using the default *Label* constructor method. By default, Java centers the text within a *Label* object. Depending on your applet's screen contents, you may want to right, left, or center justify the *Label* object's text. In such cases, you can pass an alignment parameter to the *Label* constructor, as shown:

```
Label(String label, int alignment);
```

The alignment parameter lets you specify the alignment of the label string. You can specify left, right or center alignment using *Label.LEFT*, *Label.RIGHT*, or *Label.CENTER*, as shown in Figure 489:

Left Aligned

Right Aligned

Center Aligned

Figure 489 Labels with different alignments.

490 CREATING A COMMAND BUTTON

Most graphical-user interfaces provide command buttons that let users specify simple actions. For example, one *Button* may direct the applet to print an object, while a second button may direct an applet to save an object to a file on disk. To create a *Button* object, use one of the following constructor methods:

```
Button();
Button(String label);
```

As was the case with the *Label* object, to add a *Button* object to an applet window, you use the *Container* class *add* method. The following applet, *button_test.java*, creates two buttons labeled Button A and Button B, as shown in Figure 490:

```java
import java.applet.*;
import java.awt.*;

public class button_test extends Applet {

    Button button_a = new Button("Button A");
    Button button_b = new Button("Button B");

    public void init()
      {
         add(button_a);
         add(button_b);
      }
  }
```

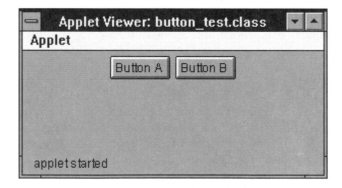

Figure 490 *An applet with two buttons.*

491 HANDLING BUTTON EVENTS

A *Button* object on the screen is not very useful unless your program can detect when the user pushes the button. As you will learn, when the user pushes a button, Java generates an *action* event. Within your applet, you can intercept the *action* event by overriding the *action* method. You can add the following *action* method to the *button_test.java* applet you created in Tip 490:

```
public boolean action(Event evt, Object arg)
  {
    if (evt.target instanceof Button)
      {
        if (arg.equals("Button A"))
            System.out.println("Button A pressed!");
        else if (arg.equals("Button B"))
            System.out.println("Button B pressed!");

        return true;   // events processed
      }
    return false;      // events not processed
  }
```

As you will learn, the *action* method processes more than just button events. The *action* method also processes other component events which include *list* events and *checkbox* events. To differentiate between the event types, you can test the *Event* object which Java passes to the *action* method as the first parameter. For example, the following statement tests if the event is a *Button* event:

```
if (evt.target instanceof Button)
```

If your applet uses more than one button, as in the case of the *button_test.java* applet, you can use the *Object* field (which is the second parameter Java passes to the *action* method) to determine which button the user pressed. The following condition, for example, is true if the button pressed is labeled "Button A."

```
if (arg.equals("Button A"))
```

One important point to remember when you process events is that other event handlers need to know if your handler actually handled the event. Therefore, your handler should return *true* if the method handled the event and *false* if it did not.

CHANGING THE BUTTON'S LABEL 492

Depending on your applet's purpose, there may be times when you need to change a button's label on the fly. For example, the following applet, *button_label.java*, uses the *setLabel* method to toggle a button's label each time the user clicks on the button:

```
import java.applet.*;
import java.awt.*;

public class button_label extends Applet {

    Button button = new Button("toggle OFF");

    public void init()
      {
        add(button);
      }

    public boolean action(Event evt, Object arg)
      {
```

```
        if (evt.target instanceof Button)
          {
            if (arg.equals("toggle ON"))
              button.setLabel("toggle OFF"); // Change label
            else if(arg.equals("toggle OFF"))
              button.setLabel("toggle ON");  // Change label

            return true;          // event processed
          }
       return false;              // event not processed
     }
  }
```

493 READING THE BUTTON'S LABEL

In Tip 492, you learned how to use the *setLabel* method to change a *Button* object's label on the fly during your program's execution. Before your applet changes a button's label, you may want to first read the current label so you can restore the label at a later time. To get a *Button* object's label, your applet uses the *Button* class *getLabel* method which returns a *String* object that contains the label:

```
String button_label = button.getLabel();
```

494 CREATING A CHECKBOX

Within a graphical-user interface, checkboxes let users specify simple on-or-off or yes-or-no selections. To create a checkbox within an applet window, you use one of the following *Checkbox* constructors:

```
Checkbox();
Checkbox(String label);
Checkbox(String label, CheckboxGroup, boolean state);
```

The *label* parameter specifies the text that Java displays next to the checkbox. The *state* parameter specifies the button's initial state: checked or unchecked. Tip 497 covers the *CheckboxGroup* parameter in detail.

To add a *Checkbox* object to an applet window, you can use the *Container* class *add* method. The companion disk that accompanies this book contains the applet *checkbox_test.java* that creates two buttons labeled "Box A" and "Box B," as shown in Figure 494:

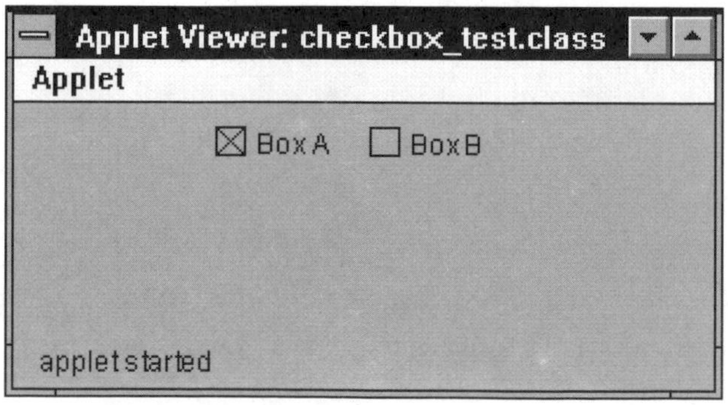

Figure 494 *An applet with two checkboxes.*

GETTING AND SETTING THE STATE OF THE CHECKBOX 495

In Tip 494, you learned how to display a checkbox within an applet window. For the *Checkbox* object to be of use, you need to determine whether the checkbox is checked or unchecked. To determine the *Checkbox* state, you use the *Checkbox* class *getState* method, the format of which is as follows:

```
public boolean getState();
```

The *getState* method returns *true* if the checkbox is checked and *false* if it is not.

As your applet executes, you may want to set a checkbox's state. For example, to initialize a checkbox, you need to set its state to checked or unchecked. Just as you use *getState* to get the state of a checkbox, you use the *setState* method set the checkbox state:

```
public void setState(boolean state);
```

HANDLING CHECKBOX EVENTS 496

Within your applet, you may want to detect when the user clicks on a checkbox. To do so, you must set up an event handler to handle the checkbox (*cbox*) event. To capture the event, your applet overrides the *action* method, much like it did to handle a button event in previous tips. To detect checkbox events, add the following *action* method to the *checkbox_test.java* applet you created in Tip 494:

```
public boolean action(Event evt, Object arg)
  {
    if (evt.target == cbox_a)
     {
        System.out.println("Box A state = " + arg);
        return true;         // events processed
     }
    else if (evt.target == cbox_b)
     {
        System.out.println("Box B state = " + arg);
        return true;         // events processed
     }

   return false;             // events not processed
  }
```

This event-handling code is a bit different from the button event-handling code you created earlier in this book. The second parameter, *arg* in this example, contains the checkbox state, as opposed to the button label. To differentiate between the two checkboxes, you must check the value of the *Event* parameter's target field: *evt.target*.

USING CHECKBOXGROUP TO CREATE AN OPTION BUTTON GROUP 497

As the number and type of options your applets present to the user become more complex, there will be times when you must provide a series of choices, which the user can select only one of at any given time. In Java, such option buttons, also known as *radio buttons*, are actually a variant of the checkbox. To create option buttons, you must first create a *CheckboxGroup* using the *CheckboxGroup* constructor, the format of which is as follows:

```
CheckboxGroup();
```

A *CheckboxGroup* object groups a set of option buttons. Within your applets, you can use multiple *CheckboxGroup* objects to group different sets of option buttons. After you create a *CheckboxGroup*, you can add option buttons to the group using the following *Checkbox* constructor:

```
Checkbox(String label, CheckboxGroup groupName, boolean state);
```

The *label* parameter specifies the *Checkbox* name, the *groupName* specifies the name of the *CheckboxGroup*, and the *state* parameter specifies its initial state, *true* for checked, *false* for unchecked.

You can also add an existing checkbox to a group using the *Checkbox* class *setCheckboxGroup* method, the format of which is as follows:

```
void setCheckboxGroup(CheckboxGroup g);
```

Therefore, you can create a *CheckboxGroup* and add a checkbox to the group by performing these steps:

```
CheckboxGroup group = new CheckboxGroup();
CheckBox box = new CheckBox();

box.setLabel("label");
box.setCheckboxGroup(g);
box.setState(true);
```

The following applet, *optionbutton.java*, illustrates the use of option buttons. When you compile and execute this program, your screen will display the buttons shown in Figure 497:

```
import java.applet.*;
import java.awt.*;

public class optionbutton extends Applet {

    CheckboxGroup group = new CheckboxGroup();
    Checkbox option_a = new Checkbox("apple");
    Checkbox option_b = new Checkbox("orange");
    Checkbox option_c = new Checkbox("banana");

    public void init() {
        option_a.setCheckboxGroup(group);
        option_b.setCheckboxGroup(group);
        option_c.setCheckboxGroup(group);
        add(option_a);
        add(option_b);
        add(option_c);
    }
}
```

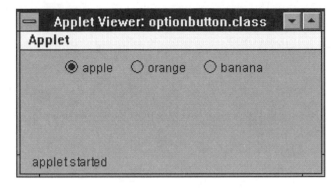

Figure 497 Displaying option buttons.

Take time to experiment with this applet. As you will find, when your applet uses option buttons, the user can only select only one button at any given time.

GETTING CHECKBOXGROUP (OPTION BUTTON) STATES

 498

When your applet uses option buttons, there will be times when you need to find out which option button the user has selected. As you have learned, one way to determine a button's state is to use the *Checkbox* class *getState* method (which you saw in Tip 495). However, to use the *getState* button to determine which button is checked, your program must examine each button's state, one by one. Another way to get the selected option button is to use the *CheckboxGroup* class *getCurrent* method, which returns the selected *Checkbox* object, as shown:

```
Checkbox getCurrent();
```

The following applet, *optionbutton_test.java*, illustrates the use of the *getCurrent* method to determine the *Checkbox* object that is currently selected:

```
import java.applet.*;
import java.awt.*;

public class optionbutton_test extends Applet {

    CheckboxGroup group = new CheckboxGroup();
    Checkbox option_a = new Checkbox("apple");
    Checkbox option_b = new Checkbox("orange");
    Checkbox option_c = new Checkbox("banana");

    Button button = new Button("Enter");

    public void init()
      {
        option_a.setCheckboxGroup(group);
        option_b.setCheckboxGroup(group);
        option_c.setCheckboxGroup(group);
```

```
        add(option_a);
        add(option_b);
        add(option_c);
        add (button);
    }


    public boolean action(Event evt, Object arg)
    {
        if (evt.target == button)
        {
            if (group.getCurrent() != null)
            {
                System.out.println ("selection = " +
                    group.getCurrent().getLabel());
            }
            return true;     // event processed
        }
        return false;          // event not processed
    }
}
```

499 CREATING A TEXTFIELD

There will be many times when you need to ask for information. For example, you may ask for the user's phone number or e-mail address. When your programs need to get a single line of text from the user, you can use a *TextField* class. To create a *TextField* class, you can use one of the following *TextField* constructor methods:

```
TextField();
TextField(int cols);
TextField(String text);
TextField(String text, int cols);
```

The *cols* parameter specifies the number of visible columns Java displays within the text field. The text parameter specifies a field's initial (default) text. The following applet, *text_field.java*, creates the *TextField* shown in Figure 499:

```
import java.applet.*;
import java.awt.*;

public class text_field extends Applet {

    Label label = new Label("Phone no.");
    TextField text_entry = new TextField(15);
    Button button = new Button("Enter");

    public void init()
    {
        add(label);
```

```
        add(text_entry);
        add(button);
    }

    public boolean action(Event evt, Object arg)
    {
        if (evt.target == button)
        {
            System.out.println("phone no = " +
               text_entry.getText());
            return true;     // event processed
        }
      return false;          // event not processed
    }
}
```

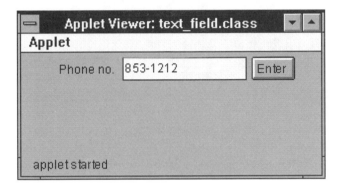

Figure 499 A TextField entry within an applet window.

As you can see, to get the text the user types into the *TextField*, you use the *TextComponent* class *getText* method. The *text_field.java* applet uses the *getText* method to get and display the text the user enters. When the user presses the ENTER button, Java returns the user entered text.

USING A TEXT FIELD FOR PASSWORD ENTRY (SETECHOCHARACTER)   500

By default, as a user types text into a *TextField*, Java displays each character the user types within the field. If the text entry the user is typing is a password, you will want to hide the typed text from prying eyes. In such cases, you can use the *TextComponent* class *setEchoCharacter* method to turn off the echo character. The format of the *setEchoCharacter* method is as follows:

```
setEchoCharacter(char c);
```

The method's *c* parameter specifies a character that Java displays for each character the user types. In many cases, programs will display the asterisk character, as shown:

```
TextField tf;
tf.setEchoCharacter('*');
```

501 DETECTING THE <ENTER> KEY IN A TEXTFIELD

Within your applets, there will be times when your program must respond as soon as the user hits the ENTER key after typing text within a *TextField*. In such cases, your program can intercept the ENTER key's event by overriding the *action* method. The following applet, *textfield_return.java*, echoes the typed text to the console window as soon as the user presses ENTER:

```java
import java.applet.*;
import java.awt.*;

public class textfield_return extends Applet {

    TextField text_entry = new TextField(20);

    public void init()
      {
        add(text_entry);
      }

    public boolean action(Event evt, Object arg)
      {
        if (evt.target instanceof TextField)
          {
              System.out.println(text_entry.getText());
            return true;   // event processed
          }
        return false;        // event not processed
      }
 }
```

As you can see, within the *action* method, the program uses the *getText* method to get the *TextField's* current contents.

502 CREATING A TEXTAREA

The *TextField* class is ideal when your applet needs to get a single line of text. When your program requires multiple lines of input, you can use the *TextArea* class. To create a *TextArea* object, you can use one of the following *TextArea* constructor methods:

```java
TextArea();
TextArea(int rows, int cols);
TextArea(String text);
TextArea(String text, int rows, int cols);
```

The *rows* and *cols* parameters specify the number of visible rows and columns Java displays within the *TextArea*. The *text* field specifies the initial text in the *TextArea*. The following applet, *text_area.java*, creates the *TextArea*, as shown in Figure 502:

```
import java.applet.*;
import java.awt.*;

public class text_area extends Applet {

    TextArea text_entry = new TextArea(5, 30);
    Button button = new Button("Enter");

    public void init()
      {
        add(text_entry);
        add(button);
      }

    public boolean action(Event evt, Object arg)
      {
        if (evt.target == button)
          {
              System.out.println(text_entry.getText());
             return true;   // events processed
          }
        return false;        // events not processed
      }
  }
```

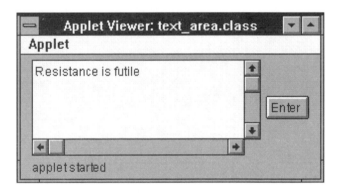

*Figure 502 A **TextArea** entry within an applet window.*

To get the text the user has typed into the *TextArea*, your program uses the *TextComponent* class *getText* method. In this case, the *text_area.java* applet captures the ENTER key to trigger its processing, and then uses the *getText* method to get the text, which it then displays.

INSERTING TEXT IN THE TEXTAREA  503

When your program uses *TextArea* fields, there may be times when you need to insert text into the *TextArea's* current contents. In such cases, you can use the *TextArea* class *insertText* method, the format of which is as follows:

```
void insertText(String str, int pos);
```

The *str* parameter specifies the text you want to insert within the *TextArea*. The *pos* parameter specifies the zero-based offset within the *TextArea's* current text. For example, the following statement inserts the text "Java" into the *TextArea* object, *text_entry*, at offset 6:

```
text_entry.insertText("Java", 6);
```

504 APPENDING TEXT TO A TEXTAREA

When your program uses *TextArea* fields, there may be times when you must append text to the end of the *TextArea's* current text. In such cases, you use the *TextArea* class *appendText* method. The following applet, *text_append.java*, counts the number of uppercase and lowercase characters in a *TextArea* field and then appends the result to the end of field using the *appendText* method to produce the output shown in Figure 504:

```java
import java.applet.*;
import java.awt.*;

public class text_append extends Applet {

    TextArea text_entry = new TextArea(5, 30);
    Button button = new Button("Count");

    public void init()
      {
         add(text_entry);
         add(button);
      }

    public boolean action(Event evt, Object arg)
      {
         String str;
         int upper, lower;

         if (evt.target == button)
           {
              str = text_entry.getText();
              upper = lower = 0;

              for (int i = 0; i < str.length(); i++)
                {
                   if (Character.isUpperCase(str.charAt(i)))
                     upper++;

                   if (Character.isLowerCase(str.charAt(i)))
                      lower++;
                }

              text_entry.appendText("\n*** " + upper + " upper and " +
                 lower + " lower ***");
              return true;                    // event processed
           }
         return false;                    // event not processed
      }
  }
```

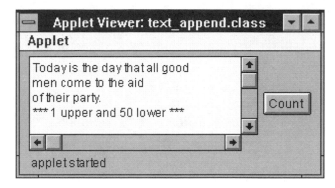

*Figure 504 An applet illustrating the **appendText** method.*

REPLACING TEXT IN A TEXTAREA

505

When your program uses a *TextArea*, there may be times when you need to replace the *TextArea's* text. To replace text within the *TextArea*, you use the *TextArea* class *replaceText*. The format of the *replaceText* method is as follows:

```
void replaceText(String str, int start, int end);
```

The following applet, *text_replace.java*, replaces all lowercase characters in a *TextArea* with uppercase letters when the user presses the Replace button:

```java
import java.applet.*;
import java.awt.*;

public class text_replace extends Applet {

    TextArea text_entry = new TextArea(5, 30);
    Button button = new Button("Replace");

    public void init()
      {
         add(text_entry);
         add(button);
      }

    public boolean action(Event evt, Object arg)
      {
         String str;

         if (evt.target == button)
           {
              str = text_entry.getText();
              for (int i = 0; i < str.length(); i++)
                {
                   if (Character.isLowerCase(str.charAt(i)))
                     {
                        text_entry.replaceText(
```

```
                        String.valueOf(
                            str.charAt(i)).toUpperCase(),i, i+1);
                }
            }
        return true;    // event processed
        }
    return false;       // event not processed
    }
}
```

506 UNDERSTANDING THE TEXTCOMPONENT CLASS

In previous tips, you learned how to get text the user has typed into a *TextField* or *TextArea* object using the *TextComponent* class *getText* method. Your applet can call the *getText* method because both *TextField* and *TextArea* are subclasses of the *TextComponent* class. In addition to the *getText* method, the *TextComponent* class provides methods for selecting text, getting the contents of the selected text, turning text editing on or off, and so on. The next few tips will show you how to use these methods within a *TextArea*.

507 GETTING SELECTED TEXT

As you have learned in previous tips, your applets can get text input using *TextField* and *TextArea* objects. If you want to enhance the text editing capability in these graphical-user interfaces, you can use one of the many editing methods you will find in the *TextComponent* class. For example, the *getSelectedText* method lets you get the selected text in a *TextField* or a *TextArea*. The following applet, *selected_text.java*, illustrates the use of the *getSelectedText* method to get the selected text from the applet window when the user presses a button:

```
import java.applet.*;
import java.awt.*;

public class selected_text extends Applet {

    TextArea text_entry = new TextArea(5, 30);
    Button button = new Button("Get text");

    public void init()
    {
        add(text_entry);
        add(button);
    }

    public boolean action(Event evt, Object arg)
    {
        if (evt.target instanceof Button)
        {
            System.out.println("selected text:" +
                text_entry.getSelectedText());
```

```
            return true;       // event processed
        }
        return false;          // event not processed
    }
}
```

Compile and run this applet. Next, type text into the *TextArea*, then highlight some of the text and press the Get Text button. Take time to experiment with this applet, selecting different text and then pressing the Get Text button.

GETTING TEXT SELECTION POSITION

508

In Tip 507, you learned that your applet can get user-selected text from a *TextField* or *TextArea* using the *getSelectedText* method. In addition, your applet can also find the position of the selected text by using the *TextComponent* class *getSelectionStart* and *getSelectionEnd* methods, whose formats are as follows:

```
int getSelectionStart();
int getSelectionEnd();
```

The *getSelectionStart* method returns the starting offset of the selected text within the current field. Likewise, the *getSelectionEnd* method returns one character position past the end of the selected text.

SELECTING TEXT

509

In Tip 507, you learned how to get selected text using the *getSelectedText* method. Normally, the end user selects the text within a *TextField* or *TextArea* field. In some cases, however, you may want the applet to select the text itself. To select text within a *TextField* or *TextArea*, you can use the *TextComponent* class *select* method, the format of which is as follows:

```
void select(int selStart, int selEnd);
```

The *selStart* and *selEnd* parameters specify the selected text's starting and ending positions. The following applet, *select_text.java*, shown in Figure 509, lets the user find a string in the *TextArea*. If the applet successfully locates the text, the applet will use the *select* method to highlight the text:

```
import java.applet.*;
import java.awt.*;

public class select_text extends Applet {

    TextArea   text_entry = new TextArea(5, 40);
    TextField find_entry = new TextField(20);
    Button button = new Button("Find");

    public void init()
      {
        add(text_entry);
        add(find_entry);
        add(button);
      }
```

```
    public boolean action(Event evt, Object arg)
    {
      if (evt.target instanceof Button)
       {
          String find_str = find_entry.getText();
          int index =
             text_entry.getText().indexOf(find_str);

          if (index >= 0)
           {
              text_entry.select(index, index +
                find_str.length());
              text_entry.requestFocus();
           }

          return true;   // events processed
       }
     return false; // events not processed
    }
 }
```

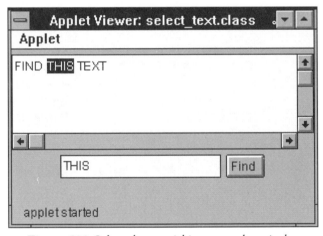

Figure 509 *Selected text within an applet window.*

510 ALLOWING AND DISALLOWING TEXT EDITING

In previous tips, you learned that both the *TextField* and *TextArea* objects let users edit a text field. Depending on your program's purpose, there may be times when you don't want the user to edit the field's text. In such cases, you can use the *TextComponent* class *setEditable* method to prevent the user from editing a field—making the field read-only. The following statement illustrates the format of the *setEditable* method:

```
void setEditable(boolean t);
```

To let the user edit the *TextField* or *TextArea* object, invoke the *setEditable* method with the value *true*. To prevent the user from editing the field, pass the value *false* to the function. Before you change a field's state, you should save the field's current state so your program can later restore the setting. To determine the field's current editing state, you can call the *isEditable* method, as shown:

```
boolean isEditable();
```

The *isEditable* method returns the value *true* if the field is editable and *false* if it is not.

CREATING A SCROLLING LIST

 511

As you know, you can provide users with a series of choices using option buttons. The option button interface is fine for a short list of choices, but as the number of items increases, you may find a scrollable list more appropriate. To create a *List* object within your applet, you can use one of the following *List* constructor methods:

```
List();
List(int rows, boolean multipleSelections);
```

The *rows* parameter specifies the number of visible rows of list options. The *multipleSelections* parameter specifies whether the user can select more than one item at a time. After you create a *List* object, you can add the object to the applet window using the *Container* class *add* method. The following applet, *list_test.java*, creates a list with five rows of visible lines that currently contains no entries:

```
import java.applet.*;
import java.awt.*;

public class list_test extends Applet {

   List  list = new List(5, false);

   public void init()
     {
        add(list);
     }
 }
```

ADDING ITEMS TO A LIST

 512

In Tip 511, you learned how to create a scroll list within your programs. After your program creates a *List* object, you add items to the object using one of the following *addItem* methods:

```
void addItem(String item);
void addItem(String item, int index);
```

The first *addItem* method appends the new item to the end of the list. The second form of the *addItem* method lets you specify the item's location within the list. The following applet, *list_add.java*, inserts ten items into a list, producing the screen shown in Figure 512:

```
import java.applet.*;
import java.awt.*;

public class list_add extends Applet {
```

```
    List list = new List(5, false);

    public void init()
      {
          for (int i = 0; i < 10; i++)
              list.addItem(String.valueOf(i));

          add (list);
      }
   }
```

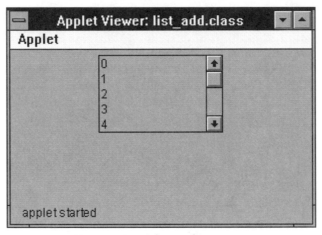

Figure 512 A list with 10 items.

513 GETTING A SELECTED ITEM FROM A LIST

When your programs work with *List* objects, your programs will need to determine which item in the *List* object is selected. To determine which list item is selected, you must use either the *List* class *getSelectedIndex* method or the *getSelectedItem* method, whose formats are as follows:

```
   int getSelectedIndex();
   String getSelectedItem();
```

The *getSelectedIndex* method returns the zero-based index of the selected item. The *getSelectedItem* method returns the selected item itself. For example, suppose the fifth item in a list contains the string "Java program." When the user selects the fifth item, the *getSelectedIndex* will return the value 4. Likewise, the *getSelectedItem* will return "Java program." The following applet, *selected_list.java*, illustrates the use of these two methods by displaying the selected item to the console window each time the user presses the Select button:

```
   import java.applet.*;
   import java.awt.*;

   public class selected_list extends Applet {

       String items[] = {"apple","banana","grape","pineapple","orange"};
```

```
   List list = new List(4, false);

   Button button = new Button("Select");

   public void init()
     {
        for(int i = 0; i < items.length; i++)
          list.addItem(items[i]);

        add(list);
        add(button);
     }

   public boolean action(Event evt, Object arg)
     {
        if (evt.target instanceof Button)
          {
             System.out.println("item " +
               list.getSelectedIndex() +
               " '" + list.getSelectedItem() + "' selected");

             return true; // event processed
          }
        return false;     // event not processed
     }
}
```

SELECTING MULTIPLE ITEMS IN A LIST  514

In Tip 513, you created a list that lets the user select only one item at a time. If your program needs to let the user select multiple items from a list, you use the *List* class *setMultipleSelections* method. Alternatively, you can allow multiple list selections using the *List* constructor (setting the *multipleSelections* parameter to *true*), as shown:

```
List(int rows, boolean multipleSelections);
```

Because the user can select more than one list item, you can no longer use the *getSelectedIndex* and the *getSelectedItem* methods you examined in Tip 513. Instead, you must use the *getSelectedIndexes* and the *getSelectedItems* methods. The following applet, *multi_list.java*, modifies the *selected_list.java* applet that you created in Tip 513, allowing the list to support multiple selections:

```
import java.applet.*;
import java.awt.*;

public class multi_list extends Applet {

    String items[] = {"apple","banana","grape","pineapple","orange"};
```

```
List list = new List(4, false);
Button button = new Button("Select");

public void init()
  {
     list.setMultipleSelections(true);
     for(int i = 0; i < items.length; i++)
        list.addItem(items[i]);

     add(list);
     add(button);
  }


public boolean action(Event evt, Object arg)
  {
     if (evt.target instanceof Button)
       {
         for(int i = 0;
             i < list.getSelectedIndexes().length; i++)
           System.out.println("item " +
             list.getSelectedIndexes()[i] +
             " '" + list.getSelectedItems()[i] +
            "' selected");

         return true;      // event processed
       }
     return false;          // event not processed
  }
}
```

515 HANDLING LIST ITEM SELECTION EVENTS

When your program works with a list of items, there may be times when you will want to detect when the user clicks on a list item. To detect the list operation, you must set up an event handler that handles the *List* events. As it turns out, Java generates a *LIST_SELECT* event when a user selects a list item. Likewise, Java generates a *LIST_DESELECT* event when the user deselects a list item. You can intercept these events by overriding the *handleEvent* method. Add the following *handleEvent* method to the *list_add.java* applet you created in Tip 512 to detect list events:

```
public boolean handleEvent(Event evt)
  {
    if (evt.target instanceof List)
      {
        if (evt.id == Event.LIST_DESELECT)
          System.out.println("item " + evt.arg + "deselected");

        if (evt.id == Event.LIST_SELECT)
          System.out.println("item " + evt.arg + "selected");
```

```
            return true;    // event processed
        }
    return false;           // event not processed
    }
```

The *Event* object *id* field indicates whether the item is selected or deselected, and the *Event* object *arg* field contains the index of the selected or deselected item.

REMOVING ITEMS FROM A LIST

 516

When your programs work with *List* objects, there may be times when you must remove one or more items from a list. To help you remove items from a list, the *List* class provides the methods listed in Table 516.

Method	Purpose
clear()	Removes all items from the list
delItem(int position)	Removes a specified item from the list
delItems(int start, int end)	Removes the list items with the specified range

Table 516 List object methods to remove items from a list.

For example, the following statement removes the third item from a list:

```
my_list.delItem(2);
```

Note again that the Java *List* objects use zero-based indexing.

REPLACING ITEMS IN A LIST

 517

In the previous tips, you have learned how to add and remove items from a *List* object. Depending on your program's purpose, there may be times when you will want to replace one list item with another. To replace a list item, you use the *List* class *replaceItem* method, the format of which is as follows:

```
void replaceItem(String newValue, int index);
```

The *newValue* parameter specifies the new list item and the *index* parameter specifies the *List* position of the item to be replaced. The following applet, *list_replace.java*, lets users replace selected items with a specified string, as shown in Figure 517:

```
import java.applet.*;
import java.awt.*;

public class list_replace extends Applet {

    String items[] =
{"apple","banana","grape","pineapple","orange"};

    List list = new List(4, false);

    TextField text_entry = new TextField(10);
```

```
Button button = new Button("Replace");

public void init()
  {
    for (int i = 0; i < items.length; i++)
        list.addItem(items[i]);

    add(list);
    add(text_entry);
    add(button);
  }

public boolean action(Event evt, Object arg)
   {
     if (evt.target instanceof Button)
       {
           if (list.getSelectedIndex() >= 0)
              list.replaceItem(text_entry.getText(),
                 list.getSelectedIndex());

           return true;                  // event processed
       }

     return false;                       // event not processed
   }
}
```

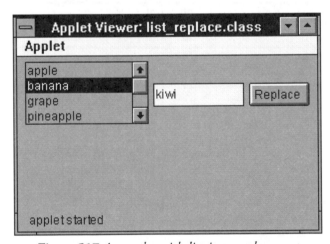

Figure 517 An applet with list item replacement.

518 GETTING ALL ITEMS IN A LIST

In previous tips, you learned that you can add and remove list items dynamically. To change list items intelligently, however, you need to know what items are in the list. To start, you can use the *countItems* method to determine the number of items in the list. Then, you can use the *getItem* method to get the string for each item in the list, one item at a time. The following code segment, for example, displays all items in a list to the console window:

```
List list;

for (int i = 0; i < list.countItems(); i++)
    System.out.println(list.getItem(i));
```

SETTING SELECTED ITEMS IN A LIST FROM THE PROGRAM

When your program works with a *List* object, there may be times when your program must select an item in a list. For example, you may want your program to set a default selection for the list. To select a list item, you use the *List* class *select* method, as shown:

```
void select(int index);
```

In the case where some of the list items are not visible, you can force the list to scroll to the selected item by using the *makeVisible* method:

```
void makeVisible(int index);
```

The following applet, *find_item.java*, lets the user find an item in the list. If the specified item is found, the program selects it and scrolls the list window to make the selected item visible:

```java
import java.applet.*;
import java.awt.*;

public class find_item extends Applet {

    String items[] = {"apple","banana","grape","pineapple",
        "orange","peach"};

    List list = new List(4, false);

    TextField text_entry = new TextField(10);
    Button button = new Button("Find");

    public void init()
      {
        for(int i=0; i<items.length; i++)
            list.addItem(items[i]);

        add(list);
        add(text_entry);
        add(button);
      }

    public boolean action(Event evt, Object arg)
      {
        if (evt.target instanceof Button)
```

```
        {
            for (int i = 0; i < items.length; i++)
                if (text_entry.getText().equals(items[i]))
                {
                    list.select(i);
                    list.makeVisible(i);
                }

            return true;    // event processed
        }
        return false;       // event not processed
    }
}
```

520 DETECTING DOUBLE-CLICKING ON A LIST ITEM

In Tip 515, you learned how to detect when a user selects or deselects a list item by overloadinng the *handleEvent* method. In addition to the *LIST_SELECT* and *LIST_DESELECT* events, Java also generates an action event when the user double-clicks a list item. Add the following code to the *list_add.java* applet that you created in Tip 515 to implement an event handler that captures the list item double-clicking event:

```
public boolean action(Event evt, Object arg)
  {
    if (evt.target instanceof List)
      {
          System.out.println("double click on " + arg);
          return true;        // event processed
      }

   return false;              // event not processed
   }
```

The *action* method's second parameter, *arg*, contains the label string of the double-clicked item.

521 CREATING A POP-UP CHOICE MENU

A pop-up menu is a menu that an applet displays on the screen on an "as needed basis." As it turns out, within your Java applet, the processing for a pop-up menu is similar to the processing for *List* objects. The difference between list interfaces and pop-up menus is that Java only displays a selected menu item until the user clicks on the menu and its options pop-up. To create a pop-up menu, your applets use a *Choice* object. To create a *Choice* object, you use the following *Choice* constructor method:

```
Choice();
```

Next, to display the *Choice* object on your screen, you use the *Container* class *add* method. The following applet, *choice_test.java*, creates a pop-up menu that contains six items, as shown in Figure 521:

```
import java.applet.*;
import java.awt.*;

public class choice_test extends Applet {

    String items[] = {"apple","banana","grape",
                      "pineapple","orange","peach"};

    Choice choice = new Choice();

    public void init()
      {
        for (int i = 0; i < items.length; i++)
          choice.addItem(items[i]);

        add(choice);
      }
}
```

The *Choice* object is initially empty, so you will need to add items to it using the *addItem* method, just as you did for the *List* interface.

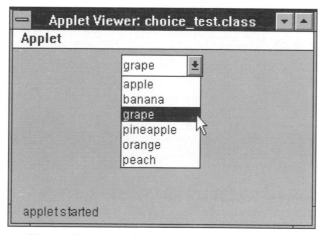

Figure 521 An applet with a pop-up choice menu.

GETTING A SELECTED ITEM FROM A POP-UP CHOICE MENU  522

As you remember, to get a choice from a *List* object, you use either the *getSelectedIndex* or the *getSelectedItem* method. Conveniently, you also use *getSelectedIndex* or *getSelectedItem* to determine which item in a pop-up choice menu is selected, as shown:

```
int getSelectedIndex();
String getSelectedItem();
```

The *getSelectedIndex* method returns the zero-based index of the selected item, and the *getSelectedItem* method returns the selected item's string. The following applet, *selected_choice.java*, illustrates the use of these two methods by displaying the selected item to the console window when the user presses the Select button:

```java
import java.applet.*;
import java.awt.*;

public class selected_choice extends Applet {

    String items[] = {"apple","banana","grape",
                         "pineapple","orange","peach"};

    Choice choice = new Choice();
    Button button = new Button("Select");

    public void init()
      {
        for(int i = 0; i < items.length; i++)
          choice.addItem(items[i]);

        add(choice);
        add(button);
      }

    public boolean action(Event evt, Object arg)
      {
        if (evt.target instanceof Button)
         {
            System.out.println("item " + choice.getSelectedIndex() +
              " '" + choice.getSelectedItem() + "' selected");
            return true;      // event processed
         }
        return false;         // event not processed
      }
}
```

523 HANDLING CHOICE EVENTS

When your program uses *Choice* objects to create a pop-up menu, there may be times when you need to know each time the user selects a different menu item. In such cases, you must set up an event handler to handle the event Java generates when a user selects an option. You can intercept the events by overriding the *action* method. Add the following *action* method to the *choice_test.java* applet that you created in Tip 521 to detect choice events:

```java
public boolean action(Event evt, Object arg)
  {
    if (evt.target instanceof Choice)
     {
        System.out.println("item " +  arg + " selected");
        return true;       // event processed
     }
    return false;          // event not processed
  }
```

The *action* method's second parameter, *arg*, contains the label for the selected choice item.

MORE ON USING THE FLOWLAYOUT

As you have learned, Java's AWT uses a layout manager to arrange components within the applet window. By default, the layout manager uses a *FlowLayout* object, which (by default) aligns the components in a row and centers them within the window. If your program requires a different alignment, you can create a *FlowLayout* object using an alignment parameter within one of the following constructor methods:

```
FlowLayout();
FlowLayout(int align);
FlowLayout(int align, int hgap, int vgap);
```

The *align* parameter specifies the component alignment: *FlowLayout.LEFT*, *FlowLayout.CENTER*, or *FlowLayout.RIGHT*, and specifies the horizontal alignment of components. The *hgap* and *vgap* parameters specify the horizontal and vertical gap spacing in pixels between components. The following applet, *flow_test.java*, places ten buttons in an applet window with a left-aligned *FlowLayout*, as shown in Figure 524:

```java
import java.applet.*;
import java.awt.*;

public class flow_test extends Applet {

    String items[] = {"one", "two", "three", "four", "five",
                        "six", "seven", "eight", "nine", "ten"};

    Button button[] = new Button[10];

    public void init()
      {
         setLayout(new FlowLayout(FlowLayout.LEFT));
       for (int i = 0; i < items.length; i++)
         {
            button[i] = new Button(items[i]);
            add(button[i]);
         }
      }
}
```

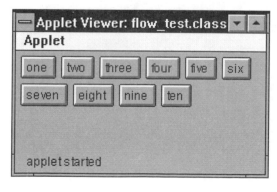

Figure 524 A left-aligned FlowLayout object.

525 USING THE BORDERLAYOUT TO MANAGE THE SCREEN LAYOUT

As you have learned, Java supports several different layouts that control how Java displays components within the applet window. The *BorderLayout* arranges components along the sides and at the center of the container. Java refers to these five areas as "*North*", "*South*", "*East*", "*West*", and "*Center*", as shown in Figure 525:

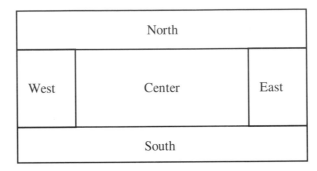

Figure 525 *Java's* **BorderLayout**.

Java lays out the "*North*", "*South*", "*East*", and "*West*" areas based on the size of their components. The "*Center*" area, in turn, gets the remaining space. To add components to the *BorderLayout*, you use the *Container* class *add* method, the format of which is as follows:

```
Component add(String name, Component comp);
```

For example, the following statement adds a button labeled "One" to the "*North*" side of the *BorderLayout*:

```
add("North", new Button("One"));
```

526 ADDING GAPS BETWEEN COMPONENTS IN A BORDERLAYOUT

By default, Java's *BorderLayout* does not leave any space between components. To add "gap" spacing between the components, your applets can use the following form of the *BorderLayout* constructor:

```
BorderLayout(int hgap, int vgap);
```

The *hgap* and *vgap* parameters specify the horizontal- and vertical-gap spacing (in pixels) between components. Figure 526 shows the difference between a *BorderLayout* with no gap spacing and one that uses 30 pixels of horizontal spacing and 10 pixels of vertical spacing:

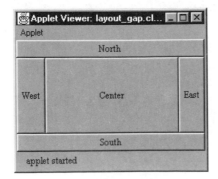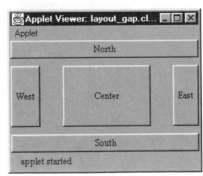

Figure 526 BorderLayouts *with and without gap spacing.*

USING GRIDLAYOUT

As you have learned, Java supports several different layouts that control how Java displays components within the applet window. The *GridLayout*, as its name implies, arranges components in a grid. You can create a *GridLayout* object using one of the following constructor methods:

```
GridLayout(int rows, int cols);
GridLayout(int rows, int cols, int hgap, int vgap);
```

The *rows* and *cols* parameters specify the number of rows and columns within the grid. Similar to the *BorderLayout* illustration in Tip 526, the *hgap* and *vgap* parameters specify the horizontal- and vertical-gap spacing (in pixels) between components. The following applet, *grid_test.java*, creates a *GridLayout* of 4 rows and 3 columns, as shown in Figure 527:

```
import java.applet.*;
import java.awt.*;

public class grid_test extends Applet {

    String items[] = {"one", "two", "three", "four", "five",
                      "six", "seven", "eight", "nine", "ten" };

    public void init()
      {
        setLayout(new GridLayout(3, 4));

        for(int i = 0; i < items.length; i++)
          add(new Button(items[i]));
      }
}
```

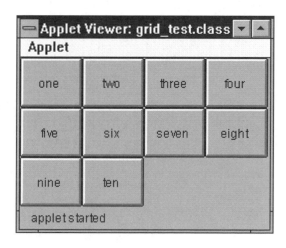

Figure 527 A 4-rows by 3-columns GridLayout

528 USING THE ADD METHOD TO ADD COMPONENTS TO A CONTAINER

As you have learned, you use the *add* method to add components to a container. In the *grid_test.java* applet that you created in the previous tip, the *add* method appends the component to the end of the layout. To insert a component to the middle of the container, you can use the following form of the *add* method:

```
synchronized Component add(Component comp, int pos);
```

The *pos* parameter specifies an index that corresponds to the new component's position. You can set the *pos* parameter to -1 to append the component to the end of the container. The following applet, *add_test.java*, creates ten buttons and arranges them using *GridLayout*. The applet's buttons differ from those in the *grid_test.java* applet that you created in the previous tip in that the applet inserts the last five buttons before the first five, as shown in Figure 528.

```java
import java.applet.*;
import java.awt.*;

public class add_test extends Applet {

    String items[] = {"one", "two", "three", "four", "five",
                      "six", "seven", "eight", "nine", "ten" };

    public void init()
      {
        setLayout(new GridLayout(3, 4));

        for (int i = 0; i < 5; i++)
           add(new Button(items[i]));

        for (int i = 0; i < 5; i++)
           add(new Button(items[i+5]), i);
      }
}
```

*Figure 528 An Applet illustrating component insertion using the **add** method.*

529 COMBINING MULTIPLE LAYOUTS TO CREATE YOUR USER INTERFACE

In previous tips, you learned that *Panels* act as a container for components such as buttons and labels. As it turns out, *Panels* can also be the container for other *Panels*, which lets you embed one layout inside another. For example, within a paint program, you can create a toolbar of drawing tools using a *GridLayout*. Then, you can place the toolbar on the "West" (left side) of the window using a *BorderLayout*.

The following applet, *multi_layout.java*, uses a *BorderLayout*. The applet places a *GridLayout* on the "West" side and a *FlowLayout* on the "South" side. Figure 529 displays the applet's output:

```java
import java.applet.*;
import java.awt.*;

public class multi_layout extends Applet {

    Panel west_panel = new Panel();
    Panel south_panel = new Panel();

    public void init()
      {
          setLayout(new BorderLayout());
          add("North", new Button("North"));
          add("East", new Button("East"));
          add("Center", new Button("Center"));

          west_panel.setLayout(new GridLayout(3,2));
          west_panel.add(new Button("Grid 1"));
          west_panel.add(new Button("Grid 2"));
          west_panel.add(new Button("Grid 3"));
          west_panel.add(new Button("Grid 4"));
          west_panel.add(new Button("Grid 5"));
          west_panel.add(new Button("Grid 6"));
          add("West", west_panel);

          south_panel.setLayout(new FlowLayout());
          south_panel.add(new Button("Flow 1"));
          south_panel.add(new Button("Flow 2"));
          south_panel.add(new Button("Flow 3"));
          south_panel.add(new Button("Flow 4"));
          add("South", south_panel);
      }
}
```

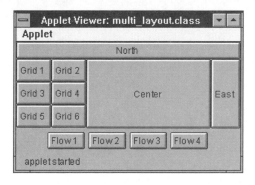

Figure 529 An Applet with multiple layout styles.

530 REMOVING COMPONENTS FROM A LAYOUT

When your applets work with component objects, there may be times when you want to remove a component from a layout. To delete an object from a layout, you can use the *Container* class *remove* and *removeAll* methods:

```
void remove(Component comp);
void removeAll();
```

The *remove* method removes a single component from the layout, whereas the *removeAll* method removes all components from the layout. The following applet, *remove_comp.java*, lets users add and remove buttons interactively. Figure 530 displays the applet's output:

```
import java.applet.*;
import java.awt.*;

public class remove_comp extends Applet {

    String items[] = {"one", "two", "three", "four", "five",
                      "six", "seven", "eight", "nine", "ten" };

    Button button[] = new Button[10];
    Panel center_panel = new Panel();
    int buttons_added = 0;

    public void init()
      {
         setLayout(new BorderLayout());
         Panel button_panel = new Panel();
         button_panel.add(new Button("Add"));
         button_panel.add(new Button("Remove"));
         button_panel.add(new Button("Remove all"));

         for(int i = 0; i < items.length; i++)
           button[i] = new Button(items[i]);

         add("Center", center_panel);
         add("South", button_panel);
      }

    public boolean action(Event evt, Object arg)
      {
        if (arg.equals("Add"))
         {
            if (buttons_added < items.length)
              {
                 center_panel.add("Center",
                   button[buttons_added++]);
                 center_panel.validate();
              }
            return true;
         }
```

```
        if (arg.equals("Remove"))
          {
            if (buttons_added > 0)
              {
                  center_panel.remove(button[-buttons_added]);
                  center_panel.validate();
              }
            return true;
          }

        if (arg.equals("Remove all"))
          {
             center_panel.removeAll();
             buttons_added = 0;
             return true;
          }
        return false; // events not processed
      }
  }
```

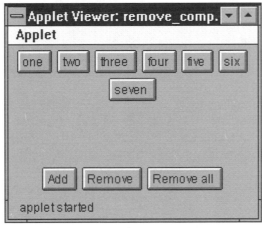

Figure 530 An Applet that allows adding and removing of components interactively.

USING CARDLAYOUT 531

If you are developing a program with a dialog box that contains pages of options, like the preference option dialog boxes in Netscape, you may want to use the *CardLayout*. The *CardLayout* lets users "flip" between multiple pages of displays, much like a stack of Rolodex cards, with only one page displayed at a time. To create a *CardLayout* object, your programs can use one of the following constructor methods:

```
CardLayout();
CardLayout(int hgap, int vgap);
```

The *hgap* and *vgap* parameters specify the horizontal- and vertical-gap spacing in pixels. Unlike other layouts, such as *BorderLayout*, Java only displays one *CardLayout* component at a time. The spacing specified, therefore, applies only to the gap between the displayed component and the border of the container.

To add components (that is, pages) to the *CardLayout*, you use the following form of the *Container* class *add* method:

```
Component add(String name, Component comp);
```

For example, the following statement adds a button to the page labeled Page 1 of the *CardLayout*:

```
add("Page 1", new Button("One"));
```

When you want your applet to switch to a new page, you use the *CardLayout* class *show* method, whose format is as follows:

```
void show(Container parent, String name);
```

The *parent* parameter specifies the parent container and the *name* parameter specifies the name of the component your applet is to display. For example, the following statements switch the display page to the component labeled "Page 1".

```
CardLayout card_layout;
Panel card_panel;
card_layout.show(card_panel, "Page 1");
```

The following applet, *card_test.java*, adds three display pages to a *CardLayout*, as shown in Figure 531. To flip between pages, use the command buttons:

```java
import java.applet.*;
import java.awt.*;

public class card_test extends Applet {

    CardLayout card_layout = new CardLayout();
    Panel card_panel = new Panel();
    Panel button_panel = new Panel();

    public void init()
      {
        setLayout(new BorderLayout());
        button_panel.add(new Button("Page 1"));
        button_panel.add(new Button("Page 2"));
        button_panel.add(new Button("Page 3"));
        add("North", button_panel);

        card_panel.setLayout(card_layout);
        card_panel.add("card 1", new Label("This is page 1"));
        card_panel.add("card 2", new Label("This is page 2"));
        card_panel.add("card 3", new Label("This is page 3"));
        add("Center", card_panel);
      }

    public boolean action(Event evt, Object arg)
      {
        if (evt.target instanceof Button)
          {
```

```
        if (arg.equals("Page 1"))
            card_layout.show(card_panel, "card 1");
        else if (arg.equals("Page 2"))
            card_layout.show(card_panel, "card 2");
        else if (arg.equals("Page 3"))
            card_layout.show(card_panel, "card 3");

        return true;          // event processed
        }
    return false;             // event not processed
    }
}
```

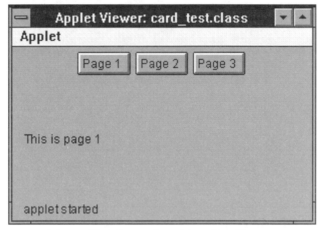

*Figure 531 An applet with a **CardLayout**.*

MORE ON FLIPPING THROUGH PAGES IN A CARDLAYOUT   532

In Tip 531, you learned that you can switch between pages in a *CardLayout* using the *show* method. In addition to the *show* method, the *CardLayout* class offers four other methods that let you navigate between pages. The *first* and *last* methods jump to (display) the first and last pages of the layout, respectively. Similarly, the *previous* and *next* methods flip to the previous and next pages. If you call the *previous* method when the first page is displayed, the display page will wrap around to the last page. Conversely, if you call the *next* method when the last page is displayed, the display page will wrap around to the first page. The following applet, *card_test2.java*, replaces the page buttons in the *card_test.java* applet of the previous tip with *first*, *prev*, *next*, and *last* buttons, as shown in Figure 532:

```
import java.applet.*;
import java.awt.*;

public class card_test2 extends Applet {

    CardLayout card_layout = new CardLayout();
    Panel card_panel = new Panel();
    Panel button_panel = new Panel();

    public void init()
      {
```

```
        setLayout(new BorderLayout());
        button_panel.add(new Button("First"));
        button_panel.add(new Button("Prev"));
        button_panel.add(new Button("Next"));
        button_panel.add(new Button("Last"));
        add("North", button_panel);

        card_panel.setLayout(card_layout);
        card_panel.add("card 1", new Label("This is page 1"));
        card_panel.add("card 2", new Label("This is page 2"));
        card_panel.add("card 3", new Label("This is page 3"));
        add("Center", card_panel);
    }

    public boolean action(Event evt, Object arg)
    {
        if (evt.target instanceof Button)
        {
            if (arg.equals("First"))
                card_layout.first(card_panel);
            else if (arg.equals("Prev"))
                card_layout.previous(card_panel);
            else if (arg.equals("Next"))
                card_layout.next(card_panel);
            else if (arg.equals("Last"))
                card_layout.last(card_panel);

            return true;      // event processed
        }
        return false;         // event not processed
    }
}
```

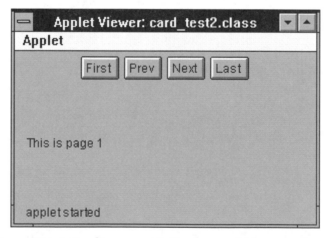

*Figure 532 A **CardLayout** with Previous and Next page buttons.*

UNDERSTANDING *GRIDBAGLAYOUT*

As you have learned, the *GridLayout* arranges components using a rectangular grid. However, all components in a *GridLayout* are set to the same size and cannot span over multiple rows or columns. To lay out components with different sizes, you can use the *GridBagLayout*, which is the most flexible layout in the AWT library, and also the most complicated one to use.

To use a *GridBagLayout*, you must first create a *GridBagLayout* object using the *GridBagLayout* constructor method. Then you must use the *setLayout* method to set the *GridBagLayout* as the layout manager:

```
GridBagLayout gb_layout = new GridBagLayout();
setLayout(gb_layout);
```

Next, you must create a *GridbagConstraints* object which contains numerous fields you use to specify the component's geometry and relationship with other components in the *GridBagLayout*. The tips that follow will examine the effect of each field in the *GridbagConstraints* class.

Then, you must set the *GridbagConstraints* fields, for each component in the *GridBagLayout* and apply them to the layout using the *SetConstraints* method, as shown:

```
void setConstraints(Component comp,
   GridBagConstraints constraints);
```

Last, you add the component itself to the container using the *add* method. The following program, *gridbag_test.java*, illustrates the use of the *GridBagLayout*. Figure 533 displays the program's output.

```
import java.applet.*;
import java.awt.*;

public class gridbag_test extends Applet {

    GridBagLayout gb_layout = new GridBagLayout();

    public void init()
      {
        GridBagConstraints constraints = new
          GridBagConstraints();

        setLayout(gb_layout);

        Label l1 = new Label("Label 1");
        constraints.gridx = 0;
        constraints.gridy = 0;
        constraints.gridwidth = 1;
        constraints.gridheight = 1;
        constraints.weightx = 0;
        constraints.weighty = 1;
         constraints.fill = GridBagConstraints.BOTH;
```

```java
            constraints.anchor = GridBagConstraints.CENTER;
            gb_layout.setConstraints(l1, constraints);
        add(l1);

        Button b1 = new Button("Button 1");
        constraints.gridx = 1;
        constraints.gridy = 0;
        constraints.weightx = 1;
         gb_layout.setConstraints(b1, constraints);
        add(b1);

        Button b2 = new Button("Button 2");
        constraints.gridx = 2;
        constraints.gridy = 0;
        constraints.gridwidth = 1;
        constraints.gridheight = 2;
         gb_layout.setConstraints(b2, constraints);
        add(b2);

        Label l2 = new Label("Label 2");
        constraints.gridx = 0;
        constraints.gridy = 1;
        constraints.gridwidth = 1;
        constraints.gridheight = 1;
        constraints.weightx = 0;
         gb_layout.setConstraints(l2, constraints);
        add(l2);

        Button b3 = new Button("Button 3");
        constraints.gridx = 1;
        constraints.gridy = 1;
        constraints.weightx = 1;
         gb_layout.setConstraints(b3, constraints);
        add(b3);

        TextField t1 = new TextField("Text Field 1");
        constraints.gridx = 0;
        constraints.gridy = 2;
        constraints.gridwidth = 4;
        constraints.gridheight = 1;
         constraints.fill = GridBagConstraints.HORIZONTAL;
         constraints.anchor = GridBagConstraints.CENTER;
         gb_layout.setConstraints(t1, constraints);
        add(t1);
    }
}
```

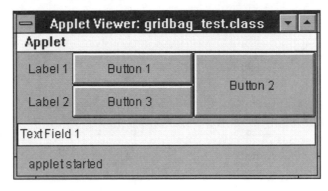

*Figure 533 An Applet with **GridBagLayout**.*

UNDERSTANDING THE GRIDBAGCONSTRAINTS FIELDS

534

As you have learned, the *GridBagConstraints* class fields define the location and size of a component in a *GridBagLayout*. The *GridBagConstraints* class *gridx* and *gridy* fields specify the row and column location of the component's upper-left corner. For example, a *gridx* value of 2 and *gridy* value of 1 specify a location at the third column and second row, as shown in Figure 534 (remember the components use zero-based indexing):

gridx = 2, gridy = 1

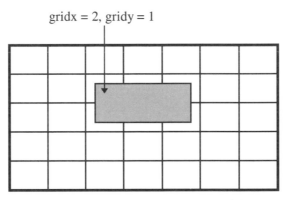

*Figure 534 Component placement with **gridx** = 2, **gridy** = 1, **gridwidth** = 3 and **gridheight** = 2.*

In addition to specifying an integer value for *gridx* and *gridy*, you can also set them to *GridBagConstraints.RELATIVE* which specifies that layout manager place a component at the right or just below the last added component.

The *GridBagConstraints* class *gridwidth* and *gridheight* fields specify the component's grid width and grid height. Figure 534 shows a component that uses a *gridwidth* of 3 and a *gridheight* of 2. When you specify the last component in a row or column, you can also set the *gridx* and *gridy* fields to *GridBagConstraints.REMAINDER* to tell the layout manager that the component should occupy the remaining grid rows or columns. In this case, you should also set the *gridwidth* and *gridheight* fields to *GridBagConstraints.RELATIVE* for the layout manager to place a component next to the last one in its column and row respectively.

UNDERSTANDING THE WEIGHTX AND WEIGHTY FIELDS

535

The *GridBagConstraints* class *weightx* and *weighty* fields specify how the layout manager distributes extra spaces are distributed among components. A larger weight value indicates a component will get a larger share of the space. A value of zero, the default setting, specifies that a component cannot get any extra spacing. If the weight fields of all components in a *GridBagLayout* object are zero, the *GridBagLayout* layout manager will place the components in a clump at the center of the container without stretching them. Figure 535 first shows the effects of setting all weight fields to zero, and then the effects of setting Button 1's weights to 1.

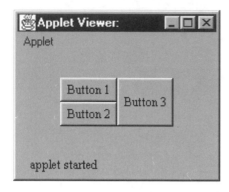 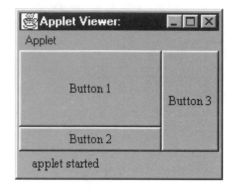

Figure 535 Layout with all button weights first set to 0, and layout with Button 1's weights set to 1.

536 UNDERSTANDING THE FILL FIELD IN GRIDBAGCONSTRAINTS

The *GridBagConstraints* class *fill* field specifies how the *GridBagLayout* layout manager should resize a component to fill the component's display area. You can assign the *fill* field any of the values specified in Table 536. Figure 536 shows the "fill button" component with no filling and vertical filling.

Setting	Result
GridBagConstraints.NONE	Do not resize to fill. This is the default setting.
GridBagConstraints.HORIZONTAL	Stretch to fill horizontally.
GridBagConstraints.VERTICAL	Stretch to fill vertically.
GridBagConstraints.BOTH	Stretch to fill both horizontally and vertically.

*Table 536 Values your applets can assign to the **GridBagConstraints** class **fill** field.*

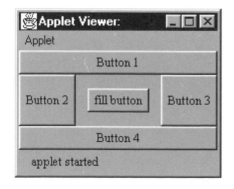 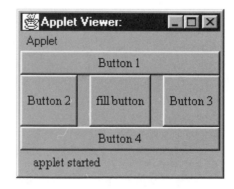

*Figure 536 The **fill button** with no filling and vertical filling in a **GridBagLayout**.*

UNDERSTANDING THE ANCHOR FIELD IN GRIDBAGCONSTRAINTS — 537

In Figure 536 of the previous tip, the layout manager positions the button labeled "fill button" at the center of its display area, and it does not fill the surrounding area up. That's because the layout manager sets the *GridBagConstraints* class *anchor* field to the default value that anchors the component to the center. The *GridBagConstraints* class *anchor* field specifies how the *GridBagLayout* layout manager should position a component inside the component's display area. You can assign the field any of the following settings:

GridBagConstraints.CENTER (the default)   GridBagConstraints.NORTH

GridBagConstraints.NORTHEAST   GridBagConstraints.EAST

GridBagConstraints.SOUTHEAST   GridBagConstraints.SOUTH

GridBagConstraints.SOUTHWEST   GridBagConstraints.WEST

GridBagConstraints.NORTHWEST

Figure 537 shows a component labeled "anchor" first set to center anchoring and then to southeast anchoring.

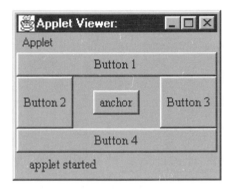 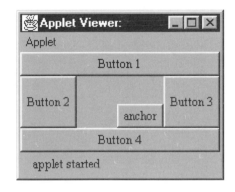

Figure 537 A Button with center anchoring and southeast anchoring within a GridBagLayout.

UNDERSTANDING THE IPADX AND IPADY FIELDS — 538

The *GridBagConstraints* class *ipadx* and *ipady* fields increase a component's size by adding internal padding to the component's width and height. Because the layout manager adds the specified padding to each side of the component, a *ipadx* value of 1 actually increases the component's width by 2 pixels. Figure 538 shows the same component, labeled "pad button", first with no padding, and then with its *ipadx* value set to 40 and its *ipady* value set to 30.

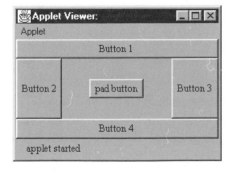 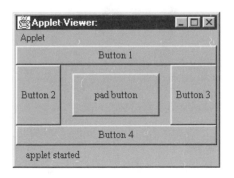

*Figure 538 A Button with no padding and a Button with its **ipadx** value set to 40 and its **ipady** value set to 30.*

539 UNDERSTANDING THE INSETS FIELD IN GRIDBAGCONSTRAINTS

The *GridBagConstraints* class *insets* field increases a component's display by adding external padding to the component. Unlike the *ipadx* and *ipady* fields that you learned about in Tip 538, the insets field does not increase the actual size of the component. Instead, it only increases the component's display area; that is, it increases the margins around the component. The *GridBagConstraints* class *insets* field is an *Insets* object which contains fields that let you specify top, bottom, left, and right spacing. Your applets assign the *Insets* object field values, as shown:

```
GridBagConstraints constraints;
constraints.insets.top = 10;
constraints.insets.bottom = 20;
constraints.insets.left = 5;
constraints.insets.right = 40;
```

Figure 539 shows the same component, labeled "pad button", with no padding and with the *insets* settings shown in the previous statements.

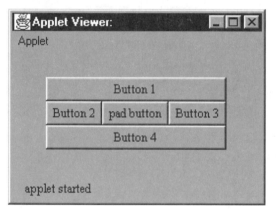 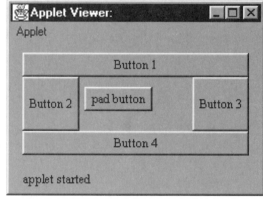

Figure 539 A Button with no insets padding and a Button with a top inset of 10, a bottom inset of 20, a left inset of 5, and a right inset of 40.

540 PLACING COMPONENTS WITHOUT USING A LAYOUT MANAGER

Several of the tips in this section have shown you how to use a layout manager to arrange components in a container. There may be times, however, when you want to place and size the components yourself. To place components without using any layout manager, your applets can use the *Container* class *setLayout* method to set the layout manager to null, as shown:

```
Panel panel_container;
panel_container.setLayout(null);
```

Because the layout manager will no longer position or size the component in the container, you can use the *Component* class *reshape* method to adjust the component's placement and dimension. The format of the *reshape* method is as follows:

```
void reshape(int x, int y, int width, int height);
```

The *x*- and *y*- parameters specify the component's location inside the container. Likewise, the *width* and *height* parameters specify the component's size. Alternatively, your applets can also use the *move* and *resize* methods to perform the same task. The format of the *move* and *resize* methods are as follows:

```
void move(int x, int y);
void resize(int width, int height);
void resize(Dimension d);
```

The following applet, *no_layout.java*, arranges its components without using a layout manager. Figure 540 displays the applet's output:

```
import java.applet.*;
import java.awt.*;

public class no_layout extends Applet {

    Button b1 = new Button("Button 1");
    Button b2 = new Button("Button 2");
    Button b3 = new Button("Button 3");

    public void init()
      {
        setLayout(null);
        add(b1);
        add(b2);
        add(b3);
        b1.reshape( 0, 0, 60, 30);
        b2.reshape(60,30, 60, 30);
        b3.reshape(120,60, 60, 30);
      }
}
```

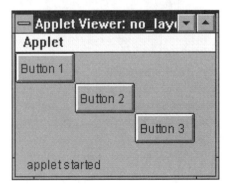

Figure 540 Component placement without using a layout manager.

CREATING A SCROLLBAR

541

In previous tips, you probably noticed the *TextArea* interface contains a horizontal and a vertical scroll bar that lets users scroll different areas of the text field into view. Within your applets, you can create standalone scroll bars using a *Scrollbar* object. To create a *Scrollbar* object, you can use one of the following *Scrollbar* constructor methods:

```
Scrollbar();
Scrollbar(int orientation);
Scrollbar(int orientation, int value, int visible, int minimum,
   int maximum);
```

To create a horizontal scroll bar, set the orientation parameter to *Scrollbar.HORIZONTAL*. Likewise, to create a vertical scrollbar, set the parameter to *Scrollbar.VERTICAL*. The *value, visible, minimum,* and *maximum* parameters set the scroll bar's initial position, page size, minimum value, and maximum value respectively. The following applet, *sbar.java*, creates the horizontal and a vertical scroll bar shown in Figure 541:

```
import java.applet.*;
import java.awt.*;

public class sbar extends Applet {

    Scrollbar horz_sb = new
Scrollbar(Scrollbar.HORIZONTAL,1,0,1,10);
    Scrollbar vert_sb = new Scrollbar(Scrollbar.VERTICAL,1,0,1,10);

    public void init()
      {
        setLayout(new BorderLayout());
        add("South", horz_sb);
        add("East", vert_sb);
      }
}
```

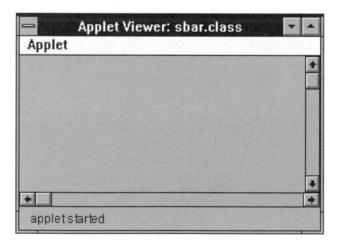

Figure 541 An applet with a horizontal and a vertical scrollbar.

542   USING SCROLLBAR EVENTS

Within your Java programs, you will normally want to detect whenever the user changes the scroll position. As it turns out, each time the user changes the scroll bar, Java generates an event. The following list briefly describes Java's scrollbar events:

- SCROLL_LINE_DOWN and SCROLL_LINE_UP events are generated when the user clicks on the arrow buttons.

- SCROLL_PAGE_UP and SCROLL_PAGE_DOWN events are generated when the user clicks on the area between the arrow buttons and the slider.

- SCROLL_ABSOLUTE events are generated when the user moves the slider to a new position.

You can intercept the action event by overriding the *handleEvent* method. You can add the following code segment to the program *sbar.java* that you created in Tip 541 to detect scrollbar events:

```
public boolean handleEvent(Event evt)
  {
    if (evt.target == vert_sb)
      {
        System.out.print(" Vertical Scroll bar ");

        switch(evt.id) {
          case Event.SCROLL_ABSOLUTE:
                      System.out.print(" moved ");
                      break;

          case Event.SCROLL_LINE_DOWN:
                      System.out.print(" scrolled down ");
                      break;
          case Event.SCROLL_LINE_UP:
                      System.out.print(" scrolled up ");
                      break;
          case Event.SCROLL_PAGE_DOWN:
                      System.out.print(" paged down ");
                      break;
          case Event.SCROLL_PAGE_UP:
                      System.out.print(" paged up ");
                      break;
        }
        System.out.println("to position " + evt.arg);
        return true;   // event processed
      }

    if (evt.target == horz_sb)
      {
        // processed the same way as vertical scroll bar
      }
    return false;         // event not processed
}
```

GETTING AND SETTING SCROLLBAR POSITION

543

Although in most cases the user will adjust the scrollbar position using the graphical-user interface, there may be times when your applet needs to set the scrollbar position itself. In such cases, your applet can use the *Scrollbar* class *setValue* method, using a parameter to specify the scrollbar block's position:

```
void setValue(int value);
```

Conversely, your applets can get the current scrollbar value by calling the *getValue* method. The following applet, *sbar_value.java*, illustrates the use of the *setValue* and *getValue* methods:

```java
import java.applet.*;
import java.awt.*;

public class sbar_value extends Applet {

    Scrollbar sbar = new
        Scrollbar(Scrollbar.HORIZONTAL,0,0,0,255);
    TextField text_entry = new TextField("0", 5);

    public void init()
    {
        setLayout(new GridLayout(1, 2));
        add(text_entry);
        add(sbar);
    }

    public boolean handleEvent(Event evt)
    {
        if (evt.target instanceof Scrollbar)
        {
            if ((evt.id == Event.SCROLL_ABSOLUTE)
                ||(evt.id == Event.SCROLL_LINE_DOWN)
                ||(evt.id == Event.SCROLL_LINE_UP)
                ||(evt.id == Event.SCROLL_PAGE_DOWN)
                ||(evt.id == Event.SCROLL_PAGE_UP))
                text_entry.setText(
                    String.valueOf(sbar.getValue()));

            return true;                      // event processed
        }
        return super.handleEvent(evt); // event not processed
    }

    public boolean action(Event evt, Object arg)
    {
        if (evt.target instanceof TextField)
        {
            int i = Integer.valueOf(
                text_entry.getText()).intValue();
            i = Math.max(0, Math.min(255, i));
            sbar.setValue(i);
            return true;                      // event processed
        }
        return false;                         // event not processed
    }
}
```

Within this applet, you can set the value of the scrollbar by entering an integer value between 0 and 255 in the *TextField*. When you adjust the value of the scrollbar, the applet will display the scrollbar's position within the *TextField*. Figure 543 displays the applet's output.

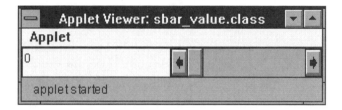

*Figure 543 An applet illustrating the use of the **setValue** and **getValue** methods.*

SETTING SCROLLBAR INCREMENTS

544

By default, when the user clicks the mouse on a scrollbar's arrow button, the scrollbar value increases or decreases by 1 line. When the user clicks on the area between the arrow buttons and the slider, the scrollbar value increases or decreases by 10 lines, which is the same as 1 page. To change the line increment, you can use the *Scrollbar* class *setLineIncrement* method, the format of which is as follows:

```
void setLineIncrement(int 1);
```

Likewise, to change the page increment, you can use the *Scrollbar* class *setPageIncrement* method, the format of which is as follows:

```
void setPageIncrement(int 1);
```

The following code segment, for example, sets a scrollbar's line increment to 5 and page increment to 40:

```
Scrollbar sbar;
sbar.setLineIncrement(5);
sbar.setPageIncrement(40);
```

SETTING NEW SCROLLBAR MAXIMUM AND MINIMUM VALUE

545

In Tip 541, you learned that you can create a scrollbar with specified minimum and maximum values using the *Scrollbar* constructor method:

```
Scrollbar(int orientation, int value, int visible, int minimum,
    int maximum);
```

However, there may be times when you need to change the minimum or maximum scroll value of an existing scrollbar. For example, users may look at drawings of various sizes, using scrollbars to move to different parts of a drawing. Because the size of the drawings may vary, your program should adjust the maximum scroll value for each image file. To change the scrollbar values, you can use the *Scrollbar* class *setValues* method, the format of which is as follows:

```
void setValues(int value, int visible, int minimum, int maximum);
```

The parameters of the *setValues* method are the same as the those defined in Tip 543 for the *Scrollbar* constructor.

546 USING THE CANVAS CLASS

Although your applets can draw directly to the applet's display area, it is often better to define a separate drawing area using a *Canvas* object. For example, assume you have a container that contains buttons and checkboxes that Java draws automatically. If you draw directly to the applet, you may draw over other AWT components or the components may overlap your drawing. The *Canvas* object, as its name implies, provides a canvas on which your applet can draw. To draw to the *Canvas* object, you must override the *paint* and *update* method. To do so, you should create a new class that extends the *Canvas* class. The following applet, *canvas_test.java*, illustrates how to create a subclass of *Canvas* and use it for drawing. Figure 546 illustrates the program's output:

```java
import java.applet.*;
import java.awt.*;

class drawing_canvas extends Canvas {
    public void paint (Graphics g) {
        g.setColor (Color.red);
        g.fillRect ( 10, 10, 50, 100);
        g.setColor (Color.blue);
        g.fillRect ( 30, 40, 100, 40);
        g.setColor (Color.yellow);
        g.fillRect ( 5,  60, 80,  30);
        g.setColor (Color.green);
        g.fillRect ( 100,50, 60,  60);
    }
}


public class canvas_test extends Applet {
    public void init()
      {
        setLayout (new BorderLayout());
        add("Center", new drawing_canvas());
        add("North", new Button("button"));
        add("South", new Button("button"));
        add("East", new Button("button"));
        add ("West", new Button("button"));
    }
}
```

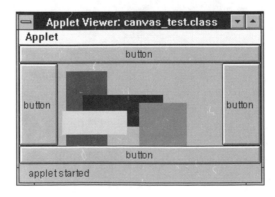

*Figure 546 Drawing on a **Canvas** subclass.*

As you know, many programs use scroll bars to help the user view documents that are too large to fit within the current viewing area. The following applet, *scroll_img.java*, uses a scroll bar to display a large image within the applet window:

```java
import java.applet.*;
import java.awt.*;
import java.net.*;

class ImgCanvas extends Canvas {

    Image canvas_image;
    int x_offset, y_offset;

    public ImgCanvas(Image img)
      {
        super();
        canvas_image = img;
        x_offset = y_offset = 0;
      }

    public void set_image_offset(int x, int y)
      {
        x_offset = x;
        y_offset = y;
        repaint();
      }

    public void paint(Graphics g)
      {
        g.drawImage(canvas_image, x_offset, y_offset, this);
      }
  }

public class scroll_img extends Applet {

    int image_width = 640;
    int image_height = 468;

    Scrollbar horz_sb = new Scrollbar(Scrollbar.HORIZONTAL);
    Scrollbar vert_sb = new Scrollbar(Scrollbar.VERTICAL);
    ImgCanvas image_canvas;

    public void init()
      {
        image_canvas = new ImgCanvas(getImage(getCodeBase(),
          "flower.jpg"));
        setLayout(new BorderLayout());
```

```
        add("South", horz_sb);
        add("East", vert_sb);
        add("Center", image_canvas);
    }


    public void start()
    {
        Dimension canvas_size = image_canvas.size();
        horz_sb.setValues(0, canvas_size.width, 0,
          image_width - canvas_size.width);
        vert_sb.setValues(0, canvas_size.height, 0,
          image_height-canvas_size.height);
    }


    public boolean handleEvent(Event evt)
    {
        if ((evt.target == vert_sb) ||
            (evt.target == horz_sb))
        {
            image_canvas.set_image_offset(
              -horz_sb.getValue(),-vert_sb.getValue());
            return true;                    // event processed
        }
        return false;                       // event not processed
    }
}
```

Figure 547 Displaying a scrollable image.

Figure 547 shows a screen shot of the applet's output. The image area is a subclass of *Canvas* and uses the *set_image_offset* method to specify the image area the applet displays. For simplicity, this applet hardcodes the size of the image. In later tips, you will learn how your applet can get an image size.

All of the AWT components, such as *Checkboxes* and *Buttons*, your applets create are initially enabled, which means the user can access the object on the screen. There may be times, however, when you want to disable an AWT component. To disable an AWT object, you use the *Component* class *disable* method. To enable a component, you use the *Component* class *enable* method. The following applet, *disable_test.java*, illustrates the use of these two methods. Figure 548 shows the program's output.

```java
import java.applet.*;
import java.awt.*;

public class disable_test extends Applet {

    Button button = new Button("Button");
    Checkbox cbox = new Checkbox("Enable button");

    public void init()
    {
        add(button);
        cbox.setState(true); // initialize to on
        add(cbox);
    }

    public boolean action(Event evt, Object arg)
    {
        if (evt.target instanceof Checkbox)
        {
            if (cbox.getState())
                button.enable();        // enable button
            else
                button.disable();       // disable button

            return true;                // event processed
        }
        return false;                   // event not processed
    }
}
```

In this case, the applet enables the button when the checkbox labeled Enable Button is checked, and disables (grays out) the button when the checkbox is not checked.

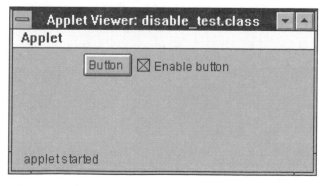

Figure 548 An applet with a Button that the user can enable or disable.

549 SHOWING AND HIDING A COMPONENT

In the previous tip, you learned how to enable and disable components. Depending on your program's processing, there may be times when you want to hide the component. To hide a component, you use the *Component* class *hide* method. To display a hidden component, you use the *Component* class *show* method. The following applet, *hide_test.java*, illustrates the use of these two methods:

```java
import java.applet.*;
import java.awt.*;

public class hide_test extends Applet {

    Button button = new Button("Button");
    Checkbox cbox = new Checkbox("Hide button");

    public void init()
      {
        add(button);
        add(cbox);
      }

    public boolean action(Event evt, Object arg)
      {
        if (evt.target instanceof Checkbox)
          {
            if (cbox.getState())
              button.hide();        // hide button
            else
              button.show();        // show button

            return true;            // event processed
          }
        return false;               // event not processed
      }
}
```

The applet hides the button when the checkbox labeled "hide button" is checked and displays the button when the checkbox in not checked.

550 SETTING THE BACKGROUND COLOR OF AN AWT COMPONENT

As you have learned, you can change an applet's background color by using the *setBackground* method. You can also use the *setBackground* method to change the background color of other AWT components. For example, the following statements illustrate how to change the background color of a *TextField* and a *Button:*

```java
Button button = new Button("Button");
TextField tfield = new TextField("TextField");
```

```
button.setBackground(Color.blue);
tfield.setBackground(Color.yellow);
```

Note: The **setBackground** *method may not work on some components on some platforms. For Java version 1.0.2 on the Windows 95 platform, the* **setBackground** *method does not change the background color of the* **Button** *in the above code, but it does change the background color of the* **TextField**. *On the Solaris platform, the* **setBackground** *method changes the background color on both the* **TextField** *and* **Button** *components.*

SETTING THE FOREGROUND COLOR OF AN *AWT* COMPONENT 551

As you have learned, by using the *setBackground* method, you can change the background color of AWT components. You can also change the foreground color of a component using the *setForeground* method. In the case of a *Button* or *TextField* components, the foreground color is for drawing the text in the components. For example, the following statements illustrate how you change the text color of *TextField* and *Button* objects:

```
Button button = new Button("Button");
TextField tfield = new TextField("TextField");
button.setForeground(Color.red);
tfield.setForeground(Color.blue);
```

Note: The **setForeground** *method may not work on some components on some platforms. For Java version 1.0.2 on the Windows 95 platform, the method does not change the foreground color of the* **Button** *in the above code, but it does change the foreground color of the* **TextField**. *On the Solaris platform, the method changes the text color on both the* **TextField** *and* **Button** *components.*

HANGING COMPONENT (BUTTON) FONTS 552

As you have learned that you can change a *Graphics* object's font using the *Graphics* class *setFont* method. There is also a method by the same name in the *Component* class, that you can use to change the font for any AWT component. Of course, not every AWT component draws text. Changing the font of a scrollbar, for instance, will have no effect. The following applet, *comp_font.java*, creates several different *Component* objects and uses the *setFont* method to change their fonts. Figure 552 illustrates the program's output.

```
import java.applet.*;
import java.awt.*;

public class comp_font extends Applet {

    Font f1 = new Font("Helvetica", Font.PLAIN, 24);
    Font f2 = new Font("TimesRoman", Font.BOLD + Font.ITALIC, 14);
    Font f3 = new Font("Helvetica", Font.ITALIC, 12);
    Font f4 = new Font("Courier",   Font.PLAIN, 12);

    Button button = new Button("Button");
    Checkbox cbox = new Checkbox("Checkbox");
    TextField tfield = new TextField("TextField", 15);
    Choice choice = new Choice();
```

```
public void init()
  {
    button.setFont(f1);
    add(button);
    cbox.setFont(f2);
    add(cbox);
    tfield.setFont(f3);
    add(tfield);
    choice.setFont(f4);
    choice.addItem("Choice 1");
    choice.addItem("Choice 2");
    choice.addItem("Choice 3");
    choice.addItem("Choice 4");
    add(choice);
  }
}
```

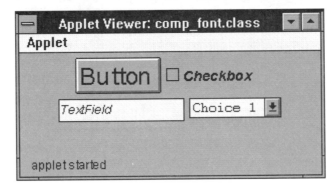

Figure 552 *AWT components with different fonts.*

553 FINDING THE SIZE AND LOCATION OF A COMPONENT

Because layout managers normally arrange and size components, you may have to rely on the *Component* class *location* and *size* methods to determine a component's position and dimension. The format of these methods are as follows:

```
Point location();
Dimension size();
```

The following applet, *comp_loc.java*, uses these two methods to determine the location and size of *Button* objects. When the user moves the mouse over one of the buttons, the applet highlights the button by drawing a red rectangle around it. Figure 553 illustrates the program's output:

```
import java.applet.*;
import java.awt.*;

public class comp_loc extends Applet {

    String items[] = {"one", "two", "three", "four"};
    Button button[] = new Button[4];
```

```
public void init()
  {
      setLayout(new FlowLayout(FlowLayout.CENTER, 10, 10));
      for(int i = 0; i < items.length; i++)
        add(button[i] = new Button(items[i]));
  }


public boolean mouseMove(Event e, int x, int y)
  {
    Graphics g = getGraphics();

    for (int i = 0; i < items.length; i++)
      {
        Point loc = button[i].location();
        Dimension dim = button[i].size();
        Rectangle rect = new Rectangle(loc, dim);
        if (rect.inside(x,y))
          g.setColor(Color.red);
        else
          g.setColor(getBackground());
        g.drawRect(loc.x-1, loc.y-1, dim.width+1, dim.height+1);
      }
    g.dispose();
    return true;
  }
}
```

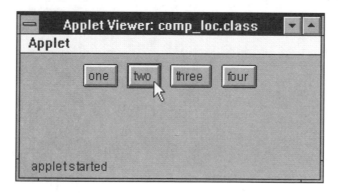

Figure 553 *An Applet that highlights a button as the mouse passes over it.*

BUILDING A LOAN CALCULATION APPLET 554

In previous tips, you learned how to use various AWT components. Now, it is time to combine what you have learned to create an actual program. The following applet, *loan_cal.java*, calculates the monthly payment for a specified interest rate, loan amount, and length of time:

```
import java.applet.*;
import java.awt.*;
```

```java
public class loan_cal extends Applet {

    TextField apr_entry = new TextField("",15);
    TextField years_entry = new TextField("",15);
    TextField amount_entry = new TextField("",15);
    Label payment_amt = new Label("", Label.LEFT);
    Button button = new Button("Calculate");

    // Method for calculating monthly loan payment
    double calc_payment(double apr, double amt, int years)
    {
        int no_of_payments = years * 12;
        double monthly_rate = 1.0 + apr / 1200;
        double pn = 1.0;
        double v0 = 0.0;

        // amount of loan for 1 dollar of monthly payment
        for (int i = 0; i < no_of_payments; i++)
        {
            pn *= monthly_rate;
            v0 += 1.0 / pn;
        }

        return(amt/v0);    // return monthly payment
    }

    public void init()
    {
        setLayout(new GridLayout(5,2,3,2));
        add(new Label("Interest Rate APR %:", Label.RIGHT));
        add(apr_entry);
        add(new Label("No. of Years:", Label.RIGHT));
        add(years_entry);
        add(new Label("Loan Amount $:", Label.RIGHT));
        add(amount_entry);
        add(new Label("Monthly Payment $:", Label.RIGHT));
        add(payment_amt);
        add(new Label());
        add(button);
    }

    public boolean action(Event evt, Object arg)
    {
        double apr, loan_amt, monthly_amt;
        int years;

        if (evt.target == button)
        { // collect user entries
            apr = Double.valueOf(apr_entry.getText()).doubleValue();
```

```
            loan_amt = Double.valueOf(
                    amount_entry.getText()).doubleValue();

        years = Integer.valueOf(years_entry.getText()).intValue();

        // calculate monthly payment
        monthly_amt = calc_payment(apr, loan_amt, years);

        // set payment label to the calculated result
         payment_amt.setText(String.valueOf(monthly_amt));
        return true;   // event processed
      }
    return false;        // event not processed
   }
 }
```

As you can see, the applet utilizes several *TextFields* for data entry, a *Button* for executing the loan calculation, and a *Label* for displaying the calculated result. Figure 554 shows the output of the loan calculation applet.

Figure 554 The loan-payment calculation applet.

CREATING AN INPUT FORM WITH DATA VALIDATION 555

In Tip 554, the loan payment calculation applet uses *TextField* interfaces to get data input from the user. However, there is nothing to stop the user from entering invalid data. For example, the loan amount entry field should only allow a positive floating-point number. If the user enters a non-numeric string, you need to catch the number format exception. You also need to check the input value to make sure it is not less than zero.

Because the applet uses the same data validation process for different entry fields, it would be useful to create a text field class that includes data checking. The following class shows you how to create a floating-point text field class:

```
class DoubleTextField extends TextField {

   double min_value, max_value;

   public DoubleTextField(String text, int cols, double min,
       double max)
```

```
    {
        super(text, cols);
        min_value = min;
        max_value = max;
    }


    public boolean isDataValid()
    {
        try {
            double value =
                Double.valueOf(this.getText()).doubleValue();

            if ((value < min_value) || (value > max_value))
                return false;
            else
                return true;
        }
        catch(NumberFormatException e)
        {
            return false;
        }
    }

    public double getDataValue()
    {
        if (isDataValid())
            return Double.valueOf(this.getText()).doubleValue();
        else
            return min_value; // returns a default valid value
    }
}
```

In addition to the normal *text* and *cols* parameters for a *TextField* constructor, the *DoubleTextField* constructor also requires the *min* and *max* parameters with which it defines the valid minimum and maximum value that the entry field allows. The *DoubleTextField* class defines the *isDataValid* method to determine whether the data in the entry field is valid. Finally, the *getDataValue* method converts the data entry and returns the *double* value.

556   UNDERSTANDING INPUT FOCUS

As was the case in the *loan_cal.java* applet, many programs contain multiple data-entry fields. In a program that has more than one data-entry field, the typed text is entered into only one data entry field at a time. The "input focus" decides which component receives keyboard events. To move the input focus from one component to another, the user can simply click on a different component.

Java applets always provide some visual indication that shows which component has the input focus. On the Windows platform, a blinking vertical bar (the cursor) indicates that a *TextField* component has the input focus. Likewise, Java displays a dotted rectangle around a *Button* component to indicate it has the input focus.

Although you can let the user change the input focus by clicking on the component, there may be times when you want your applet to set the input focus to a specific component. For example, you may want to set the focus to the *TextField* where the user entered an invalid entry. The *Component* class offers several methods for controlling and tracking the input focus, as listed in Table 556.

Method	Purpose
gotFocus	Called when the component receives the input focus
lostFocus	Called when the component loses the input focus
requestFocus	Requests the input focus for the component
nextFocus	Moves the input focus to the next component

Table 556 *Component class methods that manipulate the input focus.*

*Note: The **gotFocus** and **lostFocus** methods are not yet fully implemented in the JDK version 1.0.2.*

USING THE TAB KEY TO MOVE BETWEEN INPUT FIELDS 557

When a graphical user interface contains multiple data-input components, it is customary to let the user jump from one input field to another using the TAB key. This feature is especially useful when the user must enter many text entries. In other words, the user can enter data on all input fields without moving back and forth between the keyboard and the mouse.

In Tip 556, you learned that you can control the input focus by using the *requestFocus* and *nextFocus* methods. The following code fragment shows you how to use *requestFocus* and *nextFocus* methods to let a user cycle through input fields when using the TAB key. Add this code to the *loan_cal.java* applet you created in Tip 554 to let the user move quickly from one field to the next:

```
public boolean keyDown(Event evt, int key)
  {
    if ((char)key == '\t')
      {
         Component current_field =(Component) evt.target;

         if (current_field != button)
           current_field.nextFocus();
         else
           apr_entry.requestFocus();

         return true;
      }
    return false;
  }
```

When Java detects a TAB-key event, the applet calls the *nextFocus* method to move the input focus to the next component. When the Calculate button, which is the last component, has the input focus, the applet calls *requestFocus* to move the input focus back to the first data input field.

558 CREATING FRAMES

Each of the previous applets placed all of their graphical-user interface elements inside the original applet window, which is inside an HTML page. There may be times, however, when you want to create a separate pop-up window for such elements. For example, you may want to create a floating tool palette for a drawing applet. In such cases, you can use the *Frame* class to create a pop-up window by performing these steps:

1. Create a *Frame* object using the *Frame* class or a subclass of *Frame*. In many cases, you may want to create your own class and extend the *Frame* class to override some of the methods. You can use one of the following constructors to create a *Frame* object:

```
Frame();
Frame(String title);
```

The second form of the *Frame* constructor sets the dialog box title to the *title* parameter.

2. Call the *resize* method to set the *Frame* object's initial size. You may also add components to the *Frame* using the *add* method. Alternatively, you can call the *pack* method to let Java determine the proper window size. If you use the *pack* method, you should add all the components to the *Frame* object first before calling *pack*.

3. Call the *show* method to display the window.

The following applet, *applet_frame.java*, illustrates the process of using *Frame* objects. The applet creates a new pop-up window each time the user presses the New Frame button. Figure 558 illustrates the program's output.

```java
import java.applet.*;
import java.awt.*;

public class applet_frame extends Applet {

   public void init()
     {
        add(new Button("New Frame"));
     }

   public boolean action(Event evt, Object arg)
     {
        if (evt.target instanceof Button)
         {
            Frame f = new Frame();
            f.resize(200, 100);
             f.add("Center", new Label("A Frame", Label.CENTER));

            f.show();
            return true;   // event processed
         }
        return false;       // event not processed
     }
  }
```

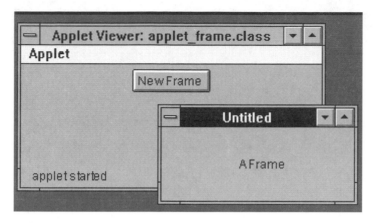

Figure 558 An applet with pop-up windows.

DESTROYING A FRAME OBJECT USING THE DISPOSE METHOD 559

One of the problems with using pop-up windows, as discussed in a previous tip, is that you cannot close the window, even when you click on the *Frame* object's close button. To destroy a pop-up window that you create using a *Frame*, you must call the *dispose* method. The *dispose* method closes the *Frame* window and releases its resources. The following applet, *frame_dispose.java*, expands on the *applet_frame.java* applet you created in Tip 558. The *frame_dispose.java* applet adds the *PopupFrame* class and extends the *Frame* class. In addition, the applet overrides the *handleEvent* method to track the *WINDOW_DESTROY* event and to dispose of the frame:

```java
import java.applet.*;
import java.awt.*;

class PopupFrame extends Frame {

    public boolean handleEvent(Event evt)
      {
         if (evt.id == Event.WINDOW_DESTROY)
           dispose();

         return super.handleEvent(evt);
      }
}

public class frame_dispose extends Applet {

    public void init()
      {
         add(new Button("New Frame"));
      }

    public boolean action(Event evt, Object arg)
      {
         if (evt.target instanceof Button)
           {
```

```
                PopupFrame f = new PopupFrame();
                f.resize(200, 100);
                 f.add("Center", new Label("A Frame", Label.CENTER));

                f.show();
                return true;    // event processed
          }
        return false;         // event not processed
      }
  }
```

560 CREATING A JAVA APPLICATION WITH GUI USING FRAME

Up to now, you have been creating graphical user interfaces for Java applets. Now, it is time to create a Java *application* with a graphical-user interface. To create a Java application with a window, you must use the *Frame* class or a subclass to create the application's top-level window. The following application, *java_app.java*, is a simple program that creates an application window and then draws a few shapes within the window. Remember that since this program is a Java application, you use the Java interpreter "java" and not the *appletviewer* to run the application. Figure 560 illustrates the application's output:

```java
import java.awt.*;

public class java_app extends Frame {

    public java_app(String title)
      {
        super(title);
      }

    public static void main(String args[])
      {
        java_app application = new java_app("java_app");
        application.resize(300, 150);
        application.show();
      }

    public boolean handleEvent(Event evt)
      {
        if (evt.id == Event.WINDOW_DESTROY)
          System.exit(0); // exit the application

        return super.handleEvent(evt);
      }

    public void paint(Graphics g)
      {
        // draw a few shapes
        g.setColor(Color.blue);
```

```
        g.fillOval(90, 50, 100, 80);
        g.setColor(Color.red);
        g.fillRoundRect(10, 10, 150, 70, 50, 25);
        g.setColor(Color.green);
        g.fillRect(150, 20, 50, 50);
    }
}
```

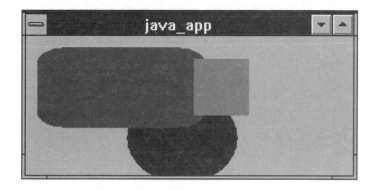

Figure 560 *A simple Java application running within a window.*

For a standalone application such as the program just shown, it is important that you provide a mechanism that lets the user quit the program. At the very least, you should track the *WINDOW_DESTROY* event of the top-level window and exit the program when the event occurs. If you do not do that, the only way to stop the program is to hit CTRL-ALT-DEL or CTRL -C within the DOS shell on a Windows-based system. On a Solaris system, you may have to resort to using the *kill* command to kill the Java application process.

LAYOUT MANAGER DIFFERS BETWEEN AN APPLET AND APPLICATION 561

As you have learned, you can add AWT components to an applet using the *add* method. You can also add components to *Frame* objects you create for a Java application. One thing to remember is that the default layout manager for an applet and an application are different. The default layout manager for an applet, as inherited from the *Panel* class, is *FlowLayout*. The default layout manager for a Java application, as inherited from the *Frame class*, is *BorderLayout*.

To change the layout manager of a *Frame*, you use the *setLayout* method the same way that you would with an applet, as shown in the following application, *flow_frame.java*:

```
import java.awt.*;

public class flow_frame extends Frame {

    String items[] = {"Mercury", "Venus", "Earth", "Mars", "Sat-
urn"};
    Button button[] = new Button[5];

    public flow_frame(String title)
    {
```

```
        super(title);
        setLayout(new FlowLayout());

        for (int i = 0; i < items.length; i++)
          {
             button[i] = new Button(items[i]);
             add(button[i]);
          }
     }

  public static void main(String args[])
     {
        flow_frame application = new flow_frame("flow_frame");
        application.resize(250, 150);
        application.show();
     }

  public boolean handleEvent(Event evt)
     {
        if (evt.id == Event.WINDOW_DESTROY)
          System.exit(0); // exit the application

        return super.handleEvent(evt);
     }
}
```

As you can see, the *flow_frame.java* application changes the layout manager to *FlowLayout* and then uses the layout manager to display several buttons.

562 BUILDING A COMPOUND INTEREST CALCULATION APPLICATION

Everything you learned about using AWT components and layout managers in a Java applet also applies to building a Java application. In Tip 554, for example, you learned how to build a loan payment calculation applet using various AWT components. In a similar way, the *savings_cal.java* application that follows combines various AWT components to build a savings-calculator application. The *savings_cal.java* application calculates the projected savings for the specified monthly contribution, interest rate, and length of the savings. Figure 562 illustrates the application's output:

```
import java.awt.*;

public class savings_cal extends Frame {

    TextField apr_entry = new TextField("",15);
    TextField years_entry = new TextField("",15);
    TextField payment_entry = new TextField("",15);
    Label total_amt = new Label("", Label.LEFT);
    Button button = new Button("Calculate");

    // Method for calculating monthly loan payment
    double calc_savings(double apr, double amt, int years)
```

```
    {
        int no_of_payments = years * 12;              // no of payments
        double monthly_rate = 1.0 + apr / 1200.0; // rate + 1.0
        double total = 0;

        // Calculate the total saving
        for (int i = 0; i < no_of_payments; i++)
         {
            total += amt;
            total *= monthly_rate;
         }

        // Return total saved amount plus interest
        return(total);
    }

public savings_cal(String title)
    {
        super(title);
        setLayout(new GridLayout(5,2,3,2));
        add(new Label("Interest Rate APR %:", Label.RIGHT));
        add(apr_entry);
        add(new Label("No. of Years:", Label.RIGHT));
        add(years_entry);
        add(new Label("Monthly Contribution $:", Label.RIGHT));
        add(payment_entry);
        add(new Label("Total Savings $:", Label.RIGHT));
        add(total_amt);
        add(new Label());
        add(button);
    }

public static void main(String args[])
    {
        savings_cal application = new savings_cal("savings_cal");
        application.pack();
        application.show();
    }

public boolean action(Event evt, Object arg)
    {
        double apr, monthly_amt, total_saving;
        int years;

        if (evt.target == button)
          { // Collect the user entries
            apr = Double.valueOf(apr_entry.getText()).doubleValue();
            monthly_amt = Double.valueOf(
                payment_entry.getText()).doubleValue();
```

```
        years=Integer.valueOf(years_entry.getText()).intValue();

        // Calculate the total savings
        total_saving = calc_savings(apr, monthly_amt, years);

        // Set payment label to the calculated result
        total_amt.setText(String.valueOf(total_saving));
       return true;   // event processed
     }
   return false;       // event not processed
 }


 public boolean handleEvent(Event evt)
   {
     if (evt.id == Event.WINDOW_DESTROY)
       System.exit(0); // exit the application

     return super.handleEvent(evt);
   }
 }
```

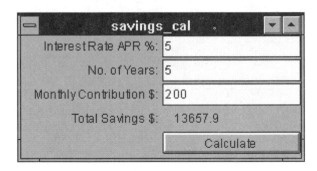

Figure 562 A savings calculator application.

563 CHANGING YOUR CURSOR

As you may have noticed, the default cursor in a *Frame* object is an arrow. Depending on your applet's purpose, there may be times when you will want to use a different cursor. For example, you may want to change to a cross-hair cursor in a CAD drawing application. Although the current version of Java's AWT does not let you create your own cursor, you can select a cursor from a set of predefined cursors. To change a *Frame* object's cursor, you use the *Frame* class *setCursor* method, the format of which is as follows:

```
void setCursor(int cursorType);
```

You set the *cursorType* parameter to one of the variables defined within the *Frame* class, such as *Frame.WAIT_CURSOR*. For example, the following statement selects the cross-hair cursor:

```
setCursor(Frame.CROSSHAIR_CURSOR);
```

The following application, *cursor.java*, lets you set the cursor using a *Choice* list. Figure 563 displays the program's output:

```java
import java.awt.*;

public class cursor extends Frame {

    String items[] = {"DEFAULT","CROSSHAIR","TEXT","WAIT",
      "SW_RESIZE", "SE_RESIZE","NW_RESIZE","NW_RESIZE",
      "NE_RESIZE", "N_RESIZE","S_RESIZE","W_RESIZE","E_RESIZE",
     "HAND", "MOVE"};

    int cursors[]={ Frame.DEFAULT_CURSOR, Frame.CROSSHAIR_CURSOR,
                    Frame.TEXT_CURSOR, Frame.WAIT_CURSOR,
                    Frame.SW_RESIZE_CURSOR, Frame.SE_RESIZE_CURSOR,
                    Frame.NW_RESIZE_CURSOR, Frame.NW_RESIZE_CURSOR,
                    Frame.NE_RESIZE_CURSOR, Frame.N_RESIZE_CURSOR,
                    Frame.S_RESIZE_CURSOR, Frame.W_RESIZE_CURSOR,
                    Frame.E_RESIZE_CURSOR, Frame.HAND_CURSOR,
                    Frame.MOVE_CURSOR };

    Choice choice = new Choice();

    public cursor(String title)
      {
          super(title);

          for (int i = 0; i < items.length; i++)
            choice.addItem(items[i]);

          add("North", choice);
      }

    public static void main(String args[])
      {
          cursor application = new cursor("cursor");
          application.resize(250, 150);
          application.show();
      }

    public boolean action(Event evt, Object arg)
      {
          if (evt.target instanceof Choice)
            {
                setCursor(cursors[choice.getSelectedIndex()]);
              return true;       // event processed
            }
           return false;         // event not processed
      }

    public boolean handleEvent(Event evt)
      {
          if (evt.id == Event.WINDOW_DESTROY)
            System.exit(0); // exit the application

          return super.handleEvent(evt);
      }
}
```

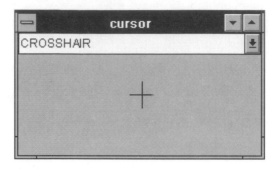

Figure 563 An application frame with a non-default cursor.

564 SETTING THE FRAME TITLE

As you know, it is customary for a Windows-based application to display its name at the top of the window, and for an application that displays files to display the name of the current file along with application name. By default, *Frame* objects use the title "Untitled." To assign a title to a *Frame* object, use the following form of the *Frame* constructor method:

```
Frame(String title);
```

If you want to change the title after the applet has constructed the *Frame*, use the *setTitle* method, the format of which is as follows:

```
void setTitle(String title);
```

For example, the following statements use the *setTitle* method to rename a *Frame* object:

```
Frame f;
f.setTitle("My Java Application");
```

565 CHANGING ICON IMAGE

When a frame is minimized, Java displays an icon image. By default, the icon image is a Java coffee cup. To differentiate one minimized application from another, you may want to change the *Frame* object's icon image. To set a new icon image, use the *Frame* class *setIconImage* method:

```
void setIconImage(Image image);
```

For example, the following statements assign a new icon image to a *Frame* object:

```
Image new_icon;

// Statements to create the icon here

Frame f;
f.setIconImage(new_icon);   // Assign the icon
```

*Note: Under Java version 1.0.2 on the Windows 95 platform, the **setIconImage** method has no effect on the icon. However, the method does work properly under Solaris.*

ADDING A PULL-DOWN MENU TO YOUR FRAME

A pull-down menu is a common element in most graphical user interfaces. Pull-down menus provide a familiar interface between different applications and greatly reduce the user's learning curve for a new application. When users see a *File* menu *Open* option within an application, they will automatically know that option lets them load an existing file into the application. To create a pull-down menu within a Java program, perform the following steps:

1. Create a *MenuBar* object by using the *MenuBar* constructor, and set the object as the *Frame* object's menu-bar using the *setMenuBar* method:

```
MenuBar menubar = new MenuBar();
setMenuBar(menubar);
```

2. Create your menus by using the *Menu* constructor, and then add the menus to the menu-bar using the *Menu* class *add* method:

```
Menu file_menu = new Menu("File");
Menu edit_menu = new Menu("Edit");
menubar.add(file_menu);
menubar.add(edit_menu);
```

3. Create and add items to each menu. The menu items can be a *MenuItem* object, a *CheckboxMenuItem* object, a separator, or submenus. You create *MenuItem* objects using the *MenuItem* constructor, and you add the object to the menu using the *Menu* class add method:

```
file_menu.add(new MenuItem("Open"));
file_menu.add(new MenuItem("Save"));
edit_menu.add(new MenuItem("Cut"));
```

Another form of the *Menu* class *add* method creates a *MenuItem* for the specified label and adds it to the menu in one step:

```
void add(String label);
```

In this way, you can add the same menu items to the menus shown previously by using the following statements:

```
file_menu.add("Open");
file_menu.add("Save");
edit_menu.add("Cut");
```

Subsequent tips in this section will show you how to create *Checkbox* menu items, separators, and submenus. The following application, *menu_test.java*, illustrates the process of adding a pull-down menu to a Java application. Figure 566 illustrates the program's output.

```
import java.awt.*;

public class menu_test extends Frame {

    MenuBar menubar = new MenuBar();
    Menu file = new Menu("File", true);
    Menu edit = new Menu("Edit", true);
```

```java
    public menu_test(String title)
    {
      super(title);
      setMenuBar(menubar);
      menubar.add(file);
      menubar.add(edit);
      file.add("New");
      file.add("Open");
      file.add("Save");
      edit.add("Cut");
      edit.add("Copy");
      edit.add("Paste");
    }

    public static void main(String args[])
    {
      menu_test application = new menu_test("menu_test");
      application.resize(250, 125);
      application.show();
    }

    public boolean handleEvent(Event evt)
    {
      if (evt.id == Event.WINDOW_DESTROY)
        System.exit(0);

      return super.handleEvent(evt);
    }
  }
```

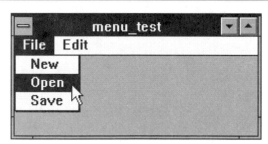

Figure 566 An application with a pull-down menu.

Keep in mind that you can only add pull-down menus to a *Frame* class object or subclass of the *Frame* class. Therefore, you cannot add a pull-down menu to an applet window directly.

567 TRACKING MENU ITEM EVENTS

In the previous tip, you learned how to create a menu within a Java program. For your program to respond when the user selects a menu item, you must be able to detect the menu item events. As it turns out, Java generates an action event each time the user selects a menu item. You can intercept the action event by overriding the *action* method. Add the following code segment to the *menu_test.java* applet that you created in Tip 566 to detect menu item events:

```
public boolean action(Event evt, Object arg)
  {
     if (evt.target instanceof MenuItem)
       {
          if (arg.equals("Open"))
             System.out.println("File open selected!");
          else if(arg.equals("Save"))
             System.out.println("File save selected!");

          // repeat comparison for other menu items
          return true;    // event processed
       }
     return false;        // event not processed
  }
```

The *action* method's second parameter, *arg*, contains the label of the selected menu item. You can use this parameter to determine which menu item the user selected.

USING A SEPARATOR LINE TO BREAK UP MENU ITEMS

When your programs use *Menu* objects, it is good practice to add separator lines to break up menu items. For example, within a File menu, you may want to separate the Open and Save options from the printing-related items. Adding a separator to a menu is similar to adding a *MenuItem* object. You create a *MenuItem* labeled "-" to make a menu separator and then add the item to the menu using the *add* method, as shown:

```
Menu menu;
menu.add(new MenuItem("-"));
```

However, a simpler way to create and add menu separators is to use the *Menu* class *addSeparator* method, as shown:

```
Menu menu;
menu.addSeparator();
```

The following application, *separator.java*, adds several separators to its pull-down menus. Figure 568 illustrates the program's output:

```
import java.awt.*;

public class separator extends Frame {

    MenuBar menubar = new MenuBar();
    Menu file = new Menu("File", true);

    public separator(String title)
      {
         super(title);
         setMenuBar(menubar);
         menubar.add(file);
         file.add("New");
         file.add("Open");
```

```
         file.add("Close");
         file.addSeparator();
         file.add("Save");
         file.add("Save As");
         file.addSeparator();
         file.add("Print");
         file.add("Printer Setup");
         file.addSeparator();
         file.add("Quit");
     }

   public static void main(String args[])
     {
        separator application = new separator("separator");
        application.resize(250, 125);
        application.show();
     }

   public boolean handleEvent(Event evt)
     {
        if (evt.id == Event.WINDOW_DESTROY)
          System.exit(0);

        return super.handleEvent(evt);
     }
 }
```

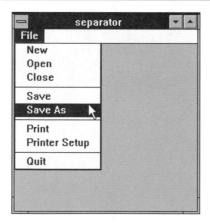

Figure 568 A menu with separators.

569 HOW TO CREATE SUBMENUS

In Tip 568, you learned that you can organize menu items into groups using separator lines. In addition, you can also use submenus to organize menu items. Submenus are particularly useful when you have a large number of menu items. Within a menu, the submenu's choices are hidden unless the user selects the submenu option. To create a submenu, you add a *Menu* object to an existing *Menu* object. For example, the following application, *submenu.java*, creates a submenu under the File menu. Figure 569 illustrates the program's output.

```
import java.awt.*;

public class submenu extends Frame {

    MenuBar menubar = new MenuBar();
    Menu file = new Menu("File", true);
    Menu save_menu = new Menu("Save", true);

    public submenu(String title)
      {
        super(title);
        setMenuBar(menubar);
        menubar.add(file);
        file.add("New");
        file.add("Open");
        file.add("Close");
        file.add(save_menu);
        save_menu.add("Save Current");
        save_menu.add("Save As");
        save_menu.add("Save All");
        file.addSeparator();
        file.add("Quit");
      }

    public static void main(String args[])
      {
        submenu application = new submenu("submenu");
        application.resize(250, 125);
        application.show();
      }

    public boolean handleEvent(Event evt)
      {
        if (evt.id == Event.WINDOW_DESTROY)
          System.exit(0);

      return super.handleEvent(evt);
      }
}
```

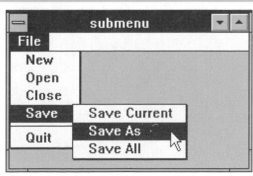

Figure 569 An application with submenus.

570 ADDING A CHECKBOX ITEM TO A MENU

Several of the previous tips have examined how you use menus within Java programs. In addition to displaying a simple labeled menu item, you can also display menu items that have check marks. To display a menu item with a check mark, you first use the *CheckboxMenuItem* constructor method to create a checkbox menu item. Next, you add the item to the menu using the *add* method:

```
Menu menu;
menu.add(new CheckboxMenuItem("check item"));
```

The check mark on the checkbox menu item toggles each time the user selects the item. The following application, *check_menu.java*, creates a checkbox menu item, as shown in Figure 570:

```
import java.awt.*;

public class check_menu extends Frame {

    MenuBar menubar = new MenuBar();
    Menu font_menu = new Menu("Font", true);

    public check_menu(String title)
      {
         super(title);
         setMenuBar(menubar);
         menubar.add(font_menu);
          font_menu.add(new CheckboxMenuItem("Bold"));
          font_menu.add(new CheckboxMenuItem("Italic"));
          font_menu.add(new CheckboxMenuItem("Underline"));
      }

    public static void main(String args[])
      {
         check_menu application = new check_menu("check_menu");
         application.resize(250, 125);
         application.show();
      }

    public boolean handleEvent(Event evt)
      {
        if (evt.id == Event.WINDOW_DESTROY)
          System.exit(0);

        return super.handleEvent(evt);
      }
}
```

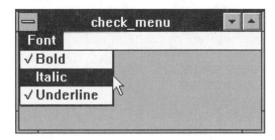

Figure 570 An application using checkbox menu items.

GETTING AND SETTING A CHECKBOX MENU ITEM'S STATE  571

As you learned in the previous tip, the user can toggle a checkbox menu item's state by selecting the menu item. To find out whether the menu item is checked or not, call the *CheckboxMenuItem* class *getState* method, whose method is shown here:

```
boolean getState();
```

The *getState* method returns *true* if the menu item is checked, and *false* otherwise.

In a similar way, there may be times when you want to set the state of the checkbox menu item. For example, you may want to set the item's initial state. In such cases, you use the *setState* method to set the state of the checkbox menu item:

```
void setState(boolean t);
```

To place a check mark next to the item, set the parameter *t* to *true*. To remove the check mark, set the parameter to *false*. The following application, *check_menu_state.java*, reports the state of the checkbox menu item each time the user selects the item:

```
import java.awt.*;

public class check_menu_state extends Frame {

    MenuBar menubar = new MenuBar();
    Menu font_menu = new Menu("Font", true);
    CheckboxMenuItem bold_item = new CheckboxMenuItem("Bold");
    CheckboxMenuItem italic_item = new CheckboxMenuItem("Italic");
    CheckboxMenuItem underline_item = new
        CheckboxMenuItem("Underline");

    public check_menu_state(String title)
      {
        super(title);
        setMenuBar(menubar);
        menubar.add(font_menu);
        font_menu.add(bold_item);
        font_menu.add(italic_item);
        font_menu.add(underline_item);
      }
```

```
    public static void main(String args[])
      {
        check_menu_state application =
            new check_menu_state("check_menu_state");
        application.resize(250, 125);
        application.show();
      }

    public boolean action(Event evt, Object arg)
      {
        if (evt.target instanceof MenuItem)
          {
            System.out.println("Bold is " + bold_item.getState());
            System.out.println("Italic is " +
                italic_item.getState());
            System.out.println("Underline is " +
                underline_item.getState());
            return true;   // event processed
          }
        return false; // events not processed
      }

    public boolean handleEvent(Event evt)
      {
        if (evt.id == Event.WINDOW_DESTROY)
          System.exit(0);

        return super.handleEvent(evt);
      }
  }
```

572 ENABLING AND DISABLING MENU ITEMS

Depending on your program's purpose, there may be times when you want to disable a menu item so that a particular option is not available to the user. When a menu item is disabled, the applet displays the label as grayed out and the user cannot select the option. To disable and enable a menu item, you use the following *MenuItem disable* and *enable* methods, as shown:

```
void disable();
void enable();
```

There is also another form of the *enable* method that lets you enable and disable a menu item based on the *boolean* parameter *cond*, as shown:

```
void enable(boolean cond);
```

In addition, you can also find out whether a menu item is enabled or not by calling the *isEnabled* method:

```
boolean isEnabled();
```

The *isEnabled* method returns *true* if the menu item is enabled, and *false* if it is disabled.

REMOVING MENU ITEMS

When your programs work with menus, there may be times you will want to remove an item from a menu. For example, in an application where the last few files accessed are stored in a menu, you need to remove an old item before you can add a new one. To remove an item from a menu, you use one of the following *Menu* class *remove* methods, as shown:

```
void remove(int index);
void remove(MenuComponent item);
```

As you can see, you can remove a menu item by specifying either the item's zero-based index or the *MenuComponent* itself. The following application, *remove_menu.java*, adds a menu item when the user selects the Add button and removes a menu item when the user selects the Remove button:

```java
import java.awt.*;

public class remove_menu extends Frame {

    MenuBar menubar = new MenuBar();
    Menu list_menu = new Menu("List", true);
    int list_menu_count;

    public remove_menu(String title)
      {
        super(title);
        setMenuBar(menubar);
        menubar.add(list_menu);
        list_menu_count = 0;
        setLayout(new FlowLayout());
        add(new Button("add"));
        add(new Button("remove"));
      }

    public static void main(String args[])
      {
        remove_menu application = new remove_menu("remove_menu");
        application.resize(250, 125);
        application.show();
      }

    public boolean action(Event evt, Object arg)
      {
        if (evt.target instanceof Button)
          {
            if (arg.equals("add"))
              list_menu.add("item " +
                String.valueOf(++list_menu_count));
            else if (arg.equals("remove"))
```

```
                    if (list_menu_count > 0)
                        list_menu.remove(--list_menu_count);


                return true;      // event processed
             }
          return false;           // event not processed
       }


    public boolean handleEvent(Event evt)
       {
          if (evt.id == Event.WINDOW_DESTROY)
            System.exit(0);

          return super.handleEvent(evt);
       }
    }
```

574 COUNTING THE NUMBER OF ITEMS IN A MENU

In the previous tips, you learned that you can add or remove menu items dynamically. To find out how many items are on a menu, you could keep a count of what you have added and removed. Fortunately, the Java AWT library offers a simpler way. To determine the number of items in a menu, use the *Menu* class *countItems* method, the format of which is as follows:

```
    int countItems();
```

575 SIMULATING MENU SELECTION WITH THE POSTEVENT METHOD

As you have learned, Java generates events when the user selects a menu item, presses a key, pushes a command button, and so on. To help you test your program, you can simulate these user-input events using the *Component* class *postEvent*. To begin, you must construct an *Event* object with the intended event parameters and deliver it to the component using the *postEvent* method.

In addition to using the *postEvent* method to test your program, you can also use it to implement keyboard shortcuts. As you know, many programs define accelerator keys for quick menu access. To implement menu accelerator keys in Java, you track the keyboard events for the accelerators. Then, you can either execute the same code as your program performs for an actual menu item selection, or you can post a simulated menu selection event. The second method offers the advantage of reducing your source code by keeping the event code in a central location.

The following application, *acc_key.java*, implements menu accelerator keys **F1**, **F2**, and **F3** for the equivalent file menu items "New," "Open," and "Save," respectively:

```
    import java.awt.*;

    public class acc_keys extends Frame {

       MenuBar menubar = new MenuBar();
       Menu file = new Menu("File", true);
```

```java
MenuItem new_item = new MenuItem("New");
MenuItem open_item = new MenuItem("Open");
MenuItem save_item = new MenuItem("Save");

public acc_keys()
  {
    setMenuBar(menubar);
    menubar.add(file);
    file.add(new_item);
    file.add(open_item);
    file.add(save_item);
  }


public static void main(String args[])
  {
    acc_keys application = new acc_keys();
    application.resize(300, 100);
    application.setTitle("acc_keys");
    application.show();
    application.requestFocus();
  }

public boolean handleEvent(Event evt)
  {
    if (evt.id == Event.WINDOW_DESTROY)
      System.exit(0);

    return super.handleEvent(evt);
  }

public boolean action(Event evt, Object arg)
  {
    if (evt.target instanceof MenuItem)
      {
        if (arg.equals("New"))
          System.out.println("File new selected!");
        else if (arg.equals("Open"))
          System.out.println("File open selected!");
        else if (arg.equals("Save"))
          System.out.println("File save selected!");

        return true;   // event processed
      }
    return false;      // event not processed
  }

public boolean keyDown(Event evt, int key)
  {
    if (key == Event.F1)
```

```
    {
        postEvent(new Event((Object) new_item,
            Event.ACTION_EVENT, (Object) new_item.getLabel()));
        return true;
    }
    else if (key == Event.F2)
    {
        postEvent(new Event((Object) open_item,
            Event.ACTION_EVENT, (Object) open_item.getLabel()));
        return true;
    }
    else if (key == Event.F3)
    {
        postEvent(new Event((Object) save_item,
            Event.ACTION_EVENT, (Object) save_item.getLabel()));
        return true;
    }
    return false;
    }
}
```

576 CREATING A DIALOG BOX

Applications commonly use dialog boxes to gather user input. There are two types of dialog boxes: modal and modeless. When a program displays a modal dialog box, the user cannot switch to other windows within the same application until the dialog box is closed. You would use a modal dialog box in a situation when the program needs immediate user response before the application can proceed. On the other hand, when the program displays a modeless dialog box, the user can switch to another window within the same application, usually by clicking on the window. For example, you can use a modeless dialog box to create a toolbar for an application, so the user can select different tools from the toolbar and apply them in another window without first closing the toolbar window. To create a dialog box, perform the following steps:

1. Create a *Dialog* object using the *Dialog* class or a subclass of the *Frame* class. In many cases, you may want to create your own class that extends the *Dialog* class. To create the *Dialog* object, use one of the following constructor methods:

```
Dialog(Frame parent, boolean modal);
Dialog(Frame parent, String title, boolean modal);
```

The first parameter is a *Frame* object that indicates the parent of the *Dialog* object. You create a modal dialog box by setting the *modal* parameter to *true*, and a modeless dialog box by setting the *modal* parameter to *false*. The second form of the *Dialog* constructor lets you set the dialog box title.

2. Call the *resize* method to set the size of the dialog box. You may also add components to the dialog using the *add* method. Alternatively, you can call the *pack* method to let Java determine the proper window. If you use the *pack* method, you should add all the components to the dialog box before calling *pack*.

3. Call the *show* method to display the dialog window.

The following application, *dialog_test.java*, illustrates the process of creating a dialog box. The application creates and displays a modeless dialog box titled "Dialog box". Figure 576 shows the application frame and the dialog box created on top of it:

```java
import java.awt.*;

class simple_dialog extends Dialog {

    public simple_dialog(Frame parent)
      {
         super(parent, "Dialog box", false);
         resize(125, 75);
      }

    public boolean handleEvent(Event evt)
      {
         if (evt.id == Event.WINDOW_DESTROY)
          {
             this.dispose();
             return true;
          }
         return super.handleEvent(evt);
      }
 }

public class dialog_test extends Frame {

    MenuBar menubar = new MenuBar();
    Menu help = new Menu("Help", true);

    public dialog_test(String title)
      {
         super(title);
         simple_dialog d = new simple_dialog(this);
         d.show();
      }

    public static void main(String args[])
      {
         dialog_test application = new dialog_test("dialog_test");
         application.resize(200, 100);
         application.show();
      }

    public boolean handleEvent(Event evt)
      {
         if (evt.id == Event.WINDOW_DESTROY)
           System.exit(0);

         return super.handleEvent(evt);
      }
 }
```

Figure 576 An application with a dialog box.

Within your program, you must provide a mechanism for closing a dialog box, such as intercepting the *WINDOW_DESTROY* event and disposing of the dialog box. Otherwise, there will be no way for users to close the dialog boxes except by quitting the entire application.

577 SETTING THE DIALOG BOX TITLE

Setting a dialog box's title is very similar to setting the title of a *Frame* object. By default, Java will title a dialog box as "Untitled." When you create a *Dialog* object, you can specify a title within the *Dialog* constructor method, as shown:

```
Dialog(Frame parent, String title, boolean modal);
```

If you need to change the title of a dialog box after you have created the *Dialog* object, you use the *Dialog* class *setTitle* method, as shown:

```
void setTitle(String title);
```

For example, the following statements change the title of an existing dialog box to "My Java Dialog Box".

```
Dialog d;
d.setTitle("My Java Dialog Box");
```

578 UNDERSTANDING THE PACK METHOD

The dialog box created by the *dialog_test.java* application in Tip 576 uses the *resize* method to set the size of the dialog box. Because the size of the components in the dialog box may vary on different platforms, setting the dialog box size using absolute values may be inappropriate. Fortunately, Java's AWT offers the *Window* class *pack* method. When you call the *pack* method, Java will automatically set the size of the dialog box based on the dimensions of the components it contains. Figure 578 shows a dialog box that is manually sized to 300x150 pixels and the same dialog box automatically sized using the *pack* method:

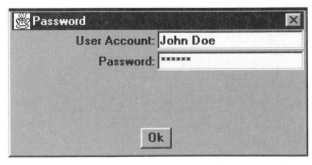
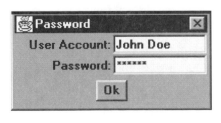

Figure 578 A manually sized and an automatically sized dialog box.

BUILDING AN ABOUT DIALOG BOX

As you have learned, you can add components to a dialog box just as you would add components to a *Frame* object. The following application, *about_dialog.java*, defines a generic About dialog box by combining several AWT components. The application displays the dialog box, as shown in Figure 579, when the user selects the Help menu About option. You can remove the About dialog box by clicking on the Ok button.

```java
import java.awt.*;

class about_box extends Dialog {

    public about_box(Frame parent, String program_title,
        String author_info, String copyright_info)
      {
        super(parent, "About", true);

        Panel info_panel = new Panel();
        Panel ok_panel = new Panel();

        info_panel.setLayout(new GridLayout(3,1));
        info_panel.add(new Label(program_title, Label.CENTER));
        info_panel.add(new Label(author_info, Label.CENTER));
        info_panel.add(new Label(copyright_info, Label.LEFT));
        add("North", info_panel);

        ok_panel.add(new Button("Ok"));
        add("South", ok_panel);
        pack();
      }

    public boolean action(Event evt, Object arg)
      {
        if (evt.target instanceof Button)
          {
            this.dispose();
            return true;        // event processed
          }
        return false;           // event not processed
      }
  }

public class about_dialog extends Frame {

    String title_str = "About dialog v1.0";
    String author_str = "Joe Doe";
    String copyright_str = "Copyright 1996";
    MenuBar menubar = new MenuBar();
    Menu help = new Menu("Help", true);
```

```java
    public about_dialog(String title)
      {
         super(title);
         setMenuBar(menubar);
         menubar.add(help);
         help.add("About");
         help.add("Quit");
      }

    public static void main(String args[])
      {
         about_dialog application = new about_dialog("about_dialog");
         application.resize(200, 100);
         application.show();
      }

    public boolean action(Event evt, Object arg)
      {
         if (evt.target instanceof MenuItem)
           {
             if (arg.equals("About"))
               {
                 about_box d = new about_box(this,
                     title_str, author_str, copyright_str);
                 d.pack();
                 d.move(10,10);
                 d.show();
               }

             if (arg.equals("Quit"))
              System.exit(0);

             return true;   // event processed
           }
         return false;        // event not processed
      }

}
```

Figure 579 An About dialog box.

PROCESSING USER INPUT FROM A DIALOG BOX 580

When a user completes the entries within a dialog box, it is often necessary for the program to respond immediately. Normally, a user signals that the dialog box is complete by clicking the mouse on an Ok button. To handle user input, such as Ok or Cancel, you can override the dialog box event-handling methods. For example, you can override the *handleEvent* and *action* methods to track the input events, and then process the data collected. In many cases, it is better to let the parent of the dialog box process the data instead of processing the data inside the *Dialog* class. The following application, *sendinfo_dialog.java*, illustrates how to respond to user inputs by overriding event-handling methods:

```java
import java.awt.*;

class entry_box extends Dialog {

    TextField tf = new TextField(15);

    public entry_box(Frame parent)
      {
        super(parent, "About", true);

        Panel entry_panel = new Panel();
        Panel ok_panel = new Panel();

        entry_panel.add(new Label("Name:", Label.LEFT));
        entry_panel.add(tf);
        add("North", entry_panel);

        ok_panel.add(new Button("Ok"));
        add("South", ok_panel);
        resize(250, 100);
      }

    public boolean action(Event evt, Object arg)
      {
        if (evt.target instanceof Button)
        {
            ((sendinfo_dialog)getParent()).dialog_entry(tf.getText());
            this.dispose();
            return true;      // event processed
        }
        return false;         // event not processed
      }
  }

public class sendinfo_dialog extends Frame {

    MenuBar menubar = new MenuBar();
    Menu help = new Menu("File", true);

    public sendinfo_dialog(String title)
```

```
    {
        super(title);
        setMenuBar(menubar);
        menubar.add(help);
        help.add("New");
        help.add("Quit");
    }

    public static void main(String args[])
    {
        sendinfo_dialog application = new
            sendinfo_dialog("sendinfo_dialog");
        application.resize(200, 100);
        application.show();
    }

    public void dialog_entry(String name)
    {
        System.out.println("Dialog entry :" + name);
    }

    public boolean action(Event evt, Object arg)
    {
        if (evt.target instanceof MenuItem)
        {
            if (arg.equals("New"))
            {
                entry_box d = new entry_box(this);
                d.show();
            }
            if (arg.equals("Quit"))
             System.exit(0);

            return true;     // event processed
        }
        return false;        // event not processed
    }
}
```

When the applet detects the Ok button event, the dialog box event handler calls the *dialog_entry* method of its parent and passes the to the method, the string it collected. Instead of storing the parent variable passed in the *Dialog* constructor method, this application uses the *getParent* method to determine the *Dialog* object's parent. Then, the *dialog_entry* method simply displays the string that the user entered in the dialog box.

581   PROCESSING USER INPUT FROM A MODAL DIALOG BOX

In Tip 580, you learned how to process user input when the user selected the Ok button within a dialog box. For a modal dialog box, as in the case of the *sendinfo_dialog.java* program that you created in the previous tip, there is a better way to handle the user input. In a modal dialog box, Java blocks the calling code when the applet calls the *show* method. In other words, the *show* method will not return to its caller until the user disposes of the dialog box.

Therefore, you can place the code to process the user's input immediately after the *show* method. The following application, *sendinfo_modal.java*, is functionally the same as the *sendinfo_dialog.java* application. However, in this case, the input processing code resides right after the dialog box creation-and-display code:

```java
import java.awt.*;

class modal_box extends Dialog {

    TextField tf = new TextField("fhbdfh", 15);

    public modal_box(Frame parent)
      {
        super(parent, "About", true);

        Panel entry_panel = new Panel();
        Panel ok_panel = new Panel();

         entry_panel.add(new Label("Name:", Label.LEFT));
        entry_panel.add(tf);
        add("North", entry_panel);

        ok_panel.add(new Button("Ok"));
        add("South", ok_panel);
        resize(250, 100);
      }

    public String getNameEntry()
      {
        return tf.getText();
      }

    public boolean action(Event evt, Object arg)
      {
        if (evt.target instanceof Button)
          {
            this.dispose();
            return true;        // event processed
          }
        return false;           // event not processed
      }
 }

public class sendinfo_modal extends Frame {

    MenuBar menubar = new MenuBar();
    Menu help = new Menu("File", true);

    public sendinfo_modal(String title)
      {
        super(title);
        setMenuBar(menubar);
```

```
        menubar.add(help);
        help.add("New");
        help.add("Quit");
  }

  public static void main(String args[])
    {
      sendinfo_modal application = new
        sendinfo_modal("sendinfo_modal");
      application.resize(200, 100);
      application.show();
    }

  public boolean action(Event evt, Object arg)
    {
      if (evt.target instanceof MenuItem)
        {
          if (arg.equals("New"))
            {
              modal_box d = new modal_box(this);
              d.show();
              System.out.println("Dialog entry :" +
                d.getNameEntry());
            }

          if (arg.equals("Quit"))
            System.exit(0);

          return true;   // events processed
        }
      return false; // events not processed
    }
}
```

When the user closes the modal dialog box, the program calls the *Dialog* class *getNameEntry* method to get the name entry string from the dialog box, displaying the string in the console window.

*Note: There is a bug in the current Windows version 1.0.2 of the Java JDK and prior versions of Java JDK on all platforms. Although the modal dialog box still blocks input to other windows, the **show** method returns immediately after the dialog box is displayed. The **sendinfo_modal.java** program will not run correctly under Windows, but will work properly under Solaris with JDK 1.0.2.*

582 USING THE FILEDIALOG CLASS FOR FILE SELECTION

Many applications let users open and save data files. It is common for applications to provide a dialog box that lets the user navigate directories and select a file from a list of available files. The Java AWT library provides a generic dialog box that your programs can use for File Open and Save selections.

To create a File Open and Save dialog box, you first create a *FileDialog* object using one of the following constructor methods:

```
FileDialog(Frame parent, String title);
FileDialog(Frame parent, String title, int mode);
```

Like the *Dialog* constructor, the *FileDialog* method's first parameter must be a *Frame* object and must indicate the *FileDialog* object's parent. The *title* parameter specifies the dialog box title. The *mode* parameter specifies the dialog box mode, which you can set to *FileDialog.LOAD* to create a File Open dialog box or to *FileDialog.SAVE* to create a File Save dialog box.

Also, like a *Frame* or *Dialog* object, the File dialog box is initially invisible. To display the dialog box, you must call the *Window* class *show* method. The following code creates and displays a File Save dialog box:

```
Frame f;
FileDialog fd = new FileDialog(f, "File Open");
fd.show();
```

THE FILEDIALOG INTERFACE IS PLATFORM DEPENDENT 583

To provide a consistent user interface, many platforms provide a standard dialog box for file access, font selection, and so on. Instead of creating a new standard dialog box, the Java AWT *FileDialog* interface utilizes each platform's standard File Access dialog box. Although using the platform's standard dialog gives the user a familiar interface, the dialog box (created by the same Java code) may look different on each platform, and the features in the dialog boxes may also vary.

For example, the *FileDialog* interface on the Windows 95 platform, as shown in Figure 583.1, lets users create new folders (directories) and delete files, while the *FileDialog* interface on Solaris, as shown in Figure 583.2, does not. Therefore, when you design your own Java program, you should only depend on the *FileDialog* interface to supply the ability to navigate directories and select files. Relying on other features will result in your program behaving inconsistently on different platforms.

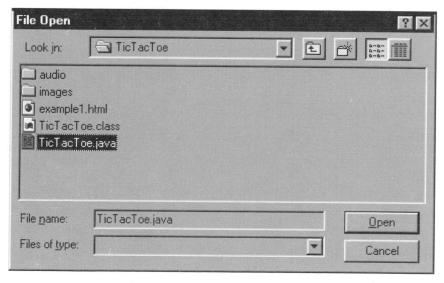

Figure 583.1 The FileDialog interface on Windows 95.

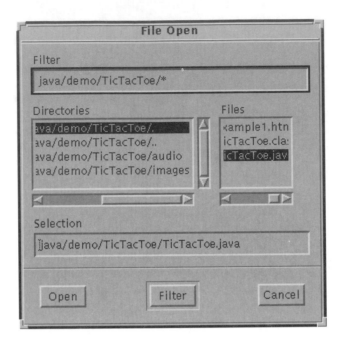

*Figure 583.2 The **FileDialog** interface on Solaris.*

584 GETTING INFORMATION FROM A FILEDIALOG INTERFACE

In Tip 583, you learned how to display a File Access dialog box. To find out which file the user has selected, you use the *FileDialog* class *getFile* and *getDirectory* methods, whose formats are as follows:

```
String getFile();
String getDirectory();
```

The *getFile* method returns the name of the file selected by the user or it returns null if the user has not selected a file. The *getDirectory* method returns the name of the directory where the selected file resides. The following application, *filedialog_test.java*, displays a File Open dialog box when the user selects the File Open menu item. Then, the applet displays the name of the file or directory that the user selects:

```
import java.awt.*;

public class filedialog_test extends Frame {

    MenuBar menubar = new MenuBar();
    Menu file_menu = new Menu("File", true);

    public filedialog_test(String title)
      {
        super(title);
        setMenuBar(menubar);
        menubar.add(file_menu);
```

```java
            file_menu.add("Open");
    }

    public static void main(String args[])
    {
        filedialog_test application = new
            filedialog_test("filedialog_test");
        application.resize(200, 100);
        application.show();
    }

    public boolean handleEvent(Event evt)
    {
        if (evt.id == Event.WINDOW_DESTROY)
          System.exit(0);

        return super.handleEvent(evt);
    }

    public boolean action(Event evt, Object arg)
    {
        if (evt.target instanceof MenuItem)
          {
            if (arg.equals("Open"))
              {
                FileDialog fd = new FileDialog(this, "File Open");
                fd.show();
                System.out.println("dialog box done" + fd.getFile());
                System.out.println("dialog box done" +
                  fd.getDirectory());
              }
            return true;   // event processed
          }
        return false;       // event not processed
    }
}
```

HOW TO CREATE A SAVE FILEDIALOG

585

In Tip 584, you learned how to create a File Open dialog box using the *FileDialog* class. You can also create a File Save dialog box using the following form of the *FileDialog* constructor method:

```java
FileDialog(Frame parent, String title, int mode);
```

To create a File Open dialog box, set the *mode* parameter to *FileDialog.LOAD*, which is the default value. To create a File Save dialog box, set the parameter to *FileDialog.SAVE*. Figure 585 shows a File Save dialog box under Windows 95.

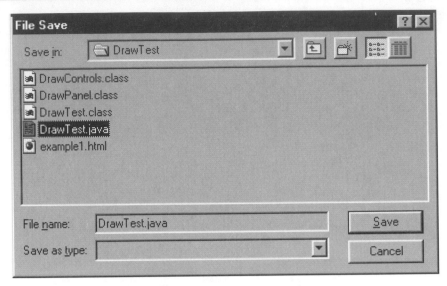

Figure 585 A File Save dialog box.

As it turns out, there is no major difference between a File Open and a File Save dialog box. Both dialog-box types simply give you the filename that the user specifies. Your program will have to provide additional code to open or save the file. You will find Tips in the I/O section of this book that will show you how to read and write files. The biggest difference between these two dialog boxes is the labels.

586   USING THE SET FILE AND SET DIRECTORY METHODS

When your programs use File Open or File Save dialog boxes, you may want to suggest a default file or a default directory. In such cases, you use the *setFile* and *setDirectory* methods, whose formats are as shown:

```
void setFile(String file);
void setDirectory(String dir);
```

For example, the following statements set the default file to a file named *myfile.java* and the default directory to *temp*:

```
FileDialog fd;
fd.setFile("myfile.java");
fd.setDirectory("temp");
```

When you use the *setDirectory* method, bear in mind that the path separator character is platform dependent. The Windows platform uses the backslash character (\) as path separator, while the Solaris platform uses the forward slash character (/).

587   SHOWING FILES OF A PARTICULAR TYPE WITH FILENAME FILTER

Because a directory can store files used by many different applications, users assign special file extensions to differentiate the files for one application from those for another. For example, a file with a *java* extension most likely contains a Java source code file. When the user selects the File Access dialog interface to open a file for a specific application, it is convenient if the dialog box filters the files in the directory and only displays ones that are usable by the application.

The *java.io* library defines the *FilenameFilter* interface class to handle file name filtering. Because this is an interface class, you cannot instantiate it (create objects of this class) directly. Instead, you should create a file name filtering class that implements this interface. The only method that you must implement is the *accept* method. Java passes file and directory names to the *accept* method, which returns *true* if the method should include the file and *false* if the method should exclude the file. The following code defines a class that filters out all files with a ".java" extension:

```
import java.io.*;

class JavaFileFilter implements FilenameFilter {

 public boolean accept(File dir, String name)
    {
       return name.endsWith(".java");
    }
}
```

After you create the file name filtering class, you can assign it to the File Access dialog box using the *setFilenameFilter* method:

```
FileDialog fd;
fc.setFilenameFilter(new JavaFileFilter());
```

*Note: The file name filtering feature is not fully implemented in the current version 1.0.2 of the Java JDK. On some platforms, including Windows 95, the **accept** method is not called and the filter has no effect. On the Window 95 platform, you can use the **setFile** method to set the default file name with a wildcard specification, such as "*.java", to display only files with the specified extension.*

FINDING THE CURRENT SCREEN SIZE AND RESOLUTION 588

Because a Java program may run on many platforms, with different types of displays, there may be times when you want to find the size and resolution of the current display. For example, you might use the display resolution to scale your drawing so that it can be displayed with the same physical size on all platforms. To find the size and resolution of the current display, use the following *Toolkit* class methods:

```
Dimension getScreenSize();
int getScreenResolution();
```

The following application, *screen_res.java*, displays the size and resolution of the display on the console window:

```
import java.awt.*;

public class screen_res {
    public static void main(String args[])
      {
        Dimension screen_size =
            Toolkit.getDefaultToolkit().getScreenSize();
        int screen_res =
            Toolkit.getDefaultToolkit().getScreenResolution();

        System.out.println("Screen size = " + screen_size.width +
            " x " + screen_size.height);
```

```
        System.out.println("Screen resolution = " + screen_res
            + " dots/inch");
        System.exit(0);
    }
}
```

589 HOW TO CENTER A DIALOG BOX ON THE SCREEN

You may have noticed that Java automatically positions the About dialog box you created in Tip 579 on the screen. At times, you may want to center the dialog box to attract the user's attention. To center a dialog box, you must override the default position and set it yourself using the *Component* class *move* method:

```
void move(x, y);
```

For example, the following statements use the *move* method to place the top-left corner of the dialog box at location (100,50):

```
Dialog d;
d.move(100,  50);
```

To position the dialog in the middle of the screen, you first must find the size of the screen by using the *getScreenSize* method you learned about in Tip 588. Next, you must find the size of the dialog box by using the *Component* class *size* method. Then, you can calculate the position of the dialog box using the following equation:

```
x position = (width_of_screen - width_of_dialog) / 2;

y position = (height_of_screen - height_of_dialog) / 2;
```

The following statements will display a dialog box in the center of the screen:

```
Dialog d;
Dimension screen_size, dialog_size;

screen_size = Toolkit.getDefaultToolkit().getScreenSize();
dialog_size = d.size();

d.move((screen_size.width-dialog_size.width)/2,
    (screen_size.height-dialog_size.height)/2);
```

Note: The previous algorithm assumes that the parameters in the **move** *method specify the absolute coordinates on the screen. This is how it works on Java JDK 1.0.2, but in future JDK versions, coordinates may be referenced to the location of the parent frame instead. In that case, you should offset the location of the dialog box by the location of its parent on the screen.*

590 UNDERSTANDING THE PEER CLASS

If you examine the Java packages, you may notice that there is a *java.awt.peer* package. If you examine the *peer* class, you will find that there is a one-to-one correspondence between the component classes in the *java.awt.peer* package and the *java.awt* package. For example, there is a *ButtonPeer* class in the *java.awt.peer* package that corresponds to the *Button* class in the *java.awt* package.

If your interest is in developing application programs, you will probably never have to use the *peer* class. Java creates *peer* objects automatically through the instantiation of AWT components. You only need the *peer* class if you are porting Java programs to a new platform.

The purpose of the *peer* class is to provide an interface between the platform independent AWT components and their corresponding platform dependent native implementations. To port Java programs to a new platform, you must implement each of the peer methods in each peer interface using the native components.

PLAYING AN AUDIO CLIP

 591

Audio can be a very powerful tool in a multimedia product. In fact, a few sound clips can really jazz up a program and draw the user's attention. The Java Developer's Kit supports the playing of Sun's AU format sound files. To play an AU sound file in an applet, you can use one of the *Applet* class *play* methods, as shown in the following statements:

```
void play(URL url);
void play(URL url, String name);
```

The first *play* method's *url* parameter should be a Uniform Reference Locator (URL) pointing to the audio file on the Web. For example, the following statement plays the audio file *sample.au* that the applet retrieves from the specified Web site:

```
play (new URL("http://www.myserver.com/audio/sample.au"));
```

Notice the hardcoded pathname in the previous example. It is good programming practice not to hardcode the server's name within your program. Should you move the program to a different server, or to a different directory, you will have to change the source code to match the new URL. Instead, you should use the *getCodeBase* method to locate the Java program, and then store the audio file in a directory related to the program file.

Using the second form of the *play* method, the *url* parameter points to the audio file's location (which you can get using the *getCodeBase* method) and the *name* parameter specifies the name of the audio file. For example, the following statement plays the audio file *sample.au*, which resides in the same directory as the Java program:

```
play(getCodeBase(), "sample.au");
```

USING THE AUDIOCLIP CLASS

 592

The *Applet* class *play* method that you examined in the previous tip provides a convenient way to get and play an audio clip. However, if you want more control over how the audio clip plays (such as whether the clip plays one time or loops), you can create an *AudioClip* reference by calling the *AudioClip* class *getAudioClip* methods, as shown in the following statements:

```
AudioClip getAudioClip(URL url);
AudioClip getAudioClip(URL url, String name);
```

The *getAudioClip* methods let you create a reference to the audio file without actually playing it. Later, you can play the audio file by calling the *AudioClip* class *play* method, as shown:

```
AudioClip sample_audio = getAudioClip(getCodeBase(), "sample.au");

sample_audio.play();   // Play the clip
```

593 STOPPING AN AUDIO CLIP

In the previous tip, you learned that you can play an audio clip by creating an *AudioClip* object and calling the *AudioClip* class *play* method. You may be wondering why you need to create an *AudioClip* object when you can use the *Applet* class *play* method. One reason is because you can use the *AudioClip* class *stop* method to stop an audio file's playback.

By default, when you start playing an audio clip, Java will play the clip until it reaches the end. There may be times, however, when you want to stop playing at some midpoint. In such cases, you call the *stop* method. For example, if you are playing a long audio clip in your applet, you may want it to stop playing when the user switches to another Web page. The following code illustrates how to stop an audio clip when the user switches Web pages:

```
public class myapplet extends Applet {

    // Other applet statements here

    public void stop()
      {
          if (long_audio_clip != null) // make sure audio clip
            {                          // reference is valid
                long_audio_clip.stop(); // stop playing the clip
            }
        }
    }
```

As you have learned, when a user switches Web pages, Java calls the *stop* method. Within the *stop* method, you can use the *AudioClip* class *stop* method to stop the audio clip. As you can see, the code first checks the *long_audio_clip* object reference to make sure it is not null, which means the variable contains an *AudioClip* object. Next, the function uses the stop method to turn off the audio clip.

594 LOOPING AN AUDIO CLIP

When your programs play audio clips, there may be times when you want to repeatedly play an audio clip. In such cases, you call the *AudioClip* class *loop* method to play the audio clip. When you call the *loop* method, Java will play the clip continuously until you call the *AudioClip* class *stop* method, or until you start to play another clip. The following applet, *splayer.java*, plays the audio clip specified by the HTML *AUDIOCLIP* parameter. To play the clip once, click the *play* button; to play the clip repeatedly, click the *loop* button.

```
import java.applet.*;
import java.awt.*;

public class splayer extends Applet {

    AudioClip aclip;

    public void init()
      {
          aclip = getAudioClip(getCodeBase(),
                    getParameter("AUDIOCLIP"));
```

```
        add(new Button ("Play"));
        add(new Button ("Stop"));
        add(new Button ("Loop"));
     }

  public void stop()
    {
      if (aclip != null)
        aclip.stop();
    }

  public boolean action(Event evt, Object arg)
    {
      if (evt.target instanceof Button)
        {
            if (arg.equals("Play"))
              aclip.play();
            else if (arg.equals("Stop"))
              aclip.stop();
            else if (arg.equals("Loop"))

            aclip.loop();

            return true;   // events processed
        }

      return false; // events not processed
    }
}
```

BUILDING A PIANO APPLET

 595

In previous tips, you learned how to play an audio clip. The following program, *piano.java*, uses a graphical user interface built from *Button* objects to create a simple piano, as shown in Figure 595. Each time the user presses a button, the applet plays the corresponding audio clip:

```
import  java.applet.*;
import  java.awt.*;

public class piano extends Applet {

    String items[] = {"C","D","E","F","G","A","B","C'"};

    public void init()
      {
        setLayout (new GridLayout(1, 8));

        for (int i = 0; i < items.length; i++)
            add (new Button(items[i]));
      }
```

```
    public boolean action(Event evt, Object arg)
  {
      if (evt.target instanceof Button)
      {
        if (arg.equals("C"))
          play (getCodeBase(), "cnote.au");
        else if (arg.equals("D"))
          play (getCodeBase(), "dnote.au");
        else if (arg.equals("E"))
          play (getCodeBase(), "enote.au");
        else if (arg.equals("F"))
          play (getCodeBase(), "fnote.au");
        else if (arg.equals("G"))
          play (getCodeBase(), "gnote.au");
        else if (arg.equals("A"))
          play (getCodeBase(), "anote.au");
        else if (arg.equals("B"))
          play (getCodeBase(), "bnote.au");
        else if (arg.equals("C'"))
          play (getCodeBase(), "c1note.au");

        return true;   // event processed
      }
      return false; // events not processed
  }
}
```

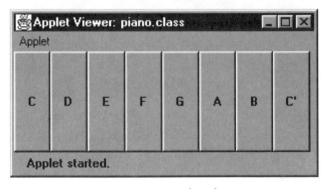

Figure 595 *A Java-based piano.*

596 CONVERTING A .WAV FILE TO A .AU FILE FORMAT

As you have learned, Java provides built-in support for playing Sun's .AU audio-file format, also known as μ-law format. However, the current release of Java's JDK does not support other formats, such as Windows .WAV format or the Sound Blaster VOC format. Until JDK supports other sound file formats, you can use one of the many sound utilities available to convert other formats to Sun's .AU format.

One such utility is *SOund eXchange* (*SOX*) created by Lance Norskog. This versatile utility lets you change between many different types of sound files. For example, to convert the .WAV file, *sample.wav*, to Sun's .AU format on a Windows platform, you can type the following command at the MS-DOS prompt:

```
C:\> sox sample.wav    sample.au   <ENTER>
```

The *SOX* utility is available on the Internet. You can download *SOX* for free and find related information on supported formats and available options at the following Websites:

```
http:/www.spies.com/SOX
http://www.hyperreal.com/tools/msdos/sound/
ftp://x2ftp.oulu.fi/pub/msdos/programming/convert/sox10dos.zip
```

CREATING A SIMPLE ANIMATION 597

Animation is the process of displaying images (sometimes called frames) in a sequence to simulate motion. When you create your first Java animation, you may be tempted to loop through the images, displaying one image after another. For example, the following code fragment uses a *for* loop to display a specific number of frame images. As you can see, the *for* loop delays one-tenth of a second between frames:

```java
public class my_animation extends Applet {

    public void start()
    {
        for (animeframe = 0; animeframe < no_of_frames;
            animeframe ++)
        {
            // set up a frame
            setup_animation_frame(animeframe);

            // redraw screen for new frame
            repaint ();

            // pause for 0.1 second (100 milliseconds)
            // between successive frames

            try {
                Thread.sleep (100);
            } catch (InterruptedException e) { };
        }
    }

    // Other applet statements here
}
```

The problem with this approach to animation is that the call to the *repaint* method does not immediately draw the screen. As it turns out, Java is an event-driven system which collects requests to paint the screen so Java can perform them when there are no other events to process. The *for* loop in the previous *start* method "locks up" Java's event message delivery system and Java cannot repaint the screen until the *for* loop completes. The solution to this problem is to create a thread, which the following code illustrates:

```java
public class my_animation extends Applet implements Runnable {

    Thread anime = null;
```

```
public void start()
  {
    anime = new Thread(this);
    anime.start();
  }

public void run()
  {
    for (animeframe = 0; animeframe < no_of_frames;
         animeframe ++)
      {
        // set up a frame
         setup_animation_frame (animeframe);

        // redraw screen for new frame
        repaint ();

        // pause for 0.1 second (100 milliseconds)
        // between successive frames

        try {
           Thread.sleep (100);
          } catch (InterruptedException e) {};
      }
  }

// Other applet statements here
}
```

The above example implements the *Runnable* interface which lets the applet run a separate thread. The program starts the *anime* thread object within the applet's *start* method. When the animation thread starts, Java automatically calls the *run* method which, in turn, uses the *for* loop that creates the animation. The section of this book that examines threads will provide a detailed discussion on thread operations.

598 SCROLLING TEXT ANIMATION

In the previous tip, you learned how to create animation using threads. In this tip, you will create a complete example of a Java animation. The following applet, *scroll_hello.java*, uses a thread object which repeatedly scrolls the string "Hello, world" from left to right across the applet window. As you will see, to move the string across the screen, the applet simply redraws the string using a different *x* coordinate each time:

```
import java.applet.*;
import java.awt.*;

public class scroll_hello extends Applet implements Runnable {

    int xpos = 0;
    Thread anime = null;
    Image file_img;
```

```java
    public void start()
      {
        if (anime == null)
          {
             anime = new Thread(this);
             anime.start();
          }
      }


    public void paint (Graphics g)
      {
         g.drawString ("hello, world", xpos, 70);
      }


    public void run()
      {
         while (anime != null)
           {
              xpos += 10;

              if (xpos > size().width)
                xpos = 0;

              repaint();

              try {
                   Thread.sleep (100);
                 }
              catch (InterruptedException e) {};
           }
      }
}
```

CREATING A SIMPLE ANIMATION WITH IMAGES 599

In the previous tip, you learned how to animate a text string by redrawing the string at different locations within the applet window. As it turns out, you can use this same technique to animate images. The following applet, *gif_anime.java*, displays a 3-D rotating "Java" logo, as shown in Figure 599, by cycling through six *GIF* images:

```java
import java.applet.*;
import java.awt.*;

public class gif_anime extends Applet implements Runnable {

    int img_index = 0;
    Thread anime = null;

    String img_names[] = {"java1.gif", "java2.gif",  "java3.gif",
                          "java4.gif", "java5.gif",  "java6.gif"};
```

```
    Image java_img[] = new Image[6];

public void init()
  {
    for (int i = 0; i < 6; i++)
      java_img[i] = getImage (getCodeBase(), img_names[i]);
  }

public void start()
  {
    if (anime == null)
      {
        anime = new Thread(this);
        anime.start();
      }
  }

public void paint (Graphics g)
  {
    g.drawImage (java_img[img_index], 0, 0, this);
  }

public void run()
  {
    while (anime != null)
      {
        img_index++;

        if (img_index > 5)
          img_index = 0;

        repaint();

        try {
            Thread.sleep (200);
          }
        catch (InterruptedException e) {};
      }
  }
}
```

The difference between this applet and the *scroll_hello.java* applet you created in the previous tip is that instead of adjusting the string position within the *run* method, the applet uses the *run* method to select which image to display. When you run this applet, you may notice a lot of screen flickering. The next tip, however, will show you how to reduce the flickering.

Figure 599 *Creating an animation using images.*

OVERRIDING THE UPDATE METHOD TO REDUCE FLICKERING

600

In the previous tip, you found that the animation in the applet *gif_anime.java* suffers from screen flickering. The reason for the flickering is that when the code calls the *repaint* method to redraw the screen, the *repaint* method in turn calls the *update* method. The default *update* method clears the drawing area with the background color and then calls the *paint* method to redraw the window contents. However, in the case of the *gif_anime.java* applet, clearing the background is unnecessary because the code in the *paint* method will draw the entire display area. Therefore, in this case, you can override the *update* method with the following code to remove the erase operation which, in turn, will reduce the flickering:

```
public void update (Graphics g)
  {
    paint(g);
  }
```

Overriding the *update* method in this way will only work in cases where the *paint* method redraws the entire display area. An alternative to overriding the *update* method is not to call the *repaint* method to redraw the screen. Instead, the applet can call the *paint* method directly, as shown:

```
Graphics g = getGraphics(); // get graphics object

paint(g);                            // replaces the repaint() call
```

IMPROVING ANIMATION USING CLIPPING AREAS

601

As your animations become more complex, one way you can improve the animation's efficiency is by redrawing only the screen area that you need to update. Consider, for example, a case where you move a small image across the screen. You could redraw the entire background and then draw the image at the new location. However, this technique is very inefficient because it redraws the screen area that does not need updating. A better way to update the screen is to define a clipping region for the area that needs updating, and then only redraw that part of the screen. The following applet, *sfish.java*, uses a clipping region to display the animation shown in Figure 601:

```java
import java.applet.*;
import java.awt.*;

public class sfish extends Applet implements Runnable {

    int xpos = 0;
    Thread anime = null;
    Image fish_img, bg_img;
    int fish_width, fish_height;

    public void init()
      {
          fish_img = getImage (getCodeBase(), "sfish.gif");
          fish_width = 100;
          fish_height = 139;

          bg_img = getImage (getCodeBase(), "fishback.gif");
      }

    public void start()
      {
        if (anime == null)
          {
            anime = new Thread(this);
            anime.start();
          }
      }

    public void paint(Graphics g)
      {
        g.drawImage (bg_img, 0, 0, this);
        g.drawImage (fish_img, xpos, 50, this);
      }

    public void run()
      {
        while (anime != null)
          {
              Rectangle old_area = new Rectangle (xpos, 50,
                  fish_width, fish_height);

            xpos += 10;

            if (xpos > size().width)
              xpos = 0;

              Rectangle new_area = new Rectangle(xpos, 50,
                  fish_width, fish_height);
```

```
          Rectangle update_area =new_area.union(old_area);

          Graphics g = getGraphics();

          g.clipRect (update_area.x, update_area.y,
             update_area.width, update_area.height);

          paint (g);

          try {
             Thread.sleep (300);
           }
          catch (InterruptedException e) {};
         }
      }
   }
```

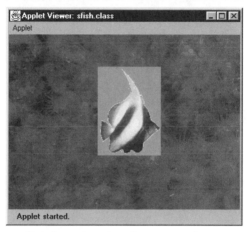

Figure 601 An animation that uses a clipping region.

USING TRANSPARENT GIF FILES   602

Quite often the objects that you want to draw within an applet window have unique shapes. However, image files can only be rectangular. When you display an image that contains a non-rectangular object, the image's background will cover up the display background. If you examine the *sfish.java* applet that you created in the previous tip, you will find that the image covers part of the background. One solution to this problem is to match the image's background color with that of your applet's background. This technique, however, is inappropriate for cases in which the image is drawn over different backgrounds. A better solution is to define an image with a transparent background. Java has built-in support for the use of transparent *GIF* files. As it turns out, loading a transparent *GIF* is no different from loading any other image files. Many graphics utilities and paint programs, such as Adobe Photoshop, let you create *GIF* images with a transparent background. The following applet, *trans_gif.java*, draws a flower image with a transparent background, as shown in Figure 602:

```
import java.applet.*;
import java.awt.*;
```

```
public class trans_gif extends Applet {

    Image bg_img, fg_img;

    public void init()
      {
         bg_img = getImage (getCodeBase(), "bgimg.jpg");
         fg_img = getImage (getCodeBase(), "tranflwr.gif");
      }

    public void paint(Graphics g)
      {
         g.drawImage (bg_img, 0, 0, this);
         g.drawImage (fg_img, 50, 40, this);
      }
}
```

Figure 602 A flower image with a transparent background.

603 ENHANCING AN ANIMATION WITH DOUBLE BUFFERING

When you run the *sfish.java* animation that you created in Tip 601, you may still notice some flickering. The reason for the flickering is that when the *paint* method draws each new frame, it draws the background first to erase the fish, and then draws the fish again in the new location. Therefore, for a brief moment, there is no fish on the screen. Unfortunately, users can detect this intermediate step. The solution to this problem is to use *double buffering*. With double buffering, you first draw your image on an off-screen buffer in memory. Then, you copy the buffer's contents to the on-screen display. In this way, the user will not see the erase process.

To create the memory-image buffer, you call the *Graphics* class *creatImage* method, as shown:

```
Image createImage(int width, int height);
```

The *width* and *height* parameters specify the dimensions of the image buffer. To draw to the image buffer, you must get a reference to a *Graphics* object by calling the *Image* class *getGraphics* method. After you have the *Graphics* object reference, drawing to the off-screen buffer is no different from drawing to the screen. The following applet, *dubf_anime.java*, improves the animation of the *sfish.java* applet by using double buffering:

```java
import java.applet.*;
import java.awt.*;

public class dbuf_anime extends Applet implements Runnable {

    int xpos = 0;
    Thread anime = null;
    Image fish_img, bg_img;
    int fish_width, fish_height;
    Image offscreen_buf = null;

    public void init()
      {
         fish_img = getImage (getCodeBase(), "tranfish.gif");
         fish_width = 100;
         fish_height = 139;

         bg_img = getImage (getCodeBase(), "fishback.gif");
      }

    public void start()
      {
         if (anime == null)
           {
              anime = new Thread(this);
              anime.start();
           }
      }

    public void paint(Graphics g)
      {
         g.drawImage (bg_img, 0, 0, this);
         g.drawImage (fish_img, xpos, 50, this);
      }

    public void run()
      {
         while (anime != null)
           {
              if (offscreen_buf == null)
                {
                    // create an offscreen buffer with the same
                    // size as the display

                    offscreen_buf = createImage (size().width,
                       size().height);
                }

                Rectangle old_area = new  Rectangle(xpos, 50, fish_width,
                     fish_height);
```

```
        xpos += 10;

        if (xpos > size().width)
          xpos = 0;

        Rectangle new_area = new  Rectangle(xpos, 50, fish_width,
              fish_height);

        Rectangle update_area =new_area.union(old_area);

        // paint to offscreen buffer
        Graphics offg = offscreen_buf.getGraphics();
        offg.clipRect(update_area.x, update_area.y,
            update_area.width, update_area.height);

        paint(offg);

        // copy image to onscreen display
        Graphics ong = getGraphics();

        ong.clipRect (update_area.x, update_area.y,
            update_area.width, update_area.height);

        ong.drawImage (offscreen_buf, 0, 0, this);

        try {
            Thread.sleep (300);
          }
        catch (InterruptedException e) {};
      }
    }
}
```

604 UNDERSTANDING THE IMAGEOBSERVER

When your program calls the *drawImage* method to display an image, Java first checks to see if the image is available (if the image has been loaded and is ready for display). If the image is unavailable, the *drawImage* method returns without drawing the image, but will notify the *ImageObserver* of its progress. Java sends the notification message to the *ImageObserver* by calling the observer's *imageUpdate* method, as shown in the following statement:

```
boolean imageUpdate(Image img, int infoflags, int x, int y,
   int width, int height);
```

The *img* parameter specifies for which image Java is sending the notification. The *infoflags* argument specifies the type of information the message contains. The *infoflags* argument is a bit-mask variable whose bits can represent a combination of the values listed in Table 604.

Bit Field	Meaning
ABORT	Image production was aborted
ALLBITS	Image is completed
ERROR	An error was encountered
FRAMEBITS	A new image frame is completed
HEIGHT	Height information is now available
PROPERTIES	Image property information is now available
SOMEBITS	Part of the image is available
WIDTH	Width information is now available

*Table 604 Flag values specified by an **imageUpdate** message.*

By default, the *imageUpdate* method calls the *repaint* method to redraw the screen area, even in the case when the image is only partially available. As you will learn in Tip 605, by overriding the *imageUpdate* method, your programs can detect when the image is loaded and ready for display.

DETECTING THE PROGRESS OF IMAGING LOADING

 605

In the previous tip, you learned that Java calls the *imageUpdate* method as it loads a graphics image. By overriding the *imageUpdate* method, you can monitor the progress of the image-loading operation. The following applet, *img_progress.java*, displays progress messages to the status window to indicate that image loading is in progress:

```java
import java.applet.*;
import java.awt.*;

public class img_progress extends Applet implements Runnable {

    int load_index = 0;
    Thread progress = null;
    Image bg_img;
    String ld_str[]  = {"loading *    ", "loading  *  ",
                        "loading    * ", "loading     *"};

    public void init()
      {
         bg_img = getImage (getCodeBase(), "bgimg.jpg");
      }

    public void start()
      {
        if (progress == null)
          {
             progress = new Thread(this);
             progress.start();
          }
      }
```

```java
public void paint(Graphics g)
  {
    g.drawImage (bg_img, 0, 0, this);
  }


public void run()
  {
    while (progress != null)
      {
        load_index++;

        if (load_index > 3)
          load_index = 0;

        showStatus (ld_str[load_index]);

        try {
            Thread.sleep (300);
          }
        catch (InterruptedException e) {};
      }
  }


public boolean imageUpdate(Image img, int flags, int x, int y,
                           int w, int h)
  {
    if (img == bg_img)
      {
        if ((flags & ALLBITS) != 0)
          {
            if ( progress != null)
              {
                showStatus ("loaded");
                progress.stop();
              }
          }
      }
    return super.imageUpdate(img, flags, x, y, w, h);
  }
}
```

606 GETTING THE SIZE OF AN IMAGE

When you use images within a Java program, there may be times you need to know the size of an image. In such cases, you use the *Image* class *getWidth* and *getHeight* methods. The formats of these methods are as follows:

```
int getWidth(ImageObserver observer);
int getHeight(ImageObserver observer);
```

These methods return the image width and height in pixels. If, for some reason, the size information is not available, such as if the image is not yet loaded, the methods return the value -1. If the information is unavailable because the image is not yet loaded, Java will call the *imageUpdate* method when the information becomes available. The following applet, *img_size.java*, illustrates the use of the *getWidth* and *getHeight* methods by displaying an image and its size, as shown in Figure 606:

```java
import java.applet.*;
import java.awt.*;

public class img_size extends Applet {

    Image file_img;
    int img_width, img_height;

    public void init()
      {
          file_img = getImage (getCodeBase(), "bgimg.jpg");
          img_width = file_img.getWidth(this);
          img_height = file_img.getHeight(this);
      }

    public void paint (Graphics g)
      {
          g.drawImage (file_img, 0, 0, this);
          g.setColor (Color.green);
          g.drawString (String.valueOf(img_width) + "x" +
              String.valueOf(img_height),30, 70);
      }

    public boolean imageUpdate(Image img, int flags, int x, int y,
                               int w, int h)
      {
        if (img == file_img)
          {
            if ((flags & HEIGHT) != 0)
              img_height = h;


            if ((flags & WIDTH) != 0)
              img_width = w;
          }
        return super.imageUpdate(img, flags, x, y, w, h);
      }
  }
```

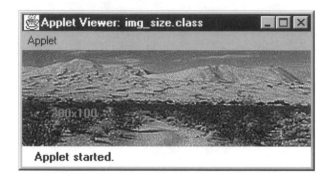

*Figure 606   Using the **getWidth** and **getHeight** methods.*

607   USING MEDIATRACKER TO PRELOAD IMAGES

As you learned in the *gif_anime.java* animation you created in Tip 599, image flickering is a problem during screen update operations. Even if your applet overrides the *update* method to remove the screen erase, flickering may still occur as the image loads. To solve this problem, your program can wait until the applet loads all of its images before it starts the animation. To help you preload images in this way, Java's AWT library provides the *MediaTracker* class. In the future, your programs may use the *MediaTracker* class to track your applet's loading of various media objects, such as images and audio clips. Currently, the *MediaTracker* only tracks the loading of images.

To use Java's *MediaTracker* to track images, you must first create a *MediaTracker* object. Then, you must call the *addImage* method to add an image to the tracker. The formats of the *addImage* methods are as follows:

```
void addImage(Image image, int id);
void addImage(Image image, int id, int w, int h);
```

The *image* parameter specifies the loading of the image that you want to track. The *id* parameter specifies an identifier which your program can use later to retrieve information about the images. The *w* and *h* parameters of the second *addImage* method specify the width and height of the area within which you want the image rendered. When you use the *addImage* method to add images to the *Media tracker*, you are not limited to assigning one *id* number to one image. In this way, you can add multiple images to the tracker with the same *id* number to form a tracking group.

Two *MediaTracker* class methods you will use to synchronize your graphics operations are *waitForAll* and *waitForId*. The formats of these two methods are as follows:

```
void waitForAll();
void waitForID(int id);
```

The *waitForID* method will not return control to the caller until the images in the tracker with the specified *id* are loaded. The *waitForAll* method will not return control to the caller until all images in the tracker are loaded. The following applet, *tracked_anime.java*, provides an improved version of the *gif_anime.java* applet that you created in Tip 599. The animation will not start until all images are loaded.

```
import java.applet.*;
import java.awt.*;
```

```java
public class tracked_anime extends Applet implements Runnable {

    int img_index = 0;
    Thread anime = null;
    String img_names[] = {"java1.gif", "java2.gif",  "java3.gif",
                          "java4.gif", "java5.gif",  "java6.gif"};

    Image java_img[] = new Image[6];

    public void init()
      {
        MediaTracker mt = new MediaTracker(this);

        for (int i = 0; i < 6; i++)
          {
              java_img[i] = getImage (getCodeBase(), img_names[i]);
             mt.addImage (java_img[i], i);
          }

        try {
            mt.waitForAll();
          }
        catch (InterruptedException e) {};
      }

    public void start()
      {
        if (anime == null)
          {
              anime = new Thread(this);
              anime.start();
          }
      }

    public void stop()
      {
        if (anime == null)
          {
              anime.stop();
          }
      }

    public void paint(Graphics g)
      {
        g.drawImage (java_img[img_index], 0, 0, this);
      }

    public void run()
      {
```

```
      while (anime != null)
        {
           img_index++;

           if (img_index > 5)
              img_index = 0;

           paint (getGraphics());

           try {
                Thread.sleep (200);
               }
            catch (InterruptedException e) {};
        }
     }
  }
```

608 SETTING TIME LIMITS WHEN LOADING AN IMAGE

In Tip 607, you learned that by using the *MediaTracker* class *waitForAll* and *waitForID* methods, you can suspend your programs until Java has loaded the specified image files. The disadvantage of the *waitForID* and *waitForAll* methods is that these methods will wait forever until the tracked images are loaded. If, for some reason, the images are never loaded because the image file does not exist or network problems prevent the file's access, your program will lock up. Therefore, you may want to use the other forms of the *waitForID* and *waitForAll* methods. The following statements illustrate the formats of the *waitForID* and *waitForAll* methods:

```
void waitForAll(long ms);
void waitForID(int id, long ms);
```

The *ms* parameter specifies the maximum time in milliseconds that the call will wait before returning control to the caller. When the function returns, you can then use the *statusID* or *statusAll* methods to determine if the images successfully loaded. The formats of the *statusID* and *statusAll* methods are as follows:

```
int statusID(int id, boolean load);
int statusAll(boolean load);
```

The *load* parameter specifies whether you want the tracker to start loading the images or not. Both of these methods return a bit-field value that can be a combination of the status bits listed in Table 608.

Bit Field	Meaning
LOADING	Still loading images
ABORTED	Loading aborted
ERROR	An error was detected
COMPLETE	Image loading completed

*Table 608 Bit field values returned by the **statusID** and **statusAll** methods.*

HOW TO BUILD ZOOM-IN ANIMATION SPECIAL EFFECTS

When your programs manipulate images, there may be times when your program needs to switch between two images. For example, within a slide-show program, you may find that switching instantly from one image to another is distracting. Rather than using an instantaneous switch from one image to the next, your programs can switch images progressively by zooming into the next image. The key to this type of special effect is your use of the *drawImage* method, which lets you stretch the image. The following applet, *zoom_in.java*, implements the fade-in special effect. Figure 609 illustrates the program's output:

```java
import java.applet.*;
import java.awt.*;
import java.awt.image.*;

public class zoom_in extends Applet implements Runnable {

    int img2_width, img2_height;
    Image img1, img2;
    Image offscreen;
    Thread anime = null;

    public void init()
      {
        img1 = getImage (getCodeBase(), "turtoise.gif");
        img2 = getImage (getCodeBase(), "sheepb.gif");

        MediaTracker mt = new MediaTracker(this);
        mt.addImage (img1, 1);
        mt.addImage (img2, 1);

        try {
           mt.waitForAll();
          }
        catch (InterruptedException e) {};

        img2_width = 0;
        img2_height = 0;
      }

    public void update (Graphics g)
      {
        paint(g);
      }

    public void paint(Graphics g)
      {
        // prepare offscreen image
        Graphics goff = offscreen.getGraphics();
        goff.drawImage (img1, 0, 0, this);
```

```java
        int x = (size().width - img2_width) / 2;
        int y = (size().height - img2_height) / 2;
        goff.drawImage (img2, x, y, img2_width, img2_height, this);

        // copy offscreen to onscreen
        g.drawImage (offscreen, 0, 0, this);
        goff.dispose();
    }

public void run()
    {
      Image tempimg;
      int width_inc, height_inc;

      while (anime != null)
        {
          // display the first image only
          img2_width = img2_height = 0;

          repaint();

          try {
             Thread.sleep (100);
           }
          catch (InterruptedException e) {};

          width_inc = img2.getWidth(null) / 16;
          height_inc = img2.getHeight(null) / 16;

          img2_width = img2.getWidth(null) - (width_inc * 15);
          img2_height = img2.getHeight(null) - (height_inc * 15);

          for (int i = 0; i < 16; i++)
            {
              repaint();
              try {
                 Thread.sleep (100);
               }
              catch (InterruptedException e) {};

              img2_width += width_inc;
              img2_height += height_inc;
            }

          // swap images
          tempimg = img1;
          img1 = img2;
          img2 = tempimg;
          tempimg = null;
        }
    }
```

```
public void start()
  {
     offscreen = createImage (size().width, size().height);

     if (anime == null)
       {
          anime = new Thread(this);
          anime.start();
       }
  }
}
```

Figure 609 *An applet illustrating the zoom-in special effect.*

UNDERSTANDING JAVA IMAGING INTERFACES 610

As you have learned, the AWT library lets your applets load and display an image from a *GIF* or *JPEG* file. However, if you need to create images from other sources, or to manipulate an existing image, you must understand Java's imaging interfaces defined in the *java.awt.image* package.

The *ImageProducer* interface lets you define an object, known as an image producer, that produces data for an image. For example, the *MemoryImageSource* class implements the *ImageProducer* interface for creating image data from an integer array. To get the image producer for an *Image* object, you call the *getSource* method.

The *ImageConsumer* interface lets you define an object, known as an image consumer, that receives image data. For example, the *PixelGrabber* class implements the *ImageConsumer* interface, which lets you extract image data and place the data in an integer array.

The *ImageFilter* class, as shown in Figure 610, takes image data from an image producer, processes the data, and then sends the data to an image consumer. For example, your applet might create an image filter to brighten the color of an image or to rotate an image.

Figure 610 *The image filtering process.*

611 UNDERSTANDING THE DEFAULT COLOR MODEL

To process image data, you must understand how programs store pixel data in memory. Java uses a color model to define how other imaging classes should interpret pixel data to extract color information. The default color model stores the color of a single pixel in a 32-bit integer, as shown in Figure 611.

Alpha	Red	Green	Blue
32	24	16	8	0

Figure 611 Java's default color mode.

The model uses eight bits to store each of the blue, green, and red colors and the alpha component. Bits 0-7 of the 32-bit integer stores the blue component, bits 8-15 store the green component, bits 16-23 store the red component, and bits 24-31 store the alpha component. The alpha component defines the pixel's transparency. An alpha value of 0 means the pixel is transparent and a value of 255 means the pixel is opaque. Using the alpha component, Java provides support for the display of transparent *GIF* images. With alpha transparency, you can even define pixels that are semi-transparent.

612 UNDERSTANDING THE DIRECT COLOR MODEL

In the previous tip, you learned that Java's default color model uses eight bits per color to store a pixel's red, green, and blue colors. Within your programs, there may be times when you will want to use a different number of bits for each component. The *DirectColorModel* class lets you define how many bits Java should use to represent each color component. To create a new direct color model, you use one of the following contructor methods:

```
DirectColorModel(int bits, int rmask, int gmask, int bmask);

DirectColorModel(int bits, int rmask, int gmask, int bmask,
   int amask);
```

The *bits* parameter specifies the number of bits required to store the color of one pixel. The *rmask, gmask, bmask,* and *amask* parameter specifies the bitmask Java uses to extract color data for the red, green, blue, and alpha components. If you do not specify the *amask* parameter, Java assumes the pixel data does not contain the alpha component. The following statement uses the *DirectColorModel* to create a direct color model that matches the default color model:

```
DirectColorModel(32,0x00FF0000,0x0000FF00,0x000000FF,0xFF000000);
```

The following statement, for example, defines a color model that uses 4 bits of red data, 6 bits of green data, 5 bits of blue, and no alpha component:

```
DirectColorModel(32, 0x00007800, 0x000007E0, 0x0000001F);
```

613 CREATING AN IMAGE USING MEMORYIMAGESOURCE

As you have learned, within your programs you can create an image using a *GIF* or *JPEG* image file. Java also lets you create an image using data in memory. The *MemoryImageSource* class produces an *Image* from an array of integer pixel values. To create an *Image* object, you can use the following *MemoryImageSource* constructor, as shown:

```
MemoryImageSource(int w, int h, int pix[], int off, int scan);
```

The *w* and *h* parameters specify the image dimensions. The *pix* parameter specifies the integer array that contains the pixel values. The *off* parameter specifies the data offset within the *pix* array. The *scan* parameter specifies the width of one line of pixel data in the *pix* array. Therefore, your program would locate the value of a pixel at the location (m, n) at the index (*n * scan + m + off*) of the pix array.

The following applet, *mem_isource.java*, creates a small (4x7 pixels) image using a *MemoryImageSource* object. The applet then displays the image as well as a scaled version within the applet window, as shown in Figure 613:

```java
import java.applet.*;
import java.awt.*;
import java.awt.image.*;

public class mem_isource extends Applet {

    int mem_pix[] = { 0x00000000, 0xFFFF0000, 0xFFFF0000, 0x00000000,
                      0xFFFF0000, 0x00000000, 0x00000000, 0xFFFF0000,
                      0xFFFF0000, 0x00000000, 0x00000000, 0xFFFF0000,
                      0x00000000, 0xFFFF0000, 0xFFFF0000, 0x00000000,
                      0xFFFF0000, 0x00000000, 0x00000000, 0xFFFF0000,
                      0xFFFF0000, 0x00000000, 0x00000000, 0xFFFF0000,
                      0x00000000, 0xFFFF0000, 0xFFFF0000, 0x00000000
                    };

    Image mem_img;

    public void init()
      {
          mem_img=createImage(new MemoryImageSource(4,7,mem_pix,0,4));
      }

    public void paint (Graphics g)
      {
         g.drawImage (mem_img,  5, 5, this);
         g.drawImage (mem_img,  20, 0, 80, 140, this);
      }
}
```

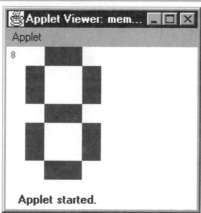

Figure 613 An image created with MemoryImageSource.

614 UNDERSTANDING THE INDEX COLOR MODEL

In Tip 611, you learned that one way Java can represent screen colors is to store RGB (red, green, and blue) color data for each pixel. The index color model provides a more compact model for storing pixel color data. Using the index model, pixel data does not represent color values directly. Instead, the pixel data is an index to a color lookup table that contains the RGB and alpha values. In fact, the 256 color standard VGA mode on IBM compatible PCs is based on an index color model. The advantage of an index color model is that it can reduce the storage size of the pixel data without limiting the colors that it can display. The disadvantage is that the index color model limits the number of simultaneous colors that the image can have. To create an index color model object, use one of the following *IndexColorModel* contructor methods:

```
IndexColorModel(int bits, int size, byte r[], byte g[],
    byte b[]);

IndexColorModel(int bits, int size, byte r[], byte g[], byte b[],
    int trans);

IndexColorModel(int bits, int size, byte r[], byte g[], byte b[],
    byte a[]);

IndexColorModel(int bits, int size, byte cmap[], int start,
    boolean hasalpha);
```

The *bits* parameter specifies the number of bits the model requires to store the index value for one pixel. The *size* parameter specifies the size of the color-lookup table and, consequently, the size of the *r*, *g*, *b*, and *a* arrays. The *trans* parameter in the second constructor specifies the index for transparent color. The *a* array in the third constructor specifies an array of alpha (transparency) settings. In the last constructor, you specify the RGB and alpha color values in sequence within the *cmap* array. The first byte in the *cmap* array stores the 8-bit red component value, the second byte stores the green component, and the third byte stores the blue component. If the *hasalpha* parameter is *true*, then the fourth byte in the *cmap* array stores the alpha transparency component.

615 CREATING AN IMAGE USING WITH THE INDEX COLOR MODEL

As you learned in Tip 614, the *MemoryImageSource* class produces an *Image* from an array of integer pixel values. To create a *MemoryImageSource* object that uses an index color model, you use the following constructor method:

```
MemoryImageSource(int w, int h, ColorModel cm, int pix[], int off,
    int scan);
```

The following applet, *index_memsource.java*, is similar to the *mem_isource.java* applet you created in Tip 613. The difference between the programs is that the *index_memsource.java* applet creates an index color model with two colors and uses it as the color model for the *MemoryImageSource* object:

```
import  java.applet.*;
import  java.awt.*;
import  java.awt.image.*;
```

```
public class index_memsource extends Applet {

    int mem pix[] = { 0x00, 0x01, 0x01, 0x00,
                      0x01, 0x00, 0x00, 0x01,
                      0x01, 0x00, 0x00, 0x01,
                      0x00, 0x01, 0x01, 0x00,
                      0x01, 0x00, 0x00, 0x01,
                      0x01, 0x00, 0x00, 0x01,
                      0x00, 0x01, 0x01, 0x00};

    /* index 0-black 1-magenta  */
    byte ra[] = {0, (byte) 255};
    byte ga[] = {0, 0};
    byte ba[] = {0, (byte) 255};

    Image mem_img;

    public void init()
      {
         IndexColorModel cm = new IndexColorModel (8, 2, ra, ga, ba);
         mem_img = createImage(new MemoryImageSource(4, 7, cm,
                    mem_pix, 0, 4)); .
      }

    public void paint(Graphics g)
      {
         g.drawImage (mem_img,  5, 5, this);
         g.drawImage (mem_img,  20, 0, 80, 140, this);
      }
}
```

USING THE PIXELGRABBER CLASS TO EXTRACT PIXEL VALUES 616

In the previous tip, you learned that you can convert an integer array into an image source (producer) object. Conversely, you can also use an integer array as the consumer of image data. For example, to brighten the current image, your program might get the image pixels and change the corresponding color values. The *PixelGrabber* class lets your programs extract pixel values from an image source. To use the *PixelGrabber*, you first need to create a *PixelGrabber* object using the following constructor method:

```
PixelGrabber(Image img, int x, int y, int w, int h, int pix[],
    int off, int scansize);

PixelGrabber(ImageProducer ip, int x, int y, int w, int h,
    int pix[], int off, int scansize);
```

You can specify the image source as an *Image* object using the *img* parameter or an *ImageProducer* object using the *ip* parameter. The *x, y, w,* and *h* parameters specify the rectangular region in the image that the *PixelGrabber* extracts. The *pix* parameter specifies the integer array that stores the pixel values. The *off* parameter specifies the offset of the data within the *pix* array, and the *scan* parameter specifies the width of the one line of pixel data in the *pix* array.

The second step to extracting pixel values is to call the *grabPixels* method, which starts the extraction process. Then, you should call the *status* method to find out whether or not the operation was successful. The following applet, *pix_grab.java*, extracts pixel values from a 30x30 rectangular region using the *PixelGrabber*. The applet then displays an ASCII version of the image in the console window, as shown in Figure 616:

```java
import java.applet.*;
import java.awt.*;
import java.awt.image.*;

public class pix_grab extends Applet {

    Image mem_img;

    public void init()
      {
          mem_img = createImage(20,20);
      }

    public void start()
      {
        // draw to offscreen buffer
        update (mem_img.getGraphics());

        int pixels[] = new int[20 * 20];

        PixelGrabber pg = new PixelGrabber(mem_img, 0, 0, 20, 20,
          pixels, 0, 20);

        // grab from offscreen buffer
        try {
          pg.grabPixels();
         }
        catch (InterruptedException e)
         {
            System.out.println("grabber error" + e);
            return;
         }

        if ((pg.status() & ImageObserver.ABORT) != 0)
         {
            System.out.println("grabber error");
            return;
         }

        for (int y = 0; y < 20; y++)
         {
            for (int x = 0; x < 20; x++)
              {
```

```
                if (pixels[y * 20 + x] == Color.red.getRGB())
                    System.out.print ("*");
                else
                    System.out.print (" ");
            }

         System.out.println();
        }
    }

    public void paint(Graphics g)
    {
        g.setColor (Color.red);
        g.drawLine (0, 0, 19, 19);
        g.drawLine (0,19, 19,  0);
    }
}
```

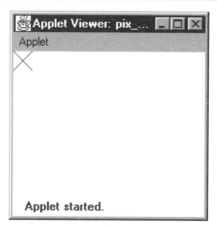

Figure 616 *Displaying an ASCII version of a pixel image.*

GETTING INDIVIDUAL COLOR COMPONENTS 617

In previous tips, you have learned that your programs can encode pixel data in many different ways based on color models. Decoding pixel data to get color components for different models can be a complex task. Fortunately, the *ColorModel* class offers several methods your programs can use to extract the color component from a pixel's data. Each method returns a specific component, as shown:

```
int getRGB(int pixel);
int getAlpha(int pixel);
int getRed(int pixel);
int getGreen(int pixel);
int getBlue(int pixel);
```

The *getRGB* method converts the pixel data into the 32-bit alpha-RGB representation, which is based on the default color model. The *getRed*, *getGreen*, *getBlue*, and *getAlpha* methods extract the 8-bit value of the red component, green component, blue component, and alpha component for a given pixel value.

618 UNDERSTANDING COLOR SPACE (RGB VS HSB)

As you know, programs specify different colors using different red, green, and blue component values. The RGB color cube, as shown in Figure 618.1, provides a graphical representation for the RGB color model.

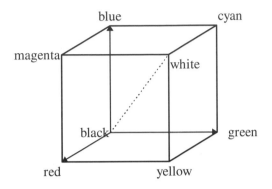

Figure 618.1 The RGB color cube model.

The RGB color model is not the only way to represent colors. For example, you can represent the same color you are expressing using RGB settings in terms of hue, saturation, and brightness. The *hue* component specifies a pure color, such as red or cyan. The *saturation* component specifies how deep or faded the color is. The *brightness* component specifies the intensity of the color. Figure 618.2 illustrates the hue, saturation, and brightness (HSB) color cone.

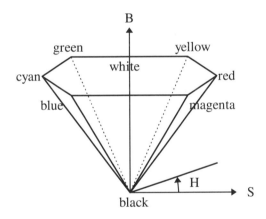

Figure 618.2 The HSB color cone model.

619 USING COLOR SPACE CONVERSION METHODS

In the previous tip, you learned that you can represent the same color in an RGB color space and in an HSB color space. When your program processes pixel data, there may be times when you want to adjust the color by hue, saturation, or brightness. In such cases, you must use the *Color* class color-space conversion methods, shown in the following statements:

```
int HSBtoRGB(float hue, float saturation, float brightness);

float[] RGBtoHSB(int r, int g, int b, float hsbvals[]);
```

The *HSBtoRGB* method returns an RGB color value for a given HSB color value. The *Color* class represents the hue parameter in terms of radians, while the saturation and brightness parameters range from 0.0 to 1.0.

The *RGBtoHSB* returns an HSB color value in a float array for a given RGB color value. You specify the *hsbvals* array parameter to store the return values or set it to null to have the *RGBtoHSB* method allocate the storage.

USING AN IMAGE FILTER

 620

As you have learned, an image filter is software that you create which takes image data from an *ImageProducer* object, processes the data, and then sends the result to an *ImageConsumer* object. To use an image filter, perform the following steps:

1. Create an image filter object by calling the filter's constructor. For example, the following statement creates an *ImageFilter* object and uses the applet-defined *MyImageFilter* class to initialize the object:

```
ImageFilter f = new MyImageFilter();
```

2. Next, you must create an image producer. In many cases, the source of the image corresponds to the image file. As such, you would create an *Image* object using the following code:

```
Image img = getImage(getCodeBase(), "image.gif");
```

You can then get a reference to the image by calling the *Image* class *getSource* method.

3. Create a *FilteredImageSource* object to connect the image producer with the image filter, as shown:

```
ImageProducer producer=new FilteredImageSource(img.getSource(),f);
```

The *FilteredImageSource* is an image producer that produces the filtered image.

4. The last step is to create the resulting image using the *createImage* method:

```
Image filtered_img = createImage(producer);
```

USING THE RGBIMAGEFILTER

 621

The *RGBImageFilter* class, a subclass of *ImageFilter*, is designed for building an image filter that calculates the new pixel color based solely on the pixel's current color value and position. However, the new pixel value that the *RGBImageFilter* class produces does not depend on the value of other pixels in the image. Color processing that only considers one pixel at a time is called *point processing*.

For each pixel in the image, the *RGBImageFilter* class calls the *filterRGB* method, passing to the method the pixel's *x*, *y* coordinates and alpha-RGB color values. When you create your own *RGBImageFilter* class, you normally override the *filterRGB* method to process the pixel data, and then return the new color value for that pixel.

The following applet, *brightness.java*, constructs a *BrightnessFilter* class to adjust the brightness of an image. When the *BrightnessFilter* receives image data in the *filterRGB* method, it converts the RGB value into an HSB value using the *Color* class *RGBtoHSB* method. The filter then adjusts the brightness components based on a specified factor, converts the colors back to the RGB format, and returns the new color. As shown in Figure 621, the applet creates a darker and a lighter version of the original image. A user can select which image to display using the selection buttons.

```java
import java.applet.*;
import java.awt.*;
import java.awt.image.*;

class BrightnessFilter extends RGBImageFilter {

    float adjustment;
    float hsb_value[] = new float[3];
    ColorModel dcm = ColorModel.getRGBdefault(); // Default model

    public BrightnessFilter(float adjustment)
      {
        canFilterIndexColorModel = true;
        this.adjustment = adjustment;
      }

    public int filterRGB (int x, int y, int rgb)
      {
        int a = rgb & 0xFF000000;
        int pixcolor = rgb & 0x00FFFFFF;

        Color.RGBtoHSB (dcm.getRed(rgb), dcm.getGreen(rgb),
                        dcm.getBlue(rgb), hsb_value);

        hsb_value[2] *= adjustment;
        hsb_value[2] = Math.max(0.0f, Math.min (hsb_value[2], 1.0f));

        return (a | Color.HSBtoRGB(hsb_value[0], hsb_value[1],
                                   hsb_value[2]));
      }
  }

public class brightness extends Applet {

    Image img, img_dark, img_light;
    int selection = 0;

    public void init()
      {
        ImageFilter lightf = new BrightnessFilter(1.25f);
        ImageFilter darkf = new BrightnessFilter(0.50f);

        img = getImage (getCodeBase(), "bgimg.jpg");
```

```
        ImageProducer lproducer =
            new FilteredImageSource (img.getSource(), lightf);

        img_light = createImage (lproducer);

        ImageProducer dproducer =
            new FilteredImageSource (img.getSource(), darkf);

        img_dark = createImage (dproducer);

        setLayout (new BorderLayout());

        Panel p = new Panel();

        p.add (new Button ("Orig"));
        p.add (new Button ("Light"));
        p.add (new Button ("Dark"));

        add ("South", p);
    }

    public boolean action(Event evt, Object arg)
    {
        if (evt.target instanceof Button)
          {
            if (arg.equals("Orig"))
              selection = 0;
            else if (arg.equals("Light"))
              selection = 1;
            else if (arg.equals("Dark"))
              selection = 2;

            repaint();
            return true;   // event processed
          }

        return false;        // event not processed
    }

    public void paint(Graphics g)
    {
        switch (selection) {
          case 0:  g.drawImage (img, 0, 0, this);
                     break;
          case 1:  g.drawImage (img_light, 0, 0, this);
                     break;
          case 2:  g.drawImage (img_dark, 0, 0, this);
                     break;
        }
    }
}
```

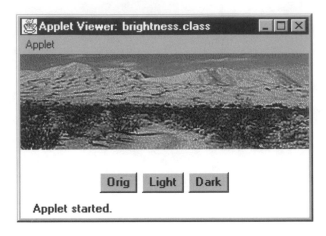

Figure 621 *Displaying an image using a brightness filter.*

622 *BUILDING A TRANSPARENT COLOR FILTER CLASS*

In previous tips, you learned that you can use an image with transparency by loading in a *GIF* file with transparent color. There may be times when you want to convert an image without transparent color into one with transparent color. To perform the conversion, you define a specific opaque color in the image to be transparent and use an *RGBImageFilter* to convert this color into a transparent color. This is similar to the "blue screen" technique special-effects people use in the movie industry. The following code, *TransFilter.java*, shows you how to build such a class. To specify the transparent color, you can simply create the filter using the *TransFilter* constructor with the specific color as an argument:

```java
import java.applet.*;
import java.awt.*;
import java.awt.image.*;

public class TransFilter extends RGBImageFilter {

    int transcolor;

    public TransFilter(int transcolor)
      {
        canFilterIndexColorModel = true;
        this.transcolor = transcolor;
      }

    public int filterRGB(int x, int y, int rgb)
      {
        int a = rgb & 0xFF000000;
        int pixcolor = rgb & 0x00FFFFFF;

        if (pixcolor == transcolor)
          a = 0x00000000;

        return (a | pixcolor);
      }
}
```

CREATING A FADE-IN ANIMATION SPECIAL EFFECT

Tip 609 showed you how to switch from the display of one image to another using a zoom-in effect. Another commonly-used special effect is the "fade-in," which slowly transforms the pixels from the first image into those of the second image.

To implement a fade-in effect, you must normally create several merged versions of the two images with different ratios for each frame of animation. In Java, however, you can take advantage of the alpha transparency feature. You create a copy of the second image using a specific alpha (transparency) value. Then, you draw the first image and overlay it with the semi-transparent version of the second image to create the merged image. By repeating the process while increasing the alpha values for each frame of animation, you can create a fade-in animation effect. The following applet, *fade_in.java*, implements the fade-in special effect. Figure 623 illustrates the applet's output:

```java
import java.applet.*;
import java.awt.*;
import java.awt.image.*;

class FadeInFilter extends RGBImageFilter {

    int transparency;

    public FadeInFilter(int transparency)
      {
        canFilterIndexColorModel = true;
        this.transparency = transparency;
      }

    public int filterRGB(int x, int y, int rgb)
      {
        int pixcolor = rgb & 0x00FFFFFF;
        int a = (transparency << 24) & 0xFF000000;

        return (a | pixcolor);
      }
  }

  public class fade_in extends Applet implements Runnable {

    Image img1, img2, fg_img;
    Image offscreen;

    Thread anime = null;

    public void init()
      {
        img1 = getImage (getCodeBase(), "turtoise.gif");
        img2 = getImage (getCodeBase(), "sheepb.gif");
```

```java
        MediaTracker mt = new MediaTracker(this);
        mt.addImage (img1, 1);
        mt.addImage (img2, 1);

        try {
           mt.waitForAll();
          }
        catch (InterruptedException e) {};

        fg_img = img2;
    }

public void update (Graphics g)
   {
      paint(g);
   }

public void paint(Graphics g)
   {
      // prepare offscreen image
      Graphics goff = offscreen.getGraphics();
      goff.drawImage (img2, 0, 0, this);
      goff.drawImage (fg_img, 0, 0, this);

      // copy offscreen to onscreen
      g.drawImage (offscreen, 0, 0, this);
      goff.dispose();
   }

public void run()
   {
      while (anime != null)
        {
          // fade In
          for (int i = 0; i < 256; i+= 32)
            {
                ImageFilter f = new FadeInFilter(i);
                ImageProducer producer =
                    new FilteredImageSource(img1.getSource(), f);

                fg_img = createImage (producer);

                 // wait until new image is ready
                 MediaTracker mt = new MediaTracker(this);
                 mt.addImage (fg_img, 1);

                 try {
                     mt.waitForID(1);
                   }
                 catch (InterruptedException e) {};
```

```java
            repaint ();

            try {
                Thread.sleep (500);
              }
            catch (InterruptedException e) {};

            fg_img.flush();
          }

       // fade Out
       for (int i = 255; i > 0; i -= 32)
         {
            ImageFilter f = new FadeInFilter(i);
            ImageProducer producer =
                new FilteredImageSource (img1.getSource(), f);

            fg_img = createImage (producer);

            // wait until new image is ready
            MediaTracker mt = new MediaTracker(this);
            mt.addImage (fg_img, 1);

            try {
                mt.waitForID(1);
              }
            catch (InterruptedException e) {};

            repaint();

            try {
                Thread.sleep (500);
              }
            catch (InterruptedException e) {};

            fg_img.flush();
          }
       }
   }

 public void start()
   {
     if (anime == null)
       {
          anime = new Thread(this);
          anime.start();
       }

     offscreen = createImage (size().width, size().height);
   }
}
```

Figure 623 Displaying images using a fade-in special effect.

624 CREATING YOUR OWN IMAGE FILTER

As you have learned, the *RGBImageFilter* class lets you build an image filter that calculates a pixel's new color based solely on the pixel's current color value and position. However, if you want to create a filter that can process a pixel's color value based on the color values of other pixels (such as surrounding pixels), you must create your own *ImageFilter* class.

To create your own *ImageFilter* class, you must first create a class that extends *ImageFilter* class. Then, you will have to override some of the following *ImageConsumer* methods:

- The *ImageFilter* class uses the *setDimensions* method to report the dimension of the image. You can override this method to find the size of the source image and to specify the size of the output image if it differs from the source.

- The image producer calls the *setColorModel* method to specify the color model of the source image.

- The image producer calls the *setHint* method to specify the order in which the image producer delivers the pixel data.

- The image producer calls the *setProperties* method if it needs to send a list of properties associated with the source image.

- The image producer calls the *setPixels* method one or more times to send the image's pixel data. You will normally override this method if you are processing any pixel data.

- When the image producer finishes sending pixel data to the *setPixels* methods, it calls the *imageComplete* method to let the consumer know that the image is complete.

If you override any of the above methods, be sure to call the consumer's methods yourself to pass the filtered information along to the image consumer.

625 SHARPENING AN IMAGE

When your applet works with images, you can use *area processing* to sharpen an image, detect edges, or remove noise. To sharpen an image, you can apply an image processing algorithm known as *convolution*. Put simply, a convolution operation calculates the color value of a pixel based on the weighted sum of the color values of its neighboring pixels. The following equation shows you how the convolution algorithm calculates the color value of a pixel :

```
P (x, y) = Σ W(w, h) * P(x + w, y + h);
```

W is the matrix that stores the pixel weights. The variable w goes from 0 to the width of the weights matrix minus one, and h goes from 0 to the height of the weights matrix minus one. The following applet, *sharp_filter.java*, implements an image-sharpening filter. The applet displays the original image at the top and the sharpened image at the bottom, as shown in Figure 625:

```java
import java.applet.*;
import java.awt.*;
import java.awt.image.*;

class SharpenFilter extends ImageFilter {

    int source_img[];
    int dest_width, dest_height;
    int source_width, source_height;

    ColorModel ocm; // output color model

    // sharpen convolution kernel
    int filter_weight[] = {-1,-1,-1,-1, 9,-1,-1,-1,-1};

    public void setDimensions(int width, int height)
      {
        source_img = new int[width * height];
        source_width = width;
        source_height = height;

        dest_width = width - 2;
        dest_height = height - 2;

          consumer.setDimensions(dest_width, dest_height);
      }
    public void setColorModel(ColorModel model)
      {
        ocm = ColorModel.getRGBdefault();
        consumer.setColorModel(ocm);
      }

    public void setPixels(int x, int y, int w, int h,
        ColorModel model, byte pixels[], int off, int scansize)
      {
        int srcoff = off;
        int dstoff = y * source_width + x;

        for (int yi = 0; yi < h; yi++)
          {
            for (int xi = 0; xi < w; xi++)
              {
```

```java
                source_img[dstoff] = model.getRGB(pixels[srcoff++] &
                    0xff);
                source_img[dstoff++] = model.getRGB(pixels[srcoff++] &
                    0xff);
            }
        srcoff += (scansize - w);
        dstoff += (source_width - w);
    }
}

public void setPixels(int x, int y, int w, int h,
    ColorModel model, int pixels[], int off, int scansize)
{
    int srcoff = off;
    int dstoff = y * source_width + x;

    for (int yi = 0; yi < h; yi++)
        {
            for (int xi = 0; xi < w; xi++)
                source_img[dstoff++] =
                    model.getRGB(pixels[srcoff++]);

            srcoff += (scansize - w);
            dstoff += (source_width - w);
        }
}

public void imageComplete(int status)
{
    int sr, sg, sb;
    int tr, tg, tb, ta;

    if (status == IMAGEERROR || status == IMAGEABORTED)
      {
        consumer.imageComplete(status);
        return;
      }

    // create output image
    int dest_img[] = new int[dest_width]; // storage for one line

    for (int yi = 0; yi < dest_height; yi++)
        {
            for (int xi = 0; xi < dest_width; xi++)
              {
                tr = tg = tb = 0;
                for (int ky=0; ky<3; ky++)
                  {
                    for (int kx=0; kx<3; kx++)
                      {
```

```
                        int rgb = source_img[(yi+ky) *
                                        source_width+xi+kx];
                    sr = ocm.getRed (rgb);
                    sg = ocm.getGreen (rgb);
                    sb = ocm.getBlue (rgb);

                    tr += sr * filter_weight[ky*3+kx];
                    tg += sg * filter_weight[ky*3+kx];
                    tb += sb * filter_weight[ky*3+kx];
                }
            }

            tr = Math.max(0, Math.min (tr, 255));
            tg = Math.max(0, Math.min (tg, 255));
            tb = Math.max(0, Math.min (tb, 255));

            dest_img [xi] = 0xFF000000 | (tr << 16) |
                            (tg << 8) | tb;
          }
        consumer.setPixels(0, yi, dest_width, 1, ocm, dest_img,
            0, dest_width);
      }

      dest_img = null;
      consumer.imageComplete(status);
    }
  }

public class sharp_filter extends Applet {

    Image orig_img, sharpened_img;

    public void init()
      {
        ImageFilter f = new SharpenFilter();

        orig_img = getImage (getCodeBase(), "tiger.jpg");

        ImageProducer producer =
            new FilteredImageSource (orig_img.getSource(), f);

        sharpened_img = createImage (producer);
      }

    public void paint(Graphics g)
      {
        g.drawImage (orig_img, 0, 0, this);
        g.drawImage (sharpened_img, 0, 200, this);
      }
}
```

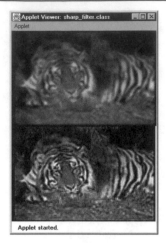

Figure 625 *Using a filter to sharpen an image.*

626 WRITING JAVA 3-D APPLETS AND APPLICATIONS

Currently, 2-D graphics and animation dominate the pictorial content of most Web sites. However, many software companies are working hard to bring 3-D to the Web. For example, VRML (Virtual Reality Modeling Language) lets browsers display interactive 3-D Web pages. Many programmers feel that VRML is to 3-D graphics what HTML is to 2-D graphics. As you will learn, Java is another way to bring 3-D images to your Web pages. Due to Java's performance, however, you have to keep your images simple.

As you have learned, Java is an interpretive language. In general, interpretive languages are much slower that compiled languages. As more just-in-time compilers become available, you will see Java's performance improve greatly. A just-in-time compiler converts Java byte code into machine code just after a browser downloads the code.

Despite Java's slow performance, you can still create simple 3-D applets and applications. For example, you can write an applet that displays different views of a 3-D object or allows a user to traverse a simple 3-D world. Java speed limits the complexity and interactivity of such 3-D scenes. However, if you stick to effects that do not require intense computation, you can still do interesting things in 3-D with Java.

627 UNDERSTANDING A 3-D COORDINATE SYSTEM

To create a 3-D application, you must first understand the 3-D coordinate system. In Tip 427, you learned about 2-D screen coordinate systems which are based on the *x*- and *y*-axes. A 3-D coordinate system is similar except that it extends into a third dimension along a *z*-axis. Figure 627.1 shows a cube defined within a 3-D coordinate system.

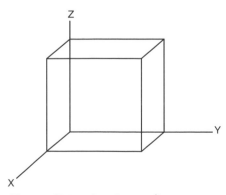

Figure 627.1 *A 3-D coordinate system.*

There are many orientations that *x-*, *y-*, and *z*-axes can have. Most people use only two of these orientations extensively. One is the right-handed coordinate system and the other is the left-handed coordinates system. Within a right-handed coordinate system, you put your thumb in the direction of the *z*-axis and your fingers in the direction of the *x*-axis. Then, when you curl your fingers, they point in the direction of the *y*-axis. You can determine a left-handed coordinate system in the same manner, except you use your left hand. Figure 627.2 demonstrates left-handed and right-handed coordinate systems.

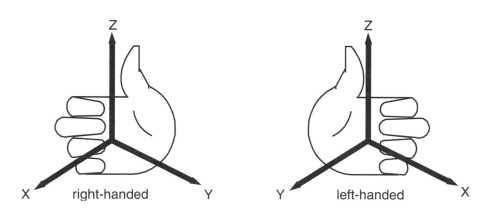

Figure 627.2 Left-handed and right-handed coordinate systems.

The advantage of 3-D graphics over 2-D graphics is that you only define objects in a 3-D coordinate system once. Then, you can display the objects from different points of view, or manipulate the objects in 3-D space mathematically. The following tips will give you the basics you need to write Java programs that work in 3-D.

Understanding Vectors 628

In 3-D graphics programs, you use vectors in many ways. For example, you use a vector to define the direction of an observer relative to the 3-D scene. You also use vectors to calculate the angle that light reflects off a surface. Also, vectors play an important role in the way objects are converted from 3-D space to the screen, a process known as *rendering*.

A vector represents a direction and magnitude and is not fixed at any particular location. You can think of a vector as a line with an arrow head at one end of it. The magnitude of a vector defines the line's size. The vector's direction defines where the vector points.

Two vectors may point in the same direction, but have different magnitudes. Physicists use vectors to denote velocity. Velocity defines both the speed and direction of an object. You know that cars on a highway can travel in the same direction, but not necessarily at the same speed. Conversely, two vectors can have the same magnitude but point in different directions. As you know, you can drive at the same speed but in many directions. Each time you turn, you are changing your velocity vector.

Calculating a Vector's Magnitude 629

Mathematicians define a 2-D vector by its length along the *x-* and *y*-axes. To calculate the magnitude of a 3-D vector, you calculate its length along the *x-*, *y-*, and *z*-axes. With a 2-D vector, as shown in Figure 629.1, the *x-* and *y*-lengths make up the sides of a right triangle.

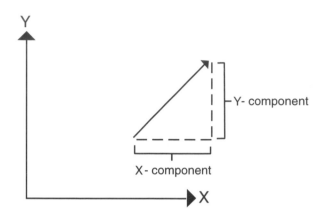

Figure 629.1 *Calculating a 2-D vector's magnitude.*

Because the sides make up a right triangle, the length of a vector is the square root of the sum of the squares. In Java, you can calculate the magnitude of a 2-D vector with the following code:

```
mag = Math.sqrt(x*x + y*y);
```

You can define a 3-D vector by its length along the x-, y-, and z-axes. Again, to calculate the magnitude of a vector, you calculate its length. To visualize how to calculate the magnitude of a 3-D vector, think about solving it in steps.

First, you must calculate the length of the shadow of the vector in the x-y plane. As you have learned, for 2-D vectors this is the square root of the sum of the x and y squares. Then, you have a right triangle with this value, the shadow of the vector in the x-y plane, and the third dimension z. To find the length, you find the sum of the squares again. Figure 629.2 shows a vector in 3-D space.

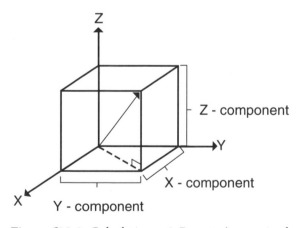

Figure 629.2 *Calculating a 3-D vector's magnitude.*

The following code demonstrates how you calculate the magnitude of a 3-D vector using Java:

```
mag = Math.sqrt(x*x + y*y + z*z);
```

ADDING VECTORS 630

You can graphically add vectors by placing the head to tail, and then drawing a vector from the first vector's tail to the last vector's head. Figure 630 shows two vectors that have been added together graphically.

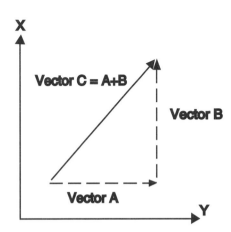

Figure 630 Adding vectors graphically.

You can also add vectors mathematically. To do this, you need to understand components. Vector components are the vector's length along each axis. You use an *i* to refer to the vector's length along the *x*-axis and a *j* to refer to the vector's length along the *y*-axis. Consider the following notation for a 2-D vector named *A*:

```
A = 2i + 2j
```

The notation says that vector *A* has a length of 3 units along the *x*-axis and 4 units along the *y*-axis. To add vectors mathematically, you add the vector's components as shown here:

```
A = 3i + 4j
B = 2i + 2j
C = A + B = (2i + 2j) + (1i + 2j) = 3i + 4j
```

For 3-D vectors, you use a third component *k* to refer to the vector's length along the *z*-axis, as shown here:

```
A = 1i + 2j + 3k
```

In this case, the vector has a length of 3 along the *z*-axis.

CALCULATING A DOT PRODUCT 631

One of the calculations that you can perform on two vectors is to compute a dot product. A *dot product* determines if two vectors are in the same direction. For example, you can use a dot product to determine if a surface is facing an observer. A *normal vector* is a vector that is perpendicular to a surface. If a surface faces an observer, then the dot product of the surface's normal vector and a vector from the center of the surface to the observer will be positive. If the dot product is negative, the back of the surface faces the observer. To calculate a dot product, you multiply the components of the vector, then add them up. You get a positive result if the vectors are in the same direction. You get a negative result if the vectors are in opposite directions. You will get zero if the vectors are ninety degrees apart. The following code defines a *Vector3d* class and a method that calculates the dot product of two vectors:

```java
public class Vector3d {

    float x = 0;
    float y = 0;
    float z = 0;

    public Vector3d(float i, float j, float k)
    {
        x = i;
        y = j;
        z = k;
    }

    public float dot(Vector3d A)
    {
        float result = A.x * x + A.y * x + A.z * z;
        return (result);
    }

    public float mag()
    {
        float result = (float)Math.sqrt(x*x + y*y + z*z);
        return (result);
    }

    public String toString()
    {
        return(new String("(" + x + "," + y + "," + z + ")"));
    }
}
```

632 CALCULATING A CROSS PRODUCT

One of the most useful vector calculations is the *cross product*. The result of the cross product of two vectors is a third vector that is perpendicular to the two vectors. For example, if you perform the cross product of the *x*-axis and *y*-axis of a right-handed coordinate system, the result is the *z*-axis. The *z*-axis is perpendicular to the *x-y* plane.

When you calculate a cross product, the result is order dependent. For example, A X B (pronounced A cross B), where A and B are vectors, is not the same as B X A. In fact, the results are two vectors that are in opposite directions. To calculate a cross product, you cross multiply the vector components. The following code demonstrates how to calculate the cross product of two vectors. The code builds upon the *Vector3d* class presented in the previous tip.

```java
public Vector3d cross(Vector3d A)
    {
        float cx = (y*A.z) - (A.y*z);
        float cy = (A.x*z) - (x*A.z);
```

```
    float cz = (x*A.y) - (A.x*y);
    return (new Vector3d(cx, cy, cz));
}
```

Understanding the Viewport

 633

Within a graphics program, a *viewport* describes a 3-D scene from an observer's point of view. As you know, a computer screen is a 2-D surface. You can use a viewport to render a 3-D object to a flat 2-D computer screen based on a particular point of view.

Think of the viewport as a porthole that sits between the observer's eyes and the viewable objects. You define a viewport by a point that defines the observer's location, a vector that determines the observer's line of sight, and a vector that defines the observer's up direction. Another important value is how far the viewport is from the observer.

Actually, a viewport is really a second 3-D coordinate system. The viewport's *x*-axis is horizontal to the observer's point of view. The viewport's *y*-axis is vertical to the observer's point of view. Finally, the *z*-axis is the observer's line of sight into the computer screen. Figure 633 shows an observer and a viewport.

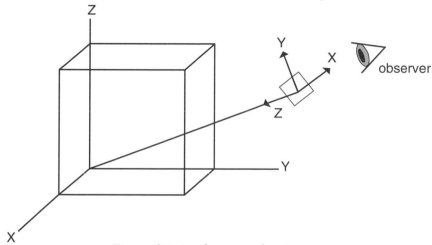

Figure 633 An observer and a viewport.

Before you can convert a 3-D object to the viewport coordinate system, you must understand matrixes. Matrixes are a convenient way to perform 3-D transformations, as the following tips will demonstrate.

Understanding Matrixes

 634

A *coordinate* is a point in space. You can transform (move or change) a point using a matrix. Matrixes let you translate (move), scale, and rotate objects. The advantage of matrixes is that you can multiply a series of matrixes together to create a single matrix. You can then use the single matrix to perform complex transformations. As you have learned, converting a 3-D point to screen coordinates is really just converting a point from one 3-D coordinate system to another. Actually, you can perform this conversion using matrixes. A series of rotations, translations, and scaling can convert any 3-D coordinate system into another so you can build a single matrix with all the steps necessary to translate a point from the 3-D world to the viewport-coordinate system.

Matrixes are also useful when you want to perform an animation. Imagine the hands of a clock that must rotate around in a circle. You can define a matrix that performs the rotation. Then, you can combine that matrix with one that transforms a coordinate from a 3-D world to viewport coordinates. This way, you will avoid performing many of the intermediate calculations. Matrixes allow for easy rotation, translation, scaling animation, and also efficient 3-D to 2-D calculations of a large list of coordinates.

If you wish to learn more about the math behind 3-D graphics, many good books are available. The following tips, however, try to give a clear explanation with an emphasis on use, not theory. These tips should give you a general understanding of how 3-D graphics work. In the following tips, you will learn how to implement and use a 3-D matrix class.

635 Implementing a 3-D Matrix

In the previous tip, you learned about matrixes. You can use matrixes to transform 3-D objects. Since there is no standard matrix class in Java, you must write your own. The following code defines the basis of a 3-D matrix class.

```java
public class Matrix3d {            // Define a 3-D Matrix class

    float e00,e01,e02,e03;
    float e10,e11,e12,e13;
    float e20,e21,e22,e23;
    float e30,e31,e32,e33;

    static final double toRad = Math.PI/180.0;
    static int REPLACE = 0;
    static int PRECONCAT = 1;
    static int POSTCONCAT = 2;

    public Matrix3d()              // Create an identity matrix
      {
        identity ();
      }

    public void identity()         // Make an identity matrix
      {
        e01 = e02 = e03 = 0.0f;
        e10 = e12 = e13 = 0.0f;
        e20 = e21 = e23 = 0.0f;
        e30 = e32 = e32 = 0.0f;
        e00 = 1.0f;
        e11 = 1.0f;
        e22 = 1.0f;
      }

    public Point3d transform(Point3d p)  // Transform a point
      {                                  // using a matrix
        float x = p.x * e00 + p.y * e01 + p.z * e02 + e03;
        float y = p.x * e10 + p.y * e11 + p.z * e12 + e13;
        float z = p.x * e20 + p.y * e21 + p.z * e22 + e23;
        return(new Point3d(x,y,z));
      }
  }
```

Notice that the *Matrix3d* class constructor makes an identity matrix. By definition, a point that is transformed by an identity matrix is left unchanged. Therefore, the matrix initially does nothing.

IMPLEMENTING A 3-D POINT 636

In the previous tip's *Matrix3d* class, the *transform* method takes a 3-D point and transforms it using the matrix. The following code demonstrates the *Point3d* class that is an argument to the transform method:

```
public class Point3d {

    float x = 0f;   // 3-D world coordinates
    float y = 0f;
    float z = 0f;

    public Point(float x0, float y0, float z0)
      {
        x = x0;
        y = y0;
        z = z0;
      }

    public String toString()
      {
          return(new String("(" + x + "," + y + "," + z + ")"));
      }
}
```

As you can see, the *Point3d* class constructor assigns three parameters to the member variables *x*, *y*, and *z* which define the point's coordinates. The *toString* function simply displays each coordinate's value.

CREATING A TRANSLATE MATRIX 637

When you translate a point, you are really just moving it in 3-D space. Within the *Matrix3d* class presented in Tip 635, you can add the following *translate* method which modifies the matrix, by adding *x*, *y*, and *z* offsets:

```
// Translate the matrix
public void translate(float x, float y, float z)
  {
    e03 += x;
    e13 += y;
    e23 += z;
  }
```

USING THE TRANSLATE MATRIX 638

In the previous tip, you created a *translate* method. The following program demonstrates how to use the *Matrix3d* class to perform a *translate* operation. The *Matrix3d* and *Point3d* class is not shown in the program code; rather, assume the classes reside in their own file:

```
public class testTranslate {

    public static void main(String args)
    {
        Matrix3d matrix = new Matrix3d();
        Point3d ptA = new Point3d(5.0f,5.0f,5.0f);

        matrix.translate(3.0f,4.0f,5.0f);          // define translate
        System.out.println("Before A" + ptA);
        ptA = matrix.transform(ptA);                // move point A
        System.out.println("After A" + ptA);
    }
}
```

639 CREATING A SCALE MATRIX

Within a graphics program, there will be times when you need to scale an object, either increasing or decreasing the object's size. To *scale* a 3-D point, you multiply the point's *x*, *y*, and *z* components by a scale factor. The scale factor may be different or the same for each component. The following *scale* method modifies the *Matrix3d* object so that it will scale a point when you call the *transform* method. If you make multiple calls to the *scale* method, the scales are multiplied together.

```
// Scale a matrix by x,y,z
public void scale(float x, float y, float z)
    {
        e00 *= x;
        e11 *= y;
        e22 *= z;
    }

// Scale a matrix by a single value
public void scale(float s)
    {
        e00 *= s;
        e11 *= s;
        e22 *= s;
    }
```

640 USING THE SCALE MATRIX

In the previous tip, you learned how to create a *scale* method with which you can increase or decrease the components of a matrix. The following program, *testScale.java*, demonstrates how to use the *Matrix3d* class to perform a scale. The *Matrix3d* class is not shown in the program code. As with the previous tips, *Matrix3d* and *Point3d* classes are assumed to reside in their own files.

```
public class testScale {

    public static void main(String args)
    {
```

```
        Matrix3d matrixA = new Matrix3d();
        Matrix3d matrixB = new Matrix3d();

        Point3d ptA = new Point3d(100.0f, 100.0f, 100.0f);
        Point3d ptB = new Point3d(100.0f, 100.0f, 100.0f);

        matrixA.scale(0.30f,0.40f,0.50f); // define scale A
        matrixB.scale(0.50f);                // define scale B
        System.out.println("Before A" + ptA + ", B" + ptB);

        ptA = matrixA.transform(ptA);        // scale point A
        ptB = matrixB.transform(ptB);        // scale point B
        System.out.println("After A" + ptA + ", B" + ptB);
    }
}
```

As you can see in the above example, there are two scale methods. One method takes three arguments and the other takes one argument. The program displays the value of the points before and after the transform calls.

CREATING X-ROTATE MATRIX

 641

When you rotate a 3-D object, you can rotate the object about the *x*-, *y*-, or *z*-axes, or a combination of all three. As it turns out, your programs can apply a 3-D rotation one axis at a time. The following method, *rotateX*, demonstrates how you would implement a rotation method about the *x*-axis, by the angle *theta*:

```
// Rotate a matrix around x-axis by theta
public void rotateX(double theta)
  {
    theta *= toRad;      // Convert angle to radians

    double theta_cos = Math.cos(theta);
    double theta_sin = Math.sin(theta);

    Matrix3d m = new Matrix3d();
    m.e11 = (float)theta_cos;
    m.e12 = (float)-theta_sin;
    m.e21 = (float)theta_sin;
    m.e22 = (float)theta_cos;
     this.multiply(m, Matrix3d.POSTCONCAT);
}
```

As you can see, the method first converts the angle *theta* into radians. Next, the method creates a new method that contains the angles of rotation, and then uses a matrix multiply operation to apply the rotation.

CREATING Y-ROTATE MATRIX

 642

In Tip 641, you created a method you can use to rotate a 3-D object about the *x*-axis rotation. In a similar way, the following method, *rotateY*, illustrates how you would rotate an object about the *y*-axis.

```
// Rotate matrix around y-axis by theta
public void rotateY(double theta)
  {
    theta *= toRad;                          // Convert to radians
    double theta_cos = Math.cos(theta);
    double theta_sin = Math.sin(theta);

    Matrix3d m = new Matrix3d();
    m.e00 = (float)theta_cos;
    m.e02 = (float)theta_sin;
    m.e20 = (float)-theta_sin;
    m.e22 = (float)theta_cos;
     this.multiply(m, Matrix3d.POSTCONCAT);
  }
```

643 CREATING Z-ROTATE MATRIX

In the previous two tips, you learned how to create methods your programs can use to rotate 3-D objects about the *x*- and *y*-axis. In a similar way, the following method, *rotateZ*, illustrates how you rotate a 3-D object about the *z*-axis.

```
// rotate matrix around z-axis by theta
void rotateZ(double theta)
  {
    theta *= toRad;                          // Convert to radians
    double theta_cos = Math.cos(theta);
    double theta_sin = Math.sin(theta);

    Matrix3d m = new Matrix3d();
    m.e00 = (float)theta_cos;
    m.e01 = (float)-theta_sin;
    m.e10 = (float)theta_sin;
    m.e11 = (float)theta_cos;
     this.multiply(m, Matrix3d.POSTCONCAT);
  }
```

644 USING THE ROTATE MATRIX

The following program demonstrates how to use the *Matrix3d* class to perform an *x*-axis rotation. The other axis rotations work in the same way. The source code assumes the *Matrix3d* and *Point3d* classes reside in separate files:

```
public class testRotate {

    public static void main(String args)
      {
        Matrix3d matrixA = new Matrix3d();
        Point3d ptA = new Point3d(100.0f, 0.0f, 0.0f);

        matrixA.rotateY(270.0f);        // define rotate
        System.out.println("Before " + ptA);
```

```
        ptA = matrixA.transform(ptA); // rotate point A
        System.out.println("After " + ptA);
    }
}
```

CREATING A MATRIX MULTIPLY METHOD

As you have learned, 3-D graphics programs use matrixes to translate, scale, and rotate coordinates. To perform a series of these operations, you can concatenate the matrixes. Then, you can modify a coordinate using a single transform call. In this way, you can avoid many redundant calculations. For example, if you want to scale and rotate an object that contains ten thousand coordinates, by combining the rotate and scale coordinates into a single matrix, you can avoid ten thousand transform calls. The following code demonstrates the *multiply* method:

```
// Concatenate this matrix with another */
void multiply(Matrix3d matrix, int concat)
  {
     Matrix3d A = null;
     Matrix3d B = null;
     if (concat == Matrix3d.PRECONCAT)
       {
          A = matrix;
          B = this;
       }
     else if (concat == Matrix3d.POSTCONCAT)
       {
          A = this;
          B = matrix;
       }
     else if (concat == Matrix3d.REPLACE)
       {
          A = this;
          A.identity();
          B = matrix;
       }

     float n00 = A.e00*B.e00 + A.e10*B.e01 + A.e20*B.e02;
     float n01 = A.e01*B.e00 + A.e11*B.e01 + A.e21*B.e02;
     float n02 = A.e02*B.e00 + A.e12*B.e01 + A.e22*B.e02;
     float n03 = A.e03*B.e00 + A.e13*B.e01 + A.e23*B.e02 + B.e03;

     float n10 = A.e00*B.e10 + A.e10*B.e11 + A.e20*B.e12;
     float n11 = A.e01*B.e10 + A.e11*B.e11 + A.e21*B.e12;
     float n12 = A.e02*B.e10 + A.e12*B.e11 + A.e22*B.e12;
     float n13 = A.e03*B.e10 + A.e13*B.e11 + A.e23*B.e12 + B.e13;

     float n20 = A.e00*B.e20 + A.e10*B.e21 + A.e20*B.e22;
     float n21 = A.e01*B.e20 + A.e11*B.e21 + A.e21*B.e22;
```

```
    float n22 = A.e02*B.e20 + A.e12*B.e21 + A.e22*B.e22;
    float n23 = A.e03*B.e20 + A.e13*B.e21 + A.e23*B.e22 + B.e23;

    e00 = n00;
    e01 = n01;
    e02 = n02;
    e03 = n03;

    e10 = n10;
    e11 = n11;
    e12 = n12;
    e13 = n13;

    e20 = n20;
    e21 = n21;
    e22 = n22;
    e23 = n23;
}
```

Notice that the second argument in the multiply method is an integer. You pass the method either *PRECONCAT* or *POSTCONCAT* constants to choose the order of the multiplication. Matrix concatenation is order dependent. For example, if you perform an *x*-axis rotation in one matrix and a *y*-axis rotation in another, the order that you concatenate these matrixes will make a difference in the transformation of a point.

For example, take a book and look at the front cover. If you rotate the book right 90 degrees around the vertical axis, you are looking at the right edge. If you then rotate it down another 90 degrees around the horizontal axis, you are looking at the top edge. The top edge will end up vertical to you. Now repeat the two rotations from the beginning, but swap the order, rotate down, then right. You will end up looking at the right edge of the book. Again, you should remember that matrix concatenation is order dependent.

646 CONCATENATING TWO MATRIXES

In the previous tip, you learned how to implement the matrix *multiply* method. You learned that you can choose to *pre* or *post* concatenate a matrix with the one that the *multiply* method belongs to. The following program demonstrates how to concatenate two matrixes. The *Matrix3d* and *Point3d* classes are assumed to be in their own files.

```java
public class testMultiply {

  public static void main(String args)
    {
      Matrix3d matrixA = new Matrix3d();
      Matrix3d matrixB = new Matrix3d();
      Point3d ptA = new Point3d(100.0f, 100.0f, 100.0f);

      matrixA.scale(0.30f,0.40f,0.50f); // define scale B
      matrixB.scale(0.50f);             // define scale A
      matrixA.multiply(matrixB, Matrix3d.POSTCONCAT);
      System.out.println("Before A" + ptA);
      ptA = matrixA.transform(ptA);     // scale point
      System.out.println("After A" + ptA);
    }

}
```

Understanding Orthogonal Transformation   647

You can observe a 3-D scene in two ways: using an orthogonal or a perspective view. An *orthogonal view* means that there is no depth perception. If you look at a road that goes off into the distance through an orthogonal view, the edges of the road will be parallel. In reality, perspective causes the parallel edges of a road to appear to converge as it goes off into the distance. Figure 647 shows a cube displayed from an orthogonal point of view. Notice that the back side has the same width as the face of the cube. Again, parallel lines in an orthogonal view remain parallel.

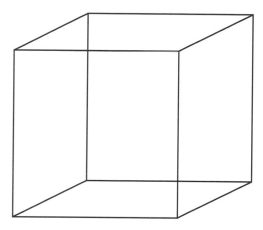

Figure 647 *The orthogonal view of a cube.*

As you have learned, a viewport defines an observer's view of a 3-D world. To display a 3-D object on a computer screen, you transform the object's coordinates from the 3-D *world* coordinate system to the 3-D viewport coordinate system. However, for orthogonal transformations, you ignore the *z*-axis of the viewport coordinate system. You only use the *x*- and *y*-axis values of the viewport coordinate system to draw the object on the screen.

Understanding Theta, Phi, and Omega angles   648

Before you can convert an object to screen coordinates, you must define the observer's position. For a orthogonal view, you can use three angles, theta, phi and omega, as shown in Figure 648.

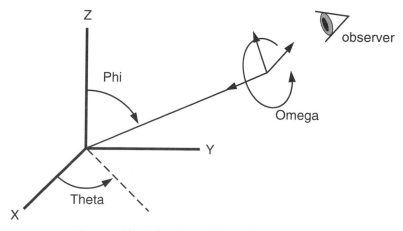

Figure 648 *The theta, phi, and omega angles.*

After you have defined the observer's position, you can create a transformation matrix that transforms points from 3-D world coordinates to viewport screen coordinates. In the following tip, you will learn how to create an orthogonal transformation matrix.

649 CREATING AN ORTHOGONAL TRANSFORMATION MATRIX

In the previous tip, you learned how to define an observer's orthogonal view using the theta, phi, and omega angles. You can use these angles to create an orthogonal matrix. When you transform a point using an orthogonal matrix, you are converting the point to the viewport coordinate system. The following *orthogonal* method demonstrates how to create an orthogonal matrix:

```java
public void orthogonal(float theta, float phi, float omega)
  {
    this.identity();
    this.rotateX(90);
    this.rotateY(90 + theta);
    this.rotateX(90 - phi);
    this.scale(1.0f, 1.0f, -1.0f);
    this.rotateZ(omega);
  }
```

650 CREATING A CUBE CLASS

In the previous tips, you learned many of the mathematical tools behind 3-D graphics programs. Next you will learn how to create the objects that go inside these programs.

When you create 3-D objects, it is important that you minimize calculations. For example, a cube has six sides. If you treat each side separately when you transform the cube, you will need to transform twenty-four coordinates. However, a better way is to have the sides of the cube share common coordinates. In this way, you only have to transform eight coordinates. To create a cube that shares coordinates, you must create a *Cube* class.

A *Cube* class contains a list of vertices and a list of surfaces. The surfaces of a cube are squares. The squares reference vertices in the cube's list. The following code demonstrates a *Cube* class:

```java
import java.awt.*;

class Square {

    int index[] = new int[4];
    Cube cube = null;

    public Square(Cube c, int v0, int v1, int v2, int v3)
      {
        cube = c;
        index[0] = v0;
        index[1] = v1;
        index[2] = v2;
        index[3] = v3;
      }
```

```java
    public void draw(Graphics g, Point offset)
      {
        Polygon poly = new Polygon();
        for (int i = 0; i < index.length; i++)
          poly.addPoint(offset.x + cube.v[index[i]].x,
              offset.y + cube.v[index[i]].y);

          poly.addPoint(offset.x + cube.v[index[0]].x,
              offset.y + cube.v[index[0]].y);
        g.drawPolygon(poly);
      }
  }


public class Cube {

    Point3d w[] = new Point3d[8];      // world
    Point v[] = new Point[8];          // viewport
    Square sides[] = new Square[6];
    Color color = Color.black;
    Matrix3d matrix = new Matrix3d();

    public Cube (float size)
      {
        /* create a cube with center at the origin */
        w[0] = new Point3d (-size, -size, -size);
        w[1] = new Point3d (-size,  size, -size);
        w[2] = new Point3d ( size,  size, -size);
        w[3] = new Point3d ( size, -size, -size);
        w[4] = new Point3d (-size, -size,  size);
        w[5] = new Point3d (-size,  size,  size);
        w[6] = new Point3d ( size,  size,  size);
        w[7] = new Point3d ( size, -size,  size);
        sides[0] = new Square(this, 0, 1, 2, 3); // top
        sides[1] = new Square(this, 7, 6, 5, 4); // bottom
        sides[2] = new Square(this, 0, 1, 5, 4); // front
        sides[3] = new Square(this, 1, 2, 6, 5); // right
        sides[4] = new Square(this, 2, 3, 7, 6); // back
        sides[5] = new Square(this, 3, 0, 4, 7); // left
      }

    public void draw(Graphics g, Point offset)
      {
        g.setColor(color);
        for (int i = 0; i < sides.length; i++)
          sides[i].draw(g, offset);
      }

    public void transform(Matrix3d toscreen)
      {
```

```
        Matrix3d m = new Matrix3d();
         m.multiply(toscreen, Matrix3d.REPLACE);
         m.multiply(matrix, Matrix3d.PRECONCAT);
         for (int i = 0; i < v.length; i++)
             v[i] = m.transform2D(w[i]);
     }
  }
```

The constructor creates a *Cube* object centered at the origin. The *Cube* contains a list of vertices and sides. The sides reference the vertices that are inside the *Cube* class. In the tips that follow, you will learn how to move, rotate, and render a 3-D cube.

651 CONVERSION FROM 3-D TO 2-D (ORTHOGONAL)

In the previous tips, you learned many of the building blocks of a 3-D graphics program. Now, you can put it all together. In the previous tip, you learned how to create a *Cube* class. And in Tip 635, you learned how to implement a *Matrix3d* class that defines an orthogonal transformation matrix. Putting these together, you can create and display a cube from an arbitrary angle, using an orthogonal view. The following program, *testOrthApplet.java*, demonstrates how to display a wireframe cube from an arbitrary *y* point of view. Figure 651 displays the program's output.

```java
import java.applet.*;
import java.awt.*;

public class testOrthApplet extends Applet {

    Cube cube = new Cube(50);
    Point xaxis = null;
    Point yaxis = null;
    Point zaxis = null;

    public void init()
      {
        Matrix3d matrix = new Matrix3d();

        matrix.orthogonal(30f, 80f, 0f);
        cube.transform(matrix);

        Point3d x = new Point3d(75f,  0f,  0f);
        Point3d y = new Point3d( 0f, 75f,  0f);
        Point3d z = new Point3d( 0f,  0f, 75f);
        xaxis = matrix.transform2D(x);
        yaxis = matrix.transform2D(y);
        zaxis = matrix.transform2D(z);
      }

    public void paint(Graphics g)
      {
```

```
        Point offset = new Point(size().width/2,size().height/2);
        cube.draw(g, offset);       // draw cube

        g.setColor(Color.red);      // draw x-axis
        g.drawLine(offset.x, offset.y,
            offset.x + xaxis.x, offset.y + xaxis.y);

        g.setColor(Color.green); // draw y-axis
        g.drawLine(offset.x, offset.y,
            offset.x + yaxis.x, offset.y + yaxis.y);

        g.setColor(Color.blue);     // draw z-axis
        g.drawLine(offset.x, offset.y,
            offset.x + zaxis.x, offset.y + zaxis.y);
    }
}
```

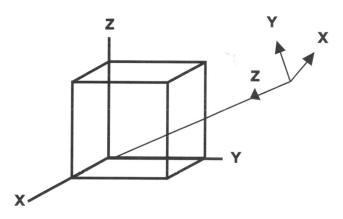

Figure 651 Displaying a cube from an arbitrary angle.

MOVING A 3-D OBJECT 652

In the previous tip, you learned how to create and display a 3-D cube. If you examine the *Cube* class presented in Tip 650, you will find that class preconcatenates its own matrix to the orthogonal transformation matrix. The following *transform* method illustrates this processing:

```
public void transform(Matrix3d toscreen)
   {
     Matrix3d m = new Matrix3d();
     m.multiply(toscreen, Matrix3d.REPLACE);
     m.multiply(matrix, Matrix3d.PRECONCAT);

     for (int i = 0; i < v.length; i++)
        v[i] = m.transform2D(w[i]);
   }
```

Initially, the cube matrix is an identity matrix. Therefore, the matrix has no effect on the transformation. You can move the cube, before it is transformed by the orthogonal matrix, by modifying the cube's own matrix. For example, the following code demonstrates how to move the cube 100 units along the *x*-axis:

```
matrix.orthogonal(30f, 80f, 0f);        // create orthogonal matrix
cube.matrix.translate(100f, 0f, 0f);    // move 100 along x-axis
cube.transform(matrix);                 // transform cube
```

653 SCALING A 3-D OBJECT

In the previous tip, you learned how to move a cube before it is transformed using the orthogonal matrix. In a similar way, you can also scale a cube. The following code demonstrates how to scale a cube by 50 percent along *x*-, *y*-, and *z*-axes:

```
matrix.orthogonal(30f, 80f, 0f);        // create orthogonal matrix
cube.matrix.scale(50);                  // scale cube 50 percent
cube.transform(matrix);                 // transform cube
```

654 ROTATING A 3-D OBJECT

In the previous two tips, you learned how to scale and move a cube before it is transformed by the orthogonal matrix. In a similar way, your programs can also rotate a cube. The following code demonstrates how to rotate a cube by 45 degrees around the *x*-axis:

```
matrix.orthogonal(30f, 80f, 0f);        // create orthogonal matrix
cube.matrix.rotateX(45f);               // rotate 45 along x-axis
cube.transform(matrix);                 // transform cube
```

655 UNDERSTANDING BACK-FACE REMOVAL

In the previous tips, your code has drawn a cube as a wireframe—an object that does not have any surfaces. Another way to draw a 3-D object is to render it as a solid. A technique that you can use to render a simple object as a solid is to draw only the sides of the object that face the observer, as the back-faces of the object are not visible anyway. To perform a back-face removal, your program must determine the object surfaces the user can see.

As you will learn, *back-face* removal is inadequate for complex objects. For example, a program will have difficulty determining what part of an object, such as a donut with a hole in the center, the user can and cannot see. However, for objects such as cubes, cones, and spheres, the back-face removal technique will do the job.

Before your program can perform back-face removal, your program needs to determine which sides of the object face the user. To do so, your program must calculate the surface's normal vector, as discussed next.

656 CALCULATING A SURFACE'S NORMAL VECTOR

To determine which sides of an object face the observer, you must create a normal vector for each surface. You calculate a normal vector by performing a cross product. The following code demonstrates how to calculate a normal vector for each side of a cube:

```
float x = cube.w[v1].x-cube.w[v0].x;
float y = cube.w[v1].y-cube.w[v0].y;
float z = cube.w[v1].z-cube.w[v0].z;
Vector3d A = new Vector3d(x, y, z);

x = cube.w[v3].x-cube.w[v0].x;
y = cube.w[v3].y-cube.w[v0].y;
z = cube.w[v3].z-cube.w[v0].z;
Vector3d B = new Vector3d(x, y, z);

normal = B.cross(A); // compute normal vector
```

The result of the cross product is a vector that is normal to the surface. By convention, the result of the cross product should face out of the surface. You can adjust the direction of the normal vector by changing the order of the cross product of a vector.

PERFORMING BACK-FACE REMOVAL 657

After all the sides of a simple object have a surface normal, you can transform the normal vector, just as you would the vertices of the cube. You can then calculate the dot product of the transformed normal vector and a vector that points to the observer. Because you are now working in the viewport coordinate system, the vector (0,0,-1) points to the observer. If the result of the dot product is positive, then the corresponding side of the object is visible.

You must calculate the dot product whenever you transform the cube. The following code demonstrates how the *Cube* class can call the *backface* method for each surface to check for back-face removal:

```
public void transform(Matrix3d toscreen)
  {
      Matrix3d m = new Matrix3d();
      m.multiply(toscreen, Matrix3d.REPLACE);
      m.multiply(matrix, Matrix3d.PRECONCAT);

      for (int i=0; i<v.length; i++)
         v[i] = m.transform2D(w[i]);

      for (int i=0; i<sides.length; i++)
         sides[i].backface(m);
  }
```

The following code demonstrates how the *backface* method performs its back-face removal:

```
public void backface(Matrix3d m)
  {
    Vector3d n = m.transform(normal);
    Vector3d o = new Vector3d(0.0f, 0.0f, -1.0f);

    if (n.dot(o) < 0.0f)
      visible = false;
    else
      visible = true;
  }
```

As you can see, the *backface* method sets the *visible* flag to *false* if the side is not visible. The following code demonstrates how the *draw* method uses the visible flag to determine if it should draw the surface:

```java
public void drawSolid(Graphics g, Point offset)
  {
    if (!visible)
      return;

    Polygon poly = new Polygon();

    for (int i = 0; i < index.length; i++)
      poly.addPoint(offset.x + cube.v[index[i]].x,
        offset.y + cube.v[index[i]].y);

    poly.addPoint(offset.x + cube.v[index[0]].x,
      offset.y + cube.v[index[0]].y);

    g.drawPolygon(poly);
  }
```

As you can see, the visible flag is *false*, so the *drawSolid* method immediately returns. Otherwise, the method draws the corresponding surface.

658 UNDERSTANDING PERSPECTIVE

For everyday experiences, you know that objects appear smaller when they are further away. Mathematically, the size of an object is inversely proportional to the object's distance from the viewer. For example, when an object is moved twice as far away from the viewer, the height and width of the object appears to be half its normal size. This effect is known as *perspective*. If you add perspective to your 3-D rendering, you add an extra level of realism.

659 CREATING A PERSPECTIVE MATRIX

To render a scene with a realistic perspective, you must create a new transformation matrix. The only difference between the perspective and orthogonal maxtrix is that for a perspective matrix, you specify the observer's distance from the origin. The *perspective* method calculates the distance in *x*, *y*, and *z* components and preconcatenates a translate matrix with the orthogonal matrix. The following code demonstrates how the *perspective* method applies its size transformation:

```java
// build perspective matrix
public void perspective(float theta,float phi,float omega,float d)
  {
    double theta_rad = theta *toRad;
    double phi_rad = phi *toRad;
    double theta_cos = Math.cos(theta_rad);
    double theta_sin = Math.sin(theta_rad);
    double phi_cos = Math.cos(phi_rad);
    double phi_sin = Math.sin(phi_rad);
    double xy_plane = d * phi_sin;
    float x = (float) (xy_plane * theta_cos);
```

```
        float y = (float) (xy_plane * theta_sin);
        float z = (float) (d * phi_cos);

        this.identity();
        this.translate(-x, -y, -z);
        this.rotateX(90);
        this.rotateY(90 + theta);
        this.rotateX(90 - phi);
        this.scale(1.0f, 1.0f, -1.0f);
        this.rotateZ(omega);
    }
```

The only thing left to do before you can render an object with perspective is to modify the *transform* method, as shown in the next tip.

A TRANSFORM METHOD FOR PERSPECIVE OBJECTS 660

To render a perspective object, you must add an extra step to the *transform* method that makes distance play a role in the object's appearance. This extra step divides the *x* and *y* coordinates by the *z* value (which contains the distance to the observer). The following code demonstrates a new *transform* method:

```
// A transform method that supports perspective display
public java.awt.Point transform2DPer(Point3d p, float d)
  {
    float xf = p.x * e00 + p.y * e01 + p.z * e02 + e03;
    float yf = p.x * e10 + p.y * e11 + p.z * e12 + e13;
    float zf = p.x * e20 + p.y * e21 + p.z * e22 + e23;

    int x = Math.round(d*xf/zf);
    int y = Math.round(d*yf/zf);
     return(new java.awt.Point(x,y));
  }
```

As you can see, the code multiplies the new *x* and *y* coordinates by a scale factor. Although the scale factor actually has a mathematical meaning, you can use half the height of the screen display (in pixels) as a scale factor.

CONVERSION FROM *3-D* TO *2-D* (*PERSPECTIVE*) 661

In the previous two tips, you created a perspective-transformation matrix. The following program, *testPerApplet.java*, demonstrates how to view the *Cube* class using a perspective view:

```
import java.applet.*;
import java.awt.*;

public class testPerApplet extends Applet {

    Cube cube = new Cube(50);

    public void init()
      {
```

```
            Matrix3d matrix = new Matrix3d();
            matrix.perspective(30f, 70f, 0f, 200f);
            cube.transformPer(matrix, 150f);
    }

  public void paint(Graphics g)
    {
        Point offset = new Point(size().width/2,size().height/2);
        cube.draw(g, offset);
    }
  }
```

Note that the example does not use the *drawSolid* method to display the object; instead, it uses the *Cube* class *draw* method. That's because the *backface* removal technique presented in this section does not work with the perspective view. However, you can still display objects using a wireframe display, as shown in Figure 661 which illustrates the program's output.

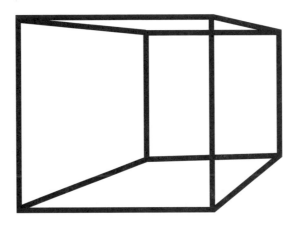

Figure 661 Displaying a wireframe 3-D cube using a perspective view.

662 UNDERSTANDING I/O STREAMS

An I/O stream provides the pathway through which your programs can send a sequence of bytes from a source to a destination. An input stream is a source (or producer) of bytes and an output stream is a destination for (or consumer of) bytes. Although I/O streams are often associated with disk file access, a program's data source and destination can also be the keyboard, mouse, memory, or display window.

The Java I/O library provides numerous stream classes. However, all input stream classes are subclasses of the *InputStream* abstract class, and all output stream classes are subclasses of the *OutputStream* abstract class. The one exception to this is the *RandomAccessFile* class that is both a source and destination. Therefore, your programs can both read from and write to a *RandomAccessFile* object.

Filters are a special group under the *InputStream* and *OutputStream* classes. The *FilterInputStream* and *FilterOutputStream* classes, along with their various subclasses, process the stream data before passing it on. For example, the *PrintStream* output filter converts numbers and other data types to a textual representation before passing on the data. Your programs can chain filter stream classes together in any length to provide the behavior you require. Figure 662 shows a buffered-file input stream that you can read and number, one line at a time.

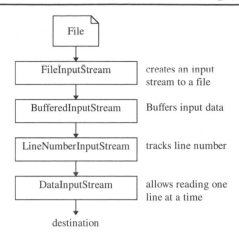

Figure 662 *Chained filter input streams.*

The following tips in this section will show you how to use the various stream classes in the library to perform I/O operations.

USING THE FILE CLASS

663

The *File* class in Java's I/O library provides a platform-independent abstraction for getting file information such as pathname, separator character, file size, and modification date. To get such file information, you must first create a *File* object using one of the following constructors:

```
File(String path);
File(String path, String name);
File(File dir, String name);
```

The *path* parameter in the first constructor specifies the path to the file, while the same parameter in the second constructor specifies the directory path. The *name* parameter specifies the name of the file. The *dir* parameter in the third constructor lets you use another *File* object as the directory. The following code, for example, determines whether or not a file named *temp.txt* exists:

```
File f = new File("temp.txt");

if (f.exists())
   System.out.println("file temp.txt exist");
else
   System.out.println("file temp.txt does not exist");
```

READING FROM A FILE USING THE FILEINPUTSTREAM

664

Many programs that you create will need to retrieve information from a file. The *FileInputStream*, a subclass of *InputStream*, provides stream access to a file. To read from a file, you use the *FileInputStream* constructor to open an input stream to the file, the format of which is shown in the following statement:

```
FileInputStream(String name);
```

For example, to read from a file named *myfile.dat*, you create a *FileInputStream* object, as shown:

```
FileInputStream istream = new FileInputStream("myfile.dat");
```

Another form of *FileInputStream* constructor lets you use a *File* object to specify which file to open, as shown:

```
FileInputStream(File file);
```

For example, the following code creates a file input stream to retrieve a file using the *FileInputStream* constructor, as shown:

```
File f = new File("myfile.dat ");
FileInputStream istream = new FileInputStream(f);
```

665 HANDLING I/O EXCEPTIONS WHEN DEALING WITH I/O OPERATIONS

When you create a stream to a file using the *FileInputStream* constructor, an I/O error, also known as an exception, may occur. For instance, the file you try to open may not exist. When an I/O error occurs, Java generates an error signal, which it represents using an *IOException* object. Your program must detect and handle the exception using a *catch* block. For example, to associate a *FileInputStream* object with a file, you would use code similar to the following:

```
try {
    FileInputStream ins = new FileInputStream("myfile.dat ");
    // read from input stream
  }
catch (IOException e)
  {
    // file I/O error
    System.out.println("File read error: " + e);
  }
```

Because I/O operations are especially susceptible to error, many other stream class constructors and methods also *throw* (create) I/O exceptions. You must *catch* (handle) these exceptions in the same way as shown in the previous code. The error handling section of this book provides a detailed discussion on exceptions.

666 READING BYTES FROM AN INPUT STREAM

The sole purpose of an input stream is to provide access to data that your programs can read. The *read* method provides your program with a basic method for reading data from an input stream. The format of the *read* method is as follows:

```
int read();
```

This *read* method reads a single byte of data from an input stream. The method returns the data read, or the value -1, if it reaches the end of the input stream. There are other forms of the *read* method that let your programs read multiple bytes into a byte array, as shown:

```
int read(byte b[]);
int read(byte b[], int off, int len);
```

The *off* parameter lets you specify where in *byte* array *b* the *read* method will store data. Likewise, the *len* parameter specifies the maximum number of bytes the method will read. Both of the *read* methods just shown return the number of bytes read, or -1 if they reach the end of the input stream. The following application, *read_bytes.java*, reads eight bytes from the file *bytedata.dat*:

```java
import java.io.*;

public class read_bytes {

   public static void main(String args[])
     {
       int b;

       try {
           FileInputStream is = new FileInputStream("bytedata.dat");

           while ((b = is.read()) != -1)
             {
                 //  do something with the data read
                 System.out.println("byte read = " + b);
             }
         }
       catch (IOException e)
         {
             System.out.println("File error: " + e);
         }
     }
}
```

CLOSING A STREAM

667

Although Java automatically closes all the opened streams when the program terminates, it is still a good idea to close any open stream explicitly when you are done using the streams. Depending on the platform and implementation, an opened stream may use up system resources. If you do not close the opened streams, these resources may not be available when this or another program tries to open another stream. Another reason to close an output stream, in particular, is to flush the stream buffer's contents (normally to a file on disk). As you will learn, the bytes your program writes to an output stream are sometimes kept in a memory buffer before the operating system writes the data to disk. By calling the *close* method, you can make certain that the operating system flushes the stream buffer to its destination. The following code illustrates the use of the *close* method:

```java
try {
    FileInputStream ins = new FileInputStream("myfile.dat ");

    // read from input stream

    ins.close(); // closing the input stream
  }
catch (IOException e)
  {
    // file I/O error
    System.out.println("File read error: " + e);
  }
```

668 SKIPPING BYTES WHEN READING FROM AN INPUT STREAM

When your programs read data from an input stream, there may be times when you want to skip over (bypass) data that you are not interested in. In such cases, you can use the *skip* method, the format of which is as follows:

```
long skip(long n);
```

The *n* parameter specifies the number of bytes within the input stream that the method will bypass. The method returns the actual number of bytes it skipped. The return value is normally the same as the number of bytes specified to skip, but could be smaller should the *skip* method reach the end of the stream. For example, the following statement skips 16 bytes within an input stream:

```
int bytes_skipped = is.skip(16);
```

669 UNDERSTANDING THE DATAINPUTSTREAM

In Tip 666, you learned how to read bytes of data from an input stream. In most cases, your programs will read specific types of data from an input stream, such as an integer value or a line of text. Using the *read* method, your programs can read the data as bytes, and you can then convert the data to the appropriate types yourself. Fortunately, the Java I/O library provides the *DataInputStream*, a filtered input stream for converting stream data into primitive types. For example, you can call the *DataInputStream* class *readInt* method to read a 32-bit integer, and the *readDouble* method to read a 64-bit double floating-point number. Table 669 provides a partial list of the methods defined in the *DataInputStream* class:

Method	Purpose
boolean readBoolean();	Reads a boolean
byte readByte();	Reads an 8-bit byte
int readUnsignedByte();	Reads an unsigned 8-bit byte
short readShort();	Reads a 16-bit short
int readUnsignedShort();	Reads an unsigned 16-bit short
char readChar();	Reads a 16-bit char
int readInt();	Reads a 32-bit integer
long readLong();	Reads a 64-bit long
float readFloat();	Reads a 32-bit floating-point number
double readDouble();	Reads a 64-bit double floating-point number
String readLine();	Reads a line
String readUTF();	Read a UTF format string

*Table 669 A partial list of the **DataInputStream** methods.*

670 READING A LINE USING THE DATAINPUTSTREAM

In addition to the *readInt* method discussed in the previous tip, you can read a line of text using the *DataInputStream* class *readLine* method. The following program, *read_ln.java*, uses the input stream methods to read the contents of the file *textfile.txt* and echos the file's contents to the console window line by line:

```
import java.io.*;

public class read_ln {

    public static void main(String args[])
    {
        try {
            String line_str;
            int line_number;
            FileInputStream is = new
FileInputStream("textfile.txt");
            DataInputStream ds = new DataInputStream(is);

            while ((line_str = ds.readLine()) != null)
             {
                 System.out.println(line_str);
             }

            ds.close();
          }
        catch (IOException e)
          {
             System.out.println("File error: " + e);
          }
       }
   }
```

UNDERSTANDING THE PROCESS OF TOKENIZATION 671

When your program reads a line of input, there may be times when your program needs to break (parse) the string apart into specific pieces (called tokens). For example, your programs might parse a filename into tokens that represent a disk drive, pathname, filename, and extension. Likewise, consider the string shown in Figure 671 that represents a stock quote on a particular date, with daily high, daily low, and closing price information.

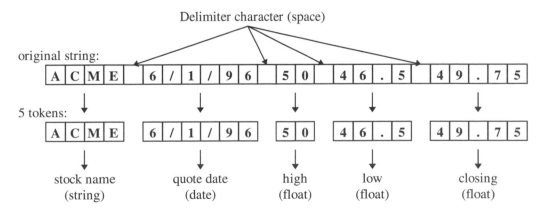

Figure 671 *Tokenizing a string.*

The information in the original string is separated by a delimiter character, which in this case is a white-space character. The *tokenization* process breaks the original string into five separate tokens, which you can then convert to the appropriate data types. The following tip will show you how to use Java's built-in tokenizer.

672 USING THE STRINGTOKENIZER

The Java *util* library defines a *StringTokenizer* class that helps you break a string into tokens. To tokenize a string, you have to create a *StringTokenizer* object, specifying your string and the special character the string uses to indicate (delimit) its components. The formats of the *StringTokenizer* constructor methods are as follows:

```
StringTokenizer(String str, String delim, boolean returnTokens);
StringTokenizer(String str, String delim);
StringTokenizer(String str);
```

The *str* parameter specifies the string that you want to tokenize. The *delim* parameter specifies a list of delimiter characters. For example, a *delim* argument of ",:" indicates that the delimiter characters are comma and colon. By default, the *StringTokenizer* class sets the delimiter character to the characters "\t\n\r" which correspond to a tab (hence the term tab-delimited file), a newline character, and a carriage-return. The *returnTokens* parameter specifies whether you want the delimiter character to be returned by the tokenizer as a token or not. By default, the method skips delimiter characters.

673 TRAVERSING THROUGH A LIST OF TOKENS

After you create a *StringTokenizer* object, you can extract each token using the *nextToken* method. The format of the *nextToken* method is as follows:

```
String nextToken();
```

Also, in order to find out whether the *StringTokenizer* object contains more tokens, you can call the *hasMoreTokens* method. The format of the *hasMoreTokens* method is as follows:

```
boolean hasMoreElements();
```

The method *hasMoreTokens* returns the value *true* if the object contains more tokens, and *false* if otherwise. Using these two methods, your programs can loop quickly through a *StringTokenizer* object, extracting the object's tokens. The following code tokenizes the string, "The quick brown fox", and breaks up the string into individual words:

```
StringTokenizer st = new StringTokenizer("The quick brown fox"," ");

while (st.hasMoreTokens())
  {
     System.out.println("token: " + st.nextToken());
  }
```

The previous code will display the following output to the console window:

```
token: The
token: quick
token: brown
token: fox
```

FINDING THE NUMBER OF TOKENS IN THE STRINGTOKENIZER

In the previous tip, you learned how to extract tokens from a string until no more tokens exist. In some cases, you may want to know the number of tokens that a *StringTokenizer* object contains. In such cases, your programs can call the *StringTokenizer* class *countTokens* method, the format of which is as follows:

```
int countTokens();
```

The following statements use the *countTokens* method to display the number of tokens in the *String*, "The quick brown fox":

```
StringTokenizer st = new StringTokenizer("The quick brown fox"," ");

System.out.println("No of tokens = " + st.countTokens());
```

In this case, the program will display the following output:

```
No of tokens = 4
```

CHANGING THE TOKEN DELIMITER ON-THE-FLY

When your program parses a string using the *StringTokenizer*, there may be times when you want to change the delimiter characters on-the-fly. For example, consider the string, "Language name: Java C Basic".

In order to extract the label "Language name", you must use the colon (":") as the delimiter. But for the rest of the tokens, "Java", "C", and "Basic", you will need to use a space character (" ") as the delimiter. Using the *StringTokenizer* class *nextToken* method lets you change the delimiter character set, as shown in the following statement:

```
String nextToken(String delim);
```

The following code illustrates how to change the delimiter character set on-the-fly:

```
StringTokenizer st = new StringTokenizer(
    "Language name: Java C Basic",":");

System.out.println("first token: " + st.nextToken());

while (st.hasMoreTokens())
  {
    System.out.println("token: " + st.nextToken(" "));
  }
```

In this case, the program will display the following output:

```
first token: Language name
token: Java
token: C
token: Basic
```

676 PARSING DATA WITH THE TOKENIZER

In previous tips, you learned how to extract string tokens using *StringTokenizer* objects. Assume, for example, the content of the file, *quote.data*, is the following:

```
ACME  6/1/96 50 46.5 49.75
SP500 6/2/96 124 122 123.5
DWMI  6/1/96 24.5 22.25 24.5
```

The program, in turn, will display the following output:

```
Stock Symbol :ACME
Quote Date :Mon Jul 01 00:00:00  1996
Price: high:50 low:46.5 close:49.75

Stock Symbol :SP500
Quote Date :Tue Jul 02 00:00:00  1996
Price: high:124 low:122 close:123.5

Stock Symbol :DWMI
Quote Date :Mon Jul 01 00:00:00  1996
Price: high:24.5 low:22.25 close:24.5

import java.io.*;
import java.util.*;
```

The following program, *stock_data.java*, extracts stock-quote data from the ASCII data file *quote.dat*:

```java
public class stock_data {

    public static void main(String args[])
      {
          String stock_name;
          Date quote_date;
          float high_p, low_p, closing_p;

          try {
             String line_str;
             int line_number;
             FileInputStream is = new FileInputStream("quote.dat");
             DataInputStream ds = new DataInputStream(is);

             while ((line_str = ds.readLine()) != null)
               {
                   StringTokenizer st = new StringTokenizer(line_str);

                   // extract tokens and convert to appropiate types
                   stock_name = st.nextToken();
```

```
                    quote_date = new Date(st.nextToken());

                    high_p = Float.valueOf(st.nextToken()).floatValue();
                    low_p = Float.valueOf(st.nextToken()).floatValue();
                closing_p =
                        Float.valueOf(st.nextToken()).floatValue();

                // display extract values
                System.out.println("Stock Symbol :" + stock_name);
                System.out.println("Quote Date :" + quote_date);
                System.out.println("Price: high:" + high_p +
                    " low:" + low_p + " close:" + closing_p);
                System.out.println();
            }
          ds.close();
        }
      catch (IOException e)
        {
            System.out.println("File error: " + e);
        }
    }
}
```

KEEPING TRACK OF LINE NUMBERS WITH LINENUMBERINPUTSTREAM 677

When your program reads text from a file, you may need to keep track of the line numbers while you are reading the file. One way to do this is to create a line number variable and increment it each time a line is read, as shown:

```
String line_str;
DataInputStream ds;
int line_number = 0;

while ((line_str = ds.readLine()) != null)
    {
       line_number++;

       // Process line read
    }
```

Another way to keep track of line numbers is to use the *LineNumberInputStream* method. This input filter stream tracks the line number as the input stream is read, and you can call the *getLineNumber* method to get the line number. The following application, *line_no.java*, illustrates the use of the *DataInputStream* class *LineNumberInputStream* method by displaying the line number each time a line is read, as shown in the following code:

```
import java.io.*;

public class line_no {
```

```
    public static void main(String args[])
    {
      try {
        String line_str;
        int line_number;

        FileInputStream is = new FileInputStream("line_no.java");
        LineNumberInputStream ls = new LineNumberInputStream(is);
        DataInputStream ds = new DataInputStream(ls);

        while ((line_str = ds.readLine()) != null)
          {
             System.out.println(ls.getLineNumber() +
               "line(s) read");
          }
        ds.close();
      }
      catch (IOException e)
      {
         System.out.println("File error: " + e);
      }
    }
}
```

678 UNDERSTANDING SEQUENCEINPUTSTREAM

There may be times when the data your program needs to read resides in multiple files, and you need to process these files one after the other. You could open a stream to the first file, read the contents, close the stream, and repeat the process with the next file. Another way to read a sequence of files is to use a *SequenceInputStream* object. The *SequenceInputStream* class lets you concatenate two or more input streams into one stream so you can access multiple files in sequence, one after another. To combine files into one stream in this way, you can use one of the following *SequenceInputStream* constructor methods:

```
SequenceInputStream(InputStream s1, InputStream s2);
SequenceInputStream(Enumeration e);
```

The first constructor method combines two input streams, *s1* and *s2,* into one stream, while the second constructor method combines all streams in the enumeration. You will examine enumeration in the data structure section of this book. For example, the following code combines two file input streams into one:

```
InputStream f1 = new FileInputStream("file1.txt");
InputStream f2 = new FileInputStream("file2.txt");

InputStream combined_stream = new SequenceInputStream(f1, f2);
```

679 WRITING TO A FILE USING THE FILEOUTPUTSTREAM

In Tip 664, you learned how to open a stream to read from a file. As you will learn, opening a stream to write to a file is a very similar process. The *FileOutputStream*, a subclass of *OutputStream*, provides stream output access to a file.

To write to a file, you can use the *FileOutputStream* constructor to open an output stream to the file. The format of the *FileOutputStream* constructor is as follows:

```
FileOutputStream(String name);
```

For example, to write to a file named *myoutput.dat*, you would create a file output stream, as shown:

```
FileOutputStream ostream = new FileOutputStream("myoutput.dat");
```

Another form of the *FileOutputStream* constructor lets you use a *File* object to specify which file to open, as shown:

```
FileOutputStream(File file);
```

For example, the following code creates a file output stream to a file using the previous constructor:

```
File f = new File("myoutput.dat");

FileOutputStream ostream = new FileOutputStream(f);
```

WRITING BYTES TO AN OUTPUT STREAM

680

The process for writing bytes to an output stream is a mirror image of reading bytes from an input stream. Just as you use the *read* method to read bytes from an input stream, you can use the *write* method to send bytes to an output stream. The format of the *write* method is as follows:

```
void write(int b);
```

This *write* method writes a single byte of data, specified by the parameter *b*, to the stream. There are other forms of the *write* method that let your programs write multiple bytes using a byte array, as shown:

```
void write(byte b[]);
void write(byte b[], int off, int len);
```

The *off* parameter lets you specify where in the byte array *b* the *write* method should locate its data. The *len* parameter specifies the number of bytes the method will write. The following application, *write_bytes.java*, writes 8 bytes of data to the file *bytewrite.dat*:

```
import java.io.*;

public class write_bytes {

    public static void main(String args[])
      {
        int p_array[] = {1, 2, 3, 5, 7, 11, 13, 17};

        try {
           FileOutputStream os =
               new FileOutputStream("bytewrite.dat");
```

```
                for (int i = 0; i < p_array.length; i++)
                    os.write(p_array[i]);
                os.close();
            }
        catch (IOException e)
            {
                System.out.println("File error: " + e);
            }
        }
    }
```

681 USING THE DATA OUTPUT STREAM

As you have learned, the *DataInputStream* lets you convert the stream data your program inputs into primitive types. In a similar way, the *DataOutputStream* lets your programs write primitive data types to an output stream. Table 681 provides a partial list of the methods defined in the *DataOutputStream* class:

Method	Purpose
void writeBoolean(boolean v) ;	Writes a boolean
void writeByte(int v);	Writes an 8-bit byte
void writeShort(int v) ;	Writes a 16-bit short
void writeChar(int v) ;	Writes a 16-bit character
void writeInt(int v) ;	Writes a 32-bit integer
void writeLong(long v) ;	Writes a 64-bit long
void writeFloat(float v) ;	Writes a 32-bit float
void writeDouble(double v) ;	Writes a 64-bit double
void writeBytes(String s) ;	Writes a string as a sequence of 8-bit byte
void writeChars(String s) ;	Writes a string as a sequence of 16-bit character
void writeUTF(String str);	Writes a UTF string

*Table 681 A partial list of the **DataOutputStream** methods.*

The following application, *data_stream.java*, illustrates the use of some of these methods by writing several primitive types to a file and then reading them back:

```
import java.io.*;

public class data_stream {

    public static void main(String args[])
      {
        // write data file

        try {
            FileOutputStream os =
                new FileOutputStream("data_stream.dat");
```

```
        DataOutputStream ods = new DataOutputStream(os);

        // write an int
        ods.writeInt(31);

        // write a float
        ods.writeFloat(3.1416f);

        // write a boolean
        ods.writeBoolean(true);

        // write a long
        ods.writeLong(725624);
        ods.close();
    }
    catch(IOException e)
    {
        System.out.println("File write error: " + e);
    }

    // read data file
    try {
        FileInputStream is =
            new FileInputStream("data_stream.dat");
        DataInputStream ids = new DataInputStream(is);

        // read an int
        int tempi = ids.readInt();
        System.out.println(tempi);

        // read a float
        float tempf = ids.readFloat();
        System.out.println(tempf);

        // read a boolean
        boolean tempb = ids.readBoolean();
        System.out.println(tempb);

        // read a long
        long templ = ids.readLong();
        System.out.println(templ);
        ids.close();
    }
    catch (IOException e)
    {
        System.out.println("File write error: " + e);
    }
  }
}
```

682 USING RANDOMACCESSFILE

Unlike other input and output streams, the *RandomAccessFile* class is neither a subclass of the *InputStream* nor the *OutputStream* classes. However, you can perform both read and write operations to a *RandomAccessFile* object at the same time. In addition, a *RandomAccessFile* object, as its name implies, also provides random access to data in a file, rather than sequential access, as is the case with the *InputStream* and *OutputStream* objects. You can use one of the following constructors to create a *RandomAccessFile* object:

```
RandomAccessFile(String name, String mode);
RandomAccessFile(File file, String mode);
```

Your programs can set the parameter *mode* to either "r" for read-only access or "rw" for read and write access.

683 FINDING INFORMATION IN A RANDOM ACCESS FILE WITH SEEK

As you have learned, a *RandomAccessFile* object provides random access to data in a file, which lets your program read or write from nonsequential locations within the file. To control the location within the file at which the program performs its read or write operation, your programs can use the *seek* method to move the file pointer. The format of the *seek* method is as follows:

```
void seek(long pos);
```

The *pos* parameter specifies the file pointer position from the beginning of the file in bytes. Just as your programs can position the file pointer within a random access file, your programs can also determine the current position of the file pointer by calling the *getFilePointer* method, the format of which is as follows:

```
long getFilePointer();
```

The following application, *random_file.java*, writes several 32-bit integers to a file named *temp.dat* and then reads the data back in reverse order by using the *seek* method:

```java
import java.io.*;

public class random_file {

    public static void main(String args[])
      {
        int data_arr[] = {12, 31, 56, 23, 27, 1, 43, 65, 4, 99} ;

        try {
            RandomAccessFile randf =
                new RandomAccessFile("temp.dat", "rw");

            // write to file
            for (int i = 0; i < data_arr.length; i++)
              randf.writeInt(data_arr[i]);
```

```
                // read back in reverse order
                for (int i = data_arr.length-1; i >= 0; i—)
                  {
                       randf.seek(i*4); // each int is 4 bytes long
                       System.out.println(randf.readInt());
                  }
                randf.close();
            }
        catch (IOException e)
            {
               System.out.println("File access error: " + e);
            }
        }
    }
```

UNDERSTANDING THE PRINTSTREAM 684

The *PrintStream* class provides a filter output stream that lets you display numbers, *boolean* values, *Strings*, and other object types in text format. For example, when your program displays the integer value 42, the *PrintStream* class converts the number to the characters "4" and "2" and then passes the characters down the stream. As it turns out, the *System.out* stream that you have used throughout this book to display messages to the console window is, in fact, a *PrintStream*.

A *PrintStream* object is not limited to just displaying output to the console window. Instead, you can also use *PrintStream* objects to output data to any stream destination, including an ASCII text file. The following application, *print_file.java*, displays a *String*, an integer, and a floating-point number to the file, *print.txt*:

```java
import java.io.*;


public class print_file {

    public static void main(String args[]) {

       try {

           PrintStream ps = new PrintStream(

              new FileOutputStream("print.txt"));

           ps.println("Hello, World!");

           ps.println(42);

           ps.println(Math.PI);


           ps.close();
```

```
        } catch (IOException e) {

            System.out.println("File write error :" + e);

        }

    }

}
```

In this case, the program will write the following content to the file:

```
Hello, World!
42
3.14159
```

685 USING THE BYTE ARRAY INPUT/OUTPUT STREAM

As you have learned, the source and destination of a stream can be computer memory as well as a file. The *ByteArrayInputStream* and *ByteArrayOutputStream* let your programs use a byte array as an input stream and output stream, respectively. After your program creates a byte-array input or output stream, you can use it just like a *FileInputStream* and *FileOutputStream*. The following application, *barr_stream.java*, illustrates the use of the *ByteArrayInputStream* and *ByteArrayOutputStream* methods:

```java
import java.io.*;

public class barr_stream {

    public static void main(String args[])
      {
        byte in_array[] = {'J', 'a', 'v', 'a', ' ', 'T', 'i', 'p', 's'};

        // ByteArrayInputStream test
        try {
           int b;
           ByteArrayInputStream is =
                new ByteArrayInputStream(in_array);
           DataInputStream datis = new DataInputStream(is);

           // verify input
           System.out.print("Input array = ");
            System.out.println(datis.readLine());
        }
        catch (IOException e)
          {
             System.out.println("Read error: " + e);
          }
```

```
        // ByteArrayOutputStream test
    try {
        ByteArrayOutputStream os = new ByteArrayOutputStream();
        DataOutputStream datos = new DataOutputStream(os);

        // write to output array
        datos.writeBytes("byte array");

        // verify output
        System.out.println("Output Array = " + os);
    }
    catch(IOException e)
      {
        System.out.println("Read error: " + e);
      }
    }
}
```

USING THE *STRINGBUFFERINPUTSTREAM*

686

As you learned in Tip 685, Java lets you use a byte array as either the source or destination for a stream I/O operation. Java also provides a *StringBufferInputStream* class which is quite similar to the *ByteArrayInputStream* class. However, instead of using a byte array to create an input stream, the *StringBufferInputStream* lets you use a *String* as an input stream. The following application, *str_stream.java*, illustrates the use of a *StringBufferInputStream*:

```
import java.io.*;

public class str_stream {

   public static void main(String args[])
     {
        String str = "String Buffer Stream";

        int b;

        // create string buffer input stream with str string
        StringBufferInputStream is =
            new StringBufferInputStream(str);

        // verify input
        while ((b = is.read()) != -1)
          {
            System.out.println((char) b);
          }
    }
}
```

687 UNDERSTANDING STREAM BUFFERED I/O STREAM

When your program accesses a file on either a local or a network disk, it is often more efficient to read or write a large block of data together, rather than reading or writing one byte at a time. The *BufferedInputStream* class lets your program load a block of data from an input stream, such as a file stream, and later read it in small chunks. By handling buffered input in this way, you reduce the overhead associated with reading data from an input stream by increasing your program's I/O efficiency. The *BufferedInputStream* class supports two constructor methods, the formats of which are as follows:

```
BufferedInputStream(InputStream in);
BufferedInputStream(InputStream in, int size);
```

The first constructor creates an input buffer using the default size of 2,048 bytes, and the second form lets you specify the buffer's size using the size parameter. Similarly, the *BufferedOutputStream* lets you build a block of data before writing the data to an output stream. There are also two forms of the *BufferedOutputStream* constructor, the formats of which are as follows:

```
BufferedOutputStream(OutputStream out);
BufferedOutputStream(OutputStream out, int size);
```

The first constructor creates an output buffer using the default size of 512 bytes, and the second form lets you specify the buffer size with the *size* parameter.

688 REREADING DATA USING THE MARK AND RESET METHODS

To provide you with better control over stream-based operations, some input stream classes let you mark a location within the stream and let you return to that location to reread the data. To specify a location within a file, you use the *mark* method to set the position in the stream, and then you use the *reset* method to move the file position back to that position:

```
void mark(int readlimit);
void reset();
```

The *readlimit* parameter specifies the maximum number of bytes back to which the program can branch within the file stream. If the program reads past this limit, the program invalidates the marked location. As discussed, not all streams support the *mark* method. To determine if a stream supports the *mark* method, you call the *markSupported* method, which returns *true* if the stream supports the *mark* method and *false* otherwise. The following application, *mark_reset.java*, illustrates the use of the *mark* and *reset* methods:

```
import java.io.*;

public class mark_reset {

    public static void main(String args[])
      {
          String str = "The quick brown fox";
          byte b[] = new byte[16];

          try {
```

```
        // create string buffer input stream with str string
        StringBufferInputStream is =
            new StringBufferInputStream(str);
        BufferedInputStream bs = new BufferedInputStream(is);

        // read 10 bytes and set mark
        bs.read(b, 0, 10);

        // echo to the console window
        System.out.println(new String(b, 0, 0, 10));

        bs.mark(16);

        // read next 6 bytes
        bs.read(b, 0, 6);

        // echo to the console window
        System.out.println(new String(b, 0, 0, 6));


        // go back and reread
        bs.reset();
        bs.read(b, 0, 9);

        // echo to the console window
        System.out.println(new String(b, 0, 0, 9));
    }
    catch(IOException e) { }
  }
}
```

USING THE PUSHBACKINPUTSTREAM 689

When your program parses an input file, there may be times when, after having read a byte from an input stream, you need to put the byte back. In such cases, the *PushbackInputStream* class lets you restore bytes to an input stream. Using a *PushbackInputStream* object, you can push back one byte of data onto the stream using the *unread* method, the format of which is as follows:

```
void unread(int ch);
```

The *ch* parameter specifies the character, or byte, that you want to push back into the stream. The character that you use to push back data into a stream is not limited to the character that you read. Instead, you can push back any single byte of data you want using the *PushbackInputStream* class *unread* method.

MORE ON PRINTING WITH PRINTSTREAM 690

Throughout this book, you have used the *println* method of the *PrintStream* class to display data to the console window followed by a line feed (new line) character. Depending on your program's requirements, there is another method named *print* that lets you display data without adding a line feed character. In this way, you can display several data items on the same line. For example, the following statements use the *print* method to display the words "Java Programming Tips" on one line:

```
System.out.print(1001);
System.out.print(" Java");
System.out.println(" Programming Tips");
```

Because Java may buffer the output of the *PrintStream* class, the result of the *print* method may not appear on the screen immediately after the method call. If you want the result to be displayed immediately, you either have to print the linefeed character "\n", as in the case of the *println* method, or call the *flush* method directly, as shown:

```
System.out.print(1001);
System.out.print(" Java");
System.out.print(" Programming Tips");
System.out.flush(); // flush the standout stream
```

691 GETTING FILE PATH INFORMATION USING THE FILE CLASS

As you have learned, the *File* class offers various methods your programs can use to get information about a file. For example, the *getName* method returns the filename, without a directory name. Likewise, the *getParent* method returns the directory name without the filename. The *getPath* method returns the file's path and the *getAbsolutePath* method returns the file's full path. The following code illustrates the use of the above methods:

```
File f = new File("data",  "temp.dat");

System.out.println("file name = "  + f.getName());
System.out.println("file directory = " + f.getParent());
System.out.println("file path = "  + f.getPath());
System.out.println("full path = "  + f.getAbsolutePath());
```

If the current directory were "C:\myprog", the code would display the following output:

```
file name = temp.dat
file directory = data
file path = data\temp.dat
full path = C:\myprog\data\temp.dat
```

692 GETTING THE PLATFORM-DEPENDENT FILE SEPARATOR CHARACTER

As you know, the operating system uses file separators to separate directory names in a file path. Unfortunately, the file separator on a Windows platform is different than the one on a UNIX platform. The Windows platform uses the backslash (\) character as the file separator, while UNIX uses the forward slash (/). Because Java is designed to be platform independent, you will have to use the appropriate separator if you need to construct a file path.

The *File* class *File.separator* and *File.separatorChar* variables contain the file separator for the platform which the Java program is currently running on. The difference between the two variables is that *File.separator* is a string and *File.separatorChar* is a character. You can use either variable when you write your program.

There may be times when you want to find the separator character between two file paths. The *File* class *File.pathSeparator* and *File.pathSeparatorChar* variables contain the path separator. Like the *File* class separator variables, the difference between the two variables is that *File.pathSeparator* is a string and *File.pathSeparatorChar* is a character.

BEWARE OF USING BACKSLASHES IN A FILE PATH

 693

As you know, on a Windows-based system, you use the backslash character (\) as the separator character within a pathname. For example, the directory path *C:\WINDOWS\FONTS\SomeFont.TTF* uses the separator to distinguish parts of a file's pathname. Remember that Java also uses the backslash character as an escape character. For example, the string "\t" represents a single tab character. Consider the following statement which creates a file input stream:

```
FileInputStream istream = new FileInputStream("data\temp.dat");
```

In this case, the file path in the previous statement specifies the string "data<tab>emp.dat" instead of the intended pathname "data\temp". Therefore, when you specify a file path with string literals, you should use double backslashes "\\" for the separator, as shown:

```
FileInputStream istream = new FileInputStream("data\\temp.dat");
```

LISTING FILES IN A DIRECTORY

 694

Although you can use the *FileDialog* interface that you learned about in the AWT section of this book to provide the user with a list of files in the directory, there may be times when you want to get the list without using the *FileDialog* interface. For example, you might want your program to display a formatted list of the files, or you may want to perform specific processing with each file. In such cases, you can use the *File* class *list* method which provides you with a list of the files that reside within a directory. The format of the *list* method is as follows:

```
String[] list();
```

To list the files that reside in a directory, you first create a new *File* object and specify the desired directory in the constructor. Then, you call the *list* method to get the file list. The following statements display the names of the files that reside in the current directory:

```
File current_dir = new File(".");
String file_list[] = current_dir.list();

for (int i=0; i<file_list.length; i++)
  {
      System.out.println(file_list[i]);
  }
```

USING A FILENAME FILTER IN THE LIST METHOD

 695

In the AWT section of this book, you learned that you can list the files with a particular extension within a *FileDialog* interface by using a filename filter. As it turns out, there is another form of the *File* class *list* method that lets you use a filename filter to access filenames within your program. The format of the *list* method is as follows:

```
String[] list(FilenameFilter filter);
```

The following application, *filter_list.java*, uses a filename filter to display the current directory files that have the *.java* extension:

```java
import java.io.*;

class JavaFileFilter implements FilenameFilter {

    public boolean accept(File dir, String name)
     {
       return name.endsWith(".java");
     }
 }

public class filter_list {

   public static void main(String args[])
    {
        File current_dir = new File(".");
        String filtered_list[] =
            current_dir.list(new JavaFileFilter());

        for (int i = 0; i < filtered_list.length; i++)
          System.out.println(filtered_list[i]);
    }
 }
```

696 GETTING THE SIZE OF A FILE

When your program performs file I/O operations, there may be times that you need to find the size of a file. For instance, if you want to load the file's contents into memory, you may need to know the file size to determine how much memory to allocate. To determine a file's size, you use the *File* class *length* method, the format of which is as follows:

```
long length();
```

The *length* method returns the size of the file in bytes. The following program, *file_size.java*, illustrates the use of the *length* method by displaying the size of all files in the current directory:

```java
import java.io.*;

public class file_size {

    public static void main(String args[])
     {
        File current_dir = new File(".");
        String file_list[] = current_dir.list();
```

```
      for (int i = 0; i < file_list.length; i++)
        {
          File current_file = new File(file_list[i]);
          System.out.println(file_list[i]+ " " +
            current_file.length());
        }
    }
}
```

GETTING THE FILE MODIFICATION TIME

 697

When your program performs file I/O operations, there may be times when you need to know when a file was last modified. To determine when a file was last modified, you can use the *File* class *lastModified* method, the format of which is as follows:

```
long lastModified();
```

The *lastModified* method returns a *long* integer value that indicates the modification time. The larger the return value, the more recently the file was modified. Although the JDK 1.0 documentation indicates the return value is meaningless as an absolute time, you can convert the result into a *Date* object and extract the actual date and time information. The following program, *file_modif.java*, displays the modification time for a given file:

```
import java.io.*;
import java.util.*;

public class file_modif {

  public static void main(String args[])
    {
      File tf = new File(args[0]);
      Date d = new Date(tf.lastModified());

      System.out.println(tf.getName() + " was last modified on:");
      System.out.println(d + " (" + tf.lastModified() + ")");
    }
}
```

CREATING A DIRECTORY

 698

When your programs store files on disk, there may be times when your program needs to create a directory to better organize your files. In such cases, your program can use the *File* class *mkdir* method, as shown:

```
boolean mkdir();
```

The *mkdir* method is equivalent to the MS-DOS MKDIR command; however, you do not specify the directory name as an argument as you would with the MKDIR command. To create a directory using the *mkdir* method, you first need to create a *File* object using the directory name you want to create. For example, the following code creates a directory named *temp* within the current directory:

```
boolean status;
File newdir = new File("temp");
status = newdir.mkdir();
```

The *mkdir* method returns *true* if it successfully creates the directory and *false* if it fails. Note, however, the method may also return *false* if the directory already exists.

699 CREATING ALL DIRECTORIES IN A FILE'S PATH

As you learned in the previous tip, you can create a directory using the *mkdir* method. The limitation of the *mkdir* method is that it can only create one directory at a time. For example, if you need to create a directory named *data* and a sub-directory named *temp* (yielding *data\temp*), you must call the *mkdir* method twice. A better alternative is to use the File class *mkdirs* method, the format of which is as follows:

```
boolean mkdirs();
```

The *mkdirs* method creates all directories in the path. To create directories using the *mkdirs* method, you create a *File* object with the directory path, and then call the *mkdirs* method to create the directories. The following program fragment creates a *data* directory and a *temp* sub-directory within the current directory:

```
boolean status;

File newdir = new File("data" + File.separator + "temp");
status = newdir.mkdirs();
```

The *mkdirs* method returns *true* if it successfully creates the directory and *false* if it fails.

700 RENAMING A FILE

Within your programs, there may be times when you need to rename an existing file. In such cases, you can use the *File* class *renameTo* method to rename the file. The format of the *renameTo* method is as follows:

```
boolean renameTo(File dest);
```

The *renameTo* method is equivalent to the MS-DOS RENAME command. To rename a file using the *renameTo* method, you must create a *File* object with the current filename and a second *File* object that contains the new name. Then, you call the *renameTo* method to rename the file. The following code fragment renames the file *oldname.txt* to *newname2.txt*:

```
boolean status;

File current_file = new File("oldname.txt");
File new_file = new File("newname.txt");
status = current_file.renameTo(new_file);
```

The *renameTo* method returns *true* if it successfully renames the file and *false* if it fails.

DETERMINING READ AND WRITE ACCESS OF A FILE

 701

When your program performs file I/O operations, there may be times when you must determine if your program has permission to read from or write to a file. In such cases, your programs can use the *File* class *canRead* and *canWrite* methods to inquire about the file access. The formats of the *canRead* and *canWrite* methods are as follows:

```
boolean canRead();
boolean canWrite();
```

The *canRead* method returns *true* if your program has permission to read the file and *false* if the file program cannot read the file. Similarly, the *canWrite* method returns *true* if your program has permission to write to the file and *false* otherwise. The following code fragment displays whether the program has read and write access to the file *temp.txt*:

```
File f = new File("temp.txt");
System.out.println("can read " + f.canRead());
System.out.println("can write " + f.canWrite());
```

DELETING A FILE

 702

As your programs create and work with files, there may be times when your program needs to delete a file. To delete a file, your programs can use the *File* class *delete* method, the format of which is as follows:

```
boolean delete();
```

The *delete* method is equivalent to the MS-DOS DEL command. However, you do not specify the filename as an argument. To delete a file using the *delete* method, you must first create a *File* object that contains the name of the file you want to delete. Then, you call the *delete* method to remove the file. The following code fragment deletes the file, *temp.txt*, from the current directory:

```
boolean status;

File f = new File("temp.txt");
status = f.delete();
```

The *delete* method returns *true* if it successfully deletes the file and *false* if it fails.

A RECURSIVE DIRECTORY LISTER

 703

In Tip 694, you learned that you can get the names of the files that reside in a directory using the *File* class *list* method. There may be times, however, when you want to list all the files in a directory and its sub-directories. To list all files in a directory tree, you traverse the sub-directories recursively using the *list* method. As you process entries within the directory list, you must determine whether a name corresponds to a directory or a file so you can alter your processing accordingly. In other words, when you encounter a directory within the list, you will recursively traverse the entries that directory contains. To determine if a name in the list corresponds to a file or a directory, you use the *File* class *isDirectory* and *isFile* methods. The formats of the *isDirectory* and *isFile* methods are as follows:

```
boolean isDirectory();
boolean isFile();
```

The *isDirectory* methods returns *true* if the pathname corresponds to a directory and *false* if it does not. Conversely, the *isFile* methods returns *true* if the pathname corresponds to a file and *false* if it does not. The following application, *recur_list.java*, lists all the files in the user-specified directory and its sub-directories, as shown in Figure 703:

```java
import java.awt.*;
import java.io.*;
import java.util.*;

public class recur_list extends Frame {

   List flist = new List();

   void add_files(File f)
     {
        File current_dir = new File(f, ".");
        String file_list[] = current_dir.list();

        for (int i = 0; i < file_list.length; i++)
          {
             File current_file = new File(f, file_list[i]);

             if (current_file.isDirectory())
               add_files(current_file);
             else
                 flist.addItem(current_file.getAbsolutePath());
          }
     }

   public recur_list(String name, String dir)
     {
        super(name);
        add("Center", flist);
        add_files(new File(dir));
     }

   public static void main(String args[])
     {
        recur_list application =
          new recur_list("recur_list", args[0]);

        application.resize(300, 150);
        application.show();
     }

   public boolean handleEvent(Event evt)
     {
```

```
        if (evt.id == Event.WINDOW_DESTROY)
          System.exit(0); // exit the application

        return super.handleEvent(evt);
      }
    }
```

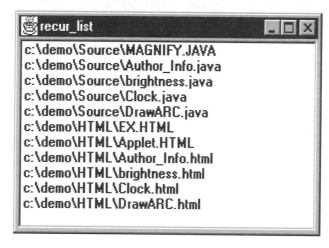

Figure 703 *Recursive file lister application.*

UNDERSTANDING RUN-LENGTH ENCODING DATA COMPRESSION  704

No matter what type of network connection you have, you will probably wish accessing data on the net could be faster. Even with the limited network bandwidth, you can increase data throughput by sending the data more efficiently using data compression. Data compression lets you send or store the same information using less space (fewer bytes). So, if you are writing data to a local disk file, you can use data compression to reduce a file's size. One such data compression algorithm is called *run-length encoding* (RLE). To understand how RLE works, consider the following data sequence:

GoooooooodTips12

As you can see, the data, in its present form, requires 16 bytes. Notice the sequence of the character "o" within the data. Instead of storing each character individually, you can represent the characters with a single "o" and a count of 8. You also need a special character to indicate the sequence is compressed. In other words, you can represent the data as follows:

G#o8dTips12

In this case, the pound sign character (#) indicates a character sequence repeats within the data. This new representation requires only 11 bytes as opposed to the 16 bytes of the original data. Identifying such sequences of repeated data is the essence of run-length encoding. As it turns out, run-length encoding is just one of many encoding algorithms available. Other encoding schemes, such as LZW, named for Lempel-Ziv and Welch,used in the popular PKZIP file compression program, can yield even greater compression ratios. The following tips discuss how you can use RLE within your programs.

705 BUILDING YOUR OWN RLE FILTER OUTPUT STREAM

As you have learned, filter streams process stream data before passing the data along. The advantage of building a filter class is that it can be plugged in to any stream. As you will learn, you can build a filter output stream that compresses data. Then, you can use the same filter class with a *FileOutputStream* to write compressed data to a disk file, or you combine the filter with a socket operation to send compressed data across a network.

The following code, *out_filter.java*, shows you how to build the *RleOutputFilter* class that compresses data using a form of the run-length encoding algorithm:

```java
import java.io.*;
import java.util.*;

// RLE data compression filter output class
class RleOutputFilter extends FilterOutputStream {

    int dcount;
    int current_b;

    void nwrite(int b, int count) throws IOException
      {
        if (count <= 0) // no data to write
          return;

        if ((count == 1) && ((current_b & 0xC0) != 0xC0))
          out.write(current_b);
        else
          {
            out.write(count | 0xC0); // turn upper 2 bits on
            out.write(current_b);
          }
      }

    public RleOutputFilter(OutputStream out)
      {
        super(out);
        dcount = 0;
        current_b = 0;
      }

    public void write(int b) throws IOException
      {
        if ((b==current_b) && (dcount < 64))
          dcount++;
        else
          {
            nwrite(current_b, dcount);
            current_b = b;
            dcount = 1;
          }
      }
```

```
public void write(byte b[], int off, int len) throws IOException
  {
    for (int i = 0 ; i < len ; i++)
      write(b[off + i]);
  }

public void flush() throws IOException
  {
    nwrite(current_b, dcount);
    dcount = 0;
    out.flush();
  }
}
```

BUILDING YOUR OWN RLE FILTER INPUT STREAM 706

In the previous tip, you learned how to create an output filter stream class that compresses data using the RLE algorithm. As you might have guessed, you must also build a companion input filter stream class to decompress the data in order to retrieve the original information. The following code, *in_filter.java*, shows you how to build the *RleInputFilter* class that decompresses data stored using the *RleOutputFilter* class you created in the previous tip:

```
import java.io.*;
import java.util.*;

// RLE data decompression filter input class
class RleInputFilter extends FilterInputStream {

  int dcount;
  int current_b;

  public RleInputFilter(InputStream in)
    {
      super(in);
      dcount = 0;
      current_b = 0;
    }

  public int read() throws IOException
    {
      if (dcount > 0)
        {
          dcount--;
          return current_b;
        }

      int b = in.read();

      if (b < 0)
        return b;
```

```java
        else
          {
            if ((b & 0xC0) != 0xC0)
              return b;
            else
              {
                dcount = (b & 0x3F) - 1;
                current_b = in.read();
                return current_b;
              }
          }
      }

    public int read(byte b[]) throws IOException
      {
        return read(b, 0, b.length);
      }

    public int read(byte b[], int off, int len) throws IOException
      {
        int i;

        for (i = 0; i < len ; i++)
          {
            int c = read();

            if (c == -1)
              break;

            if (b != null)
              b[off + i] = (byte)c;
          }

        if (i==0)
          return -1;
        else
          return i;
      }
  }

public class in_filter {

    public static void main(String args[])
      {
        byte buf[] = new byte[8];
        int readcount;

        try {
            FileInputStream ins =
                new FileInputStream("compressed.dat");
```

```
            RleInputFilter ifs = new RleInputFilter(ins);
            DataInputStream dais = new DataInputStream(ifs);

            // read data 8 bytes at a time till the end of the file
            while ((readcount = dais.read(buf, 0, 8)) != -1)
                System.out.print(new String(buf, 0, 0, readcount));

            System.out.println();
            dais.close();
        }
        catch (IOException e)
        {
            System.out.println("File read error :" + e);
        }
    }
}
```

As you have learned, you can access the standard output stream through the *System* class. Likewise, you can also access the standard input stream through the *System* class. The standard input stream lets you direct user input through the console window. Although you have already seen that the AWT class lets you create a graphical user interface for user input, for a simple program you can use the standard input stream to collect user input without having to create a GUI interface. The following application, *std_in.java*, illustrates the use of the standard input stream. The application asks the user to enter his or her name and then prints a message that reflects the entry:

```java
import java.io.*;

public class std_in {

    public static void main(String args[])
    {
        InputStream istream = System.in;
        DataInputStream distream = new DataInputStream(istream);

        try {
            System.out.println("Enter your name and hit <Enter>:");
            String name_str = distream.readLine();
            System.out.println("Your name is " + name_str);
        }
        catch (IOException e)
        {
            System.out.println("input error " + e);
        }
    }
}
```

708 PRINTING TO THE STANDARD ERROR STREAM

In addition to the standard output stream, *System.out*, you can also use the standard error stream, *System.err*, to display messages on the console window. The standard error stream, as its name implies, is designed for displaying error messages. As you may know, programs can redirect the output from the standard output stream to another destination such as a file. For example, the following command, when executed within an MS-DOS window, redirects the program's standard output to the file *run.log*:

```
C:\> java myprogram > run.log   <ENTER>
```

To display error messages that the user cannot redirect, you can use the standard error stream. The standard error stream, *System.err*, is a *PrintStream* object, just like *System.out*. You send output to the *System.err* stream in the same way that you would to the *System.out* stream. For example, the following statement uses the *System.err* stream to display an error message:

```
System.err.println("Error Message!");
```

709 UNDERSTANDING EXCEPTIONS

As your programs become more complex, you will need to handle a variety of error conditions. As you have learned, the Java creators worked hard to reduce the possible things that can go wrong within a program. For example, Java has no pointers or explicit memory-release operations. Unfortunately, not all problems can be avoided. Sometimes errors just happen. For example, suppose a user tries to connect across a network that is down, or open a file that does not exist. Your program will have to dynamically detect and take care of these types of error conditions. To help your program detect and respond to errors, Java provides *exceptions*.

Using exceptions, your programs instruct Java to watch for errors during a specific operation. If the error occurs, Java notifies your program which, in turn, can respond to the error.

710 UNDERSTANDING THROW AND CATCH

In C, as well as many other programming languages, you perform error detection by checking a function's return value or a function's error-status parameter. To detect and handle the error condition, you must place *if* statements throughout your program. Unfortunately, a large number of such *if* statements can make a program complex and difficult to understand.

Java's built-in exception-based error handling protocol is built on the throw-and-catch concept. When a method returns an error condition, it *throws* the condition. Conversely, when the calling method tries to detect an error condition, it *catches* the condition. As you will learn, to detect the exceptions that Java throws, your programs use the *catch* statement.

711 UNDERSTANDING THE EXCEPTION SUBCLASSES

As briefly discussed, Java generates an *Exception* object to flag that an error has occurred. Java derives *Exception* objects from the *Throwable* class. As you can see in Figure 711.1, the *Throwable* class has two immediate subclasses:

Error and *Exception*. You generally do not need to concern yourself with the *Error* subclass—it is used by the Java run-time system to *throw* non-recoverable errors to the Java interpreter.

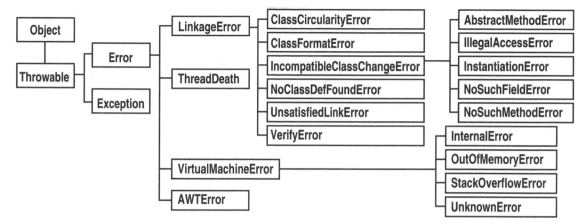

*Figure 711.1 The **Throwable** class hierarchy.*

As you can see in Figure 711.2, the *RuntimeException* class is a subclass of the *Exception* class. *RuntimeExceptions* are avoidable errors that you can prevent by following good programming practices. For example, the *IndexOutOfBoundsException*, a subclass of the *RuntimeException,* is an exception that Java throws when your program tries to access an array index that is out of bounds (outside of the array's boundaries). Trying to access an index outside of the bounds of an array is a program bug and not a dynamic-error condition. A *RuntimeException* is a red flag which indicates that you must fix your program.

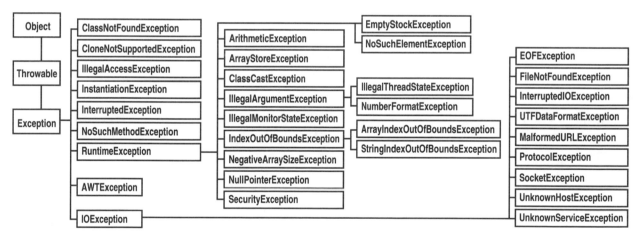

*Figure 711.2 The **Exception** class hierarchy.*

The other *Exception* subclasses, such as *IOExceptions*, indicate error conditions that you must catch dynamically because they are not preventable. For example, if a user tries to open a file that does not exist, Java will throw the *FileNotFoundException*, which your program must handle on the fly (dynamically).

THROWING AN EXCEPTION

712

In Java, you can think of an exception as a second type of value a method returns. To return an exception, a method must create an object derived from the *Exception* class and call the *throw* method. The calling method can either *catch* the exception and handle it, or allow the exception to pass through to its calling method. The following program demonstrates how to create and *throw* an *InterruptedException* object:

```
void myExceptionTest (boolean error)
 {
    // Statements here

    if (some_error_occurs)
      throw (new InterruptedException());
 }
```

As you can see, if an error occurs, the method uses the *new* operator to create an *InterruptedException* object, and the *throw* statement to generate the exception. In Tip 713, you will learn how your program can *catch* and handle the exception.

713 CATCHING AN EXCEPTION

In Tip 712, you learned how to *throw* an exception object. To *catch* (detect) an exception, you must call the method that *throws* the exception within a *try* block:

```
try {
    some_method();
 }
```

A *try* block tells Java to execute the statements that follow unless an exception occurs. If an exception is thrown, Java breaks out of the *try* block, bypassing the remainder of the block's statements, and looks for a matching *catch* block. If an exception does not occur, Java executes all the statements within the block, and continues its execution with the first statement that follows the *try* block.

Java programs follow *try* blocks with *catch* blocks. A *catch* block uses the *catch* keyword and specifies a particular exception the program is trying to detect, as shown:

```
catch (someException object)
  {
     System.out.println("caught someException");
  }
```

If Java throws an exception that matches the one specified within a *catch* statement, Java will execute the corresponding *catch* block's corresponding statements. As you can see, Java passes an *Exception* object to the *catch* block which provides the block with details about the exception.

For example, at many sandwich shops, after customers place an order, they receive a ticket with a number on it. When an order is ready, the clerk might call out, "Number 17!" The customers all check their tickets. The customer who has the matching ticket receives the order.

In this example, the number that the clerk calls out is similar to an exception that a *try* block throws, and the number on the ticket is similar to the argument Java passes to the *catch* block. Just as the customer with the matching number picks up the order, the *catch* block with the matching argument handles the exception.

If Java does not find a match for an exception, Java passes the exception up the calling hierarchy (to the method that called the current method, and so on). If the exception reaches the top of the calling hierarchy without being handled, the program writes an error message and exits. The following code demonstrates the syntax of the *try* and *catch* statements:

```
try {
    myExceptionTest();
}

catch (InterruptedException e)
  {
      System.out.println("catch InterruptedException");
  }
```

CATCHING MULTIPLE EXCEPTIONS

714

In the previous tip, you learned how to *throw* and *catch* an exception. Within a *catch* block, Java matches the exception if it is a subclass of the *catch* block argument. By letting you detect subclasses in this way, you gain some flexibility as to how your program handles exceptions. Assume, for example, a method returns three different types of *IOExceptions*. Within your applet, you could define three *catch* blocks to handle these errors separately:

```
try {
    myExceptionTest();
}

catch (EOFException e)
  {
      System.out.println("catch EOFException");
  }

catch (FileNotFoundException e)
  {
      System.out.println("catch FileNotFoundException");
  }

catch (InterruptedIOException e)
  {
      System.out.println("catch InterruptedIOException");
  }
```

As an alternative, your code can simply *catch* the superclass *IOException*, which will funnel all three exceptions into a single *catch* block:

```
try {
    myExceptionTest();
}

catch (IOException e)
  {
      System.out.println("catch IOException");
  }
```

715 Understanding the try Block

You have learned that if a method throws an exception, you must call the method from within a *try* block if you want your program to *catch* the exception. If you place a *try/catch* pair around each method that throws an exception, your code can get very big and become very difficult to read. However, you can avoid writing too many *try-catch* pairs by putting more than one method that throws an exception inside a single *try* block.

There is no limit to the number of program statements you can place inside of a *try* block, but you should group statements that perform related processing. In this way, if an exception occurs, the *catch* block can take proper action more easily. The following code demonstrates a *try* block that opens a file and writes the content of an array:

```
try {
    FileOutputStream fos = new FileOutputStream(filename);
    PrintStream ps = new PrintStream(fos);

    for (int i = 0; i < array.length; i++)
        ps.println(array[i]);
 }

catch (IOException e)
  {
    System.out.println("Can't open:" + filename);
  }
```

In this case, should the method that opens the file stream fail, there is no reason to continue with the rest of the *try* block. Because this *try* block is concise, the *catch* block can write a clear message of what went wrong.

716 Understanding the Implicit throw

In the previous tips, you have learned how to create and *throw* an exception. Sometimes, though, an exception occurs without a corresponding *throw* call. For example, if you accidentally index an array out of bounds, Java will generate an *ArrayIndexOutOfBoundsException*. Indexing an array out of bounds is a program bug and, therefore, it is something you want to fix and prevent, not *catch*.

Another type of throwable object that Java generates behind the scenes is the *Error* class. Java generates *Error* class exceptions when the run-time system encounters a very serious error that will prevent the program from continuing. For example, when a network breaks, the run-time system throws an *Error* class exception. The point is, not all exceptions are generated by explicit *throw* statements or, for that matter, from within a method that you use.

717 Understanding Code Bypassing

When you *throw* an exception, Java bypasses the rest of the code within the method and tries to find the *catch* statement that will handle the error. In the program code that follows, the applet will not display the "No error" message if the program throws the *InterruptedException* object:

```
if (error)
   throw(new InterruptedException ());

System.out.println("No error");
```

When a method in a *try* block throws an exception, not only is the rest of the code in the *try* block bypassed, but also the code after the *catch* block. In the program code that follows, neither of the "No error" messages will appear if the *myExceptionTest* method throws an exception:

```
try {
   myExceptionTest();
   System.out.println("No error");
 }

catch (InterruptedException e)
  {
      System.out.println("catch InterruptedException");
  }

System.out.println("No error");
```

In other words, when the *myExceptionTest* method throws the exception, its processing ends, returning control to the first statement that follows the *try* block. If the *catch* statement processes the exception, the *catch* statement will execute its statements and then return control to the current method's caller.

USING THE FINALLY BLOCK 718

As you have learned, when an exception is thrown within a *try* block, Java executes only the code in the matching *catch* block, bypassing the rest of the method. Assume, however, that your applet has created a resource that it must dispose of should an exception occur. One way to dispose of the resource would be to duplicate the disposal code within every *catch* block. A better solution, however, is to use a *finally* block. As it turns out, Java executes the code in a *finally* block whether or not an exception is thrown. The following code fragment demonstrates how your program might dispose of a *Graphics* object should an exception occur (or not occur):

```
try {
   Graphics g = getGraphics();
   myExceptionTest();
 }

catch (InterruptedException)
  {
     System.out.println("caught myExceptionTest");
  }

catch (IOException e)
  {
     System.out.println("caught IOException");
  }
```

```
finally()
  {
    g.dispose();      // Java executes this statement whether an
  }                   // exception occurs or does not occur
```

719 SPECIFYING AN EXCEPTION

As you have learned, a Java *throw* statement is somewhat like a *return* statement. You also know that a method must declare the type of object it will *return*. Similarly, a method must also declare the type of exceptions it might *throw*. If a method does not specify all the exceptions it throws, the Java compiler will generate a compile error. To declare exception types, you list the exceptions after the *throws* keyword within the method declaration. The following *mytest* method, for example, demonstrates how to specify the exceptions thrown by an exception:

```
void mytest() throws InterruptedException
  {
    // Statements here

    if (error)
      throw (new InterruptedException ());
     System.out.println("No error");
  }
```

You can also list more that one exception, separated by commas, within a method's declaration, as shown:

```
void mytest() throws IOException InterruptedException
  {
    // Statements here

    if (some_error)
      throw (new InterruptedException ());
    else if (some_other_error)
      throw (new IOException ());
  }
```

Note that there are two throwable classes that are exempt from having to be declared: the *RuntimeException* and the *Error* classes. As you will recall, Java uses the *RuntimeException* class for errors due to program bugs. Likewise, the Java run-time system throws the *Error* class. If Java did not exempt these two classes, your program would need to execute just about every method within a try block.

720 SENDING EXCEPTIONS UP THE HIERARCHY TREE

As you have learned, if a method does not provide a *catch* block that matches an exception, Java passes the exception up the calling hierarchy. However, you have learned that you must declare all exceptions that a method throws. Therefore, it is an error to let an exception pass up the hierarchy tree if it is not listed in that method's declaration. In other words, you cannot just ignore exceptions; you need to either handle them, or at least know that they are listed in the method's declaration. In the following code, the *writeIt* method ignores the *IOException* thrown by *FileOutputStream*. However, because the *IOException* is listed in *writeIt's* declaration, an error does not occur:

```
import java.io.*;

class testApplication {

    public void writeArray(String f, int a[]) throws IOException
    {
        FileOutputStream fos = new FileOutputStream(f);
        PrintStream ps = new PrintStream(fos);

        for (int i = 0; i < a.length; i++)
            ps.println(a[i]);

        System.out.println("File written: " + file);
    }

    public static void main(String args[])
    {
      testApplication t = new testApplication();
      int myarray[] = { 1, 2, 3, 4, 5 };

      try {
            t.writeArray("array.txt", myarray);
        }

      catch (IOException e)
        {
            System.out.println("Can't open: array.txt");
        }
    }
}
```

In this case, if the *IOException* occurs, the program will *catch* the exception within the *main* method.

UNDERSTANDING EXCEPTIONS AND INHERITANCE 721

In the previous tips, you learned that you must declare the exceptions a method might *throw*. However, if you extend a class and override one of its methods, that method's declaration has already been defined in the parent class. This is an important point; if you are overriding a method, you may only throw exceptions that are listed in the method's original declaration. You must not allow exceptions not listed to pass up the calling hierarchy, because you will get a compile error.

DON'T SUPPRESS ALL EXCEPTIONS 722

To simplify your programming, you may find it tempting to just *catch* the *Exception* class which, in turn, suppresses all other exceptions. Don't do it. You should either handle an exception or let it pass up the exception hierarchy. If you generically suppress all exceptions, your program might ignore important dynamic errors. The reason you should take the time to handle exceptions is because exceptions allow large complex programs to behave well. A large program with poor dynamic-error checking can crash and be very difficult to debug. The following code demonstrates how you should *NOT* suppress exceptions:

```
try {
    FileOutputStream fos = new FileOutputStream(file);
}

catch (Exception e) {} // Do Not catch Exception simply
                       // to surpress other handlers
```

723 CREATING YOUR OWN EXCEPTIONS

So far, the exceptions that you have created, thrown, or caught in the previous tips have been standard exception types. Sometimes, it is useful to create your own exceptions. Suppose, for example, that you have written routines that interface with a new type of database. You may want to have an exception class that can distinguish between different types of database-insertion errors. To create a new exception class, you must extend one of the standard execution types, as the following code demonstrates:

```
class myDatabaseException extends Exception {

  public myDatabaseException() { }
}
```

As shown in the following code, you can *throw* your own exceptions just as you would the standard types:

```
throw new myDatabaseException();
```

724 USING THE getMESSAGE METHOD

In the previous tips, you learned how to *throw* and *catch* an exception. You also know that you can easily write an error message inside of a *catch* block. However, sometimes you may want to provide additional information within the *catch* block. In such cases, you can get a message out of the method that throws the exception into the method that catches it. Java provides a constructor method for all exception classes which receive a *String* argument. A *catch* block can use the *getMessage* method to access this *String*. The following code demonstrates how to create an exception that includes a *String* message:

```
class myDatabaseException extends Exception {

  public myDatabaseException(String message)
   {
      super(message);
   }
}
```

When a program *throws* the exception, the program passes the *String* message to the class constructor, as shown:

```
throw new myDatabaseException("Error in file open");
```

As it turns out, most of the standard exceptions create messages in this way. For example, the *FileOutputStream* throws an *IOException* with a message that contains the file name which caused the error. The last statement of the following program uses the *getMessage* method to display the name of a file that the program could not open:

```java
import java.io.*;

class testApplication {

    public void writeIt(String file, int a[]) throws IOException
    {
        FileOutputStream fos = new FileOutputStream(file);
        PrintStream ps = new PrintStream(fos);

        for (int i = 0; i < array.length; i++)
            ps.println(a[i]);

        System.out.println("File written: " + file);
    }

    public static void main(String args[])
    {
        testApplication t = new testApplication();

        int myarray[] = { 1, 2, 3, 4, 5 };

        try {
            // write the array to three files
            t.writeIt("array1.txt", myarray);
            t.writeIt("array2.txt", myarray);
            t.writeIt("array3.txt", myarray);
        }

        catch (IOException e)
        {
            System.out.println("Can't open: " + e.getMessage());
        }
    }
}
```

PASSING DATA IN AN EXCEPTION

725

In Tip 724, you learned how to create a *catch* block that uses the *getMessage* method to obtain an exception's *String* message. Sometimes, though, you may want to add more than just a message to an exception object—you may want to add data. To add data to an exception, you first create your own exception, which you learned to do in Tip 723. Then, you add member variables to your exception class. When the *catch* method gets an exception, it can then access the variables, use the data, for example, to build a complex message, or show debug data. The following code demonstrates how to add data to an exception:

```
class myDatabaseException extends Exception {
    double data;
    int table;

    public myDatabaseException(double d, int t)
      {
        data = d;
        table = t;
      }
}
```

When the program later *throws* the exception, it passes values to the exception's class constructor method, as shown in the following code:

```
throw new myDatabaseException(25.1, 2);
```

726 EXTENDING THE CORRECT EXCEPTION

When you create your own exception, you must choose which class in the exception hierarchy to extend. Your choice is important because you may want to *catch* a family of exception types. For example, if you want to *catch* all exceptions that have to do with input and output stream errors, you can catch the *IOException* class. If you are going to create a new exception that is related to the *IOException* class, you should extend this class.

If you need to create a new family of exceptions, you should first make a generic parent exception. Then, you can create related exceptions that are subclasses of this parent class. By creating a family of exceptions with a single parent, you have the option of catching all these exceptions at once, or each individually. It is not good practice to force a user of your methods to handle a lot of exceptions.

727 WHAT IS A THREAD OF CONTROL?

A *thread of control*, usually referred to as *thread*, is a sequence of executable program statements. You may not realize it, but the *main* method is just a thread. It is a very important thread, but a thread nonetheless. When you write the simple Java application "Hello, world," you define the contents of the main thread of control. When the main thread dies, the program quits.

Unlike programming languages such as C/C++, Java lets your programs use multiple threads of control. In other words, your program can execute (appear to execute) two or more different operations at one time. Assume, for example, that you are creating a simple word-processing program. Your program might use one thread or execution to process the user's keystrokes, while a second thread of execution spell checks the document behind the scenes, and a third thread of execution periodically saves the user's document to a file on disk.

Although threads of execution give the illusion of two or more events occurring at the same time, in actuality, your computer can only execute one of the threads at any given time. To create the illusion that the threads are executing simultaneously, Java rapidly switches control from one thread to another—letting each thread execute for a brief period of time before passing control to the next thread. The following tips will examine how your programs use threads of control.

UNDERSTANDING MULTITHREADING

As you learned in Tip 727, Java lets your programs execute multiple threads at the same time. *Multithreading* is the process of using two or more threads of control within the same program. For example, in Tip 600, you learned that the *repaint* method returns almost immediately to its caller after it is called to update the screen. As it turns out, within the *repaint* method, Java creates a thread that updates the screen. In this way, while the thread updates the screen display, the rest of your program can continue independently.

One of the definitive examples of a multithreaded application is the Web browser. As you know, most browsers let you open more than one window and perform multiple downloads at the same time. To let you perform multiple tasks in this way, the browser takes advantage of multiple threads.

In Java, multithreading is not only powerful, it is also easy to implement. Basically, threads give your program the ability to chew gum and walk at the same time. The following program, *myThread.java*, demonstrates the use of multiple threads within a program that both chews gum and walks at the same time:

```java
import java.applet.*;

class myThread extends Thread {

public void run()
  {
    for (int i = 0; i < 4; i++)
      {
         System.out.println(getName() + " " + i);

         try {
             sleep(400);
           } catch (InterruptedException e) {}
      }
  }

public class ChewWalk extends Applet {

    myThread chew = new myThread("Chewing");
    myThread walk = new myThread("Walking");

    public void init() {
       chew.start();
       walk.start();
    }
}
```

As you can see, this program has two threads, one for chewing and the other for walking. These threads run in parallel. Don't worry about the details just yet; they will be covered by the tips that follow. When you compile and execute this program, your screen will display the following output.

```
Chewing  0
Walking  0
Chewing  1
```

```
Walking 1
Chewing 2
Walking 2
Chewing 3
Walking 3
```

Your output may vary a little due to the fact that multithreading in Java is machine dependent. We will cover why later. For now, just take note how the threads appear to run at the same time.

729   UNDERSTANDING A THREAD'S STATES

As your program runs, a *Thread* object can be in one of four states: new, runnable, blocked, and dead. Figure 729 illustrates the states of a *Thread* object.

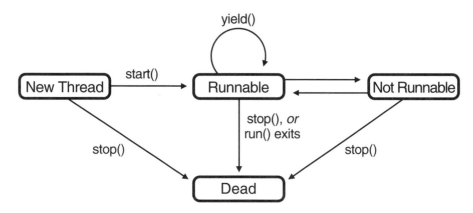

*Figure 729 The four states of a **Thread** object.*

When you create a thread, it enters the *new* state. In this state, the thread is waiting for you to call the thread's *start* method. No code is running yet.

In the runnable state, a thread executes the code in its *run* method. The *run* method is the main body of a thread. To move a thread from the new state to the *runnable* state, you execute its *start* method. You never call the *run* method directly; the *start* method calls it for you.

When a thread is idle, it is in the *not runnable* state. It is a temporary condition. A thread enters the not runnable state if you call a thread's *suspend, sleep,* or *wait* method, or after certain I/O methods that must wait for completion. As you will learn, each of these methods has a different mechanism for getting a thread back to the runnable state.

The final thread condition is the *dead* state. As you can guess, it means the thread is done. A thread enters the dead state if you call the *stop* method or when the *run* method completes normally.

730   IMPLEMENTING A THREAD (THE MORE COMMON METHOD)

You can implement threads within a Java program in two ways. In this tip, you will use the more common approach; the other method is covered in the next tip. Normally, you implement a thread by creating an object that extends the *Thread* class. As you have learned, extending a class lets the new object inherit the properties of the parent (in this case, the *Thread* class). After you extend the *Thread* class, you override the *run* method, as the following program code shows:

```
class Chew extends Thread {

    public void run()
    {
        // Place thread code here
    }
}
```

IMPLEMENTING A THREAD (THE LESS COMMON METHOD)

 731

As you learned in the previous tip, to implement a thread, you can extend the *Thread* class. But, if your class already extends a different class, you have a problem because Java does not support multiple inheritance. The solution is to implement the *Runnable* interface, which happens to be the second method of creating a thread. You learned how to implement interfaces in Tip 200. You also learned that interfaces are how Java provides the benefits of multiple inheritance without many of the problems.

The *Runnable* interface declares only the *run* method. Just as when you extend the *Thread* class, you must override the *run* method. The following program code demonstrates how to implement the *Runnable* interface:

```
class Walk implements Runnable {

    public void run()
    {
        // Place thread statements here
    }
}
```

STARTING A THREAD

 732

One of the key differences between extending the *Thread* class and implementing the *Runnable* interface is how you start the threads. The *Thread* class has a *start* method which your program simply calls to start the thread. The following statements demonstrate the use of the *start* method:

```
Chew chew = new Chew(); // Chew extends class Thread
Chew().start();
```

In Tip 729, you learned that when you create a thread, it enters the new state and waits for you to call its *start* method. Because the thread waits for you to start it, you have the flexibility of creating threads before you need them. Later, you can start the threads as they are required. You can also create and start a thread in one statement, as shown:

```
new Chew().start();    // Chew extends class Thread
```

The *Runnable* interface does not have a *start* method. Instead, to start a thread, you must create a second *Thread* object and pass your thread to its constructor method. Then, you use the start method of the second *Thread* object, as shown:

```
Thread walk = new Thread(new Walk()); // Walk implements the
                                      // Runnable interface
walk().start();
```

Note: You never call the run method directly. This is done for you by the thread's start method.

733 Using the run Method

As you have learned, the *run* method allows a *Thread* object to do its work. To have the *run* method perform the *Thread* object's desired task, you must override the *run* method for each object. The following *Chew* class defines a *run* method that executes a *for* loop four times:

```java
class Chew extends Thread {

    public void run()
      {
        for (int i = 0; i < 4; i++)
          System.out.println(getName() + " " + i);
      }
}
```

After the fourth time through the loop, the *run* method will exit normally causing the thread to enter the dead state. Since the thread is dead, you cannot reuse it. Think of the *run* method as a one shot rifle. If you want to shoot again, you will have to reload, that is, create a new copy of the thread.

734 Putting a Thread to Sleep

As your program executes, there will be times when you will want to suspend one or more threads. For example, if you have a thread that flashes an icon, you may want to control how fast the thread blinks the icon. To do so, you suspend the thread's execution briefly each time the thread updates the icon. To pause a thread for a specific time period, you can put it to sleep using the *sleep* method. The argument to the *sleep* method specifies the number of milliseconds (one thousandth of a second) for which you want to suspend the thread's execution. For example, if you want a thread to sleep for a half a second, then you pass the value 500 (500 milliseconds is one-half of a second) to the *sleep* method, as shown:

```java
sleep(500);
```

In previous tips, you learned how to *catch* an exception. The *sleep* method throws an exception named *InterruptedException* which your program must *catch*. The following program code demonstrates a thread that sleeps for a half of a second between writing two strings to the console window:

```java
class sleepTest extends Thread {

    public void run()
      {
        System.out.println("Time zero");
        try {
            sleep(500);
         }
        catch (InterruptedException e) {}
        System.out.println("half of a second later!");
      }
}
```

CALLING SLEEP OUTSIDE OF A THREAD 735

In Tip 734, you learned how to use the *Thread* class *sleep* method to suspend a thread's execution for a specific number of milliseconds. The *sleep* method is *static*, which means you can call *sleep* by referencing the *Thread* class by name. For example, assume your program needs a delay between frames of an animation sequence. In such cases, you can simply call the *sleep* method by name: *Thread.sleep*. However, remember that you still must *catch* the *InterruptedException*. The following program, *sleepApplet.java*, demonstrates how a program calls the *sleep* method from outside of a thread:

```java
import java.applet.*;

public class sleepApplet extends Applet {

    public void init()
      {
        repaint();
      }

    public void paint()
      {
        System.out.println("Time zero");

        try {
           Thread.sleep(500);
         }
        catch (InterruptedException e) {}

        System.out.println("Time 500 miliseconds");
      }
}
```

CHANGING THREAD PRIORITY 736

As you have learned, Java creates the illusion that multiple threads are running at the same time by rapidly switching control of the processor between the threads. Depending on your program's purpose, there may be times when you want to give processing preference to specific threads. In such cases, your programs can change the priority value that Java uses to determine which thread runs next.

A thread's priority provides a way of giving a thread an advantage over other threads competing for processor time. In Java, a thread's priority can range from 1 to 10, where 1 is low priority and 10 is high priority. To simplify thread priority processing, Java defines three constants that you can use to select common thread priorities: *MIN_PRIORITY* (which is equal to 1), *NOM_PRIORITY* (equal to 5), and *MAX_PRIORITY* (equal to 10). A thread inherits a default priority from its parent thread, and is usually *NOM_PRIORITY*.

To change a thread's priority, you call the *Thread* class *setPriority* method. You can also find out a thread's priority using the *Thread* class *getPriority* method. The following program, *threadPriority.java*, demonstrates how to get and set a thread's priority:

```java
import java.applet.*;

class myThread extends Thread {

    public mythread(String name) { super(name) };

    public void run()
    {
        for (int i = 0; i < 8; i++)
        {
            System.out.println(getName() + " " + i);
            try {
                sleep(400);
             }
            catch (InterruptedException e) {}
        }
    }
}

public class threadPriority extends Applet {

    myThread min_thread = new myThread ("Thread Min");
    myThread max_thread = new myThread ("Thread Max");

    public void init()
    {
        min_thread.setPriority(Thread.MIN_PRIORITY);
        max_thread.setPriority(Thread.MAX_PRIORITY);
        min_thread.start();
        max_thread.start();
    }
}
```

As you can see, the applet creates two *Thread* objects, *max_thread* and *min_thread*, and assigns the objects the corresponding thread priorities. The program then starts each thread which loops, repeatedly displaying a message to the system console. If you examine the program's output, you will find that the higher priority thread will monopolize the console output.

737 UNDERSTANDING THE THREAD QUEUE

The Java developers did not specify how threads are to be implemented at the system level. On most operating systems, like Windows 95, Windows NT, and Macintosh, each thread in the runnable state receives a separate slice of time to execute its code. On other operating systems, like Sun's Solaris, the behavior is quite different. Of all the threads in the runnable state, only one is actually executing code. The other threads sit in a queue. The thread that has control executes until it completes or yields, or a higher priority thread moves from the not runnable state to the runnable state. At that point, the thread-scheduler chooses the highest priority thread from the runnable queue.

UNDERSTANDING SELFISH AND NICE THREADS 738

In Tip 737, you have learned that on some operating systems, the threads sit within a runnable queue and compete for processor time. In such environments, your program can exhibit inconsistent behavior if the threads do not behave nicely. A nice thread sleeps or yields the processor's control often, to give other threads a chance to run. A thread that does not yield processor control is said to be *selfish*. If a selfish thread has a high priority, the thread may be able to shut other threads out from receiving processor time.

SHARING TIME WITH OTHER THREADS 739

In Tip 735, you learned how to suspend a thread's execution using the *sleep* method. Suspending a thread's execution using the *sleep* method provides one way to share processor time. An alternative way for a thread to share processor time is to call the *Thread* class *yield* method. Using the *yield* method in this way simply gives other threads on the runnable queue an opportunity to run. For any loop inside a *run* method, you should include a call to the *sleep* or *yield* method. The following program code demonstrates how your program should share processor time:

```
class foreverThread extends Thread {

   public void run()
     {
       int i=0;

       while (true)        // Loop forever
         {
           System.out.println("Loop " + i++);
           yield();         // Yield processor to other threads
         }
     }
}
```

HOW TO SUSPEND AND RESUME A THREAD 740

In Tip 734, you learned how to pause a thread for a specific amount of time by using the *Thread* class *sleep* method. However, there may be times you will want to pause a thread until a specific condition occurs, such as a user keystroke or mouse operation. In such cases, your programs can use the *Thread* class *suspend* method. The *suspend* method puts a thread into the not runnable state until you call the *resume* method. For example, using the *suspend* method, you can let users pause an animation while they hold the mouse down, and then resume the animation when they release the mouse button. The following program, *suspendResume.java*, demonstrates how your program suspends and later resumes a thread:

```
import java.applet.*;
import java.awt.*;

class myThread extends Thread {
```

```
public void run()
  {
    while (true)
      {
        try {
            sleep(400);
          }
        catch (InterruptedException e) {}
        System.out.println("Thread Running!");
      }
  }
}

public class suspendResume extends Applet {

    myThread mythread = new myThread ();

    public void init()
      {
          mythread.start();
      }

    public boolean mouseDown(Event evt, int x, int y)
      {
        mythread.suspend();
        System.out.println("Thread Suspended.");
        return(true);
      }

    public boolean mouseUp(Event evt, int x, int y)
      {
          System.out.println("Thread Resumed.");
        mythread.resume();
        return(true);
      }
}
```

741 SYNCHRONIZING DATA SHARING BETWEEN THREADS

Data sharing is one pitfall of the thread system. If two threads have *shared* access to the same variable (that is, they both have read and write access), strange results can occur if your programs don't take special care to coordinate the thread's data access.

For example, suppose a husband and wife each have a check book to a single account. Each might be careful in updating their own check book. But unless they are careful together, the combination of checks might exceed their balance. To eliminate the problem, suppose instead that they have one check book, and both are diligent in keeping it up to date. They should never overdraw their account because they access the check book one at a time. This is the essence of synchronized data sharing. Only one thread has access to the data at a time; the data's integrity is never compromised.

To synchronize data sharing, you create a method to access the shared data element, and use the *synchronized* key in the method's declaration. Java will then restrict the method's access so that only one thread at a time can access the method. The following program, *synchronize.java*, demonstrates a synchronized method access:

```java
import java.applet.*;

class Account {

  static int balance = 1000;
   static int expense = 0;

   static public synchronized void withdraw(int amount)
     {
       if (amount <= balance)
         {
            System.out.println("check: " + amount);
           balance -= amount;
           expense += amount;
           System.out.print("bal: " + balance);
           System.out.println(", spent: " + expense);
         }
       else
         {
            System.out.println("bounced: " + amount);
         }
     }
 }


class myThread extends Thread {
    public void run()
      {
        for (int i = 0; i < 10; i++)
          {
            try {
               sleep(100);
              }
            catch (InterruptedException e) {}
            Account.withdraw((int) (Math.random() * 500 ));
          }
      }
 }


public class synchronize extends Applet {

  public void init()
    {
      new myThread().start();
      new myThread().start();
    }
}
```

742 ANOTHER WAY TO SYNCHRONIZE DATA

In Tip 741, you learned that you can use the *synchronized* keyword in a method declaration to restrict a method's access to one thread at a time. You can also declare an object and a block of code as *synchronized*, which lets only one thread execute class methods and modify any class data at any time. The following program, *synchronizedObject.java*, demonstrates a *synchronized* object and code block:

```java
import java.applet.*;

class myThread extends Thread {

    static Integer balance = new Integer(1000);
    static int expense = 0;
    static {
        System.out.print("Starting balance: " + balance);
     }

    public void run()
      {
        int amount;

        for (int i = 0; i < 10; i++)
          {
            try {
                sleep(100);
              }
            catch (InterruptedException e) {}

            bill = ((int) (Math.random() * 500 ));
            synchronized (balance)
              {
                if (bill <= balance.intValue())
                  {
                    System.out.println("check: " + bill);
                    balance = new Integer(balance.intValue()-bill);
                  expense += bill;
                    System.out.print("bal: "+balance.intValue());
                    System.out.println(",spent: " + expense);
                  }
                else
                  {
                    System.out.println("bounced: " + bill);
                  }
              }
          }
      }
  }
```

```
public class synchronizedObject extends Applet {


   public void init()
     {
        new myThread().start();
        new myThread().start();
     }
 }
```

The argument to the *synchronized* code block must be an object which, in this example, is an *Integer* object, named *balance*. As you have learned, in Java, arrays are objects; therefore, you can use an array as an argument to a *synchronized* code block.

WAITING FOR SYNCHRONIZED DATA 743

As you have learned, you must synchronize code that shares data between threads. But, there are cases when synchronizing data is not enough. The classic case of shared data is the "producer consumer" problem within which a producer and consumer share data. Imagine, for example, you are at the drive through window of a fast-food restaurant. If you get up to the window and your food is not ready, you must wait. If five orders are done, the server cannot just give them to the first car that pulls up. Instead, the consumer and the server must wait until the appropriate car pulls up to the window. In this case, both the consumer (you) and producer (the waiter) are stuck, waiting on each other.

Now, assume you have one thread within your program that must create (produce) a data item and a second thread that must process (consume) it. The threads must use a protocol similar to the drive-through etiquette. When a thread arrives at a *synchronized* method and finds that it has arrived too early, the thread should wait. Note that either the producer or the consumer thread might arrive too early.

When a thread calls the *wait* method inside a *synchronized* method or code block, another thread is allowed to access the code. When a thread is finished processing *synchronized* data, the thread calls the *notify* method to tell other threads to stop waiting. Using *wait* and *notify* methods, you can program the drive through etiquette described above.

USING THE WAIT AND NOTIFY METHODS 744

In Tip 743, you learned the importance of synchronizing data, and also the possibility of having to wait for the data to be ready. To notify another thread that data is ready for processing, the producer thread simply calls the *notify* method. The following program, *waitNotify.java*, demonstrates the producer and consumer threads using the *wait* and *notify* methods:

```
import java.applet.*;

class Dealer {
   int goods = 0;

   public synchronized int consume()
     {
        int temp;
```

```java
      while (goods == 0)
        {
          try {
              wait();
           }
          catch (InterruptedException e) {}
        }

      temp = goods;
      goods = 0;
       System.out.println("Consumed: " + temp);
      notify();
      return temp;
    }

  public synchronized void produce(int amount)
    {
      while (goods != 0)
        {
          try {
              wait();
           }
           catch (InterruptedException e) {}
        }

      goods = amount;
      notify();
       System.out.println("Produced: " + goods);
    }
 }

class myThread extends Thread {

    boolean producer = false;
    Dealer dealer;

    public myThread(Dealer d, String type)
      {
        dealer = d;

        if (type.equals("Producer"))
          producer = true;
      }

    public void run()
      {
        for (int i = 0; i < 10; i++)
          {
            try {
                sleep((int)(Math.random() * 200 ));
             }
```

```
              catch (InterruptedException e) {}

          if (producer)
            dealer.produce((int)(Math.random() * 10 ) + 1);
          else // must be a consumer
            dealer.consume();
        }
      }
    }

  public class waitNotify extends Applet {

    Dealer dealer = new Dealer();

    public void init()
      {
        new myThread(dealer, "Consumer").start();
        new myThread(dealer, "Producer").start();
      }
    }
```

Note: You must call the **wait** and **notify** methods within a **synchronized** method or code block.

The *notify* method only makes one thread stop waiting. If you have many threads that are waiting, you can use the *notifyAll* method which will cause all threads that are waiting to try to execute one at a time. Within your applet, you must make sure that you have one *notify* method for each *wait* method. If you don't, you may have threads that never stop waiting.

UNDERSTANDING THREAD STARVATION

 745

Thread synchronization comes at a price. You could probably guess that if you use synchronization, you also take a hit in performance. When a thread spends more time waiting for *synchronized* data than it spends working, the thread is said to be *starving*. You should try to minimize thread starvation as much as possible. Otherwise, your program can become sluggish and act erratic. To reduce the potential of starving threads, you should use synchronization only when necessary.

UNDERSTANDING DEADLOCK

 746

In Tip 745, you learned that when your programs synchronize data access, you run the risk of thread starvation. The ultimate in thread starvation is *deadlock*, which occurs when several threads are waiting for a condition to occur that can never be satisfied. One method of dealing with deadlock is to fix it as it occurs. However, detecting deadlock can require very complex code. Instead, you should write your own code to prevent deadlock from ever happening. Consider the following example to understand why preventing deadlock is better than correcting it.

Suppose our husband and wife of the original synchronized data example in Tip 741 have one check book and one pen. Now, assume the husband's rule for writing a check is to take the pen first, take the check book second, write a check, and then put the pen and checkbook down. On the other hand, the wife's rule is to take the *check book* first, take the *pen* second, write a check, and then put the pen and checkbook down. The problem arises when the husband takes the pen and the wife takes the checkbook. In this situation, they are both hopelessly deadlocked. Each will wait for the other to finish, but each holds a key resource. The solution is to have one procedure for writing a check and for both to follow that procedure.

To prevent deadlock, you must serialize not only the resources, but the process of acquiring those resources. This will prevent multiple threads from waiting for a common resource.

747 CHECKING THE STATE OF A THREAD

In Tip 729, you learned about the four different states of a thread. To check a thread's state within your program, you use the *Thread* class *isAlive* method. If a thread is in the runnable or not runnable state, the *isAlive* method returns *true*; if the thread is in the new or dead state, the *isAlive* method returns *false*. Remember, a thread is in the new state when its *start* method has not been called yet. The following program, *threadState.java*, demonstrates the *isAlive* method:

```java
import java.applet.*;

class myThread extends Thread {

    public void run() {
        for (int i=0; i<10; i++) {
          try {
              sleep(200 );
          } catch (InterruptedException e) {}
        }
    }
}


public class threadState extends Applet {

    myThread mythread = new myThread();

    public void init()
      {
          System.out.println("isAlive: " + mythread.isAlive());
          mythread.start();
          System.out.println("isAlive: " + mythread.isAlive());
      }
}
```

748 UNDERSTANDING THREADS IN AN APPLET

As you have learned, when a Web browser leaves an HTML page that contains an applet, Java calls the applet's *stop* method. However, if a running thread is inside that applet, the thread will continue even though the applet stops. Users would be very disappointed to know that valuable processor time is still being spent on a page that they have probably long forgotten.

To prevent threads from continuing after their applet has stopped, you should *suspend* the threads within the *stop* method. By suspending threads in this way, you prevent the threads from consuming limited processor resources. If a user returns to the HTML page which contains your applet, the applet's *start* method is called. Within the *start* method, you can *resume* any threads that you had suspended. The following program, *suspendResume.java*, demonstrates the *suspend* and *resume* method:

```java
import java.applet.*;

class myThread extends Thread {
    public void run() {
        while (true) {
            try {
                sleep(100);
            } catch (InterruptedException e) {}
            System.out.println("Thread Running!");
        }
    }
}


public class suspendResume extends Applet {
    myThread mythread = null;

    public void start() {
        if (mythread == null) { // does thread exist?
            mythread = new myThread();
            mythread.start();
            System.out.println("Thread Initialized.");
        } else {
            mythread.resume();
            System.out.println("Thread Resumed.");
        }
    }


    public void stop() {
        mythread.suspend();
        System.out.println("Thread Suspended.");
    }
}
```

HANDLING A WEB BROWSER RESIZE OPERATION 749

In the previous tips, you have just learned about how important it is to *suspend* your threads when Java calls an applet's *stop* method. Normally, Java calls the *stop* method when a browser leaves the corresponding Web page. However, in some cases, a Web browser will unexpectedly call an applet's *stop* method. When a browser window is resized, the browser may first call the *stop* method and then the *start* method. If you only *stop* a thread when its applet stops, and create a new thread when the applet restarts, the applet will probably not behave the way that a user expects. To prevent unwanted behavior after resizing the browser, your program should suspend threads when the applet stops, and *resume* the threads when the applet starts.

750 CREATING A THREAD GROUP

Within your Java program, there may be times when you have multiple threads working on a similar task. In such cases, you may find it convenient to group threads by type, which then lets you manipulate the group as a single entity. For example, suppose you have a number of animation threads that you need to pause based on user input. You can group these threads into a single-thread group and then suspend them all with one function call. The following code fragment shows you how to group threads:

```
ThreadGroup all = new ThreadGroup("all threads");
myThread mythread1 = new myThread(all, "child thread1");
myThread mythread2 = new myThread(all, "child thread2");
```

In this example, the *myThread* class must have a constructor that takes a *ThreadGroup* and *String* as arguments. Inside the *myThread* class constructor, you must call the *Thread* superclass's constructor. The constructor adds the thread to the *ThreadGroup* class which, in this case, is named "all threads". The following *myThread* constructor method uses the *super* method to call the *Thread* class constructor method with the thread-group name and thread object to add to the group:

```
public myThread(ThreadGroup group, String name)
  {
     super(group, name);
  }
```

751 ACCESSING THREADS INSIDE A THREAD GROUP

In the previous example, you learned that you can treat a set of threads as a single group. You also learned that the constructor method that adds a thread to a group requires a *String* argument. The string argument names the thread. Java stores a thread group as an array of *Thread* objects. To access a specific *Thread* object from within the group, you can search the thread-group array using the *ThreadGroup* class *getName* method. The following code fragment demonstrates how you would search the *ThreadGroup* array for a *Thread* object named "my thread":

```
int thread_cnt = thread_group.activeCount();
Thread found = null;
Thread threads[] = new Thread[thread_cnt];

thread_group.enumerate(threads, true); // Entire hierarchy

for (int i=0; i< thread_cnt; i++)
    if (threads[i].getName().equals("my thread"))
      {
         found = threads[i];                 // Assign thread object
         break;
      }
  }
```

As you can see, the code first uses the *ThreadGroup* class *activeCount* method to determine the number of threads in the group. Within the *for* statement, the code searches the array of *Thread* objects for the *Thread* object named "my thread".

USING THE DEFAULT THREAD GROUP

Actually, all threads are ultimately a member of a default thread group. Within your programs, you can use the default thread group to list all your program's threads. You obtain the default thread group by calling the *Thread* class *static* methods *currentThread* and *getThreadGroup*. You must traverse up the thread group hierarchy to obtain the default thread. The following program, *showThreads.java*, demonstrates how to list all the threads in an *applet*:

```java
import java.applet.*;

class myThread extends Thread {

    public myThread(String name)
      {
        super(name);
      }

    public void run() {}
}

public class showThreads extends Applet {

    ThreadGroup top_group;
    ThreadGroup parent;
    Thread my_thread = new myThread("my thread");

    public void print_threads(ThreadGroup g, String indent)
      {
        int thread_cnt = g.activeCount();
        int group_cnt = g.activeGroupCount();

        Thread threads[] = new Thread[thread_cnt];
        ThreadGroup groups[] = new ThreadGroup[group_cnt];

        System.out.println("Thread Group : " + g.getName());

        g.enumerate(threads, false);

        for (int i = 0; i < thread_cnt; i++)
          if (threads[i] != null)
              System.out.println(indent + "Thread:" +
                threads[i].getName());

        g.enumerate(groups, false);
        for (int i = 0; i < group_cnt; i++)
          if (groups[i] != null)
              print_threads(groups[i], indent + " ");
    }
```

```
    public void init()
      {
        top_group = Thread.currentThread().getThreadGroup();

        while ((parent = top_group.getParent()) != null)
          top_group = parent;

        print_threads(top_group, "");
      }
  }
```

In this example, the *activeCount* method returns the number of threads within the entire thread-group hierarchy. There is no way to get the number of threads that are immediately below the thread group. That is why the applet tests for *null* in the *for* loop inside the *print_threads* method.

753 LIVING WITH A THREAD'S PLATFORM DEPENDENCY

You have learned that many of the most popular operating systems, such as Windows NT, Windows 95, and Macintosh 7.5, use time slicing to give each runnable thread a chance to execute even though some threads may be selfish. On the other hand, other operating systems, such as Sun's Solaris, do not implement time slicing. Even though you may carefully create threads that yield often, they may behave very differently on time slicing and non-time slicing systems. To ensure that your multithreaded Java program behaves predictably regardless of platform differences, you must test your program on both time slicing and non-time slicing platforms.

754 AVOIDING I/O BLOCKING

Many system I/O methods wait (suspending the program) until they are done. This means that a single-threaded program will freeze until the I/O method is complete. An alternative approach is to create a thread that calls the I/O method. If a thread that calls the I/O method is waiting, the rest of the program can continue processing. You can pass the thread the information required for the I/O method through its constructor. The following statement, for example, creates a new thread object that writes an array's contents to a specified file:

```
new IO_write_array_thread(myarray, "filename").start();
```

In this case, you must implement the code that writes the array's contents within the *IO_write_array_thread* class *run* method.

755 UNDERSTANDING DAEMON THREADS

If you have some understanding of client-server processing, you may already know something about *daemon* threads. As you know, a *server* is simply a computer with a continuously running program, the sole purpose of which is to provide a service to other programs. A *client* is a program that receives service. For example, a print server is a software program that waits until other programs (the clients) send it files to print.

Inside a Java program, a daemon thread is like a server. Daemon threads run continuously with the sole purpose of providing a service to other threads. Unlike other threads, if daemon threads are the only threads that are running, the program will exit because the daemons have no other threads to serve. Depending on your program's purpose, there may be times when you need to create your own daemon thread. In such cases, you use the *Thread* class *setDaemon* method to inform Java that a specific thread object will serve as a daemon thread:

```
myThread mythread = new myThread();
mythread.setDaemon(true);
```

MAKING A TIMER THREAD

756

A *timer* is an object that calls another object after a regular time interval. You would find a timer object very useful to drive an animated clock or delay the frames of a movie, for example. The *Thread* class makes it easy to implement such timers. A timer uses an interface that lets you specify which object to call after each time interval. You have learned that a Java interface lets you create the equivalent of a callback function. The following program, *stopWatch.java*, demonstrates a digital stop watch that displays how long the program has been running:

```
import java.applet.*;
import java.util.*;
import java.awt.*;

interface timerObject
  {
    public void do_update();
  }

class myClock extends Canvas implements timerObject {

    int zero;
    int seconds;

    public myClock()
      {
        Date now = new Date();
        zero = (now.getHours() * 3600 + now.getMinutes() * 60 +
                now.getSeconds());
      }

    public void do_update()
      {
        Date now = new Date();

        seconds = now.getHours() * 3600 + now.getMinutes() * 60 +
                  now.getSeconds() - zero;
        repaint();
      }
```

```java
    public void paint(Graphics g)
      {
          String buffer = new String(Integer.toString(seconds));
          g.drawString(buffer, 20, 20);
      }
  }

class myTimer extends Thread {

    int time;
    timerObject timer_object;

    public myTimer(timerObject to, int t)
      {
          timer_object = to;
          time = t;
      }

    public void run()
      {
        while (true)
          {
            try {
                sleep(time);
              }
            catch (InterruptedException e) {}
            timer_object.do_update();
          }
      }
  }

public class stopWatch extends Applet {

    myClock myclock = new myClock();
    myTimer mytimer = new myTimer(myclock, 1000);

    public void init()
      {
         setLayout(new GridLayout(2, 3));
         add(myclock);
         mytimer.start();
      }

    public void repaint()
      {
      }
  }
```

UNDERSTANDING LINKED LISTS

Almost every program must store data as it executes, and the choice of data structure you use to store the data plays an important role in the efficiency of data access and storage. A well-defined data structure gives you quicker data searches, simpler programming, and requires less memory space. In previous tips, you learned that you can store a list of data using an array. However, for cases in which you cannot determine the number of data entries at compile time, you may allocate too many array locations and waste valuable memory resources. Or worse, you may not allocate enough locations, and your program will run out of storage space. When you need to store data sets that grow and shrink dynamically at run-time, you can use a link list instead of an array.

A linked list consists of a list of nodes. A *node*, or element, contains the data and one or more links (a reference) that connect one node to another. Figure 757 shows a simple linked list:

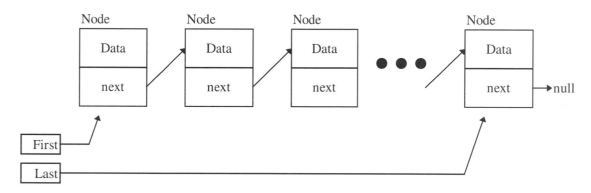

Figure 757 A simple linked list.

More specifically, the above illustration is known as a singly-linked list because each node contains a single link that points to the next node. The next few tips will show you how to implement a singly-linked list in Java.

BUILDING A SINGLY-LINKED LIST

To build a singly-linked list in Java, you define a class for the node which will contain the data and a link to the next node. As illustrated in the following code, the *IntNode* class stores an integer value:

```java
class IntNode {

  int value;        // data storage
  IntNode next;     // link to the next node

  IntNode(int node_value)
    {
      value = node_value;
      next = null;
    }
}
```

As you will learn, it is convenient to build a link list class that stores the link to the list's *first* and *last* nodes and that provides a method named *append_node* which adds a new node to the list:

```
// A singly-liked list class

class S_LinkList {

    IntNode first, last; // link to the first and last node
    int number_of_nodes;

    S_LinkList()
     {
       first = last = null;
       number_of_nodes = 0;
     }

    void append_node(IntNode new_node)
      {
        new_node.next = null;

        if (first == null)  // This is the first entry
          first = new_node;

        if (last != null)
          last.next = new_node;

        last = new_node;
        number_of_nodes++;
      }
  }
```

For example, using the *S_LinkList* class, the following statements create a singly-linked list with nodes that contain the data 7, 3, and 0.

```
S_LinkList llist = new S_LinkList();
llist.append_node(new  IntNode(7));
llist.append_node(new  IntNode(3));
llist.append_node(new  IntNode(0));
```

759 TRAVERSING A SINGLY-LINKED LIST

To find an item in a singly-linked list, you must start with the first element in the list and then traverse through the elements, one by one, using the link until the item is found or you reach the end of the list. The following code illustrates the process of traversing the *IntNode* linked list you created in Tip 758 to find a specified node:

```
int  find_node(IntNode  target)
  {
     int i = 0;
     IntNode temp_node = first;

     while (temp_node != null)
       {
```

```
        if (temp_node == target)
          return i;                      // Target found

        i++;

        temp_node = temp_node.next;  // Get the next node
    }
  return -1;                          // Target not found
}
```

The *find_node* method returns a zero-based index to the list item if the element is found and returns the value -1 if it does not find the element in the list.

INSERTING AN ITEM INTO THE MIDDLE OF A SINGLY-LINKED LIST 760

If your linked list is order dependent, such as an employee list sorted by last name, there will be times when you must insert an item within the middle of the list. Inserting a node in the middle is a little more complex than appending it to the end because you must disconnect the chain in the middle and then reconnect the list with the new node inserted, as shown in Figure 760.

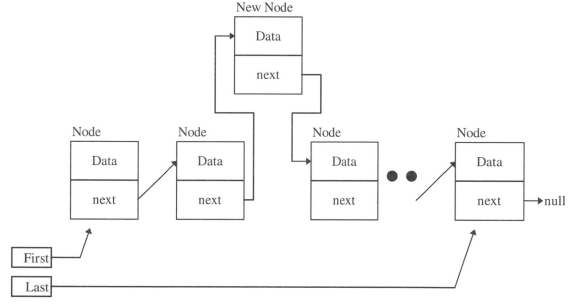

Figure 760 Inserting a node in the middle of a singly -linked list.

The following code implements the *insert_node* method which inserts a node within the middle of a list:

```
void insert_node(IntNode new_node, int location)
  {
    if (location == 0)
      {
        new_node.next = first;
        if (last == first)
          last = new_node;

        first = new_node;
      }
```

```
        else
          {
            // find location to insert
            IntNode temp_node = first;
            while ((location > 1) && (temp_node != null))
              {
                 temp_node = temp_node.next;
                 location--;
              }
            new_node.next = temp_node.next;
            temp_node.next = new_node;
            if (new_node.next == null)
              last = new_node;
          }
     }
```

As you can see, the *insert_node* method inserts an element at the specified zero-based index location it receives as a parameter.

761 REMOVING AN ITEM FROM A SINGLY-LINKED LIST

As you have seen, inserting a node into a linked list involves disconnecting and reconnecting links. When you remove a node from a list, you must also disconnect and reconnect links. To remove a node, you must change the link of the previous node to point to the next node in the list, as shown in Figure 761. In some languages, such as C/C++, you have to free the memory that the program previously allocated for the node you are removing. In Java, however, you do not have to explicitly free the allocated memory. Instead, Java's garbage collection software automatically frees the node's memory because it is no longer referenced.

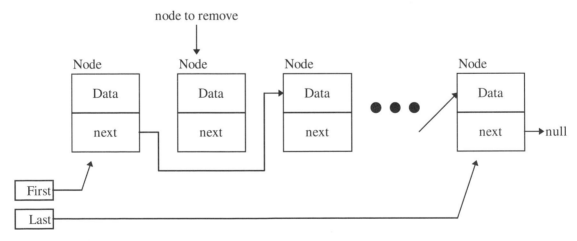

Figure 761 Removing a node from a singly -linked list.

The following code implements the *remove_node* method, which removes a node from a singly-linked list:

```
void remove_node(int location)
  {
    if (location==0)
      {
```

```
         if (last == first)
            last = first.next;
         first = first.next;
      }
    else
      {
         // find location to insert
         IntNode temp_node = first;
         while ((location > 1) && (temp_node != null))
           {
              temp_node = temp_node.next;
              location—;
           }
         temp_node.next = temp_node.next.next;
         if (last == temp_node.next)
             last = temp_node;
      }
  }
```

As you can see, the *remove_node* method removes the element at the specified zero-based index location.

BUILDING A DOUBLY-LINKED LIST 762

As you have learned, you can only traverse singly-linked lists in one direction, from the beginning to the end. A doubly-linked list is similar to a singly-linked list, except that the doubly-linked list maintains a link to the previous and next nodes, as shown in Figure 762.

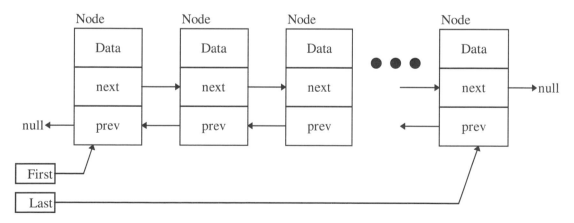

Figure 762 A doubly-linked list.

A doubly-linked list lets you traverse the list in both directions. The following code shows the Java implementation of a doubly-linked list:

```
// Class for integer data storage

class DLinkIntNode {

    int value;
    DLinkIntNode prev;       // Link to previous node
```

```java
    DLinkIntNode next;      // Link to next node

    DLinkIntNode(int node_value)
     {
         value = node_value;
         prev = next = null;
     }
  }

// Class for singly-link list operations
class D_LinkList {

   DLinkIntNode first, last;
   int number_of_nodes;

   D_LinkList()
    {
        first = last = null;
        number_of_nodes = 0;
    }

// append a node to the linked list

void append_node(DLinkIntNode new_node)
  {
     new_node.next = null;
     new_node.prev = last;

     if (first == null)
        first = new_node;

     if (last != null)
        last.next = new_node;

     last = new_node;
     number_of_nodes++;
  }

// Find a node using a zero-based index

DLinkIntNode get_node(int index)
  {
     DLinkIntNode temp_node = first;

     for (int i = 0; (i < index) && (temp_node != null); i++)
        temp_node = temp_node.next;

     return temp_node;
  }
}
```

Inserting an Item in the Middle of a Doubly-Linked List

Conceptually, inserting a node in a doubly-linked list is similar to inserting a node in a singly-linked list, as shown in Tip 760. The only difference is that you must also disconnect and later connect the link to the previous node. In practice, inserting a node into a given position of a doubly-linked list is actually simpler than a singly-linked list because you no longer have to search the list to find the previous node. The following code inserts a new node to a given position of a doubly-linked list:

```
void insert_node(DLinkIntNode new_node, int index)
  {
     DLinkIntNode temp_node = get_node(index);

     new_node.next = temp_node;
     if (new_node.next != null)
       {
          new_node.prev = temp_node.prev;
          new_node.next.prev = new_node;
       }
     else
       {
          new_node.prev = last;
          last = new_node;
       }

     if (index == 0)
        first = new_node;
     else
        new_node.prev.next = new_node;
     number_of_nodes++;
  }
```

Removing an Item from the Middle of a Doubly-Linked List

When your programs work with linked lists, there will be times when you must remove an item from the list. In such cases, you must first locate the item and then update the nodes that precede and follow the item's node so that they point to each other, as opposed to the item's node (the node you want to remove). As you have learned, for a doubly-linked list, once you find the item, you don't have to search the list again to find the previous node. That's because the doubly-linked list maintains a link to the previous and next nodes. After you find the item in the list, you immediately have links to the nodes you need to update. Therefore, the process for removing a node from a doubly-linked list is simpler than removing a node from a singly-linked list. The following code removes a node from a doubly-linked list:

```
void remove_node(int index)
  {
     if (index == 0)
       {
          first = first.next;
```

```
        if (first != null)
           first.prev = null;
    }
  else
    {
       DLinkIntNode temp_node = get_node(index);
       temp_node.prev.next = temp_node.next;

       if (temp_node != last)
          temp_node.next.prev = temp_node.prev;
       else
          last = temp_node;
    }
  number_of_nodes—;
}
```

765 BUILDING A GENERIC DOUBLY-LINKED LIST CLASS

A limitation of the doubly-linked list you implemented in Tip 762 is that it can store only a single integer in each node. If you want to store a different set of data, you not only must modify the node storage class, you must also modify the linked list class. Also, consider the case where you have linked lists of different types of data in the same program. You will have to build a different linked list class for each node class.

To build a generic linked list class with which you can build a linked list of different data elements, you can store the reference to the data in the node, instead of storing the actual data, as shown in Figure 765.

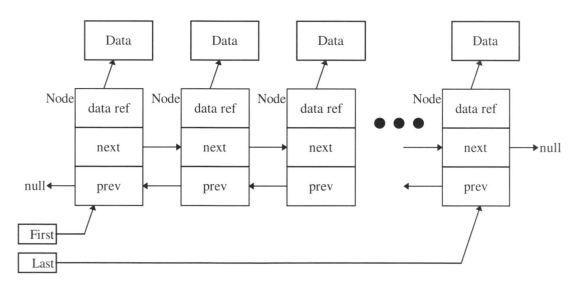

Figure 765 *A generic doubly-linked list.*

The following application, *genlist.java*, illustrates the use of the generic doubly-linked list by creating two linked lists, an integer list, and a *String* list, using the same linked list class:

```
import java.io.*;

// class for generic data storage
class DLinkNode {
```

```
    Object data;
    DLinkNode prev;
    DLinkNode next;

    DLinkNode(Object new_data) {
       data = new_data;
       prev = next = null;
    }
}

// class for doubly-linked list operations
class DLinkList {

    DLinkNode first, last;
    int number_of_nodes;

    DLinkList()
      {
         first = last = null;
         number_of_nodes = 0;
      }

    void append_node(Object new_data)
      {
         DLinkNode new_node = new DLinkNode(new_data);

         new_node.next = null;
         new_node.prev = last;
         if (first == null)
            first = new_node;
         if (last != null)
            last.next = new_node;
         last = new_node;
         number_of_nodes++;
      }

    DLinkNode get_node(int index)
      {
         DLinkNode temp_node = first;

         for (int i = 0; (i < index) && (temp_node != null); i++)
            temp_node = temp_node.next;
         return temp_node;
      }

    Object get_data(int index)
      {
         return get_node(index).data;
      }
```

```java
    void insert_node(Object new_data, int index)
      {
        DLinkNode temp_node = get_node(index);
        DLinkNode new_node = new DLinkNode(new_data);

        new_node.next = temp_node;
        if (new_node.next != null)
          {
            new_node.prev = temp_node.prev;
            new_node.next.prev = new_node;
          }
        else
          {
            new_node.prev = last;
            last = new_node;
          }
        if (index == 0)
          first = new_node;
        else
          new_node.prev.next = new_node;
        number_of_nodes++;
      }


    void remove_node(int index)
      {
        if (index == 0)
          {
            first = first.next;
            if (first != null)
              first.prev = null;
            else
              {
                DLinkNode temp_node = get_node(index);
                temp_node.prev.next = temp_node.next;
                if (temp_node != last)
                  temp_node.next.prev = temp_node.prev;
                else
                  last = temp_node;
              }
            number_of_nodes--;
          }

    void show_list()
      {
        int i = 0;
        DLinkNode temp_node = first;

        while (temp_node != null)
          {
```

```
                System.out.println("element " + i + " = " +
                    temp_node.data);
                i++;
                temp_node = temp_node.next;
            }
        }
    }

public class genlist {

    public static void main(String args[])
    {
        DLinkList llist1 = new DLinkList();
        DLinkList llist2 = new DLinkList();

        llist1.append_node(new Integer(4));
        llist1.append_node(new Integer(3));
        llist1.append_node(new Integer(12));
        llist1.append_node(new Integer(6));

        llist2.append_node(new String("One"));
        llist2.append_node(new String("Three"));
        llist2.append_node(new String("Five"));
        llist2.append_node(new String("Seven"));

        System.out.println("Integer list:");
        llist1.show_list();
        System.out.println();

        System.out.println("String list:");
        llist2.show_list();
        System.out.println();
    }
}
```

For the data reference to reference different data types, it has to be defined as an *Object*, as shown by the *data* variable in this program's *DLinkNode* class. As you have learned, all classes in Java are a subclass of the *Object* class. Even in the case where you do not use the *extends* keyword in the class definition, the class inherits from the *Object* class by default. When your program retrieves data from a linked list, it is important to remember that you must explicitly cast the data *Object* back to the original class type.

SAVING A LINKED LIST TO A FILE 766

To say the least, if users had to reenter a program's information every time they ran a program, they would quit running the program. To avoid such problems, programs use files to store data from one user session to the next. When your program works with linked lists, your program can save and retrieve the link's data to and from a file as the program starts and ends. As you have learned, Java provides numerous output stream classes you can use to write data to a file. But regardless of which output stream you use, the process of saving a linked list is the same. You must traverse the linked list and write the information one node at a time. It may also be convenient to write the number of nodes you are saving at the start of the file, so you later know how many records there are when you read the list information back from the file.

The following application, *llist_save.java*, creates a linked list of *Integer* objects and saves it to the data file, *intlist.dat*. The tip that follows will show you how to read data back from the file into the linked list.

```java
import java.io.*;

public class llist_save {

    public static void main(String args[])
    {
        DLinkList llist = new DLinkList();

        llist.append_node(new Integer(2));
        llist.append_node(new Integer(5));
        llist.append_node(new Integer(4));
        llist.append_node(new Integer(3));
        llist.append_node(new Integer(12));
        llist.append_node(new Integer(6));

        try {
            DataOutputStream ostream = new DataOutputStream(
                new FileOutputStream("intlist.dat"));

            ostream.writeInt(llist.number_of_nodes);
            for (int i = 0; i < llist.number_of_nodes; i++)
            {
                Integer value = (Integer) llist.get_data(i);
                ostream.writeInt(value.intValue());
            }
        }
        catch (IOException e)
        {
            System.out.print("File Write Error:" + e);
            System.exit(1);
        }
    }
}
```

767 LOADING A LINKED LIST FROM A FILE

The previous tip showed you how to save a linked list to a file. Likewise, this tip will show you how to read the data back from a file into a list. When the *llist_save.java* program saves the linked-list data to a file, the program does not save the node links. So when you read the data back from the file, you must reconstruct the links. It would not do much good for the program to save the links to the data file because these links correspond to memory locations. When you rebuild the nodes with data from the file, the nodes will occupy different memory locations, so you must set the links accordingly. In the case of a simple singly- or doubly-linked list, you can rebuild the list based on the order in which the node data was saved in the file.

The following application, *llist_load.java*, reads the data from the *intlist.dat* data file created by the *llist_save.java* application in the previous tip. As the program reads the data, it rebuilds the *Integer* object linked list.

```
import java.io.*;

public class llist_load {

    public static void main(String args[])
      {
          DLinkList llist = new DLinkList();

          try {
              DataInputStream istream = new DataInputStream(
                  new FileInputStream("intlist.dat"));

              int sets = istream.readInt();
              for (int i = 0; i < sets; i++)
                {
                    int value = istream.readInt();
                    llist.append_node(new Integer(value));
                }
          }
          catch (IOException e)
            {
                System.out.print("File Read Error:" + e);
                System.exit(1);
            }

          System.out.println("Integer list read from file:");
          llist.show_list();
      }
}
```

UNDERSTANDING QUEUES 768

A *queue* is a list of elements that a program normally handles in the "first come, first serve" order. In other words, the program adds new elements to the end of the list and removes old elements from the front. This type of data structure is also known as a FIFO (First In, First Out) list. Figure 768 shows an illustration of a queue data structure.

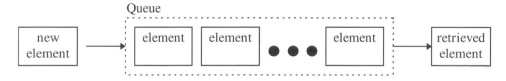

Figure 768 A queue data structure.

A queue is useful for keeping track of data that the program cannot process immediately. For example, you can implement a printer queue so the file at the front of the queue prints first and additional files will print when the printer is ready (in other words, when the printer is ready to handle them).

769   IMPLEMENTING A QUEUE

Within your programs, implementing a *queue* is quite similar to building a linked list. In fact, you can build a queue class by extending the generic *DLinkList* doubly-linked list class that you created in Tip 765. Specifically, you must add a *get_front* method that retrieves the element at the front of the queue:

```
// queue class
class Queue extends DLinkList{

    public Object get_front()
     {
       DLinkNode front = first;
       if (first != null)
         first = first.next;

       return front.data;
     }
  }
```

The *get_front* method not only returns the element at the front of the list, it also removes that element from the list so that the second element is now the first. The *append_node* method, defined in the *DLinkList* class, appends a new element to the end of the queue.

The following application, *queue_test.java*, adds several file names to a queue and retrieves them, one at a time, using the *get_front* method:

```
public class queue_test {

  public static void main(String args[])
    {
      String f;
      Queue queue = new Queue();

       queue.append_node(new String("file1.txt"));
       queue.append_node(new String("file2.txt"));
       queue.append_node(new String("file3.txt"));

       f = (String) queue.get_front();
       System.out.println("retrieved " + f);
       f = (String) queue.get_front();
       System.out.println("retrieved " + f);

       queue.append_node(new String("file4.txt"));
       f = (String) queue.get_front();
       System.out.println("retrieved " + f);
       f =(String) queue.get_front();
       System.out.println("retrieved " + f);
    }
  }
```

UNDERSTANDING BINARY TREES   770

As you have learned, you can connect data nodes using links to create linked lists. Linked lists are well suited for dynamic lists whose size may change during your program's execution. However, as you have learned, to locate an item in the list, you search through the list elements, starting with the first item in the list. Depending on the size of your list, finding an item can become a time-consuming task. Luckily, you can also use nodes to create other types of data structures which, depending on your application, may store your data in a format which lets you locate elements much more quickly. For example, consider the following sequence of 15 different numbers:

7, 8, 12, 14, 27, 30, 45, 58, 65, 69, 71, 77, 83, 96

Assume you store these numbers in a linked list. Next, assume the program must search for the node that contains the value 96. In this "worst case," you must access all 15 nodes to find the element 96. On the other hand, if you organized the numbers in a structure called a *binary tree*, as shown in Figure 770, you start your search for a number at the root. If the target number is smaller than the one in the current node, you continue the search on the left side. Conversely, if the target number is bigger than the one in the current node, you continue the search on the right side. You repeat the process with each node until you find the target number. As you can see, you can find the target value 96 by comparing 4 elements in this structure, rather than 15 in a linked list.

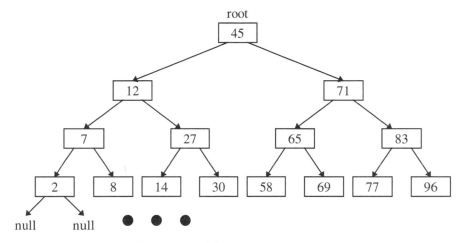

***Figure 770** A binary tree structure.*

In a binary tree data structure, each node element contains the stored data, a left link, and a right link. The left link points to another node with smaller data and the right link points to another node with larger data. By using the binary tree data structure, you can greatly improve the search efficiency.

BUILDING A BINARY TREE   771

To build a binary tree in Java, you should first define a class for the node. The node class of a binary tree is quite similar to the one for a doubly-linked list. The node contains the data and two links. In the case of the binary tree, the links point to a right and a left node. The following *BIntNode* class contains the code for a binary tree that stores an *IntNode* class object and its two nodes:

```
class BIntNode
  {
    int value;              // data storage
    IntNode left, right;    // link to the next node
  }
```

Next, you must define a binary tree class. The binary tree class should contain a reference to the root of the tree and a method for adding nodes to the tree. The binary tree is a recursive structure, which means you perform the same processing at each node (if the value is smaller, move left—if the value is larger, move right). You can implement the *add_node* method using recursion (using a method that calls itself), as shown in the following code:

```java
void addnode(BIntNode node, BIntNode new_node)
  {
    if (node.value == new_node.value)
     {
         // int data already exist - do nothing
     }
    else if(node.value > new_node.value)
     {
        if (node.left != null)
           addnode(node.left, new_node); // go to left branch
        else
           node.left = new_node; // added to left branch
     }
    else if(node.value < new_node.value)
     {
        if (node.right != null)
           addnode(node.right, new_node); // go to right branch
        else
           node.right = new_node; // added to right branch
     }
  }
```

772 A BINARY TREE EXAMPLE

In the previous tips, you have learned about the binary tree structure. This tip provides a complete implementation of a binary tree class, *WordBinaryTree*, that stores the number of occurrences of the same word within a document:

```java
import java.io.*;
import java.util.*;

// class for word count binary tree data storage
class BtreeNode {

    int word_count;
    BtreeNode left;
    BtreeNode right;

    BtreeNode(String new_word)
      {
        word = new_word;
        word_count = 1;
        left = right = null;
      }
  }
```

```java
// class for binary tree operations
class BtreeLinkList {
   BtreeNode root;

   BtreeLinkList()
     {
       root = null;
     }

   void insert(BtreeNode node, String new_word)
     {
        int compare = node.word.compareTo(new_word);
        if(compare == 0) // word already exist
          node.word_count++;
        else if(compare > 0)
          {
            if(node.left != null)
               insert(node.left, new_word);
            else
              node.left = new BtreeNode(new_word);
          }
        else if(compare < 0)
          {
            if(node.right != null)
               insert(node.right, new_word);
            else
               node.right = new BtreeNode(new_word);
          }
     }

   void insert_word(String new_word)
     {
        if(root == null)
          root = new BtreeNode(new_word);
        else
           insert(root, new_word);
     }

   BtreeNode find(BtreeNode node, String keyword)
     {
        int compare = node.word.compareTo(keyword);
        if(compare == 0) // keyword found
          return node;
        else if(compare > 0)
          {
            if(node.left != null)
               return find(node.left, keyword);
            else
              return null; // keyword not found
          }
```

```java
            else if(compare < 0)
              {
                if(node.right != null)
                  return find(node.right, keyword);
                else
                  return null;
              }
            return null;
        }


    int count_word(String keyword)
      {
        if(root != null)
          {
            BtreeNode node = find(root, keyword);
            if(node != null)
              return node.word_count;
            else
              return 0;
          }
        return 0; // tree empty
      }
  }


public class word_btree {

  public static void main(String args[])
    {
      BtreeLinkList btree = new BtreeLinkList();

      // open file and insert words into binary tree
      try {
          DataInputStream istream = new DataInputStream(
            new FileInputStream("sshare.txt"));
          String thisLine;
          while((thisLine = istream.readLine()) != null)
            {
              StringTokenizer st =
                new StringTokenizer(thisLine," \t\n\r");
              while(st.hasMoreTokens())
                btree.insert_word(new String(st.nextToken()));
            }
        }
      catch(Exception e)
          System.out.println("Error: " + e);

      // get word count for several words
      System.out.println("count of the word 'of' = " +
          btree.count_word("of"));
```

```
        System.out.println("count of the word 'there' = " +
            btree.count_word("there"));
        System.out.println("count of the word 'Java' = " +
            btree.count_word("Java"));
    }
  }
```

UNDERSTANDING VECTORS

 773

You have learned that you can build a dynamic list of data using a linked list. You can also use the built-in Java class *Vector* to store your data. The *Vector* object is an adjustable array that can increase or decrease its size in response to the number of elements it needs to store. Unlike C/C++, where you must call the *realloc* run-time library function to increase an array's storage size, a vector increases its size automatically, as necessary. The *Vector* class also provides methods that let you insert, remove, and search for elements.

With the *Vector* class, you may wonder why you would ever need to build your own linked list. In many cases, you can indeed use the *Vector* class rather than creating your own linked list. But with your own linked list, you have direct access to the node links; therefore, you may find that node insertion and removal operations are much more efficient with a link list than with a *Vector* object.

USING VECTORS IN JAVA

 774

To create a *Vector* object, you use the *Vector* constructor. Then, you can add elements to the vector using the *addElement* method, the format of which is as follows:

```
    void addElement(Object obj);
```

The following code creates a vector and adds several *String* elements to it using the *addElement* method:

```
Vector strlist = new Vector();

strlist.addElement(new String("Java"));
strlist.addElement(new String("C++"));
strlist.addElement(new String("Pascal"));
```

COUNTING THE NUMBER OF ELEMENTS IN A VECTOR

 775

When you store information within a *Vector* object, there may be times when you need to know how many items the object contains. In such cases, you can use the *Vector* class *size* method. The following code illustrates the use of the *size* method by displaying the number of items in the *strlist Vector* object to the console window:

```
Vector strlist = new Vector();

strlist.addElement(new String("apple"));
strlist.addElement(new String("orange"));
strlist.addElement(new String("banana"));
System.out.println("Number of items in the list = " +
    strlist.size());
```

In this case, the program statements will display the following output:

```
Number of items in the list = 3
```

776  GETTING A PARTICULAR ITEM WITH THE *elementAt* METHOD

Although a *Vector* object is an array of elements, you cannot access a vector element using the square brackets syntax as you would with a normal array. To retrieve an item from a *Vector* object, you can call the *elementAt* method, the format of which is as follows:

```
Object elementAt(int index);
```

The *index* parameter specifies a zero-based array offset for the item you are trying to get. You can also call the *firstElement* and the *lastElement* methods to retrieve the array's first and the last item, respectively.

All three of these item-retrieval methods return an *Object*, like the generic doubly-linked list class. Therefore, you need to cast the returned *Object* to the element's class type. The following application, *employee_vector.java*, stores three sets of employee information in a vector and then retrieves them using the *elementAt* method:

```java
import java.util.*;

// class for employee data storage
class Employee {

    String name;
    String phone;
    int employee_id;

    Employee(String new_name, String new_phone, int new_id)
      {
         name = new String(new_name);
         phone = new String(new_phone);
         employee_id = new_id;
      }

    public String toString()
      {
         return("Name: " + name +
                "\nPhone: " + phone +
                "\nID No: " + employee_id);
      }
 }

public class employee_vector {

    public static void main(String args[])
      {
         Vector emplist = new Vector();

         emplist.addElement(new Employee("John Doe",
            "555-1234",101));
```

```
        emplist.addElement(new Employee("Mary Jones",
           "555-4832",102));
        emplist.addElement(new Employee("Bill Smith",
           "555-2730",130));

        for(int i = 0; i < emplist.size(); i++)
          {
            Employee current =(Employee) emplist.elementAt(i);
            System.out.println("Employee " + i + ":");
            System.out.println(current);
          }
      }
   }
```

STORING PRIMITIVE DATA TYPES IN A VECTOR 777

Although a *Vector* object stores objects of any type, it cannot directly store primitive types such as *int*, *float*, *double*, or arrays of primitive types. Primitive data types like *int* are not objects; therefore, they cannot be referenced by the *Vector* class. To store primitive values within a *Vector* object, you must put the primitive data type in an object wrapper. If you want to store *int* values in a *Vector* object, for example, you can wrap the values within an *Integer* object. The following application, *int_vector.java*, illustrates the storage of *int* values in a *Vector* object:

```
import java.util.*;

public class int_vector {

   public static void main(String args[])
     {
        int intarray[] = { 1, 3, 2, 5, 7, 0 };
        Vector intlist = new Vector();

        for(int i = 0; i < intarray.length; i++)
           intlist.addElement(new Integer(intarray[i]));

        for (int i = 0; i < intlist.size(); i++)
          {
            int value =((Integer) intlist.elementAt(i)).intValue();
            System.out.println("Element " + i + ": " + value);
          }
      }
   }
```

SETTING AND INCREMENTING VECTOR STORAGE CAPACITY 778

As your program executes, a *Vector* object automatically increases its size when it needs more storage. By default, a *Vector* object doubles its size each time it runs out of space. This algorithm of space allocation can be wasteful if you just need a small additional space. In addition to the *Vector* constructor with no argument, there are two other forms of the *Vector* constructor that let you control the initial size of the vector and the size of the memory reallocation increment, as shown:

```
Vector(int initialCapacity);
Vector(int initialCapacity, int capacityIncrement);
```

By specifying the *Vector* object's initial capacity, you can reduce the amount of time it takes to reallocate the object's storage memory. The *Vector* class also provides the *capacity* method that you can use to find the current space available for the *Vector* object and the *ensureCapacity* method which lets you specify the minimum storage space the object will require:

```
int capacity();
ensureCapacity(int minCapacity);
```

779 INSERTING AN ELEMENT IN THE MIDDLE OF A VECTOR

If you are building a list of ordered elements using a Vector object, you may need to insert an element in the middle of the vector. In such cases, you can use the *Vector* class *insertElementAt* method to insert a new element. The format of the *insertElementAt* method is as follows:

```
insertElementAt(Object obj, int index);
```

The *obj* parameter specifies the element you are storing. The *index* parameter specifies the zero-based offset within the *Vector* object at which you want to insert the object. For example, the following statements create a *Vector* object that contains the number sequence 0, 3, 8:

```
Vector intlist = new Vector();

intlist.addElement(new Integer(0));
intlist.addElement(new Integer(3));
intlist.addElement(new Integer(8));
```

To insert a new *Integer* object with value 5 at position 2, you would use the following statement:

```
intlist.insertElementAt(new Integer(5), 2);
```

Following this statement, the *Vector* object's contents becomes: 0, 3, 5, 8.

780 REMOVING ELEMENTS FROM A VECTOR

Just as you must add elements to a *Vector* object, there may be times when you must remove an element. For such cases, the *Vector* class offers several methods you can use to remove elements, as shown:

```
boolean removeElement(Object obj);
void removeElementAt(int index) ;
void removeAllElements();
```

The *removeElement* method removes the specified object from the vector. The *removeElement* method returns the value *true*, if the operation is successful, and *false*, if the operation failed The *removeElementAt* method removes the element at the specified zero-based index location, whereas the *removeAllElements* methods removes every element from the vector.

SEARCHING FOR AN OBJECT IN A VECTOR 781

When you store elements within a *Vector* object, you must later be able to locate the element quickly. The *Vector* class offers a good set of methods for finding an object in a vector. First, you can call the *contains* method to see whether or not the specified element exists in the *Vector* object. The format of the *contains* method is as follows:

```
boolean contains(Object elem);
```

The *elem* parameter is the actual object, not just a field within the object, such as a name. If the *contains* method locates the object, the method will return the value *true*. If the *Vector* does not contain the object, the *contains* method returns the value *false*.

There may be times when you want to know whether or not a *Vector* contains an object, as well as the object's location within the *Vector*. To determine an object's position within a *Vector*, you use the *indexOf* methods, the formats of which are as follows:

```
int indexOf(Object elem);
int indexOf(Object elem, int index);
```

The *indexOf* methods begin their searches at the start the *Vector* object and return the object's position if a match is found, or the value -1 to indicate the object is not in the *Vector*. You can use the *int* parameter with the second form of the *indexOf* method to specify the starting offset at which the method begins its search.

There may be times when you want to locate the last occurrence of an object within a vector. In such cases, you can perform the search operation starting at the end of the *Vector* object. In such cases, you uses the *lastIndexOf* methods, as shown:

```
int lastIndexOf(Object elem);
int lastIndexOf(Object elem, int index);
```

Like the *indexOf* methods, the *lastIndexOf* methods search the *Vector* object. However, the *lastIndexOf* methods start their search at the last *Vector* element and then search forward to the first element. Also like the *indexOf* methods, the *lastIndexOf* methods return an object's position if they find a match, and the value -1 otherwise. With the second form of the *lastIndexOf* methods, you can use the *index* parameter to specify that the method start its search at a specific offset.

STORING OBJECTS OF DIFFERENT TYPES IN THE SAME VECTOR 782

In the previous examples, the objects you have stored within a *Vector* class have always been the same type, however, that is not a *Vector* class requirement. As you have learned, *Vector* objects use an *Object* reference to point to their elements. As such, you can use a *Vector* object to store any type of objects. In fact, you can store different types of objects within the same vector. The only requirement is that you must be able to determine what object types the vector is storing, and how the vector is organizing the objects. In that way, your program can cast the element to the correct type when you retrieve the element. The following application, *mixed_vector.java*, stores three Integer objects, three *String* objects, and three floating-point numbers within the same vector:

```java
import java.util.*;

public class mixed_vector {

    public static void main(String args[])
      {
        Vector mixedlist = new Vector();

        // add 3 integers to the vector
        mixedlist.addElement(new Integer(4));
        mixedlist.addElement(new Integer(2));
        mixedlist.addElement(new Integer(0));

        // add 3 strings to the vector
        mixedlist.addElement(new String("Jack"));
        mixedlist.addElement(new String("Jill"));
        mixedlist.addElement(new String("Joe"));

        // add 3 floating point numbers to the vector
        mixedlist.addElement(new Float(1.1));
        mixedlist.addElement(new Float(2.2));
        mixedlist.addElement(new Float(4.4));

        // retrieve the integers
        System.out.print("The 3 integers are :");
        for (int i = 0; i < 3; i++)
          {
            Integer int_value =(Integer) mixedlist.elementAt(i);
            System.out.print(" " + int_value);
          }

        System.out.println();
        // retrieve the strings
        System.out.print("The 3 strings are :");
        for (int i = 3; i < 6; i++)
          {
            String str_value =(String) mixedlist.elementAt(i);
            System.out.print(" " + str_value);
          }
        System.out.println();
        // retrieve the floats
        System.out.print("The 3 floats are :");
        for (int i = 6; i < 9; i++)
          {
            Float float_value =(Float) mixedlist.elementAt(i);
            System.out.print(" " + float_value);
          }
        System.out.println();
    }
}
```

EXTENDING THE VECTOR CLASS TO PROTECT DATA FIELDS 783

As you learned in Tip 782, the *Vector* class does not discriminate the type of data it stores. You may, however, want to build your own vector class that allows storage of only a single type, perhaps to protect yourself from casting the retrieved data to the wrong type. You can create such a class by extending the *Vector* class and adding your own insertion and retrieval methods. The following code extends the *Vector* class to store only *String* objects:

```
import java.util.*;

public class StringVector extends Vector {

    public void addStringElement(String new_element)
    {
        addElement(new_element);
    }

    public void insertStringElementAt(String new_element, int index)
    {
        insertElementAt(new_element, index);
    }


    public String stringElementAt(int index)
    {
        return(String) elementAt(index);
    }
}
```

You use these methods in place of the *Vector* class *addElement, insertElementAt,* and *elementAt* methods.

UNDERSTANDING HASHTABLES 784

A *hashtable* is a data structure that lets you look up stored items using an associated key. With an array, you can quickly access an element by specifying an integer index. The limitation of an array is that the look up key can only be an integer. With a hashtable, on the other hand, you can associate an item with a key and then use the key to look up the item. You can use an object of any type as a key in a hashtable. For example, you might specify the license-plate number as the key, and use the key to look up the vehicle owner's record. To distinguish one item from the next, the associated key that you use must be unique for each item, as in the case of a vehicle's license plate number. The following tips describe how you create a hashtable within Java.

USING HASHTABLES IN JAVA 785

To build a hashtable in Java, you must first create a *Hashtable* object using the *Hashtable* constructor. Then, you add new elements to your hashtable using the *Hashtable* class *put* method, the format of which is as shown:

```
Object put(Object key, Object value);
```

To retrieve the item using the key, you call the *Hashtable* class *get* method:

```
Object get(Object key);
```

Like the *Vector* class, the *get* method returns an *Object*, which you must cast to the element's original class. To remove an item from within the hashtable, you call the *Hashtable* class *remove* method, the format of which is as follows:

```
Object remove(Object key);
```

The following application, *student_hash.java*, creates a hashtable of student records, using student IDs as keys:

```java
import java.util.*;

// class for student data storage
class StudentRec {

    String name;
    String phone;
    float gpa;

    StudentRec(String new_name, String new_phone, float new_gpa)
    {
        name = new String(new_name);
        phone = new String(new_phone);
        gpa = new_gpa;
    }

    public String toString()
    {
        return("Name: " + name +
               "\nPhone No: " + phone +
               "\nGrade Point Avg.: " + gpa);
    }
}

public class student_hash {

    public static void main(String args[])
    {
        Hashtable studentlist = new Hashtable();

        studentlist.put("575-17-2351",
            new StudentRec("John Doe",  "555-2310", 4.0f));
        studentlist.put("243-67-0201",
            new StudentRec("Mary Jones", "555-6104", 3.1f));
        studentlist.put("923-55-9124",
            new StudentRec("Bill Smith","555-3434", 2.7f));
        studentlist.put("123-95-7934",
            new StudentRec("Jane Lee","555-0017", 3.9f));
```

```
        // retrieve a student record
        StudentRec student =
            (StudentRec) studentlist.get("243-67-0201");
         System.out.println("Student id 243-67-0201:");
         System.out.println(student);
    }
}
```

SETTING HASHTABLE STORAGE CAPACITY AND LOAD FACTOR

 786

A hashtable automatically increases its size when it needs more storage. As was the case with the *Vector* class constructor, you can control the capacity of the hashtable and how it grows. In addition to the *Hashtable* constructor with no argument, there are two other forms of the constructor that let you control the hashtable's initial size. In addition, you can specify a fraction of that size the object uses to determine when it should resize itself:

```
Hashtable(int initialCapacity);
Hashtable(int initialCapacity, float loadFactor);
```

Unlike the *Vector* class, *Hashtable* objects normally resize themselves before they reach their capacity. By default, a hashtable doubles its size when it reaches the fraction of capacity you specify with the *loadFactor* parameter. The *loadFactor* parameter is a floating-point number between 0.0 and 1.0. The default *loadFactor* is 0.75, which means that the hashtable resizes itself when it reaches 75% of its capacity because it stores the elements in a table and creates an integer number for each key to index the table like an array. The hashtable calculates this integer number for each key and the value must be unique and within the hashtable's capacity. When a hashtable is close to reaching its capacity, the algorithm for finding the index number becomes less efficient and the performance of the hashtable suffers. In most cases, the default *loadFactor* of 0.75 is appropriate.

ACCESSING HASHTABLE ELEMENTS USING ENUMERATION

 787

As you have learned, you can retrieve an item from the hashtable by calling the *Hashtable* class *get* method with a specified key. There may be times, however, when you need to access all the elements in the hashtable. In such cases, you can use the *Hashtable* class *element* method which returns an *Enumeration* object. An *Enumeration* interface lets you count through the elements one by one. For example, you can add the following code to the *student_hash.java* application in Tip 785 to go through all elements in the hashtable, displaying the elements one at a time:

```
// retrieve all student records

Enumeration enum = studentlist.elements();

while(enum.hasMoreElements())
    {
       StudentRec student =(StudentRec) enum.nextElement();
       System.out.println(student);
    }
```

The *Enumeration* class *hasMoreElements* method indicates whether or not there are more elements to process. The *nextElement* method retrieves the next element in the enumeration. Please note that you can go through the elements in an enumeration only once. For the above example, you will have to call the *elements* method again to create a new *Enumeration* object if you want to go through the elements a second time. You can also get an enumeration of the keys of the hashtable by calling the *keys* method.

788 UNDERSTANDING STACKS

In Tip 768, you examined a queue(also known as a FIFO, or First In, First Out list) data structure. Conversely, your programs can also store values within a *stack*, which is a LIFO(Last In, First Out) data structure. A stack places the first data you store at the bottom and places subsequent data on top of your existing data, as shown in Figure 788. Since you retrieve data from the top of the stack, the last data you place on the stack will be the first data you retrieve—hence, the terms Last In, First Out. Placing data on the top of the stack is called *pushing* and retrieving data from the top of the stack is called *popping*.

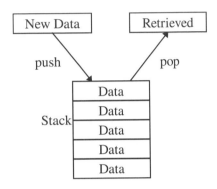

Figure 788 A stack structure.

Although it is quite simple to extend the linked-list structure to create a stack, you can use the built-in *Stack* class to create a stack data structure. The next few tips will show you how to use Java's *Stack* class.

789 USING STACKS IN JAVA

To build a stack in Java, you must first create a *Stack* object using the *Stack* constructor. Then, you add new elements to the stack using the *push* method, the format of which is as follows:

```
void push(Object obj);
```

To retrieve an item from the stack, you can call the *pop* method, the format of which is as follows:

```
Object pop();
```

When you add and remove items from a stack, you should test whether or not the stack contains data. To do so , you call the *Stack* class *empty* method. The empty method returns *true* if the stack is empty and *false* when the stack contains data. The following application, *stack_test.java*, creates a stack, pushes several integers onto it, and retrieves them back:

```
import java.util.*;

public class stack_test {

    public static void main(String args[])
      {
        String s;
        Stack strstack = new Stack();
```

```
         strstack.push(new String("one"));
         strstack.push(new String("two"));
         strstack.push(new String("three"));

         s =(String) strstack.pop();
         System.out.println("Popped element = " + s);
         s =(String) strstack.pop();
         System.out.println("Popped element = " + s);

         strstack.push(new String("four"));
         s =(String) strstack.pop();
         System.out.println("Popped element = " + s);
         s =(String) strstack.pop();
         System.out.println("Popped element = " + s);
      }
   }
```

When you retrieve an item from the stack using the *pop* method. In addition to returning the stack's top value, the *pop* method removes the item from the top of the stack. Before you *pop* an item off the stack, you may want to examine the item's value. In such cases, you can use the *Stack* class *peek* method to view the item without removing it from the stack.

SEARCHING FOR AN ITEM IN THE STACK 790

When you store data within a *Stack* object, there may be times when you need to find out whether or not an item is on the stack. In such cases, you can use the *Stack* class *search* method, the format of which is as follows:

```
int search(Object o);
```

The *search* method returns the(zero-based) distance of the object from the top of the stack, or the value -1 if the specified item is not in the stack. For example, the *search* method returns 0 if the specified item is on the top of the stack. The *Stack* class is a subclass of the *Vector* class which implements the *Enumeration* interface. Thus, you can use the same technique you learned in Tip 787 to enumerate the items in a *Stack*, as shown:

```
Stack stack_list;

Enumeration enu = stack_list.elements();

while(enum.hasMoreElements())
  {
     Object stackitem = enum.nextElement();
     // do something with the stackitem
  }
```

BUILDING A STACK-BASED CALCULATOR 791

In the previous tips, you have learned how to use the *Stack* class. This tip presents a Java applet that uses the *Stack* class to build a basic calculator. The applet, as shown in Figure 791, uses reverse Polish notation(RPN); therefore, the operands are entered and placed on the stack. When one of the operation keys are pressed, the applet retrieves the first two operands on the stack to perform the operation and displays the result. For example, to calculate the result of 2 + 3 - 5 + 4, you would key in the following sequence:

2 Ent 3 + 5 - 4 +

The following code, *st_cal.java*, implements the stack-based calculator. Please note that the applet does not include much error checking. For an actual application, you may want to add additional checking for input error, overflow, and underflow conditions:

```java
import java.applet.*;
import java.util.*;
import java.awt.*;

public class st_cal extends Applet {

    boolean new_entry;
    Label display = new Label("0", Label.RIGHT);
    Stack st = new Stack();

    public void init()
      {
         setLayout(new BorderLayout());
         Panel key_panel = new Panel();
         display.setBackground(Color.white);
         add("North", display);
         key_panel.setLayout(new GridLayout(4,4));
         key_panel.add(new Button("7"));
         key_panel.add(new Button("8"));
         key_panel.add(new Button("9"));
         key_panel.add(new Button("X"));
         key_panel.add(new Button("4"));
         key_panel.add(new Button("5"));
         key_panel.add(new Button("6"));
         key_panel.add(new Button("/"));
         key_panel.add(new Button("1"));
         key_panel.add(new Button("2"));
         key_panel.add(new Button("3"));
         key_panel.add(new Button("-"));
         key_panel.add(new Button("0"));
         key_panel.add(new Button("."));
         key_panel.add(new Button("Ent"));
         key_panel.add(new Button("+"));
         add("Center", key_panel);
         new_entry = true;
      }

    public boolean action(Event evt, Object arg)
      {
         double arg1, arg2;
```

```java
if (evt.target instanceof Button)
 {
    arg1 = arg2 = 0.0;
     char keypress =((String) arg).charAt(0);
     if (((keypress >= '0') &&(keypress <= '9'))
         ||(keypress == '.'))
      {
         if (new_entry)
          {
              display.setText((String) arg);
              new_entry = false;
          }
         else
            display.setText(display.getText() +((String) arg));
      }
     else if (keypress == 'E')
       {
          st.push(new Double(display.getText()));
          new_entry = true;
       }
     else if((keypress == '+')  ||(keypress == '-')  ||
            (keypress == 'X')  ||(keypress == '/'))
       {
          if (!new_entry)
             st.push(new Double(display.getText()));
          if (!st.empty())
             arg1 =((Double) st.pop()).doubleValue();
          if (!st.empty())
             arg2 =((Double) st.pop()).doubleValue();

          new_entry = true;
       }

    if (keypress == '+')
      {
          display.setText(String.valueOf(arg1 + arg2));
          st.push(new Double(display.getText()));
      }
    else if(keypress == '-')
      {
          display.setText(String.valueOf(arg2 - arg1));
          st.push(new Double(display.getText()));
      }
    else if(keypress == 'X')
      {
          display.setText(String.valueOf(arg2 * arg1));
          st.push(new Double(display.getText()));
      }
```

```
                else if(keypress == '/')
                  {
                      display.setText(String.valueOf(arg2 / arg1));
                    if (arg1 != 0.0)
                        st.push(new Double(display.getText()));
                  }
              return true;
            }
        return false;
      }
  }
```

Figure 791 A stack-based calculator.

792   UNDERSTANDING BITSETS

As your programs become more complex, there may be times when you need a set of bits to store on-and-off conditions. To store such bit values, you can use Java's built-in *BitSet* class. Although you can represent such settings using a *Vector* class object or an array of *boolean* values, in general, neither of these techniques is as space efficient as a *Bitset* object. A *Bitset* object packs the bits into bytes, hence, you can use a single byte to store 8 settings. Another common technique to represent bit settings is to use an integer or some other primitive type—however, that technique requires that you create bit masks to set or get the state of an individual bit, which can yield code that is hard to understand.

The *BitSet* class lets you create a data structure for a set of bits that automatically grows in size, as needed. The *BitSet* class provides methods for setting a bit, clearing a bit, and performing logical operations. The following tip will show you how to use Java's *BitSet* class.

793   USING BITSETS IN JAVA

As you have learned, a *BitSet* object lets your programs store and manipulate bit settings. Within a Java program, you create a *BitSet* object using one of the following *BitSet* constructor methods:

```
BitSet();
BitSet(int nbits);
```

The second form of the *BitSet* constructor lets you specify the *Bitset* object's initial size. To specify whether a bit within the set is on or off, you use the *set* and *clear* methods, respectively:

```
void set(int bit);
void clear(int bit);
```

The *bit* parameter specifies which bit in the object to set or clear. To find out whether or not a bit in the object is set, you use the *get* method:

```
boolean get(int bit);
```

The *get* method returns *true* if the bit is set and *false* if the bit is clear.

APPLYING LOGICAL OPERATORS TO BITSETS

 794

In addition to setting and clearing bits, the *BitSet* class also lets you perform logical operations with another *Bitset* object. For example, assume that your program uses two *Bitset* objects to track the state of two aircraft controls. In this case, your program may need to compare the state of both controls using one or more of the three *BitSet* class logical operations. The formats of the *BitSet* class logical operations are as follows:

```
void and(BitSet set);
void or(BitSet set);
void xor(BitSet set);
```

The following application, *bitset_invert.java*, illustrates the use of the *xor* method to invert the bits in a *Bitset*:

```java
import java.util.*;

public class bitset_invert {

    public static void main(String args[])
      {
          BitSet bset1 = new BitSet(4);
          BitSet bset2 = new BitSet(4);

          // bitset set to true,false,true,true
          bset1.set(0);
          bset1.clear(1);
          bset1.set(2);
          bset1.set(3);
          System.out.println(bset1);

          // create a biset with all bits set
          for (int i = 0; i < 4; i++ )
            bset2.set(i);

          // invert bset1 by xored it with bset2
          bset1.xor(bset2);
          System.out.println(bset1);
      }
  }
```

795 UNDERSTANDING PROPERTIES LISTS

When your programs work with *Hashtable* objects, there may be times when you need to store and later retrieve the table's contents to and from a file. As it turns out, Java's *Properties* class extends the *Hashtable* class to let your programs read or write the table's contents to or from a file. A property list also lets you store default values. For example, if a program cannot find a particular property within the list, the list can load the default value from the properties file. The limitation of a properties list is that both the key and the stored value in the table must be *String* objects.

Possible applications of the properties list are customizing applications and saving settings between program execution. Java's properties list file is equivalent to an *.INI* file used with Microsoft Windows. In fact, the syntax of the files is quite similar. Java's properties list file uses the following format:

```
PROPERTY_KEY=PROPERTY_VALUE
```

The following is an example of a properties list file:

```
#my properties list - app_prop.ini
#Sun Sep 01 04:48:47  1996
Foreground=0000FF
Background=FF8888
FontSize=12
Font=Courier
```

796 CREATING A PROPERTIES LIST

To build a properties list in Java, you first create a *Properties* object using the *Properties* constructor. Then, you can add properties to the list using the Hashtable class *put* method:

```
Object put(Object key, Object value);
```

Your program can call the *Hashtable* class *put* method because *Properties* is a subclass of the *Hashtable* class. One word of caution: the *put* method accepts objects of any type for the key and stored values; however, when used in a properties list, you should only use *String* objects. The following statements create a property list and add several properties to it:

```
Properties property_list = new Properties();

property_list.put("ForegroundColor",  "blue");
property_list.put("BackgroundColor",  "grey");
property_list.put("FontSize",  "12");
```

797 GETTING A PROPERTY FROM A PROPERTIES LIST

To retrieve a property value from a properties list, you call one of the *Properties* class *getProperty* methods, using the specific property name. The formats of the *getProperty* method are as follows:

```
String getProperty(String key);
String getProperty(String key, String defaultValue);
```

The *key* parameter specifies the property name and the *defaultValue* parameter specifies the default return value if the method cannot find the specified property within the list. For example, the following statements return the value of the "UserID" property if it is found in the list or the string "619" if the key "UserID" is not found:

```
Properties property_list;
property_list.getProperty("UserID", "619");
```

ACCESSING PROPERTIES USING ENUMERATION

 798

When your programs work with property lists, there may be times when you want to go through the entire list of properties. As you have learned, you can go through the elements in a *Hashtable* object using enumeration. Likewise, you can enumerate the property keys by calling the *Properties* class *propertyNames* method, the format of which is as follows:

```
Enumeration propertyNames();
```

The *propertyNames* method returns an enumeration of the property keys, which you can then use to access each property value using the *getProperty* method. The following application, *prop_enum.java*, creates a properties list with several properties and displays the properties to the console window one at a time using key enumeration:

```java
import java.util.*;

public class prop_enum {

    public static void main(String args[])
      {
        Properties program_prop = new Properties();

        program_prop.put("one", "1");
        program_prop.put("two", "2");
        program_prop.put("three", "3");
        program_prop.put("four", "4");
        program_prop.put("five", "5");

        // display the properties
        Enumeration enum = program_prop.propertyNames();
        while (enum.hasMoreElements())
          {
            String prop_key =(String) enum.nextElement();
            System.out.println(prop_key + ": " +
              program_prop.getProperty(prop_key));
          }
      }
  }
```

When you run this program, the console window will display the following output:

```
five: 5
one: 1
three: 3
four: 4
two: 2
```

Bear in mind that the enumerated list is not guaranteed to be in the same order in which you added the properties—as in the case of enumerating a *Hashtable* object.

799 LOADING PROPERTIES FROM A PROPERTIES LIST FILE

The Java *Properties* class greatly simplifies the process of reading a properties file. All you have to do is open an input stream to the properties file and call the *Properties* class *load* method. The *load* method, in turn, will read and parse the properties file, placing the information into the *Properties* object. The following application, *load_prop.java*, loads the properties file *app_prop.ini* and displays the properties information to the console window:

```java
import java.util.*;
import java.io.*;

public class load_prop {

   public static void main(String args[])
    {
       Properties program_prop = new Properties();
       try {
           FileInputStream istream =
              new FileInputStream("app_prop.ini");
           program_prop.load(istream);
        }
       catch(IOException e)
         {
           System.out.println("File Read Error:" + e);
           System.exit(1);
         }

        // display the properties
        Enumeration enum = program_prop.propertyNames();
        while(enum.hasMoreElements())
          {
             String prop_key =(String) enum.nextElement();
             System.out.println(prop_key + ": " +
                program_prop.getProperty(prop_key));
          }
     }
  }
```

SAVING A PROPERTIES LIST TO A FILE **800**

In the previous tip, you learned how to load a *Properties* object using the *load* method. In a similar way, after you set up a properties list, you can save the list to a file using the *Properties* class *save* method:

```
void save(OutputStream out, String header);
```

The *out* parameter specifies an output stream that corresponds to the file to which you want to save the properties data. The header string appears as a comment line at the top of the properties list file and is for documentation purposes only. The following application, *save_prop.java*, illustrates the process of saving properties to a file:

```java
import java.util.*;
import java.io.*;

public class save_prop {

    public static void main(String args[])
      {
          Properties program_prop = new Properties();

          program_prop.put("Account No", "231-24523-12");
          program_prop.put("User Name", "MarkoC");
          program_prop.put("IP Address", "252.60.138.0");

          try {
             FileOutputStream ostream =
                 new FileOutputStream("saved_prop.ini");
             program_prop.save(ostream, "Account properties list");
          }
          catch(IOException e)
            {
               System.out.print("File Write Error:" + e);
               System.exit(1);
            }
      }
  }
```

SETTING PROPERTY DEFAULTS **801**

As you have learned, the *Properties* class lets you specify default values for a property. One way to specify a default value is to use the *defaultValue* parameter in the *getProperty* method as shown in Tip 797. Another way is to define the default value when you create a new *Properties* object using the *Properties* constructor, as shown:

```
Properties(Properties defaults);
```

The constructor's *default* parameter lets you specify an entire list of defaults, which is especially useful when you have a default properties file for general use, and a custom properties file which individual users can customize to override defaults. The following application, *def_prop.java*, loads a default properties list and then a custom user properties list. The program then displays the merged property values in the console window:

```java
import java.awt.*;
import java.util.*;
import java.io.*;

public class def_prop {

    public static void main(String args[])
      {
        // load default properties
        Properties default_prop = new Properties();
        try {
           FileInputStream istream =
               new FileInputStream("default_prop.ini");
           default_prop.load(istream);
         }
        catch(IOException e)
          {
            System.out.println("File Read Error:" + e);
            System.exit(1);
          }

         // create program properties and set defualts
         Properties program_prop = new Properties(default_prop);

         // load custom properties
         try {
            FileInputStream istream =
                new FileInputStream("custom_prop.ini");
            program_prop.load(istream);
          }
         catch(IOException e)
           {
             System.out.println("File Read Error:" + e);
             System.exit(1);
           }

         // print out all properties
         Enumeration enum = program_prop.propertyNames();
         while(enum.hasMoreElements())
           {
             String prop_key =(String) enum.nextElement();
             System.out.println(prop_key + ": " +
                 program_prop.getProperty(prop_key));
           }
      }
  }
```

USING A PROPERTIES LIST TO CUSTOMIZE YOUR APPLICATION

802

As you know, one application of the properties list is to customize your application. This tip provides an example that illustrates that use. The following application, *custom_app.java*, lets the user change the background color, text color, font type, and font size of the application using a properties list file, *app_prop.ini*:

```java
import java.awt.*;
import java.util.*;
import java.io.*;

public class custom_app extends Frame{

    TextArea txtarea = new TextArea("1001 Java\nProgrammer's Tips");
    Font f;

    public custom_app(String name)
      {
        super(name);
        add("Center", txtarea);

        Properties program_prop = new Properties();
        try {
           FileInputStream istream =
               new FileInputStream("app_prop.ini");
           program_prop.load(istream);
         }
        catch(IOException e)
          {
            System.out.println("File Read Error:" + e);
            System.exit(1);
          }

        String arg = program_prop.getProperty("Background");
        int ColorVal = Integer.valueOf(arg, 16).intValue();
        txtarea.setBackground(new Color(ColorVal));

        arg = program_prop.getProperty("Foreground");
        ColorVal = Integer.valueOf(arg, 16).intValue();
        txtarea.setForeground(new Color(ColorVal));

        String fontstyle = program_prop.getProperty("Font");
        arg = program_prop.getProperty("FontSize");
        int fsize = Integer.valueOf(arg).intValue();
        f = new Font(fontstyle, Font.PLAIN, fsize);
        txtarea.setFont(f);
      }
```

```
    public boolean handleEvent(Event evt)
    {
       if (evt.id == Event.WINDOW_DESTROY)
         System.exit(0); // exit the application

       return super.handleEvent(evt);
    }

    public static void main(String args[])
    {
       custom_app application = new custom_app("custom_app");
       application.resize(300, 100);
       application.show();
    }
}
```

803 GETTING A PARTICULAR SYSTEM VARIABLE USING getPROPERTY

In the previous tips, you learned to work with property lists. As it turns out, Java has a set of system properties, and there may be times when you want to access them. For example, you can find the name of the current user by getting the "user.name" property. You can get the system properties by calling the *System* class *getProperty* method. The formats of the *getProperty* method are as follows:

```
String getProperty(String key);
String getProperty(String key, String def);
```

The *key* parameter specifies the property you want to find and the optional *def* parameter specifies the default value if the specific property cannot be found. The following code uses the *getProperty* method to display the name of the current user:

```
String user_name = System.getProperty("user.name");
System.out.println("user name = " + user_name);
```

804 GETTING ALL SYSTEM PROPERTIES USING getPROPERTIES

As you learned in Tip 803, you can get Java's system properties by calling the *System* class *getProperty*. To get the entire list of system properties, you can call the *getProperties* method which returns the system properties list. You can then go through the list using enumeration. The following application, *system_prop.java*, displays your system's properties to the console window:

```
import java.util.*;

public class system_prop {

    public static void main(String args[])
    {
        Properties sysprop = System.getProperties();

        Enumeration enum = sysprop.propertyNames();
```

```
            while (enum.hasMoreElements())
              {
                 String prop_key =(String) enum.nextElement();
                 System.out.println(prop_key + ": " +
                    sysprop.getProperty(prop_key));
              }
         }
    }
```

The program's actual output will vary depending on the settings of your system. On a Windows 95 system, the output may look like this:

```
java.home: C: \JAVA
awt.toolkit: sun.awt.win32.Mtoolkit
java.version: 1.0.2
user.name: johndoe
os.name: Windows 95
  .
  .
  .
```

IMPLEMENTING AN ENUMERATION INTERFACE

805

As you have learned, you can use enumeration to go through the items in a *Vector*, *Hashtable*, or *Properties* list. There may be times when you want to implement the *Enumeration* interface in your own data structure. Using enumeration is particularly useful for data structures, such as binary trees, where sequential access is not possible. To create a class that implements an *Enumeration* interface, you have only to define the following methods:

```
boolean hasMoreElements();
Object nextElement();
```

For example, to enumerate the binary tree structure you used in the word count example in Tip 772, you first must create an enumeration class:

```
// Binary tree enumeration class

class BtreeEnumeration implements Enumeration {

    Stack st = new Stack();

     BtreeEnumeration(BtreeNode root)
       {
          st.push(root);
       }

    public boolean hasMoreElements()
       {
          return !st.empty();
       }

    public Object nextElement()
       {
          BtreeNode element =(BtreeNode) st.pop();
```

```
        if(element.right != null)
           st.push(element.right);

        if(element.left != null)
           st.push(element.left);

        return element;
     }
   }
```

The next step is to add a method to the *BtreeLinkList* class to create and return the enumeration:

```
class BtreeLinkList {

   BtreeNode root;

   Enumeration elements()
     {
         return new BtreeEnumeration(root);
     }

         .
         .
         .
   }
```

The following code displays all the words in the tree and the word count:

```
Enumeration enum = btree.elements();

while(enum.hasMoreElements())
  {
     BtreeNode tree_element =(BtreeNode) enum.nextElement();
     System.out.println(tree_element.word + ": " +
        tree_element.word_count);
  }
```

806 UNDERSTANDING NETWORKS

A network is a set of computers and peripherals, such as modems and printers, that are physically connected together. A particular network has a unique set of hardware and software that enables various computers and peripherals to communicate. The power of networks enables computers to share resources. For example, a small computer on a network can access and use other computers that are much more powerful.

One Java design goal was to support the development of complex programs that are small, bug free, and easy to understand. One of the areas in which Java's creators have succeeded with this goal is in the *Network* class. In other programming languages, performing the simplest network task can require pages of code. With Java, in contrast, many of these tasks have been reduced to a single statement. For example, opening a file across a network in Java is not much more complicated than opening a local file. Because of this ease in programming, Java should make network programming commonplace. In the following tips, you will learn how to write Java programs that work across networks.

UNDERSTANDING THE INTERNET 807

The generic term *internet* refers to a network of networks. The Internet is just one particular *internet*. However, it is the ultimate network of networks. Because you are interested in Java, you have certainly used a Web browser to "surf" the Internet. As you probably know, a Web browser is only one of many Internet applications.

Other Internet applications include e-mail, network news, file transfers, and telnet. Other than e-mail, some users on the Web aren't aware of these other applications. Each has played an important role in getting the Internet where it is today. For example, network news, also called Usenet, is still a popular way for users to exchange information using a bulletin-board like media. Usenet lets users discuss a wide range of topics.

In the early days, the Internet was developed by the academic community. Usenet and e-mail were ideal for researchers to communicate with each other across the country. Today, Usenet topics cover all aspects of human interest, and e-mail is an indispensable business tool.

When you consider creating your own Internet-based programs, you should study existing Internet-based applications, such as newsgroups, to better understand the Internet's rules of communication, or *protocols*.

UNDERSTANDING *TCP/IP* 808

To communicate across the Internet, a program must follow a specific set of rules, called protocols. These protocols may specify the size and format of the program's electronic messages, or how programs synchronize messages. In short, who sends the first message and what type of reply the sender expects.

The primary protocol on the Internet is TCP/IP (the Transmission Control Protocol/Internet Protocol). The TCP/IP protocols define the rules that computers and peripherals on the Internet use to communicate. For example, TCP/IP's protocols define how a program finds a particular device on a network, the format the program must use to send the device data, how the program should check for errors, and so on. Many good books describe TCP/IP networks in detail, such as *Internet Programming*, Jamsa Press, 1994. The information provided in the following tips will give you the basic understanding to begin writing your own simple Java network programs.

UNDERSTANDING CLIENT-SERVER APPLICATIONS 809

Networks make many new types of applications possible because a single machine no longer has to do everything. Within a network, some computers, called *servers*, perform specialized tasks on behalf of other programs. A program that uses a server is a *client*.

A *server* is simply a computer that runs a specific program continuously whose sole purpose is to provide a service to other programs. A *client*, on the other hand, is a program that receives service from the server. For example, a print server is a software program that waits until other programs (the clients) send it files to print. The server then prints the files on behalf of the client. There are many types of servers across the Internet with which you may familiar, such as mail servers, file servers and, of course, World Wide Web (or HTTP) servers.

810 UNDERSTANDING PROTOCOLS

To write a client-server application, you must create two programs: the client and the server. Within these programs, you must define how the two applications will communicate—the rules each program must follow. As you have learned, the rules the client and server programs must follow to communicate are *protocols*. In short, protocols define how client-server programs interact.

Most programmers implement protocols using a series of layers, where each layer deals with a particular task. For example, the lowest layer might deal with the actual communication across the network hardware. The next layer might check the bits sent across the network for communication errors. Likewise, the next layer might package the bits into a message format your program understands. Client-server applications use upper-layer protocols that are normally based on a specific application (such as printing a file or transferring a file). The upper-layer protocol defines a strict set of rules on how two applications exchange data.

811 UNDERSTANDING *TCP/IP* PROTOCOLS

As you have learned, across the Internet, the primary protocol is TCP/IP. You can visualize most Internet-based applications as sitting on top of the TCP/IP protocol; in other words, the applications layer their own protocols on top of TCP/IP. For example, the SMTP (Simple Mail Transfer Protocol) is the protocol that uses TCP/IP to communicate with other computers across the Internet.

Other common protocols that reside on top of TCP/IP are FTP (File Transfer Protocol), HTTP (the HyperText Transport Protocol which lets users surf the Web), and NNTP (which supports newsgroups such as Usenet) and Telnet. Table 811 lists some of the most popular Internet protocols that sit on top of TCP/IP.

Upper-Layer Protocol	Description
HTTP (HyperText Transport Protocol)	World Wide Web
NNTP (Network News Transfer Protocol)	Newsgroups
SMTP (Simple Mail Transfer Protocol)	Sending electronic mail
POP3 (Post Office Protocol)	Reading mail stored on a server
FTP (File Transfer Protocol)	Transferring files between computers
TELNET	Controlling a computer remotely

Table 811 Popular TCP/IP-based protocols.

812 UNDERSTANDING INTERNET ADDRESSES

Every computer within a TCP/IP network has a unique address. You should be comfortable with the idea of addresses because you are surrounded with examples. For instance, every phone has a unique phone number and every house has a unique mailing address. An Internet address, or IP (Internet Protocol) address, is a 32-bit number. Programs represent IP addresses using four numbers that are separated by periods. Each number has a range from 0-255, or one byte. Figure 812 shows an Internet address.

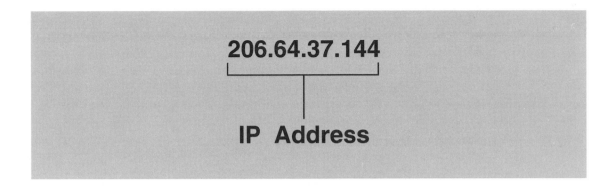

206.64.37.144

IP Address

Figure 812 An Internet Address.

If you use a dial-in connection through an Internet service provider to access the Internet, your provider will assign your computer a temporary IP address dynamically each time you connect. The temporary IP address that you receive is usually dependent on which of your provider's modems you happen to call into. If your computer is connected directly to the Internet, you will have a fixed IP address.

UNDERSTANDING DOMAIN NAMES 813

As you can imagine, if users had to specify an IP address for each computer to which they wanted to connect, the Internet would be a very confusing place. Luckily, most systems have a character-based name, such as *microsoft.com* or *jamsa.com*. The character-based names represent the computer's *domain name*. Across the Internet, a domain name must be unique. To control domain names, users must register their name with the InterNIC (*www.rs.internic.net*). The InterNIC is a cooperative effort between the National Science Foundation, Network Solutions, Inc., and AT&T.

When a user (or a program) uses a domain name, the program must convert the character-based name into a 32-bit IP address. In other words, the program must convert the domain name *jamsa.com* into an IP address such as 123.221.111.012. To convert a domain name into an IP address, your programs take advantage of a special program called a *Domain Name Server* (DNS) which "looks up" the domain name and returns the corresponding IP address. Across the Internet, there are several domain name servers your programs can use to look up IP addresses. Depending on your Internet software, you may have had to specify the IP address of a DNS server when you set up your computer's Internet connection.

UNDERSTANDING THE INETADDRESS CLASS 814

Within your Java programs, you use *InetAddress* objects to store Internet addresses. The *InetAddress* class resides within the *java.net* package. You will use this class to specify the computers to which you want to connect across the Internet. To create an *InetAddress* object, you do not use an *InetAddress* constructor method. You just declare a variable and use one of the *InetAddress* class methods that return an *InetAddress* object. The following two tips demonstrate how your programs use the *InetAddress* class.

815 GETTING A LOCAL HOST IP ADDRESS

In Tip 814, you learned that your programs use the *InetAddress* class to store Internet addresses. Suppose, for example, you want to determine the IP address of your own computer. You can use the *InetAddress* class *static getLocalHost* method to return an *InetAddress* object that contains your computer's IP address. The following program, *getLocalHostTest.java*, displays the IP address for your local computer. For the program to work, you must be connected to the Internet:

```java
import java.net.*;

public class getLocalHostTest {

    public static void main(String args[])
     {
        InetAddress myIPaddress = null;

        try {
             myIPaddress = InetAddress.getLocalHost();
          }
        catch (UnknownHostException e) {}

        System.out.println(myIPaddress);
     }
}
```

Note that there is no *new* keyword in the code and that the *InetAddress* class has no public constructor method. In this example, the *getLocalHost* method creates an *InetAddress* for you. Also note, because the *getLocalHost* method might throw an *UnkownHostException*, your program code must *catch* the exception.

816 GETTING AN IP ADDRESS FROM A DOMAIN NAME

In Tip 813, you learned that domain name servers convert domain names, such as *microsoft.com*, into IP addresses. The *InetAddress* class *getByName* method creates an *InetAddress* object from a domain name. When your program calls the *getByName* method, the method connects to a domain name server and gets the IP address for the specified domain name. The method then returns the IP address as an *InetAddress* object. The following program, *getIPFromDNSTest.java*, demonstrates how to get the IP address for the Jamsa Press Web site:

```java
import java.net.*;

public class getIPFromDNSTest {

    public static void main(String args[])
     {
        InetAddress jamsa = null;

        try {
             jamsa = InetAddress.getByName("www.jamsa.com");
          }
```

```
      catch (UnknownHostException e)
        {
           System.out.println(jamsa);
        }
      System.out.println(jamsa);
    }
  }
```

This Java program works across the Internet. As you can see, Java reduces the program's interaction with the DNS server to a single line.

UNDERSTANDING PORT NUMBERS 817

As you have learned, an IP address identifies a specific computer on the Internet. You also know that a server is just a computer running a specific software program that provides a service to other programs. If there are two copies of the same type of server software running on one computer, each server program is an independent application. For example, two companies, Website and Netscape each make an HTTP server with different features. You can run both these server applications on a single machine to take advantage of various features. However, for the two programs to run on the same system, a client application must be able to distinguish between each HTTP server process. A client tells the difference between server applications using port numbers.

A *port number* is a way to distinguish between the processes that are running on the same computer. A port number is not a physical connector on a computer. Instead, it is an imaginary port that only has meaning in software. A server computer associates server software, such as FTP and HTTP, to a specific port. A server can run two HTTP servers using two different port numbers. To explicitly identify a service that a computer is providing, you append the port number to the IP address of that machine. Figure 817 illustrates an Internet address with a port number.

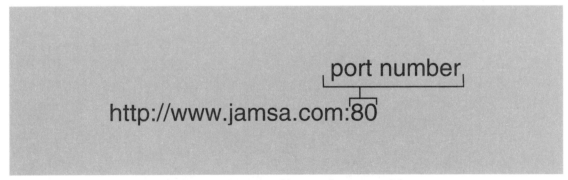

Figure 817 An IP address and port number.

You have probably noticed that you don't often see port numbers appended to IP addresses. The reason is that there exists a set of default port numbers for the common Internet protocols. For example, the default port number for an HTTP server software is port 80. If you do not specify a port number explicitly, your browser will specify port 80 by default. The default port numbers are reserved by the Internet Assigned Numbers Authority (IANA) and are called the *well-known ports*. Table 817 lists some of the most common default port numbers.

Default Port Numbers	Service
20	FTP Data
21	FTP Control
23	TELNET
53	DNS
80	HTTP
110	POP3
119	NNTP

Table 817 *Some well-known port numbers.*

818   UNDERSTANDING THE UNIVERSAL RESOURCE LOCATOR (URL)

A Universal Resource Locator (URL) points to resource files on the Internet. A resource file may be one of many types, from text to multimedia. The URL also specifies the type of protocol programs used to retrieve the file from a server. In Figure 818 below, note that the URL is made up of two parts, the protocol prefix and the Universal Resource Identifier (URI).

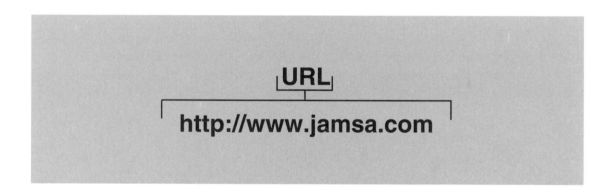

Figure 818 *The Universal Resource Locator (URL).*

The protocol prefix specifies how the client software communicates with the server software to access the resource. For example, if the protocol prefix is *ftp*, the client software should use FTP protocol to access the file. If *http* is the protocol prefix, the client software should use the HTTP protocol. The URI contains the Internet address of the server and the location of a file on that server.

819   UNDERSTANDING THE UNIVERSAL RESOURCE IDENTIFIER (URI)

In the previous tip, you learned that a URL is made up of a protocol prefix and a universal resource identifier (URI). The URI points to a specific resource. The URI consists of an Internet address, an optional port number, and a directory path to the resource. The IP address and port number completely define a particular server process on the Internet. The directory path defines where the file resides on the server.

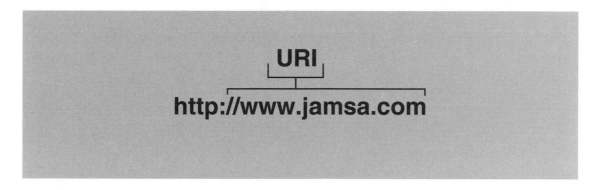

Figure 819 *The Universal Resource Identifier. (URI)*

A URI cannot contain white-space characters, such as space, tabs, or carriage returns. A URI can, however, use the reserved characters which have the special meanings listed in Table 819.

URI Reserved Characters	Description
/	Directory separator
?	Followed by query arguments
#	Argument separator
+	White space
%	Encode special characters
!	Reserved
*	Reserved

Table 819 URI reserved characters.

Should you need to specify a white-space character within a URI, you can use a special syntax that encodes the character. To include a special character, you use the percent character (%) followed by the hexidecimal ASCII code for the special character. The following line demonstrates a URI with a white-space character (the hexidecimal ASCII value, 20) encoded:

```
http://www.jamsa.com/one%20space.html
```

In the previous example, the file is actually named "one space.html".

ENCODING URL STRINGS 820

In the previous tip, you learned about the URI special characters. If you extensively use *URIs* within the *URL* class, there may be times when you have to encode URLs. In Java, you can encode URLs with the *URLEncoder* class. For example, suppose you want to create a URL from a string that contains blanks. In such cases, you can use the *URLEncoder* class to encode the blanks, as demonstrated in the following code:

```
String encoded = URLEncoder("http://www.jamsa.com/one blank.htm");
```

The *URLEncoder* method will assign the *String* the URL *http://www.jamsa.com/one%20blank.htm*.

821 CREATING A URL IN JAVA

In the previous tips, you have learned about Internet-based URLs. You know that URLs point to resources across the Internet. Within your Java programs, you can create a *URL* object using the *URL* constructor method. The following statement, for example, demonstrates how to create a *URL* object:

```
URL jamsa = new URL("http://www.jamsa.com");
```

After you create a *URL* object, you may want to create a second *URL* object that specifies a file that is relative to the URL. To create a relative URL object, you use a different form of the *URL* constructor. The following statement demonstrates how you create a *URL* object for a file which is relative to the *URL* object you created in the previous statement:

```
URL cover = new URL(jamsa, "index.html");
```

In this case, the *URL* constructor method receives a *URL* object and a *String* as arguments. The URL constructors do not actually download the resource. To download the object, you use other *URL* class methods. If the syntax of your URL is incorrect, the *URL* constructor will throw a *MalformedURLException*. Therefore, you need to create the *URL* object inside a *try/catch* block, as shown:

```
try {
    URL jamsa = new URL("http://www.jamsa.com");
    URL home = new URL(jamsa, "index.html");
  }
catch (MalformedURLException e)
  {
    System.out.println("URL not valid:" + e.getMessage());
  }
```

822 DISPLAYING A NEW DOCUMENT WITH SHOWDOCUMENT

To display a Web page that corresponds to a *URL* object, your program calls the *showDocument* method. You might, for example, find the *showDocument* method useful to link graphical items to an HTML document within a Java applet's window. The program, *showDocumentTest.java*, demonstrates the use of the *showDocument* method:

```
import java.applet.*;
import java.net.*;
import java.awt.*;

public class showDocumentTest extends Applet {

   URL jamsa = null;

   public void init()
     {
       try {
             jamsa = new URL("http://www.jamsa.com");
         }
       catch (MalformedURLException e)
         {
```

```
            System.out.println("Error:" + e.getMessage());
        }
    }

  public boolean mouseDown(Event evt, int x, int y)
    {
      // when user clicks, go to Jamsa Press Home page
       getAppletContext().showDocument(jamsa);
      return(true);
    }
}
```

When you run the applet, click your mouse button and the browser window will display the Jamsa Press Web site, as shown in Figure 822.

*Figure 822 Displaying an HTML document using the **showDocument** method.*

DIFFERENT WAYS TO DISPLAY AN HTML DOCUMENT IN A BROWSER 823

In the previous tip, you learned how to use the *showDocument* method to display an HTML document within an applet window. The problem with the example is that if you call *showDocument* with only a URL as an argument, the browser will replace the page that contains your applet with the new HTML page. To direct the browser to open a new window in which to display the new HTML page, pass the string "_blank" as a second argument to *showDocument*, as shown:

```
getAppletContext().showDocument(jamsa, "_blank");
```

Table 823 lists other strings that you can pass to *showDocument* to display an HTML page in different ways.

Target String	Description
"_self"	Display document in current frame
"_blank"	Display document in new window
"_top"	Display document in top frame
"_parent"	Display document in parent frame
other string	Display document in frame with this name

Table 823 Target String arguments for the showDocument method.

824 GETTING THE URL OF AN APPLET'S HTML PAGE

In the previous tips, you have learned how to explicitly create a *URL* object in Java. Within your programs, there may be times when you need the URL that corresponds to the HTML page that contains an applet. In such cases, you call the *getDocumentBase* method, which returns a *URL* object that corresponds to the applet's HTML page. The following program, *getDocumentBaseTest.java*, demonstrates how to use the *getDocumentBase* method to get the URL for the HTML page that contains the applet:

```java
import java.applet.*;
import java.net.*;
import java.awt.*;

public class getDocumentBaseTest extends Applet {

    public void init()
      {
         URL html = getDocumentBase();
         System.out.println(html);
      }
 }
```

825 GETTING THE URL OF AN APPLET'S CODEBASE

In Tip 824, you learned how to use the *getDocumentBase* to determine the URL that corresponds to the HTML Web page that contains your applet. There may be times, however, when you need the URL of your applet itself. In such cases, your program can use the *getCodeBase* method. The following program, *getCodeBase.java*, uses the *getCodeBase* method to display the applet's URL:

```java
import java.applet.*;
import java.net.*;

public class getCodeBaseTest extends Applet {

    public void init()
      {
         URL codebase = null;
         codebase = getCodeBase();

         System.out.println(codebase);
      }
 }
```

826 READING A FILE ACROSS THE INTERNET

In the previous tips, you have learned how to create a URL for a file on the Internet. To actually read the file's contents, you must connect to a server and retrieve the file. Fortunately, Java does most of the hard work for you. All you need to do is call the *DataInputStream* class *openStream* method.

In Tip 670, you learned how to read the contents of a stream using the *DataInputStream* class. However, the *openStream* method returns an *InputStream* object which you must convert to a *DataInputStream* object. The following program, *readURLTest.java*, uses a data stream to read an HTML file's contents. The program displays the file's contents to the console window.

```
import java.net.*;
import java.io.*;

public class readURLTest {

   public static void main(String args[])
     {
       try {
          URL homeJamsa = null;
          DataInputStream dis = null;

          homeJamsa = new URL("http://www.jamsa.com");
          dis = new DataInputStream(homeJamsa.openStream());

          String line = dis.readLine();

          while (line != null)
            {
               System.out.println(line);
               line = dis.readLine();
            }
        }
      catch (IOException e)
        {
           System.out.println("Error:" + e.getMessage());
        }
     }
}
```

As you can see, Java makes the process of reading a file across the Internet as easy as reading a file on a local disk. Again, this is because Java does a lot of work for you behind the scenes.

In previous tips, you learned that a URL has a protocol prefix. Java uses the protocol prefix so that it knows how to communicate with the server and gain access to a file. In the previous example, the *http* protocol prefix tells Java that it must use the HTTP protocol to communicate with the server to access the Web site's default file. If the protocol prefix was *ftp*, Java would use the FTP protocol to communicate with the server and to access the file. All you would have to do is create a URL and open a stream.

UNDERSTANDING CONTENT TYPES AND SUBTYPES 827

In the previous example, you learned how to read a file across the Internet. However, certain applications, such as Web browsers, have to handle files with a variety of *content types*. A Web browser, for example, must be able to load text, image, video, audio, and other content types. But the content type alone does not determine what a file contains. You also need to know the file's *subtype*. A subtype tells you how to interpret the content of a file. For example, a text file may contain HTML or plain ASCII, and an image file may contain *GIF* or *JPEG* image. All these files have a content type and a subtype.

828 UNDERSTANDING THE CONTENT HANDLER

A content handler is software that lets you deal with a large number of content types and subtypes. Java has a content handler built into it, but the current release supports only a limited number of content types and subtypes. However, you will still find the content handler useful should you write applications that must handle a large number of file formats. In addition, Java's content handler is designed to be extensible. You can add methods that load your own file formats. The goal of the *contentHandler* class is to create a generic object loader.

829 USING THE getCONTENT METHOD

In Tip 828, you learned that Java provides a built-in content handler to help your programs deal with various document types and subtypes. You call Java's *URL* class *getContent* method to load many different types of files. The *getContent* method, in turn, determines a content type and subtype by examining the file's extension. After it determines a file's type, it calls an intermediate method to choose the appropriate parser. The method that chooses the parser is referred to as a *factory* in Java. Finally, after a file is parsed, the *getContent* method returns an *Object* which your program can cast to the appropriate object type. The following program demonstrates how to read in a text and image (*GIF*) file using the *URL* class *getContent* method:

```java
import java.applet.*;
import java.net.*;
import java.io.*;
import java.awt.*;
import java.awt.image.*;

public class getContentTest extends Applet {

    String str;
    Image  image;

    public void init()
      {
        try {   // load a text file
            URL filetxt = new URL(getDocumentBase(), "simple.txt");
            str = (String) filetxt.getContent();

            // load an image file
            URL u = new URL(getDocumentBase(), "simple.gif");
            image = this.createImage((ImageProducer)
                    u.getContent());
          }
        catch (MalformedURLException e)
          {
            System.out.println("Error:" + e.getMessage());
          }
        catch (IOException e)
          {
```

```
            System.out.println("Error:" + e.getMessage());
        }
      repaint();
  }

  public void paint(Graphics g)
    {
      g.drawImage(image, 0, 0, this);
      g.drawString(str, 75, 75);
    }
}
```

FINDING THE CONTENT TYPE OF A FILE   830

In the previous tip, you learned how to use Java's content handler to load a file. However, before you can load a file, you must know the file's content type before you can use the *getContent* method. Then, you can prepare a variable to receive the file's contents.

To find the content type using a "more generic" method, you can use the *URLConnection* class. The *URLConnection* class provides methods your program can use to find information about a URL such as its content type, length, modify date, expiration, and content encoding (subtype). The following code fragment uses the *URLConnection* class to display the file's content to the screen:

```
URL fileimage = new URL(getDocumentBase(), "simple.gif");
URLConnection connect = fileimage.openConnection();
System.out.println(connect.getContentType());
```

CREATING YOUR OWN CONTENT HANDLER   831

In the previous tips, you have learned how to use the *URL* class *getContent* method for text and image files. When the *getContent* method does not support a content type or subtype that you need, you can add your own parser to the ones that *getContent* uses. You might, for example, find the ability to add a parser convenient if you are writing a client-server application that must handle many different content types.

UNDERSTANDING THE RELATIONSHIP BETWEEN SERVERS AND PORTS   832

As you have learned, an IP address identifies a computer on the Internet. You also learned that a port number identifies a process (a program) that is running on a computer. As it turns out, programs use port numbers for client and server applications. Because IP addresses are unique and, on a given computer, port numbers are unique, a port number combined with an IP address completely distinguishes an application running on the Internet. The combination of port number and IP address yields a *socket* and provides an end point of a communication path. As you will learn, the same application (IP address and port number) may use multiple sockets, each having a different value. Thus, a socket's value combines an application-specific value with the IP address and port number.

833   UNDERSTANDING A SOCKET CONNECTION

When two applications need to communicate, they must find each other on the Internet. When two applications know each other's socket, they can create a *socket connection*. Usually it is the client's responsibility to find the server. For example. when you call to have a pizza delivered to your home, you need to know the phone number of a local pizzeria. The same is true for client applications. A client tries to connect to a server by initiating a socket connection. The client application does this by sending a message (its socket number) to a server's socket.

The pizzeria, on the other hand, just sits and waits for customers to make the contact. The same is true for server applications. The server does not initially need to know where the client is because it waits for a client to make contact. However, after you have ordered your pizza, the pizzeria usually will ask for your phone number. Now both parties have a way to initiate communication. If something goes wrong, such as the driver gets lost or you want to change your order, corrective action can be taken. A reliable communication path has been set up. The first message that a client application sends to a server contains the client's socket.

The server, in turn, creates a socket it will use to communicate with the client and sends its socket address to the client within its first return message.

834   HOW A JAVA CLIENT CREATES A SOCKET CONNECTION

You learned that a client initiates a socket connection with a server. To initiate a socket connection in Java, you use the *Socket* class. To start, you first create a *Socket* object by specifying a server's IP address and port number. If you specify a domain name, Java will connect to a DNS server to get the equivalent IP address. The following code demonstrates how a Java client connects to a server:

```
try {
    socket = new Socket("www.jamsa.com", 80);
}
catch (IOException e)
  {
    System.out.println("Error: " + e);
  }
```

In the above code, the domain name is "www.jamsa.com" and the server's port number is 80 (the HTTP port number).

835   CREATING A SERVERSOCKET

In previous tips, you have learned that a client application is responsible for finding the server. The server must wait for the client to make first contact, which means the server must be running on a port. To create a server in Java, you create a *serverSocket*. The constructor method takes the port number of the server as an argument. A server then calls the *accept* method to wait for a client to make first contact. When a client makes a request, the *accept* method returns the client's socket. The following code fragment demonstrates how a server creates a *serverSocket* and waits for a client to connect:

```
try {
    server = new ServerSocket(2525);
  }
```

```
catch (IOException e)
  {
    System.out.println("Error: " + e);
  }

try
  {
    socket = server.accept(); // wait for client to connect
  }
catch (IOException e)
  {
    System.out.println("Error: " + e);
  }
```

STREAMS ACROSS SOCKET CONNECTIONS

 836

After a client and server have established a connection, they will need to send data back and forth. In previous tips, you have learned how to write and receive data from input and output streams. Both the client and server can use the *Socket* class *getInputStream* and *getOutputStream* methods to establish streams. Then, the client and server can each convert the streams to *DataInputStream* and *DataOutputStream* or *PrintStream* objects so that they can communicate with each other in the same way as they would write and read local files. The following two tips provide examples of how client-server applications exchange data.

HOW A SERVER SENDS A STRING TO A CLIENT

 837

A server calls the *Socket* class *getOutputStream* method to establish a way to send data to a client. In previous tips, you have learned that you can convert any *OutputStream* to a *PrintStream* so your programs can treat the stream as an output file. The following code fragment shows how a server sends a "Hello World" string to a client. After the server sends the string, the server disconnects the socket:

```
try {
    ServerSocket server = new ServerSocket(2525);
    s = server.accept(); // wait for client to connect
    PrintStream ps = new PrintStream(s.getOutputStream());
    ps.println("Hello World!");
    ps.flush();
  }
catch (IOException e)
  {
    System.out.println("Error: " + e);
  }
```

Again, Java has reduced the complexity of performing a network task to a few lines of code that are almost identical to those the program would use to write a local file.

838 HOW A CLIENT RECEIVES A STRING FROM A SERVER

A client calls the Socket *getInputStream* method to establish a way to receive data from a server. In previous tips, you have learned that your program would convert any *InputStream* to a *DataInputStream*, which your program can treat as a file. The following code fragment shows how a client receives a string from a server and prints it to the screen:

```java
try {
    s = new Socket("www.jamsa.com", 2525);
    DataInputStream dis = new DataInputStream(s.getInputStream());
    String msg = dis.readLine(); // get a string from server
    System.out.println(msg);
  }
catch (IOException e)
  {
    System.out.println("Error: " + e);
  }
```

If the client needs to send data to the server, it creates a *getOutputStream* method, just as the server did in the previous tip. Then, to receive data from a client, the server would create a *getInputStream*.

839 HOW TO CLOSE A SOCKET CONNECTION

When a client or server is done communicating, it can close the socket using the *Socket* class *close* method. A well-behaved client or server will always formally close a connection. The following code fragment is from a simple server that sends "Hello World" to a client and then closes the socket connection:

```java
try {
    server = new ServerSocket(2525);   // Create server socket
  }
catch (IOException e)
  {
    System.out.println("Error: " + e);
  }

while (true)
  {
    Socket s = null;

    try {
        s = server.accept();            // Wait for a client
      }
    catch (IOException e)
      {
        System.out.println("Error: " + e);
      }

    try {
        PrintStream ps = new PrintStream(s.getOutputStream());
        ps.println("Hello World!");
```

```
         ps.flush();
         s.close();                        // Close the socket
      }
   catch (IOException e)
      {
         System.out.println("Error: " + e);
      }
}
```

TESTING CLIENT-SERVER APPLICATIONS ON A LOCAL MACHINE 840

If you would like to test the example code in the previous tips using only your own computer, you can connect to your own machine. To connect to your own computer, use the *InetAddress* class to get your machine's IP address. As you have learned, every machine on the Internet has an IP address. Even if you use a dial up service, your provider will give you a temporary IP address each time you call in. To dynamically determine your local computer's IP address, you can use the *InetAddress* class *getLocalHost static* method.

In addition, to test your network applications, Java requires that you are connected to the Internet even though you are running both the client and server on your local machine. Therefore, you must have access to the Internet before you can debug your network applications.

USING THE LOCAL LOOP-BACK ADDRESS 841

In the previous tip, you learned that you can use the *InetAddress* class to get your machine's IP address. Another way to test your client-server applications is to use the *loop-back address*. The loop-back address is a reserved IP address (127.0.0.1) that always points to the local host. The following code fragment demonstrates a client that uses the loop-back address to connect to a server running on the same machine:

```
try {
    s = new Socket("127.0.0.1", 2525);   // use loopback port
    DataInputStream dis = new DataInputStream(s.getInputStream());

    String msg = dis.readLine(); // get a string from server
    System.out.println(msg);        // display the message
  }
catch (IOException e)
  {
    System.out.println("Error: " + e);
  }
```

UNDERSTANDING APPLET CLIENT RESTRICTIONS 842

In Tip 35, you learned about the restrictions Java places on an applet. One restriction is that an applet cannot make a *Socket* connection to any server other than the one it came from (the server from which the browser downloaded the applet). Therefore, you cannot, for example, make a generic mail tool applet unless you plan to support it with SMTP and POP3 mail servers on the same machine that stores the applet. Also, because of this restriction, you cannot have two applets connect directly together, so that two users can play a game. Consequently, you should always take applet restrictions into consideration when you design a Java client-server application with applets.

843 TESTING YOUR APPLET CLIENT WITH THE APPLETVIEWER

In Tip 840, you learned how to test Java client and server applications. Due to the restrictions that Java places on applets, the default *appletviewer* settings will not let you connect to a server that is running on your local host. To directly connect to a server program that is running on your computer, you must change the default appletviewer *network property* setting in the Properties menu to Unrestricted. Otherwise, you will get a security violation exception. When you test an applet client inside a browser, you can only connect to the computer that the applet was downloaded from.

844 UNDERSTANDING WHY SERVERS SHOULD BE MULTITHREADING

In Tips 727 through 756, you learned about Java threads of control. As you know, multithreading lets your Java program perform tasks in parallel. A server is a great example of a program that should be multithreaded. If a server has a single thread of control, only one client can interact with the server at any one time. If you write your server to support multithreading, the server can process many client-server connections simultaneously.

845 IMPLEMENTING A MULTITRHEADING SERVER

To write a multithreaded server, you create a loop that waits for a new client connection. Each time a client requests a connection, the server creates a new thread. The following code fragment demonstrates a server class that extends the *Thread* class to support multithreading. In this case, the server simply returns any messge that a client sends it.

```java
class serverThread extends Thread {

    Socket socket;
    DataInputStream dis;
    PrintStream ps;

    public void send(StringBuffer msg)
      {
        ps.println(msg);
        ps.flush();
      }

    public serverThread(Socket s)
      {
        socket = s;

        try {
              dis = new DataInputStream(s.getInputStream());
              ps = new PrintStream(s.getOutputStream());
          }
        catch (IOException e)
          {
              System.out.println("Error: " + e);
          }
      }
```

```
    public void run()
      {
        while (true)
          {
            String line = null;

            try {
                line = dis.readLine();
              }
            catch (IOException e)
              {
                System.out.println("Error: " + e);
              }

            if (line == null) // client is gone
              return;

            send(line);
          }
      }
  }
```

UNDERSTANDING WHY A CLIENT SHOULD BE MULTITHREADING 846

In Tip 844, you learned why a server should support multiple threads. In many types of client applications, support for multiple threads is also useful. A Web browser, for example, is a multithreaded application. Within a browser, you can have multiple windows open and perform multiple downloads at the same time. To perform each download operation, the browser simply starts a new thread which performs the corresponding processing.

When your program writes information to or receives information from a stream, a program that uses a single thread of control must wait for the I/O operation to complete—a process called *I/O blocking*. If you use multiple threads to perform the stream read and write operations, your application can continue to perform other operations. When you write client applications, take advantage of Java's multithreading to make your program's interface more user-friendly and more responsive.

A CLIENT-SERVER EXAMPLE WITHIN A SINGLE FILE 847

An interesting thing you can do with multithreading is to write a client and server within a single application. To do this, you create a thread for the client and another for the server. You must, however, make sure the server is established before the client tries to make a socket connection. Also, you must use either the loop-back address or find the local host IP address for the client to connect to the server. The following program, *clientAndServerTest.java*, demonstrates a client and server in the same program:

```
import java.awt.*;
import java.net.*;
import java.io.*;
```

```java
class clientThread extends Thread {

    DataInputStream dis = null;
    Socket s = null;

    public clientThread()
      {
        try {
            s = new Socket("127.0.0.1", 2525);
            dis = new DataInputStream(s.getInputStream());
          }
         catch (IOException e)
           {
             System.out.println("Error: " + e);
           }
      }

    public void run()
      {
        while (true)
          {
            try {
                String msg = dis.readLine();

                if (msg == null)
                  break;

                System.out.println(msg);
              }
            catch (IOException e)
              {
                System.out.println("Error: " + e);
              }
          }
      }

  }

public class clientAndServerTest extends Frame {

    static ServerSocket server = null;

    public boolean handleEvent (Event evt)
      {
        if (evt.id == Event.WINDOW_DESTROY)
          {
            System.exit(0);
          }
        return super.handleEvent (evt);
      }
```

```
public boolean mouseDown(Event evt, int x, int y)
  {
      new clientThread().start(); // start client thread
      return(true);
  }

public static void main(String args[])
  {
    clientAndServerTest f = new clientAndServerTest();
    f.resize (200, 200);

    f.show();

    try {
        server = new ServerSocket(2525);
      }
    catch (IOException e)
      {
        System.out.println("Error: " + e);
      }

    while (true)
      {
        Socket s = null;

        try {
            s = server.accept();
          }
        catch (IOException e)
          {
            System.out.println("Error: " + e);
          }

        try {
            PrintStream ps = new PrintStream(s.getOutputStream());
            ps.println("Hello World!");
            ps.flush();
            s.close();
          }
        catch (IOException e)
          {
            System.out.println("Error: " + e);
          }
      }
  }
}
```

Many network games are designed so that each player has a client and server in one application. In this way, each player has the potential to be a server, but only one player is a server at any one time. If the player who is acting as the server drops out of the game, some other player must become the server. Usually the server part of the application can be done in the background and is hidden from the players of the game. A player only sees and interacts with the client part of the application.

848 UNDERSTANDING THE SMTP PROTOCOL

In previous tips, you have learned how to write Java clients that connect to Java servers. Actually, connecting to any standard TCP/IP protocol server is no different from what you have already learned. However, to communicate with a TCP/IP server, you will need to understand the protocol for that server.

You may recall, the SMTP protocol (a protocol for communicating with a mail server) is one protocol that sits on top of TCP/IP. The SMTP server waits for clients to send it e-mail that needs to be delivered. To write a very simple SMTP client, you need to understand the SMTP protocol. Table 848 shows the steps required to send an e-mail to an SMTP server.

Protocol	Description
HELO localhost.domain.name	Initiate communication with SMTP server.
MAIL FROM: user@emailadress.com	Specify who is sending the e-mail.
RCPT TO: user@emailadress.com	Specify who is to receive the e-mail.
DATA	Specify that the e-mail data is next.
(your e-mail message)	Specify data of the e-mail (any number of lines).
.	A period alone specifies the end of the e-mail.
QUIT	Close the connection nicely.

Table 848 SMTP protocol.

The first step tells the SMTP server who you are. The second step tells the SMTP server who is sending the e-mail. Next, you tell the SMTP server who is to receive the e-mail. Finally, you send the DATA keyword to signify that the data of the e-mail will be sent next. You then send the body of the e-mail followed by a period on a line by itself. Implementing a Java application that uses the SMTP protocol is demonstrated in the following tip.

849 SENDING E-MAIL FROM A JAVA APPLICATION

In the previous tip, you learned that a client application can follow the SMTP protocol to send e-mail to someone's e-mail account. The following program, *JavaMailTest.java*, demonstrates how to send e-mail in a Java application:

```java
import java.io.*;
import java.net.*;

public class JavaMailTest {

    static PrintStream ps = null;        // send messages
    static DataInputStream dis = null;   // recieve messages

    public static void send(String str) throws IOException
      {
        ps.println(str); // send SMTP a string
        ps.flush();      // flush the string

        System.out.println("Java sent: " + str);
    }
```

```java
public static void receive() throws IOException
  {
     String readstr = dis.readLine(); // get SMTP response
     System.out.println("SMTP response: " + readstr);
  }


public static void main (String args[])
  {
     String HELO = "HELO ";
     String MAIL_FROM = "MAIL FROM: user@emailadress.com ";
     String RCPT_TO = "RCPT TO: user@emailadress.com ";
     String SUBJECT = "SUBJECT: Java is cool!";
     String DATA = "DATA"; // begining of message

     // Note: "\r\n.\r\n" indicates the end of the message
     String BODY     = "Java sent this!\r\n.\r\n";

     Socket smtp = null;    // SMTP socket

     try {  // Note: 25 is the SMTP default port number
         smtp = new Socket("smtp.any.com", 25);
         OutputStream os = smtp.getOutputStream();
         ps = new PrintStream(os);
         InputStream is = smtp.getInputStream();
         dis = new DataInputStream(is);
     }
     catch (IOException e)
       {
         System.out.println("Error connecting: " + e);
       }

     try {       // tell SMTP helo
         String loc = InetAddress.getLocalHost().getHostName();
         send(HELO + loc);
         receive();          // get SMTP response
         send(MAIL_FROM);    // send SMTP from address
         receive();          // get SMTP response
         send(RCPT_TO);      // send SMTP who address
         receive();          // get SMTP response
         send(DATA);         // send SMTP begin
         receive();          // get SMTP response
         send(SUBJECT);      // send SMTP subject
         receive();          // get SMTP response
         send(BODY);         // send message body
         receive();          // get SMTP response
         smtp.close();       // close connection
     }
```

```
    catch (IOException e)
      {
         System.out.println("Error sending:" + e);
      }


    System.out.println("Mail sent!");
   }
 }
```

You should note that the data portion of the e-mail message has two sections, a header and the body. In the header you can specify additional information about the message. In the previous example, the code sets the subject of the message. To run the code above, you must change the SMTP domain name, as well as the sender and recipient e-mail addresses. You might, for example, simply send an e-mail message to yourself.

850 HOW TO USE A PROXY SERVER

If you are desperate to implement a client applet for a server that is not the server from which the applet came, you can implement a *proxy server*. Think of a proxy server as a messenger for two parties that are not allowed to talk to each other. The proxy server relays the messages a client sends it to another server. In turn, the proxy server relays all messages it receives from the server to the client. Using a proxy server, you do pay a price in performance, and you also slow down your own server, but for a simple protocol and a limited number of hits, a proxy server can get the job done. Figure 850 shows a proxy server.

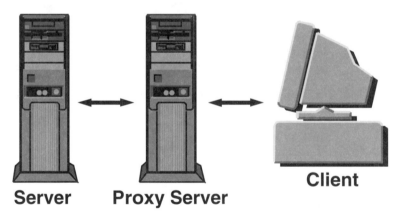

Server   **Proxy Server**   **Client**

Figure 850 A proxy server.

851 UNDERSTANDING CHAT AREAS

Ever since the first computers were connected, people have been using them to talk. A *chat area* is an interface that lets a group of people talk by typing messages. Like all Internet-based programs, chat programs must follow a specific protocol. Specifically, chat programs rely on the Internet Relay Chat (IRC) protocol. However, chatting on a Web page has been ad-hoc at best, until Java.

With Java, a Web page can have a fully featured chat area. Features such as instant messages and membership rooms are not difficult to implement. Due to the applet restrictions, chat applets on the same page will have to communicate through a server on the computer where they reside.

HANDLING THE CHAT APPLET'S EVENTS

In the previous tip, you learned how to create a *chatApplet's* interface. Now, you can write the code that goes beneath the interface. The chat applet is an event-driven program. You must implement the applet's *action* method to capture the button-down events. When the user clicks on the Connect button, the chat applet tries to connect to the *chatServer*. After the applet establishes a socket connection, the chat applet sends its name to the server. When the user clicks on the disconnect button, the chat applet closes the connection.

In addition, if the *chatApplet* is connected to a server, the user's selection of the Send button causes the applet to send the contents of the message-text area to the chat server. The following code demonstrates how to process a *chatApplet's* events:

```java
public boolean action(Event evt, Object obj)    // event handler
  {
    if (evt.target instanceof Button)
     {
       String label = (String) obj;

       if (label.equals(CONNECT))
         {
           if (soc == null)
            {
              try {
                   soc = new Socket(InetAddress.getLocalHost(),2525);
                   ps = new PrintStream(soc.getOutputStream());
                   ps.println(name_txt.getText());
                   ps.flush();
                   listen = new Listen(this,name_txt.getText(),soc);
                   listen.start();
                 }
              catch (IOException e)
                 {
                    System.out.println("Error: " + e);
                    disconnect();
                 }
            }
         }
       else if (label.equals(DISCONNECT))
         {
             disconnect();
         }
       else if (label.equals(SEND))
         {
             if (socket != null)
              {
                 StringBuffer msg = new StringBuffer("MSG:   ");
                 ps.println(msg.append(msg_txt.getText()));
                 ps.flush();
              }
         }
     }
  }
```

```
      return true;
   }

public void stop()
   {
      disconnect();
   }

public void disconnect()
   {
      if (soc!= null)
        {
          try {
                listen.suspend();
                ps.println("QUIT");
                ps.flush();
                soc.close();
             }
          catch (IOException e)
             {
                System.out.println("Error: " + e);
             }
          finally
             {
                listen.stop();
                listen = null;
                soc = null;
                list.clear();
             }
        }
   }
```

You may have noticed the *Listen* class within the code. The *Listen* class is a thread that listens to the *chatServer*. You will learn how to implement the *Listen* class in the following tip.

855   *Processing Messages Received from a chatServer*

In previous tips, you learned how to handle user-generated events. As you will also learn, an event-driven program can also receive events from other programs. For the *chatApplet* program, you must handle messages received from the chat server. There are three messages that the *chatApplet* might receive from the chat server.

When someone enters or leaves the chat area, the *chatServer* sends the *PEOPLE* keyword followed by a list of names. When a client sends a message to the chat area, the *chatServer* sends a *MSG* keyword followed by the message. Finally, when the *chatServer* is going to disconnect, it sends the *QUIT* keyword. The following code demonstrates how to handle messages received from a *chatServer*.

```
class Listen extends Thread {

    String name = null;
    DataInputStream dis = null;
```

```
PrintStream ps = null;
Socket socket = null;
chatApplet parent = null;

public Listen(chatApplet p, String n, Socket s)
  {
    parent = p;
    name = n;
    socket = s;

    try {
        dis = new DataInputStream(s.getInputStream());
        ps = new PrintStream(s.getOutputStream());
      }
    catch (IOException e)
      {
        System.out.println("Error: " + e);
        parent.disconnect();
      }
  }

public void run()
  {
    String msg = null;

    while (true)
      {
        try {
            msg = dis.readLine();
          }
        catch (IOException e)
          {
            System.out.println("Error: " + e);
            parent.disconnect();
          }

        if (msg == null)
          {
            chatApplet.listen = null;
            chatApplet.socket = null;

            chatApplet.list.clear();
            return;
          }

          StringTokenizer st = new StringTokenizer(msg, ":");
          String keyword = st.nextToken();
```

```
                    if (keyword.equals("PEOPLE"))
                      {
                          chatApplet.list.clear();

                          while (st.hasMoreTokens())
                            {
                               String str = st.nextToken();
                               chatApplet.list.addItem(str);
                            }
                      }
                    else if (keyword.equals("MSG"))
                      {
                          String usr = st.nextToken();
                          chatApplet.chat_txt.appendText(usr);
                          chatApplet.chat_txt.appendText(
                             st.nextToken("\0"));

                          chatApplet.chat_txt.appendText("\n\n");
                      }
                    else if (keyword.equals("QUIT"))
                      {
                          chatApplet.listen = null;
                          chatApplet.socket = null;

                          chatApplet.list.clear();
                          return;
                      }
                }
            }
      }
```

The *Listen* class extends the *Thread* class to simplify the design of the *chatApplet* and also to improve the response to user input. Using threads, the *chatApplet* can detect new messages being sent from the server and take input from the user at the same time.

856 HOW A CHATSERVER ACCEPTS CLIENTS

The first task of a chat server is to create a server socket on a specific port. Then, the chat server must wait for clients to connect. When a client requests a connection, the chat server creates a thread for that client, saves the client with a client list, and then waits for the next client. The following code demonstrates a *chatServer's main* method, where a *chatServer* waits for new clients:

```
public class chatServer extends Frame {

    static Vector clients = new Vector(10);
    static ServerSocket server = null;
    static int active_connects = 0;
    static Socket socket = null;
```

```
public boolean handleEvent (Event evt)
  {
    if (evt.id == Event.WINDOW_DESTROY)
      {
         sendClients(new StringBuffer("QUIT"));
        closeAll();
        System.exit(0);
      }
    return super.handleEvent (evt);
  }

public static void main(String args[])
  {
    Frame f = new chatServer();
    f.resize (200, 200);
    f.show();

    try {
        server = new ServerSocket(2525);
      }
    catch (IOException e)
      {
        System.out.println("Error: " + e);
      }

    while (true)
      {
        if (clients.size() < 10)
          {
            try {
                socket = server.accept();
              }
            catch (IOException e)
              {
                System.out.println("Error: " + e);
              }

            for (int i = 0; i < chatServer.clients.size(); i++)
              {
                Client c = new Client(socket);
                clients.elementAt(i) = c;

                if (checkName(c))
                  {
                    c.start();
                    notifyRoom();
                  }
```

```
                        else
                          {
                              c.ps.println("TAKEN");
                              disconnect(c);
                          }

                        break;
                   }

             }
           else
             {
                try {
                    Thread.sleep(200);
                 }
                catch (InterruptedException e) { }
             }
         }
      }
   }
```

Some of the methods in this code are not implemented. For example, the *notifyRoom* and *disconnect* methods are used but their implementation is not shown. A *chatServer* must perform a number of tasks. The following two tips will show you how to perform them in Java.

857 CREATING A CHATSERVER'S CLIENT THREAD

In the previous tip, you learned how to create a chat server that lets multiple clients make a connection. For each of these clients, the chat server must be able to accept messages. The best way to do this in Java is to create a separate thread per client. The following code demonstrates a class that extends the *Thread* class. The chat server in the previous tip can use this class to monitor any messages sent from each individual client:

```
class Client extends Thread {

    Socket socket;
    String name;
    DataInputStream dis;
    PrintStream ps;

    public void send (StringBuffer msg)
      {
         ps.println(msg);
         ps.flush();
      }

    public Client(Socket s, int i)
      {
         socket = s;
```

```java
        try {
            dis = new DataInputStream(s.getInputStream());
            ps = new PrintStream(s.getOutputStream());
            name = dis.readLine();
        }
      catch (IOException e)
      {
         System.out.println("Error: " + e);
      }
  }

public void run()
  {
    while (true)
      {
        String line = null;

        try {
           line = dis.readLine();
         }
        catch (IOException e)
          {
             System.out.println("Error: " + e);
             chatServer.disconnect(this);

             chatServer.notifyRoom();
             return;
          }

        if (line == null) // Client is gone
          {
             chatServer.disconnect(this);
             chatServer.notifyRoom();

             return;
          }

        StringTokenizer st = new StringTokenizer(line, ":");
        String keyword = st.nextToken();

        if (keyword.equals("MSG"))
          {
             StringBuffer msg = new StringBuffer("MSG:");
             msg.append(name);

             msg.append(st.nextToken("\0"));

             chatServer.sendClients(msg);
          }
```

```
            else if (keyword.equals("QUIT"))
              {
                  chatServer.disconnect(this);
                  chatServer.notifyRoom();
                  this.stop();
              }
          }
      }

  }
```

As you can see, a client may send two types of messages which the *Client* class processes. Clients precede each message they send with a keyword, which distinguishes the message type. The *MSG* keyword specifies that the client wants the server to send the *String* that follows to every client. The *QUIT* message informs the server that the client is going to disconnect. The example code above uses the *chatServer* class *disconnect*, *sendClients*, and *notifyRoom* methods. The following tips will discuss these methods.

858 IMPLEMENTING CHATSERVER METHODS

In the previous tip, you learned how to respond to client requests. Some of the requests require the server to send the messages to all other clients that are connected to the chat server. For example, if a client sends a *QUIT* message, the chat server must notify all other clients that one of the clients has left. Likewise, if a client sends a *MSG*, the chat server must send all other clients that message.

When a chat server gets a connection request from a new client, the chat server must make sure that the name is not already taken by another client. The following code illustrates the processing the server must perform. Note that because the server uses multiple threads, you implement the synchronized methods to ensure that only one thread executes the critical methods at any given time:

```java
public static void notifyRoom()
  {
     StringBuffer people = new StringBuffer("PEOPLE");

     for (int i = 0; i < clients.size();i++)
       {
          Client c = clients.elementAt(i);
          people.append(":" + c.name);
       }
     sendClients(people);
  }

public static synchronized void sendClients(StringBuffer msg)
  {
     for (int i=0; i < clients.size(); i++)
       {
          Client c = clients.elementAt(i);
          c.send(msg);
       }
  }
```

```java
public static void closeAll()
  {
    while (clients.size())
      {
        Client c = clients.firstElement();

        try {
            c.socket.close();
         }
        catch (IOException e)
         {
            System.out.println("Error: " + e);
         }
        finally
         {
            clients.removeElement(c);
         }
      }
  }

public static boolean checkName(Client newclient)
  {
    for (int i=0; i < clients.size(); i++)
      {
        Client c = clients.elementAt(i);

        if ((c != newclient) && c.equals(newclient.name))
          return(false);
      }
    return(true);
  }

public static synchronized void disconnect(Client c)
  {
    try {
        c.send(new StringBuffer("QUIT"));
        c.socket.close();
      }
    catch (IOException e)
      {
        System.out.println("Error: " + e);
      }
    finally
      {
        clients.removeElement(c);
      }
  }
```

859 UNDERSTANDING CGI-BIN SCRIPTS

Even without Java, HTML Web pages have been interactive. For example, search engines on the Web take user input and provide a list of search results. An HTML page that a user fills out is called a form. An HTML form can contain elements such as text fields, radio buttons, checkboxes, lists, and other graphical user interface (GUI) components. When the user clicks on the form's Submit button, the browser sends the information from the form's elements to the HTTP server. In turn, the HTTP server calls a program that processes the information. The program can return a dynamically generated HTML page as a result, which the browser displays to the user.

The program that the HTTP server executes is called a CGI (Common Gateway Interface) script. The Common Gateway Interface defines how the HTTP server sends and receives information to and from a CGI. The use of the term *script* is just customary. A CGI script can be written in just about any programming language, compiled or scripted. You can even write a CGI script in Java. For security reasons, a CGI script must reside in a special directory, usually named "cgi-bin," so that the HTTP cannot be tricked into running a program that might cause damage or compromise a system.

CGI scripts increase the capabilities of the Web by interfacing with other programs, such as databases, or hardware, such as video cameras. You may want to take advantage of some of the many CGIs that exist today by calling one from an applet. To do this, you cannot execute the CGI script directly. Instead, you must emulate a Web browser and tell an HTTP server to do it for you. The following tips will show you the two methods used to execute a CGI script from an applet.

860 RUNNING CGI-BIN SCRIPTS FROM AN APPLET (GET)

To execute a CGI script from an applet, you must first connect to an HTTP server. You cannot execute a CGI script directly. Fortunately, the HTTP protocol is straightforward, and it is not difficult to tell an HTTP server to execute a CGI-Bin script. To connect to an HTTP server, you need to open a socket connection. As you have learned, you open a socket connection by executing the following line of code:

```
Socket http = new Socket("www.jamsa.com", 80);
```

Next, you need to open a stream to send strings to the HTTP server. You do this by executing the following lines of code:

```
OutputStream os = http.getOutputStream();
ps = new PrintStream(os);
```

There are two methods to invoke a CGI script: *GET* and *POST*. Each method passes data to the script differently. The *GET* method passes data to the script as command-line arguments. As you have learned, Java programs receive command-line arguments through the *main* method's *String* argument. Regardless of the language in which the CGI script is written, it will receive data in a similar manner. The following code demonstrates how to tell the HTTP server to execute a CGI script using the *GET* method:

```
ps.println("GET /cgi-bin/websearch.pl?say+Hello%20World");
```

The string that specifies the CGI script in the previous statement is the second half of a URI. The first part of a URI is normally an IP address and port number. Since you have already connected to the HTTP server, that piece of information is not necessary. The path name specified in the code above must follow the URI special character rules that you already learned. The forward slash (/) is the directory separator. The question mark (?) character separates the script from the program arguments. The plus (+) character specifies a blank. The percent sign (%) encodes special characters. Therefore, the previous statement is equivalent to being on the server, going to the "cgi-bin" directory, and typing the following command:

```
C:\> websearch.pl say "Hello World"
```

To receive data back from the script, you must read the input stream of the HTTP server socket.

RUNNING CGI-BinScripts FROM AN APPLET (POST) 861

In the previous tip, you learned how to invoke a CGI script from an applet using the *GET* method. You learned that the *GET* method passes data to a CGI script through command-line arguments. The *POST* method passes data to the CGI script through standard input. To use the *POST* method, you must still connect to the HTTP server and open streams as you learned in the previous tip. The following code demonstrates how to tell the HTTP server to execute a CGI script using the *POST* method:

```
ps.println("POST /cgi-bin/websearch.pl");
```

At this point, you have not specified any data. To specify data, you must first tell the HTTP server the type of data you plan to send. In Tips 827through830, you learned about content type. The following statement demonstrates how to specify the type of data you plan to send:

```
ps.println("Content-type: plain/text");
```

Next, you must specify the length of the data, in bytes, that you plan to send,. Java automatically converts the *String* from UNICODE to ASCII before it sends the *String's* contents through the stream. Therefore, if your data is a *String*, you can just specify the length of the string, as the following program code demonstrates:

```
String data = "Hello World";
ps.println("Content-length: " + data.length + "\n");
```

Note the additional new-line at the end of the content-length string. Actually, there are two new-lines: one is provided by the *println* method; the second, you must specify manually. It is a requirement that the content-length statement be followed by two new lines. Finally, all that is left is to send the data. The following code demonstrates the complete *POST* method:

```
ps.println("POST /cgi-bin/websearch.pl");
ps.println("Content-type: plain/text");
String data = "Hello World";
ps.println("Content-length: " + data.length + "\n");
ps.println(data);
```

UNDERSTANDING JAVA CGI-BinScripts 862

In the previous two tips, you learned how to invoke a CGI script from an applet. You also learned that CGI scripts may be written in many different languages. Because Java makes it easy to perform network connections, Java is a good language for some CGI applications. One drawback is that Java is much slower than compiled languages. However, when Java compilers become available, it should make Java's speed comparable to those of normal compiled languages. Since CGI scripts just sit on a single machine, there is no benefit to running them through the interpreter.

To write a CGI script, you need to support either the *GET* or *POST* invocation. You learned that *GET* passes data as arguments to a program. For a Java CGI, the data would be passed through the *main* method's *args* argument. The *POST* invocation passes data to the CGI through standard input. In Java, you read standard input through an *InputStream*. Finally, a Java CGI returns data to the HTTP server by writing to standard output.

863　UNDERSTANDING THE GARBAGE COLLECTION PROCESS

When you allocate memory in a language such as C/C++, it becomes your responsibility to free, or return, the memory back to the system when your program no longer needs it. If your program does not return memory after it is done using it, the program suffers from what is known as a *memory leak*. In other words, the program now has less memory to work with than it did when it started. Memory leaks are a serious problem in many programs, and they can be very difficult to find. Memory leaks can be so severe as to cause your program to crash suddenly.

Java solves the problem of memory leaks. As a programmer, you no longer have to track the life of each object your program allocates,and free the object when your program no longer needs it. Instead, Java does this for you automatically through a process known as *garbage collection*. For example, consider the following code which allocates memory, uses it, and then no longer needs it:

```
String item_1= "Originally occupy several bytes of memory";
System.out.println("Use original: " + item_1);
item_1= "Some other memory";
System.out.println("Using other: " + item_1);
```

As you can see, the code initializes the *item_1 String* object and then displays the object to the screen. However, after the assignment *item_1 = "Some other memory"*, the original memory occupied by the string *"Originally occupy several bytes of memory"* is no longer referenced (and no longer accessible). Fortunately, Java will take care of this situation by freeing up the memory.

Java performs its garbage collection by periodically scanning for unreferenced memory. When it finds memory that is no longer in use, it will free it for you. In addition, the garbage collection process runs as a thread in the background. Normally, you will not notice it running as it cleans up memory.

864　FINDING THE AMOUNT OF FREE MEMORY

As you allocate memory for large objects, there may be times when you need to know how much memory your system has available (not in use). To determine how much memory (in bytes) is available for your program to use, you may use the *Runtime* class *freeMemory* method, as shown:

```
Runtime info = Runtime.getRuntime();
System.out.println("freeMemory= " + info.freeMemory());
```

In this case, the program uses the *getRuntime* method to display the amount of available memory to the console window.

865　FINDING THE AMOUNT OF TOTAL MEMORY

In Tip 864, you learned how to determine how much free memory was available to your program. There may be times, however, when you want to know the total amount of memory in the Java Virtual Machine, that is, the total amount of memory currently available (free) and unavailable (in use for objects). Your programs can use the *Runtime* class *totalMemory* method, which returns the total memory in bytes. The following statements, for example, display the amount of total memory to the console window:

```
Runtime info = Runtime.getRuntime();
System.out.println("totalMemory= " + info.totalMemory());
```

HELPING THE GARBAGE COLLECTOR

866

As you have learned, the Java garbage collector works by freeing memory that the program no longer references. Java's garbage collector works in the background as a low priority thread. Normally, the garbage collector does not need any special assistance from you, the programmer. However, there may be situations in which the garbage collector could use some help. For example, consider the case where you temporarily need a large array, use it once, and never again. After you are done using the array, you can assign the *null* value to the array reference. In that way, the garbage collector knows it can free the array's memory. The following code, for example, assigns the *null* value to the array when the program is done using the array:

```
public static void main(String argv[ ])
  {
    int giant_array[ ]= new int[1000000];    // allocate the array
    process_it(giant_array);                 // use the array

    // make the array reference nothing
    // to help the garbage collector
    giant_array= null;

    // other code goes here
  }
```

FORCING GARBAGE COLLECTION

867

Normally, Java will take care of garbage collection for you. However, there may be times when you have just released a very large resource (by assigning the *null* value, as shown in Tip 866). In such cases, you can use the *System* class *gc* (garbage collection) method to direct Java to perform its garbage collection, as shown:

```
System.gc();
```

TURNING OFF GARBAGE COLLECTION USING THE JAVA INTERPRETER

868

When you test your programs within the Java interpreter, there may be times when you need to turn off garbage collection. In such cases, to stop garbage collection from occurring, invoke the Java interpreter's *-noasync gc* switch by typing the following command:

```
C:\> java -noasynch gc some_program    <ENTER>
```

UNDERSTANDING THE FINALIZE METHOD

869

As you have learned, the Java garbage collector releases an object's memory when the object is no longer needed. Depending on your object's purpose, there may be times when you want Java to perform specific processing before it releases the object. In such cases, you can create a special class-based *finalize* method, which Java calls when your program no longer uses or references an object. The *finalize* method is Java's closest counterpart to a C++ destructor method.

Java calls the *finalize* method just before it calls the garbage collector to reclaim the object. The purpose of the *finalize* method is to clean up resources that the garbage collector cannot. For example, your *finalize* method may do things such as close files, terminate network connections, delete temporary files, and so on. The following statements illustrate the format of the *finalize* method:

```
protected void finalize()
  {
     // close whatever remaining resources exists
  }
```

If the object is not garbage collected, for whatever reason, Java will not call the object's *finalize* method. In addition, your program has no control over the order in which Java calls the *finalize* method for different objects.

870 FORCING FINALIZE METHODS

As you have learned, before Java's garbage collector frees an object's memory, it calls the object's *finalize* method. As you have also learned, you normally have little control over when Java performs its garbage collection. Depending on your program's processing, there may be times when you will want the system to run the *finalize* method for all the objects the garbage collector has found and plans to discard. In such cases, your programs can call to the *Runtime* class *runFinalization* method, as shown:

```
Runtime mem = Runtime.getRuntime();
mem.runFinalization();
```

871 CHAINING FINALIZERS

As you learned in Tip 869, your programs can define class-based *finalize* methods that Java calls before the Java garbage collector releases the object's memory. As you learned, the purpose of the *finalize* method was to perform class-specific processing. Depending on an object's purpose, you may want the object to call its superclass finalizers. In such cases, you should include a call to the superclass *finalize* method at the end of your finalizer, as shown:

```
super.finalize();
```

872 WHAT IS A RELATIONAL DATABASE?

Either as a programmer or a user, you have probably interacted with a database before. A database is simply a program that makes it easy to store and retrieve data. The data can be numeric, string, or more complex objects, such as a video database. A *relational database* is one implementation of a database—one that organizes data in tables.

A table is made up of rows and columns. In relational database terminology, the table is called a *file*, a row is called a *record*, and a column is called a *field*. One of the features of a relational databases is that you can retrieve the data by its content. For example, assume you have a relational database with a table made up of two fields, one for names and another for phone numbers. To retrieve data by content means that you can simply ask the database to retrieve a phone number for a particular name. You do not have to specify an explicit row and column to get a data element.

The Role Relational Databases Play on the Net   873

As you surf the World Wide Web, one thing will become apparent—there is a lot of information out there. Already, many companies are using relational databases to manage data on their Web sites. For example, most of the major search engines use relational databases. A relational database is an ideal place to store large amounts of information that must be accessible by many users.

If, for example, you need to create an on-line catalog, store locator, or Internet white pages, a relational database is a good choice for storing your data. Today, most relational databases use HTML interfaces. For some applications, HTML does a good job. However, for more complex queries, HTML does not lend itself to a nice interface. Sometimes, programmers must make compromises because of the limitations of HTML. In such cases, programmers can turn to Java, using a Java program to "front end" the database. Using a Java-based program to access the database, you do not have to make any compromises. Java can do just about anything you will need.

For intranets, you can use Java with a relational database back-end to create sophisticated business applications. You can do everything with Java from time-card processing, to document control, to other business applications. However, it will take some time before applications become robust enough to compete head on with current business software applications. Still, part of the excitement over intranets is that intranets use open system standards; thus, there is room for many products from a variety of vendors.

Understanding SQL   874

SQL (Structured Query Language) is a high-level language that hides a particular relational database's implementation. SQL provides a standard database interface. Using SQL, your program is not stuck with one particular vendor's database management system (DBMS). Ideally, you can change from one DBMS to another without changing your application. In reality, however, each vendor's interpretation of SQL is slightly different, so switching from one DBMS to another normally requires some work.

SQL is officially pronounced "ess-cue-ell," but most people call it "sequel." You use SQL to interact with relational databases. There are three main operations that you may want to perform with a database: database manipulation, definition, and administration. The tips this book presents will focus on database manipulation, that is, data retrieval and modification. The other operations, database definition and administration, correspond to database creation and management, which most users are not in a position to perform.

Many books describe SQL in detail. However, the following tips should provide you with enough information to perform simple database operations using Java.

Understanding the SQL SELECT Statement   875

In Tip 872, you learned that a relational database organizes its data in a table. The columns of the table are *fields* and the rows are *records*. When you search a database, you actually search through a table's records for specific fields. To perform a search in SQL, you use the SELECT keyword. A simple definition of the SELECT syntax is as follows:

```
SELECT <select list> FROM <table list> WHERE <search condition>
```

You follow the SELECT keyword with a list of fields that you want to retrieve. The FROM keyword specifies the list of tables that you want to search, and you follow the optional WHERE keyword with a search condition. The SELECT statement can span multiple lines. To demonstrate the SQL query syntax, suppose you have an employee database, as shown in Table 875.

id	name	shift
75	Greg	1
77	Marcia	1
80	Peter	2
82	Jan	2
93	Bobby	3
95	Cindy	3

Table 875 Database table of employees.

If you need to retrieve all the records in a database, you would use the asterisk (*) wildcard character as shown in the following SQL SELECT statement:

```
SELECT * FROM employees
```

In this case, the name of the table is *employees.* The asterisk (*) is a wildcard that directs the database to retrieve every column in the table. Thus, SQL's response to the previous query will be to retrieve every record in the table. The following tips demonstrate more sophisticated query statements.

876 EXAMPLE OF SQL DATABASE RETRIEVAL WITH COLUMN SELECTION

In Tip 875, you learned the syntax for the SQL SELECT statement. Suppose you have the database table shown in Table 875. To extract the employee ids and names from the table, you must specify the fields in the SELECT statement. Selecting specific fields is called *projection.* The following SQL statement demonstrates projection of the *employees* database:

```
SELECT id, name FROM employees
```

In this case, your query will contain the following search results:

```
75 Greg
77 Marcia
80 Peter
82 Jan
93 Bobby
95 Cindy
```

877 EXAMPLE OF SQL DATABASE RETRIEVAL WITH ROW SELECTION

In the previous tips, you learned how to retrieve a specific database field using an SQL SELECT statement. Suppose, for example, you want to retrieve the employee id and name for all third-shift employees. Using the database shown in Table 875, you can perform the following SQL query:

```
SELECT id, name FROM employees WHERE shift = '3'
```

The following is the search results:

```
93 Bobby
95 Cindy
```

EXAMPLE OF THE SQL JOIN OPERATION

878

In the previous tips, you have only searched through a single database table. There may be times, however, when you need to search multiple databases. For example, assume that the phone company uses one database to track the names and phone numbers for people who live in Los Angeles, and a second database tracks people who live in San Diego. If you want to search both cities for all listings with the name "Smith," you might first join the databases. In SQL, a *join* query lets you combine two tables.

As you will learn, the power of relational databases is that you can save data in different tables. For example, you might store employee names, addresses, and phone numbers in one database, and health-care information about employee families in a different database. You can retrieve combinations of data by combining (joining) the tables. For example, in addition to Table 875, suppose you have another table that lists a shift to shift schedule, as shown in Table 878.

Shift	Start	Stop
1	7:30am	3:30pm
2	3:30pm	11:30pm
3	11:30pm	7:30am

Table 878 A database table of work schedules.

Assume that you want to find the start time for each employee. To start, you can join the two tables. The following SQL SELECT statement combines the two tables, and then returns the name and start time for each employee:

```
SELECT name, shift_start
   FROM employees, schedule
      WHERE employee.shift = schedule.shift
```

Given the previous tables, the query would display the following search results:

```
Greg      7:30am
Marcia    7:30am
Peter     3:30pm
Jan       3:30pm
Bobby     11:30pm
Cindy     11:30pm
```

EXAMPLE OF SQL DATABASE UPDATING

879

As you have learned, using a SELECT statement you can retrieve a specific field using SQL. Suppose you want to update a specific field within a specific row. In such cases, you can use the SQL UPDATE statement. A simple definition of the SQL UPDATE syntax is as follows:

```
UPDATE <table> SET <column>=<expression> WHERE <search condition>
```

Notice that you must include the table name after the UPDATE keyword. Also, you must specify a column name and its assigned expression after the SET keyword. Finally, you need to include the search condition after the optional WHERE keyword. To demonstrate the SQL UPDATE syntax, suppose you want to change the name of an employee. You can use the following SQL UPDATE statement:

```
UPDATE employee SET name = 'Johnny' WHERE name = 'Greg'
```

Now, suppose that you want to make a more global change. If you want to change all employees to first shift, you can use the following SQL statement:

```
UPDATE employee SET shift = '1'
```

880   EXAMPLE OF SQL DATABASE INSERTION

You have learned how to query data in a database. You have also learned how to update a record. Sometimes, you will want to insert brand new data into a database. To do this, you can use the INSERT statement. A simple definition of the SQL INSERT syntax is as follows:

```
INSERT INTO <table list> [(<field list>)] VALUES (<data list>)
```

Within the INSERT statement, you follow the INTO keyword by a table name. You follow the table name by an optional list of field names, separated by commas. Finally, you follow the VALUES keyword with a list of data. If you do not specify field names in the optional field list, the database inserts the data into the fields starting from the first column. For example, the following SQL INSERT statement adds an employee name, shift, and id to a database:

```
INSERT INTO employee VALUES ('98', 'Tiger', '1')
```

If you want to add only the name and id of a new employee, without specifying a shift, you would use an SQL statement similar to the following:

```
INSERT INTO employee (id, name) VALUES ('99', 'Fluffy')
```

881   CREATING A TABLE

The previous tips show how to manipulate a database. To begin, you may need to create a table from scratch. To do so, you use the CREATE TABLE statement. On most systems, before you can create a table, you must make sure you have the appropriate privileges.

Normally, you don't create database tables on the fly. Instead, the person who creates a table must be sure to allocate sufficient disk space. In addition, professional database programmers go through a rigorous process to design tables that use disk space efficiently. You should use the following only example to create small tables for brief periods of time. A simple definition of the SQL CREATE TABLE syntax is as follows:

```
CREATE TABLE <table name> ( <column name> <datatype>
                   [, <column name> <datatype>] )
```

Notice that you need to include the table name after the CREATE TABLE keywords. Then, you specify a column name and its data type. For additional columns, you add a comma, followed by another column name and type. You can use the following SQL CREATE TABLE statement to create the employee table:

```
CREATE TABLE employee ( id NUMBER, name CHAR(20), shift NUMBER )
```

WHAT IS JDBC? 882

Programmers and users refer to relational databases as DBMS (DataBase Management System). JDBC which stands for Java Database Connectivity is an Application Program Interface (API) developed by Sun that lets a Java program access a DBMS. The JDBC is currently in alpha release; however, it should be part of the Java 1.1 release. You can think of a DBMS as just another server. JDBC makes it easy to connect to a database, submit SQL statements, and get results. In the following tips, you will learn how to use the JDBC API to access a relational database.

UNDERSTANDING THE JDBC DRIVER 883

JDBC is built in layers. The top layer is the Java application. The Java application uses the JDBC API to communicate with the JDBC Manager. The JDBC Manager relays information from the Java application to a JDBC driver—the third layer. Different DBMS software may have different drivers. The driver can convert SQL statements into a particular DBMS proprietary-access protocol. However, as far as the application programmer is concerned, the API is consistent no matter what the DBMS or JDBC drivers are. The JDBC API and JDBC Manager shield the application from the implementation of the DBMS. Figure 883 shows the layers that make up the JDBC protocol.

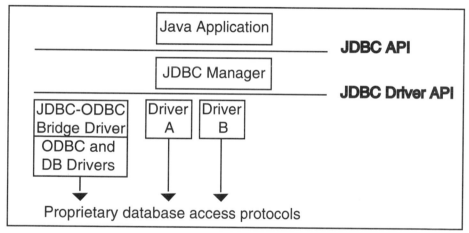

Figure 883 Layers of the JDBC Protocol.

WHAT IS A JDBC SUB-PROTOCOL NAME? 884

As briefly discussed in Tip 883, the JDBC drivers do the low-level work of connecting and communicating with a particular DBMS. The JDBC API is your way of telling the JDBC Manager the operations you want to perform. In turn, the JDBC Manager tells the JDBC Driver what to do.

A JDBC driver accesses a particular DBMS by using a connectivity protocol. JDBC uses a sub-protocol name to distinguish between DBMS connectivity mechanisms. For example, you can use Microsoft's ODBC (open database connectivity) protocol to use Microsoft Access, which is a relational database. JDBC has given ODBC the sub-protocol name *odbc*.

As software companies create new connectivity mechanisms, they must register their sub-protocol with JavaSoft, who assigns a unique name to the software. In this way, the name will not collide with an existing sub-protocol name.

885 UNDERSTANDING HOW APPLET RESTRICTIONS AFFECT JDBC

As you have learned, a Java applet can only connect to the server from which the user downloaded the applet. In addition, some browsers, such as Netscape, do not let an applet write or read local files. Therefore, a database applet cannot write search results to a file or insert data into a database. You must take these restrictions into consideration when you design an applet that is going to access a database.

886 HOW TO SPECIFY A JDBC URL

In previous tips, you learned how to specify a URL within your applets. As you know, a URL points to resources on the Internet. JDBC has come up with its own syntax to point to a database to which you want to connect. The syntax is similar to that of a URL. As you learned, the first part of a URL specifies the protocol prefix. JDBC has defined *jdbc* as a protocol prefix. For example, the following illustrates the syntax of a JDBC URL:

```
jdbc:<sub-protocol>:<subname>
```

In Tip 885, you learned that a sub-protocol specifies how a JDBC Driver connects and communicates with a particular DBMS. The sub-protocol uses the *subname* string to connect to a particular DBMS. The subname syntax varies based on the specified sub-protocol.

887 AN EXAMPLE OF A JDBC URL FOR A ODBC DATABASE

In Tip 886, you learned the syntax for a JDBC URL. For example, the following URL specifies a JDBC database that you can access with ODBC, such as that supported by Microsoft Access:

```
jdbc:odbc:some_database
```

In this example, *some_database* is the name of a local database (the fact that no IP address is specified indicates a local address). When you pass this string to the JDBC to connect to a database, the JDBC Manager will try to find a JDBC driver that supports the ODBC connectivity protocol. The driver uses the name *some_database* to find the database. The Java developers have implemented the JDBC ODBC driver, which is actually a bridge between the JDBC Manager and the ODBC.

888 USING A NAME SERVER IN A JDBC URL

In previous tips, you learned about domain names. Specifically, you learned that a domain name is a string that corresponds to an IP address. The domain name indirection lets you change a server's IP address without having to notify every user. Instead, you simply notify the domain-name server of the change.

The JDBC URL syntax allows for indirection. Within a JDBC URL, you can specify a *name service* that the JDBC will use to get a sub-protocol name and a subname. That way, a Java application does not have a particular hard-coded database. For example, if you must change the database server, you do not have to upgrade your JDBC programs. Instead, you only have to update the name server.

There are many network name services available, such as NIS (Network Information Service). For example, you could have your database administrator set up NIS on a local network. If you change your database server, you only have to update the NIS server with the new sub-protocol and subname string.

CONNECTING TO A DATABASE

889

In previous tips, you have learned how to create a JDBC URL. To connect to a database, you use the *getConnection* method that is defined in the *java.sql.DriverManager* class. The *getConnection* method takes a URL object and two strings as arguments. The two strings specify a database account name and password. Normally, users have different levels of access to a database. The following code demonstrates how to connect to a database that is running on a local machine:

```java
java,net,*;
java.sql.*;


public class databaseTest {

   public static void main (String args[])
     {
        URL url = "jdbc:odbc:trex";
        Connection db = DriverManager.getConnection(url,"mcg","");
     }
   }
```

HOW TO MAKE AN SQL QUERY

890

In Tip 875, you learned the syntax of the SQL SELECT statement. To make a query in JDBC, you first make a SQL statement by creating a *Statement* object. Java defines the *Statement* class within the *java.sql* package. After you create a *Statement* object, you execute an SQL string by calling the *Statement* class *executeQuery* method. The following statements demonstrate the use of the *executeQuery* method:

```java
Statement sq_stmt = db.createStatement();
String sql_str = "SELECT name FROM employees";
ResultSet rs = sq_stmt.executeQuery(sql_str);
```

As you can see, to perform a database operation, you simply pass an SQL string to the *executeQuery* constructor. Notice that the *executeQuery* returns a *ResultSet* object. After you execute an SQL query, you process the result by getting the contents of the *ResultSet* object.

GETTING A QUERY'S RESULTS USING RESULTSET

891

In the previous tip, you learned how to make an SQL query. Some SQL statements return search results. The *executeQuery* method returns a *ResultSet* object that contains search results. To extract the data, you loop through the *ResultSet* object until the *next* method returns *false*. Inside the loop, you call a *getxxx* method, in this case *getString*, to get different fields of the current record. (See the following tip for a description of these methods.) Remember, you have learned that a record is a row and a field is a column of a database table. The following code demonstrates how to get the fields for every record of a table:

```java
java,net,*;
java.sql.*;
```

```
public class databaseTest {

    public static void main (String args[])
      {
        URL url = "jdbc:odbc:trex";
        Connection db = DriverManager.getConnection(url,"mcg","");
        Statement sq_stmt = db.createStatement();

        String sql_str = "SELECT * FROM employees";
        ResultSet rs = sq_stmt.executeQuery(sql_str);

        while (rs.next())
          {
            int id = rs.getInt("id");
            String name = rs.getString("name");
            int shift = rs.getInt("shift");

            System.out.println("ID: " + id);
            System.out.println("Name: " + name);
            System.out.println("Shift: " + shift + "\n");
          }
      }
}
```

892 HOW TO ACCESS DIFFERENT DATA TYPES USING GETXXX

In the previous tip, you learned how to loop through all the records from an SQL query. In the previous tip's example, you called the *getString* method to retrieve the data value of the record's fields. Actually, there are many *getxxx* methods, as shown in Table 892.

ResultSet Class getxxx Methods		
getByte	getNumeric	getTimestamp
getShort	getBoolean	getAsciiStream
getInt	getString	getUnicodeStream
getLong	getBytes	getBinaryStream
getFloat	getDate	getObject
getDouble	getTime	

Table 892 ResultSet class getxxx methods.

The Java developers have chosen to provide a large number of *getxxx* methods. The idea is that it is better to have a large number of methods with descriptive names than a generic method with an argument that modifies the method's behavior.

893 UNDERSTANDING THE READ LEFT-TO-RIGHT AND ONCE-ONLY RULE

In Tip 891, you learned how to retrieve the results of an SQL query. You also learned how to use the *getxxx* methods. Some databases, however, require that you read query search results from left to right. In addition, they may only let you read each field once. These two requirements stem from the low-level implementation of how a driver extracts data from a database. To make your Java JDBC program portable to a variety of databases, you should follow the read left-to-right and only-once rule.

HOW TO DETECT A NULL USING WASNULL 894

In the previous tips, you have learned how to retrieve data from an SQL query. For some fields in relational databases, the *null* is a valid value. You can think of *null* as an empty data element. To detect *null*, you cannot just examine the return value from a *getxxx* method. For example, if a field is an integer, a *null* will cause the *getInt* method return value to be zero. However, zero is a valid numeric value. In fact, when there is a *null*, all numeric types from *getxxx* return zero. In addition, the *getBoolean* method returns *false*.

To detect *null* in these cases, you call the *ResultSet* class *wasNull* method immediately after calling a *getxxx* method. When the value is *null*, the *wasNull* returns a *true*. The following code demonstrates a call to the *wasNull* method:

```
Statement sq_stmt = db.createStatement();
String sql_str = "SELECT id FROM employees";

ResultSet rs = sq_stmt.executeQuery(sql_str);

while (rs.next())
  {
    int id = rs.getInt("id");

    if (rs.wasNull())
      System.out.println("Error: ID is null!");
    else
      System.out.println("ID: " + id);
  }
```

UNDERSTANDING SQL TO JAVA DATA TYPE MAPPING 895

Tip 892 listed the *getxxx* methods which perform an SQL to Java type conversion. However, because you dictate what field is converted by a particular *getxxx* method, you must be careful not to call a *getxxx* method that can't properly convert an SQL data type. For example, it does not make sense to call the *getDate* method for an SQL *FLOAT* field. A bad type conversion will cause the *getxxx* method to throw an *SQLException*. Table 895 shows the SQL to Java type conversion that the JDBC Specification recommends.

SQL Type	Java Type
CHAR	String
VARCHAR	String
LONGVARCHAR	String
NUMERIC	java.sql.Numeric (new type)
DECIMAL	java.sql.Numeric (new type)
BIN	boolean
TINYINT	byte

Table 895 SQL to Java type conversion. (Continued on following page.)

SQL Type	Java Type
SMALLINT	short
INTEGER	int
BIGINT	long
REAL	float
FLOAT	double
DOUBLE	double
BINARY	byte[]
VARBINARY	byte[]
LONGVARBINARY	byte[]
DATE	java.sql.Date (new type)
TIME	java.sql.Time (new type)
TIMESTAMP	java.sql.Timestamp (new type)

Table 895 SQL to Java type conversion. (Continued from previous page.)

896 USING INPUTSTREAM TO READ LARGE DATA ELEMENTS

In the previous tips, you learned how to retrieve individual fields from a database. Sometimes, however, a field may contain a large data element. For example, suppose you have a very large ASCII file stored as a field in a record. You may find it easier to handle the large data in smaller chunks. To let you do so, the JDBC lets you read a field through an *InputStream* stream. In fact, the JDBC provides three methods you can use to get an *InputStream* for a field's data: *getAsciiStream*, *getBinaryStream*, and *getUnicodeStream*. To demonstrate, the following code fragment reads a large ASCII text file from a database:

```
Statement sq = db.createStatement();
String sql_str = "SELECT summary FROM books";


ResultSet rs = sq_stmt.executeQuery(sql_str);
byte[] buffer = new byte[4096];


OutputStream fos = new FileOutputStream("tmp");

while (rs.next())
  {
    InputStream is = rs.getAsciiStream("summary");

    while (true)
      {
        int len = is.read(buffer);

        if (len != 0)
          {
            // do something with data
          }
```

```
        else
          {
              break; // done
          }
       }
  }
```

After you call the next *getxxx* method, the *InputStream* is no longer valid.

USING THE PREPAREDSTATEMENT

897

Within your programs, there may be times when you interact with a database, and you end up making many calls that differ by only a parameter or two. For example, suppose you must update a list of student's test scores within a database. To change the scores, the majority of the UPDATE calls remain unchanged, only changing the name and score for each student. To perform the update more efficiently, you can use the *preparedStatement* method. To start, you create a parameterized UPDATE statement using the *preparedStatement* method. Then, within a loop, you can set the parameters using a *setxxx* method. After you fill in the parameters, you call the *executeUpdate* method. The following program fragment demonstrates the use of the *preparedStatement*:

```
String sql_str = "UPDATE students SET score = ? WHERE name=?";

PreparedStatement ps = db.preparedStatement(sql_str);

for (int i = 0; i < class.length; i++)
  {
     ps.setString(1, class[i].score);
     ps.setString(2, class[i].name);
     int result = stmt.executeUpdate();
  }
```

As you can see from the example, the *preparedStatement* is useful if you have to create a very complex SQL statement and have to execute it multiple times with minor modifications.

UNDERSTANDING THE SETXXX METHOD

898

In the previous tip, you learned how to use a *setxxx* method to set a parameter within a *prepareStatement*. As you know, the *setxxx* method maps a Java type to an SQL type. The JDBC supports many *setxxx* methods, as shown in Table 898.

prepareStatement Class setxxx Methods		
setByte	setNumeric	setTimestamp
setShort	setBoolean	setAsciiStream
setInt	setString	setUnicodeStream
setLong	setBytes	setBinaryStream
setFloat	setDate	setObject
setDouble	setTime	

*Table 898 JDBC prepareStatement class **setxxx** methods.*

899   CHOOSING THE RIGHT SETXXX METHOD

In the previous tips, you learned how to use the *getxxx* method to convert a database field from an SQL type to a Java type. In a similar way, the *setxxx* methods maps a Java type to the SQL type of a field. You should ensure that the conversion makes sense. Table 899 shows the Java to SQL type conversion that the JDBC Specification recommends.

Java Type	SQL Type
String	VARCHAR or LONGVARCHAR
java.sql.Numeric	NUMERIC
boolean	BIT
byte	TINYINT
short	SMALLINT
int	INTEGER
long	BIGINT
float	REAL
double	DOUBLE
byte[]	VARBINARY or LONGVARBINARY
java.sql.Date	DATE
java.sql.Time	TIME
java.sql.Timestamp	TIMESTAMP

Table 899 Java to SQL data type conversion.

900   SETTING A PARAMETER TO NULL

As you have learned, within a database, the *null* value is a valid field value. Sometimes, depending on your database contents, you will want to set a parameter within a prepare statement to *null*. There are two ways that you can do this. First, you can pass *null* as an argument to any of the *setxxx* methods. The JDBC, in turn, will set the data field to *null*. Second, you can call the *setNull* method.

901   UNDERSTANDING DATA TRUNCATION

When you work with databases, there may be times when you will encounter data truncation which occurs when you impose a limit by calling the *Connection* class *setMaxFieldSize* method. If you later read or write data larger than the limit that you set, the JDBC will simply truncate the data to the *maxFieldSize* value, rather than generating an exception or displaying a warning.

Also, a driver may truncate data because of an artificial limit due to the buffer size that the driver uses during low-level communication with the database. In addition, a database may truncate your database because of its implementation. For example, a database designer can place limits on field sizes. If you get a truncation because of a write, it is an error and JDBC will *throw* an *SQLException*. A truncation because of a read is a warning.

UNDERSTANDING THE JAVA.SQL.NUMERIC PACKAGE

 902

As you have learned, values within a database may be numeric. To provide you with better control over fields that represent monetary values, SQL provides the DECIMAL and NUMERIC types. In a similar way, the JDBC developers created a complimentary *Numeric* class. You can access the *Numeric* class from the *java.sql.Numeric* package. The NUMERIC type extends the *Number* class. Therefore, you can perform the usual math operations with the *Numeric* class as you would with any other Java number class.

UNDERSTANDING THE JAVA.SQL.DATE PACKAGE

 903

Within a database, SQL uses DATE fields to store a date value. The Java developers found that the SQL DATE type did not map well to the Java *Date* class that resides within the *java.util.Date* package. As you have learned, the Java *Date* class is a mixture of date and time information. As such, the JDBC developers created a new *Date* class within the *java.sql.Date* package. This new *Date* class only has date information (no time information). Actually, the *java.sql.Date* class extends the *java.util.Date* class, however, it holds the time values of seconds, minutes, and hours to zero.

UNDERSTANDING THE JAVA.SQL.TIME CLASS

 904

The Java developers found that the SQL TIME type did not map well to the Java *Date* class. Specifically, the *Date* class contained in the *java.util.Date* class contains a mix of date and time information. The SQL TIME type, on the other hand, does not have date information. The JDBC developers created a new *java.sql.Time* class that extends the *java.util.Date* class. Specifically, this new class holds the date information in the *Date* superclass to January 1, 1970, the epoch year. The Java time-and-date system stores all date information relative to the epoch year.

UNDERSTANDING THE JAVA.SQL.TIMESTAMP CLASS

 905

Within a Java database, you can use the TIMESTAMP type to store a time with a resolution in nanoseconds. Java's *Date* class, on the other hand, only measures to milliseconds. Therefore, the JDBC developers have made a *java.sql.Timestamp* class. This new *Timestamp* class extends the *java.util.Date* class by adding a *nanosecond* variable to store the time-stamp information.

UNDERSTANDING OBJECT SERIALIZATION

 906

Within your programs, there will be many times when you need to write objects to a stream. For example, if you write a drawing program, you must let users save their work to a file. Before you can write an object to a stream, you must serialize the object. Think of object serialization as breaking down an object into smaller pieces so you can write it to a byte stream. The term for this process is called *object serialization*.

At the time of this writing, the Java developers have released an alpha version of an object serialization library that supports the generic writing of objects to a stream. The library's serialization interface is an extensible methodology that recursively traverses a data structure and serializes objects. In the following tips, you will learn how to create your own methods to serialize an object and write it to a stream. Also, you will learn how to use the serialization library so that, when it becomes available, you will be able to use it.

907 WRITING AN OBJECT TO A STREAM

In Tip 746, you learned that to write an object to a stream, you must serialize the object. To do so, you can create a method inside the object that serializes the object's data. In Tip 681, you learned about the *DataOutputStream*. At that time, you learned that you can use the *DataOuputStream* class methods to write primitive data types to a stream. The following code fragment demonstrates a method that writes an object's variables to a stream:

```java
class myClass {

    int    my_int = 0;
    double my_double = 0.0;
    String  my_string = null;

    public myClass() { }

    public myClass(int i, double d, String s)
      {
        my_int = i;
        my_double = d;
        my_string = s;
      }

    public void writeData(DataOutputStream dos)
      {
        try {
            dos.writeInt(my_int);
            dos.writeDouble(my_double);
            dos.writeUTF(my_string);
          }
        catch (IOException e)
          {
            System.out.println("Error: " + e);
          }
      }
}
```

908 READING AN OBJECT FROM A STREAM

In Tip 907, you learned that to serialize an object, you must create a method that writes the method's data to an output stream. In a similar way, to read an object from a stream, you create a method inside the object that reads the serialized data from the file and loads the object's variables. In Tip 670, you learned about the *DataInputStream*. Specifically, you learned that you can use the *DataInputStream* class methods to read primitive data types from a stream. The following code fragment demonstrates a method that reconstructs a serialized object from a stream:

```java
public void readData(DataInputStream dis)
  {
    try {
```

```
            my_int = dis.readInt();
            my_double = dis.readDouble();
            my_string = dis.readUTF();
        }
    catch (IOException e)
        {
            System.out.println("Error: " + e);
        }
    }
```

WRITING A LIST OF OBJECTS TO A STREAM 909

Often, your programs must save a list of objects to a stream. For example, to write an array of objects to a file, you first save an integer value to the file that specifies the number of objects in the array. Then, you can write each array element to the file. The following program fragment demonstrates how to write an array of objects to a stream:

```
try {
    FileOutputStream fos = new FileOutputStream("tmp");
    DataOutputStream dos = new DataOutputStream(fos);

    dos.writeInt(A.length); // write length of array

    for (int i = 0; i < A.length; i++)
      {
          A[i].writeData(dos);
      }
    }
catch (IOException e)
    {
        System.out.println("Error: " + e);
    }
```

READING A LIST OF OBJECTS FROM A STREAM 910

In the previous tip, you learned how to write a list of objects to a stream. As you may have noticed, the first thing that the program did was to write the list size to the file. Consequently, to reconstruct a list of objects from a stream, the first thing that your program should read is the size of the list. After that, you simply reconstruct the objects as your code reads them from the input stream. The following code demonstrates how read an array of objects from a stream:

```
try {
    FileInputStream fis = new FileInputStream("tmp");
    DataInputStream dis = new DataInputStream(fis);

    int length = dis.readInt(); // read length of array
    B = new myClass[length];
```

```
    for (int i = 0; i < B.length; i++)
      {
        B[i] = new myClass();
        B[i].readData(dis);
      }
    }
  catch (IOException e)
    {
      System.out.println("Error: " + e);
    }
```

911 WRITING A LIST OF OBJECTS OF DIFFERENT TYPES

In the previous two tips, you learned how to read and write a list of objects. However, the technique presented only works if all the objects are of the same type. In Tip 782, you learned how to create an array of different types of objects. In the previous tip, however, your program has no way to know what type of object it will read from the input stream. To get around this, you write the class name of each object before you save it, as the following code demonstrates:

```
Serialize A[] = new Serialize[9];
Serialize B[] = null;

int j;

for (j = 0; j < A.length/2; j++)
  {
    A[j] = new myClass(j, (double) j*1.5, "test" + j);
  }

for (; j < A.length; j++)
  {
    A[j] = new myClass2(j*3);
  }

try {
    FileOutputStream fos = new FileOutputStream("tmp");
    DataOutputStream dos = new DataOutputStream(fos);
    dos.writeInt(A.length);

    for (int i = 0; i < A.length; i++)
      {
        dos.writeUTF(A[i].getClass().getName());
        A[i].writeData(dos);
      }
    }
  catch (IOException e)
    {
      System.out.println("Error: " + e);
    }
```

In this example, you declare the arrays as type *Serialize*. Then, you add objects to the arrays. As it turns out, *Serialize* is an interface that declares the *writeData* and *readData* methods. The objects that you want to add to the array must implement the *Serialize* interface so that you can call the *writeData* and *readData* methods generically. The following code fragment demonstrates the *Serialize* interface. In the tips that follow, you will learn how to serialize objects of different types.

```
abstract interface Serialize {
    public abstract void writeData(DataOutputStream dos);
    public abstract void readData(DataInputStream dis);
}
```

READING A LIST OF OBJECTS OF DIFFERENT TYPES

 912

When you read a list of objects,of different types,from a stream, your program first reads an unknown object from a file. Then, your program must be able to create a corresponding object based on a class name. If your program knows the object's name, your program can call the *Class forName* method to create an object from a specific type of class. Then, you can call the *newInstance* method to create an object of a class from its name. The *newInstance* method is a way to create an object of a class without calling the *new* keyword. The following code fragment demonstrates how to reconstruct a list of objects of different types:

```
try {
    FileInputStream fis = new FileInputStream("tmp");
    DataInputStream dis = new DataInputStream(fis);

    int length = dis.readInt();
    B = new Serialize[length];

    for (int i = 0; i < B.length; i++)
      {
         Class c = Class.forName(dis.readUTF());
         B[i] = (Serialize) c.newInstance();
         B[i].readData(dis);
      }
    }
catch (IOException e)
   {
      System.out.println("Error: " + e);
   }
catch (InstantiationException e)
   {
      System.out.println("Error: " + e);
   }
catch (IllegalAccessException e)
   {
      System.out.println("Error: " + e);
   }
catch (ClassNotFoundException e)
   {
      System.out.println("Error: " + e);
   }
```

As you can see, performing a generic read requires that a program *catch* a lot of exceptions.

913 SERIALIZING OBJECTS THAT REFERENCE OTHER OBJECTS

In the previous four tips, you learned how to read and write objects that only contain primitive data types. The tips did not show you how to handle objects that reference other objects. To write an object that references another object, you simply call the other object's write method. The following code fragment demonstrates this:

```java
class myClass {

    int       my_int = 0;
    double    my_double = 0.0;
    String     my_string = null;
    myClass2   my_class2 = null;

    public myClass() { }

    public myClass(int i, double d, String s, int n)
      {
        my_int = i;
        my_double = d;
        my_string = s;
        my_string = s;
        my_class2 = new myClass2(n);
      }

    public void writeData(DataOutputStream dos)
      {

      try {
          dos.writeInt(my_int);
          dos.writeDouble(my_double);
          dos.writeUTF(my_string);
          my_class2.writeData(dos);
        }
      catch (IOException e)
        {
          System.out.println("Error: " + e);
        }
      }
    }
```

914 DESERIALIZING OBJECTS THAT REFERENCE OTHER OBJECTS

In the previous tips, you learned how to write objects that reference other objects to an output stream. To reconstruct these objects, you simply call the referenced object's data-input methods. The following program fragment, for example, demonstrates how to reconstruct the object that was written to an output stream in the previous tip:

```
public void readData(DataInputStream dis)
  {

   try {
        my_int = dis.readInt();
        my_double = dis.readDouble();
        my_string = dis.readUTF();
        my_class2 = new myClass2();  // create new object
        my_class2.readData(dis);     // load object
      }
   catch (IOException e)
      {
        System.out.println("Error: " + e);
      }
  }
```

UNDERSTANDING PERSISTENCE

 915

There is a problem with the methodology you used in the previous two tips to serialize and deserialize objects. Assume, for example, that your program references an object more than once. The previous tips would generate multiple copies of an object, instead of having two references to the same object. Therefore, the reconstructed object would not be equivalent to the one that you wrote. To get around this, you must write objects only once. Conversely, you must also reconstruct objects only once. The ability to read and write objects that have multiple references is referred to as *persistence*.

SERIALIZING OBJECTS WITH MULTIPLE REFERENCES

 916

When you serialize objects that your program references multiple times, you should write the object only one time. To do this, you can use a hashtable, as discussed in Tip 784, to keep track of the objects that you have written. When you write an object for the first time, you add its reference to the hashtable along with a unique ID value. The ID can be any numeric value. You write the object's class name and ID value to the stream, followed by the object itself. If your program encounters the object a second time, you only write the name of the object and ID value to the stream.

DESERIALIZING OBJECTS WITH MULTIPLE REFERENCES

 917

When you deserialize objects that you have referenced multiple times, you should reconstruct the objects only once. As in previous tips, you should use a hashtable to keep track of objects that you must reconstruct. When you read an object for the first time, you add the reference to the hashtable along with the object's ID value. If you encounter the object a second time, you use the reference that is stored in the hashtable.

USING THE JAVA OBJECT SERIALIZATION LIBRARY

 918

In the near future, you will not have to write your own methods to read and write objects. The Java developers soon plan to release the Java Object Serialization library with which your programs can write and read persistent objects. In the background, the library follows similar steps as those described in the previous tips. However, as with all Java libraries, the developers will hide the underlying code from you. In fact, the library lets your programs write complex data structures to a stream with a single statement. Conversely, your programs can also reconstruct the data structure just as easily. The following tips demonstrate the Object Serialization library.

919 INSTALLING THE OBJECT SERIALIZATION LIBRARY

An alpha version of the Object Serialization library is available at the Javasoft Web site, *http://chatsubo.javasoft.com/ current/serial/*. You will also find an Object Serialization Specification at that Web site. You simply download the library and install it. You should find a help file in the documentation directory for your particular platform. In Tip 37, you learned about the CLASSPATH entry that specifies where Java will locate your class files. The only real trick to initializing object serialization is to make sure that your CLASSPATH entry points to the object serialization class library.

If you install the object serialization library in the same directory as your Java Development Kit (JDK), you won't have to change your CLASSPATH entry. Don't be afraid to install the Object Serialization library in the same directory as the JDK, because the installation only adds files. However, if you install it in a separate directory, it will be easier for you to update the library when Sun releases their next version of the Object Serialization library.

920 UNDERSTANDING THE OBJECTOUTPUTSTREAM

The Object Serialization library defines an *ObjectOutputStream* that you can use to write objects to a stream. To create an *ObjectOutputStream*, you must first create a subclass of the *OutputStream* class. For example, to save an object to a file, you can easily create a *FileOutputStream* object. Because *FileOutputStream* is a subclass of the *OutputStream* class, you can pass the *FileOutputStream* object to the *ObjectOutputStream* constructor, as shown:

```
FileOutputStream fos = new FileOutputStream("tmp");
ObjectOutputStream oos = new ObjectOutputStream(fos);
```

To send an object to another program across a socket connection, you can use the socket's *getOutputStream* to create the *ObjectOutputStream*, as shown:

```
OutputStream os = socket.getOutputStream();
ObjectOutputStream oos = new ObjectOutputStream(os);
```

921 USING THE WRITEOBJECT METHOD

After you have established an *ObjectOutputStream*, you can call the *writeObject* method to serialize the object so you can write it to the stream. If the object is a data structure, the *writeObject* method will correctly write the data structure and all its members, even if those elements themselves are objects. The method will also maintain object persistence. The following code demonstrates a call to the *writeObject* method:

```
try {
    FileOutputStream f = new FileOutputStream("tmp");
    ObjectOutput s = new ObjectOutputStream(f);
    s.writeObject(new Date);
    f.flush();
}
```

```
catch (IOException e)
    {
        System.out.println("Error: " + e);
    }
```

As you can see, the *writeObject* method can *throw* an *IOException*, which your code must *catch*.

UNDERSTANDING THE OBJECTINPUTSTREAM CONSTRUCTOR

922

To read an object from a stream, you have to create an *ObjectInputStream*. To do so, you must first create a subclass of the *OutputStream* class. For example, to read an object from a file, you must create a *FileInputStream* object. Then, you pass the *FileInputStream* object to the *ObjectInputStream* constructor method, as shown:

```
FileInputStream in = new FileInputStream("tmp");
ObjectInputStream oos = new ObjectInputStream(fos);
```

To read an object from another program across a socket connection, you can use the *getInputStream* of the socket class to create the *ObjectInputStream*, as follows:

```
InputStream is = socket.getInputStream();
ObjectInputStream ois = new ObjectInputStream (is);
```

USING THE READOBJECT METHOD

923

In the previous tips, you have learned how to write objects using the *writeObject* method. To reconstruct the object, you simply call the *readObject* method. Again, if the object is a data structure, the *readObject* method will correctly reconstruct it. The method will also maintain object persistence. The following code demonstrates a call to the *readObject* method:

```
try {
    FileInputStream in = new FileInputStream("tmp");
    ObjectInputStream ois = new ObjectInputStream(in);
    Date dates = (Date)s.readObject();
}
catch (IOexception e)
    {
        System.out.println("Error: " + e);
    }
```

As you can see, the *readObject* method can *throw* an *IOException* which your program must *catch*. Also, the *readObject* method returns an *Object* type. You must cast the return value to the object type you expect to receive. For example, the previous code casts the value to a *Date* object.

TESTING THE OBJECT SERIALIZATION LIBRARY

924

The current version of the Object Serialization library does not contain many examples. To gain a better understanding of the library, you can use the following program, *objSerialLibTest.java*:

```
import java.io.*;
import java.util.*;

class myChild {

    Integer data = null;

    public myChild() { }

    public myChild(int i)
      {
         data = new Integer(i);
      }

    public String toString()
      {
         return(new String(data.toString()));
      }
 }

class myParent {

    myChild child1 = null;
    myChild child2 = null;

    public myParent() { }

    public myParent(myChild c)
      {
         child1 = c;
         child2 = c;
      }

    public String toString()
      {
         return(new String("child1="+child1+",child2="+child2));
      }
 }

public class objSerialLibTest {

    public static void main (String args[])
      {
        try {
             // Serialize a multi-ref object from a file
             FileOutputStream f = new FileOutputStream("tmp");

             ObjectOutput s = new ObjectOutputStream(f);
             myParent parent = new myParent(new myChild(42));
```

```
            System.out.println("Before: " + parent);
            s.writeObject(parent);
            f.flush();
        }
        catch (IOException e)
        {
            System.out.println("Error: " + e);
        }

        try {
            // Deserialize a multi-ref object from a file
            FileInputStream in = new FileInputStream("tmp");
            ObjectInputStream s = new ObjectInputStream(in);
            myParent parent = (myParent)s.readObject();
            System.out.println("After: " + parent);
            parent.child1.data = new Integer(99);
            System.out.println("Persistence Test: " + parent);
        }
        catch (IOException e)
        {
            System.out.println("Error: " + e);
        }
        catch (ClassNotFoundException e)
        {
            System.out.println("Error: " + e);
        }
    }
}
```

Initially, the *child1* and *child2* fields of the *myParent* class reference the same object. After the program reads the *myParent* object back from a file, the program performs a test to see if the two fields still reference a single object. When you execute the program, you get the following output:

```
Before: child1=42,child2=42
After:  child1=42,child2=42
Persistence Test:  child1=99,child2=99
```

WHAT IS THE OBJECT SERIALIZATION LIBRARY GOOD FOR? 925

As you have learned, object serialization lets your program read and write objects from and to a stream. You have also learned that client-server network communication in Java is no different than writing to and reading from a file. Therefore, it should be apparent that you can use object serialization to send objects from one program to another, even if the other program is across the world on a different computer. The one requirement is that both programs have the same class definition of the object that is being sent and received.

926 SUMMARY OF APPLET SECURITY RESTRICTIONS

Throughout many of this book's tips, you have had to take applet restrictions into consideration. For example, if an applet is a client program, it can only make a network connection to the host that it came from. If an applet is run under Netscape, there are additional applet restrictions. For example, the restriction that an applet cannot load a local file is a Netscape restriction. Netscape has decided that the Java security model restrictions are not enough to protect its users. If you are writing an applet for the Internet, you must abide by the Netscape restrictions if you want to support the widest audience. Table 926 summarizes some of the more important Java security restrictions.

Action	appletviewer	Netscape from File	Netscape from URL	Java Applet
Connect to foreign host	Yes	No	No	Yes
Connect to local host	Yes	Yes	No	Yes
Read a local file	Yes	No	No	Yes
Write a local file	Yes	No	No	Yes
Delete a file within Java	No	No	No	Yes
Launch external programs	Yes	No	No	Yes
Load a library	Yes	Yes	No	Yes

Table 926 Java security restrictions table.

927 WHY APPLET RESTRICTIONS ARE STRICT

Tip 926 examined the restrictions Java applies to an applet, as well as those imposed by Netscape. The applet restrictions exist to protect a user from accidental "buggy" code and from intentional attacks by hackers. At first glance, you may think the restrictions are harsh. If you look more closely, you will understand why the restrictions are strict. For example, you can see in Table 926 that an applet running from an *appletviewer* cannot delete a file. However, the *appletviewer* lets an applet launch external programs. An applet could execute a standard-operating system command that would, in turn, delete a file. On UNIX, the command is */urs/bin/rm*. Thus, the *appletviewer's* security restrictions are loose. The Java developers really had no choice other than to make their restrictions harsh. Programmers will always find a way to get around loose restrictions.

928 DETECTING IF AN APPLET CAN CONNECT TO A HOST

You have learned that an applet can only make a network connect to the host that it came from. Usually, you will not have to check whether an applet can connect to a specific host. That's because Java generates an exception if an applet violates this restriction. However, if you are writing low-level Java code, such as a driver, you may want to test wether an applet can connect to a particular host. To do this, you can use the *SecurityManger* class *checkConnect* method. The following code demonstrates how to detect if a Java program can connect to a specific host:

```
SecurityManger sm = System.getSecurityManger();

if (security != null)
{
```

```
    try {
        sm.checkConnect("www.jamsa.com", 80);
    }
    catch (SecurityException e)
    {
        // statements
    }
}
```

As you can see, the *checkConnect* method takes a host name and a port number as an argument. If the applet cannot connect to the server, the *checkConnect* method throws the *SecurityException*.

DETECTING IF A JAVA PROGRAM CAN READ A FILE

 929

When a Java program attempts to access a file for which the applet does not have access, Java will generate an exception. To determine if a program has read access to a file, you can use the *Security* class *checkRead* method. If the program cannot access the file, the method throws a *SecurityException*. The following code fragment demonstrates how to test whether or not a program has read access to a file referenced by a file descriptor:

```
SecurityManger  sm = System.getSecurityManger();

if (security != null)
 {
  try {
        sm.checkRead(file_descriptor);
      }
   catch (SecurityException e)
     {
        // statements
     }
 }
```

As you can see, the *checkRead* method takes a file descriptor as an argument. If the applet cannot read from the file, the *checkRead* method throws the *SecurityException*.

DETECTING IF AN APPLET CAN WRITE A FILE

 930

In Tip 929, you learned how to use the *Security* class *checkRead* method to determine if a program has read access to a file. In a similar way, there may be times when you must determine if a program has write access to a file. In such cases, your program can use the *Security* class *checkWrite* method. The following code demonstrates how to determine whether or not a program has write access to a file:

```
SecurityManger  sm = System.getSecurityManger();

if (security != null)
 {
  try {
        sm.checkWrite(file_descriptor);
      }
```

```
   catch (SecurityException e)
    {
       // statements
    }
}
```

As you can see, the *checkWrite* method takes a file descriptor as an argument. If the applet cannot write to the file, the *checkWrite* method throws the *SecurityException*.

931 DEBUGGING JAVA WITH JDB

Sun's Java Developer's Kit, includes a debugger, which you can use, named *jdb*. The Java Debugger, *jdb*, is a command-line debugger for Java classes. It uses the Java Debugger API to provide inspection and debugging of a local or remote Java interpreter. If you are using an Integrated Development Environment (IDE), you may want to investigate the debugging options which that software provides. Although *jdb* is a powerful debugger, the current version does lack a friendly interface.

There are two ways you can use *jdb* for debugging. The most frequently used way is to have *jdb* start the Java interpreter with the class to be debugged. The second way is to attach *jdb* to a Java interpreter that is already running. In the following tips, you will learn how to start and use *jdb*.

Sun Microsystems, Inc., offers a wealth of additional information about the *jdb* debugger. If you need more help with the *jdb* debugger, visit Sun's JavaSoft Web site at *http://www.javasoft.com*. Sun has several examples and references to sites as well as user groups that you may find helpful.

932 STARTING JDB ON A CLASS

As briefly discussed in Tip 931, you direct *jdb* to start the Java interpreter with the class you want to debug. To do so, you invoke the class using *jdb* within the command line. For example, the following command starts the *jdb* debugger using the *MyTest.class* file:

```
C:\> jdb MyTest     <ENTER>
```

When you run *jdb* this way, *jdb* will invoke a second Java interpreter with the necessary parameters. Then, *jdb* will load the specified class and will prepare to execute the first instruction within the class.

933 ATTACHING JDB TO AN ALREADY RUNNING APPLET

As briefly discussed in Tip 931, you can attach *jdb* to a Java interpreter that is already running. For security reasons, Java interpreters can only be debugged if they have been started with the *-debug* option. When you start *java* with the *-debug* option, the Java interpreter prints out a password for *jdb's* use. After you know this password, you can attach *jdb* to a running Java interpreter as follows:

```
C:\> jdb -host <hostname> -password <password>    <ENTER>
```

BASIC JDB COMMANDS

The *jdb* debugger supports several basic commands which Table 934 briefly describes. To get a complete list of the latest commands, you can use *jdb's help* command.

Command	Description
help, or ?	Displays the list of supported commands with a brief description.
print	Calls the object's *toString)* method to display the object's value. You specify classes either by their object ID or by name. If a class is already loaded, you can use a substring, such as *Thread* for *java.lang.Thread*. If a class is not loaded, you must specify its full name, and *jdb* will load the class. The *print* command supports Java expressions, such as *print MyClass.clsVar*.
dump	Displays an object's instance variables. You specify objects by their object ID (a hexadecimal integer). You specify classes either by their object ID or by name. If a class is already loaded, you can use a substring, such as *Thread* for *java.lang.Thread*. If a class is not loaded, you must use its full name, and *jdb* will load the class. The *dump* command supports Java expressions such as *dump 0x12345678.myCache[3].foo*.
threads	Lists the current threads in the default threadgroup, which is normally the first non-system group. Threads are referenced by their object ID, or if they are in the default thread group, with the form *t@<index>*, such as *t@3*.
where	Dumps the stack of either a specified thread or the current thread (which is set with the *thread* command). If that thread is suspended (either because it's at a breakpoint or via the suspend command), local (stack) and instance variables can be browsed with the *print* and *dump* commands. The *up* and *down* commands select which stack frame is current.

*Table 934 Summary of the basic **jdb** commands.*

HOW JDB HANDLES EXCEPTIONS

When an exception occurs for which there is no corresponding *catch* statement, the Java run-time normally dumps an exception trace to the console window and exits. When running under *jdb*, however, *jdb* treats the exception as a non-recoverable breakpoint, and *jdb* stops at the offending instruction. In this case, you can print the instance and local variables to determine the cause of the exception (but only if you compiled the class using the *-g* option).

You may debug specific exceptions by using the *catch* command. The Java debugging facility keeps a list of these exceptions and, when one is thrown, it is treated as if a breakpoint were set on the instruction which caused the exception. The *ignore* command removes exception classes from this list. However, the *ignore* command does not cause the Java interpreter to ignore specific exceptions, only the debugger.

JDB OPTIONS

As you have learned, there are two ways in which you can run *jdb*. As you may expect, there are also two sets of options that you can use. When you use *jdb* in place of the Java command-line interpreter, *jdb* accepts the same options as the *java* command. When you use *jdb* to attach to a running Java interpreter session, *jdb* accepts the following options:

-host <hostname>   Sets the name of the host machine on which the interpreter session that you will attach *jdb* to is running.

-password <password> Lets you connect to the active interpreter session. This is the password printed by the Java interpreter when invoked with the *-debug* option, as discussed in Tip 933.

937   JDB ENVIRONMENTAL VARIABLES

Like the Java compiler and interpreter, the *jdb* debugger uses the CLASSPATH environment variable to locate user-defined classes. Within the CLASSPATH entry, you separate directories with semicolons. For example, the following SET command defines a CLASSPATH entry:

```
SET CLASSPATH=.;C:\users\sample\classes;C:\tools\java\classes  <ENTER>
```

938   INVOKING THE JAVA DEBUGGER USING THE APPLETVIEWER

To invoke the Java debugger using the *appletviewer*, you must specify the *-debug* switch along with the HTML file of the applet you want to debug. When you start the *appletviewer* in debug mode, *jdb* will start as well. The following command starts the *appletviewer* in debug mode:

```
C:\> appletviewer -debug some_file.html   <ENTER>
```

939   DISASSEMBLING A JAVA CLASS WITH JAVAP

If you have a class file which has been compiled, and you do not have the source code for the class, you can use the *javap* disassembler to "reverse compile" the class file and regenerate useful information about the original source. Depending on which options you use, you can view local variables, as well as *private* and *protected* variables and methods in addition to the *public* ones. You can also view the Java bytecodes which make up the executable code part of the class.

If you don't specify any options, *javap* displays the public fields and methods of the classes contained in the file it receives. The *javap* disassembler displays its output to the console window. If you are using an IDE, consult your system documentation to determine how to disassemble your program.

940   JAVAP OPTIONS

As you learned in Tip 939, you can use the *javap* command to disassemble a Java program to produce source code. When you run *javap*, you can tell it exactly which components of the compiled class file you are interested in viewing. There are three basic components that you can disassemble: variables, methods, and bytecodes. Table 940 summarizes the *javap* options.

Option	Description
-l	Displays line and local variable tables.
-p	Displays the private and protected methods and fields of the class, in addition to the public ones.
-c	Displays disassembled code—the instructions that comprise the bytecodes for each of the methods in the class.
-classpath path	Specifies the path *javap* uses to look up classes. Overrides the default or the CLASSPATH environment variable if it is set.

Table 940 Command-line options for javap.

JAVAP ENVIRONMENTAL VARIABLES

941

As you have learned, the *javap* command lets you disassemble a Java class. By default, *javap* uses the CLASSPATH environmental variable to provide the system a path to user-defined classes. However, if you use the *-classpath* command-line switch, you can specify alternate directories. When you use this switch, you must separate directories using colons, as shown:

```
C:\> javap -classpath .:/usr/local/java/classes <ENTER>
```

SECURITY AND JDB

942

The mechanism that allows communications between the debugger and the Java interpreter may have you raising a few questions about Java security. It would appear that if the debugger can intercept a running Java program, other programs may be able to do the same. However, Java was designed so that security is not compromised under normal operation.

The debugger communicates with the Java interpreter via a socket-based, proprietary protocol. This protocol is neither public nor extensible by debugging clients, and it is implemented this way for security reasons.

In addition, the Java Runtime class can only be debugged if you start it with the *-debug* switch. When you start *java* this way, the interpreter prints out a password to be used by the debugger and begins listening on a dynamically allocated port. The debugger must specify the correct host and password before debugging can occur. Also, only one debugger may connect to a Java interpreter while in debug mode.

SAMPLE JDB SESSION

943

To help you get started, this tip provides you with a set of steps you may want to use to familiarize yourself with the *jdb* debugger:

1. Start *jdb* from the command line. You will see a ">" prompt after *jdb* starts, indicating that there is currently no default thread.

2. To list the commands supported by your version of *jdb*, type **help** and press ENTER.

3. To display the list of currently running threadgroups, type **Threadgroups** and press ENTER. The *system* and *main* threadgroups should be present.

4. To display the *system* threadgroup, type **print** followed by the **object_id**, which is the eight digit hexadecimal number following the class name, *java.lang.ThreadGroup*.

5. To list the threads in the current threadgroup, *main*, type **threads** and press ENTER. You should see only one thread currently running in this threadgroup. By typing **threads system**, you can list all the threads.

6. To dump the *main* thread, use the **dump** command with either the thread's **object_id**, or the shorthand notation for threads: **t@<thread_number>** (in this case, **t@1**).

7. To display object variables with the **print** command, print the *main* threadgroup using the command **print t@1.group**. To see how many threads that threadgroup supports, issue the command **print t@1.group.nthreads**.

8. Next, list the currently loaded classes by entering the **classes** command.

9. Use the **dump Thread** command to display a class, its class variables, and constants. Technically, that class name is really *java.lang.Thread*, but *jdb* will make its best guess if you specify a partial name.

10. Dump the *main* thread's stack by specifying **where t@1**. Each line is a separate stack frame whose display varies slightly depending on how that file was compiled. Every line displays the full method name and signature. The first line then shows a stack frame where the class was optimized and has no line number information, while the next line shows one with line numbers.

11. Type **quit** to exit *jdb*.

944 DEBUGGING A SAMPLE APPLET USING JDB

To help you get started, this tip provides the steps you would perform in a typical debugging session with an applet using *jdb*:

1. First, you must start your *appletviewer* using the *-debug* switch and specifying the HTML file that corresponds to the applet you want to debug. When the *appletviewer* starts in debug mode, *jdb* will start also.

2. After *jdb* reports within the console window that the *sun.applet.AppletViewer* class is loaded, you can type **threads** to show which thread is running at startup.

3. Type **run** to start the *appletviewer*.

4. After your applet is displayed, type **threads** again. This time, two threadgroups will be displayed: one for the *appletviewer*, and one for the applet being debugged.

5. To set a breakpoint at a specific method, you can use the **stop at <class:method>** command, where *class* is the name of the class, and *method* is the name of the method. You can also use a line number instead of a method, in which case the debugger will stop at the first bytecode generated by a particular line in a Java source file.

6. When you try to run the method that contains the breakpoint, *jdb* will stop the applet's execution at that breakpoint. To find out the applet's current stack, type **where**. To see that the current thread is at a breakpoint, type **threads**.

7. Use the **step** command to execute individual lines. Type **step** to execute a line in the method. Type **step** again to execute additional lines.

8. To see the path list _jdb_ uses to find source files (by default, the classpath), type **use**. To view the current source, type **list**. You can change the source path list by using **use <path list>**.

9. To examine the previous stack frame, type **up**. To view that frame's source, type **list**. To go back to the original stack frame, type **down**.

10. To see the local variables, type **locals**, or the name of the variable (type **this** to print the object whose method you are stopped in). If you are having trouble seeing local variables, make sure that the applet was compiled using the _-g_ option.

11. To continue execution from the breakpoint, type **cont**.

12. You can clear breakpoints by using the command **clear <class> <line number>**.

If you need more help with the _jdb_ debugger, you may want to access Sun's JavaSoft Web site at _http://www.javasoft.com_. They have several other examples and include references to sites and user groups that you may find helpful.

USING TRACE*INSTRUCTIONS*

945

Within your programs, you can direct the Java Virtual Machine to display a listing of those instructions it executes to the console window. The _Runtime_ class _traceInstructions_ method asks the Java Virtual Machine to display a detailed trace of each instruction as it executes. The virtual machine may ignore this request if it does not support this feature. The destination of the trace output is system dependent. If the _boolean_ argument is _false_, this method causes the Java Virtual Machine to stop performing a detailed instruction trace it is performing. You may use this method in your program, as follows:

```
Runtime mem = Runtime.getRuntime();
mem.traceInstructions(true);     // turn it on
   // other statements
mem.traceInstructions(false);    // turn it off
```

USING TRACE*METHODCALLS*

946

As you learned in Tip 945, using the _Runtime_ class, your programs can request that the Java Virtual Machine display a listing of the instructions it executes to the console window. In a similar way, there may be times when you want to know the methods your program calls. In such cases, your program can use the _Runtime_ class _traceMethodCalls_. The Java Virtual Machine may ignore this request if it does not support this feature. The destination of the trace output is system dependent. If the _boolean_ argument is _false_, this method causes the Java Virtual Machine to stop performing the detailed method trace. You may use the _traceMethodCalls_ method in your program, as follows:

```
Runtime mem= Runtime.getRuntime();
mem.traceMethodCalls(true);     // turn it on
   // other statements
mem.traceMethodCalls(false);    // turn it off
```

947 DEBUGGING USING THE STACK TRACE

When you develop complicated programs, there will be times when you would like to know what the calling order is of the various methods within your program. The calling order, also known as the *stack trace*, helps you to determine which method is calling, and what other methods are calling it.

Your IDE probably has this feature in an optional window. Look for the menu command "Stack trace" or "History window". If you are using the *Java Developer's Kit* (JDK), you can use the *-t* option when running the java interpreter. For example:

```
C:\> java -t MyClass   <ENTER>
```

948 UPDATING AND RELOADING JAVA APPLETS IN NETSCAPE

To increase performance, Netscape Navigator caches Web pages, including Java applets. This means that the page is not reloaded and updated if you leave it and come back moments later. Netscape does provide a *Reload* button to force the Web page to be redrawn. Unfortunately, the *Reload* button does not reload the Java applet. If you are testing your applets, you will want to reload your applet so that changes made to it can be immediately seen. Fortunately, the Netscape Navigator provides a secret way for you to forcibly reload your applet. You can do this by holding down the SHIFT key while clicking on the Reload button.

Some implementations do not have this hidden feature. If your applet does not reload after trying the SHIFT-Reload method, you will have to try another, less convenient method. Select the *Cache* tab after selecting the *Network Preferences* command found in the Options menu. Within the dialog box, there should be two buttons: Clear Memory Cache Now and Clear Disk Cache Now. If you click these, your applet should reload. You may also want to set the *Disk Cache* size to 0 which forces reloads every time. Just remember to restore it when you are done testing your applet.

949 UNDERSTANDING HOW TO BUILD CUSTOM CONTROLS

In the previous tips, you learned how to use many of the AWT controls such as scroll bars, buttons, and checkboxes. Sometimes, you will want to create you own controls. For example, you might want to create a new type of control, or perhaps you just want to spice up the usual controls. To do this, you extend the *Canvas* class. Your control, in turn, will inherit all the methods the various layout classes need from the *Canvas* class. In particular, you should also implement the *minimumSize* and *preferredSize* methods. The various layout classes call these methods to determine how much space to allocate to a control.

If your control will draw images, you should implement the *ImageObserver*. As you have learned, Java uses an *ImageObserver* to load images. For example, the *getHeight* and *getWidth* methods require an *ImageObserver* object as an argument. If your control implements *ImageObserver*, you can pass your control as an argument to various *Image* class methods. The following tips demonstrate how to build various custom controls. They also illustrate the use of many of the tips that you have learned.

UNDERSTANDING THE GRAPHICAL BUTTON 950

As you have learned, the *Button* class creates a button with a text label. Sometimes, however, you will want to create buttons that have pictures instead of text. You are probably familiar with many programs that use pictures on buttons. To do this in Java, you can create a *graphicalButton* class. Figure 950 shows a graphical button in an applet window.

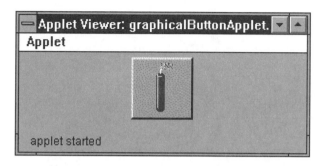

*Figure 950 A graphical **ButtonControl** object.*

At this time, the AWT library does not contain a *graphicalButton* class; you have to create one yourself. The simple implementation of a graphical button uses two images. The code displays one image when the button is up and the other image when the button is down. The code generates an *ACTION_EVENT* when a user presses the button. Actually, the code only generates an *ACTION_EVENT* if the mouse is over the button when the user releases it. That way, the code gives the user a chance to abort the button selection. The following tip demonstrates how to implement a graphical button.

IMPLEMENTING A CUSTOM GRAPHICAL BUTTON 951

In the previous tip, you learned about graphical buttons. The following program, *graphicalButton.java*, shows you how to implement a button object. In this case, the *graphicalButton* class implements the *Canvas* class so you can use it with the standard layout classes. Also, the *graphicalButton* implements the *minimumSize* and *preferredSize* methods so that the layout class can properly size it. The *getHeight* and *getWidth* methods require an *ImageObserver* object; therefore, the *graphicalButton* class also implements the *ImageObserver* interface.

The *graphicalButton* uses the *mouseDown* and *mouseUp* methods to detect when a user clicks on the button. In addition, the *graphicalButton* class uses the *deliverEvent* method to send an *ACTION_EVENT* to its parent. Again, the reason the *graphicalButton* can use these methods is because it extends the *Canvas* class which, in turn, extends the *Component* class—a superclass for all controls.

```
import java.awt.*;
import java.awt.image.*;

public class graphicalButton extends Canvas implements
ImageObserver {

  Image   image_up;
  Image   image_down;
```

```java
String   name;
static boolean DOWN = false;
static boolean UP = true;
boolean is_up = true;

public graphicalButton(String n, Image up, Image down)
 {
   image_up = up;
   image_down = down;
   name = n;
 }

public Dimension minimumSize()
 {
    return(new Dimension(image_up.getWidth(this),
     image_up.getHeight(this)));
 }

public Dimension preferredSize()
 {
   return(minimumSize());
 }

public boolean mouseDown(Event evt, int x, int y)
 {
   is_up = graphicalButton.DOWN;
   repaint();
   return(true);
 }

public boolean mouseUp(Event evt, int x, int y)
 {
   if (inside(x,y))
    {
      deliverEvent(new Event(this, evt.when,
       Event.ACTION_EVENT, x, y, evt.key,
                evt.modifiers, name));
      }
     else
       {
          is_up = graphicalButton.UP;
         repaint();
         System.out.println(name + " Abort");
       }

     return(true);
   }
```

```java
public void setButton(boolean state)
  {
    is_up = state;
    repaint();
  }

public void update(Graphics g)
  {
    paint(g);
  }

public void paint(Graphics g)
  {
    if (is_up)
      g.drawImage(image_up, 0, 0, this);
    else
      g.drawImage(image_down, 0, 0, this);
  }
}
```

USING A CUSTOM GRAPHICAL BUTTON 952

In the previous tip, you learned how to create a graphical button class. The following applet, *graphicalButtonApplet.java*, demonstrates how to create a graphical button within an applet. As you will see, the applet must set the button after processing the *ACTION_EVENT*. The applet can choose to make the button toggle or stay down. Also, the applet uses a *MediaTracker* object to load the images before it creates the buttons. The *graphicalButton* class expects that you have finished loading the images before calling its constructor method:

```java
import java.awt.*;
import java.applet.*;

public class graphicalButtonApplet extends Applet {

    graphicalButton button1 = null;
    Image up = null;
    Image down = null;

    public void init()
      {
        up = getImage(getCodeBase(), "up.gif");
        down = getImage(getCodeBase(), "down.gif");

        MediaTracker tracker = new MediaTracker(this);
        tracker.addImage(up, 0);
        tracker.addImage(down, 0);

        try {
            tracker.waitForAll();
          }
```

```
            catch(InterruptedException e)
              {
                  System.out.println("Interrupted: " + e);
              }


            button1 = new graphicalButton("Dynamite1", up, down);
            add(button1);
        }

    public boolean action(Event evt, Object obj)
        {
            if (evt.target instanceof graphicalButton)
              {
                String label = (String)obj;

                if (label.equals("Dynamite1"))
                  {
                      button1.setButton(graphicalButton.UP);
                  }

                System.out.println(label);
                return true;
              }
            return false;
        }
    }
```

953   UNDERSTANDING CUSTOM CONTROLS IN APPLETS

In the previous tip, you learned how to use a custom graphical button in an applet. You should understand that there are penalty applications for using controls that draw images in applets. Assume, for example, a browser downloads an applet from across a network. If the applet uses controls that require images, the applet's download time increases. If the controls make up the interface of an applet, the browser must download all the images before the user can do anything with the applet. Therefore, to manage your applet's download time, you should be careful of how many images you use in an applet interface.

If you use the controls in the AWT library, users do not have to download the classes for those controls with your applet. The AWT package already resides on each user's machine. In addition, using a custom control increases the size of an applet. You may decide that a custom control is worth the penalty in download time. You should make a conscious effort to evaluate the value of each custom control.

954   UNDERSTANDING THE TRACKBALL CONTROL

A trackball is not a standard control, however, it can be an intuitive interface for some applications. For example, if you want to allow a user to rotate a 3-D object, a trackball makes a nice interface. Simply, a trackball behaves like a *mouseDrag* operation that must start on an icon that looks like a trackball. Figure 954 shows a trackball control inside an applet window.

Figure 954 A trackball control.

To implement a *Trackball* object, you extend the *Canvas* class and implement the *ImageObserver* as you did for the *graphicalButton* in Tip 951. You still need the *ImageObserver* because the *Trackball* uses images to make a simple animation.

Instead of creating an event, the *Trackball* class uses an interface to tell its parent when events happen. As you have learned, Java duplicates the benefits of multiple inheritance without many of the problems. In addition, you learned that interfaces are how Java creates the equivalent of a C programming language callback function. The following tip demonstrates how to create a *Trackball* control.

IMPLEMENTING A CUSTOM TRACKBALL CONTROL 955

In the previous tip, you learned about a *Trackball* control. The following program, *Trackball.java*, shows you how to implement one. You can later use the *Trackball* class within your applets, as shown in the following tips.

```
import java.awt.*;
import java.awt.image.*;

public class Trackball extends Canvas implements ImageObserver {

    Image frames[];
    trackballCalls calls = null;
    int x_start;
    int y_start;
    int index = 0;

    public Trackball(Image f[], trackballCalls c)
      {
        frames = f;
        calls = c;
      }

    public Dimension minimumSize()
      {
        return(new Dimension(frames[0].getWidth(this),
          frames[0].getHeight(this)));
      }
```

```java
    public Dimension preferredSize()
      {
        return(minimumSize());
      }


    public boolean mouseDown(Event evt, int x, int y)
      {
        x_start = x;
        y_start = y;
        calls.start();
        return(true);
      }


    public boolean mouseDrag(Event evt, int x, int y)
      {
         calls.drag(x-x_start, y-y_start);
        index++;
        repaint();
        return(true);
      }


    public boolean mouseUp(Event evt, int x, int y)
      {
        calls.stop();
        index = 0;
        repaint();
        return(true);
      }


    public void update(Graphics g)
      {
        paint(g);
      }


    public void paint(Graphics g)
      {
        g.drawImage(frames[index % frames.length], 0, 0, this);
      }
}
```

956   UNDERSTANDING THE CUSTOM TRACKBALL INTERFACE

In Tip 955, you learned how to create a *Trackball* class. The *Trackball* class constructor method requires a *trackballCalls* object. Actually, *trackballCalls* is an interface. The class that creates a *Trackball* object must pass an object that implements the *trackballCalls* interface as an argument to the *Trackball* constructor. The following code implements the *trackballCalls* interface:

```
public abstract interface trackballCalls {
   public abstract void start();
   public abstract void drag(int x, int y);
   public abstract void stop();
}
```

The *Trackball* class calls the *trackballCalls* class *start* method when the user first clicks on the *Trackball* control. When the user drags the mouse, the *Trackball* calls the *trackballCalls* object's *drag* method. Finally, when the mouse is released, the *Trackball* calls the *trackballCalls* object's *stop* method.

USING THE CUSTOM TRACKBALL CONTROL 957

In the previous tips, you have learned how to create a *Trackball* control. The following program, *myTrackBalls.java*, demonstrates how to use a *Trackball* control within an applet. As you will see, *myTrackballCalls* implements the *trackballCalls* interface. When the user uses the *Trackball* object, the *Trackball* calls the various *myTrackballCalls* methods.

```
import java.awt.*;
import java.applet.*;

class myTrackballCalls implements trackballCalls {

   public void start()
     {
        System.out.println("Trackball Start");
     }

   public void drag(int x, int y)
     {
        System.out.println("Trackball Drag " + x + ", " + y);
     }

   public void stop()
     {
        System.out.println("Trackball Stop");
     }
   }

 public class trackballApplet extends Applet {

    Trackball trackball = null;

    public void init()
      {
         Image track[] = new Image[3];
         track[0] = getImage(getCodeBase(), "track0.gif");
         track[1] = getImage(getCodeBase(), "track1.gif");
         track[2] = getImage(getCodeBase(), "track2.gif");
```

```
MediaTracker tracker = new MediaTracker(this);
tracker.addImage(track[0], 0);
tracker.addImage(track[1], 0);
tracker.addImage(track[2], 0);

try {
    tracker.waitForAll();
  }
catch (InterruptedException e)
  {
    System.out.println("Interrupted: " + e);
  }

trackball = new Trackball(track, new myTrackballCalls());
add(trackball);
  }
}
```

958 UNDERSTANDING THE GAUGE CONTROL

A gauge is a simple control which provides feedback to a user. For example, the car's speedometer is a gauge. A car's driver can look at the speedometer and quickly determine the car's speed. Within a Java applet, you can use a *Gauge* control in a similar manner. For example, you can use a *Gauge* control to show the number of threads that a program is running. A *Gauge* control is especially good at showing how close a parameter is to a specific limit. Figure 958 shows a *Gauge* control inside an applet window.

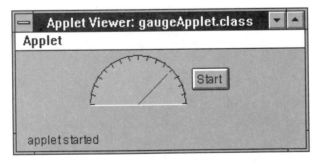

*Figure 958 A **Gauge** control.*

959 BUILDING A CUSTOM GAUGE CONTROL

Tip 958 briefly describes *Gauge* controls. Within a Java program, you implement a *Gauge* much like you would implement a *Trackball*. The following code implements a *Gauge* control that does not draw any images; therefore, it does not have to implement the *ImageObserver* interface. However, just like the previous controls, the *Gauge* control has to extend the *Canvas* class so that you can add it to the various layout classes. The following code demonstrates how to implement a custom *Gauge* control in Java:

```java
import java.awt.*;
import java.awt.image.*;

public class Gauge extends Canvas {

    int     width;
    int     height;
    float   mag;
    int     progress = 0;
    int     x_coord = 0;
    int     y_coord = 0;

    static Color   back_color = new Color(207,207,255);
    static final double toRad = Math.PI;

    public Gauge(int w)
      {
        width = w;
        height = w/2;
        mag = (float) height - 7;
      }

    public Dimension minimumSize()
      {
         return(new Dimension(width+1,height+2));
      }

    public Dimension preferredSize()
      {
         return(minimumSize());
      }

    public void setProgress(float percent)
      {
        float angle = percent * (float)Math.PI;

        int y = Math.round(mag * (float)Math.sin(angle));
        angle = (float)Math.PI - angle;
        int x = Math.round(mag * (float)Math.cos(angle));

        Graphics g = getGraphics();
        g.setColor(back_color);         // erase old hand
          g.drawLine(width/2,height,width/2+x_coord,height-y_coord);

        x_coord = x;
        y_coord = y;
```

```java
            g.setColor(Color.darkGray); // draw new hand
             g.drawLine(width/2,height,width/2+x_coord,height-y_coord);
          g.dispose();
    }

  public void drawMarks(Graphics g)
    {
        g.setColor(Color.black);

        for (float p = 0.0f; p < 1.25f; p+=0.0625f)
          {
            float a = p * (float)Math.PI;

            int y1 = Math.round((float) (height -4)*
                (float) Math.sin(a));

            int y2 = Math.round((float) height *
                (float)Math.sin(a));

            a = (float) Math.PI - a;

            int x1 = Math.round((float)(height -4) *
                (float) Math.cos(a));

            int x2 = Math.round((float) height *
                (float) Math.cos(a));

             g.drawLine(width/2+x1, height-y1, width/2+x2,
                height-y2);
          }
    }

  public void update(Graphics g)
    {
      paint(g);
    }

  public void paint(Graphics g)
    {
      g.setColor(back_color);
      g.fillArc(1,1, width-2, 2*height-2, 0, 180);
      g.setColor(Color.darkGray);
       g.drawLine(width/2,height,width/2+x_coord,height-y_coord);
      g.setColor(Color.black);
      g.drawArc(0,0, width-1, 2*height-1, 0, 180);
      g.setColor(Color.white);
       g.drawLine(0,height+1,width-1,height+1);
      drawMarks(g);
    }
}
```

In the previous tip, you learned how to implement a custom *Gauge* class. The following program, *gaugeApplet.java*, demonstrates how to use the custom *Gauge* control in an applet:

```java
import java.awt.*;
import java.applet.*;

public class gaugeApplet extends Applet {

    Gauge gauge = null;
    Button button = null;

    public void init()
      {
         gauge = new Gauge(100);
         add(gauge);

         button = new Button("Start");
         add(button);
      }

    public boolean action(Event evt, Object obj)
      {
         if (evt.target instanceof Button)
           {
              String label = (String)obj;

              if ( label.equals("Start"))
                {
                   gauge.setProgress(0f);

                   for (float p = 0.0f; p < 1.01f; p+=0.01f)
                     {
                        try {
                             Thread.sleep(25);
                             gauge.setProgress(p);
                          }
                        catch(InterruptedException e)
                          {
                             System.out.println("Interrupted: " + e);
                          }
                     }
                }
           return true;
           }
        return false;
      }
}
```

961 UNDERSTANDING THE SLIDER CONTROL

A *Slider* control is very similar to a scrollbar. However, you can make a *Slider* control look much different. For example, most sliders look like a bead on a rod rather than a thumb in a groove. You may want to do this simply for cosmetic reasons, or you may wish to make a special slider for a specific task. Figure 961 shows a *Slider* control inside an applet window.

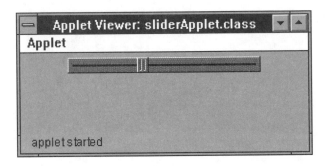

Figure 961 *The **Slider** control.*

A *Slider* control can behave differently than a scroll bar. For example, you could have a slider that creates events as a user moves the control. You can then make real-time updates to the screen. The following tip will show you how to implement a horizontal slider.

962 BUILDING A CUSTOM SLIDER CONTROL

In Tip 961, you examined a *Slider* control. In this tip, you will implement such a control. The *Slider* class extends the *Canvas* class and implements the *ImageObserver* like the other custom controls that draw images, such as *Trackball* or a graphical button. The following code, *Slider.java*, shows how to implement a custom slider:

```java
import java.awt.*;
import java.awt.image.*;

public class Slider extends Canvas implements ImageObserver {

    sliderCalls calls = null;
    int min = 0;
    int max = 0;
    int pixels = 0;
    int bead_loc;
    int offset;
    float percent = 0.0f;
    Image bead = null;
    Image rod = null;
    Image erase = null;
    boolean slide = false;
    Rectangle bead_rect;
```

```
public Slider(Image b, Image e, Image r, sliderCalls c)
  {
    bead = b;
    rod = r;
    erase = e;
    calls = c;

    min = bead.getWidth(this)/2;
    pixels = rod.getWidth(this)-2 * min - bead.getWidth(this);
    max = pixels + min;
    bead_rect = new Rectangle(0,0,2*min,bead.getHeight(this));
    bead_loc = pixels/2 + min;
  }

public Dimension minimumSize()
  {
    return(new Dimension(rod.getWidth(this),
      rod.getHeight(this)));
  }

public Dimension preferredSize()
  {
    return(minimumSize());
  }

public boolean mouseDown(Event evt, int x, int y)
  {
    bead_rect.move(bead_loc,0);

    if (bead_rect.inside(x,y))
     {
       calls.start();
       slide = true;
       offset = x - bead_loc;
     }

    bead_rect.move(-bead_loc,0);
    return(true);
  }

public boolean mouseDrag(Event evt, int x, int y)
  {
    if (slide)
     {
       int new_loc = x - offset;

       if (new_loc < min)
         new_loc = min;

       if (new_loc > max)
         new_loc = max;
```

```java
            if (new_loc != bead_loc)
              {
                  eraseBead(bead_loc, new_loc);
                  drawBead(new_loc);
                  percent = ((float)(new_loc - min))/(float)pixels;
                  calls.drag(percent);
                  bead_loc = new_loc;
              }
          }
        return(true);
    }

public boolean mouseUp(Event evt, int x, int y)
  {
     if (slide)
       {
           calls.stop();
           slide = false;
       }
     return(true);
  }

public void eraseBead(int old, int loc)
  {
      Graphics g = getGraphics();

      if (old < loc)   // avoid flicker
        g.clipRect(old, 0, loc - old, bead_rect.height);
      else
        {
           int left = loc + bead_rect.width;
           g.clipRect(left, 0, old - loc, bead_rect.height);
        }

      g.drawImage(erase, old, 0, this);
      g.dispose();
  }

public void drawBead(int x)
  {
     Graphics g = getGraphics();
     g.drawImage(bead, x, 0, this);
     g.dispose();
  }

public void update(Graphics g)
  {
     paint(g);
  }
```

```
    public void paint(Graphics g)
      {
        g.drawImage(rod, 0, 0, this);
        g.drawImage(bead, bead_loc, 0, this);
      }
  }
```

UNDERSTANDING THE SLIDER BEAD ANIMATION

 963

In the previous tip, you learned how to implement a custom *Slider* class. As the Slider class moves its bead, it calls the *eraseBead* method, as shown:

```
  public void eraseBead(int old, int loc)
    {
      Graphics g = getGraphics();

      if (old < loc) // avoid flicker
        g.clipRect(old, 0, loc - old, bead_rect.height);
      else
        {
          int left = loc + bead_rect.width;
          g.clipRect(left, 0, old - loc, bead_rect.height);
        }

      g.drawImage(erase, old, 0, this);
      g.dispose();
    }
```

At first, you may think the method seems overly complex, but a basic implementation of the *eraseBead* method simply draws the *Slider's* background where the bead was previously located. However, to create a smooth animation, you should avoid flicker as much as possible. Flicker usually happens when a program draws two different bead positions to one area of the screen in succession. When the user moves a slider a half-bead length, the new bead position and the old bead position overlap. If you erase the old bead area and draw a new one, the portion where the two positions overlap will flicker. The code in the *eraseBead* method avoids the flicker by erasing the old bead area only where the new and old bead positions do not overlap.

UNDERSTANDING THE CUSTOM SLIDER INTERFACE

 964

Like the custom *Trackball* control, the *Slider* class uses an interface to pass events back to its parent. The following code demonstrates the *sliderCalls* interface:

```
  public abstract interface sliderCalls {
     public abstract void start();
     public abstract void drag(float percent);
     public abstract void stop();
  }
```

The *Slider* will call the *start* method when the user presses the mouse button down on the *Slider* bead. When the user slides the bead, the *Slider* calls the *drag* method. The slider passes to the *drag* method a percentage that represents the position of the bead on the slider. Finally, the *Slider* calls the *stop* method when the user releases the mouse.

965 USING THE CUSTOM SLIDER CONTROL

In the previous tips, you have learned how to implement a custom *Slider* class. The following program, *mySliderCalls.java*, demonstrates how to use a *Slider* object within an applet:

```java
import java.awt.*;
import java.applet.*;

class mySliderCalls implements sliderCalls {

    public void start()
      {
        System.out.println("Slider Start");
      }

    public void drag(float percent)
      {
        System.out.println("Slider Drag " + percent);
      }

    public void stop()
      {
        System.out.println("Slider Stop");
      }
  }

public class sliderApplet extends Applet {

    Slider slider = null;

    public void init()
      {
        Image bead = getImage(getCodeBase(), "bead.gif");
        Image rod = getImage(getCodeBase(), "rod.gif");
        Image erase = getImage(getCodeBase(), "erase.gif");

        MediaTracker tracker = new MediaTracker(this);
        tracker.addImage(bead, 0);
        tracker.addImage(rod, 0);
        tracker.addImage(erase, 0);

        try {
           tracker.waitForAll();
         }
```

```
     catch (InterruptedException e)
       {
          System.out.println("Interrupted: " + e);
       }

     slider = new Slider(bead, erase, rod,
          new mySliderCalls());
     add(slider);
   }
 }
```

UNDERSTANDING THE PROGRESS METER

 966

Many times, your programs must perform time-consuming tasks. For example, to download large images from across the Internet takes time. To give the user feedback on how the operation is moving along, you can use a progress meter. A progress meter shows the user how much longer it is going to take the program to finish an operation. You have probably seen progress meters in other programs. Just about every set-up program uses one. Most browsers, for example, use a progress meter to provide feedback on how long it will take to download a page. The following tip demonstrates how to create a custom progress meter.

BUILDING A CUSTOM PROGRESS METER

 967

Within a Java program, you implement a progress meter much like you implement a *Gauge* control. The progress meter implemented by the code below does not draw any images; therefore, it does not have to implement the *ImageObserver* interface. However, just like the previous controls, the *progressMeter* extends the *Canvas* class so that you can use it with the various AWT layout classes. The following code demonstrates how to implement a custom *progressMeter* class in Java:

```
import  java.awt.*;
import  java.awt.image.*;

public class progressMeter extends Canvas implements ImageObserver
{

   int     width;
   int     height;
   int     progress = 0;

   Color    back_color = new Color(207,207,255);

   public progressMeter(int w)
     {
       width = w - 1;
       height = 12;
     }
```

```java
    public Dimension minimumSize()
      {
         return(new Dimension(width+1,height+1));
      }


    public Dimension preferredSize()
      {
         return(minimumSize());
      }


    public void setProgress(float percent)
      {
         progress = (int)(percent * (width - 2));
         repaint();
      }


    public void update(Graphics g)
      {
         paint(g);
      }


    public void paint(Graphics g)
      {
          g.setColor(Color.darkGray);        // draw progress
          g.fillRect(1,1,progress,height - 2);
          g.setColor(back_color);            // draw background
          g.fillRect(1+progress, 1, width-2-progress, height-2);
          g.setColor(Color.white);           // draw bottum,right edge
          g.drawLine(width-1,1,width-1,height-1);
          g.drawLine(1,height-1,width-1,height-1);
          g.setColor(Color.black);           // draw top,left edge
          g.drawLine(0,0,width-1,0);
          g.drawLine(0,0,0,height-1);
      }
 }
```

968 USING THE CUSTOM PROGRESS METER

In the previous tip, you learned how to implement a custom *progressMeter* class. The following program, *progressMeterApplet.java*, demonstrates how to use the custom progress meter in an applet:

```java
import java.awt.*;
import java.applet.*;


public class progressMeterApplet extends Applet {
```

```
    public void init()
      {
          progressMeter meter = new progressMeter(200);
          add(meter);

          Button button = new Button("Start");
          add(button);
      }


    public boolean action(Event evt, Object obj)
      {
          if (evt.target instanceof Button)
            {
               String label = (String)obj;

               if (label.equals("Start"))
                 {
                    meter.setProgress(0.0f);

                    for (float p = 0.0f; p < 1.01f; p+=0.01f)
                       {
                          try {
                              Thread.sleep(25);
                              meter.setProgress(p);
                          }
                          catch (InterruptedException e)
                            {
                                System.out.println("Interrupted: " + e);
                            }
                       }
                 }
            }
          return true;
      }
}
```

UNDERSTANDING A SIMPLE 2-D DRAWING PROGRAM 969

To illustrate many of the things that you have learned, the following tips will build a very simple 2-D drawing program. A 2-D drawing program must provide a toolbar from which a user can select various types of drawing objects. To do this, you can use the AWT library to create a toolbar. Also, the program must be able to store the various objects that a user draws, so that it can update the drawing area. To store the objects, you can use the *Vector* class. A 2-D drawing program must also be able to interactively show users what they are drawing. Again, you can use the drawing methods of the AWT library to provide users with interactive feedback.

970 *IMPLEMENTING A FLOATING TOOLBAR CLASS*

A floating toolbar is simply a window with a set of buttons. The buttons are *radio buttons* because a user can only select one of them at a time. Like a car radio, if you press a new button, the last selected button will pop out. The toolbar saves its current setting in a *mode* field. If another window object uses the *floatToolBar* class, the program only has to call the *getMode* method to determine what the current selected button is. The following code demonstrates how to implement a floating toolbar:

```java
import java.awt.*;
import java.awt.image.*;

public class floatToolBar extends Frame {

    int mode = 0;
    graphicalButton buttons[] = null;
    String id[] = null;

    floatToolBar(String title, String labels[], String files[][])
      {
        super(title);
        id = labels;
        buttons = new graphicalButton[labels.length];
        Image imgs[][] = new Image[files.length][2];
        Toolkit tk = Toolkit.getDefaultToolkit();

        for (int i = 0; i < files.length; i++)
          {
            imgs[i][0] = tk.getImage(files[i][0]);
            imgs[i][1] = tk.getImage(files[i][1]);
          }

        MediaTracker tracker = new MediaTracker(this);

        for (int i = 0,id = 0; i < imgs.length; i++)
          {
            tracker.addImage(imgs[i][0], id++);
            tracker.addImage(imgs[i][1], id++);
          }

        try {
           tracker.waitForAll();
           }
        catch (InterruptedException e)
          {
            System.out.println("Interrupted: " + e);
          }

        setLayout(new GridLayout(id.length, 1));
```

```
        for (int i = 0; i < id.length; i++)
          {
              buttons[i] = new graphicalButton(id[i],imgs[i][0],
                                      imgs[i][1]);
              add(buttons[i]);
          }

       buttons[0].setButton(graphicalButton.DOWN);
      pack();
      show();
   }

   public int getMode()
   {
      return(mode);
   }

   public boolean action(Event evt, Object obj)
   {
       if (evt.target instanceof graphicalButton)
         {
             String label = (String) obj;

             for (int i = 0; i < id.length; i++)
               {
                   if (label.equals(id[i]))
                   {
                       if (mode != i)
                           buttons[mode].setButton(graphicalButton.UP);
                       mode = i;
                       break;
                   }
               }
         }
       return true;
   }
}
```

USING THE FLOATING TOOLBAR CLASS

 971

In the previous tip, you learned how to create a floating-toolbar class. The following code demonstrates how to create a *toolbar* object that has two buttons: one to select an arrow tool and another to select a rectangle tool.

```
String labels[] = {"Select", "Rectangle"};

String gifs[][] = {{"sel_up.gif", "sel_down.gif"},
                   {"rect_up.gif", "rect_down.gif"}};
```

```
int SELECT = 0;
int RECTANGLE = 1;

toolbar = new floatToolBar("Tools", labels, gifs);
```

To check the state of the *toolbar* object, you call the *toolbar* class *getMode* method, as the following code demonstrates:

```
if (toolbar.getMode() == RECTANGLE)
    System.out.println("Mode equals Rectangle!");
```

972 IMPLEMENTING A BOUNDBOX CLASS

If you have worked with graphics-based programs, you have probably seen a bound-box before. Just about every graphical drawing program uses an XOR-mode box to let the user select an area on the screen. You have learned that when you draw a line in XOR mode one time, you get a line. If you draw the line in XOR mode a second time, you erase the line. Within your programs, you can use XOR mode to perform fast interactive drawing. Using XOR mode, you do not have to worry about overriding complex graphics. In a 2-D drawing program, for example, you can use a bound-box to allow the user to interactively draw rectangles. The following program code demonstrates how to implement a *boundBox* class which draws the box using XOR mode:

```java
import java.awt.*;

public class boundBox {

    static int x_anchor, y_anchor;
    static int x_mouse, y_mouse;

    public static void mouseDown(Component c, int x, int y)
      {
        x_anchor = x;
        y_anchor = y;
        x_mouse = x;
        y_mouse = y;

        drawbox(c); // draw box
      }

    public static Rectangle mouseUp(Component c, int x, int y)
      {
        drawbox(c); // erase box

        int xc = Math.min(x_anchor, x);
        int yc = Math.min(y_anchor, y);

        if ((x == x_anchor) || (y == y_anchor))
          return(null); // invalid
        else
            return(new Rectangle(xc, yc, Math.abs(x-x_anchor),
                                  Math.abs(y-y_anchor)));
      }
```

```
public static void mouseDrag(Component c, int x, int y)
  {
    drawbox(c); // erase box

    x_mouse = x;
    y_mouse = y;

    drawbox(c); // draw box
  }

public static void drawbox(Component c)
  {
    Graphics g = c.getGraphics();
    g.setXORMode(Color.lightGray);

    int x = Math.min(x_anchor, x_mouse);
    int y = Math.min(y_anchor, y_mouse);

    g.drawRect(x, y, Math.abs(x_mouse-x_anchor),
               Math.abs(y_mouse-y_anchor));
    g.dispose();
  }
}
```

DRAWING A RECTANGLE WITH THE BOUNDBOX CLASS   973

In the previous tip, you learned how to create a *boundBox* class. To use the *boundBox* class, your program calls the class methods when it receives mouse events. The *boundBox* class will return a *RECTANGLE* object for a *mouseUp* event, provided the user has drawn a valid box. The following code demonstrates how to use the *boundBox* class to interactively draw a rectangle.

```
public boolean mouseDown(Event evt, int x, int y)
  {
    if (toolbar.getMode() == RECTANGLE)
    {
      boundBox.mouseDown(this, x, y);
    }
    return(true);
  }

public boolean mouseDrag(Event evt, int x, int y)
  {
    if (toolbar.getMode() == RECTANGLE)
    {
      boundBox.mouseDrag(this, x, y);
    }
    return(true);
  }
```

```
public boolean mouseUp(Event evt, int x, int y)
  {
    if (toolbar.getMode() == RECTANGLE)
     {
        Rectangle r = boundBox.mouseUp(this, x, y);

        if (r != null)
         {
            rects.addElement(r); // insert into datastructure
            repaint(r.x, r.y, r.width+1, r.height+1);
         }
     }
    return(true);
  }
```

When the user is finished drawing a rectangle, the program adds a *Rectangle* object to a *Vector* object.

974 IMPLEMENTING A GRIDAREA CLASS

Within a 2-D drawing program, it is often convenient to draw a grid within which users can place objects precisely. When a user moves an object around a grid, at least one vertex or, perhaps, the center of the object, always stays on the grid. To draw a grid, you should first prepare the grid behind the scenes. That way you can draw the grid on the screen quickly, rather than drawing the grid's coordinates in front of the user's eyes. The following code demonstrates how to implement a *gridArea* class that you can use in a drawing program:

```
import java.awt.*;
import java.awt.image.*;

public class gridArea extends Canvas implements ImageObserver {

    int width, height;
    Image grid;
    int spacing = 5;
    int half = spacing/2;

    public gridArea(Component c, int x, int y, int size)
      {
        super();

        width = x;
        height = y;
        spacing = size;

        grid = c.createImage(x,y);
        Graphics g = grid.getGraphics();
        g.setColor(Color.white);
```

```
            g.fillRect(0,0,width,height);
            g.setColor(Color.black);

            for (int j = 0; j < height; j += spacing)
              for (int k = 0; k < width; k += spacing)
                  g.drawLine(k,j,k,j);

            g.dispose();
        }

    public int snap(int x)
      {
          return((x + half)/spacing * spacing);
      }

    public void draw(Graphics g)
      {
          g.drawImage(grid, 0, 0, this);
      }
    }
```

USING THE gridArea CLASS TO DRAW A GRID  975

In Tip 974, you learned how to create a *gridArea* class. To draw a grid using the *gridArea* class, you simply create a *gridArea* object with the current window size. Then, inside the *paint* method, you draw the grid before any other objects. The following code demonstrates how to draw a grid that uses five-pixel spacing:

```
public void paint(Graphics g)
  {
    if (grid == null)
      {
          grid = new gridArea(this,size().width,size().height,5);
      }

    grid.draw(g);

    g.setColor(Color.red);

    for (int i = 0; i < rects.size(); i++)
      {
          Rectangle r = (Rectangle) rects.elementAt(i);
          g.drawRect(r.x, r.y, r.width, r.height);
      }
  }
```

If the user resizes the window, the program simply sets the grid variable to *null*. The next time there is a *paint* call, the *paint* method will create a new grid.

976   DRAWING A BOX THAT SNAPS TO A GRID

In the previous tips, you learned how to create and use a *gridArea* object. In Tip 973, you learned how to create an interactive boundbox for drawing rectangles. To fully implement a grid, you have to make sure the boundbox stays on the grid points. To do this, you have to "snap" the end points of the boundbox to the grid before you draw it. To do so, you can use the *gridArea* class *snap* method, as shown:

```java
public boolean mouseDown(Event evt, int x, int y)
  {
    x = grid.snap(x);
    y = grid.snap(y);

    if (toolbar.getMode() == RECTANGLE)
      {
          boundBox.mouseDown(this, x, y);
      }

    return(true);
  }

public boolean mouseDrag(Event evt, int x, int y)
  {
    x = grid.snap(x);
    y = grid.snap(y);

    if (toolbar.getMode() == RECTANGLE)
      boundBox.mouseDrag(this, x, y);

    return(true);
  }

public boolean mouseUp(Event evt, int x, int y)
  {
    x = grid.snap(x);
    y = grid.snap(y);

    if (toolbar.getMode() == RECTANGLE)
      {
          Rectangle r = boundBox.mouseUp(this, x, y);

        if (r != null)
          {
              rects.addElement(r); // insert into datastructure
              repaint(r.x, r.y, r.width+1, r.height+1);
          }
      }
    return(true);
  }
```

EXTENDING THE RECTANGLE CLASS 977

If the user can only draw rectangles in one color, your drawing program will not be very exciting. Long gone are the days of monochrome monitors. To allow the user to use different colors, you can create a color palette. You could implement a color palette just like the toolbar in Tip 970. Then, when a user draws a rectangle, you simply save the current color for that object. To do this, you can extend the *Rectangle* class so that you can add your own data. The following code demonstrates how to extend the *Rectangle* class to support colors. Notice that the new class knows how to draw itself:

```java
import java.awt.*;

public class colorRect extends Rectangle {

    Color color;

    public colorRect(int x, int y, int w, int h, Color c)
    {
        super(x, y, w, h);
        color = c;
    }

    public void draw(Graphics g)
    {
        g.setColor(color);
        g.fillRect(x, y, width+1, height+1);
        g.setColor(Color.black);
        g.drawRect(x, y, width, height);
    }
}
```

DRAWING THE NEW colorRect CLASS 978

In the previous tip, you extended Java's *Rectangle* class to support color information. Now, with the new rectangle object, the drawing area's *repaint* method only has to call the object's *draw* method. The *repaint* method does not have to worry about setting the color of individual rectangles. Instead, the *colorRect* objects know how to draw themselves. The following code demonstrates how to draw all the rectangles in the *rects* data structure:

```java
public void paint(Graphics g)
{
    if (grid == null)
        grid = new gridArea(this,size().width,size().height, 5);

    grid.draw(g);

    for (int i = 0; i < rects.size(); i++)
    {
        colorRect r = (colorRect) rects.elementAt(i);
        r.draw(g);
    }
}
```

979 SELECTING AND DESELECTING RECTANGLES

Most drawing programs require a user to select objects before the user can edit them. To implement drawing-object selection, you can wait for the drawing area to receive a *mouseDown* event. Then, you can traverse the list of *Rectangle* objects and call the *inside* method. The *inside* method will return *true* if the user clicked inside the rectangle. You can assume the first rectangle that returns *true* is the only one that is selected. The following program demonstrates how to select a *Rectangle* object in this way:

```
public void select(int x, int y)
  {
  // deselect
  if (selection != null)
    {
      if (selection.inside(x,y))
        return; // selected the same one again
      else
        {
          colorRect r = selection;
          selection = null;
          repaint(r.x, r.y, r.width+1, r.height+1);
        }
    }

  // select from newest to oldest
  for (int i = rects.size(); i->0; )
    {
      colorRect r = (colorRect) rects.elementAt(i);

      if (r.inside(x,y))
        {
          selection = r;
          repaint(r.x, r.y, r.width+1, r.height+1);
          break;
        }
    }
  }
```

Notice that the program can only select one rectangle at a time.

980 DELETING A RECTANGLE FROM THE LIST OF DRAWN OBJECTS

Within a drawing program, there are times when you create things that don't look the way you want them to look. For such mishaps, the program must provide you with a way to delete objects. To implement a delete operation, you can let the user select an object, and then press the **D** key to signal the delete operation. Your program, in turn, can detect the **D** key using the *keyDown* event. The following code demonstrates how to delete a *Rectangle* object:

```
public boolean keyDown(Event evt, int key)
  {
    if ((selection != null) && (key == 'd'))
      {
        rects.removeElement(selection);
        colorRect r = selection;
        selection = null;
        repaint(r.x, r.y, r.width+1, r.height+1);
      }
    return(true);
  }
```

Notice that after the code deletes the *Rectangle*, the code calls the *repaint* method, which updates only the area of the *Rectangle* deleted. By minimizing your screen-update area, you can reduce screen flicker.

IMPLEMENTING THE MOVERECT CLASS 981

In Tip 970, you learned how to implement a floating toolbar. When a toolbar's arrow button is down, it means that the user wants to edit objects that are already drawn. One of the simplest things that a user can do to an object is move it. To do this, you first have to detect if a user has clicked on a selected object. Then, to perform a move, you use an interactive XOR-mode box to show the rectangle's new position around the screen. You must make sure that one corner of the rectangle remains on the grid. The following code demonstrates how to create a *moveRect* class that can interactively move a *Rectangle* object:

```
import java.awt.*;

public class moveRect {

  static Rectangle rect;
  static int x_last;
  static int y_last;
  static int x_orig;
  static int y_orig;

  public static void mouseDown(Component c, int x,int y,
                                   Rectangle r)
    {
      x_orig = x;
      y_orig = y;
      x_last = x;
      y_last = y;

      rect = new Rectangle(r.x, r.y, r.width, r.height);
      drawbox(c); // draw box
    }

  public static Rectangle mouseUp(Component c, int x, int y)
    {
```

```
        drawbox(c); // erase box
        rect.translate(x - x_last,y - y_last);

        if ((x == x_orig) && (y == y_orig)) // did it move?
            return(null);
        else
            return(rect);
    }

public static void mouseDrag(Component c, int x, int y)
    {
        drawbox(c); // erase box
        rect.translate(x - x_last,y - y_last);

        x_last = x;
        y_last = y;

        drawbox(c); // draw box
    }

public static void drawbox(Component c)
    {
        Graphics g = c.getGraphics();
        g.setXORMode(Color.lightGray);
        g.drawRect(rect.x, rect.y, rect.width, rect.height);
        g.dispose();
    }
}
```

982 USING THE MOVERECT CLASS

In the previous tip, you learned how to create a class with which your programs can interactively move a rectangle around the screen. After the move operation is complete, your program must update the *Rectangle* object in the data structure that contains the list of drawn objects. Then, your program must call the *repaint* method to update the screen. The following code demonstrates how to perform these update operations:

```
public boolean mouseDown(Event evt, int x, int y)
    {
        if (toolbar.getMode() == RECTANGLE)
        {
            x = grid.snap(x);
            y = grid.snap(y);
            boundBox.mouseDown(this, x, y);
        }
        else
        {
            select(x,y);
            x = grid.snap(x);
            y = grid.snap(y);
```

```
            if (selection != null)
                moveRect.mouseDown(this, x, y, selection);
        }
      return(true);
  }

public boolean mouseDrag(Event evt, int x, int y)
  {
     x = grid.snap(x);
     y = grid.snap(y);

     if (toolbar.getMode() == RECTANGLE)
       boundBox.mouseDrag(this, x, y);
     else if (selection != null)
       moveRect.mouseDrag(this, x, y);

     return(true);
  }

public boolean mouseUp(Event evt, int x, int y)
  {
     x = grid.snap(x);
     y = grid.snap(y);

     if (toolbar.getMode() == RECTANGLE)
       {
         Rectangle r = boundBox.mouseUp(this, x, y);

         if (r != null)
           {
             rects.addElement(new colorRect(r.x, r.y, r.width,
                    r.height, colors[colorbar.getMode()]));

             repaint(r.x, r.y, r.width+1, r.height+1);
           }
       }
     else if (selection != null)
       {
         Rectangle r = moveRect.mouseUp(this, x, y);

         if (r != null)
           {
             int index = rects.indexOf(selection);
             colorRect new_r = new colorRect(r.x, r.y, r.width,
                    r.height, selection.color);

             rects.setElementAt(new_r, index);

             r = selection;
             selection = new_r;
```

```
                repaint(r.x, r.y, r.width+1, r.height+1); // old
                r = selection;
                repaint(r.x, r.y, r.width+1, r.height+1); // new
            }
        else
            {
                r = selection;
                repaint(r.x, r.y, r.width+1, r.height+1); // fix
            }
        }
    return(true);
}
```

Notice that to reduce flicker, the above code tries to minimize the amount of area that it passes to the *repaint* method.

983 CHANGING THE CURSOR

Within your drawing program, when the user clicks the mouse on a toolbar arrow button, the main drawing area should change the cursor to an arrow cursor. If the user clicks on the toolbar rectangle tool, the drawing area should use a cross-hair cursor. To perform these cursor operations, you can create an interface that the *floatToolBar* class calls to notify its parent of a new mode. The parent-class object can then change its cursor. The following code shows such an interface for the *floatToolBar* class:

```
public abstract interface floatToolBarCall
  {
     public void notify(int mode);
  }
```

The following code demonstrates how to implement the interface for a drawing area that needs to change its cursor.

```
class draw2DCursor implements floatToolBarCall {

    draw2D parent;

    static int cursors[] = { Frame.DEFAULT_CURSOR,
                             Frame.CROSSHAIR_CURSOR };

    public draw2DCursor(draw2D p)
      {
        parent = p;
      }

    public void notify(int mode)
      {
         parent.setCursor(cursors[mode]);
      }
 }
```

Finally, the following code demonstrates how the *floatToolBar* class receives the interface object, and how it calls the *notify* method when the user has pressed a button:

```
public void setCallBack(floatToolBarCall c)
{
    callback = c;
}

public boolean action(Event evt, Object obj)
{
    if (evt.target instanceof graphicalButton)
      {
        String label = (String) obj;

        for (int i = 0; i < id.length; i++)
          {
            if (label.equals(id[i]))
              {
                if (mode != i)
                    buttons[mode].setButton(graphicalButton.UP);

                mode = i;

                if (callback != null)
                   callback.notify(mode);

                break;
              }
          }
      }
    return true;
}
```

IMPLEMENTING UNDO AND REDO IN A DRAWING PROGRAM 984

Within a drawing program, you need to provide users with a way to undo their previous operations. There are many ways to implement undo and redo in a drawing program. One approach simply copies the list of objects just before a user performs any action. If the user hits *undo*, you can simply backup and replace the list data structure with an older copy. You save the replaced data structure in case the user hits *redo*.

Another approach for implementing undo and redo operations is for you to save all selected items just before the user performs any edit. Then, after the user performs an edit, you must mark all new and selected items. To do this, you can keep track of the end of the object list before the user does any edits. Since you append the new items at the end of the list, you will know where the new items are. When the user hits *undo*, you remove all the new and selected items. You add back the old selected items that you saved before the edit.

The second approach is more complicated than simply backing up an entire list of data structures; however, you save memory use with the second approach. Also, the second approach runs much faster. You should notice that the type of edit the user has made makes no difference in either approach. The edit can be a draw, move, or color change.

985 TECHNIQUES FOR BUILDING A DIGITAL CLOCK

As you know, within a Java applet, you can use Java's *Date* class to get the current time. To display the time on the screen, however, you need to use the *Graphics* class. The *Graphics* class provides a method called *drawString*, which will print any desired character string in an applet window. After you represent the time as a *String* object, you can call the *drawString* method to display the current time. But, before you start to build your new clock, you have one more thing to think about. Because the time changes every second (that is, if you display the seconds), you need a way to refresh the screen and display the new digits. To do this, you can use a thread which sleeps for a second and redraws the current time every time the thread comes out of its sleep.

Another clock feature you need to consider is to override the *update* method for smoother screen redraws. If your applet defines an *update* method, your redraws will use *update* instead of the *paint* method. However, Java will still call the *paint* method whenever your entire screen needs to be redrawn (as in a resize operation). You can customize the *update* method to draw only the portions of the screen that have been changed, resulting in cleaner redraws. The following tip implements a digital clock applet, as shown in Figure 985.

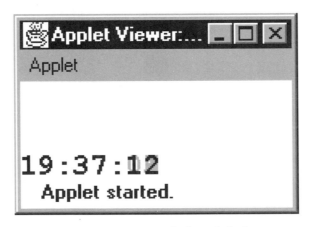

Figure 985 A simple digital clock.

986 SAMPLE DIGITAL CLOCK

The following code is a complete applet (from the book *Java Programmer's Library*, Jamsa Press, 1995) which displays a digital clock in your applet window. The applet updates the time every second by using a thread which sleeps for one second intervals. When the applet redraws the time, it erases the old digits by displaying the previous time string using the background color, which effectively erases the previous time.

```
import java.applet.*;
import java.awt.*;
import java.util.Date;

public class Clock extends Applet implements Runnable {
    Graphics g;
    Font font;
    Thread my_thread;
    int width, height;
```

```java
Date current_time;
String time = " ";

public void init( ) {
    g = getGraphics();
    current_time = new Date();
    set_defaults();
 }


void set_defaults()
  {
    width  = size().width;
    height = size().height;
    font = new Font("Courier", Font.BOLD, 18);
    g.setFont(font);
  }


public void start()
  {
    if (my_thread == null)
      {
         my_thread = new Thread(this);
         my_thread.start();
      }
  }


public void stop()
  {
    my_thread.stop();
    my_thread = null;
  }


public void run()
  {
    while (my_thread != null) {
        repaint();
        try {
            Thread.sleep(1000);
          }
        catch (InterruptedException e) {
          }
      }
  }


public void update(Graphics g)
  {
    g.setPaintMode();
    current_time = new Date();
    int hours   = current_time.getHours();
```

```
      int minutes = current_time.getMinutes();
      int seconds = current_time.getSeconds();
      String prev_time= time;  // store old time
      if (hours < 10)
        time = "0" + hours;
      else
        time = "" + hours;
      if (minutes < 10)
        time += ":0" + minutes;
      else
        time += ":" + minutes;
      if (seconds < 10)
        time += ":0" + seconds;
      else
        time += ":" + seconds;
      g.setColor(Color.lightGray);
      g.setFont(font);
      g.drawString(prev_time, 0, height); // erase old
      g.setColor(Color.black);
      g.drawString(time, 0, height); // draw new
    }

   public void paint(Graphics g)
     {
       set_defaults();
       update(g);
     }
 }
```

To run this applet, create an HTML file that contains the following contents:

```
<applet code=clock.class width=100 height=30> </applet>
```

987 CREATING PROGRAM DOCUMENTATION WITH JAVADOC

The Java Developer's Kit includes a utility called *javadoc* that helps you generate program documentation automatically. The *javadoc* program extracts class, methods, and other information from a Java source code file and creates documentation in HTML format. In fact, the on-line Java API documentation was generated using *javadoc*. For example, you can create program documentation for a file named *mycode.java* by typing the following command line:

```
C:\> javadoc mycode.java   <ENTER>
```

The *javadoc* program will process the specified Java source file and create an HTML documentation file for each class it finds in the specified Java source file. The *javadoc* program will also create a package list file, an index file, a class hierarchy file, and an alphabetical listing of all methods. Figure 987 shows the HTML document generated for a *TransFilter* class.

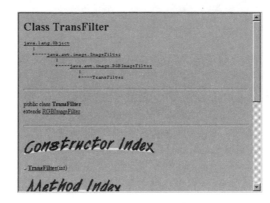

Figure 987 Documentation for the TransFilter class generated by javadoc.

ADDING COMMENTS TO DOCUMENTATION GENERATED BY JAVADOC 988

As you learned in the previous tip, you can generate program documentation using the *javadoc* utility for the class methods, class hierarchy, and so on. The *javadoc* utility can also extract comments from within your source code that begin with the characters /** and end with */. You can also include any valid HTML tags within the comment block. The following code shows a valid *javadoc* comment block:

```
/**
 * This is a class for building a
 * generic <B>binary tree</B> structure.
 */
```

Note that *javadoc* only extracts comments that begin with /** and end with */. The *javadoc* program does not extract comment blocks that begin with /* or a single-line comments that begin with //.

USING SPECIAL TAGS WITH JAVADOC 989

As you have learned, the *javadoc* utility lets you generate program documentation automatically. The *javadoc* utility also lets you use special tags, also known as keywords, to provide additional information such as a "See Also" reference. The following is a list of some of the tags that you can use with *javadoc*:

@see	Create a see also reference
@param	Document the method's parameters
@return	Document the method's return value
@exception	Document exceptions thrown by the method

The following code shows an example of a comment block that uses *javadoc* tags:

```
/**
 * This method finds an element in the binary tree
 * @see GLinkList
 * @see DLinkList
 * @param obj target element to search for
```

```
 * @return method returns the node found
 * @exception NoSuchElementException  element not found
 */
```

For more information on the *javadoc* keywords, visit the Web site, *http://java.sun.com/JDK-1.0/tools/win32/javadoc.html*.

990 WHY THE JAVA VIRTUAL MACHINE IS IMPORTANT

When you compile your Java program (presumably using *javac*, or your IDE compiler), you actually create a *.class* file that contains bytecode instructions. These bytecode instructions are used by another program (usually the Java interpreter or even an *appletviewer*) to actually run your program. Each computer may have its own interpreter, but they all are able to read a common bytecode, or *.class*, file.

To accomplish the goal of providing a single bytecode file that is runnable on any computer, the Java designers developed the Java Virtual Machine (JVM). In the same way that your computer uses a hardware CPU (Central Processing Unit) to read a compiled program and execute actions, the JVM uses software (instead of a CPU) to read your bytecode file and execute actions. Of course, since the JVM is program, it uses the CPU. The key point to understand is that the JVM is an additional layer between the CPU and the bytecode file.

If you are somewhat familiar with hardware CPUs, you know that they are composed of several components, including a set of registers, an instruction set, on-board memory, and so on. It turns out that the Java Virtual Machine also has these elements. More specifically, the JVM includes a bytecode instruction set, a set of registers, a stack, a garbage-collection heap, and an area for storing methods.

By putting the Java processor in software, rather than in hardware, you can run the same program on any computer—a feat that has up to now been nearly impossible.

991 UNDERSTANDING REMOTE METHOD INVOCATION (RMI)

As you develop more complicated Java applets, and as other developers publish their own applets, you may find that you need to have your Java objects invoke other Java object methods residing on other computers. This is a natural extension of Java—you are able to use Java-based resources throughout the Web to give your own applet additional functionality. Remote Method Invocation (RMI) lets methods within your Java objects be invoked from Java code that may be running in a different virtual machine, often on another computer.

992 THE DETAILS BEHIND REMOTE METHOD INVOCATION (RMI)

To make use of Remote Method Invocation, you must make the methods within your objects callable from other objects. Objects that can have their methods invoked in this way are called *remote objects*. You can implement a remote object by following these guidelines:

- You define an interface that extends *Remote* and each method in the interface must declare that it throws a *RemoteException*.

- You must define a class that implements the interface and provides a remote reference to the object. Sun provides the *UnicastRemoteServer* class which you can extend for this purpose.

- Run Sun's *rmic* program to generate stubs and skeletons for your remote implementations. These stubs and skeletons are loaded when clients use RMI to talk to your remote objects.

RMI treats parameters passed to your method in the following ways:

- Primitive types (*int*, *boolean*, *long*, and so on) are passed by value, as normal.

- Remote object references are passed as references, allowing the recipient to invoke methods on the remote object. Local object references are passed to local Java methods in this way.

- Non-remote objects are passed as complete copies, also known as passing by value. This is how primitive types are passed in Java.

RMI COMPATIBILITY PROBLEMS WITH NETSCAPE 993

If you are having trouble using RMI, it may be because you are not using the latest JDK and Netscape browser. RMI relies on object serialization which, in turn, requires changes made in the JDK 1.0.2 that may not be reflected in your version of Netscape. However, RMI and Object Serialization are expected to be finalized in the JDK 1.1. There have also been several bugs in the early DLLs for the separate RMI components. Again, these fixes are expected in JDK 1.1. To check on the current status of Netscape browser compatibility, you may want to visit the JavaSoft site at:

```
http://www.javasoft.com
```

FINDING OUT MORE ABOUT REMOTE METHOD INVOCATION (RMI) 994

Finding more information about this newly emerging technology may be illusive. The best place to start is from the JavaSoft Web site.

You can find a variety of topics in the hypermail archive at:

```
http://chatsubo.javasoft.com/email/rmi-
```

There are some additional resources. You can subscribe (or unsubscribe) to the RMI-users list server by sending e-mail to *listserv@java.sun.com* with the following contents in the mail body (NOT the subject line):

```
subscribe rmi-users
```

```
unsubscribe rmi-users
```

Sun has also been offering RMI support by e-mail at:

```
rmi-support@jse.east.sun.com
```

UNDERSTANDING THE MAC OS RUNTIME FOR JAVA (MRJ) 995

The Mac OS Runtime for Java (MRJ) is Apple's Java execution environment based on technology from Sun Microsystems, Inc. Apple plans to build both the interpreter and the Just-In-Time compiler into a future version of the operating system, thereby ensuring that all Macintosh computers can execute applets. For now, you can obtain a copy of the current version of MRJ, which comes with several demonstration utilities, from Apple's *ftp* site:

```
ftp://devtools.apple.com/mrj/mrj-1.0a1-installer.hqx
```

996 JAVA JIT COMPILERS

When your Java-enabled browser connects to a server and tries to view a Web page that contains a Java applet, the server transmits the bytecode for that applet to your computer. Before your browser can run the applet, it must interpret the bytecode data. The Java interpreter performs the task of interpreting the bytecode data.

As you have learned, using an interpreter to read bytecode files makes it possible for the same bytecode to run on any computer (such as a Windows-based or Mac-based computer) that supports Java. The big drawback is that interpreters can be 20 to 40 times slower than code that was custom compiled, or *native*, for a specific computer.

As it turns out, a new type of browser-side software, called a *Just-In-Time compiler* (JIT), can convert (*compile*) the bytecode file directly into native code optimized for the computer that is browsing it. The JIT compiler will take the bytecode data sent by the server and compile it just before the applet needs to run. The compiled code will execute as fast as any application you already use on your computer. As you might expect, the major compiler and IDE manufacturers, such as Borland, Microsoft, Symantec, and Metrowerks, are all developing JIT compilers.

997 WHAT IS THE JAVA2C TRANSLATOR?

Sun has been experimenting with a translator called *java2c* (pronounced Java two C) which simply takes the bytecode file sent by a server and converts it into C code. The C code is then compiled resulting in fast, native code. The only shortcoming is that *java2c* runs only on computers that have a C compiler. Along with JIT compilers, *java2c* promises to be yet another possible solution for Java's current poor performance.

998 WHERE TO FIND SUN'S OFFICIAL BUG LIST

If you are having difficulty getting a program to work, the problem may not be your program, it could (although not likely) be an error within your version of Java. Before you blame the compiler, you should find out about the documented bugs and incompatibilities by visiting Sun's Web page which exists specifically for such bug reports. For release of the JDK1.0.2, you should visit:

`http://java.sun.com/java.sun.com/products/JDK/1.0.2/KnownBugs.html`

As Java is a developing language, there is a good possibility that you may find a bug or other problem. Sun is very interested in finding out about these things, and they have a special address for you to e-mail your problem to:

`java-bugs@java.sun.com`

Before you submit your bug report, however, you should first consult the instructions on Sun's bug report page at:

`http://java.sun.com/GettingInTouch/BugReport.html`

999 UNDERSTANDING THE JAVA IDL SYSTEM

The Interface Definition Language (IDL) is an industry standard format useful for letting a Java client transparently invoke existing IDL objects that reside on a remote server. In addition, it allows a Java server to define objects that can be transparently invoked from IDL clients. The Java IDL system lets you define remote interfaces using the IDL interface definition language which you can then compile with the *idlgen* stub generator tool to generate Java interface definitions and Java client and server stubs. For more information on IDL, you can subscribe (or unsubscribe) to the IDL-users list server by sending e-mail to *listserv@java.sun.com* with the following contents in the mail body (NOT the subject line):

```
subscribe idl-users

unsubscribe idl-users
```

In addition, Sun offers IDL support by e-mail at:

```
idl-support@java.sun.com
```

UNDERSTANDING JAVA BEANS  1000

Java Beans is the name of a project at JavaSoft to define a set of standard component software APIs (Application Programmers Interface) for the Java platform. By developing these standards, it becomes possible for software developers to develop reusable software components that end-users can then hook together using application-builder tools. In addition, these API's make it easier for developers to bridge to existing component models such as Microsoft's ActiveX, Apple's OpenDoc, and Netscape's LiveConnect. For more information on Java Beans, visit the Web site, *http://splash.javasoft.com/beans/*, shown in Figure 1000.

Figure 1000 *Information on Java Beans.*

JAVA RESOURCES ON THE INTERNET  1001

The Internet is perhaps one of the best resources for gaining access to the latest developments involving Java, including actual sample code, newsgroups, educational information, and on-line magazines. If you don't like typing in long URLs, you can simply start either from the JavaSoft Web site, or be adventurous and use a search engine, such as Yahoo or Lycos, to search for the word *Java*. You will get an immense list of sites to explore and add to your own bookmarks.

YAHOO'S JAVA LISTING

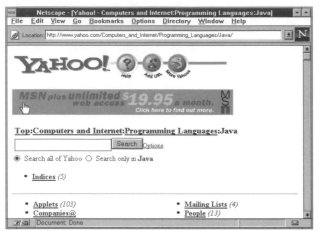

http://www.yahoo.com/Computers_and_Internet/ Programming_Languages/Java/

THE PRIMARY JAVASOFT HOME PAGE

http://www.javasoft.com

SUN'S JAVA LANGUAGE TUTORIAL

http://www.javasoft.com/tutorial/index.html

NETSCAPE'S APPFOUNDRY STARTER APPLETS

http://home.netscape.com/one_stop/intranet_apps/ index.html

JAVAWORLD MAGAZINE

http://www.javaworld.com

JAVA IDE REVIEWS

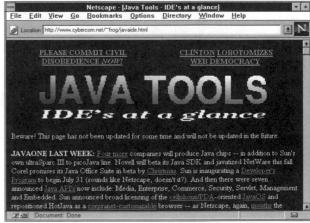

http://www.cybercom.net/~frog/javaide.html

INFORMATION ON USING JAVASCRIPT WITH JAVA

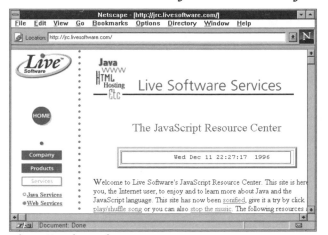

http://jrc.livesoftware.com

TUTORIAL ON USING THREADS

http://g.oswego.edu/dl/pats/aopintro.html

JAVA CLASS HIERARCHY DIAGRAMS

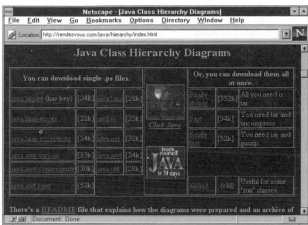

http://rendezvous.com/java/hierarchy/index.html

THE JAVA REPOSITORY

http://java.wiwi.uni-frankfurt.de

JAVA APPLET RATING SERVICE

http://www.jars.com

THE JAVA CENTRE

http://www.java.co.uk

APPLE FLAVORED JAVA-MACINTOSH RELATED JAVA

http://www.mbmdesigns.com/macjava

THE AUTHOR'S OWN WEB SITE

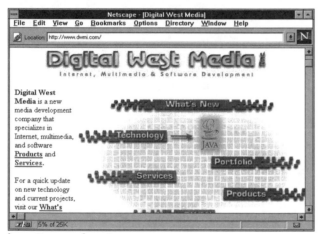

http://www.dwmi.com

THE JAMSA PRESS WEB SITE

http://www.jamsa.com

JAVA LAUNCHING PAD

http://ng.netgate.net/~aronoff/JavaLinks.html

JAVA OASIS: FREE SOFTWARE

http://www.oasis.leo.org/java/

JAVA LINKS FROM TEAMJAVA

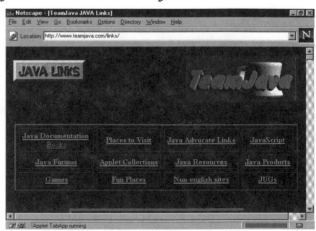

http://www.teamjava.com:80/links/

Index